EDITION 5

Intercultural
Communication

Intercultural Communication
A Contextual Approach

EDITION 5

James W. Neuliep
St. Norbert College

Los Angeles | London | New Delhi
Singapore | Washington DC

Los Angeles | London | New Delhi
Singapore | Washington DC

FOR INFORMATION:

SAGE Publications, Inc.

2455 Teller Road

Thousand Oaks, California 91320

E-mail: order@sagepub.com

SAGE Publications Ltd.

1 Oliver's Yard

55 City Road

London EC1Y 1SP

United Kingdom

SAGE Publications India Pvt. Ltd.

B 1/I 1 Mohan Cooperative Industrial Area

Mathura Road, New Delhi 110 044

India

SAGE Publications Asia-Pacific Pte. Ltd.

33 Pekin Street #02-01

Far East Square

Singapore 048763

Acquisitions Editor: Matthew Byrnie

Associate Editor: Nathan Davidson

Editorial Assistant: Elizabeth Borders

Production Editor: Eric Garner

Copy Editor: Megan Granger

Typesetter: C&M Digitals (P) Ltd.

Proofreader: Susan Schon

Indexer: Kathy Paparchontis

Cover Designer: Janet Kiesel

Marketing Manager: Liz Thornton

Permissions Editor: Karen Ehrmann

Printed in the United States of America

Library of Congress Cataloging-in-Publication Data

Neuliep, James William, 1957-

Intercultural communication: a contextual approach/James W. Neuliep. — 5th ed.

p. cm.
Includes bibliographical references and index.

ISBN 978-1-4129-7689-3 (pbk. : acid-free paper)

1. Intercultural communication. 2. Culture. I. Title.

HM1211.N48 2012
303.48'2—dc23   2011031177

This book is printed on acid-free paper.

11 12 13 14 15 10 9 8 7 6 5 4 3 2 1

Brief Contents

Preface   xiii

Chapter 1. The Necessity of Intercultural Communication   1

Chapter 2. The Cultural Context   45

Chapter 3. The Microcultural Context   93

Chapter 4. The Environmental Context   131

Chapter 5. The Perceptual Context   167

Chapter 6. The Sociorelational Context   205

Chapter 7. The Verbal Code: Human Language   235

Chapter 8. The Nonverbal Code   267

Chapter 9. Developing Intercultural Relationships   311

Chapter 10. Intercultural Conflict   351

Chapter 11. Intercultural Communication in Organizations   373

Chapter 12. Acculturation, Culture Shock, and Intercultural Competence   405

Glossary   G-1

Photo Credits   P-1

Name Index   NI-1

Subject Index   SI-1

About the Author   A-1

Detailed Contents

Preface   xiii

1 The Necessity of Intercultural Communication   1

The Need for Intercultural Communication   4
    Benefits of Intercultural Communication   6
    Diversity in the United States   8
Human Communication   9
    The Nature of Human Communication   10
    Human Communication Apprehension   15
    The Nature of Culture   18
    Microcultural Groups   22
    The Study of Intercultural Communication   22
    A Contextual Model of Intercultural Communication   24
Fundamental Assumptions About Intercultural Communication   32
The Ethics of Intercultural Communication   36
Chapter Summary • Discussion Questions • Key Terms • References   41

2 The Cultural Context   45

Individualism–Collectivism   48
    Individualism   48
    Collectivism   49
    Individualism Versus Collectivism?   50
    So, Who's an Individualist and Who's a Collectivist?   51
An Intercultural Conversation: Individualistic and Collectivistic Cultures   52
    Patterns of Individualism and
        Collectivism Across the United States   54
    Communication Consequences of Individualism–Collectivism   55
    Measuring Individualism–Collectivism   56
    Vertical and Horizontal Individualism and Collectivism   56
The Pancultural Self   60
High- and Low-Context Communication   61
    Characteristics of High- and Low-Context Cultures   62
    Communication Consequences of
        Low- and High-Context Cultural Orientations   64
An Intercultural Conversation: High- and Low-Context Cultures   64
    Assessing High- and Low-Context Communication   65

Value Orientations   67
    Schwartz's Universal Values   71
    Kluckhohn and Strodtbeck's Value Orientations   71
Power Distance   76
    Measuring Power Distance   79
    Communication and Power Distance   80
An Intercultural Conversation: Large and Small Power Distance Cultures   83
Uncertainty Avoidance   83
A Theory of Uncertainty Orientation   84
An Intercultural Conversation: Weak and Strong Uncertainty Avoidance   86
Chapter Summary • Discussion Questions • Key Terms • References   87

3 The Microcultural Context   93

Microcultural Group Status   95
Muted Microcultural Groups   97
Microcultures in the United States   99
    Hispanics/Latinos   100
    African Americans   105
    The Amish   109
    The Hmong   114
    Arab Americans   118
    Lesbian, Gay, Bisexual, and Transgendered Microcultural Groups   121
Chapter Summary • Discussion Questions • Key Terms • References   125

4 The Environmental Context   131

Environments and Information Load   133
Culture and the Natural Environment   135
    Worldviews of the Natural Environment   136
Culture and Natural Disasters   137
    Natural Disasters as Cultural and Social Events   138
The Built Environment   139
Cross-Cultural Comparisons of Housing   141
    Japanese Housing   142
    American Navajo Housing   144
    Marakwet Housing   146
Privacy   148
    Assessing Dimensions of Privacy   150
    Perceptions of Privacy in the United States   151
    Cross-Cultural Variations on Privacy   153
    Online Privacy Across Cultures   155
Monochronic Versus Polychronic Time Orientation   156
    Consequences of Monochronic and Polychronic Orientations   158
An Intercultural Conversation: Monochronic and Polychronic Cultures   159
Chapter Summary • Discussion Questions • Key Terms • References   162

5 The Perceptual Context   167

Culture and Cognition   170
     The Geography of Thought   170
     A Model of Human Information Processing   172
     Cross-Cultural Differences in Sensation and Perception   174
     Cross-Cultural Differences in Memory and Retrieval   179
     Categorization and Mental Economy   181
Stereotyping   182
     Racial and Ethnic Stereotypes   184
     American Stereotypes   185
     Stereotype Content Model   188
     Why Stereotype?   191
     Stereotypes and Expectations   193
An Intercultural Conversation: Stereotyping   194
Ethnocentrism   195
     A Contemporary Conceptualization of Ethnocentrism   196
     Ethnocentrism, Intercultural Communication, and Interpersonal Perception   196
     Ethnocentrism and Communication in the Workplace   197
     Ethnocentrism and Racism   198
Chapter Summary • Discussion Questions • Key Terms • References   199

6 The Sociorelational Context   205

Dimensions of Group Variability   207
     Membership and Nonmembership Groups   207
     In-Groups and Out-Groups   208
     Reference Groups   209
Role Relationships   210
An Intercultural Conversation: Student/Teacher Role Positions   213
     Role Differentiation and Stratification   213
An Intercultural Conversation: Cross-Cultural Role Positions   216
     Family Groups   217
     Sex and Gender Groups   219
     Gender Stereotypes   221
Sex and Gender Roles Across Cultures   223
     Morocco   223
     Japan   224
     India   225
     Saudi Arabia   226
     Egypt   226
     China   228
     Mexico   229
Chapter Summary • Discussion Questions • Key Terms • References   230

7 The Verbal Code: Human Language 235

The Relationship Between Language and Culture   237
    Sapir-Whorf Hypothesis   237
The Structure of Human Language   238
    Sounds and Symbols   239
    Syntax and Universal Grammar   240
    Universals of Language   244
    Generative Grammar   245
Elaborated and Restricted Codes   247
Cross-Cultural Communication Styles   248
    Direct and Indirect Styles   249
An Intercultural Conversation: Direct and Indirect Speaking   250
    Elaborate, Exacting, and Succinct Styles   251
    Personal and Contextual Styles   252
An Intercultural Conversation: Personal and Contextual Speaking   253
    Instrumental and Affective Styles   254
An Intercultural Conversation:
  Instrumental and Affective Speaking   256
Language and Ethnic Identity   257
    Do You Speak American?   259
Chapter Summary • Discussion Questions • Key Terms • References   263

8 The Nonverbal Code 267

Definitions of Nonverbal Communication   269
The Relationship Between Verbal and Nonverbal Codes   270
    Formal Versus Informal Code Systems   271
Channels of Nonverbal Communication   272
    Kinesics   272
    Paralanguage   283
    Proxemics   287
    Haptics   288
    Olfactics   290
    Physical Appearance and Dress   296
    Chronemics   297
Nonverbal Communication and Dimensions of Cultural Variability   298
    Individualism–Collectivism   299
    Power Distance   299
    High and Low Context   300
    Nonverbal Expectancy Violations Theory   300
    Cultural Contexts and Nonverbal Expectancies   303
An Intercultural Conversation: Violation of Nonverbal Expectancies   304
Chapter Summary • Discussion Questions • Key Terms • References   305

9 Developing Intercultural Relationships 311

Communication and Uncertainty   313
Anxiety Uncertainty Management Theory of Effective Communication   316
Uncertainty Reduction and Intercultural Communication Apprehension   320
An Intercultural Conversation: Uncertainty Reduction and Sociocommunicative Style   322
    Assessing Sociocommunicative Orientation/Style   324
Empathy and Similarity in Relationship Development   324
    Empathy   324
    Similarity   327
Perceptions of Relational Intimacy Across Cultures   329
    Eastern and Western Cultures and Relationships   329
    Intercultural and Interracial Relationships and Marriage   332
    Intercultural Relational Maintenance   334
    The Internet as Relational Maintenance   337
    Mate Selection and Desirability Across Cultures   338
    Arranged Marriages   344
    Marital Dissolution and Divorce Across Cultures   345
Chapter Summary • Discussion Questions • Key Terms • References   347

10 Intercultural Conflict 351

Definition of Intercultural Conflict   352
    A Model of Intercultural Conflict   353
An Intercultural Conversation: Kim's Model of Intercultural Conflict   355
The Concept of Face, Facework, and Communication Conflict Styles   357
    Face   357
    Facework   357
    Conflict Communication Styles   360
An Intercultural Conversation: Dominating and Third-Party Conflict Styles   361
The Intercultural Conflict Style Inventory   362
A Culture-Based Situational Model of Conflict   364
Individualistic and Collectivistic Approaches to Conflict   366
Conflict Resolution in High- Versus Low-Context Cultures   368
Chapter Summary • Discussion Questions • Key Terms • References   370

11 Intercultural Communication in Organizations 373

Intercultural Management   375
    The Cultural Context   377
An Intercultural Conversation: Clashing Cultural Concepts on the Job   378
    The Environmental Context   380
    The Perceptual Context   381
    The Sociorelational Context   381
    Verbal and Nonverbal Codes   382

An Intercultural Conversation: Misinterpretation of Common U.S. Phrases   383
Intercultural Relations   385
    Japanese Management Practices   386
    German Management Practices   391
    Mexican Management Practices   394
    Chinese Management Practices   396
    Commerce in the Middle East   398
An Intercultural Conversation: Business Communication in the Middle East   400
Chapter Summary • Discussion Questions • Key Terms • References   402

12 Acculturation, Culture Shock, and Intercultural Competence 405

Acculturation   406
    Acculturative Stress   407
    A Model of Acculturation   408
    Modes of Acculturation   410
    Acculturation in the United States   411
Culture Shock   417
    W-Curve Models of Reentry Culture Shock   422
    Strategies for Managing Culture Shock   422
Intercultural Communication Competence   424
A Model of Intercultural Competence   425
    The Knowledge Component   426
    The Affective Component   427
    The Psychomotor Component   429
    Situational Features   430
An Integrated Model and Measure of Intercultural Communication Competence   431
Chapter Summary • Discussion Questions • Key Terms • References   433

Glossary   G-1

Photo Credits   P-1

Name Index   NI-1

Subject Index   SI-1

About the Author   A-1

Preface to the Fifth Edition

*I*ntercultural Communication: A Contextual Approach (5th ed.) is designed for undergraduate students taking their first course in intercultural communication. The purpose of the book is to introduce students to the fundamental topics, theories, concepts, and themes at the center of the study of intercultural communication.

The overall organizational scheme of the book is based on a *contextual model of intercultural communication*. The model is based on the idea that whenever people from different cultures come together and exchange verbal and nonverbal messages, they do so within a variety of contexts, including a cultural, microcultural, environmental, sociorelational, and perceptual context. The model is conceptually and graphically consistent and is presented in Chapter 1.

The organizational scheme of this new edition remains essentially unchanged from the fourth edition, but many substantive revisions have been incorporated. Each chapter has been revised and updated to include the most recent research. A new and exciting feature of this edition is Student Voices Across Cultures. Each chapter (with the exception of Chapter 11) includes an essay from a student applying a concept from that chapter to his or her life experiences. Students from China, Saudi Arabia, Mexico, Germany, Colombia, and the United States have contributed to this feature. Many of the U.S. students discuss their experiences from studying abroad. These essays provide the reader with real-life applications of theoretical concepts.

A second new feature is the addition of discussion questions focusing on ethics at the close of most chapters. Here, readers are asked to consider the ethical implications of what they have read and learned about intercultural communication and cultural differences. Several chapters now include discussions of lesbian and gay culture and communication. The role of modern technology and its impact on intercultural communication has also been added to many chapters. Other revisions include an expansion of Chapter 10, on intercultural conflict, and many new photographs. Like earlier editions, this edition contains an assortment of reliable and valid self-assessment instruments designed to help students measure theoretical concepts.

Chapter 1 alerts students to the importance and necessity of intercultural communication in the 21st century. A new discussion of the role of modern technology has been included here. The argument is that modern technology has decentralized information. This means that billions of people across the planet now have access to information that was not available to them only a few years ago. Such information empowers them. In addition, the most current data from the U.S. Census Bureau are reviewed and point to the growing diversity of the U.S. population. The chapter continues with extended discussions of the nature of human communication and culture. While reading Chapter 1, students can complete and score the Personal Report of Communication Apprehension (PRCA-24), the Generalized Ethnocentrism (GENE) Scale, and the Personal Report of Intercultural Communication Apprehension (PRICA). The chapter closes with a delineation of five fundamental assumptions of intercultural communication. The Student Voices Across Cultures profile in this chapter presents one young woman's experiences with cultural differences while studying abroad in Spain.

In Chapter 2, culture is defined as an accumulated pattern of values, beliefs, and behaviors shared by an identifiable group of people with a common history and verbal and nonverbal code system. The outer circle of the contextual model of intercultural communication represents the cultural context. This is the largest circle because culture permeates every aspect of the communicative exchange, even the physical geography. All communicative exchanges between persons occur within some cultural context. The cultural context is the focus of Chapter 2. Well-recognized topics such as individualism–collectivism, high–low context, weak–strong uncertainty avoidance, value orientations, and high–low power distance are discussed. Self-report scales measuring each of these topics are included in the chapter, and a new scale that measures vertical and horizontal individualism and collectivism has been added. Although most textbooks present individualism and collectivism as opposite dimensions of cultural variability, they are not mutually exclusive; that is, they can coexist within a person of any culture. Moreover, individuals can be characterized by specific combinations of individualistic and collectivistic tendencies. An expanded discussion of the behavioral traits shown to be associated with individualism and collectivism is also included. Two Student Voices Across Cultures profiles are included in this chapter: one from a Chinese student who discusses collectivism in China and the other from a Saudi Arabian student who explains power distance in his family.

The focus of Chapter 3 is the microcultural context. Within most cultures are groups of people that differ in some significant way from the general macro culture. These groups are sometimes called minorities, subcultures, or co-cultures. In this book, the term *microculture* is used to refer to those identifiable groups of people that share a set of values, beliefs, and behaviors and possess a common history and verbal and nonverbal symbol system that is similar to, but systematically varies from, the larger, often dominant cultural milieu. Microcultures can be different from the larger culture in a variety of ways—most often because of race, ethnicity, language, religion, or even their behavioral practices. Such microcultures develop their own language for communicating outside the dominant or majority culture's context or value system. Chapter 3 includes an updated and revised discussion of four U.S. microcultures: Hispanics, African Americans, the Amish, and the Hmong. In this new edition, a fifth microculture—lesbian, gay, bisexual, and transgendered groups—is also profiled. Included in this chapter is a Student Voices Across Cultures profile written by a gay college professor who discusses personal examples of being silenced as a member of a microculture.

Chapter 4 focuses on the environmental context. Whereas culture prescribes the overall rules for communication, the environmental context prescribes when and what specific rules apply. The environmental context includes the physical geography, architecture, landscape design, housing, perceptions of privacy, time orientation, and even climate of a particular culture. These environmental factors play a key role in how people communicate. In this chapter, students are given the opportunity to assess their privacy preferences and monochronic/polychronic time orientations. Chapter 4 includes coverage of the nature of privacy in the United States, with a special focus on the perceptions of privacy among U.S. students. A new discussion of natural disasters as cultural and social events has been added. Although natural disasters are triggered by natural events (e.g., tsunamis, earthquakes, floods, etc.), the effects of such disasters vary considerably across cultures because they take place within particular social and cultural systems of laws and values. In the Student Voices Across Cultures profile included at the end of this chapter, a young man from Germany discusses his country's monochronic time orientation.

Chapter 5 focuses on the perceptual contexts of the interactants and includes a revised and simplified model of human information processing. The perceptual context refers to the individual characteristics of the interactants, including their cognitions, attitudes, dispositions, and motivations. How an individual gathers, stores, and retrieves information is uniquely human but also culturally influenced. An individual's attitudes about others, including stereotypes, are culturally influenced. Also included in Chapter 5 is a discussion of American racism as a parallel to ethnocentrism. A new feature of this chapter is a discussion of the geography of thought—that is, how geographical differences among cultures have a dramatic influence on how humans in those distinct geographical areas perceive the world. Here, the focus is on how Asians (Eastern cultures) and Westerners think differently and why. Another new feature of this chapter is a fascinating discussion of the Stereotype Content Model, which explains how and why people stereotype and the essential content of those stereotypes. This model is applicable across cultures. In one of the Student Voices Across Cultures profiles included in this chapter, a young woman who has won beauty pageants discusses the long-held stereotypes applied to beauty queens. In another profile, a student from the United States discusses being stereotyped while studying abroad in Ecuador.

The sociorelational context is the focus of Chapter 6. Whenever two people come together and interact, they establish some sort of social relationship based on their group memberships. Within such relationships, each person assumes a role. Roles prescribe with whom, about what, and how to communicate. Roles vary from culture to culture. For example, in just about every culture, there are student and teacher role relationships, but how student–teacher roles are defined varies significantly from culture to culture. For example, the U.S. American definition of student varies significantly from the Japanese definition of student. What it means to be a mother or father varies considerably from one culture to another as well. One's roles prescribe the types of verbal and nonverbal symbols that are exchanged. Chapter 6 contains a revised and updated discussion of family groups and sex groups. In addition, the contextual model of intercultural communication represents the sociorelational context as defined by the verbal and nonverbal codes. In the Student Voices Across Cultures profile included in this chapter, a young woman from Saudi Arabia discusses sex roles in her family and culture.

Chapter 7 focuses on the verbal code and human language. Throughout much of the book, cultural *differences* are highlighted. In Chapter 7, however, language is characterized as essentially *human* rather than cultural. Based on the ideas of Noam Chomsky and other contemporary linguists, Chapter 7 points out that regardless of culture, people are born with the capacity for language. Humans are born with universal grammar and, through culture, are exposed to a subset that constitutes their particular culture's language (e.g., English, French, and so on). The language of a particular culture is simply a subset of universal language. To be sure, culture certainly affects how we use language. Thus, Chapter 7 outlines several styles of language and how they vary across cultures. An expanded discussion of uniquely American accents, including a section addressing whether or not such a thing as a Midwestern accent exists, closes the chapter. In this chapter's Student Voices Across Cultures profile, a student from China explains how her native language emphasizes nonverbal tones that dramatically change the meanings of words.

Chapter 8 focuses on the nonverbal code. After a discussion of the relationship between the verbal and nonverbal codes, seven channels of nonverbal communication are discussed: kinesics, paralanguage, proxemics, haptics, olfactics, physical appearance/dress, and chronemics. In the section on kinesics, the use of gestures across cultures and an extended discussion of affect displays across cultures are presented. In the coverage of paralanguage, cultural uses of silence and tonal languages are discussed. A new discussion of accents is also included. Cultural variations of space are covered in the section on proxemics. High- and low-contact cultures are the focus of the section on haptics. An extended discussion of olfactics across cultures is presented, and students can assess their perception of smell by completing the Personal Report of Olfactic Perception and Sensitivity (PROPS) scale. A discussion of physical appearance and dress looks at cultural variations in Muslim and Japanese cultures, among others. The discussion of chronemics reviews Hall's monochronic/polychronic distinction, in addition to a discussion of the use of calendars across cultures. Finally, the chapter closes with a cross-cultural application of nonverbal expectancy violations theory. In this chapter's Student Voices Across Cultures essay, a U.S. student discusses her trip to Zambia, Africa, and her experience with haptics/touch.

Chapter 9 discusses the development of intercultural relationships. This chapter focuses on five factors that affect relationships: uncertainty reduction, intercultural communication apprehension, sociocommunicative style, empathy, and similarity. Each factor is discussed with an emphasis on intercultural relationships. The chapter also presents an expanded discussion of relationship differences among Eastern and Western cultures, marital relationships across cultures, interracial and intercultural relationships, arranged marriages, mate selection practices across cultures, and divorce. A new discussion of the Internet as relational maintenance looks at the role of social media outlets. Also included is a discussion of the research associated with lesbian and gay relational maintenance. In this chapter, students can complete the Sociocommunicative Orientation/Style and Factors in Choosing a Mate instruments and compare their preferences with other cultures. In the two Student Voices Across Cultures profiles, a young man from Saudi Arabia discusses marriage in Saudi, and a young woman explains relationship building in Colombia.

Chapter 10, which focuses on intercultural conflict, has been significantly expanded. The chapter begins with a definition of intercultural conflict and describes three levels of conflict as described by Young Kim's model. The chapter also includes an extended discussion of face-negotiation theory, where students can assess their degree of self-face, other-face, and mutual-face concerns after exposure to a conflict situation. The chapter also includes a discussion of facework and facework strategies. A new feature of this chapter is a discussion of the Intercultural Conflict Style Inventory. This inventory is a theoretical model and assessment tool used by professional mediators and trainers to diagnose and manage intercultural conflicts. Also added to this chapter is Ting-Toomey and Oetzel's culture-based situational model of conflict, which highlights four main factors that come into play during an intercultural conflict episode: individual factors, conflict process factors, situational features, and conflict outcomes. The chapter closes with a discussion of conflict communication styles and how culture affects one's preference for conflict styles. In the Student Voices Across Cultures profile, a young man from Mexico describes how people in his culture approach interpersonal conflict.

Chapter 11's focus is intercultural communication in organizations. In this chapter, all the contexts presented earlier are applied to the organizational context. Organizational examples from the cultural, microcultural, environmental, perceptual, and sociorelational contexts have been updated. An interesting case study of Wal-Mart's failure in some countries has been added here. Because they are three of our largest trade partners, management perspectives in Japan, Germany, and Mexico are highlighted, along with business practices in the Middle East. A new feature of this chapter is a discussion of Chinese management practices. Economic and trade data from each of these countries has been updated.

Chapter 12 presents a discussion of acculturation, culture shock, and intercultural competence. The central theme of this chapter is the practical aspects of traveling or moving to a new culture. A model of assimilation/acculturation is presented, along with factors that influence the acculturation process, such as perceived similarity and host culture attitudes. A four-stage "U-curve" model of culture shock is outlined. In addition, the chapter includes a discussion of the "W-curve" model of reentry culture shock. The chapter also includes a variety of self-report inventories to help students prepare for their journeys abroad. The chapter closes with a model of intercultural competence as four interdependent components—knowledge, affective, psychomotor, and situational features. The chapter now includes a discussion of Arasaratnam's integrated model and measure of intercultural communication competence. Like others, Arasaratnam maintains that being a competent intercultural communicator involves knowing about other cultures, an approach tendency, and the application of appropriate and effective communication behaviors. A new scale that measures intercultural competence is now included. The Student Voices Across Cultures profile features a young woman's experiences with culture shock during her semester in Spain.

As mentioned above, most chapters contain a number of self-assessment instruments. These are designed to help students learn about themselves as they learn about important concepts in intercultural communication. The instruments included in the chapters are documented as being valid and reliable. As in the earlier editions, most of the chapters in this newly revised edition of the book contain *intercultural conversations*. These hypothetical scripts illustrate how the various concepts discussed in the chapters manifest themselves in human interactions. Each chapter also includes a set of learning objectives, a chapter summary, key terms, discussion questions, and an extensive reference list.

A number of people have been instrumental in the revision of this book. As in the earlier editions, the late William B. Gudykunst has strongly influenced the writing and research of this book. I am blessed, truly blessed, with the people at Sage Publications. My former editors, Todd Armstrong and Deya Saoud, and my new editorial and production staff at Sage deserve much of the credit for what is good in this book. They have been incredibly patient with me, and I wish to express my gratitude publicly. My new editor, Matt Byrnie, is a welcome addition to this project. Very special thanks to my assistant editor, Nathan Davidson. Nathan has been charitable and forgiving of my numerous missed deadlines. I appreciate his attention to detail. He kept me on task. Thanks also to Eric Garner, the senior project editor. Also, thanks to Elizabeth Borders, who came on late but is a welcome addition. A very, very personal and warm thanks goes to Megan (Ms. Meg) Granger, copy editor extraordinaire, who spent so many hours editing the manuscript.

I hope Meg is aware of how much I will miss her late-night/early-morning e-mails, her sharp wit, and her relentless pursuit of excellence. Thanks, Meg, for enduring my sense of humor. I think I'll write another book just so I can work with you again. Although she is pursuing a new career outside publishing, I wish to also thank Aja Baker, former assistant editor at Sage, for her diligent work in securing the reviews and planning the revisions for this new edition. I hope she reads this. Thanks, Aja. Thanks to the following reviewers of the book, whose many suggestions were incorporated into the revision. I much appreciate their constructive comments and recommendations:

James Honeycutt, *Louisiana State University*

Katie Neary Dunleavy, *La Salle University*

Jean L. Bush-Bacelis, *Eastern Michigan University*

Deborah Whitt, *Wayne State College*

Kathryn Toelken, *University of South Alabama*

Patricia S. Hill, *The University of Akron*

Sheila Cuffy, *IPFW Fort Wayne*

Hsiu-Jung "Mindy" Chang, *Western New England College*

Rachel Alicia Griffin, *Southern Illinois University at Carbondale*

Parthenia Hilliard Franks, *Morehouse College*

Sudeshna Roy, *Stephen F. Austin State University*

A sincere thank you goes to my students, from whom I have learned a great deal about culture. One of the great pleasures of my life is the relationships I have initiated and maintained with my students. In the case of this edition, the students who contributed to the Student Voices Across Cultures essays deserve a special thanks. These students are Ahmed and Mohammad Alshaya, Ala Aldahneem, Jennifer Seidemann, Jessica Bahrke, Rodrigo Villalobos Arevalo, Lindsey Novitzke, Pengfei (Jack) Song, Chen Chen, Karen Henao Carbonell, Sebastian Friedemann, Amanda Garrity, and Morgan Johnson. Also, thanks to my colleague and friend Stephen Rupsch for his contribution.

Finally, to Stephanie, Becket, and Ellie—my family—who played such a significant role in my mental well-being while revising this new edition, they each deserve an out-of-the-ordinary thank you. They share with me the best and worst of times. I want all of them to know how important they are to me and how much I love them.

—J.W.N.
—DePere, WI

ANCILLARIES

The password-protected instructor's site at **www.sagepub.com/neuliep5e** contains an electronic test bank, powerpoints, sample syllabi, discussion questions, class activities, video and film resources, and a variety of paper assignments for use in the classroom.

The open-access student study site at **www.sagepub.com/neuliep5e** contains flascards, web quizzes, web resources, internet exercises, self-assessments from the chapters and key terms to enhance student learning.

CHAPTER 1

The Necessity of Intercultural Communication

CHAPTER OBJECTIVES

After reading this chapter, you should be able to

1. list and discuss the benefits of intercultural communication;

2. recognize the increasing racial and ethnic diversity in the U.S. population;

3. identify and discuss the eight dimensions of communication;

4. assess your degree of communication apprehension;

5. define and discuss the nature of culture;

6. identify and discuss the five contexts of intercultural communication;

7. discuss the relationship between intercultural communication, uncertainty, and anxiety;

8. assess your degree of intercultural communication apprehension;

9. identify and discuss the five fundamental assumptions of intercultural communication; and

10. assess your degree of ethnocentrism.

The history of our planet has been in great part the history of the mixing of peoples.

—Arthur M. Schlesinger, Jr.[1]

In 1804, the number of people on planet earth was one billion. In 1927, 123 years later, it was two billion. By 1960, 33 years later, it was three billion. By 1974, 14 years later, it was four billion. In the year 2012, there will be nearly seven billion (i.e., 7,000,000,000) people on planet earth. Of these, approximately 1.3 billion, or nearly 20%, are Chinese, and 1.2 billion, just over 17%, are East Indian. Approximately 310 million, about 4.5%, reside in the United States; about 3.5% are Indonesian; and just less than 3% are Brazilian. The next largest countries, in order, include Pakistan, Bangladesh, Nigeria, Russia, and Japan. The annual world population growth rate has declined in the past few decades and now hovers at about 1.1%. Over the past 200 years, the growth rate, distribution, and density of the world population has not been spread equally. Certain regions of the world have grown disproportionately in terms of the number of people, while other regions vary considerably in terms of population density (i.e., number of people per square mile). As seen in the above statistics, China and India account for nearly 40% of the world's population. African countries make up nearly 15% of the world's population, while Europe constitutes about 11%. Monaco, Singapore, Vatican City, Maldives, and Malta are the world's five most densely populated countries. Monaco, for example, has nearly 43,000 people per square mile, while the United States has about 76 people per square mile, and Canada has just over 9 people per square mile.[2]

The purpose of the above paragraph is to point out that the world's population is growing disproportionately. Along with that, something else has grown disproportionately—technology and its decentralizing role in information dissemination. In 1948, the painter and writer Wyndham Lewis wrote about a global village in his book titled *America and Cosmic Man.* Several years later, his friend Marshall McLuhan also used the term to describe how technological advances of mass media would eventually disintegrate the natural time and space barriers inherent in human communication. McLuhan predicted that through the elimination of such barriers, people would continue to interact and live on a global scale but one that would have been virtually transformed into a village.[3]

Twelve years into the 21st century, Marshall McLuhan's vision of a global village is no longer considered an abstract idea but a near certainty. Technological changes have made the world a smaller planet to inhabit. The technological feasibility of the mass media and the Internet to bring events from across the globe into our homes, businesses, and schools dramatically reduces the distance between people of different cultures and societies. Telecommunication systems, including e-mail, texting, and social networking sites such as Facebook, connect people throughout the world via satellites and fiber optics. Skype links people together from across the planet in seconds.

The essential effect of this technology is its decentralizing role in disseminating information across local, regional, national, and international borders. This means that billions of people across the planet now have access to information that was not available to them only a few years ago. Information empowers people. The ease and speed with which people of differing cultures can now communicate is stunning. In 1780—some 230 years ago—when John Adams, the second president of the United States, corresponded with his European counterparts in France, it would take as long as 6 months to send and receive letters as they traveled by ship across the Atlantic Ocean. Imagine sending a text message to a friend that takes half a year to be received! Today, it takes less than a second. Moreover, the sheer frequency and quantity of messages sent is baffling compared with what it was only a few years ago. Some sources estimate that in 2009, more than 90 trillion e-mails were sent via the Internet, averaging 250 billion e-mails a day sent by more than a billion e-mail users worldwide! And, although one in five humans on the planet can speak English, use of English is not nearly as dominant on the Internet. Of all Internet users, only about 27% use English, 23% Chinese, 8% Spanish, 5% Japanese, and about 4% each for Portuguese and German.[4]

Of course, e-mail is only one of the technological advances facilitating communication across cultures. The technological revolution has reached even remote places such as rural India. Writing in *The New York Times,* Anand Giridharadas notes that in 2009, India added more cell phone connections than any other country on the planet, with more than 15 million added per month. In addition, in India, where more than 700 million people (more than twice the number of people in the United States) live on less than $2 a day, the cost of calling is among the lowest in the world. According to Giridharadas, cell phones play a socially significant role in India, more so than in the wealthy countries where they were invented. Why? Because they give quick and easy access to the rest of the world in a place where 40% of the 1.3 billion people are illiterate and unbelievably poor. Yet there are more cell phone owners/ users in India (i.e., more than 500 million) than there are people in the United States. More importantly, cell phone technology has reached into historically impoverished slums and small towns and villages where communicating with outsiders was virtually impossible only a few years ago. According to Giridharadas, cell phones allow a class of people to cross the barriers of a rigid caste system where communicating with others outside one's level in the social hierarchy is heavily restricted. The majority of subscribers are now outside the major cities and wealthiest states. Indeed, so valued is the technology that the average cell phone bill of less than $5 per month, which represents 7% of the average Indian's income, is well worth the economic sacrifice to most Indians. If these trends continue, in 5 years, every Indian will own a cell phone.[5] And while many may think that the United States is the cell phone capital of the world, it actually ranks 72nd among 212 countries in terms of the number of cell phones per capita. The top 10 countries for number of cell phones per capita are, in order, the United Arab Emirates, Bahrain, Macau, Hong Kong, Estonia, Qatar, Israel, Lithuania, Bulgaria, and Italy.[6] Technology has linked the world.

Many college students in the United States have a Facebook account or are at least familiar with the social networking site. But unlike e-mail or cell phones, social networking sites such as Facebook are actually intentionally designed to establish and maintain relationships. So initiating a relationship with someone from across the globe is much easier now than it was only a few years ago. According to its own Factsheet, Facebook maintains that is has 500 million active users and that 70% of these (i.e., 350 million) are outside the United States. More than 70 translations are available for the site's content.[7]

Although the technological advances mentioned above facilitate the initiation and maintenance of cross-cultural relationships, the late noted historian and Pulitzer Prize winner Arthur Schlesinger warns us that history tells an ugly story of what happens when people of diverse cultural, ethnic, religious, or linguistic backgrounds converge in one place. The hostility of one group of people against another, *different* group of people is among the most instinctive of human drives. Xenophobia, the fear or contempt of that which is foreign or unknown, especially of strangers or those perceived as foreigners, is believed by many to be an innate biological response to intergroup competition. Indeed, Schlesinger contends that unless a common goal binds diverse people together, tribal hostilities will drive them apart. By replacing the conflict of political ideologies that dominated in the 20th century, ethnic, religious, and racial strife will usher in the new millennium as the explosive issue.[8]

Throughout the first decade of the new century, we witnessed ethnic, racial, and religious violence, and we continue to see such conflict today. In just the year 2011, thousands of people have died in violent religious and ethnic clashes in central Nigeria, where the mostly Muslim north region meets the predominantly Christian south. In late 2010, in Moscow, flare-ups of ethnic violence threatened Russia's stability. Russian President Medvedev announced over state television, "Crimes aimed at fanning hatred and animosity based on race, ethnic origin, or religion are especially dangerous. Such actions threaten the stability of the state." Tibet has been the scene of periodic religious and ethnic strife for 50 years. A report issued by Human Rights Watch, released in 2010, said Chinese security forces violated international law by indiscriminately beating, detaining, and fatally shooting Tibetan civilians in towns across Tibet in western China. In France, the French Senate voted overwhelmingly to ban the wearing of Islamic headscarves in public buildings and schools. Moreover, by a margin of four to one, the French people agreed with the ban. In October of 2010, German Chancellor Angela Merkel was greeted by a standing ovation from a crowd of supporters after she asserted:

> The approach [to build] a multicultural [society] and to live side by side and to enjoy each other . . . has failed, utterly failed. . . . We feel tied to Christian values. Those who don't accept them don't have a place here.

That same month, the premier of Bavaria and a member of Merkel's ruling coalition called for a halt to Turkish and Arab immigration. The results of a survey of native Germans showed that about one third of them believed the country was overrun by foreigners and that more than half believed Arabs are unpleasant people. In her speech, Merkel said the education of unemployed Germans should take priority over recruiting workers from abroad. The United Kingdom's prime minister, David Cameron, also criticized state multiculturalism in a recent speech. At a February 2011 security conference in Germany, he argued that the United Kingdom needed a stronger national identity to prevent people from turning to all kinds of extremism. These are just a few instances of the ethnic, racial, and religious conflicts across our planet.[9] But the good news is that, through intercultural communication, such conflict can be managed and reduced. To be sure, only by competently and peacefully interacting with others who are different from us can our global village survive.

THE NEED FOR INTERCULTURAL COMMUNICATION

International tensions around the globe, the most noticeable to U.S. Americans being those in the Middle East, are striking examples of the need for effective and competent intercultural communication. As mentioned above, such conflicts are often fueled by political, ethnic, and religious differences. Indeed, national conflicts within our own borders, often ignited by racial and ethnic tensions, underscore the necessity for skillful intercultural communication.

Perhaps more importantly, the need for competent intercultural communication is felt intrapersonally, within our own personal, social, and professional relationships. Consider the following situations that Jim, an undergraduate student at a Midwestern university, has faced in the past few days.

Situation #1

Jim has just met Bridget, an exchange student from England. They are talking in Jim's dorm room.

Jim: So, Bridget, are you enjoying your first few days in the U.S.?

Bridget: Yes, but I am a bit paggered, you know. Got pissed last night.

Jim: Oh . . . sorry . . . are you having problems with someone? Can I help?

Bridget: Not a'tall, oh no, nothing traumatic, just farty things, you know. Nothing to have a dicky fit over.

Jim: Ah, yeah, right.

(Jim's girlfriend, Betsy, enters the room.)

Betsy: Hello.

Jim: Hi, Betsy! Hey, this is Bridget. She's from England.

Betsy: Hi, Bridget.

Bridget: Hello. Nice to meet you. Jim and I were just having a bit of intercourse. Won't you join us?

Betsy: You were what? (leaves the room)

Jim: (Running after her) No! Betsy, that's not true! We were just talking! I swear!

Situation #2

Later that same day, Jim is trying to explain to Betsy that nothing was happening between him and Bridget when Jahan, an exchange student from India, enters the room unannounced.

Jim: (To Betsy) So, I swear we weren't doing anything except talking.

(Jahan enters)

Jahan: Hello, Jim. Who is this with you?

Jim: Oh, hi, Jahan. This is Betsy. Betsy, this is Jahan; he lives just down the hall.

Betsy: Hi, Jahan.

Jahan: Is this your girlfriend, Jim?

(Continued)

(Continued)

Jim: Ah . . . yeah, she is.

Jahan: Are you two going to marry? Have children?

Jim: Ah, well . . .

Betsy: Uh . . . we really haven't discussed that.

Jahan: Oh, I see. Is your family not wealthy enough for her, Jim? What is your father's occupation?

Jim: What?

Unfortunately, Jim has found himself in some rather awkward situations here. The misinterpretations in each of the situations above are due mostly to cultural and linguistic differences. In Bridget's England, for example, the word *paggered* means tired. The colloquialism *pissed* means to get drunk, *farty* refers to something insignificant, a *dicky fit* is an emotional outburst, and *intercourse* simply means to have conversation. Translated in terms Jim can understand, Bridget was tired because she had been drunk the night before, but she did not think it significant enough to complain. Upon meeting Betsy, she simply invited her into the conversation.

The second conversation is a bit more complicated. The late Dr. Pittu Laungani, the well-known Indian-born psychologist, has written extensively about the culture of his native India. In his writings, Laungani asserts that Indians tend to initiate social conversations with complete strangers quite easily. According to Laungani, Indians often ask, without embarrassment, very personal and delicate questions concerning one's age, marital status, occupation, income, religious beliefs, and so on. Laungani professes that Westerners need to learn that these questions are not to be taken with any offense.[10]

Benefits of Intercultural Communication

Although the challenges of an increasingly diverse world are great, the benefits are even greater. Communicating and establishing relationships with people from different cultures can lead to a whole host of benefits, including healthier communities; increased international, national, and local commerce; reduced conflict; and personal growth through increased tolerance (see Table 1.1).

Table 1.1   Benefits of Intercultural Communication

1. Healthier communities
2. Increased commerce
3. Reduced conflict
4. Personal growth through tolerance

Healthy Communities. Joan England argues that genuine community is a condition of togetherness in which people have lowered their defenses and learned to accept and celebrate their differences. England contends that we can no longer define equality as "sameness" but, instead, must value our differences—whether they be in race, gender, ethnicity, lifestyle, or even occupation or professional discipline.[11] Healthy communities are made up of individuals working collectively for the benefit of everyone, not just their own group. Through open and honest intercultural communication, people can work together to achieve goals that benefit everyone, regardless of group or culture, including the global community in the home, business, or neighborhood. Healthy communities support all community members and strive to understand, appreciate, and acknowledge each member.

Increased Commerce. Our ability to interact with persons from different cultures, both inside and outside our borders, has immense economic benefits. The top 10 countries with which the United States trades—in terms of both imports and exports—are, in order, Canada, China, Mexico, Japan, Germany, the United Kingdom, South Korea, France, Taiwan, and Brazil. In 2010, U.S. trade with these countries accounted for nearly $3 trillion (i.e., $3,000,000,000,000). Only through successful intercultural communication can such economic potentials be realized.[12]

Reduced Conflict. Conflict is inevitable; we will never be able to erase it. We can, however, through cooperative intercultural communication, reduce and manage conflict. Often, conflict stems from our inability to see another person's point of view, especially if that person is from a different culture. We develop blatant negative generalizations about the person, which are often incorrect and which lead to mistrust. Table 1.2 summarizes some of the most common stereotypes of different racial and ethnic groups in the United States, documented by researchers. Such feelings lead to defensive behavior, which fosters conflict. If we can learn to think and act cooperatively by engaging in assertive (not aggressive) and responsive intercultural communication, we can effectively manage and reduce conflict with others.

Personal Growth Through Tolerance. As you communicate with people from different cultures, you learn more about them and their way of life—including their values, history, and habits—and the substance of their personality. As your relationship develops, you start to understand them better, perhaps even empathizing with them. One of the things you will

Table 1.2 Common Stereotypes[13]

. . . About Blacks	. . . About Whites	. . . About Asians
"They're lazy."	"They think they know everything."	"They're sneaky."
"They live on welfare."	"They're all arrogant."	"They're good at math."
"They like to dance."	"They're all rich."	"I wouldn't trust them."
"They smoke crack."	"They're materialistic."	"They're really shy."

learn (eventually) is that although your cultures are different, you have much in common. As humans, we all have the same basic desires and needs; we just have different ways of achieving them. As we learn that our way is not the only way, we develop a tolerance for difference. This can be accomplished only when we initiate relationships with people who are different from ourselves. We could learn far more about Japanese culture by initiating and maintaining a relationship with a Japanese student at our college or university than we would by traveling to Japan for a 2- or 3-week vacation. Moreover, although this may sound contradictory, the more we learn about others and other cultures, the more we begin to learn about ourselves. When we observe how others conduct their lives, we begin to understand how we conduct our own lives.

Diversity in the United States

One need not travel to faraway countries to understand the need for and experience the benefits of intercultural communication. Largely because of immigration trends, cultural and ethnic diversity in the United States is a fact of life. Immigrants, in record numbers, are crossing U.S. borders. According to the latest available U.S. government statistics (i.e., 2008), just over 37 million persons living in the United States, about 12.5%, were not U.S. citizens at birth. More than half of these people were born in Latin America (i.e., the Caribbean, Central America, Mexico, and South America).[14]

Every 10 years, at the beginning of a new decade, the U.S. Department of Commerce conducts a census. The results of the 2010 census, although still being analyzed, profile the remarkable racial and ethnic diversity that has been a hallmark of American society. In 2010, there were approximately 308 million people in the United States (i.e., roughly 4.5% of the world's population). Of these people, just over 65% were White non-Hispanics, approximately 15.5% were Hispanic (any race), 12% were Black non-Hispanic, 4% were Asian or Pacific Islander, and 1% were American Indian.[15]

Both the 2000 and 2010 census point out that different racial and ethnic groups in the United States grow at different rates. For example, in 2000, White non-Hispanics made up nearly 70% of the U.S. population. In 2010, White non-Hispanics made up 65%. By the year 2050, the non-Hispanic White population will shrink to approximately 50% of the population. Conversely, the Hispanic population in 2000 made up 12.5% of the population, while in 2010, it grew to 15.5%. The Black population has remained stable at 12% in both 2000 and 2010.[16]

One of the most significant population trends in the United States is the growth of the Hispanic population. In 2010, there were 46 million Hispanics living in the United States, of which 34 million were citizens. The federal government uses the terms *Hispanic* and *Latino* interchangeably and classifies Hispanics/Latinos as an ethnic group but *not* a racial group. According to the U.S. Census Bureau, Hispanics are a heterogeneous group composed of Mexicans, Cubans, Puerto Ricans, persons from Central and South America, and persons of other Hispanic origin. Mexicans account for 66% of all Hispanics in the United States. In 2010, nearly 80% of all Hispanics/Latinos lived in the southern or western areas of the United States. In fact, 62% of all Hispanics in the United States live in just two states, California and Texas. Just over 8% live in the Midwest, and about 14% live in the Northeast. But that trend is likely to change in the upcoming decades as the Hispanic population expands geographically.[17]

In addition to the rapid growth of non-White populations in the United States, another trend is emerging: an increasing number of groups are revitalizing their ethnic traditions and promoting their cultural and ethnic uniqueness through language. Language is a vital part of maintaining one's cultural heritage, and many people become very protective of their native language. For example, in July 2002, in Brown County, Wisconsin—a county with a sizable Hmong and Hispanic community—the county Board of Commissioners made English the official language of its government and called for more spending to promote English fluency. The all-White Brown County board voted 17 to 8 to approve the measure. "It's saying this is our official language. This is what we believe in, and we should encourage English," said then Board Supervisor John Vander Leest. On the other hand, in August 2004, the Texas border town of El Cenizo—whose population is heavily Hispanic—adopted Spanish as its official language. Mayor Rafael Rodriguez said that he and most of the town's residents speak only Spanish. According to Rodriguez, "In past administrations, the meetings were done in English and they did not explain anything." The vote means that town business will be conducted in Spanish, which then will be translated into English for official documents to meet the requirements of Texas law. Rodriguez said the city council's intent was not to usurp English or create divisions but to make local government more accessible to the town's residents. "What we are looking for is that the people of the community who attend the meetings and who only speak Spanish be able to voice their opinions," Rodriguez said.[18]

According to 2009 data, nearly one in five people in the United States speaks a language other than English at home. Interestingly, more than half of these people report that they speak English very well. When these people are combined with those who speak only English at home, the overwhelming majority of the U.S. population has no difficulty speaking English.[19]

Although the United States prides itself on being a nation of immigrants, there is a growing sense of uncertainty, fear, and distrust between different cultural, ethnic, and linguistic groups. These feelings create anxiety that can foster separatism rather than unity. Arthur Schlesinger alerts us that a cult of ethnicity has arisen both among non-Anglo Whites and among non-White minorities to denounce the idea of a melting pot; to challenge the concept of "one people"; and to protect, promote, and perpetuate separate ethnic and racial communities.[20] Many Americans are frustrated, confused, and uncertain about these linguistic and definitional issues. Only through intercultural communication can such uncertainty be reduced. Only when diverse people come together and interact can they unify rather than separate. Unity is impossible without communication. Intercultural communication is a necessity.

Human Communication

Communication is everywhere. Everywhere, every day, people are communicating. Even when they are alone, people are bombarded with communication. Communication professor Charles Larson estimates that, in 2010, most Americans were exposed to more than 5,000 persuasive messages every day.[21] Most people would be miserable if they were not allowed to communicate with others. Indeed, solitary confinement is perhaps the worst form of punishment inflicted on humans. Human communication—that is, the ability to symbolize and use language—separates humans from animals. Communication with others is the essence of what it means to be human. Through communication, people conduct their lives. People define themselves via their communication with others. Communication is the vehicle by which people initiate, maintain, and terminate their relationships with others. Communication is the means by which people influence and persuade others. Through communication, local, regional, national, and international conflicts are managed and resolved.

Ironically, however, communication, and particularly one's *style* of communication, can be the source of many problems. Marriage counselors and divorce lawyers indicate that a breakdown in communication is one of the most frequently cited reasons for relational dissolution in the United States.[22] A specific kind of communication—that is, public speaking—is one of the most frequently cited fears, even more feared than death.

This book is about the ubiquitous subject labeled "communication." Specifically, this is a book about *intercultural* communication—that is, communication between people of different cultures and ethnicities. Throughout the course of this book, you will be introduced to a whole host of concepts and theories that explain the process of people of differing cultural backgrounds coming together and exchanging verbal and nonverbal messages. Chapter 1 is designed as an introductory chapter and is divided into four parts. The first part of the chapter outlines and discusses the nature of communication. This part will examine communication variables that apply to everyone, regardless of cultural background. The second part outlines and discusses culture. Culture is seen as a paradox; that is, culture is simultaneously a very subtle and clearly defined influence on human thought processes and behavior. The third part of the chapter presents a brief history of the study of intercultural communication. Finally, the last part of the chapter introduces a contextual model of intercultural communication that will serve as the organizing scheme for the rest of this book.

The Nature of Human Communication

Because of its ubiquitous nature, communication is very difficult to define. If you were to go to your university library and select 10 different introductory communication texts, the probability is that each would offer a different definition of communication. Although there is no universally agreed-on definition of communication, most communication scholars agree on certain dimensions of communication that describe its nature. Outlined below are eight of these dimensions along with eight definitions of communication (see Table 1.3). These definitions come from a variety of scholars with diverse backgrounds in the communication field.

Dimension 1: Process. Almost all communication scholars concur that communication is a process. A **process** is anything that is ongoing, ever changing, and continuous. A process does not have a specific beginning or ending point. A process is not static or at rest; it is always moving. The human body is a process; it is always aging. Communication is always developing; it is never still or motionless. There is no exact beginning or ending point of a communication exchange. Although individual verbal messages have definite beginning and ending points, the overall process of communication does not. For example, Jose and Juan meet in the hallway and greet each other. Jose says, "What up, Juan?" and Juan says, "Not much,

Table 1.3	Eight Dimensions and Definitions of Communication

1. Process	"Communication theory reflects a process point of view . . . you cannot talk about the beginning or the end of communication." (Berlo)[23]
2. Dynamic	"Communication is a transaction among symbol users in which meanings are dynamic, changing as a function of earlier usages and of changes in perceptions and metaperceptions. Common to both meanings is the notion that communication is timebound and irreversible." (Bowers & Bradac)[24]
3. Interactive–Transactive	"Communication occurs when two or more people interact through the exchange of messages." (Goss)[25]
4. Symbolic	"All the symbols of the mind, together with the means of conveying them through space and preserving them in time." (Cooley)[26]
5. Intentional	"Communication has as its central interest those behavioral situations in which a source transmits a message to a receiver(s) with conscious intent to affect the latter's behavior." (Miller)[27]
6. Contextual	"Communication always and inevitably occurs within some context." (Fisher)[28]
7. Ubiquitous	"Communication is the discriminatory response of an organism to a stimulus." (Stevens)[29]
8. Cultural	"Culture is communication . . . communication is culture." (Hall)[30]

man." Both Jose's and Juan's verbal messages have exact beginning and ending points. But to determine exactly when and where their nonverbal communication begins and ends is virtually impossible. They may not be verbally communicating with each other, but they are still communicating nonverbally. Even if they walk away from each other, they are communicating that they are no longer talking with each other. A process is something that continues to develop and change; it does not stop, nor can it reverse itself. Because communication is irreversible, it affects future communication. How Jose and Juan interact with each other today is very much influenced by how they interacted yesterday, last week, or even years ago. Think about your own relationships with your friends and how what you have said to one another in the past influences what you say today. Imagine the last time you had an argument with your boyfriend or girlfriend, for example. You may have said some things you now regret. Such interaction influences your relationships and how you interact today.

Dimension 2: Dynamic. Inextricably bound to the notion that communication is a process is that communication is dynamic. The terms process and dynamic are closely related. Part of what makes communication a process is its dynamic nature. Something that is **dynamic** is considered active or forceful. Unfortunately, communication is typically discussed as if it were some physical entity that people can hold or touch. Because communication is a dynamic process, it is impossible to capture its essence in a written definition or graphic model. This problem is not unlike that faced by a photographer who tries to capture the dynamic essence of a running horse. Certainly, the photograph can be very informative about the horse, but the camera cannot make a complete reproduction. The relationship between the fore and hind legs, the beautiful "dynamic" muscular motions, cannot be truly represented in a photograph. Any discussion of communication as a dynamic process is subject to the same kinds of limitations as is the photographer.[31] To fully appreciate the process, one must be a part of it or witness it in motion. As a dynamic process, communication is flexible, adaptive, and fluid; thus, it is impossible to identically replicate in a picture, drawing, or model.

Dimension 3: Interactive–Transactive. Communication is interactive and transactive because it occurs between people. While some might argue that people can communicate with themselves (what is called intrapersonal communication), most scholars believe that interaction between people is a fundamental dimension of communication. Communication requires the active participation of two people sending and receiving messages. Active participation means that people are consciously directing their messages to someone else.[32] This means that communication is a two-way process, or **interactive**. Likewise, to say that communication is **transactional** means that while Jose is sending messages to Juan, Juan is simultaneously sending messages to Jose. Juan's eye contact, facial expression, and body language are nonverbal messages to Jose informing him how his message is being received. Each person in an interactional setting simultaneously sends (encodes) and receives (decodes) messages. For example, when you listen to your friends talk about the great party they went to last night, it is obvious to you that they are sending you messages. At the same time as they describe the party to you, you are sending messages to them, too. Your eye contact, smiles, and other nonverbal reactions are communicating to them your interest in their story. Hence, both you and your friends are sending and receiving messages at the same time.

Dimension 4: Symbolic. That communication is symbolic is another fundamental assumption guiding most communication scholars. A **symbol** is an arbitrarily selected and learned stimulus that represents something else. Symbols can be verbal or nonverbal. Symbols are the vehicle by which the thoughts and ideas of one person can be communicated to another person. Messages are constructed with verbal and nonverbal symbols. Through symbols, meanings are transferred between people. Symbols (i.e., words) have no natural relationship with what they represent (they are arbitrarily selected and learned). For example, the verbal symbols "C.A.T." have no natural connection with cute, fuzzy animals that purr and like to be scratched. The symbols "C.A.T." have no meaning in other languages besides English (see Figure 1.1).

Nonverbal symbols are arbitrary as well. Showing someone your upright middle finger may not communicate much in some cultures. Verbal and nonverbal symbols are meaningful only to people who have learned to associate them with what they represent. People can allow just about any symbols they want to represent just about anything they want. For example, you and your friends probably communicate with one another using private symbols that no one else understands. You have your own secret code. You have words, phrases, gestures, and handshakes that only you and your friends know, understand, and use. This allows you to communicate with one another in your own "foreign" language. Drug dealers and users, for example, have an elaborate and highly rule-governed language that allows them to communicate about their illegal activities. In drug language, the phrase

Figure 1.1   Different languages use different codes.

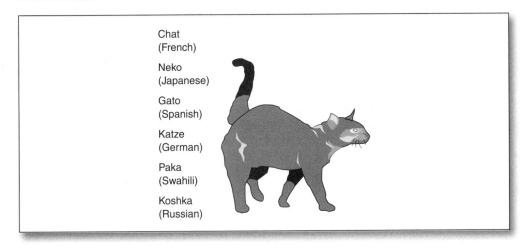

Chat
(French)

Neko
(Japanese)

Gato
(Spanish)

Katze
(German)

Paka
(Swahili)

Koshka
(Russian)

"blow a spliff" is symbolic code for "smoke a marijuana cigarette." Any verbal language (e.g., English, Chinese, Russian) is a code made up of symbols. The letters of the English alphabet (e.g., *A, B, C, . . .*) are a set of symbols that represent sounds. When we combine the individual symbols (e.g., *C + A + T*), they become meaningful. By using symbols, people can represent their thoughts and ideas through writing or speaking. Once an idea has been encoded with symbols, it becomes a message. During communication, people encode their thoughts and send them to someone else. The other person listens to the message and translates or decodes it. When Jose saw Juan, he encoded a greeting. Juan decoded (i.e., translated) the message and encoded a response. Interaction, then, is the process of encoding and decoding messages. People who speak different languages are simply using different codes.

Dimension 5: Intentional. Perhaps one of the most debated issues regarding the communication process centers on **intentionality**. On one side of the debate are those who argue that communication is intentional. On the other side are those who insist that communication can occur unintentionally. Intentional communication exists whenever two or more people consciously engage in interaction with some purpose.[33] For example, if Kyoko says to Akira, "Hey, you wanna go out to eat tonight?" and Akira responds by saying, "Yeah, that sounds like a good idea!" intentional communication surely has taken place. Unintentional **communication** may exist, however. For example, at a party, Kyoko thinks that Akira is consciously ignoring her because he interacts with several other people. Kyoko senses that Akira is consciously sending her a message when, in fact, Akira's intention is simply to talk with new friends. Akira is not intentionally ignoring Kyoko, but she thinks that he is indeed sending her a message (i.e., a nonverbal message). Since a response has been elicited in Kyoko, some communication scholars argue that communication has occurred. Three interpretations can be drawn from the above discussion. To many communication scholars, intentionality is a central property of the communication process. Others insist that any message interpreted by a person qualifies as communication whether or not the message was intentionally sent. Still others insist that all behavior, intentional or not, is informative and meaningful and, thus, is communicative. Thus, whenever a person (e.g., Kyoko in the above example) responds to some stimulus (e.g., Akira talking with other people), communication has occurred. In this book, the type of communication that will be discussed is intentional communication. This book takes the position that intentional communication, either verbal or nonverbal, is more informative than unintentional communication.

Dimension 6: Contextual. Communication is dependent on the context in which it occurs. The effects and outcomes, styles and fashions, and the resulting meaning are all dependent on the context. In this book, **context** is the cultural, physical, relational, and perceptual environment in which communication occurs. In many ways, the context defines the meaning of any messages. For example, the context of the classroom defines the kind of communication that will occur. Most students sit quietly while the professor psychologically stimulates them with a brilliant lecture. Essentially, four different kinds of context influence the process of communication: (a) the cultural and microcultural context, (b) the physical context, (c) the sociorelational context, and (d) the perceptual context. The cultural context includes all the factors and influences that make up one's culture. This context will be discussed in detail in the next section of this chapter. The physiological context is the actual geographical space or territory in which the communication takes place. For example, communication between Juan and Jose will be different when they are interacting on a busy street in a big city compared with when they are in their university library. The sociorelational context refers to social roles and group memberships (e.g., demographics). Sex, age, religious affiliation, education level, and economic status affect how one communicates and relates with others. Finally, the **perceptual context** includes all the motivations, intentions, and personality traits people bring to the communication event. When you are interacting with your professor about an examination that you just failed, you have a very different set of motivations and intentions from when you are asking someone out on a date.

Dimension 7: Ubiquitous. That communication is ubiquitous simply means that communication is everywhere, done by everyone, all the time. Humans are constantly bombarded with verbal and nonverbal messages. Wherever one goes, there is some communication happening. In fact, some scholars in the field of communication argue that it is impossible not to communicate. In their classic writings, Paul Watzlawick, Janet Beavin, and Don Jackson have argued that *one cannot not communicate*. The logic of their argument is that (a) behavior has no opposite—one cannot not behave; (b) in an interactional setting, all behavior has informational value or message value; (c) behavior is informative, and since it is informative, it is communicative; and (d) if behavior is communicative, and one cannot not behave, then one cannot not communicate.[34]

Dimension 8: Cultural. Culture shapes communication, and communication is culture bound. People from different cultures communicate differently. The verbal and nonverbal symbols we use to communicate with our friends and families are strongly influenced by our culture. Perhaps the most obvious verbal communication difference between two cultures is language. Even cultures speaking the same language have different meanings for different symbols, however. For example, although English is the dominant language spoken in the United

States and England, many words and phrases have different meanings between these two cultures. In England, to "bomb" an examination is to have performed very well. When in London, do not bother to ask for directions to the nearest bathroom or restroom; in England, it is called the "water closet" or the "WC." Australians also speak English but have a variety of colloquialisms not well understood by persons from the United States (see Table 1.4).

Table 1.4	Australian Colloquialisms

Amber Fluid = beer

Bag of Fruit = slang for men's clothing

Barbie = barbeque

Bickie = cookie

Bottler = expression for a person who performs well

Off = to describe rotten food

Tucker = food

Culture also has a dramatic effect on nonverbal communication. Nonverbal symbols, gestures, and perceptions of personal space and time vary significantly from culture to culture. In the United States, for example, people generally stand about 2 1/2 feet, or an arm's length, away from others when communicating. In many Middle Eastern cultures, people stand very close to one another when interacting, especially men (see Figure 1.2). They do this in order to smell one another's breath. In Saudi Arabia, two men walking together are likely to hold hands as a sign of trust. **Communication**, then, is the dynamic process of encoding and decoding verbal and nonverbal messages within a defined cultural, physiological, sociorelational, and perceptual context. Although many of our messages are sent intentionally, many others—perhaps our nonverbal messages—can unintentionally influence other people.

Human Communication Apprehension

Although communication is difficult to define, we know that people begin to communicate at birth and continue communicating throughout their lives. We also know that many people experience fear and anxiety when communicating with others, particularly in situations such as public speaking, class presentations, a first date, or during a job interview. The fear or anxiety people experience when communicating with others is called **communication apprehension**. In the past 40 years, a substantial body of research has accumulated regarding the nature and prevalence of communication apprehension. Jim McCroskey, considered the father of this concept, argues that nearly everyone experiences some kind of communication apprehension sometimes, but roughly one in five adults in the United States suffer from communication apprehension every time they communicate with others. McCroskey argues that experiencing communication apprehension is normal; that is, all of us experience it occasionally.

| Figure 1.2 | In many Middle Eastern cultures, men typically stand very close to one another when interacting. |

McCroskey argues that there are four types of communication apprehension: traitlike, context based, audience based, and situational. Traitlike communication apprehension is an enduring general personality predisposition where an individual experiences communication apprehension most of the time across most communication situations. Of all adults in the United States, 20% experience traitlike communication apprehension.

Context-based communication apprehension is restricted to a certain generalized context, such as public speaking, group meetings, or job interviews. Persons with context-based communication apprehension experience anxiety only in certain contexts. Audience-based communication apprehension is triggered not by the specific context but by the specific person or audience with whom one is communicating. Hence, persons with audience-based communication apprehension may experience anxiety when communicating with strangers or their superiors. College students with audience-based communication apprehension may experience anxiety when communicating with professors but not when communicating with other students. Finally, situational-based communication apprehension, experienced by virtually everyone, occurs with the combination of a specific context and a specific audience. For example, students may feel anxious interacting with professors only when they are alone with the professor in the professor's office. At other times, perhaps in the hallways or in the classroom, interacting with the professor may not be a problem.[35] To repeat, virtually everyone experiences communication apprehension at some time; if you experience such anxiety, it does not mean you are abnormal or sick. What follows is the **Personal Report of Communication Apprehension (PRCA-24)**, a scale designed to measure your degree of communication apprehension. Take a few moments and complete the scale.

Self-Assessment 1.1

Personal Report of Communication Apprehension

Directions: This instrument is composed of 24 statements concerning your feelings about communicating with other people. Please indicate in the space provided the degree to which each statement applies to you by marking whether you (1) strongly agree, (2) agree, (3) are undecided, (4) disagree, or (5) strongly disagree with each statement. There are no right or wrong answers. Many of the statements are similar to other statements. Do not be concerned about this. Work quickly; just record your first impressions.

_____ 1. I dislike participating in group discussions.

_____ 2. Generally, I am comfortable while participating in group discussions.

_____ 3. I am tense and nervous while participating in group discussions.

_____ 4. I like to get involved in group discussions.

_____ 5. Engaging in group discussion with new people makes me tense and nervous.

_____ 6. I am calm and relaxed while participating in group discussions.

_____ 7. Generally, I am nervous when I have to participate in group discussions.

_____ 8. Usually, I am calm and relaxed while participating in meetings.

_____ 9. I am very calm and relaxed when I am called upon to express an opinion at a meeting.

_____ 10. I am afraid to express myself at meetings.

_____ 11. Communicating at meetings usually makes me uncomfortable.

_____ 12. I am very relaxed when answering questions at a meeting.

_____ 13. While participating in a conversation with a new acquaintance, I feel very nervous.

_____ 14. I have no fear of speaking up in conversations.

_____ 15. Ordinarily, I am very tense and nervous in conversations.

_____ 16. Ordinarily, I am very calm and relaxed in conversations.

_____ 17. When conversing with a new acquaintance, I feel very relaxed.

_____ 18. I am afraid to speak up in conversations.

(Continued)

(Continued)

_____ 19. I have no fear of giving a speech.

_____ 20. Certain parts of my body feel very tense and rigid while giving a speech.

_____ 21. I feel relaxed while giving a speech.

_____ 22. My thoughts become confused and jumbled when I am giving a speech.

_____ 23. I face the prospect of giving a speech with confidence.

_____ 24. While giving a speech, I get so nervous I forget facts I really know.

Scoring: The PRCA-24 allows you to compute a total score and four subscores. The total score represents your degree of traitlike communication apprehension. Total scores may range from 24 to 120. McCroskey argues that any score above 72 indicates general communication apprehension. Scores above 80 indicate a very high level of communication apprehension. Scores below 59 indicate a very low level of communication apprehension.

Total PRCA Score:

Step 1. Add what you marked for Items 1, 3, 5, 7, 10, 11, 13, 15, 18, 20, 22, and 24.

Step 2. Add what you marked for Items 2, 4, 6, 8, 9, 12, 14, 16, 17, 19, 21, and 23.

Step 3. Subtract the score from Step 1 from 84 (i.e., 84 minus the score of Step 1).

Then add the score of Step 2 to that total. The sum is your PRCA score. The subscores indicate your degree of communication apprehension across four common contexts: group discussions, meetings, interpersonal conversations, and public speaking. For these scales, a score above 18 is high and a score above 23 is very high.

Subscores for Contexts:

Group Subscore: 18 + scores for Items 2, 4, and 6, minus scores for Items 1, 3, and 5.

Meeting Subscore: 18 + scores for Items 8, 9, and 10, minus scores for Items 7, 10, and 11.

Interpersonal Subscore: 18 + scores for Items 14, 16, and 17, minus scores for Items 13, 15, and 18.

Public Speaking Subscore: 18 + scores for Items 19, 21, and 23, minus scores for Items 20, 22, and 24.

The Nature of Culture

Like communication, culture is ubiquitous and has a profound effect on humans. Culture is simultaneously invisible yet pervasive. As we go about our daily lives, we are not overtly conscious of our culture's influence on us. How often have you sat in your dorm room or classroom, for example, and consciously thought about what it means to be an American? As you stand in the lunch line, do you say to yourself, "I am acting like an American"? As you sit in your classroom, do you say to yourself, "The professor is really acting like an American"?

Yet most of your thoughts, emotions, and behaviors are culturally driven. One need only step into a culture different from one's own to feel the immense impact of culture.

Culture has a direct influence on the physical, relational, and perceptual contexts. For example, the next time you enter your communication classroom, consider how the room is arranged *physically,* including where you sit and where the professor teaches, the location of the chalkboard, windows, and so on. Does the professor lecture from behind a podium? Do the students sit facing the professor? Is the chalkboard used? Next, think about your *relationship* with the professor and the other students in your class. Is the relationship formal or informal? Do you interact with the professor and students about topics other than class material? Would you consider the relationship personal or impersonal? Finally, think about your *perceptual disposition*—that is, your attitudes, motivations, and emotions about the class. Are you happy to be in the class? Do you enjoy attending? Are you nervous when the instructor asks you a question? To a great extent, the answers to these questions are contingent on your culture. The physical arrangement of classrooms, the social relationship between students and teachers, and the perceptual profiles of the students and teachers vary significantly from culture to culture.

Like communication, culture is difficult to define. To be sure, more than 50 years ago, two well-known anthropologists, Alfred Kroeber and Clyde Kluckhohn, found and examined 300 definitions of culture, no two of which were the same.[36] Perhaps too often, people think of culture only in terms of the fine arts, geography, or history. Small towns or rural communities are often accused of having no culture. Yet culture exists everywhere. There is as much culture in Willard, New Mexico (population 240), as there is in New York City, New York (population 8,400,197). The two cultures are just different. Simply put, culture is people.

Although there may not be a universally accepted definition of culture, there are a number of properties of culture that most people would agree describe its essence. In this book, **culture** is defined as *an accumulated pattern of values, beliefs, and behaviors, shared by an identifiable group of people with a common history and verbal and nonverbal symbol systems.*

Accumulated Pattern of Values, Beliefs, and Behaviors

Cultures can be defined by their value and belief systems and by the actions of their members. People who exist in the same culture generally share similar values and beliefs (see Table 1.5). In the United States, for example, individuality is highly valued. An individual's self-interest takes precedence over group interests. Americans believe that people are unique. Moreover, Americans value personal independence. Conversely, in Japan, a collectivistic and homogeneous culture, a sense of groupness and group harmony, is valued. Most Japanese see themselves as members of a group first, as individuals second. Where Americans value independence, Japanese value interdependence. The values of a particular culture lead to a set of expectations and rules prescribing how people should behave in that culture. Although many Americans prefer to think of themselves as unique individuals, most Americans behave in similar ways. Observe the students around you in your classes. Although you may prefer to think that you are very different from your peers, you are really quite similar to them. Most of your peers follow a similar behavioral pattern to your own. For example, on a day-to-day basis, most of your peers attend classes, take examinations, go to lunch, study, party, and write papers.

Table 1.5 Values Across Cultures

Saudi Arabia	Maori (New Zealand)
Islam	Land
Hospitality	Kinship
Cleanliness	Education
India	**Yemen**
Family lineage	Islam
Supernatural guidance	Self-respect and honor
Sexual inequality	Family

Americans share a similar behavioral profile. Most Americans work an average of 40 hours a week, receive some form of payment for their work, and pay some of their earnings in taxes. Most Americans spend their money on homes and cars. Almost every home in the United States has a television. Although Americans view themselves as unique individuals, most of them have very similar behavioral patterns.

An Identifiable Group of People With a Common History

Because the members of a particular culture share similar values, beliefs, and behaviors, they are identifiable as a distinct group. In addition to their shared values, beliefs, and behaviors, the members of a particular culture share a common history. Any culture's past inextricably binds it to the present and guides its future. At the core of any culture are traditions that are passed on to future generations (see Figure 1.3). In many cultures, history is a major component of the formal and informal education systems. To learn a culture's history is to learn that culture's values. One way that children in the United States develop their sense of independence, for example, is by learning about the Declaration of Independence, one of this country's most sacred documents. Elementary school children in Iran learn about the historical significance of the political and religious revolution that took place in their culture in the 1970s and 1980s. Russian children learn about the arts in Russian history—for example, famous Russian composers, including Tchaikovsky, Rachmaninoff, and Stravinsky. The art of the past helps Russians remember their culture and history as they face disruptive social and political crises. Such historical lessons are the glue that binds people together.

Verbal and Nonverbal Symbol Systems

One of the most important elements of any culture is its communication system. The verbal and nonverbal symbols with which the members of a culture communicate are culture bound. Seeing the difference between the verbal codes of any two cultures is easy. For instance, the dominant verbal code in the United States is English, whereas the dominant verbal code in Mexico is Spanish. But although two cultures may share the same verbal code,

Figure 1.3 Children learn the values, norms, and behaviors of their culture at an early age.

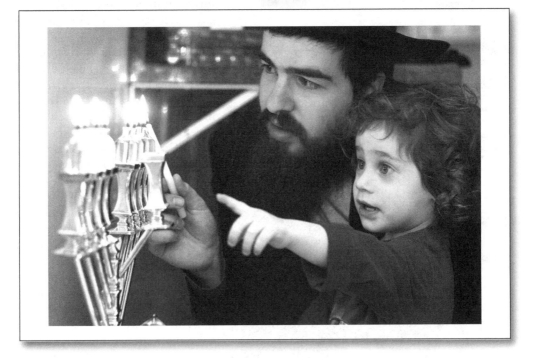

they may have dramatically different verbal styles. Most White Americans, for example, use a direct, instrumental, personal style when speaking English. Many Native Americans who also speak English use an indirect, impersonal style and may prefer the use of silence over words.[37]

Nonverbal code systems vary significantly across cultures as well. Nonverbal communication includes the use of body language, gestures, facial expressions, voice, smell, personal and geographical space, time, and artifacts (see Figure 1.4). Body language can communicate a great deal about one's culture. When an adult interacts with a young child in the United States, for example, it is not uncommon for the adult to pat the child's head. This nonverbal gesture is often seen as a form of endearment and is culturally acceptable. In Thailand, however, where the head is considered the seat of the soul, such a gesture is unacceptable. Belching during or after a meal is viewed by most Americans as rude and impolite, perhaps even disgusting. But in parts of Korea and the Middle East, belching after a meal might be interpreted as a compliment to the cook.[38]

People communicate nonverbally through smell also. Americans, in particular, seem obsessed with the smell of the human body and home environment. Think of all the products you used this morning before you left for class that were designed to mask the natural scent of your body, including soap, toothpaste, mouthwash, deodorant, and cologne and/or perfume. Persons from other cultures often complain that Americans tend to smell antiseptic.

| Figure 1.4 | Nonverbal communication, including body language, can communicate a great deal about one's culture. |

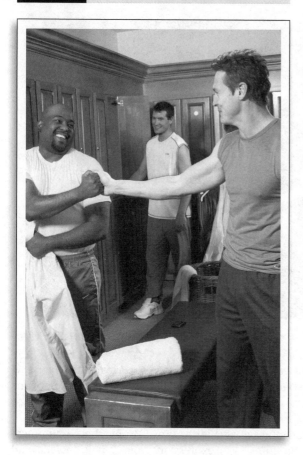

Microcultural Groups

Within most cultures, groups of people—or **microcultures**—coexist within the mainstream society. Microcultures exist within the broader rules and guidelines of the dominant cultural milieu but are distinct in some way, perhaps racially or linguistically, or via their sexual orientation, age, or even occupation. In some ways, everyone is a member of some microcultural group. Microcultures often have histories that differ from the dominant cultural group. In many cases, microcultural groups are subordinate in some way, perhaps politically or economically.

In the United States, Native American tribes might be considered microcultures. The Amish of Lancaster County, Pennsylvania, also can be considered a microcultural group. Although the Amish are subject to most of the same laws as any other group of citizens, they have unique values and communication systems that differentiate them from mainstream American life. For example, Amish children are exempt from compulsory attendance in public schools after eighth grade. Although almost all Amish speak English, when they interact among themselves, they speak German. During church services, a form of High German is used. Hence, most Amish of Lancaster County speak three languages.

The Study of Intercultural Communication[39]

Hopefully, we now have an understanding of the word communication and the idea of culture. So, what happens when people from different cultures come together and communicate with one another? We call that process intercultural communication. Compared with many other academic disciplines, the study of intercultural communication is very young. The histories of other academic fields such as math, biology, philosophy, and psychology date back hundreds and, in some cases, thousands of years. But the academic discipline of intercultural communication can be traced back only a few decades, specifically to the year 1959 and the publication of Edward T. Hall's book *The Silent Language*. Edward T. Hall is generally recognized as the founder of the academic discipline we call intercultural communication. Although the term intercultural had been used prior to Hall's work, it is thought that Hall was the first to use the term intercultural communication.

Edward Hall held three university degrees (i.e., BA, MA, and PhD) in anthropology. Anthropology is the study of the origin, the behavior, and the physical, social, and cultural development of humans. Hall earned his doctorate in anthropology in 1942 when the United States was involved in the Second World War. During this period, traditional approaches in anthropology focused on studying a single culture at a time. So a particular anthropologist might focus his or her studies on, say, the Navajo or Hopi Indians of the American Southwest, as did Hall. Hall often referred to this as a macrolevel approach to culture. Among the many significant influences on Hall's approach to his studies was anthropologist Franz Boas. The term *cultural relativism* is often attributed to him.

Boas believed, as did Hall, that humans are inherently ethnocentric (i.e., believing that one's native culture is the standard by which other cultures are observed and judged) and that our observations of other cultures are necessarily biased in favor of our native cultural background. For example, a child raised in Germany, Iran, or China is taught that his or her cultural traditions, values, and customs are the preferred and accepted standards by which one should conduct his or her life. Consequently, an individual from a particular culture cannot draw conclusions about some other culture's traditions, values, and customs without some inherent bias. Moreover, Boaz believed that any particular culture is an adaptation to and a distinctive product of a unique set of historical, social, and environmental conditions. As these conditions vary, cultures vary accordingly, and in this sense, there is no correct culture.

Following World War II, the U.S. Congress established the Foreign Service Institute (FSI). FSI is the federal government's primary training institution for officers and support personnel of the U.S. foreign affairs community, preparing American diplomats and other professionals to advance U.S. foreign affairs interests overseas and in Washington. In the early 1950s, Hall taught at FSI and soon discovered that the traditional ways of teaching about macrolevel culture, from an anthropological perspective, were not effective in training FSI personnel how to interact with persons from different cultures. So Hall and others began to rethink how to teach about culture and soon developed a new curriculum that eventually became known as intercultural communication.

In this new curriculum, scholars focused on intercultural communication—that is, how people from different cultures interact *with one another*—rather than on how members of a particular culture interact within their culture. This new curriculum also emphasized the nonverbal elements of intercultural communication. Hall was especially interested in the study of how cultures manage the nonverbal channels of time (chronemics), space (proxemics), and body language (kinesics). One of Hall's most fascinating insights was how *invisible* culture is to its own members—that is, how most people are so unaware of their own cultural ways of living. This new approach also embraced Boas's idea of cultural relativism in that cultures should be judged only from within their specific cultural context and that cultural traditions, beliefs, and behaviors are to be evaluated on that culture's unique set of historical, social, and environmental conditions.

In 1959, Hall published *The Silent Language,* which sold more than 500,000 copies in its first 10 years and is considered the seminal work in the field. In the book, Hall asserted that *culture is communication.* By the late 1960s, we saw the first intercultural communication courses being offered at universities. In 1970, the International Communication Association established a Division of Intercultural Communication. L. S. Harms's 1970 book, titled *Intercultural Communication,* is thought to be the first textbook on the subject. By 1975, the

Speech Communication Association established the Division of Intercultural Communication, and in 1977, the *International Journal of Intercultural Relations* began publication.

A Contextual Model of Intercultural Communication

Intercultural communication occurs whenever a minimum of two persons from different cultures or microcultures come together and exchange verbal and nonverbal symbols. A central theme throughout this book is that intercultural communication is contextual. A contextual model of intercultural communication is presented in Figure 1.5. According to the model, intercultural communication occurs within and between a variety of interconnected contexts, including cultural, microcultural, environmental, perceptual, and sociorelational contexts.

The term *context* refers to the setting, situation, circumstances, background, and overall framework within which communication occurs. For example, when you interact with your friends, you interact in some *physical context,* such as your dorm room. You also interact within a *social context*—that is, friend to friend. You also interact within a *psychological context*—your thoughts and emotions about your friend. The contextual model of intercultural communication attempts to identify the various contexts that define what happens when a person from Culture A communicates with a person from Culture B. As we walk through the contextual model of intercultural communication, please note that the model is both conceptually and graphically consistent.

Figure 1.5 A Contextual Model of Intercultural Communication

The largest, outer circle of the model represents the cultural context. All communicative exchanges between persons occur within some culture. The cultural context represents *an accumulated pattern of values, beliefs, and behaviors, shared by an identifiable group of people with a common history and verbal and nonverbal symbol systems*. So, whenever you and someone from a different culture come together and interact, you are within a cultural context. In this textbook, the cultural context is the focus of Chapter 2.

The next largest circle in the model is the microcultural context (Figure 1.6). As mentioned earlier, within most cultures, separate groups of people coexist. These groups, called microcultures, are in some way different from the larger cultural milieu. Sometimes the difference is via ethnicity, race, or language. Conceptually, microcultures exist within a larger culture; notice that in the model, the microculture is within the cultural context. Often, microcultures are treated differently by the members of the larger culture. Some people refer to microcultural groups as *minority groups* or *subcultures*. But those terms will not be used here. Microcultures are the focus of Chapter 3.

The next largest circle in the model is the **environmental context** (Figure 1.7). This circle represents the physical, geographical location of the interaction. While culture prescribes the overall rules for communication, the physical location indicates when and where the specific rules apply. For example, in the United States there are rules about yelling. Depending on the physical location, yelling can be prohibited or encouraged. In a church, yelling is generally prohibited, whereas at a football game, yelling is the preferred method of communicating.

Figure 1.6   The Cultural and Microcultural Contexts

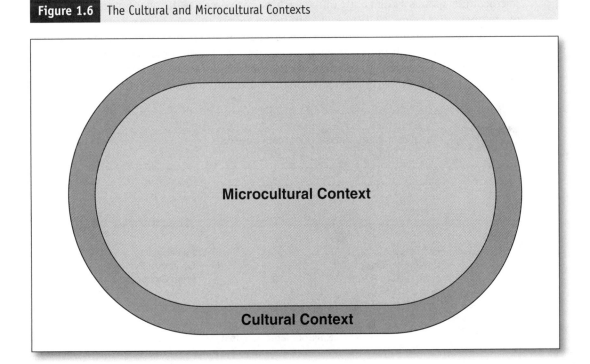

Figure 1.7   The Cultural, Microcultural, and Environmental Contexts

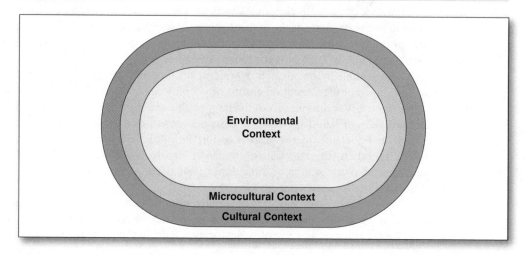

The environmental context includes the physical geography, architecture, landscape design, and even the climate of a particular culture. All these environmental factors play a key role in how people communicate. In the model, the environmental context is within the microcultural and cultural contexts. Conceptually, this is because one's culture and membership in microcultural groups significantly influence how one perceives the environment. For example, temperatures below 32 degrees (i.e., freezing) are not thought of as extreme to a person raised in International Falls, Minnesota. But to a person raised in Tucson, Arizona, they may seem unbearable. In this book, the environmental context is discussed in Chapter 4.

The two circles within the environmental context represent the perceptual context(s) (Figure 1.8). The perceptual context refers to the individual characteristics of each interactant,

Figure 1.8   The Environmental and Perceptual Contexts

Figure 1.9   A Contextual Model of Intercultural Communication

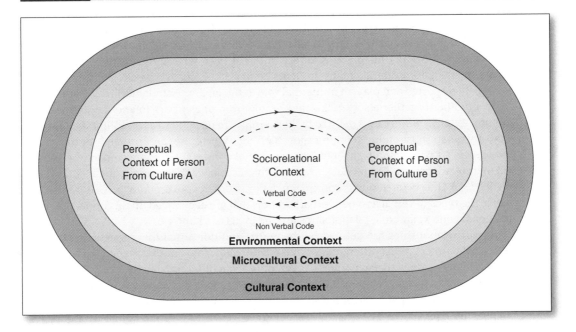

including cognitions, attitudes, dispositions, and motivations. Specifically, the perceptual context refers to how an individual gathers, stores, and retrieves information. Humans gather information via their senses—that is, through sight, sound, taste, touch, and smell. We then store the information in our memories and retrieve it for later use. Although the ability to gather, store, and retrieve information is fundamentally human, it is also affected by culture. Many of the attitudes, beliefs, and values that you hold were taught to you by your culture. For example, what smells good to you is cultural. The music you listen to is also largely a cultural by-product. Moreover, how an individual develops attitudes about others, including stereotypes, varies from culture to culture. The perceptual context is the emphasis of Chapter 5.

The circles connecting the perceptual contexts in the model form the **sociorelational context** (Figure 1.9). This refers to the relationship between the interactants. Whenever two people come together and interact, they establish a relationship. Within this relationship, each person assumes a role. Right now, you are assuming the role of student; the person teaching your communication class is assuming the role of teacher. So, in a very real sense, you are having a relationship with your teacher—that is, a student-teacher relationship. Roles prescribe how people should behave. Most of the people with whom you interact are related to you via your role as student. The reason you interact with so many professors is because you are a student. What you interact about—that is, the topic of your interaction—is also defined by your role as student; you and your professors interact about courses. How you interact with your professor—that is, the style of talk (e.g., polite language)—is also prescribed by your role as student. The language and style of your talk with your professor is probably very different from the language and style of talk you use when you go back to your dorm room and interact with your friends. Probably the last 10 people with whom you interacted were directly related to you via your role as student. When you go back to your hometown during semester break and step into the role of son/daughter or brother/sister, you are assuming a different role and your interaction changes accordingly. Your interaction varies as a function of what role you are assuming.

Roles vary from culture to culture. Although in just about every culture there are student and teacher role relationships, how those roles are defined varies significantly. What it means to be a student in the United States is very different from what it means to be a student in Japan. In Japan, for example, many students go to school 6 days a week. Japanese teachers are highly respected and play an influential role in the Japanese student's life. What it means to be a mother or father also varies considerably from one culture to another. In the Masai culture of Kenya, a woman is defined by her fertility. To be defined as a mother in Masai culture, a woman must endure circumcision (i.e., clitoridectomy), an arranged marriage, and wife beating.[40] Conceptually, people (i.e., perceptual contexts) are connected to one another via their relationships. The model shows this connection via the sociorelational context (see Figure 1.9). The sociorelational context links the two perceptual contexts. One's roles prescribe the types of verbal and nonverbal symbols that are exchanged. In this book, the sociorelational context and role relationships are the focus of Chapter 6.

All our relationships are defined by the verbal and nonverbal messages we send to our relational partners. What differentiates one relationship from another is the verbal and nonverbal things we do with each other. For example, what differentiates your relationship with your teacher from your relationship with your best friend is the verbal and nonverbal things you do with each other. Notice that in the contextual model, the sociorelational context is graphically represented by two circles labeled nonverbal and verbal code (see Figure 1.9). Again, the verbal and nonverbal messages define the relationship, and the relationship connects the perceptual contexts.

The nonverbal circle is the larger of the two and is represented by a continuous line. The verbal circle is smaller and is represented as a series of dashes in the shape of a circle. The nonverbal message circle is larger than the verbal message circle because the majority of our communicative behavior is nonverbal. Whether we are using words or not, we are communicating nonverbally through eye contact, body stance, and space. In addition, our nonverbal behavior is ongoing; we cannot *not* behave. The verbal message circle is formed by a series of dashes to represent the *digital* quality of verbal communication.[41] By digital, we mean that, unlike our nonverbal communication, our verbal communication is made up of words that have recognizable and discrete beginning and ending points. A word is like a digit. We can start and stop talking with words. However, our nonverbal behavior goes on continuously. Chapter 7 concentrates on verbal communication codes, and Chapter 8 centers on nonverbal codes.

The general theme of this book, as represented in the model, is that intercultural communication is defined by the interdependence of these various contexts. The perceptual contexts combine to create the sociorelational context, which is defined by the verbal and nonverbal messages sent. The sociorelational context is influenced by the environmental context and defined by the microcultural and cultural contexts. These contexts combine in a complex formula to create the phenomenon of intercultural communication.

Intercultural Communication and Uncertainty

When we interact with someone from a different culture, we are faced with a lot of **uncertainty**. We may not know anything about the person's culture, values, habits, behavior, dress, and so on. We may not know what to say or do in such circumstances. This uncertainty about the other person may make us feel nervous and anxious. Communication theorist Charles Berger contends that the task of interacting with someone from a different culture who may look, act, and communicate differently presents the intercultural communicator with some complex predictive and explanatory problems. To some extent, to effectively interact with someone from a different culture, we must be able to predict how our interaction partner is likely to behave and, based on those predictions, select our appropriate verbal and nonverbal messages.[42]

Berger theorizes that whenever we come together and interact with a stranger, our primary concern is to reduce uncertainty, especially when the other person is someone with whom we will interact again. Often, when we are faced with high levels of uncertainty, we experience anxiety. In high-uncertainty situations, our primary goal is to reduce uncertainty and to increase the predictability about the other. This can be accomplished via specific verbal and nonverbal communication strategies such as question asking and appropriate nonverbal expressiveness.[43]

Some types of communication situations may be more anxiety producing than others. For example, Buss argues that situations that are novel, unfamiliar, or dissimilar lead to increased anxiety. Those situations containing new, atypical, or conspicuously different stimuli are likely to increase our sense of anxiety. Based on these criteria, initial interaction with someone, or interacting with someone from a different culture, may produce heightened anxiety.[44]

Intercultural communication experts William Gudykunst and Young Kim have argued that when we interact with people from different cultures, we tend to view them as strangers. Strangers are unknown people who are members of different groups. Anyone entering a relatively unknown or unfamiliar environment falls under the rubric of "stranger." Interaction with people from different cultures tends to involve the highest degree of "strangerness" and the lowest degree of familiarity. Thus, there is greater uncertainty in initial interaction with strangers than with people with whom we are familiar. According to Gudykunst and Kim, actual or anticipated interaction with members of different groups (e.g., cultures or ethnic groups different from our own) leads to anxiety.[45] If we are too anxious about interacting with strangers, we tend to avoid them. Communication researchers Jim Neuliep and Jim McCroskey state that this type of communication anxiety can be labeled **intercultural communication apprehension**—that is, the fear or anxiety associated with either real or anticipated interaction with people from different groups, especially different cultural or ethnic groups.[46]

Intercultural Communication Apprehension

Successfully interacting with someone from a different culture requires a degree of communication competence. According to Brian Spitzberg, most models of communication competence include cognitive, affective, and behavioral components. The cognitive component refers to how much one knows about communication. The affective component includes one's motivation to approach or avoid communication. The behavioral component refers to the skills one has to interact competently. An interculturally competent communicator is *motivated* to communicate, *knowledgeable* about how to communicate, and *skilled* in communicating. In addition, an interculturally competent communicator is *sensitive* to the expectations of the context in which communication occurs. Competent communicators interact effectively by adapting messages appropriately to the context. Competent communicators understand the rules, norms, and

STUDENT VOICES ACROSS CULTURES

Jennifer Seidemann

St. Norbert College 2010

Elementary Education and Spanish

Studied Abroad in Toledo, Spain, Fall 2008

During my experience in Spain, I learned a lot about the Spanish culture and how it compares and contrasts with my own culture in the United States. I found that Spanish natives tend to avoid eye contact and relations with people they do not know. Back at home, I was used to being able to walk down the street and smile or say hello to anybody who walked by, regardless of whether or not I knew them personally. In Spain, this was not the common custom. Eye contact was diverted from the unknown. I found that if I did smile or say hello to people I did not know, the response from them was somewhat cold and confused. The only time eye contact was acceptable was if the person was familiar or if the eye contact was made with a sexual intention. It was not that the people were unfriendly, because if I asked a question about locations or directions, they always seemed helpful. But my initial attempt for interaction through eye contact and greetings was met with skepticism and insecurity.

After studying abroad and taking the course about intercultural communication, I learned that the differences in willingness to make eye contact and communicate with the unknown were based on the culture's uncertainty avoidance. Here in the United States, we have a much weaker uncertainty avoidance than they do in Spain. The unknown or the uncertain aspects of our lives are better tolerated here than in other cultures with a strong uncertainty avoidance. Both the experience in Spain and the course taught me how to embrace and understand the differences between cultures in our world, and I feel much more comfortable in my relationships with people from abroad.

expectations of the relationship and do not significantly violate them. Communicators are effective to the degree that their goals are accomplished successfully.[47]

According to Neuliep and McCroskey, a person's affective orientation toward intercultural communication involves the individual's degree of motivation to approach or avoid a given intercultural context or person. Communication studies indicate that at least 20 % of the U.S. adult population experiences high levels of fear or anxiety even when communicating with members of their own culture. Other studies indicate that 99 % of Americans experience communication apprehension at some time in their lives, perhaps during a job interview, a first date, and so on. One outcome of communication apprehension is to avoid communication. When people feel anxious about communicating with others, they tend to avoid such situations.

Given that intercultural communication may be more anxiety producing than other forms of communication, the number of people suffering from intercultural communication apprehension may be considerable. Identifying such individuals may be the first step toward more effective and successful intercultural communication. Self-Assessment 1.2 is an instrument called the Personal Report of Intercultural Communication Apprehension (PRICA). This scale was developed by communication researchers Neuliep and McCroskey. The PRICA is similar to the Personal Report of Communication Apprehension that you completed earlier in this chapter. The difference between these two scales is that the PRICA assesses your degree of apprehension about communicating with someone from a culture different from yours. After completing each scale, you can compare your scores.

The PRICA instrument is composed of 14 statements concerning your feelings about communication with people from other cultures. Please indicate in the space provided the degree to which each statement applies to you by marking whether you (1) strongly agree, (2) agree, (3) are undecided, (4) disagree, or (5) strongly disagree with each statement. There are no right or wrong

Self-Assessment 1.2

Personal Report of Intercultural Communication Apprehension[48]

(1) strongly agree, (2) agree, (3) undecided, (4) disagree, or (5) strongly disagree

_____ 1. Generally, I am comfortable interacting with a group of people from different cultures.

_____ 2. I am tense and nervous while interacting in group discussions with people from different cultures.

_____ 3. I like to get involved in group discussions with others who are from different cultures.

_____ 4. Engaging in a group discussion with people from different cultures makes me tense and nervous.

_____ 5. I am calm and relaxed when interacting with a group of people who are from different cultures.

_____ 6. While participating in a conversation with a person from a different culture I feel very nervous.

_____ 7. I have no fear of speaking up in a conversation with a person from a different culture.

_____ 8. Ordinarily, I am very tense and nervous in conversations with a person from a different culture.

_____ 9. Ordinarily, I am very calm and relaxed in conversations with a person from a different culture.

_____ 10. While conversing with a person from a different culture, I feel very relaxed.

_____ 11. I'm afraid to speak up in conversations with a person from a different culture.

_____ 12. I face the prospect of interacting with people from different cultures with confidence.

_____ 13. My thoughts become confused and jumbled when interacting with people from different cultures.

_____ 14. Communicating with people from different cultures makes me feel uncomfortable.

Scoring: To score the instrument, reverse your original response for Items 2, 4, 6, 8, 11, 13, and 14. For example, for each of these items $1 = 5$, $2 = 4$, $3 = 3$, $4 = 2$, and $5 = 1$. If your original score for Item 2 was 1, change it to a 5. If your original score for Item 4 was a 2, change it to a 4, and so on. After reversing the score for these 7 items, sum all 14 items. Scores cannot be higher than 70 or lower than 14. Higher scores (e.g., 50–70) indicate high intercultural communication apprehension. Low scores (e.g., 14–28) indicate low intercultural communication apprehension.

answers, and many of the statements are designed to be similar to other statements. Do not be concerned about this. Work quickly and record your first impressions. Responding to these statements as honestly as possible is very important; otherwise, your score will not be valid.

To the degree that you answered the items honestly, your score is a fairly reliable and valid assessment of your motivation to approach or avoid intercultural communication. Spitzberg argues that as your motivation increases, so does your confidence. As confidence increases, intercultural communication competence also is likely to increase. People who are nervous and tense about interacting with people from different cultures are less likely to approach intercultural communication situations and probably are not confident about encountering new people from different cultures.[49]

FUNDAMENTAL ASSUMPTIONS ABOUT INTERCULTURAL COMMUNICATION

A central premise of this book is that intercultural communication is a complex combination of the cultural, microcultural, environmental, perceptual, and sociorelational contexts between two people who are encoding and decoding verbal and nonverbal messages. Because of the complexity of this process, a fundamental assumption about intercultural communication is that, during intercultural communication, the message sent is usually not the message received.

Assumption #1: During intercultural communication, the message sent is usually not the message received. Whenever people from different cultures come together and exchange messages, they bring with them a whole host of thoughts, values, emotions, and behaviors that were planted and cultivated by culture. As we have said, intercultural communication is a symbolic activity where the thoughts and ideas of one person are encoded into a verbal or nonverbal message format and then transmitted through some channel to another person who must decode it, interpret it, and respond to it. This process of encoding, decoding, and interpreting is filled with cultural noise. Noted intercultural communication scholar William Gudykunst has asserted that, during intercultural communication, culture acts as a filter through which all messages, both verbal and nonverbal, must pass. To this extent, all intercultural exchanges are necessarily, to a greater or lesser extent, charged with ethnocentrism. Hence, during intercultural communication, the message sent is not the message received.[50]

Ethnocentrism refers to the idea that one's own culture is the center of everything and all other groups (or cultures) are scaled and rated with reference to it. Sociologist W. G. Sumner argued that ethnocentrism nourishes a group's pride and vanity while looking on outsiders, or out-groups, with contempt.[51] Although culture may mediate the extent to which we experience ethnocentrism, it is thought to be universal. One of the effects of ethnocentrism is that it clouds our perception of others. We have a tendency to judge others, and their communication, based on the standards set by our own culture. Neuliep and McCroskey have argued that the concept of ethnocentrism is essentially descriptive and not necessarily pejorative. Ethnocentrism may serve a valuable function when one's in-group is under attack or threatened. Moreover, ethnocentrism forms the basis for patriotism, group loyalty, and the willingness to sacrifice for one's own group. To be sure, however, ethnocentrism can be problematic. In not looking past their own culture, people see little importance in understanding other cultures. At high levels, ethnocentrism is an obstacle to effective intercultural communication.[52]

Neuliep and McCroskey have developed the **GENE** Scale, which is designed to measure ethnocentrism. This scale and the directions for completing it are presented below.

Self-Assessment 1.3

GENE (Generalized Ethnocentrism) Scale

Directions: The GENE Scale is composed of 22 statements concerning your feelings about your culture and other cultures. In the space provided to the left of each item, indicate the degree to which the statement applies to you by marking whether you (5) strongly agree, (4) agree, (3) are neutral, (2) disagree, or (1) strongly disagree with the statement. There are no right or wrong answers. Some of the statements are similar. Remember, everyone experiences some degree of ethnocentrism. Fortunately, as we will see in Chapter 5, ethnocentrism can be managed and reduced. Be honest! Work quickly and record your first response.

_____ 1. Most other cultures are backward compared to my culture.

_____ 2. My culture should be the role model for other cultures.

_____ 3. People from other cultures act strange when they come into my culture.

_____ 4. Lifestyles in other cultures are just as valid as those in my culture.

_____ 5. Other cultures should try to be more like my culture.

_____ 6. I'm not interested in the values and customs of other cultures.

_____ 7. People in my culture could learn a lot from people of other cultures.

_____ 8. Most people from other cultures just don't know what's good for them.

_____ 9. I respect the values and customs of other cultures.

_____ 10. Other cultures are smart to look up to our culture.

_____ 11. Most people would be happier if they lived like people in my culture.

_____ 12. I have many friends from other cultures.

_____ 13. People in my culture have just about the best lifestyles of anywhere.

_____ 14. Lifestyles in other cultures are not as valid as those in my culture.

_____ 15. I'm very interested in the values and customs of other cultures.

_____ 16. I apply my values when judging people who are different.

_____ 17. I see people who are similar to me as virtuous.

_____ 18. I do not cooperate with people who are different.

_____ 19. Most people in my culture just don't know what is good for them.

(Continued)

(Continued)

_____ 20. I do not trust people who are different.

_____ 21. I dislike interacting with people from different cultures.

_____ 22. I have little respect for the values and customs of other cultures.

Scoring: To determine your ethnocentrism score, complete the following steps:

Step 1: Add your responses to Items 4, 7, and 9.

Step 2: Add your responses to Items 1, 2, 5, 8, 10, 11, 13, 14, 18, 20, 21, and 22.

Step 3: Subtract the sum from Step 1 from 18 (i.e., 18 minus Step 1 sum).

Step 4: Add the results of Step 2 and Step 3. This sum is your generalized ethnocentrism score (note that not all items are used in scoring). Higher scores indicate higher ethnocentrism. Scores above 55 are considered high ethnocentrism.

Assumption #2: Intercultural communication is primarily a nonverbal act between people. Some foreign language teachers might have us believe that competency in a foreign language is tantamount to effective and successful intercultural communication in the culture that speaks that language. To be sure, proficiency in a foreign language expedites the intercultural communication experience, but intercultural communication is primarily and fundamentally a nonverbal process. The expression of intimacy, power, and status among communicators is typically accomplished nonverbally through paralinguistic cues, proxemics, haptics, oculesics, and olfactics. In Korea, for example, one's hierarchical position is displayed via vocal tone and pitch. When a subordinate is offered an important piece of paper, such as a graded exam from a respected professor, he or she grasps it with both hands (not just one), accompanied with a slight nod of the head and indirect eye contact—all nonverbal signs of deference.

The well-known anthropologist Edward Hall has argued that people from different cultures live in different sensory worlds. Hall claims that people from different cultures engage in a selective screening of sensory information that ultimately leads to different perceptions of experience.[53] Regarding olfactics (smell), most cultures establish norms for acceptable and unacceptable scents associated with the human body. When people fail to fit into the realm of olfactic cultural acceptability, their odor signals others that something is wrong with their physical, emotional, or mental health. In the United States, we are obsessed with masking certain smells, especially those of the human body. In Western and Westernized cultures, body odor is regarded as unpleasant and distasteful, and great efforts are expended in its removal. Many Muslims believe that cleanliness of the body and purity of the soul are related. Muslim women are told to purify themselves after menstruation. Cleanliness is prescribed before and after meals. As we will see in Chapter 8, our nonverbal messages complement, augment, accent, substitute for, and repeat our verbal messages.

Assumption #3: Intercultural communication necessarily involves a clash of communicator style. In the United States, talk is a highly valued commodity. People are routinely evaluated by their speech. Yet silence—that is, knowing when *not* to speak—is a fundamental prerequisite for linguistic and cultural competence.[54] The use and interpretation of silence varies dramatically across cultures. In many collectivistic cultures, such as Japan and Korea, silence can carry more meaning than words, especially in the maintenance of intimate relationships. In fact, the Japanese and some Native American tribes in the United States believe that the expression of relational intimacy is best accomplished nonverbally. They believe that having to put one's thoughts and emotions into words somehow cheapens and discounts them.

In the United States, we value, and employ, a direct and personal style of verbal communication. Personal pronouns are an essential ingredient to the composition of just about any utterance. Our motto is "Get to the point," "Don't beat around the bush," "Tell it like it is," "Speak your mind." Many cultures, however, prefer an indirect and impersonal communication style. In these cultures, there is no need to articulate every message. True understanding is implicit, coming not from words but from actions in the environment where speakers provide only hints or insinuations. The Chinese say, "One should use the eyes and ears, not the mouth" and "Disaster emanates from careless talk." The Chinese consider the wisest and most trustworthy person to be the one who listens, watches, and restricts his or her verbal communication.[55]

Assumption #4: Initial intercultural communication is a group phenomenon experienced by individuals. Whenever we interact with a person from a different culture, especially early in our relationship with him or her, we carry with us assumptions and impressions of that other person. The specific verbal and nonverbal messages that we exchange are usually tailored for the person based on those assumptions and impressions. Often, these are based on characteristics of the other person by virtue of his or her membership in groups such as culture, race, sex, age, and occupation. In other words, we have a tendency to see others not as individuals with unique thoughts, ideas, and goals but, rather, as "an Asian" or "a woman" or "an old person" or "a cab driver." In other words, we do not see the person—we see the groups to which the person belongs. The problem with this is that group data may not be a reliable source on which to construct our messages. Because someone belongs to a specific racial, ethnic, sex, or age group does not necessarily mean that he or she takes on the thoughts, behaviors, and attitudes associated with such groups. Thus, the potential for miscommunication is great. So, during initial intercultural communication, we have to be mindful that, while the person with whom we are interacting is from a different cultural group, he or she is also an individual. Once we further develop a relationship with that person, we will start to see the relationship as interpersonal rather than intercultural. We will further discuss this in Chapter 9.[56]

Assumption #5: Intercultural communication is a cycle of stress and adaptation. As mentioned earlier in this chapter, when we come together with a person from a different culture, we may feel uncertain, apprehensive, and anxious. Such feelings are stressful. Hence, sometimes intercultural communication is stressful. The good news is that we can learn and adapt to such stress and eventually grow. During intercultural communication, we have to be mindful that the communication strategies we use with persons with whom we are familiar may not be effective with persons from other cultures. Thus, we have to learn to adapt and adjust our communication style. We have to recognize that we will make mistakes, learn from them, adapt, and move on. A good beginning point is to recognize that people from different cultures are different—not better or worse, but simply different. Once we are able to do this, we can adjust and adapt our verbal and nonverbal messages accordingly and become competent interactants.[57]

The Ethics of Intercultural Communication

A recurring theme throughout this book is ethics. Ethics involve judgments about what is right and wrong in the course of human conduct. Ethics set a standard by which judgments of right and wrong are decided. Although some scholars distinguish between ethics and morals, we will treat the two terms interchangeably. Ethics become salient (i.e., particularly relevant) whenever human behavior and decision making are conscious, voluntary, and impact others. Ethics should not be confused with, nor are they necessarily linked to, religion. While most religions profess and advocate strict ethical standards, ethics apply to non-religious people as well as religious people. One need not be religious to act ethically. Moreover, ethics are not synonymous with whatever is legal. While legal codes integrate ethical standards into laws that guide and control the behavior of citizens, they may not necessarily be ethical. For example, slavery was legal in the United States for more than a hundred years.[58]

If we define culture as an accumulated pattern of values, beliefs, and behaviors held by an identifiable group of people and if we assume that cultures are different from one another, then intercultural communication takes on a necessary ethical dynamic because communication is a conscious, voluntary act that influences others. Consider the following situation:

An Intercultural Conversation: Where Should We Eat Dinner?

Tommy is from the Chicago suburbs. He is studying abroad in Seoul, South Korea. His host-national friend, Kwan, is a native South Korean student and is serving as his mentor. They are joined by another fellow student, Dinesh, their friend from India.

Tommy:	Hey, guys, I'm starved. Where should we eat dinner?
Kwan:	I know a great place not far from here where they serve *poshintang*. You guys should try it.
Tommy:	Poshintang? What's that?
Kwan:	It's dog meat soup. A lot of people eat it in the summer.
Tommy:	Seriously?
Kwan:	Yeah, for sure.
Tommy:	No way am I eating dog.
Dinesh:	Me either. I don't eat any meat anyway. Is there a vegetarian restaurant nearby?
Tommy:	I'm not doing vegetarian, either. I have to have meat, but not dog.
Kwan:	Why don't you just try poshintang and see what you think. You'll probably like it.

Tommy:	No way, man. Not me.
Dinesh:	I can't. My parents would be very disappointed in me if I did.
Kwan:	Listen, you guys, you are in Korea now. You need to adapt, ya know . . . *when in Rome?* Do as we do!
Tommy:	No way.
Dinesh:	No, I can't.
Kwan:	If I were in the U.S. now, you'd probably make me eat something I don't like.
Dinesh:	Yeah, would you make me eat beef, Tommy?
Tommy:	Sure, you should eat beef, it's natural, and it's full of iron and protein. It's good for you.

Here's a simple example of the ethics involved in communicating with people from different cultures. Although we may not think about it much, people express and create meaning through the shared food they eat. In any culture, food serves a communicative function. Many important cultural and social rituals are conducted around and with food. In the United States, for example, Thanksgiving is a food-centered holiday. Meals are a central feature of birthday parties, weddings, and funerals. First dates often occur in restaurants. Sporting events (e.g., the Super Bowl) are regularly thought of as much as eating events as sporting ones. In her research on the food and eating habits in South Asian cultures, Saunders observes that in many, the preparation, serving, and consumption of food are often enacted in heightened contexts that create symbolic meanings for both the performers and the audience. Saunders maintains that in Indian culture, the substance and symbol of the food one eats are clearly defined. She notes that the act of eating reveals participants' ethics and character. Each bite of food, she argues, communicates how that person understands himself or herself and how the food will contribute to his or her moral and emotional state.[59]

In 2009, in the United States, nearly 27 billion pounds of beef were consumed—the retail equivalent value of $73 billion. Americans like to eat beef. On the other hand, many Hindus regard cows as sacred and abstain from eating beef, although buffalo beef is consumed by some. And while Americans enjoy eating beef, most are disgusted by the thought of eating a horse, dog, or cat. Yet in parts of South Korea, people still eat dogs, although selling dog meat has been illegal in South Korea since 1984. Some statistics show that dog is the fourth most popular meat in South Korea after pork, beef, and chicken. According to a British Broadcasting Corporation report, there may be as many as 6,000 restaurants across South Korea selling dog meat soup, or what is called *poshintang,* using up to 8,500 tons of dog meat a year. According to the same report, another 94,000 tons is used to produce a medical tonic called *kaesoju.*[60]

So Tommy, Kwan, and Dinesh are faced with an ethical dilemma within the social/communicative ritual of eating a meal. All three young men have their own cultural ethics guiding their eating habits. Kwan wants Tommy and Dinesh to eat dog meat soup. Neither wants to eat it. Dinesh wants to eat vegetarian. Tommy admits that if they were in his native culture, he would sway them to eat beef. Who is right?

A central question about intercultural ethics is whether the same ethical principles apply to all cultures, a concept sometimes referred to as meta-ethics, or whether unique ethical standards apply to each culture individually, sometimes referred to as cultural relativism. There is no easy answer to this question. If we argue from a culturally relativistic perspective, then we must be willing to tolerate behaviors that many of us would find abhorrent, such as dowry deaths. In India, marriages are often arranged between the parents of the future bride and groom. In virtually all marital arrangements, the bride's family is required to pay a dowry—that is, a gift of some sort or financial grant to be paid to the groom's family. If the bride's family cannot meet the dowry arrangements, or if the groom's family sees the given dowry as unacceptable, the bride suffers; she is often abused, beaten, and sometimes murdered. The typical cause of dowry deaths is particularly brutal: the bride is chained to the kitchen stove, doused in kerosene, and set afire. Official Indian government agencies estimate the number of dowry deaths at 6,000 every year. And this is believed to be an understatement. Legislation outlawing dowries in India was enacted in 1961, but such laws are typically ignored. The point here is that few persons would condone the practice of dowry deaths. There is likely not a single anthropologist who, after immersing him/herself in Indian culture, would come away and justify or excuse such a cultural custom under the guise of cultural relativism.[61]

On the other hand, are there universal standards that everyone on the planet must obey? And who decides on these standards? If Tommy decides, then Dinesh must eat beef. If Kwan decides, then Tommy must eat dog. Historically, scholars from across a variety of academic fields have recognized five approaches to determining which behaviors are ethical: the utilitarian approach, the rights approach, the social justice and fairness approach, the common good approach, and the virtues approach.[62]

The utilitarian approach, sometimes called utilitarianism, posits that ethical actions are those that provide the greatest balance of good over evil. Some act is deemed ethical if it provides the greatest good for the greatest number (of people). To apply such an approach, one must first identify the courses of action available, determine who is affected by such actions in terms of who benefits or who is harmed, and then select the action that produces the greatest benefits and least harm. This approach is called utilitarianism because it emphasizes the consequences that actions have on the well-being—that is, the utility—of all persons directly or indirectly benefiting from or harmed by the act.[63]

The rights approach focuses on an individual's right to choose for her/himself. Advocates of a rights approach maintain that humans are distinct from other living beings on the planet because they have the free will to choose their course of action, and that such free will leads to dignity. Moreover, humans have a basic moral right to have their free choices respected, and it is a violation of human dignity to use people (e.g., hurt, manipulate) in ways they do not freely choose. Other fundamental human rights include the right to the truth, the right to privacy, the right not to be injured, and the right to what is agreed on. From this perspective, all humans have the right to be respected and treated as free, rational, and capable of making their own decisions. Thus, in this view, acts are ethical to the extent that they respect the rights of others. Acts are wrong to the extent that they violate the rights of others.[64]

The fairness or social justice approach is based on the Aristotelian dictum that "equals should be treated equally and unequals unequally." In this case, the ethical question is whether an act treats everyone in the same way or whether it shows favoritism and/or discrimination—that is, treats some unequally. Advocates of this approach maintain that favoritism benefits some people without a justifiable reason. Discrimination burdens people who should be treated equally. Hence, an act that shows favoritism and/or discrimination is unethical. This approach requires that people be treated with consistency.[65]

The common good approach is based on the idea that community life is, in and of itself, good and that people within the community and their subsequent actions should contribute to the community good. This approach has a more societal orientation than does utilitarianism in that it emphasizes that one's actions affect everyone's welfare, including a society's system of just laws, public safety, affordable healthcare, an effective education system, a clean environment, and even public recreation areas. Thus, an ethical act is one that ensures that such social policies are not violated, especially those that may inordinately affect vulnerable members of the society. This approach differs from the rights approach in that, while respecting and championing the rights of societal members to follow their individual goals, the common good approach also challenges societal members to recognize and advance the goals shared by the community.[66]

The virtues approach asserts the idea that there are certain ideals, principles, or standards (i.e., virtues) toward which every individual should strive in order to reach his or her highest potential. Individuals realize such virtues through conscious reflection on what kind of people they have the potential to become. Virtues such as truth, beauty, honesty, courage, compassion, generosity, tolerance, love, fidelity, integrity, fairness, self-control, and prudence are encouraged. Actions manifested in such virtues are considered ethical. In dealing with an ethical problem using the virtue approach, individuals should ask themselves, "What kind of person should I be? What will promote the development of character within me and my community?"[67]

Although the five approaches to ethics listed above are applicable to a large group of people and an array of different cultures, all of them have their roots in Western ideology and philosophy and may not be applicable to all cultures. To be sure, Shuter asserts that many of the fundamental tenets of the above five approaches are, in fact, not a part of the ethics that guide many Eastern cultures.[68] For example, Shuter points out that implicit in most of these classical approaches is the tenet that human acts are considered ethical to the extent that they contribute to the happiness and general well-being of the individual—that truthfulness, equality, choice, and fairness are paramount in defining an ethical act. Moreover, Shuter points out that these perspectives place the free will of the individual at the center of ethics, above all else. Such focus assumes that humans are naturally reasonable and intellectual. But, as Shuter points out, the ethical principles of some major Eastern ethical codes do not follow the same assumptions. Two traditions, including Confucianism and Hinduism, have very different perspectives on what is ethical.

Confucianism prescribes an ethical and philosophical scheme of living developed from the writings of Confucius. Cultures and countries strongly influenced by Confucianism include China, Korea, Japan, Taiwan, and Vietnam. Unlike many of the Western approaches to ethics that stress free choice and equality, Confucianism prescribes a set of rituals and conventional social habits to guide humans to appropriate and ethical acts. The wisest of humans is competent at ritual and practicing ritual in all circumstances. By definition, rituals restrict, rather than free, human action. In addition, where many of the Western approaches elevate humans above all else, Confucianism prescribes social rituals designed so that the natural world, social institutions, and humans all flourish interdependently.[69] In Confucianism, there are five basic virtues: *ren* (benevolence/altruism), *yi* (integrity/ sense of rightness), *li* (rite and propriety), *chi* (moral understanding), and *shin* (trust).[70] Within these five virtues is the recurring theme that humans are defined by their obedience to their place in the social hierarchy of relationships. By definition, social hierarchies rank order people and prescribe rules for proper conduct within each level of the hierarchy. In Confucianism, the five principal relationships are (1) ruler and subject, (2) parent and child, (3) husband and wife, (4) older sibling and younger sibling, and (5) friend and friend. Peace and harmony can be achieved only if people know, understand, and practice their proper place in society.[71] Some scholars maintain that Confucianism fosters inequality. You states that Confucianism has fostered gender biases by promoting the belief that a son is preferred over a daughter and a man is inherently superior to a woman in society . . . a woman who is as talented and educated as a man also faces great discrimination in the society because of the portrayal of a man being superior to a woman, which is deeply rooted in Confucianism.[72]

Hinduism is an inegalitarian practice-based religion and is the third largest religion after Christianity and Islam, with more than one billion followers. Unlike Christianity and Islam, Hinduism lacks a specific doctrine, is not monotheistic (i.e., believing in a singular God), has no recognized set of Holy Scriptures, and has no organized worship. Hinduism is practice based rather than faith based, which means that practices—which are often social—are more important than belief. Spinner-Halev writes that

> Hinduism is concerned with legitimizing hierarchical social relationships and mollifying deities, not with faith or belief. A Hindu may be a theist, pantheist, atheist, communist and believe whatever he likes, but what makes him into a Hindu are the ritual practices he performs and the rules to which he adheres, in short, what he does.[73]

Unlike most of the Western approaches to ethics, Hinduism categorically denies that people are equal and practices a rigid caste system. A caste is a social-ordering hierarchical system in which people are ranked. Hinduism prescribes strict rules and regulations about how one is to act within his or her caste level. In some cases, the lower caste may not be allowed to even interact with the higher caste. In India's caste system, there are four levels: (1) the Brahmins, the learned, educated elites, priests; (2) the Kshatriyas, the noble, warriors; (3) the Vaishyas, the traders, businessmen, and farmers; and (4) the Sudras, those who serve the needs of the upper caste members. The Sudras are further divided into the touchables and untouchables. The touchables take on jobs that are considered demeaning and polluting by the upper caste, such as being barbers, hairdressers, or cleaners. The untouchable Sudras are considered spiritually polluting and occupy jobs such as garbage collecting. Hinduism prescribes that one is born into a caste level and it is virtually impossible to move from one caste level to the next—that is, from lower to higher levels. In Hindu society, men and women are clearly not equal. The birth of a son is a blessing, while the birth of a daughter is met with misgivings. She is a financial burden to the family.[74]

So, we can see from the above discussion that Tommy, Kwan, and Dinesh have themselves an ethical dilemma. The answer to where they will lunch is not an easy one, since each comes from a very different set of ethical standards.

CHAPTER SUMMARY

The purpose of this chapter is to emphasize the necessity of intercultural communication and to define and clarify the terms *communication* and *culture*. The first part of this chapter argued that recent technological, political, and sociological advancements have created a global village only dreamed about 20 years ago. While the dream of a global village holds great promise, the reality is that diverse people have diverse opinions, values, and beliefs that clash and too often result in violence. Only through intercultural communication can such conflict be managed and reduced.

The second part of this chapter offered some definitions of communication and culture. Both terms are difficult to define. Communication involves the simultaneous encoding and decoding of verbal and nonverbal messages with someone else within some context. Culture, in part, can be defined as an accumulated pattern of values, beliefs, and behaviors shared by an identifiable group of people with a common history and verbal and nonverbal symbol system. Intercultural communication is essentially contextual. The cultural, microcultural, and environmental contexts surround the communicators, whose sociorelational contexts are defined by the exchange of verbal and nonverbal messages that are encoded and decoded within each interactant's perceptual context.

The final part of this chapter lets you discover something about yourself—in this case, your intercultural communication apprehension. Competent intercultural communicators are willing to approach intercultural situations and are sensitive to the differences in those situations.

Visit the student study site at **www.sagepub.com/neuliep5e** *for e-flashcards, web quizzes, web resources and more.*

DISCUSSION QUESTIONS

1. In what ways is the United States changing demographically? What will the population look like in 50 years?

2. Why are so many people afraid of communication?

3. Why are so many people afraid to communicate with people from cultures different from their own?

4. Using the definition of culture presented in this chapter, how would you describe your culture?

5. How do the various contexts of the contextual model of intercultural communication relate to one another?

6. Why is it that "the message sent is rarely the message received"?

KEY TERMS

communication   13

communication apprehension   15

context   14

culture   19

dynamic   11

environmental context   25

ethnocentrism   32

GENE   33

intentionality   13

interactive   12

intercultural communication   24

intercultural communication
    apprehension   29

microculture   22

perceptual context   14

Personal Report of Communication
    Apprehension (PRCA)   17

process   10

sociorelational context   27

symbol   12

transactional   12

uncertainty   28

REFERENCES

1. Schlesinger, A. M. (1993). *The Disuniting of America: Reflections of a Multicultural Society.* New York: Norton, p. 10.

2. These data come from a variety of sources: Rosenberg, M. (2011, March 2). *Population Density.* (http://geography.about.com/od/populationgeography/a/popdensity.thm); U.S. Census Bureau. *U.S. and World Population Clocks.* (http://www.census.gov/main/www/popclock.html); *World Population.* (http://en.wikipedia.org/wiki/World_population); *World Population Prospects: The 2008 Revision Population Database.* (http://esa.un.org/unpp/).

3. Lewis, W. (1948). *America and Cosmic Man.* London: Nicholson & Watson.

4. *Internet 2009 in Numbers.* (2010, January 22). Retrieved from http://royal.pingdom.com/2010/01/22/internet-2009-in-numbers/; *Internet World Users by Language: The Top 10 Languages.* (2010). Internet World Stats: Usage and Population Statistics. Retrieved from http://www.internetworldstats.com/stats7.htm.

5. Canadian Broadcasting Corporation. *Cellphones in India.* Retrieved from http://www.cbc.ca/doczone/cellphones/india.html; Giridharadas, A. (2009, May 9). A Pocket-Size Leveler in an Outsize Land. *New York Times.* Retrieved from http://www.nytimes.com/2009/05/10/weekinreview/10giridharadas.html.

6. *Media Statistics: Telephones: Mobile Cellular (per Capita) (Most Recent) by Country.* Retrieved from http://www.nationmaster.com/graph/med_tel_mob_cel_per-cap-telephones-mobile-cellular-per-capita.

7. Facebook. (2011). *Statistics.* Retrieved from http://www.facebook.com/press/info.php?statistics; Facebook. (2011). *Facebook Factsheet.* Retrieved from http://www.facebook.com/press/info.php?factsheet.

8. Schlesinger, *The Disuniting of America: Reflections of a Multicultural Society;* van den Berghe, P. L. (1987). *The Ethnic Phenomenon.* New York: Praeger; Waller, J. (2002). *Becoming Evil: How Ordinary People Commit Genocide and Mass Killing.* New York: Oxford University Press.

9. Carroll, J. (2010, October 25). The Rising Tides of Xenophobia. *Boston Globe.* Retrieved from http://www.boston.com/bostonglobe/editorial_opinion/oped/articles/2010/10/25/the_rising_tides_of_xenophobia/; Reuters. (2010, December 25). Nigerian Villages and Churches Are Struck in Deadly Attacks. *New York Times.* Retrieved from http://www.nytimes.com/2010/12/26/world/africa/26nigeria.html?scp=2&sq=ethnic%20clashes&st=cse; Schwirtz, M., & Barry, E. (2010, December 13). Medvedev Warns Against Ethnic Attacks. *New York Times.* Retrieved from http://www.nytimes.com/2010/12/14/world/europe/14russia.html?scp=6&sq=ethnic%20clashes&st=cse; *State multiculturalism has failed, says David Cameron.* BBC News UK Politics. Retrieved from http://www.bbc.co.uk/news/uk-politics-1237199; Tibet. (2010, July 26). *New York Times.* Retrieved from http://topics.nytimes.com/top/news/international/countriesandterritories/china/tibet/index.html?scp=13&sq.

10. Laungani, P. (2007). *Understanding Cross-Cultural Psychology.* London: Sage.

11. England, J. T. (1992). *Building Community for the 21st Century.* Ann Arbor, MI: ERIC. (ERIC Document Reproduction Service No. ED347489)

12. U.S. Census Bureau. *Top Ten Countries With Which the U.S. Trades.* Retrieved from http://www.census.gov/foreign-trade/top/dst/2010/10/balance.html; *Top Trading Partners: Total Trade, Exports, Imports.* Retrieved from http://www.census.gov/foreign-trade/statistics/highlights/top/top1010yr.html.

13. These stereotypes are reported in the following sources: Credit Union National Association. *Credit Unions Serving Hispanics: A National Perspective.* Available from www.cuna.org/initiatives/download/hisp_bndr1.pdf; Lee, Y. T., Vue, S., Seklecki, R., & Ma, Y. (2007). How Did Asian Americans Respond to Negative Stereotypes and Hate Crimes? *American Behavioral Scientist, 51,* 271–293; Welch, K. (2007). Black Criminal Stereotypes and Racial Profiling. *Journal of Contemporary Criminal Justice, 23,* 276–288.

14. U.S. Census Bureau. (2009). *Statistical Abstract of the United States: 2010* (129th ed.). Washington, DC: Author. Retrieved from http://www.census.gov/statab/www/ and http://www.census.gov/compendia/statab/2010/tables/10s0043.pdf.

15. Ibid.

16. Pew Hispanic Center. (2010). *Statistical Portrait of Hispanics in the United States, 2008.* Washington, DC: Author; Pew Research Center. (2010). *Fact Sheet 2010: Hispanics of Mexican Origin in the United States, 2008.* Washington, DC: Author; U.S. Census Bureau. (2008). *American Community Survey.* Retrieved from http://www.census.gov/acs/www/.

17. Ibid.

18. County: English Is Official Language. (2002, July 18). *Associated Press;* Shin, H. B., & Bruno, R. (2003). *Language Use and English-Speaking Ability: 2000.* Washington, DC: U.S. Department of Commerce, U.S. Census Bureau; Texas Town Adopts Spanish as Official Language. (2004, August). *Reuters News Service.*

19. U.S. Census Bureau. (2009). *Language Spoken at Home:* 2005–2009 *American Community Survey.* Retrieved from http://factfinder.census.gov/servlet/STTable?_bm=y&-geo_id=01000US&-qr_name=ACS_2009_5YR_G00_S1601&-ds_name=ACS_2009_5YR_G00_&-redoLog=false.

20. Schlesinger, *The Disuniting of America,* p. 15.

21. Larson, C. U. (2010). *Persuasion: Reception and Responsibility* (12th ed.). Boston: Wadsworth.

22. McCloud, L. (2006). *Top Reasons People Divorce: Is Divorce on the Back of Your Mind as You Are Saying "I Do."* Retrieved from www.associatedcontent.com/article/35097/top_reasons_people_divorce.html.

23. Berlo, D. K. (1960). *The Process of Communication.* New York: Holt, Rinehart, & Winston, p. 24.

24. Bowers, J. W., & Bradac, J. J. (1982). Issues in Communication Theory: A Metatheoretical Analysis. In M. Burgoon (Ed.), *Communication Yearbook 5* (p. 3). New Brunswick, NJ: Transaction Books.

25. Goss, B. (1983). *Communication in Everyday Life.* Belmont, CA: Wadsworth.

26. Cooley, C. (1909). *Social Organization.* New York: Scribner, p. 61.

27. Miller, G. R. (1966). On Defining Communication: Another Stab. *Journal of Communication, 16,* 92.

28. Fisher, B. A. (1994). *Interpersonal Communication: Pragmatics of Human Relationships.* New York: Random House, p. 22.

29. Stevens, S. S. (1950). Introduction: A Definition of Communication. *Journal of the Acoustical Society of America, 22,* 689.

30. Hall, E. T. (1959). *The Silent Language.* New York: Doubleday.

31. Berlo, D. K. (1960). *The Process of Communication.* New York: Holt, Rinehart, & Winston, p. 24.

32. Motley, M. T. (1990). On Whether One Can(not) Not Communicate: An Examination via Traditional Communication Postulates. *Western Journal of Communication, 54,* 1–20.

33. Ibid.

34. Watzlawick, P., Beavin, J., & Jackson, D. (1967). *Pragmatics of Human Communication: Patterns, Pathologies, and Paradoxes.* New York: Norton.

35. McCroskey, J. C. (2006). *An Introduction to Rhetorical Communication* (9th ed.). Boston: Allyn & Bacon.

36. Kroeber, A. I., & Kluckhohn, C. (Eds.). (1954). *Culture: A Critical Review of Concepts and Definitions.* New York: Random House; Seelye, H. N. (1993). *Teaching Culture: Strategies for Intercultural Communication.* Lincolnwood, IL: National Textbook Company.

37. Basso, K. (1990). "To Give Up on Words": Silence in Western Apache Culture. In D. Carbaugh (Ed.), *Cultural Communication and Intercultural Contact* (pp. 303–320). Hillsdale, NJ: Erlbaum.

38. Axtell, R. (1991). *Gestures: Dos and Taboos of Body Language Around the World.* New York: Wiley.

39. Franz Boas: retrieved from www.nnnd.com/people/861/000097570/ This discussion of the history of intercultural communication is based on the following sources: Hall, E. T. (1959). *The Silent Language.* New York: Doubleday; Kitao, K. (1985). *A Brief History of Intercultural Communication in the United States.* Education Resources Information Center. (ERIC Document Reproduction Service No. ED278212); Leeds-Hurwitz, W. (1990). Notes in the History of Intercultural Communication: The Foreign Service Institute and the Mandate for Intercultural Training. *Quarterly Journal of Speech, 76,* 262–281; Neuliep, J. W. (2010). Ethical and Cultural Relativism. In R. L. Jackson II (Ed.), *Encyclopedia of Identity* (pp. 252–254). Thousand Oaks, CA: Sage; Rogers, E. M., Hart, W. B., & Miike, Y. (2002). Edward T. Hall and the History of Intercultural Communication: The United States and Japan. *Keio Communication Review, 24,* 3–26.

40. Angeloni, E. (Ed.). (1995). *Mystique of the Masai.* Guilford: Dushkin.

41. Watzlawick et al., Pragmatics of Human Communication.

42. Berger, C. R. (1992). Communicating Under Uncertainty. In W. B. Gudykunst & Y. Y. Kim (Eds.),

Readings on Communicating With Strangers (pp. 5–15). New York: McGraw-Hill.

43. Berger, C. R., & Calabrese, R. (1975). Some Explorations in Initial Interaction and Beyond. *Human Communication Research, 1,* 99–112.

44. Buss, A. H. (1980). *Self-Consciousness and Social Anxiety.* San Francisco: W. H. Freeman.

45. Gudykunst, W. B., & Kim, Y. Y. (1997). *Communicating With Strangers: An Approach to Intercultural Communication.* New York: McGraw-Hill.

46. Neuliep, J. W., & McCroskey, J. C. (1997). The Development of Intercultural and Interethnic Communication Apprehension Scales. *Communication Research Reports, 14,* 145–156.

47. Spitzberg, B. H. (1997). A Model of Intercultural Communication Competence. In L. A. Samovar & R. E. Porter (Eds.), *Intercultural Communication: A Reader* (8th ed., pp. 379–391). Belmont, CA: Wadsworth.

48. Neuliep & McCroskey, The Development of Intercultural and Interethnic Communication Apprehension Scales.

49. Spitzberg, A Model of Intercultural Communication Competence.

50. Gudykunst, W. (1997). Cultural Variability in Communication: An Introduction. *Communication Research, 24,* 327–348.

51. Sumner, W. G. (1906). *Folkways.* Boston: Ginn.

52. Neuliep, J. W., & McCroskey, J. C. (1997). The Development of a U.S. and Generalized Ethnocentrism Scale. *Communication Research Reports, 14,* 385–398.

53. Hall, The Silent Language.

54. Braithwaite, C. (1990). Communicative Silence: A Cross-Cultural Study of Basso's Hypothesis. In D. Carbaugh (Ed.), *Cultural Communication and Intercultural Contact* (pp. 321–328). Hillsdale, NJ: Erlbaum.

55. Gudykunst, W. B., & Ting-Toomey, S. (1988). Verbal Communication Styles. In W. B. Gudykunst & S. Ting-Toomey (Eds.), *Culture and Interpersonal Communication* (pp. 427–441). Newbury Park, CA: Sage.

56. Gudykunst, W. B., & Kim, Y. Y. (2003). *Communicating With Strangers: An Approach to Intercultural Communication.* New York: McGraw-Hill; Kim, Y. Y. (2005). Association and Disassociation: A Contextual Theory of Interethnic Communication. In W. B. Gudykunst (Ed.), *Theorizing About Intercultural Communication* (pp. 323–350). Thousand Oaks, CA: Sage.

57. Kim, Y. Y. (2005). Adapting to a New Culture: An Integrative Communication Theory. In W. B. Gudykunst (Ed.), *Theorizing About Intercultural Communication* (pp. 375–400). Thousand Oaks, CA: Sage.

58. Valasquez, M., Andre, C., Thomas-Shanks, S. J., & Meyer, M. J. (1987). What is ethics? *Issues in Ethics, 1,* N1.

59. Saunders, J. B. (2007). "I don't eat meat": Discourse on food among transnational Hindus. *Contributions to Indian Sociology, 41,* 302–323.

60. *South Korea's dog day.* (1999, August 17). BBC News. Retrieved from http://news.bbc.co.uk/2/hi/asia-pacific/422338.stm.

61. Hitchcock, A. (2001). Rising number of dowry deaths in India. World Socialist Web Site. Retrieved from www.wsws.org/articles/2001/jul2001/ind-j04shtml

62. This discussion of the five classical approaches to ethics is based largely on Velasquez, M., Andre, C., Shanks, T., & Meyer, S. J. & M. J. (1996). Thinking Ethically: A Framework for Moral Decision Making. *Issues in Ethics, 7*(1), 2–5.

63. Based on Valasquez, et al.

64. Based on Valasquez, et al.

65. Based on Valasquez, et al.

66. Based on Valasquez, et al.

67. Based on Valasquez, et al.

68. Shuter, R. (2003). Ethics, Culture, and Communication: An Intercultural Perspective. In L. A. Samovar & R. E. Porter (Eds.), *Intercultural Communication: A Reader* (10th ed., pp. 449–455). Belmont, CA: Wadsworth/Thomson.

69. Billington, R. (1997). Chinese Philosophy III: Confucianism. In R. Billington (Ed.), *Understanding Eastern Philosophy* (pp. 118–133). New York: Routledge.

70. Cua, A. S. (2000). Confucian Philosophy, Chinese. In E. Craig (Ed.), *Concise Routledge Encyclopedia of Philosophy* (pp. 162–163). New York: Routledge.

71. Park, M., & Chesla, C. (2007). Revisiting Confucianism as a Conceptual Framework for Asian Family Study. *Journal of Family Nursing, 13*(3), 293–311.

72. You, Y. (2009). Injustice: It Is Confucianism. *Qualitative Inquiry, 15*(7), 1290–1292.

73. Spinner-Halev, J. (2005). Hinduism, Christianity, and Liberal Religious Toleration. *Political Theory, 33,* 28–57.

74. Laungani, Understanding Cross-Cultural Psychology.

CHAPTER 2

The Cultural Context

CHAPTER OBJECTIVES

After reading this chapter, you should be able to

1. recognize that cultures are dynamic, fluid, and not static entities;

2. compare and contrast individualism and collectivism;

3. identify some cultures that are individualistic and some that are collectivistic;

4. recognize that no culture is purely individualistic or purely collectivistic;

5. compare and contrast high- and low-context cultures;

6. identify some cultures that are high context and some that are low context;

7. compare value orientations among cultures;

8. compare and contrast large and small power distance cultures;

9. identify some cultures that are large power distance and some that are small power distance;

10. compare and contrast large and small uncertainty avoidant cultures;

11. identify some cultures that are weak uncertainty avoidant and some that are strong uncertainty avoidant; and

12. assess your degree of individualism/collectivism, vertical and horizontal individualism/collectivism, high/low context, and power distance.

Cultural Context

Culture hides more than it reveals, and strangely enough what it hides, it hides most effectively from its own participants.

—Edward T. Hall[1]

The cultural context in which human communication occurs is perhaps the most defining influence on human interaction. Culture provides the overall framework wherein humans learn to organize their thoughts, emotions, and behaviors in relation to their environment. Although people are born into a culture, it is not innate. Culture is learned. Culture teaches one how to *think,* conditions one how to *feel,* and instructs one how to *act,* especially how to *interact* with others—in other words, how to communicate. In many respects, the terms *communication* and *culture* can be used interchangeably. Yet the influence of culture on human interaction is paradoxical. As we conduct our daily lives, most of us are unaware of our culture; however, culture influences our every thought, feeling, and action. As the late internationally recognized anthropologist Edward Hall asserts in the quote at the beginning of this chapter, culture hides more than it reveals, particularly from its own members. Australian anthropologist Roger Keesing argues that culture provides people with an implicit theory about how to behave and how to interpret the behavior of others. People from different cultures learn different implicit theories. These theories are learned through socialization. And through socialization, individuals also learn the dominant values of their particular culture and their self-identities.[2]

We often think of a culture in terms of its geography; for example, we think of Saudi Arabia as a hot, desert culture and of Siberia as a cold, mountainous one. But culture is more a human phenomenon than a geographic one. And while geography certainly affects how people live within a particular culture, it is the people, more than the geography, that constitute culture. So when you think of a culture, think about the people. That being said, it is also important to understand that cultures of people are not static but, rather, dynamic. This means that cultures change; they are fluid, always moving. For example, a dramatic change we have seen in China is the implementation of the one-child policy, which was established in 1979 to limit that country's population explosion (recall from Chapter 1 that China has 1.3 billion people). Although originally intended to be a temporary measure, the policy limiting couples to one child each continues today. Fines, taxes, forced abortions, and sterilization may result if a couple violates the policy. This policy has dramatically changed China's culture; to be sure, it is thought to have reduced the population growth by as many as 300 million people since its inception. To provide some perspective on that change, there are about 310 million people in the United States.[3]

Over the past few decades, anthropologists, communication researchers, psychologists, and sociologists have isolated several dimensions of cultural variability that can be used to differentiate cultures. This chapter will focus on five dimensions of cultural variability: individualism–collectivism, high–low context, value orientations, power distance, and uncertainty avoidance. Each of these dimensions affects how people communicate.

The five dimensions of cultural variability will be presented along cultural continua:

Low [_____] High

The cultural continua allow us to represent the dimensions of cultural variability as continuous and varying in magnitude by degree. In other words, no culture is purely and absolutely individualistic or collectivistic. Instead, a culture may be more individualistic or more collectivistic than some other culture. Another important point to make is that these cultural dimensions of variability are not opposites; that is, a culture where a large power distance is practiced should not be thought of as the opposite of a culture where small power distance is practiced. In some cases, dimensions of cultural variability may coexist in cultures. In addition, as mentioned above, cultures are not static or fixed in time; many cultures are in a state of great transition. Thus, a culture that was once considered collectivistic may now be considered individualistic. For example, Japan is considered a collectivistic, group-oriented society. However, since the 1950s, Japan has been strongly influenced by Western culture. Many Japanese scholars have observed that the younger generation of Japanese, while still considered collectivistic, is more individualistic than their parents and especially their grandparents. Likewise, although the United States is considered very individualistic, many U.S. businesses and corporations employ collectivistic management models in the workplace, focusing on teamwork and cooperation.

Finally, and this is an important point, when we label a culture as individualistic—or large power distance and so forth—that does not mean that every person in that culture is an individualist. The United States, for example, is considered an individualistic culture, yet groups within the United States are collectivistic. While reading through this chapter, remember that cultures are not static. Cultures are dynamic, continuously developing and evolving.

INDIVIDUALISM–COLLECTIVISM

Perhaps the single most studied dimension of cultural variability used to compare and contrast cultures and microcultures is individualism–collectivism (see Figure 2.1).

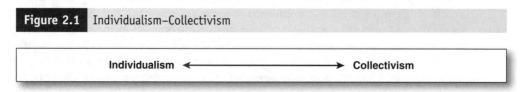

| Figure 2.1 | Individualism–Collectivism |

Cultures falling on one side of the continuum are individualistic, while those falling toward the other side are collectivistic. Cultures falling at the midpoint might possess both individualistic and collectivistic characteristics. Gayle and Knutson write that Norwegians, for example, possess both individualistic and collectivistic tendencies. Norwegians are taught to put the needs of society above their own and to embrace a classless society. Simultaneously, however, Norwegians value personal independence. While they conform to social norms, the individual Norwegian rebuffs traditional rules and standards. They strive for independence yet do not depend on others to recognize their individual achievements. They believe that they must recognize their own good qualities in order to gain self-esteem.[4]

Perhaps Norway is unusual in that its people carry collectivistic and individualistic tendencies, but regardless of culture, most persons carry both individualistic and collectivistic tendencies to some degree. The difference is that in some cultures individualistic tendencies dominate while in others collectivistic tendencies dominate.[5]

Individualism

Researchers at the University of Michigan recently analyzed more than 250 studies that investigated individualism, collectivism, or both.[6] They found that the most relevant feature of **individualism**, as defined in the majority of the studies they reviewed, was valuing personal independence. Researchers at the University of Auckland in New Zealand point out that valuing personal independence involves putting an emphasis on personal responsibility and freedom of choice, personal autonomy, and achieving self-fulfillment. Moreover, individualists strive to maintain distinctive personal attitudes and opinions and prefer self-directed behavior and independence of groups. Individualists tend to see themselves as unique from others.[7]

Harry Triandis, from the University of Illinois, is well known for his work on individualism and collectivism. Triandis discusses four defining attributes of individualism–collectivism:

1. How individuals perceive themselves (e.g., "I am distinct and unique" vs. "I am a member of a family, tribe")

2. How individuals relate to others (e.g., "How/what do I gain from this act?" vs. "How will this act affect others?")

3. The goals they follow (e.g., "I want to win" vs. "I'm a team player to help the group win")

4. What drives their behavior (e.g., "It is my right to do this" vs. "My duty is to my group")

Triandis writes that in individualistic cultures, emphasis is placed on individuals' goals over group goals. Social behavior is guided by personal goals, perhaps at the expense of other types of goals. Individualistic cultures stress values that benefit the individual person. The self is promoted because each person is viewed as uniquely endowed and possessing distinctive talent and potential. Individuals are encouraged to pursue and develop their abilities and aptitudes. In many individualistic cultures, people are taught to be creative, self-reliant, and assertive.[8]

Triandis and others have pointed out that an important ingredient of individualistic cultures is that the individual is emotionally disconnected from in-groups such as the family. Because the individual has been taught to be independent, social control depends more on personal guilt than on shame or other social norms or conformity. Ironically, members of individualistic cultures tend to belong to many groups, but their affiliation with them is short-lived. Many of the groups to which an individualist belongs are designed to enhance self-worth. Such groups might include self-help groups, therapy groups, or occupational groups.[9]

The origins of individualism have been traced to ancient Greece, where literature (e.g., *The Iliad* and *The Odyssey*) celebrates the accomplishments of individuals. Oyserman, Coon, and Kemmelmeier point out that the term *individualism* may have its roots in the French Revolution (1789–1799), where the word was used to describe the negative influence of individual rights on the well-being of the French commonwealth.[10] Triandis also notes that ecology (i.e., features of geography, resources, and the history of a society) can shape the level of individualism in a culture. For example, modern, industrial-urban, fast-changing cultures tend to be individualistic.

In many cases, individualistic cultures are highly complex and affluent. Complex cultures have heterogeneous populations and economies based on occupational specialization, where individuals do different jobs. Cultural complexity also occurs in cultures where people are separated from one another either geographically or through migration patterns. Many individualistic cultures have a history of colonization, for example.[11]

Collectivism

Oyserman, Coon, and Kemmelmeier point out that the central ingredient of **collectivism** is the assumption that groups bind and mutually obligate individuals.[12] In their extensive review of literature, they found that collectivism is linked to a sense of duty to group, interdependence, harmony, and working with the group. Triandis asserts that in collectivistic societies, group goals take precedence over individual goals. Collectivistic cultures stress values that serve the in-group by subordinating personal goals for the sake of preserving the in-group. Collectivistic societies are characterized by extended primary groups such as the family, neighborhood, or occupational group in which members have diffuse mutual obligations and expectations based on their status or rank. In collectivistic cultures, people are not seen as isolated individuals. People see themselves as interdependent with others (e.g., their in-group), where responsibility is shared and accountability is collective. A person's identity is defined by his or her group memberships.[13]

Triandis points out that while collectivistic cultures stress the importance of the group over the individual, their members tend to belong to fewer groups than do persons in individualistic cultures. Unlike the individualist, the collectivist is emotionally connected to the in-group. A collectivist's values and beliefs are consistent with and reflect those of the in-group. Moreover, a collectivist's association with his or her in-groups may last a lifetime. In many collectivistic cultures, the primary value is harmony with others. Triandis observes that because group harmony is so highly valued, obedience to and compliance with in-group pressures is routine. One's behavior is role based, and deviations from the prescribed role are discouraged and often negatively sanctioned. In this sense, a person's behavior is guided more by shame than by personal guilt. A collectivist who stands out from the group disrupts the harmony and may be punished. Most collectivistic cultures value social reciprocity, obligation, dependence, and obedience. But by far, the primary value stressed by many collectivistic cultures is harmony.[14]

STUDENT VOICES ACROSS CULTURES

Personal Understanding of Collectivism in China

My name is Pengfei Song, and I'm a 25-year old guy from China. I was raised in Qiqihaer, a city located in the northeast part of the country. Before I came to the United States to get my bachelor's degree, I had received my education in China from kindergarten through the first 2 years in university.

As far as I can recall, the idea of collectivism has been introduced to me since I was in elementary school. I was told that serving your country and people should be your priority regardless of what you want to do in the future. The reason is that we, as Chinese, believe that individuals, to a large extent, cannot have a peaceful life without the prosperity of our nation. Put in another way, our nation is defined as the big family, whereas each household is a small family within this big family. As a result, it is very common to see the Chinese people emphasize group goals over individual goals and think more in terms of "we."

Dating back to the sports meeting in my high school, I remember that I signed up to compete in the 200-meter race with other students from other classes in my grade. I decided to do it not because I had the ability to be the winner but because my class needed someone to represent it and I wanted to be that person for my class. To me, the reputation of my class meant more than anything. I could feel that I was not myself. I stood for all my classmates. So if I failed, my class failed. Fortunately, I won the competition eventually, which meant victory for the whole class. Therefore, the repute apparently belonged to my class, not to myself.

Individualism Versus Collectivism?

Although they sound as though they're opposite dimensions of cultural variability, individualism and collectivism are not mutually exclusive; that is, they can coexist within a person of any culture. Green, Deschamps, and Páez point out that the degree of individualism or collectivism within someone may be triggered by the social context and one's social relations. They suggest that individuals can be characterized by specific combinations of individualistic and collectivistic tendencies. For example, a person may find that individualistic relations are motivated in particular situations, such as in business relationships, whereas with family members, the relationship is collectivistic.[15] To be sure, Hui has shown variation in individualistic and collectivistic attitudes in different types of relationships, such as with one's spouse, parent, neighbor, or coworker.[16]

Competitiveness often has been associated with individualism. Instruments that measure individualism often include items that tap into one's competitive nature (e.g., "It's important to me that I win"). Recent research suggests that competitiveness is not a necessary feature of individualism, however. In their research, Oyserman, Coon, and Kemmelmeier found that Americans generally score higher in individualism than do Japanese. But when competitiveness is included in the measurement of individualism, the difference between Americans and Japanese disappears (i.e., they score the same on measures of individualism).[17] Green, Deschamps, and Páez note that, in any culture, people compete for scarce resources in economically adverse contexts and that scarcity triggers competitiveness, which leads to active individualism aimed at achieving economic success and material well-being. In contexts of affluence, in contrast, other individualistic values such as individual freedom, personal development, quality of life, and relational interdependence become salient.[18] In a Taiwanese sample, Yu and Yang found that achievement motivation as a form of competitiveness can be driven by individual or collective concerns. These findings support the idea that competitiveness is associated with individualism as well as with collectivism.[19]

So, Who's an Individualist and Who's a Collectivist?

Because there can be considerable within-country variation, labeling a particular country or culture as individualistic or collectivistic is difficult and may lead to overgeneralizations. However, in their landmark analysis of more than 250 research articles on individualism and collectivism, Oyserman and her colleagues were able to draw some conclusions.[20] The central focus of the Oyserman study was to answer the question, Are Americans (i.e., European Americans) more individualistic and less collectivistic than others groups? In general, the answer was yes, Americans are more individualistic and less collectivistic than other groups. In comparison with nearly 50 other countries, European Americans were more individualistic than all but 12. European Americans were generally lower in collectivism as well. There were exceptions, though; Americans were higher in collectivism than were people in New Zealand, France, Singapore, Tanzania, Egypt, Costa Rica, and Venezuela. Oyserman notes that one of the most remarkable findings was that Americans were slightly more collectivistic than Japanese and no difference was observed between Americans and Koreans on collectivistic measures.

However, in her recent research, Toshi Imada found that the stories in American textbooks highlighted themes of individualism such as self-direction and achievement, whereas Japanese stories highlighted themes of collectivism, such as conformity and group harmony. Her study also found cultural differences in story characteristics (e.g., the narrator, attribution of the outcome, picture content) that are related to individualism and collectivism.[21] Oyserman has pointed out that although as a group East Asians were simultaneously lower in individualism and higher in collectivism than were Americans, there was notable variety within East Asian countries regarding individualism and collectivism. For example, Chinese were highest in collectivism but lowest in individualism, whereas Japanese were highest in individualism but lowest in collectivism. South Koreans were between Chinese and Japanese on these measures. This may be because South Korean culture has unique features that distinguish it from traditional Confucian-based collectivistic cultures—that is, a strong emphasis on family. In a more recent study, Fischer and a number of his colleagues examined 11 countries and found that among these countries, the United States ranked highest in overall individualism.[22]

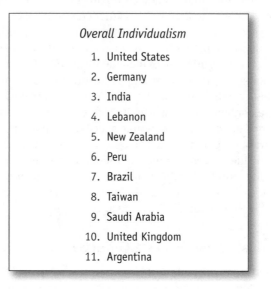

Overall Individualism

1. United States
2. Germany
3. India
4. Lebanon
5. New Zealand
6. Peru
7. Brazil
8. Taiwan
9. Saudi Arabia
10. United Kingdom
11. Argentina

Individualism and collectivism also have been studied among Middle Eastern and African cultures. Sagy, Orr, Bar-On, and Awwad found that both Israeli-Jewish and Palestinian-Arab groups were more collectivistic than individualistic. However, the Palestinians scored higher than the Israeli group on items measuring and emphasizing an in-group collectivistic orientation (e.g., my nationality, my country). Pirttilä-Backman, Kassea, and Ikonen found that Cameroonians were shown to be more collectivistic than individualistic. They also found that Cameroonian women were more individualistic than were the men. Cameroon provides an interesting context for the study of individualism and collectivism because of the vast ethnic differences there. For example, although the country is officially bilingual—with about 20% speaking English and the rest speaking French—more than 200 languages are spoken there. Religious diversity abounds as well, with indigenous beliefs held by about 40% of the population, Christian beliefs held by another 40%, and Muslim beliefs by about 20%.[23]

AN INTERCULTURAL CONVERSATION: INDIVIDUALISTIC AND COLLECTIVISTIC CULTURES

To be sure, one's individualistic or collectivistic disposition will affect communication. In the following exchange, Mr. Patterson, an American manager working in Korea, is meeting with his supervisor, Mr. Wyman, who is also American. The United States is considered more individualistic than Korea. In this scenario, Mr. Patterson reports to Mr. Wyman about some changes he has made within several of his sales teams. Later, Park Young Sam, their Korean counterpart, enters into the dialogue.[24]

Mr. Patterson:	Good morning, Mr. Wyman, thanks for meeting with me this morning. As you know, our division has been doing very well this quarter. In fact, our numbers are up across the board.
Mr. Wyman:	Yes, I've seen your quarterly reports. Nice job!
Mr. Patterson:	Thanks. In order to recognize their hard work, I've made some changes in our sales teams. I've created team leaders in each group. In our product group, I promoted Lee Young-sam. In the marketing group, I promoted Chun Tae-woo, and in the technology group, I promoted Choi Mino. All of them have been real leaders. I think this idea will really motivate them. In fact, I met with the groups individually and announced the promotions.
Mr. Wyman:	Good job, Patterson. I can see you're really on top of things. Good work.

Two Months Later

Mr. Patterson, Mr. Wyman, and Park Young Sam, a Korean manager, are discussing the poor performance of Mr. Patterson's sales teams.

Mr. Wyman:	Well, just look at these dismal results. The numbers for this quarter are way down from last quarter. What's happened?
Mr. Patterson:	I don't know. Ever since I introduced the team leader concept, the groups' productivity has really plummeted. I thought it was a great idea. I guess I chose the wrong people to lead the teams. I'll assign new leaders tomorrow.
Park Young Sam:	Well . . . you may select new leaders if you desire, but the men you chose were all very capable. However, by elevating them, you made them stand out and disrupted the harmony of each group. In Korea, we all work hard for the group . . . not just one person.
Mr. Patterson:	I guess I should have just left things as they were.

Following their individualistic orientations, Mr. Patterson and Mr. Wyman were perfectly comfortable with the idea of appointing team leaders within the individual sales groups. However, as Park Young Sam mentioned, doing so upset the harmony of the groups, which in turn led to poor performance. In the United States, workers are often motivated by the opportunity for promotion and advancement, as this serves the individualistic drive for individual achievement. In less individualistic cultures, however, workers may be motivated by being a part of a cohesive and productive team. Mr. Patterson and Mr. Wyman could have consulted with Mr. Sam prior to making the promotions. He probably would have advised against it.

Patterns of Individualism and Collectivism Across the United States

As mentioned above, although the United States is considered individualistic, considerable regional variation exists. Because of ecological, historical, and institutional practices, the Deep South is the most collectivistic region of the United States. Defeat in the Civil War, the institution of slavery, relative poverty, and the prominence of religion all contribute to the collectivistic tendencies of the South. In addition, the Southwest, having been settled by Mexican and Spanish populations before White settlers entered the area, is also considered fairly collectivistic. Hawaii, too, has a culture different from the rest of the United States, with approximately 65% of its population coming from Asian cultures. Hence, much of the culture has collectivistic characteristics, and Hawaii would be considered collectivistic. On the other hand, the Mountain West and Great Plains is thought to be the most individualistic region in the United States.[25]

In their research, Vandello and Cohen created an index designed to measure collectivism in different regions of the United States. Their index was composed of eight items, including the percentage of people living alone, percentage of elderly people living alone, percentage of households with grandchildren in them, divorce-to-marriage ratio, percentage of people with no religious affiliation, average percentage of those voting Libertarian over the past four presidential elections, ratio of people carpooling to work to people living alone, and percentage of self-employed people. Their index showed a general pattern of relative collectivism in the South, particularly in the former slave states, with maximum individualism in the Great Plains and Mountain West. Montana was the most individualistic state, and Hawaii was the most collectivistic (see Table 2.1).[26]

The point has been made several times now that variations of individualism and collectivism can be seen within any culture. No culture is purely and entirely individualistic or collectivistic. To account for this phenomenon, Triandis and other cross-cultural researchers distinguish between individualism and collectivism at the *cultural* level and idiocentrism and allocentrism at the individual *psychological* level. Many cross-cultural researchers believe that

Table 2.1   The Most Collectivistic States and the Most Individualistic States

Most Collectivistic States	Most Individualistic States
Hawaii	Montana
Louisiana	Oregon
South Carolina	Nebraska
Mississippi	Wyoming
Maryland	South Dakota
Utah	Colorado
Virginia	North Dakota
Georgia	Washington
California	Kansas
New Jersey	Iowa

individualism–collectivism cannot be measured at the cultural level. We should not label entire cultures as individualistic or collectivistic, because persons within those cultures may vary considerably. We can, however, measure an individual degree of individualism–collectivism.

When people carry individualistic tendencies, we call them *idiocentric*. When people carry collectivistic tendencies, we call them *allocentric*. Idiocentrism and allocentrism are the individual equivalents of cultural individualism–collectivism. Allocentrics tend to define themselves with reference to social entities (e.g., families, hometowns) more so than do idiocentrics. Allocentrics internalize the norms of the in-group and enjoy behavior along in-group expectations. Allocentrics are less likely to be lonely than idiocentrics. The self-esteem of allocentrics tends to be based on getting along with others, compared with idiocentrics, whose self-esteem is often based on getting ahead of others.[27]

Communication Consequences of Individualism–Collectivism

A given culture's orientation toward individualism or collectivism has important behavioral consequences for that culture's members. Among collectivists, social behavior is guided by the group. Along with group membership come prescribed duties and obligations. Among individualists, social behavior is guided by one's personal attitudes, motivations, and other internal processes. To be sure, individualistic cultures value and reward an individual's uniqueness. The United States, for example, is replete with contests and ceremonies that recognize individual accomplishment. People are publicly rewarded for being the most beautiful, thinnest, strongest, fastest, tallest, smartest, youngest, oldest, funniest, or the "best" at whatever they aspire to. Collectivistic cultures, on the other hand, stress harmony and cooperation. Collectivists strive for the approval of the in-group, which is accomplished not by standing out but by conforming to the group's norm. From the collectivist's perspective, an individual who stands out from the group disrupts harmony. In the United States, "the squeaky wheel gets the grease," but in Japan, "the tallest nail gets hammered down."[28]

Triandis maintains that a culture's individualistic or collectivistic orientation will likely affect child-rearing practices. In individualistic cultures, child rearing emphasizes independence, exploration, creativity, and self-reliance. Individualistic parents encourage their children to be unique, express themselves, and be independent. The children of individualistic parents understand that they are to leave home once they reach a certain age or education level. In fact, it is thought odd or unusual if children past the age of about 21 still live at home with their parents. Though rank order exists in the individualist's family, decisions are often made democratically. In collectivistic cultures, child rearing emphasizes conformity, obedience, security, and reliability. Collectivistic parents teach their children the importance of family lineage and ancestry. Typically, the father dominates the collectivist's home, where rank in the family is often determined by sex and age.[29]

Collectivists are more conscious of in-group/out-group distinctions than are individualists. According to Gudykunst and his colleagues, individualists tend to initiate and maintain specific friendships based on desirable qualities of the other person. Collectivists form friendships that are determined by their hierarchical role in society. Collectivists perceive and rate their in-group friendships as more intimate than do individualists. On the other hand, individualists tend to apply the same value standards to all, whereas collectivists tend to apply different value standards to members of their in-groups and out-groups. For example, collectivists are likely to use the equality norm (i.e., equal distribution of resources) with in-group members and the equity norm (i.e., unequal distribution of resources) with out-group members.[30]

Finally, in their exhaustive review of studies, Oyserman, Coon, and Kemmelmeier summarized behavioral traits that have been shown to be associated with individualism and collectivism (Table 2.2).[31]

Measuring Individualism–Collectivism

Over the past decades, cross-cultural researchers have spent considerable effort developing instruments designed to measure one's relative degree of individualism and collectivism. Researchers at the University of Auckland in New Zealand recently developed the Auckland Individualism and Collectivism Scale.[32] (See Self-Assessment 2.1.)

Vertical and Horizontal Individualism and Collectivism

While it is clear that individualistic cultures differ from collectivistic cultures, individualistic cultures can, and do, differ from other individualistic cultures. The same can be said of collectivistic cultures. Some individualistic cultures, for example, link self-reliance with competition, while other individualistic cultures do not. Some collectivistic cultures emphasize in-group harmony above all else, while other collectivistic cultures do not. To account for some of these finer distinctions among individualistic and collectivistic cultures, Triandis and his colleagues differentiate between vertical and horizontal individualism and collectivism.

According to Singelis, Triandis, Bhawuk, and Gelfand, horizontal individualism is a cultural orientation where an autonomous self is valued but the individual is more or less equal in status to others. The self is perceived as independent but nevertheless the same as others. Vertical individualism is the cultural orientation where an autonomous self is also valued but

Table 2.2   Behavioral Traits Associated With Individualism and Collectivism

Individualism	Collectivism
Optimism	Social self-concept
High self-esteem	Need for affiliation
Lower social anxiety	Sensitivity to rejection
Emotional expression	Sensitivity to embarrassment
Satisfaction with self	In-group relationship preferences
Satisfaction with freedom	Indirect communication style
Ease of interacting with strangers	Valuing of social networks
Direct communication style	
Lower relational commitment	
Preference to work alone	

Self-Assessment 2.1

Individualism and Collectivism Scale

Directions: Below are 20 statements that may or may not reflect how you act within your relationships with others. For each statement, indicate the *frequency* with which you engage (or not) in the behaviors described.

5 = always, 4 = usually, 3 = sometimes, 2 = rarely, 1 = never

_____ 1. I discuss job or study-related problems with my parents.

_____ 2. I consult my family before making an important decision.

_____ 3. Before taking a major trip, I consult with most members of my family and many friends.

_____ 4. It is important to consult close friends and get their ideas before making a decision.

_____ 5. Even when I strongly disagree with my group members, I avoid an argument.

_____ 6. I hate to disagree with others in my group.

_____ 7. In interacting with superiors, I am always polite.

_____ 8. I sacrifice my self-interest for the benefit of my group.

_____ 9. I define myself as a competitive person.

_____ 10. I enjoy working in situations involving competition with others.

_____ 11. Without competition, it is impossible to have a good society.

_____ 12. Competition is the law of nature.

_____ 13. I consider myself as a unique person, separate from others.

_____ 14. I enjoy being unique and different from others.

_____ 15. I see myself as "my own person."

_____ 16. It is important for me to act as an independent person.

_____ 17. I take responsibility for my own actions.

_____ 18. Being able to take care of myself is a primary concern for me.

_____ 19. I consult with my superior on work-related matters.

_____ 20. I prefer to be self-reliant rather than depend on others.

Scoring: To compute your *collectivism* score, sum your responses for Items 1 through 8. Your sum must be between 8 and 40. Higher sums (e.g., > 30) indicate a prevalence for collectivism. To compute your *individualism* score, sum your responses for Items 9 through 20. Your sum must be between 12 and 60. Higher sums (e.g., > 45) indicate a prevalence for individualism.

the self is seen as different from and perhaps unequal to others. Status and competition are important aspects of this orientation. The United States and France are examples of vertical individualism, whereas Sweden and Austria are examples of horizontal individualism.[33] **Horizontal collectivism** is the cultural orientation where the individual sees the self as a member of an in-group whose members are similar to one another. The self is interdependent and the same as the self of others. Equality is expected and practiced within this orientation. China is probably a good example of horizontal collectivism. Theoretical communism is an example of extreme horizontal collectivism. **Vertical collectivism** is the cultural orientation in which the individual sees the self as an integral part of the in-group but the members are different from one another, some having more status than others. The self is interdependent, and inequality within the group is valued. In this orientation, serving and sacrifice are important. Japan, India, and rural traditional Greece are examples of vertical collectivism.

In a recent comparison of U.S., Thai, and Japanese students on horizontal and vertical individualism and collectivism, McCann, Honeycut, and Keaton found significant differences among the three groups and within each group. Regarding horizontal individualism, the U.S. students scored higher than the Japanese, who scored higher than the Thai students. Interestingly, there were no significant differences among the three groups on vertical individualism, where we might have expected the U.S. students to score higher than the other groups. Finally, the Japanese scored higher on horizontal and vertical collectivism than the U.S. and Thai students. Within each culture, the U.S. students scored highest on horizontal individualism, then, in order, horizontal collectivism, vertical collectivism, and

---

Measuring Horizontal and Vertical Individualism–Collectivism[35]

Consider the following situations. Place a check next to the response that most closely fits how you would act.

1. You and your friends decided spontaneously to go out to dinner at a restaurant. What do you think is the best way to handle the bill?

   A. _____ Split it equally, without regard to who ordered what.

   B. _____ Split it according to how much each person makes.

   C. _____ The group leader pays the bill or decides how to split it.

   D. _____ Compute each person's charge according to what that person ordered.

2. Which of the four books are you more likely to find the most interesting?

   A. _____ How to make friends

   B. _____ How to succeed in business

   C. _____ How to make sure you are meeting your obligations

   D. _____ How to enjoy yourself inexpensively

3. When you buy clothing for a major social event, you would be most satisfied if . . .

   A. _____ your friends like it.

   B. _____ it is so elegant it will dazzle everyone.

    C. _____ your parents like it.

    D. _____ you like it.

4. When people ask me about myself, I . . .

    A. _____ talk about my friends and what we like to do.

    B. _____ talk about my accomplishments.

    C. _____ talk about my ancestors and their traditions.

    D. _____ talk about what makes me unique.

5. Suppose your boy/girlfriend and your parents do not get along very well. What would you do?

    A. _____ Tell my boy/girlfriend that he/she should make a greater effort to "fit in with my family"

    B. _____ Tell my boy/girlfriend that I need my parents' financial support and he/she should learn to handle them

    C. _____ Remind my boy/girlfriend that my parents and family are very important to me and he/she should submit to their wishes

    D. _____ Nothing

6. Suppose you had one word to describe yourself. What would it be?

    A. _____ Cooperative

    B. _____ Competitive

    C. _____ Dutiful

    D. _____ Unique

7. Happiness is attained by . . .

    A. _____ linking with a lot of friendly people.

    B. _____ winning in competition.

    C. _____ gaining a lot of status in the community.

    D. _____ keeping one's privacy.

8. You are at a pizza restaurant with a group of friends. How should you decide what kind of pizza to order?

    A. _____ We select the pizza that most people prefer.

    B. _____ We order the most extravagant pizza available.

    C. _____ The leader of the group orders for everyone.

    D. _____ I order what I like.

Scoring: Indicate the number of times you selected letters A, B, C, and D. The frequency that is the highest represents your general HC, VI, VC, or HI orientation.

    A. _____ Horizontal Collectivism (HC)

    B. _____ Vertical Individualism (VI)

    C. _____ Vertical Collectivism (VC)

    D. _____ Horizontal Individualism (HI)

vertical individualism. The Japanese students scored highest on horizontal collectivism, virtually the same on vertical collectivism and horizontal individualism, then lowest on vertical individualism. Finally, the Thai students scored highest on horizontal collectivism, then, in order, horizontal individualism, vertical individualism, and vertical collectivism.[34]

There are advantages and disadvantages to being an individualist, just as there are to being a collectivist. Neither approach is "better" than the other; they are simply different orientations. The goal is to recognize and understand the differences, thereby increasing your intercultural competence. To be sure, the individualism–collectivism dimension of cultural variability has been used extensively in describing cultural differences—perhaps too much. Asian cultures, in particular, are often branded as collectivistic. Recently, the individualism–collectivism dichotomy has been the subject of criticism. In her analysis of the Chinese, Hui-Ching Chang argues that by describing cultures as only collectivistic—which focuses on the structure of society—much of the creativity of individual Asian cultures, including very rich histories, has been ignored. As Chang asserts,

> Although it is through the lens of the metaphor "collectivism" that we are allowed to focus on group membership and patterns of relationships in Asian cultures, at the same time, we lose sight of other aspects of delicate cultural reasoning that underlie manifested behavior patterns.[36]

The essence of Chang's argument is that we cannot rely on single metaphorical distinctions such as individualism–collectivism if we really want to accurately describe and ultimately understand other cultures.

THE PANCULTURAL SELF

As mentioned above, in individualistic cultures, emphasis is placed on individual goals over group goals, values that benefit the self are championed, the self is promoted, and individuals are encouraged to pursue and develop their individual abilities and aptitudes. In these cultures, people are taught to be creative, self-reliant, competitive, and assertive. The *individual self* is the most fundamental basis for self-definition. In contrast, in collectivistic cultures, group goals take precedence over individual goals, values that serve the in-group are stressed, and people are not seen as isolated individuals but as interdependent with others. In these cultures, the *collective self* is the most fundamental basis of self-definition.

Yet there is a growing body of literature that suggests that the individual self is pancultural—that is, that the individual self is more fundamental to self-definition across all cultures than is the collective self. In other words, people in all cultures strive to maintain and achieve positive self-regard as a primary motivation. Current research suggests that both individualistic and collectivistic cultures sanction and even endorse self-enhancement, but via different means. Collectivism is just another way to promote the self. For example, in individualistic cultures of the West (i.e., the United States, Canada, Great Britain), it is accepted and tolerated to show off one's success. In Eastern cultures (e.g., Japan, Korea, China), it is accepted and tolerated to expect reciprocity based on seniority. In other words, in both types of cultures, a person's motivations for behavior and self-definition stem primarily from one's personal identity and an independent sense of self. Moreover, research demonstrates that on self-description tasks, people generate more aspects of their individual self than of their collective self, regardless of their cultural individualism or collectivism. Some researchers have even suggested that social harmony, a primary value among collectivists, often serves as a means through which to accomplish individual goals. Other researchers have argued that collectivism is explainable not in terms of a fundamentally different cognitive organization of the self but because it is advantageous to the self in the long run. Still others maintain that in collectivistic cultures individuals may temporarily sacrifice their self-interest for the group as long as they expect to receive rewards from the group eventually. Finally, in both individualistic and collectivistic cultures, self-enhancement is sanctioned through upward mobility, status seeking, and general promotions of the self. In both types of cultures, people engage in strategic efforts to self-enhance.

Oyama points out that collectivism has long been used to describe Japanese culture. But, as Oyama asserts, Japanese society is changing and Japanese values also have changed, especially since World War II. Oyama argues that the Japanese collectivistic orientation has been decreasing and that many Japanese now have an individualistic orientation. To be sure, collectivism remains as a cultural system in Japan, especially in decision making in companies or government and in cases of company loyalty or village exclusiveness, but such an expression of collectivism is sometimes just a means of achieving an individually oriented goal. In such circumstances, Oyama contends, seeming collectivistic is a false appearance produced by individually oriented people using collectivistic methods for the realization of personal goals. For example, to value hard work in order to get rich or to study hard to make a name for oneself indicates an individual orientation that depends on a social system. People are obedient to the social system as a means to get money or honor. In behavioral terms, obedience to a social system resembles the behavior of persons with a collective orientation, but the real value orientation underlying the behavior is individual. According to Oyama, this means that individualism and collectivism, at least as practiced and valued in Japan, are not so different.[37] As Gaertner, Sedikides, and Graetz note,

> Given a choice, however, most persons would opt to stay home rather than go to war, save their hard-earned money rather than pay taxes, and relax in the company of their favorite music than engage in community volunteer work. At the same time, most persons would cherish the protection of the group when attacked individually, seek the financial support of the group when experiencing individual financial troubles, and call on the aid of the community in times of individual disaster. The individual self is the primary basis for self-definition.[38]

HIGH- AND LOW-CONTEXT COMMUNICATION

Human communication is dependent on the context in which it occurs. In addition to the verbal and nonverbal codes that are exchanged between interactants, the salient features of a communicative context include the cultural, physical, sociorelational, and perceptual environments (see Table 2.3).

Table 2.3 Human communication is dependent on the context in which it occurs.

Contextual Features

Culture (race, language)

Physical environment (office, church)

Sociorelational (superior/subordinate) $\rightarrow$ **Communication Decisions** $\rightarrow$ **Message**

Perceptual (attitudes, emotions)   Verbal choices

     Nonverbal choices

The cultural context includes, among myriad other variables, such features as individualism and collectivism. The physical environment includes the actual geographical location of the interaction (e.g., office, classroom, bedroom). The sociorelational environment encompasses the relationship between the interactants (e.g., superior/subordinate, teacher/student, husband/wife). The perceptual environment consists of the attitudes, motivations, and cognitive dispositions of the interactants. Each of these environments provides a wealth of information to the interactants about how to communicate. Here's the important point: *The degree to which interactants focus on these contexts while communicating varies considerably from culture to culture.*

Depending on contextual features present during communication, some persons choose to focus more on the verbal codes than on the nonverbal elements while others actively monitor the nonverbal elements of the context. Edward Hall describes the former as low context and the latter as high context. Hall asserts that

a high-context (HC) communication or message is one in which most of the information is either in the physical context or is internalized in the person, while very little is in the coded, explicit, transmitted part of the message. A low-context (LC) communication is just the opposite; i.e., the mass of information is vested in the explicit code.[39]

Like individualism and collectivism, high–low context is best conceptualized along a cultural continuum (see Figure 2.2). No culture exists exclusively on one end of the continuum.

Figure 2.2 High- and Low-Context Continuum

Low Context $\longleftrightarrow$ High Context

Characteristics of High- and Low-Context Cultures

Hall argues that the environmental, sociorelational, and perceptual contexts have an immense impact on communication. High-context cultures generally have restricted code systems. Users of a restricted code system rely more on the contextual elements of the communication setting for information than on the actual language code. In restricted-code cultures, communication is not general across individuals in content but is specific to particular people, places, and times. Within a **high-context** transaction, the interactant will look to the physical, sociorelational, and perceptual environment for information. Of particular importance is the social relationship between the interactants, especially their status. As Hall notes,

> Twins who have grown up together can and do communicate more economically (HC) than two lawyers in a courtroom during a trial (LC), a mathematician programming a computer, two politicians drafting legislation, two administrators writing a regulation, or a child trying to explain to his mother why he got into a fight.[40]

Because interactants in a high-context culture know and understand each other and their appropriate role, words are not necessary to convey meaning. One acts according to one's role. Words and sentences may be collapsed and shortened. In this sense, restricted codes are not unlike local dialects, vernacular, or even jargon used by a well-defined group. Users of restricted codes interpret messages based on their accumulation of shared experiences and expectations.

Hall contends that persons communicating in high-context cultures understand that information from the physical, sociorelational, and perceptual environment already exists and need not be codified verbally. Therefore, high-context communication is fast, proficient, and gratifying. Unlike low-context communication, the burden of understanding in high-context communication rests with each interactant. The rules for communication are implicit, and communicators are expected to know and understand unspoken communication. High-context communication involves using and interpreting messages that are not explicit, minimizing the content of verbal messages, and being sensitive to the social roles of others. Although there are exceptions, many high-context cultures have collectivistic tendencies, including China, Japan, North and South Korea, Vietnam, and many Arab and African cultures.[41]

According to Hall, in a **low-context** transaction, the verbal code is the primary source of information. Low-context cultures generally rely on elaborated codes. Unlike users of restricted codes, users of elaborated codes rely extensively on the verbal code system for creating and interpreting meaning. Information to be shared with others is coded in the verbal message. Although persons in low-context transactions recognize the nonverbal environment, they tend to focus more on the verbal context. Moreover, the rules and expectations are explicitly outlined. Users of elaborated codes are dependent on words to convey meaning and may become uncomfortable with silence. In low-context transactions, the communicants feel a need to speak. People using low-context communication are expected to communicate in ways that are consistent with their feelings. Hence, low-context communication typically involves transmitting direct, explicit messages. Although there are exceptions, many low-context cultures are individualistic, including Switzerland, Germany, Scandinavia, the United States, France, and the United Kingdom.[42]

Communication Consequences of Low- and High-Context Cultural Orientations

Members of high- and low-context cultures communicate differently, especially with the use of silence. Charles Braithwaite argues that one of the fundamental components of cultural and linguistic competence is knowing how and when to use silence as a communicative tactic.[43] During a high-context communicative exchange, the interactants generally are content with silence because they do not rely on verbal communication as their main source of information. Silence, in fact, communicates mutual understanding. Much of the meaning in communication is expected to be interpreted by the receiver. In communicative exchanges between persons of differing status, the person with lower status may recognize the higher status of the other through silence. Steven Pratt and Lawrence Weider contend that many Native American tribes use silence as a way of recognizing "Indianness." A "real" Indian recognizes another real Indian with silence rather than speech. A recognizable Indian knows that neither he nor the others has an obligation to speak and that silence on the part of all conversants is permissible.[44] In her book on the contemporary Japanese woman, Sumiko Iwao writes that most Japanese feel that expressing especially personal or intimate details is best done nonverbally or intuitively—that is, without words. Iwao writes,

> There is an unspoken belief among the Japanese in general that putting deep feelings into words somehow lowers or spoils their value and that understanding attained without words is more precious than that attained through precise articulation.[45]

Unlike in high-context communication, during most low-context transactions, silence is uncomfortable. Persons who do not talk are often perceived negatively. When someone is quiet in a low-context transaction, others may suspect that something is amiss. Silence somehow communicates a problem. Low-context communicators are expected to be direct and to say what they think. Persons in low-context cultures typically separate the issue of communication from the person with whom they are interacting. A manager might say to an employee, "Don't take it personally," as he or she reprimands the person. High-context cultures, on the other hand, tend to see the topic of communication as intrinsic to the person. A person is seen as a role. If the issue is attacked, so is the person. This results in low-context cultures that deliver a direct style of communication, whereas a high-context person prefers indirectness typified by extreme politeness and discretion.

AN INTERCULTURAL CONVERSATION: HIGH- AND LOW-CONTEXT CULTURES

In the following exchange, Mr. Hutchinson is the head of Information Technology within his organization. Mr. Wong is lead computer programmer. Mr. Wong was born and raised in Malaysia, a high-context culture. The two are discussing when Mr. Wong will put a computer program into production. Note that Mr. Hutchinson's speech is direct and to the point while Mr. Wong's is indirect and subtle. In simple frequency, Mr. Hutchinson uses four times as many words as Mr. Wong.[46]

Mr. Hutchinson:	The program looks good and passed the test run with only minor errors. When do you think you can put it into production? I don't see any production schedule here. The changes need to go into the system by the end of the month. Is that possible? When do you want to go with this?
Mr. Wong:	Maybe I should review the requirements.
Mr. Hutchinson:	The errors were minor. Quality Control needs to know when it will go into production. Let's set the production date now. Just tell me when you'll fix the errors. I'll tell QC.
Mr. Wong:	Perhaps I can e-mail you an estimate. I'll talk to the team.
Mr. Hutchinson:	Couldn't you just tell me when you'll have them fixed? Here, it's no big deal. (Hands Mr. Wong the program) Don't they seem like easy fixes?
Mr. Wong:	(Looks at the program but says nothing—as if not hearing Mr. Hutchinson's suggestion)
Mr. Hutchinson:	Mr. Wong? Just give me a date.
Mr. Wong:	Yes. Whenever you prefer is fine. (Hands the program back to Mr. Hutchinson)
Mr. Hutchinson:	I don't need this. (Hands it back to Mr. Wong) Well, it's got to go in by the first of next month. OK?
Mr. Wong:	Yes, that is fine.

In the above dialogue, Mr. Hutchinson misses the hint that Mr. Wong is unable to set a production date. When Mr. Wong indicates that setting a date is difficult and will require some expertise, he is indirectly telling Mr. Hutchinson that he is not in a position to make the decision on his own and would prefer to discuss it with the team. Mr. Wong further signals his discomfort by telling Mr. Hutchinson that he could e-mail him the date.

Mr. Hutchinson ignores Mr. Wong's status in the organization and further complicates the issue by handing Mr. Wong the program. Trying to avoid any disagreement, Mr. Wong simply asks Mr. Hutchinson to set the date for production and agrees to whatever he says.

Assessing High- and Low-Context Communication

Communication researcher William Gudykunst and his colleagues have developed a survey designed to measure low- and high-context communication styles. The instrument that follows is an adaptation of Gudykunst's scale.[47]

Self-Assessment 2.2

Low- and High-Context Communication Scale

Directions: Below are 32 statements regarding how you feel about communicating in different ways. In the blank to the left of each item, indicate the degree to which you agree or disagree with each statement. If you are unsure or think that an item does not apply to you, enter a 5 in the blank.

Strongly Disagree	1	2	3	4	5	6	7	8	9	Strongly Agree

_____ 1. I catch on to what others mean, even when they do not say it directly.

_____ 2. I show respect to superiors, even if I dislike them.

_____ 3. I use my feelings to determine whether to trust another person.

_____ 4. I find silence awkward in conversation.

_____ 5. I communicate in an indirect fashion.

_____ 6. I use many colorful words when I talk.

_____ 7. In argument, I insist on very precise definitions.

_____ 8. I avoid clear-cut expressions of feelings when I communicate with others.

_____ 9. I am good at figuring out what others think of me.

_____ 10. My verbal and nonverbal speech tends to be very dramatic.

_____ 11. I listen attentively, even when others are talking in an uninteresting manner.

_____ 12. I maintain harmony in my communication with others.

_____ 13. Feelings are a valuable source of information.

_____ 14. When pressed for an opinion, I respond with an ambiguous statement/position.

_____ 15. I try to adjust myself to the feelings of the person with whom I am communicating.

_____ 16. I actively use a lot of facial expressions when I talk.

_____ 17. My feelings tell me how to act in a given situation.

_____ 18. I am able to distinguish between a sincere invitation and one intended as a gesture of politeness.

_____ 19. I believe that exaggerating stories makes conversation fun.

_____ 20. I orient people through my emotions.

_____ 21. I find myself initiating conversations with strangers while waiting in line.

_____ 22. As a rule, I openly express my feelings and emotions.

_____ 23. I feel uncomfortable and awkward in social situations where everybody else is talking except me.

_____ 24. I readily reveal personal things about myself.

_____ 25. I like to be accurate when I communicate.

_____ 26. I can read another person "like a book."

_____ 27. I use silence to avoid upsetting others when I communicate.

_____ 28. I openly show my disagreement with others.

_____ 29. I am a very precise communicator.

_____ 30. I can sit with another person, not say anything, and still be comfortable.

_____ 31. I think that untalkative people are boring.

_____ 32. I am an extremely open communicator.

Scoring: Reverse your score for Items 4, 6, 7, 10, 16, 19, 21, 22, 23, 24, 25, 28, 29, 31, and 32. If your original score was 1, reverse it to a 9; if your original score was a 2, reverse it to an 8; and so on. After reversing the score for those 15 items, simply sum the 32 items. Lower scores indicate low-context communication. Higher scores indicate high-context communication.

SOURCE: Reprinted from Gudykunst, Matsumoto, Ting-Toomey, Nishida, Kim, & Heyman, "The Influence of Cultural Individualism–Collectivism, Self Construals, and Individual Values on Communication Styles Across Cultures," in *Human Communication Research, 22,* 1996, pp. 510–543. Reproduced with permission of Oxford University Press, Inc. via Copyright Clearance Center.

At this point in the chapter, you have been given the opportunity to assess your own level of individualism–collectivism and the degree to which your communication style is high or low context. Whatever the outcome on these surveys, one style is not better than the other; they are simply different. The goal is for you to have a better understanding of yourself and those persons with different cultural backgrounds. Individualism–collectivism and high/low context are two dominant ways in which cultures differ. But perhaps what guides cultural behavior more than anything else is the values held by large collectives.

VALUE ORIENTATIONS

In his seminal book on values, Milton Rokeach argues that

the value concept, more than any other, should occupy a central position across all social sciences. . . . It is an intervening variable that shows promise of being able to unify the apparently diverse interests of all sciences concerned with human behavior.[48]

Values affect intercultural communication. When people from different cultures come together to interact, their messages are guided by and reflect their fundamental value orientations. People who strongly value individuality will likely interact differently than will people who strongly value collectivism. An understanding of cultural value systems can help identify similarities and differences between people from different cultures from which intercultural communication can proceed. Like culture, values are learned; they are not innate or universal. Rokeach argues that values guide us in the selection and justification of social behavior. Values prescribe what is preferred or prohibited. Values are the evaluative component of an individual's attitudes and beliefs. Values guide how we think about things in terms of what is right/wrong and correct/incorrect. Values trigger positive or negative emotions. Values also guide our actions.[49]

Israeli psychologist Shalom Schwartz asserts that values are concepts or beliefs that pertain to outcomes and behaviors, guide the selection and evaluation of behaviors, and are rank ordered according to their relative importance to the individual.[50] Although any individual probably has a unique set of values, there are also sets of values that are representative of a particular culture. Francis Hsu, an anthropologist who has lived much of his life in China and the United States, has outlined what he thinks are the nine basic values of Americans. His list was generated from his personal experiences, American literature and prose, social science research, and studies of criminal behavior in the United States.[51]

Hsu's Postulates of Basic American Values

1. An individual's most important concern is self-interest, self-expression, self-improvement, self-gratification, and independence. This takes precedence over all group interests.

2. The privacy of the individual is the individual's inalienable right. Intrusion into it by others is permitted only by invitation.

3. Because the government exists for the benefit of the individual and not vice versa, all forms of authority, including government, are suspect. Patriotism is good.

4. An individual's success in life depends on acceptance among his or her peers.

5. An individual should believe in or acknowledge God and should belong to an organized church or other religious institution. Religion is good. Any religion is better than no religion.

6. Men and women are equal.

7. All human beings are equal.

8. Progress is good and inevitable. An individual must improve himself/herself (minimize efforts and maximize returns); the government must be more efficient to tackle new problems; institutions such as churches must modernize to make themselves more attractive.

9. Being American is synonymous with being progressive, and America is the utmost symbol of progress.

Most of the values listed above reflect America's individualistic tendencies. In addition, they echo our emphasis on equality (which is discussed later under power distance) and our determination to push toward the future.

An interesting contrast to the values of America—an individualistic, low-context culture—are those of China—a collectivistic, high-context culture. A group of cross-cultural researchers calling themselves the Chinese Culture Connection (CCC) constructed a list of 40 dominant Chinese values. The CCC is an international network of social scientists under the direction of Michael Bond, a professor in the Department of Psychology at Chinese University of Hong Kong. The members of the CCC approached a number of Chinese social scientists and asked each of them to prepare a list of 10 fundamental and basic Chinese values. Although their procedure resulted in considerable overlap, they were able to eliminate redundancy by creating a master list of 40 values.[52]

The Chinese Value Survey

1. Filial piety (obedience to parents, respect for parents, honoring of ancestors)

2. Industry (working hard)

3. Tolerance of others

4. Harmony with others

5. Humbleness

6. Loyalty to superiors

7. Observation of rites and social rituals

8. Reciprocation of greetings, favors, and gifts

9. Kindness

10. Knowledge (education)

11. Solidarity with others

12. Moderation, following the middle way

13. Self-culturation

14. Ordering relationships by status and observing this order

15. Sense of righteousness

16. Benevolent authority

17. Non-competitiveness

(Continued)

(Continued)

18. Personal steadiness and stability

19. Resistance to corruption

20. Patriotism

21. Sincerity

22. Keeping oneself disinterested and pure

23. Thrift

24. Persistence

25. Patience

26. Repayment of both the good and evil that another person has caused you

27. A sense of cultural superiority

28. Adaptability

29. Prudence (carefulness)

30. Trustworthiness

31. Having a sense of shame

32. Courtesy

33. Contentedness with one's position in life

34. Being conservative

35. Protecting your "face"

36. A close, intimate friend

37. Chastity in women

38. Having few desires

39. Respect for tradition

40. Wealth

In related research, Zhang and Bond affirmed the dominance of filial piety in China. They argue that filial piety surpasses all other cultural ethics in Chinese culture. Specifically, filial piety prescribes how children should behave toward their parents, living or dead, as well as toward their ancestors. Chinese children are taught to provide for their parents' material and mental well-being, perform ceremonial ancestral worship, ensure the continuity of the family line, and conduct themselves in a way that brings honor to and avoids shaming the family name. Zhang and Bond assert that Chinese filial piety extends beyond the limits of one's direct nuclear family. Chinese filial piety prescribes not only absolute parental authority over children but also, by extension, the authority of those senior in rank (i.e., age) over those junior in rank. Zhang and Bond maintain that Chinese filial piety influences myriad social behaviors—even in modern China, where Western, individualistic culture has been introduced.[53]

In their research on Chinese values in work organizations, Kao and Sek-Hong discovered that the Chinese values of trust, fidelity, altruism, and unspecified obligations of reciprocity norms are an important source of strategic advantage giving Chinese corporations resilience and flexibility to cope with change.[54] Researchers Domino and Hannah argue that Chinese values are taught early and can be seen in the stories told by Chinese children. In comparison with stories told by American children, the Chinese stories demonstrated greater social orientation, greater emphasis on public shame, fewer interpersonal confrontations, more instances of teamwork, more concern for the role of authority, greater preoccupation with moral and ethical rectitude, more expressions of sorrow and happiness, fewer instances of physical aggression, and less economic orientation.[55]

Schwartz's Universal Values

Shalom Schwartz and his colleagues have studied values across cultures. Schwartz's goal is to create a comprehensive classification scheme of the substantive content of human values that are shared across cultures. Although some disagree with his position, Schwartz argues that there is a universal structure to values recognized by all cultures. Schwartz's work focuses on the structure of values, not on the universality of their relative importance. Schwartz argues that values represent goals or motivations. He contends that values represent, in the form of goals, three universal requirements for human existence to which all cultures must be responsive: (a) the biological needs of individuals, (b) the need for social coordination, and (c) the survival and welfare needs of groups. From these three universal human requirements, Schwartz derived 11 distinct motivational value types (listed on p. 72). These motivational types lead to the formation of specific values and their priorities. To make the meaning of each motivational type more concrete and explicit, the specific values used to measure the motivational type are listed in parentheses.[56]

Kluckhohn and Strodtbeck's Value Orientations

In the early 1960s, Florence Kluckhohn and Fred Strodtbeck developed the concept of value orientations. They argued that in every culture there are universal problems and conditions that must be addressed. For example, every culture must deal with the natural environment. All cultures must feed themselves. All cultures must face the issues of child rearing, and so on. For a given culture, however, there are a limited number of solutions to these problems. These possible solutions are motivated by the values of the culture. Initially, Kluckhohn and Strodtbeck created five sets of value orientations.[57] Several years later, communication researchers John Condon and Fathi Yousef extended the set to a total of 25 value orientations. Condon and Yousef organized the value orientations around six dominant themes: the self, the family, society, human nature, nature, and the supernatural.[58]

Schwartz's Motivational Types of Values

1. *Self-Direction:* The defining goal of this value type is independent thought and action. (freedom, creativity, independent, choosing own goals, curious, self-respect)

2. *Stimulation:* The goal is derived from the need for variety and stimulation in order to maintain an optimal level of activation. Some of these needs are biological, while others are learned/cultural. (an exciting life, a varied life, daring)

3. *Hedonism:* The need and motivation for pleasure. (pleasure, enjoying life)

4. *Achievement:* The need and value of personal success and prestige. (ambitious, influential, capable, successful, intelligent, self-respect)

5. *Power:* Attainment of social status. (social power, wealth, authority, preserving my public image, social recognition)

6. *Security:* Need for safety, harmony, and the stability of society and relationships. (national security, reciprocation of favors, family security, sense of belonging, social order, healthy, clean)

7. *Conformity:* Restraint of actions, inclinations, and impulses. (obedient, self-discipline, politeness, honoring of parents and elders)

8. *Tradition:* The value of religious rites, beliefs, and norms of behavior that, over time, are valued and passed on by a collective. (respect for children, devout, accepting of my portion in life, humble, moderate)

9. *Spirituality:* The goal of inner harmony through the transcendence of everyday life. (a spiritual life, meaning in life, inner harmony, detachment)

10. *Benevolence:* The need and motivation for positive interaction and affiliation. (helpful, responsible, forgiving, honest, loyal, mature love, true friendship)

11. *Universalism:* The value of understanding, appreciation, tolerance, and protection for the welfare of all people and for nature. (equality, unity with nature, wisdom, a world of beauty, social justice, broad-minded, protecting the environment, a world at peace)

The Condon and Yousef set of value orientations provides a structure and vocabulary that can be used to compare cultures. Although there are exceptions, many of the values on the left of the continuum are representative of individualistic, low-context cultures, while those on the right are representative of collectivistic, high-context cultures (see Table 2.4).

The Self

In all cultures, people develop their self-identity. How that identity is fostered is influenced by the culture's values. For example, people in individualistic societies, such as the United States, tend to view their accomplishments and failures very personally. Conformity is viewed negatively. Hsu notes that in China, however, conformity and cooperation are highly valued. In the United States, a person is seen as a unique individual and strives for independence

Table 2.4   The Condon and Yousef Set of Value Orientations

	Individualistic Low Context		Collectivistic High Context
THE SELF			
1. Individualism	Individualism	Individuality	Interdependence
2. Age	Youth	Middle years	Old age
3. Sex	Equality of sexes	Female superiority	Male superiority
4. Activity	Doing	Being-in-becoming	Being
THE FAMILY			
1. Relational orientations	Individualistic	Collateral	Lineal
2. Authority	Democratic	Authority centered	Authoritarian
3. Positional role behavior	Open	General	Specific—prescribed
4. Mobility	High mobility	Phasic mobility	Low mobility—stasis
SOCIETY			
1. Social reciprocity	Independence	Symmetrical—obligatory	Complementary—obligatory
2. Group membership	Many—brief membership	Balanced	Few—prolonged membership
3. Intermediaries	Few	Specialist only	Essential
4. Formality	Informal	Selective formality	Pervasive formality
5. Property	Private	Utilitarian	Communal
HUMAN NATURE			
1. Rationality	Rational	Intuitive	Irrational
2. Good/evil	Good	Mixture	Evil
3. Happiness/pleasure	Happiness as goal	Inextricable bond of happiness and sadness	Life is mostly sad
4. Mutability	Change, growth, learning	Some change	Unchanging
NATURE			
1. Relationship between humans and nature	Humans dominate nature	Harmonious	Nature dominates humans
2. Ways of knowing nature	Abstract	Circle of induction and deduction	Specific—direct
3. Structure of nature	Mechanistic	Spiritual	Organic
4. Concept of time	Future	Present	Past
THE SUPERNATURAL			
1. Relationship between humans and the supernatural	Humans as God	Pantheism	Humans controlled by supernatural
2. Meaning of life	Physical/material goals	Intellectual goals	Spiritual goals
3. Providence	Good is unlimited	Balance of good and misfortune	Good in life is limited
4. Knowledge of cosmic order	Order is comprehensible	Faith and reason	Mysterious and unknowable

from others. When individuals succeed or win, they receive a great deal of attention and adulation, as in the case of winning an Olympic gold medal or an Academy Award. The individual is "put on a pedestal." Likewise, when individuals lose, they are often left to suffer alone. No one wants to be seen with a loser. Whether on the top or on the bottom, the individual experiences intense emotions. Hsu contends that strong emotions are unavoidable because they are concentrated in one individual. The Chinese, however, are interdependent with others, and for them, responsibility and accountability are shared and divided among the group members. If the group wins, everyone in the group wins; there is no "most valuable player," so to speak. Therefore, the intense emotions experienced by winning or failing are tempered and moderated because they are shared.[59]

The second variation on the self continuum is age. Western, individualistic, low-context cultures tend to value youth. Conversely, old age is valued in many cultures, such as Nigeria, where it is associated with wisdom. According to Harris and Moran, in Nigeria the elderly are respected because they have much experience and can pass on family history and tradition. Harris and Moran suggest that when conducting business with Nigerians, a company would be wise to send an older person to meet with prospective businesspersons, as this will show a certain amount of respect for Nigeria's emphasis on age.[60]

The third variation on the self is activity. Americans identify themselves in terms of their activities, usually professions and occupations. Condon and Yousef hold that many English names indicate "doers," such as Baker, Smith, and Carpenter, for example. In the United States, people are often asked about what they "do" for a living. Some non-Western cultures emphasize being, a form of self-actualization. In this view, life is an organic whole; it is human to embrace life and to become one with the universe and oneself.[61]

The Family

Familial relationships differ across cultures. Harris and Moran write that in Nigeria, for example, the family is the core group of society. Nigerians value their family lineage through the male head of the household. A Nigerian is known by his or her family lineage and may have privileges and responsibilities based on family name. Furthermore, marriage is seen as a way of producing more children to contribute to this lineage. If one's spouse is sterile, it is grounds for divorce. Nigerians also practice polygamy. Wives are often acquired through the payment of a bride price to the bride's parents.[62]

Positional role behavior within families refers to how strictly roles are prescribed among family members. The Guatemalan Ladinos (a term used to refer to people born through interracial relationships or those who have Spanish and Indian blood) define a man's and woman's role within the family quite differently. Mike Keberlein, who grew up in Guatemala, argues that machismo is a Spanish concept that deals mainly with how male and female roles are performed in the home. Ladinos view the men as protectors and providers and women as child rearers and homemakers. Children are taught early by their mother to recognize their responsibilities as men and women. A boy may be sent to work in the fields when he is as young as 5 years old. A young girl might start household chores at the same age, where she is taught to care for younger children of the house and to cook. Young boys are expected never to cry or show signs of pain, whereas young girls are taught to show emotion whenever appropriate.[63]

Society

According to Condon and Yousef, social reciprocity refers to the mutual exchanges people make in their dealings with others. What is perceived as a relatively innocuous request in one country may be interpreted quite seriously in others. In the United States, a request to do a favor (e.g., "Can I borrow your car?") may imply no necessary reciprocity. In other cultures, one is required to return favors and obligations in kind. Equal exchanges are expected and obligatory.[64]

The second value orientation, group membership, differs greatly among individualistic and collectivistic cultures. According to Condon and Yousef, members of individualistic cultures tend to join many groups throughout their lifetime, yet their affiliation with any particular group may be quite brief. The group is subordinate to the individual's needs. In the United States, for example, people join political groups, social groups, hobby groups, occupational groups, self-help groups, fraternal groups, and so on. In collectivistic cultures, people tend to belong to fewer groups (e.g., family and occupational) but belong for a lifetime.[65]

An intermediary is a go-between; intermediaries are more common in collectivistic than in individualistic cultures. Many Chinese prefer to work through an intermediary. The concept of *mian-zi,* or "face," is a critical ingredient for Chinese. The Chinese believe that respect for others binds society together. Mian-zi is a sort of social status, or how a person is ranked in relation to others. This is sometimes referred to as one's "face." A person's face is determined by such things as wealth and power. Chinese are very conscious of their face as well as the face of others. The higher in rank a person is, the more critical the concern with face. In business dealings and in personal relationships, it is critical to the Chinese that they maintain face and avoid offending the face of others. Hence, it is difficult for the Chinese to be straightforward and open in their daily interactions with others. Intermediaries are, therefore, essential in both personal and business relationships. Accordingly, the notion of losing face means that an individual loses his or her social position or prestige in front of others. When local senior executives perceive the local staff to be incompetent, they may feel that they risk "losing face" vis-à-vis headquarters' management and expatriates. To save face, these executives may think about quitting or involving an intermediary.[66]

Human Nature

The human nature orientation deals with how cultures perceive human character and temperament. In Western cultures such as the United States, people are viewed as essentially rational. American children are taught to "use their heads" when making decisions. Americans frequently tell their friends to "stop being so emotional," as if being emotional implied some character flaw. Japanese children, on the other hand, are often taught to follow their intuition or to lead with their hearts. Condon and Yousef note that in the United States, happiness is viewed as a practical goal, even the primary goal—hence the popular song titled "Don't Worry, Be Happy." Moreover, the Declaration of Independence states that people "are endowed by their creator with certain inalienable rights, that among these are life, liberty, and the pursuit of happiness." Other societies and cultures view happiness and sadness as inseparable, as in the yin–yang philosophy of many Asian cultures. A Chinese proverb reads, "If a man's face does not show a little sadness, his thoughts are not too deep." Another one reads, "One should not miss the flavor of being sick, nor miss the experience of being destitute."[67]

Nature

In the United States, high school students learn about the structure of nature in their biology, geography, and physics classes, among others. Students learn about things they may never actually see, such as the structure of DNA. The models they see are not literal reproductions but, rather, dramatic abstractions. Much of the education taught in the United States is based on abstract concepts and constructs. Condon and Yousef maintain that in other cultures, perhaps those with little formal education, what a person knows about nature is learned through direct experience. Many Western cultures view nature as mechanistic, meaning that nature is structured much like a machine or clock. The brain, for example, is explained using computer analogies. Models of DNA look like double helixes. The organic orientation likens nature to a plant, where nature is seen as an organic whole that is interdependent with all other natural forces.[68]

The Supernatural

Condon and Yousef assert that a culture's perspective on the cosmos reflects its philosophy about its people's relationship with the supernatural and spiritual world. In many Western cultures, the supernatural is studied almost scientifically. Scientists study the structure of space and seek, through scientific means, to find the origins of the universe. We send out satellites equipped with printed messages and recordings in an (perhaps vain) attempt to communicate with extraterrestrials. Most Western cultures believe that the order of the cosmos is knowable. Conversely, other cultures view the cosmos with a great deal of fear and uncertainty. Condon and Yousef point to a farmer in Peru who relies on the phases of the moon and the cycles of the seasons to tell him when to plant or harvest his fields. The farmer thinks of the cosmos with a great deal of superstition and fear. To him, these mysteries are unexplainable.[69]

The organization of the value orientations presented above is neither mutually exclusive nor exhaustive. They are representative of the kinds of values held by cultures and the differences in those values. They also serve as a starting point for researchers to compare and contrast the myriad cultures that cohabit the planet.

POWER DISTANCE

According to Hofstede, while many cultures declare and even legislate equality for their members, all cultures must deal with the issue of human inequality. A fundamental tenet expressed in the beginning of the Declaration of Independence, the document on which the United States was founded, states that "we hold these truths to be self-evident, that all men are created equal." In the United States, we generally try to treat others as equal, in both our personal and professional lives. Although some cultures, like the United States, affirm equality for their members, some form of inequality exists in virtually every culture. Inequality can occur in areas such as prestige, wealth, power, human rights, and technology, among others. Issues of inequality fall within the rubric of what Hofstede calls "power distance." In his landmark survey research, Geert Hofstede defined **power distance** as "the extent to which the less powerful members of institutions and organizations within a country expect and accept that power is distributed unequally."[70] Power distance can be seen in families, in bureaucracies, and even in friendships. Inequality of power within organizations is inevitable and desirable in many cases for organizations to function effectively. For example, military organizations are defined by power distance.

Hofstede categorizes cultures as possessing either large or small power distance. Cultures with a smaller power distance emphasize that inequalities among people should be minimized and that there should be interdependence between less-powerful and more-powerful people. In cultures with small power distance (e.g., the United States, Canada, Austria), family members are generally treated as equal and familial decisions are reached democratically. According to Hofstede, in small power distance schools, teachers expect a certain amount of initiative and interaction with students. The overall educational process is student oriented. In class, students are expected to ask questions and perhaps even challenge their teachers. In organizations, decentralization is popular, where subordinates engage in participative decision making. The organizational power hierarchy is mostly for convenience, where the persons who occupy powerful roles may change regularly. In fact, workers are expected to try to "climb the ladder of success" to more power and prestige. In this sense, persons in small power distance cultures may recognize "earned" power—that is, power that people deserve by virtue of their drive, hard work, and motivation. Moreover, small power distance cultures tend to resent those whose power is decreed by birth or wealth (i.e., positional power).[71]

Hofstede maintains that in cultures with a larger power distance, inequalities among people are both expected and desired. Less powerful people should be dependent on more powerful people.

In larger power distance cultures (e.g., the Philippines, Mexico, India), children are expected to be obedient. In many larger power distance cultures, there is a strict hierarchy among family members where typically the father rules authoritatively, followed by the eldest son and moving down the ladder by age and sex (see Figure 2.3). In educational settings, teachers are treated as parents—with respect and honor—especially older teachers. Students who disobey may be punished severely. In the workplace, power is usually centralized, and workers and bosses are treated unequally. In many large power distance cultures, Hofstede observed that workers are generally uneducated and superiors are entitled to special privileges and status—in some cultures, by law.[72]

There appears to be a direct link between power distance and the latitude of the country. In a study conducted at 40 universities in the United States, Peter Andersen and his colleagues found a strong correlation between latitude and authoritarianism. Residents in the northern U.S. states were less authoritarian than those in the southern United States. The population of a country may be another predictor of power distance. Generally, larger cultures tend to have larger power distance (see Table 2.5). As the size of any group increases, it becomes unwieldy and difficult to manage informally.[73]

Large and small power distance cultures may value different types of power. Large power distance cultures tend to emphasize positional power. Positional power is based on formal authority (e.g., family rank). Persons with positional power have control over rewards, punishments, and information. Small power distance cultures recognize and respect earned power. Earned power is based on an individual's accomplishments, hard work, and effort.

Figure 2.3   In many cultures, there is a strict hierarchy among family members.

Table 2.5   Small and Large Power Distance Cultures

Small Power Distance Cultures	Large Power Distance Cultures
Austria	Malaysia
Denmark	Guatemala
New Zealand	Panama
Ireland	Philippines
Sweden	Mexico
Norway	Venezuela
Finland	Ecuador
Switzerland	Indonesia
Great Britain	India
Germany	Brazil

STUDENT VOICES ACROSS CULTURES

Power Distance

My name is Ahmed I. Alshaya, and I am from Riyadh, Saudi Arabia. I graduated from St. Norbert College with a major in business administration.

Saudi Arabia is a large power distance country for reasons concerned with favorability of outcomes. The culture merely focuses on the outcomes that do not disturb the harmony of the people. Power distance in Saudi Arabia is defined by age and sex. There is a hierarchical structure in almost all families. In a typical Saudi family, since there is a hierarchical structure, obviously the father is the head of the house. He is the one in charge of the house in all aspects. The father has some responsibilities that he must provide to his house. The father is responsible for teaching his offspring the moral traits. That is, the family must obey the father and treats him with respect and honor. The role then goes to the elder son if the father is not available. There is, of course, a dependence on the one in charge, and usually the family depends on him in making decisions.

Moving to a bigger scale, society plays a big role in shaping the people of Saudi Arabia. The elderly are always seen as people who are wise and are capable of leading the community to prosperity. Usually, people are expected to treat the elderly with respect. For example, at a time of conflict, the elderly would always step in to resolve a problem, and all the parties involved have to acknowledge the issue and have some respect for the decision that has been made. The "self-face" and the "other-face" are concerns for people who are involved. The "face" is a concern because if not properly maintained, it will bring disgrace to the family. The "face" is recognized in many ways. It is present during all social gatherings; the elderly are always treated with respect because the host and his sons must save their "self-face" by properly making the elderly feel comfortable.

In the workplace, Saudi is considered to be power distance oriented especially in the relationship between subordinates and their employees. There is a strong hierarchical structure. Employers must be treated with respect because they have authority in the organization. Different organizations have different approaches, but most commonly, employees do not participate in the decision-making role.

Measuring Power Distance

If we know the position of a culture on the power distance scale relative to our own culture, then we have a starting point from which to proceed in our understanding of that culture. In large power distance cultures, subordinates are extremely submissive, whereas in small power distance cultures, subordinates are confrontational. Power distance tells us about dependence relationships in a given culture. In those countries where a small power distance is observed (e.g., Austria, Norway), there is limited dependence. Workers in these cultures prefer managers who consult with them in decision making. Here, subordinates are generally comfortable approaching and interacting with their superiors. In cultures with large power distance (e.g., Malaysia, Mexico, India), there is considerable dependence of subordinates on superiors.

Self-Assessment 2.3

Power Distance Scale

Directions: Below are 10 statements regarding issues we face at work, in the classroom, and at home. Indicate in the blank to the left of each statement the degree to which you (1) strongly agree, (2) agree, (3) are unsure, (4) disagree, and (5) strongly disagree with the statement. For example, if you strongly agree with the first statement, place a 1 in the blank. Work quickly and record your initial response.

_____ 1. Within an organization, employees should feel comfortable expressing disagreements to their managers.

_____ 2. Within a classroom, students should be allowed to express their points of view toward a subject without being punished by the teacher/professor.

_____ 3. At home, children should be allowed to openly disagree with their parents.

_____ 4. The primary purpose of a manager is to monitor the work of the employees to make sure they are doing their jobs appropriately.

_____ 5. Authority is essential for the efficient running of an organization, classroom, or home.

_____ 6. At work, people are more productive when they are closely supervised by those in charge.

_____ 7. In problem-solving situations within organizations, input from employees is important.

_____ 8. Generally, employees, students, and children should be seen and not heard.

_____ 9. Obedience to managers, teachers, and parents is good.

_____ 10. Managers, teachers, and parents should be considered equal to their workers, students, and children.

Scoring: For Items 4, 5, 6, 8, and 9, reverse your responses. That is, if your original response was a 1, reverse it to a 5. If your original response was a 2, reverse it to a 4 and so on. Once you have reversed your responses for these items, sum your 10 responses. This sum is your power distance score. Lower scores equal smaller power distance.

SOURCE: Reproduced by permission. Copyright © Geert Hofstede.

Communication and Power Distance

Power distance affects the verbal and nonverbal behavior of a culture. Several studies have investigated power distance and communication during conflict. In their research, Tyler, Lind, and Huo found that power distance influences the way that people react to third-party authorities in conflict situations. Specifically, they found that when making evaluations of authorities, persons in small power distance cultures placed more value on the quality of their treatment by authorities. In contrast, those with larger power distance values focused more strongly on the favorability of their outcomes. Tyler, Lind, and Huo suggest that the degree to which authorities can gain acceptance for themselves and their decisions through providing dignified, respectful treatment is influenced by the cultural values of the disputants. Specifically, they found that dispute resolution methods, such as mediation, are more likely to be effective among those who have small power distance values.[74]

In another study, Smith, Dugan, Peterson, and Leung examined how managers handled disagreement with their subordinates. Their results showed that the larger the power distance, the more frequent are reports of out-group disagreements; and the smaller the power distance, the more likely managers are to ask peers to handle disagreements and to use subordinates to handle disagreements. The authors conclude that in small power distance cultures, managers minimize status differences during conflict and rely on peers and subordinates to assist in mediating conflict.[75]

Ting-Toomey has examined power distance and the concepts of *face* and *facework* in conflict situations. Ting-Toomey and others argue that persons in all cultures have face concerns. Face represents an individual's sense of positive self-image in the context of communication. According to Ting-Toomey, everyone, in all cultures, has face concerns during conflict. *Self-face* is the concern for one's own image, *other-face* is concern for another's image, and *mutual-face* is concern for both parties. *Facework* is used to manage these face concerns during conflict. Ting-Toomey's research has shown that small power distance cultures have a greater self-face concern, have lesser other- and mutual-face concerns, use more dominating facework, and use less avoiding facework.[76]

Other research has investigated how power distance affects reactions to messages about alcohol warnings. Perea and Slater examined the responses of Mexican American and Anglo young adults to four televised drinking and driving warnings. The messages were manipulated into large and small power distance appeals by attributing or not attributing them to the Surgeon General—that is, an authority with power. Anglos (small power distance) rated the warnings without the Surgeon General as more believable than warnings with the Surgeon General; the opposite was true for Latinos (large power distance).[77]

Student–teacher relationships exist in virtually every culture. Generally, teachers possess more legitimate and expert power than do their students (see Figure 2.4). In an interesting examination of student–teacher relationships in small (i.e., Britain) and large (i.e., China) power distance cultures, Spencer-Oatey found that Chinese students reported a larger power differential between themselves and their Chinese teachers than did the British students with their British teachers. Yet the Chinese reported their relationships with their teachers to be interpersonally closer than did the British. Moreover, the Chinese students reported that the power differential between them and their teachers was acceptable. Consistent with their value of filial piety, one Chinese student commented that one should "treat teachers as you would treat your elders." On the other hand, the British students were significantly less accepting of the power differential between them and their teachers, even though that differential was small. One British student reported that teachers "certainly have these powers, but shouldn't have."[78]

Figure 2.4 In many cultures (especially large power distance cultures), teachers may hold more power over students than do parents.

In another interesting study, Michael Bond and his colleagues found that persons in large power distance cultures respond differently to verbal insults than do persons in small power distance cultures. In their comparison of Chinese and American students, they found that the Chinese were less critical of an insulter as long as the insulter had higher status than the in-group. Americans, on the other hand, made no distinction as a function of the insulter's status.[79]

Power distance also affects the nonverbal behavior of a culture. In many large power distance cultures, persons of lower status are taught not to give direct eye contact to a person of higher status. Indirect eye contact from a subordinate signals to the superior that the subordinate recognizes his or her lower status. In large power distance cultures, when a person of high status hands something to a person of lower status (e.g., a book), the lower status person will often use both hands to receive the item, again recognizing his or her lower status. Andersen, Hecht, Hoobler, and Smallwood have observed that many large power distance cultures prohibit interclass dating, marriage, and contact. They also suggest that persons of lower power must become skilled at decoding nonverbal behavior and that persons of lower status must show only positive emotions to those of higher status. Moreover, in large power distance cultures, persons of lower status smile more in an effort to appease those of higher status.[80]

AN INTERCULTURAL CONVERSATION: LARGE AND SMALL POWER DISTANCE CULTURES

Different power distance orientations manifest themselves in interaction. In the dialogue below, Jim Neuman is a U.S. high school exchange student in Guatemala. Coming from a smaller power distance culture, Jim is accustomed to interacting with his teachers. Raising one's hand in a U.S. classroom is not only acceptable but encouraged. In Guatemala, a larger power distance culture, the classroom is teacher centered. In Mr. Gutierrez's classroom, there is to be strict order, with Mr. Gutierrez initiating all the communication. Teachers are to be treated with deference.

Mr. Gutierrez:	This morning I will be discussing some points about Guatemala's geography. Guatemala is the northernmost country of Central America. (Jim Neuman raises his hand) To the north it borders the countries of El Salvador and Honduras. To the west, its natural border is the Pacific Ocean. In the east is another natural border, the Atlantic Ocean, as well as the country of Belize.
Jim Neuman:	(Raising his hand and waving it slightly) Mr. Gutierrez?
Mr. Gutierrez:	Guatemala is called the "Land of the Eternal Spring." There are all the same kinds of natural land forms as in Mexico but are (Jim Neuman interrupts)
Jim Neuman:	Mr. Gutierrez, I have a question.
Mr. Gutierrez:	Jim, stop interrupting, please.
Jim Neuman:	May I ask a question?
Mr. Gutierrez:	No! If you continue to disobey, I will punish you! Be quiet!

In the above dialogue, Jim does not understand Mr. Gutierrez's harsh reprimand. Coming from a small power distance culture, Jim recognizes that teachers have more power than students but does not see their power as absolute. Jim sees himself as an active participant of the class. After all, for most of his life Jim's teachers have encouraged him to speak up in class. Mr. Gutierrez, on the other hand, sees the classroom as his domain, one that he rules absolutely. By raising his hand, Jim demonstrates his insolence toward Mr. Gutierrez. To some extent, a certain degree of power distance is essential if cultures are to survive. Legitimate power is a necessity of civil life. Yet independence from power, liberation, and freedom of choice are politically attractive alternatives. Perhaps the ideal situation is one where individual families operate with internally driven large power distances while the larger cultural milieu restricts overbearing, omnipotent, and intimidating governments.

UNCERTAINTY AVOIDANCE

Gudykunst and Kim state that communicating with someone from an unknown culture can be uncomfortable because such situations are replete with uncertainty and unpredictability. When uncertainty is high, anxiety is usually high, and communication can be difficult and awkward. This may account for why some people avoid interacting with people from other cultures. By reducing uncertainty, however, anxiety can be reduced, which, in turn, facilitates effective and successful communication. Although uncertainty is probably a universal feature of initial intercultural communication, one's level of tolerance for uncertainty and ambiguity varies across cultures. In addition, argue Gudykunst and Kim, the communicative strategies for reducing uncertainty also vary across cultures. Persons in high-context cultures, for example, look to the environmental, sociorelational, and perceptual contexts for information to reduce uncertainty. People in low-context cultures tend to rely on verbal information-seeking strategies, usually by asking lots of questions.[81]

Hofstede asserts that although the extent to which an individual experiences uncertainty and the subsequent strategies for reducing it may be unique to that person, a general orientation toward uncertainty can be shared culturally. According to Hofstede, tolerance for uncertainty is learned through cultural socialization. Hofstede notes that a culture's technology, system of laws, and religion are markers for how that culture addresses and attempts to avoid or reduce uncertainty. For example, some kinds of technology help a culture manage natural uncertainty (e.g., weather), systems of law are designed to prevent and account for behavioral uncertainties (e.g., crime), and religion can help a culture cope with supernatural uncertainty (e.g., death). A culture's technology, law, and religion are ingrained in the individual through socialization, education, and occupation. Hence, they lead to collective patterns of tolerance for ambiguity and uncertainty.[82]

Uncertainty avoidance is the degree to which the members of a particular culture feel threatened by uncertain or unknown situations. Hofstede contends that this feeling is expressed through nervous stress and in a felt need for predictability and for written and unwritten rules. Cultures possess either a weak or a strong uncertainty avoidance orientation. In cultures with a weak uncertainty avoidance orientation, uncertainty is seen as a normal part of life, where each day is accepted as it comes. The people are comfortable with ambiguity and are guided by a belief that what is different is curious. In school settings, students are comfortable with open-ended learning situations and enjoy classroom discussion. In the workplace, time is needed only as a guide, not as a master. Precision and punctuality are learned because they do not come naturally. Workers are motivated by their achievements and personal esteem or belongingness. There is also a high tolerance for innovative ideas that may conflict with the norm.[83]

Conversely, cultures with a strong uncertainty avoidance orientation sense that uncertainty in life is a continuous threat that must be fought. Life can be stressful where a sense of urgency and high anxiety are typical. Hofstede maintains that strong uncertainty avoidant cultures are guided by the belief that what is different is dangerous. Uncertainty avoidant cultures evade ambiguity in most situations and look for structure in their business organizations, home life, and relationships. At school, students are most comfortable in structured environments. The teachers are supposed to have all the right answers. On the job, time is money; punctuality and precision are expected. There is generally a resistance to innovative ideas, and workers are motivated by job security.[84]

A THEORY OF UNCERTAINTY ORIENTATION

Related to Hofstede's concept of uncertainty avoidance is the theory of uncertainty orientation. According to this variation of Hofstede's ideas, some individuals are considered uncertainty oriented and others are considered certainty oriented. Uncertainty-oriented individuals have a weak uncertainty avoidance tendency, while certainty-oriented individuals have a strong uncertainty avoidance tendency. Uncertainty-oriented persons' preferred method of handling uncertainty is to seek out information and to engage in activity that will directly resolve the uncertainty. These people try to understand and discover aspects of the self and the environment about which they are uncertain.

Certainty-oriented people, on the other hand, develop a self-regulatory style that circumvents uncertainty. Given the choice, persons who are certainty oriented will undertake activity that maintains clarity; when confronted with uncertainty, they will rely on others or on heuristic devices more than on more direct methods of resolving uncertainty (see Figure 2.5).

Generally, Eastern cultures have a preference for certainty, whereas Western cultures are uncertainty oriented (see Table 2.6). The tendency to be individualistic or self-oriented in Western populations exists because uncertainty-oriented people like to find out new information about the self. The more personally relevant or uncertain the situation, the more

---

Figure 2.5   Uncertainty and Certainty Orientations

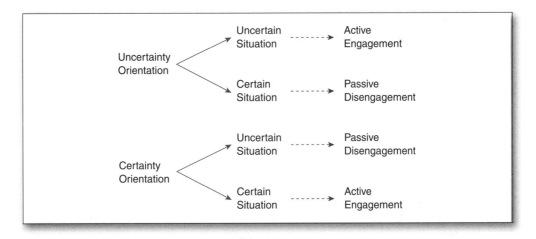

Table 2.6   Certainty- and Uncertainty-Oriented Cultures

Certainty-Oriented Cultures	Uncertainty-Oriented Cultures
Japan	United States
Guatemala	Canada
Portugal	New Zealand
Peru	Sweden
El Salvador	Ireland
Panama	Great Britain
Chile	Denmark
Spain	South Africa
Uruguay	Norway

uncertainty-oriented persons will be actively engaged in the situation. Certainty-oriented people, however, are more group oriented, as the group provides a clear standard for norms and behavior, a standard that can be embraced by the certainty oriented. Western societies tend to be more uncertainty oriented because of their self-oriented and individualistic approaches to life than do people in Eastern societies, who, in turn, should be more certainty oriented as a function of their heavy reliance on groups.[85]

AN INTERCULTURAL CONVERSATION: WEAK AND STRONG UNCERTAINTY AVOIDANCE

One's uncertainty avoidance orientation may manifest itself in interaction in any number of ways. In the dialogue presented below, Kelly and Keiko are interacting about a dinner invitation. Kelly, from the United States, possesses a relatively weak uncertainty avoidance index, while Keiko, from Japan, comes from a culture with a relatively strong uncertainty avoidance index.

Keiko:	Hey, Kelly, let's do something tonight.
Kelly:	All right.
Keiko:	Please come over to my house and I'll cook dinner for you.
Kelly:	I have invited some friends over to my house for dinner tonight, but I don't know if they're coming.
Keiko:	Well . . . as soon as you know if they're coming, let me know.
Kelly:	I won't know until tonight.
Keiko:	What time?
Kelly:	I won't know until they call me. They'll probably call later this afternoon.
Keiko:	How will you know whether or not to cook enough for everyone?
Kelly:	Oh, I'll make up something on the spot. I like to cook. I'll whip up something fast.
Keiko:	But . . . what if they don't come? Won't they call and let you know?
Kelly:	No . . . if they don't come, I'll know that something else came up. I'll let you know as soon as I can.
Keiko:	Maybe we should plan my dinner for some other night.

In the above dialogue, Keiko is confused by Kelly's easygoing attitude toward the evening's plans. Coming from a strong uncertainty-avoidant culture, Keiko would prefer to plan ahead to avoid uncertainty and prepare her script for the evening. Kelly, on the other hand, is perfectly comfortable making plans based on how the evening progresses. Without a plan, how will Keiko know how to act? Although the feelings associated with uncertainty are personal and subjective, they can be shared by whole cultures. Although anxiety creates the same physiological responses in humans, what triggers anxiety and one's level of tolerance for it is learned. A culture's orientation toward uncertainty can be found in its families, schools, and institutions. But uncertainty avoidance ultimately manifests itself in human interaction.

CHAPTER SUMMARY

In the contextual model of intercultural communication, culture is the largest context, surrounding all the other contexts. This chapter has presented the paradox of culture. On one hand, culture is amorphous; it is shapeless, vague, and nebulous. Most of us are not aware of its influence on our daily behaviors. On the other hand, culture is arguably the strongest influence on an individual's cognitive, affective, and behavioral choices. Over the past few decades, anthropologists, psychologists, and sociologists have isolated several dimensions of cultural variability by which cultures can be compared. This chapter has focused on five of these dimensions, including the extent to which we place individual goals over those of the group (i.e., individualism) or the degree to which we see ourselves as members of a group first, then as an individual (i.e., collectivism). Another dimension is high–low context, which refers to the extent to which we gather information from the physical, social, and psychological context (i.e., high context), or the extent to which we gather information from the verbal code (i.e., low context). One of the most influential features of our lives is our value orientation. A culture's values guide its decisions as to what is right or wrong, decent or indecent, moral or immoral. Cultures also differ regarding the extent to which people accept and expect that power is distributed unequally (i.e., large power distance) or believe that people are inherently equal (i.e., small power distance). And finally, cultures differ in the extent to which people accept and tolerate uncertainty and unpredictability in their lives (i.e., weak uncertainty avoidance) or the extent to which uncertainty should be fought and conquered (i.e., strong uncertainty avoidance). These dimensions provide a starting point for our future examination of intercultural communication.

Visit the student study site at **www.sagepub.com/neuliep5e** *for e-flashcards, web quizzes, web resources and more.*

DISCUSSION QUESTIONS

1. Do you feel that you belong to an individualistic or collectivistic culture? Why? What are the signs?

2. What are some of the ways that you use high-context communication? What are some of the ways that you use low-context communication? Which do you prefer?

3. Is your relationship with your professors indicative of large or small power distance?

4. Is your relationship with your parents indicative of large or small power distance?

5. If you have no plans for the upcoming weekend, does that make you feel anxious, or are you comfortable with not knowing? Depending on your answer, are you certainty or uncertainty oriented?

ETHICAL CONSIDERATIONS WITHIN THE CULTURAL CONTEXT

If you were born and raised in the United States, you are probably relatively individualistic, low context, small power distance, and have a weak uncertainty avoidance tendency. Seeing the various dimensions of cultural variability discussed in this chapter, consider the following situations and how you might address them.

1. A Saudi working in the United States wakes up ill. He sends his younger brother to work for him that day. The U.S. employer sends the brother home. What happened?

   The Saudi has not yet learned that in the United States, relatives usually cannot substitute for one another. Perhaps in other cultures, it is acceptable to have one's siblings or even friends fill in on the job. If the job is done, what difference does it make? What would you do? How would you handle the situation?

2. You are at a social gathering and meet Dr. Dinesh Mammen, a local physician from India who has been living and practicing medicine in the United States for many years. You meet his wife, who has her bachelor's degree in biology and a master's degree in chemistry. You ask about her career and what she does for a living. Dr. Mammen pauses, smiles, and asserts that she stays home and takes care of his needs. How do you react? Do you think Mrs. Mammen should be following a career path related to her college degrees?

KEY TERMS

collectivism   49

high context   63

horizontal collectivism   58

horizontal individualism   56

individualism   48

low context   63

power distance   76

uncertainty avoidance   84

vertical collectivism   58

vertical individualism   56

REFERENCES

1. Hall, E. T. (1959). *The Silent Language*. Greenwich, CT: Fawcett, p. 39.

2. Keesing, R. M. (1974). Theories of Culture. In B. J. Siegel (Ed.), *Annual Review of Anthropology* (pp. 73–97). Palo Alto, CA: Annual Reviews.

3. Rosenberg, M. (2011, March 2). *China's One Child Policy: One Child Policy in China Designed to Limit Population Growth*. Retrieved from http://geography .about.com/od/populationgeography/a/onechild.htm.

4. Gayle, A. R., & Knutson, K. P. (1993). Understanding Cultural Differences: Janteloven and Social Conformity in Norway. *Et Cetera, 49,* 449; Yurkovich, D., Pliscott, K., & Halverson, R. (1996). *The Norwegian Culture*. Unpublished student manuscript, St. Norbert College, De Pere, WI.

5. Triandis, H. C. (1990). Cross-Cultural Studies of Individualism and Collectivism. In J. J. Berman (Ed.), *Nebraska Symposium on Motivation: 1989* (pp. 41–133). Lincoln: University of Nebraska Press; Triandis, H. C. (1993). Collectivism and Individualism as Cultural Syndromes. *Cross Cultural Research, 27,* 155–180; Triandis, H. C. (1995). *Individualism and Collectivism.* Boulder, CO: Westview; Triandis, H. C. (2001). Individualism–Collectivism and Personality. *Journal of Personality, 69,* 907–924.

6. Oyserman, D., Coon, H. M., & Kemmelmeier, M. (2002). Rethinking Individualism and Collectivism: Evaluation of Theoretical Assumptions and Meta-Analyses. *Psychological Bulletin, 128,* 3–72.

7. Shulruf, B., Hattie, J., & Dixon, R. (2005). Development of a New Measurement Tool for Individualism and Collectivism. *Journal of Psychoeducational Assessment, 25,* 385–401.

8. Triandis, Individualism–Collectivism and Personality; Triandis, *Individualism and Collectivism.*

9. Shulruf, Hattie, & Dixon, Development of a New Measurement Tool for Individualism and Collectivism; Triandis, Individualism–Collectivism and Personality; Triandis, *Individualism and Collectivism.*

10. Oyserman, Coon, & Kemmelmeier, Rethinking Individualism and Collectivism: Evaluation of Theoretical Assumptions and Meta-Analyses; Triandis, Individualism–Collectivism and Personality; Triandis, *Individualism and Collectivism.*

11. Triandis, Individualism–Collectivism and Personality; Triandis, *Individualism and Collectivism.*

12. Oyserman, Coon, & Kemmelmeier, Rethinking Individualism and Collectivism: Evaluation of Theoretical Assumptions and Meta-Analyses.

13. Hsu, F. L. K. (1986). *Americans and Chinese: Passage to Differences.* Honolulu: University of Hawai'i Press; Triandis, *Individualism and Collectivism.*

14. Triandis, Cross-Cultural Studies of Individualism and Collectivism.

15. Green, E. G. T., Deschamps, J.-C., & Páez, D. (2005). Variation of Individualism and Collectivism Within and Between 20 Countries. *Journal of Cross-Cultural Psychology, 36,* 321–339.

16. Hui, C. H. (1988). Measurement of Individualism–Collectivism. *Journal of Research in Personality, 22,* 17–36.

17. Oyserman, Coon, & Kemmelmeier, Rethinking Individualism and Collectivism: Evaluation of Theoretical Assumptions and Meta-Analyses.

18. Green, Deschamps, & Páez, Variation of Individualism and Collectivism Within and Between 20 Countries.

19. Yu, A.-B., & Yang, K.-S. (1994). The Nature of Achievement Motivation in Collectivist Societies. In U. Kim, H. C. Triandis, C. Kagitçibasi, S.-C. Choi, & G. Yoon (Eds.), *Individualism and Collectivism: Theory, Method, and Applications* (pp. 239–250). Thousand Oaks, CA: Sage.

20. Oyserman, Coon, & Kemmelmeier, Rethinking Individualism and Collectivism: Evaluation of Theoretical Assumptions and Meta-Analyses.

21. Imada, T. (2010). Cultural Narratives of Individualism and Collectivism: A Content Analysis of Textbook Stories in the United States and Japan. *Journal of Cross-Cultural Psychology, 41,* 1–16.

22. Fischer, R., Ferreira, M. C., Assmar, E., Redford, P., Harb, C., Glazer, S., et al. (2009). Individualism–Collectivism, as Descriptive Norms: Development of a Subjective Norm Approach to Culture Measurement. *Journal of Cross-Cultural Psychology, 40,* 187–213.

23. Pirttilä-Backman, A. M., Kassea, B. R., & Ikonen, T. (2004). Cameroonian Forms of Collectivism and Individualism. *Journal of Cross-Cultural Psychology, 35,* 481–498; Sagy, S., Orr, E., Bar-On, D., & Awwad, E. (2001). Individualism and Collectivism in Two Conflicted Societies: Comparing Israeli-Jewish and Palestinian-Arab High School Students. *Youth Society, 33,* 3–30.

24. This dialogue is adapted from a scene in Copeland, L. (Producer). (1983). *Managing the Overseas Assignment* [Motion picture]. San Francisco: Copeland Griggs.

25. Vandello, J. A., & Cohen, D. (1999). Patterns of Individualism and Collectivism Across the United States. *Journal of Personality and Social Psychology, 77*(2), 279–292.

26. Ibid.

27. Triandis, Individualism–Collectivism and Personality; Triandis, *Individualism and Collectivism.*

28. Hsu, *Americans and Chinese: Passage to Differences;* Triandis, *Individualism and Collectivism.*

29. Triandis, Individualism–Collectivism and Personality; Triandis, *Individualism and Collectivism.*

30. Gudykunst, W. B., Matsumoto, Y., Ting-Toomey, S., Nishida, T., Kim, K. S., & Heyman, S. (1994, July). *Measuring Self-Construals Across Cultures.* Paper presented at the International Communication Association Convention, Sydney, Australia; Gudykunst, W. B., Matsumoto, Y., Ting-Toomey, S., Nishida, T., Kim, K. S., & Heyman, S. (1996). The Influence of Cultural Individualism–Collectivism, Self-Construals, and Individual Values on Communication Styles Across Cultures. *Human Communication Research, 22,* 510–543.

31. Oyserman, Coon, & Kemmelmeier, Rethinking Individualism and Collectivism: Evaluation of Theoretical Assumptions and Meta-Analyses.

32. Shulruf, Hattie, & Dixon, Development of a New Measurement Tool for Individualism and Collectivism.

33. Singelis, T. M., Triandis, H. C., Bhawuk, D. P. S., & Gelfand, M. J. (1995). Horizontal and Vertical Dimensions of Individualism and Collectivism: A Theoretical and Measurement Refinement. *Cross-Cultural Research, 29,* 240–275; Triandis, Cross-Cultural Studies of Individualism and Collectivism.

34. McCann, R. M., Honeycutt, J. M., & Keaton, S. A. (2010). Toward Greater Specificity in Cultural Value Analyses: The Interplay of Intrapersonal Communication Affect and Cultural Values in Japan, Thailand, and the United States. *Journal of Intercultural Communication Research, 39*(3), 157–172; Singelis, Triandis, Bhawuk, & Gelfand, Horizontal and Vertical Dimensions of Individualism and Collectivism: A Theoretical and Measurement Refinement.

35. This scale for measuring horizontal and vertical individualism and collectivism is adapted from

Triandis, H. C., Chen, X. P., & Chan, D. K. S. (1998). Scenarios for the Measurement of Collectivism and Individualism. *Journal of Cross-Cultural Psychology, 29,* 275–289.

36. Chang, H.-C. (1996). *"Collectivism" or "Competitive Bidding": An Alternative Picture of Chinese Communication.* Paper presented at the annual convention of the Speech Communication Association, San Diego, CA, p. 10.

37. Chang, H., & Holt, R. (1991). More Than a Relationship: Chinese Interaction and the Principle of Kuanhis. *Communication Quarterly, 39,* 251–271; Gaertner, L., Sedikides, C., Vevea, J. L., & Iuzzini, J. (2002). The "I," the "We," and the "When": A Meta-Analysis of Motivational Primacy in Self-Definition. *Journal of Personality and Social Psychology, 83,* 574–591; Mortenson, S. T. (2005). Clarifying the Link Between Culture and Self-Construal Through Structural Equation Models. *Journal of Intercultural Communication Research, 34,* 1–22; Oyama, N. (1990). Some Recent Trends in Japanese Values: Beyond the Individual–Collective Dimension. *International Sociology, 5,* 445–459; Sedikides, C., Gaertner, L., & Toguchi, Y. (2003). Pancultural Self-Enhancement. *Journal of Personality and Social Psychology, 84,* 60–79; Voronov, M., & Singer, J. A. (2002). The Myth of Individualism–Collectivism: A Critical Review. *Journal of Social Psychology, 142*(4), 461–480; Yamaguchi, S. (1994). Collectivism Among the Japanese: A Perspective From the Self. In U. Kim, H. C. Triandis, C. Kagitcibasi, S. H. Choi, & G. Yoon (Eds.), *Individualism and Collectivism: Theory, Method, and Applications* (pp. 175–188). Thousand Oaks, CA: Sage.

38. Gaertner, L., Sedikides, C., & Graetz, K. (1999). In Search of Self-Definition: Motivational Primacy of the Individual Self, Motivational Primacy of the Collective Self, or Contextual Primacy? *Journal of Personality and Social Psychology, 76,* 5–18.

39. Hall, E. T. (1976). *Beyond Culture.* Garden City, NY: Anchor Press/Doubleday, p. 79.

40. Ibid. (quote on p. 79).

41. Ibid.

42. Ibid.

43. Braithwaite, C. A. (1990). Communicative Silence: A Cross-Cultural Study of Basso's Hypothesis. In D. Carbaugh (Ed.), *Cultural Communication and Intercultural Contact* (pp. 321–328). Hillsdale, NJ: Erlbaum.

44. Weider, D. L., & Pratt, S. (1990). On Being a Recognizable Indian Among Indians. In D. Carbaugh (Ed.), *Cultural Communication and Intercultural Contact* (pp. 45–64). Hillsdale, NJ: Erlbaum.

45. Iwao, S. (1993). *The Japanese Woman: Traditional Image and Changing Reality.* Cambridge, MA: Harvard University Press, p. 98.

46. Although different, the model for this dialogue is adapted from Storti, C. (1994). *Cross-Cultural Dialogues: 74 Brief Encounters With Cultural Differences.* Yarmouth, ME: Intercultural Press.

47. Gudykunst, Matsumoto, Ting-Toomey, Nishida, Kim, & Heyman, The Influence of Cultural Individualism–Collectivism, Self Construals, and Individual Values on Communication Styles Across Cultures.

48. Rokeach, M. (1973). *The Nature of Human Values.* New York: Free Press, p. 3.

49. Ibid.

50. Schwartz, S. H. (1992). Universals in the Content and Structure of Values: Theoretical Advances and Empirical Tests in 20 Countries. In M. P. Zanna (Ed.), *Advances in Experimental Social Psychology* (Vol. 25, pp. 1–66). San Diego, CA: Academic Press.

51. Hsu, F. L. K. (1969). *The Study of Literate Civilizations.* New York: Holt, Rinehart, & Winston; Hsu, F. L. K. (1970). *Americans and Chinese: Reflections on Two Cultures and Their People.* Garden City, NY: Doubleday; Hsu, *Americans and Chinese: Passage to Differences;* Seelye, H. N. (1993). *Teaching Culture Strategies for Intercultural Communication.* Lincolnwood, IL: National Textbook Company.

52. Chinese Culture Connection. (1987). Chinese Values and the Search for Culture-Free Dimensions of Culture. *Journal of Cross-Cultural Psychology, 18,* 143–164.

53. Zhang, J., & Bond, M. H. (1998). Personality and Filial Piety Among College Students in Two Chinese Societies: The Added Value of Indigenous Constructs. *Journal of Cross-Cultural Psychology, 29,* 402–417.

54. Kao, H. S. R., & Sek-Hong, N. (1995). Chinese Values in Work Organization: An Alternative Approach to Change and Development. *Journal of Human Values, 1,* 173–189.

55. Domino, G., & Hannah, M. T. (1987). A Comparative Analysis of Social Values of Chinese and American Children. *Journal of Cross-Cultural Psychology, 18,* 58–77.

56. Schwartz, S. H., Universals in the Content and Structure of Values: Theoretical Advances and Empirical Tests in 20 Countries.

57. Condon, J. C., & Yousef, F. (1975). *An Introduction to Intercultural Communication.* Indianapolis, IN: Bobbs-Merrill; Kluckhohn, F., & Strodtbeck, F. (1961). *Variations in Value Orientations.* Evanston, IL: Row, Peterson.

58. Condon & Yousef, *An Introduction to Intercultural Communication;* Hsu, *Americans and Chinese: Passage to Differences.*

59. Hsu, *Americans and Chinese: Passage to Differences;* Hsu, *Americans and Chinese: Reflections on Two Cultures and Their People.*

60. Harris, P. R., & Moran, R. T. (1996). *Managing Cultural Differences* (4th ed.). Houston, TX: Gulf.

61. Condon & Yousef, *An Introduction to Intercultural Communication.*

62. Harris & Moran, *Managing Cultural Differences.*

63. Keberlein, M. (1993). *A Cultural Profile of the Guatemalan Ladinos.* Unpublished student manuscript, St. Norbert College, De Pere, WI.

64. Condon & Yousef, *An Introduction to Intercultural Communication.*

65. Ibid.

66. De Menthe, B. (1992). *Chinese Etiquette and Ethics in Business.* Lincolnwood, IL: NTC; Zhang, Y., George, J. M., & Chan, T.-S. (2006). The Paradox of Dueling Identities: The Case of Local Senior Executives in MNC Subsidiaries. *Journal of Management, 32,* 400–425.

67. Condon & Yousef, *An Introduction to Intercultural Communication.*

68. Ibid.

69. Ibid.

70. Hofstede, G. (1980). *Culture's Consequences: International Differences in Work-Related Values.* Beverly Hills, CA: Sage; Hofstede, G., Hofstede, G. J., & Minkov, M. (2010). *Culand Organizations: Software of the Mind.* New York: McGraw-Hill.

71. Ibid.

72. Ibid.

73. Andersen, P. A., Hecht, M. L., Hoobler, G. D., & Smallwood, M. (2003). Nonverbal Communication Across Cultures. In W. B. Gudykunst (Ed.), *Cross-Cultural and Intercultural Communication* (pp. 73–90). Thousand Oaks, CA: Sage; Andersen, P. A., Lustig, M. W., & Andersen, J. F. (1990). Changes in Latitude, Changes in Attitude: The Relationship Between Climate and Interpersonal Communication Predispositions. *Communication Quarterly, 38,* 291–311; Lustig, M. W., & Koester, J. (2003). *Intercultural Competence.* Boston: Allyn & Bacon.

74. Tyler, T. R., Lind, E. A., & Huo, Y. J. (2000). Cultural Values and Authority Relations: The Psychology of Conflict Resolution Across Cultures. *Psychology, Public Policy, and Law, 6*(4), 1138–1163.

75. Smith, P. B., Dugan, S., Peterson, M. F., & Leung, K. (1998). Individualism–Collectivism and the Handling of Disagreement: A 23 Country Study. *International Journal of Intercultural Relations, 22,* 351–367.

76. Oetzel, J., Ting-Toomey, S., Chew-Sanchez, M. I., Harris, R., Wilcox, R., & Stumpf, S. (2003). Face and Facework in Conflicts With Parents and Siblings: A Cross-Cultural Comparison of Germans, Japanese, Mexicans, and U.S. Americans. *Journal of Family Communication, 3,* 67–93; Ting-Toomey, S., & Oetzel, J. G. (2003). Cross-Cultural Face Concerns and Conflict Styles. In W. B. Gudykunst (Ed.), *Cross-Cultural and Intercultural Communication* (pp. 127–147). Thousand Oaks, CA: Sage.

77. Perea, A., & Slater, M. D. (1999). Power Distance and Collectivistic/Individualistic Strategies in Alcohol Warnings: Effects by Gender and Ethnicity. *Journal of Health Communication, 4,* 295–310.

78. Spencer-Oatey, H. (1997). Unequal Relationships in High and Low Power Distance Societies: A Comparative Study of Tutor–Student Role Relations in Britain and China. *Journal of Cross-Cultural Psychology, 28,* 284–302.

79. Bond, M. H., Wan, K.-C., Leung, K., & Giacalone, R. A. (1985). How Are Responses to Verbal Insult Related to Cultural Collectivism and Power Distance? *Journal of Cross-Cultural Psychology, 16,* 111–127.

80. Andersen, P. A., Hecht, M. L., Hoobler, G. D., & Smallwood, M. (2003). Nonverbal Communication Across Cultures. In W. B. Gudykunst (Ed.), *Cross-Cultural and Intercultural Communication* (pp. 73–90). Thousand Oaks, CA: Sage.

81. Gudykunst, W. B., & Kim, Y. Y. (1997). *Communicating With Strangers: An Approach to Intercultural Communication.* New York: McGraw-Hill.

82. Hofstede, *Cultures and Organizations: Software of the Mind.*

83. Ibid.

84. Ibid.

85. Shuper, P. A., Sorrentino, R. A., Otsubo, Y., Hodson, G., & Walker, A. M. (2004). A Theory of Uncertainty Orientation: Implications for the Study of Individual Differences Within and Across Cultures. *Journal of Cross-Cultural Psychology, 35,* 460–480.

CHAPTER 3

The Microcultural Context

CHAPTER OBJECTIVES

After reading this chapter, you should be able to

1. define and explain the concept of a microculture,

2. list and illustrate the five criteria for membership in a microculture,

3. recount the fundamental assumptions of the muted group theory,

4. provide examples of the various microcultures in the United States,

5. identify and discuss two cultural values of the Hispanic microculture,

6. identify and discuss at least three aspects of African American communication,

7. identify and discuss at least three aspects of Amish communication,

8. identify and discuss at least three aspects of Hmong communication, and

9. identify and discuss at least three aspects of LGBT communication.

For those of us who live in/between, being required, on the one hand, to cast off our cultural selves in order to don the worldview and ethos of an alien culture, on the other hand to cast off the influences of the alien culture as a means of purification and identification is more than a personal dilemma; it is always and most of all a condition of living in/between.

—Richard Morris[1]

Within most cultures, there are groups of people who differ from the general societal culture in some custom, habit, or practice. These groups are sometimes called minorities, subcultures, or co-cultures. In this book, the term **microculture** is used to refer to those identifiable groups of people who share the set of values, beliefs, and behaviors of the macroculture, possess a common history, and use a common verbal and nonverbal symbol system. In some way, however, the microculture varies from the larger, often dominant cultural milieu. Most microcultural groups are groups of individuals who have much in common with the larger macroculture yet are bonded together by similar experiences, traits, values, or in some cases, histories. Hence, the term *microculture* includes different types of groups that could be classified by age, class, geographic region, sexual preference, disability (e.g., the deaf), ethnicity, race, size, or even occupation. Most people, regardless of culture, are likely members of some kind of microcultural group.

Microcultures can be different from the larger culture in a variety of ways, often because of race or ethnicity. In the United States, for example, approximately 65% of the population is classified as White or Caucasian.[2] In this context, African Americans, Hispanics, and Hmong might be considered microcultural groups. Microcultures can also differ from the larger culture on account of language or religion. For example, Protestants, Catholics, Jews, or Muslims (persons of Islamic faith) might be considered microcultural groups. Finally, persons might be classified as members of microcultures because of their behavioral practices. Persons who use drugs are often said to belong to a "counter" or "drug" culture, not because of their race, ethnicity, or religion but because they use drugs. Gays or lesbians could be considered a microculture because of their sexual orientation.

In any culture, microcultural groups often develop their own language for communicating outside the dominant or majority culture's context or value system. Indeed, deaf persons, who communicate using sign language, can be considered a microculture. Though not always, microcultural groups generally have less power than the majority or "macro" culture. The majority group's power may be legal, political, economic, or even religious. The group with the most power is considered the dominant or majority group, while the less powerful groups have been known as minority groups. Sociologist Richard Schaefer argues that the term *minority group* is a misnomer, however, in that it does not refer to the relative size of a group. According to Schaefer, **minority groups** are subordinate groups whose members have significantly less power and control over their own lives than do members of the dominant or majority group.[3] Although defined as a minority, such groups may actually be larger (in population) than the majority group. A classic example is South Africa. From 1948 to 1994, Whites, who were greatly outnumbered by Blacks, ruled in South Africa under the political system of apartheid. In many countries colonized by Europeans, the indigenous people outnumbered the dominant Europeans. And in parts of the United States, certain ethnic/cultural groups outnumber the "dominant" group.

The term *subculture* is sometimes used to refer to microcultural groups. Like *minority group,* the term *subculture* carries negative connotations. By definition, *sub-* means "beneath," "below," and "inferior." The perspective of this book is that no cultural group is beneath or below any other cultural group. To be sure, some cultures are subordinate (i.e., have less power) to other groups, but such groups should not be considered inferior. Hence, for the reasons cited above, the term *microcultural group* has been chosen as the most appropriate label for these groups.

MICROCULTURAL GROUP STATUS

In many cultures, including the United States, microcultural group status is determined by one's membership in sex, racial, ethnic, or religious groups. Schaefer notes that social scientists generally recognize five characteristics that distinguish microcultural groups from the dominant culture. The first characteristic is that members of the group possess some physical or cultural trait that distinguishes them from others. Two obvious physical properties that distinguish one group from another are skin color and sex. In the United States, for example, Blacks and women are considered minorities (even though women constitute about 51% of the population). White males are considered the most powerful political and economic group in the United States. Blacks are also considered a minority in Brazil, which depended on slave trading much more than did the United States. In fact, Brazil imported eight times the number of African slaves brought to the United States.[4]

Other traits that can distinguish a microcultural group include language or distinctive dress habits. A microcultural group in Jamaica is the Rastafarians. According to Barrett, the Jamaican Rastafarian movement is the largest, most identifiable indigenous group in Jamaica. Rastas are recognizable by their dreadlock hair and unique dress habits. Barrett argues that their appearance is the most distinguishing mark of the Rastafarians.[5] Regardless of culture, the dominant group decides, perhaps arbitrarily, on what characteristics afford a group its microcultural status. Such traits vary considerably across cultures.

The second distinguishing characteristic is that minority group/microcultural membership is usually not voluntary. Though not always, people are generally born into their microculture. For example, people cannot choose to be of a certain race, ethnicity, or gender. Although people can choose their religion, most people are born into a religion and find it difficult to leave. In tracing its history, Schaefer notes that the roots of the violence in Northern Ireland are based in religion. Northern Ireland is two-thirds Protestant and one-third Catholic. The Catholics in Northern Ireland, a minority in both numbers and power, complain of inadequate housing and education, low income, and high unemployment. They often blame the Protestant majority for their problems. Armed conflict has been the result. Laungani notes that a unique feature of India's society is the caste system—that is, a rigid social hierarchy. In India, one is born into a given caste level, and it is virtually impossible to move from one caste level to another.[6]

The third property that distinguishes a microcultural group from the macroculture is that microcultural group members generally practice endogamy (i.e., marrying within the in-group). In many cultures, the dominant group staunchly discourages or even prohibits exogamy (i.e., marrying out of one's own group). Ethnologist Suzan Ilcan of the University of Windsor writes that majority groups believe that endogamy strengthens familial ties, preserves family property through inheritance, and upholds cultural and group traditions. Ilcan's work has focused on marital practices in Turkey, where endogamous marriages are viewed as a family or community affair. According to Ilcan, in the village of Sakli in the northwestern region of Turkey, spousal selection and all aspects of marriage are controlled by certain members of the family. Couples have little to do with the arrangements. Moreover, any meaningful romance between unmarried persons is not valued. Love and mutual attraction are expected to come after marriage and, even then, are not considered necessities. In Sakli, people are considered suitable marriage partners based on the compatibility of their families. Familial reputation and comparable economic and social classes are the crucial elements of a marriage.[7] In cultures such as those of Pakistan, China, India, and Laos, among others, endogamous marriages are often arranged.

The fourth characteristic that distinguishes a microcultural group from the dominant group is that the group members are aware of their subordinate status. Because they know that they are less powerful within a particular culture, some microcultural groups are very cohesive. In the United States, for example, Blacks have gained significant political and economic strength and are arguably the most powerful microcultural group in the country.

Finally, perhaps the most disturbing aspect of microcultural group membership is that such groups often experience unequal treatment from the dominant group in the form of segregation and discrimination. Women in Saudi Arabia, Blacks and Hispanics in the United States, and the Sudras in India are all vivid examples of how membership in a microculture can affect one's life negatively.[8]

MUTED MICROCULTURAL GROUPS

Another type of power that most microcultural groups lack is linguistic power—that is, the power of language. In all cultures, language is the vehicle for representing and expressing experience. And the experiences and perceptions of subordinate microcultural groups are often different from those of the dominant cultural group. For example, microcultural groups often are not able to communicate as freely as the dominant group does. In the United States, for example, historically, women and Blacks could not vote or join the armed services. Only since 1994 have Black South Africans been allowed to vote in their country; for decades, they had no legal voice or representation. Today, Saudi women, under strict Islamic law, suffer severe restrictions on daily life: they are not allowed to be anywhere with an unrelated man, cannot drive, cannot appear before a judge without a male representative, and cannot travel abroad without a male guardian's permission.[9]

In many cultures, the subordinate microcultural groups do not contribute to the construction of the language of the dominant group. In this sense, the language of a particular culture does not benefit its members equally. Yet the language of the dominant group may not provide the words and symbols representative of the microcultural group's perceptions and experiences. Thus, because such groups are forced to communicate within the dominant mode of expression, they become "muted." In essence, the language of the dominant cultural group, which is the preferred language, contributes to the microcultural group's subordination. This idea is known as the muted group theory.[10]

The manifestation of the muted group theory is that microcultural groups' speech and writing are not valued by the dominant cultural group. Moreover, microcultural groups experience difficulty expressing themselves fluently within the dominant mode of expression; that is, they may not speak the same language as the dominant group, and hence "micro–macro" interaction is difficult. However, because the microcultural groups must communicate within the dominant mode, they must achieve some level of linguistic competence to survive. The same is not true of the dominant group, however. In fact, the dominant cultural group experiences more difficulty than the microcultural groups in understanding the communication of the microcultural groups because the dominant group is not required to learn the microcultural groups' codes. Indeed, the communication style of the microcultural group is often considered substandard or inferior by the dominant group and is rejected as a legitimate form of communication.

Shirley Weber contends that microcultural groups may respond to the dominant mode of expression in two ways. Some will refuse to live by the standards set forth by the dominant group and will try to change the dominant mode of expression. In the United States, for example, the replacement of words such as *chairman* with simply *chair* or *mailman* with *mail carrier* is demonstrative of this phenomenon. Another way subordinate groups respond is by using their own "private" language. They create symbols that are not understood or used by the dominant group. They use their own language in order to express their unique experiences. Weber argues that sometimes the language of the subordinate group serves as a political statement that the microcultural group has not relinquished or abandoned its political or social identity. The group's ability to sustain a living language indicates that the members have control over a certain aspect of their lives and are determined to preserve their culture. As Weber notes, one's language is a model of his or her culture's adjustment to the world.[11]

Many social scientists consider the hip-hop/rap music generation a microcultural group that has been muted by mainstream culture. Christopher Tyson argues that hip-hop/rap has been the defining African American cultural movement in the United States over the past 35 years.[12] Terri Adams and Douglas Fuller of Howard University point out that rap music emerged as an artistic cultural expression of urban African American youth in the Bronx, New York, in the late 1970s. They describe rap as the poetry of the youth who are often disregarded as a result of their race and class status—that is, as members of a microcultural group. Adams and Fuller maintain that rap has gone through a number of phases and has been used as a primary outlet for microcultural groups to express a variety of ideas, feelings, and emotions. They argue that hope, love, fear, anger, frustration, pride, violence, and misogyny (i.e., hatred or strong prejudice against women) have all been expressed through the medium of rap.[13]

As most college students know, rap is a fast, rhythmical, and accentuated singing and speaking style. Christopher Tyson contends that rap music reflects the growing flux of non-conformity among young African Americans (and, now, other microcultural groups) in mainstream culture and the backlash against middle-class values.[14] Aino Konkka asserts that one of the most recognized styles of rap music is called *gangsta rap*. This style originated on the West Coast, where inner-city gangs are prominent. Gangsta rap lyrics often tell the story of the desperate situation faced by many inner-city youths who feel rejected and alienated by the dominant culture. Because the lyrics of gangsta rap are often profane—dealing with drugs and violence, especially violence against women and law enforcement—gangsta rap music has received a great deal of criticism from mainstream cultural critics.[15]

To be sure, Edgar Tyson, a professor at Florida State University, agrees that a major criticism of some rap music is its noticeable appetite for violent, sexist, and misogynistic images, and what many view as glorification of drugs and alcohol. Tyson argues that such a negative perception of rap music could be explained by the disproportionate media attention given to "gangsta" rap. Tyson argues that with a similar level of exposure on radio and television to that currently given to its negative counterpart, greater awareness of "positive and constructive" rap music would create a more balanced public perception of rap music.[16] Finally, Konkka argues that it is the language young African Americans understand. According to Konkka, "Using language that children can relate to, added with humor and catchy rhythms, helps getting the message through."[17] Consistent with the tenets of the muted group theory, rappers have created and developed a unique vocabulary that they use in their music and to communicate with one another. Although rappers speak English, the vocabulary and its meanings differ considerably from mainstream culture. Table 3.1 lists some examples of rap vocabulary.

Another example of a microcultural group is the Amish. Many Amish groups in the United States are trilingual. They speak low German at home, high German at church, and English at school or with outsiders. High German is more formal, whereas low German is a relaxed oral dialect spoken at home. Koslow notes that in Canada, the people of Quebec define themselves as culturally unique from the rest of the country because they speak French. In Quebec, the

Table 3.1   Rap Vocabulary

Rap Vocabulary	Meaning
"Ace boon coon"	Your best friend, your nigga. But it is rude (and grounds for a beat down in some circles) for someone of another ethnicity to use it.
"All that"	In possession of all good qualities
"Ay yo trip"	Phrase to seek attention, similar to "check this out"
"Bang"	To fight or kill
"Be geese"	To leave: "Yo, we be geese."
"Bitch"	Label generally used for females but not necessarily derogatory and not necessarily limited to women, as in "All yo niggas be bitches."
"Biscuit"	Genitals: "Gals, if you see a man you like, just grab him in the biscuits . . . and doowutchalike."
"Bone"	To have sexual intercourse: "Your aim is to bone."
"Cave boy"	A white person
"Chill"	To relax
"Coconut"	A Hispanic person trying to be white (like a coconut, they are "brown" on the outside but "white" on the inside)
"Homeboy"	Close friend
"Hood"	The neighborhood, usually a poor community
"Nigga"	Originally considered racist and profane, now used by rappers to express pride; my friend, as in "my nigga"
"Peckerwood"	Derogatory term for a white person
"Roll up"	To arrive on the scene
"Shank"	A custom-made knife used in prisons
"Strawberry"	Someone who willingly exchanges sexual services for drugs
"Tag"	The act of writing graffiti, as in "tagging up"
"Tight"	Feeling really good at the moment

SOURCE: Atoon, P. "Tricky." (2010). *The Rap Dictionary*. Retrieved from www.rapdict.org.

language debate is so great and emotional that many Quebecers are pushing for sovereignty. Quebecois (those who speak French) use French as a model and insist on keeping French in the home and on the street signs throughout the province.[18]

MICROCULTURES IN THE UNITED STATES

Many microcultures exist in the United States. The formation of microcultural groups is often the result of immigration, annexation, or colonization.[19] In this chapter, six U.S. microcultures will be explored, with particular attention paid to the communication of each and how it differs from the dominant macroculture.

The first microcultural group to be examined is the Hispanic/Latino group. Hispanics/Latinos represent the largest microcultural group in the United States. The second group consists of African Americans, whose ancestors were brought to the United States mainly as slaves. This group was selected because it represents perhaps the most powerful microcultural group in the United States. And although African Americans have made strides in social, legal, economic, and political power in the United States in the past century, they remain socially disenfranchised by many in the dominant culture. The third group is the Amish. The Amish immigrated to the United States from Europe to escape religious persecution. The Amish were chosen for this discussion because, perhaps more than any other microcultural group, they have managed to maintain their cultural traditions in the face of immense pressure from the dominant culture to conform and yet have managed to coexist successfully within the dominant cultural milieu.

The fourth group to be explored is the Laotian Hmong (pronounced "mung"), who began their immigration to the United States after the end of the Vietnam War in 1975. This group was chosen because its members represent perhaps the newest microculture. They are also a relatively powerless group who lack social, political, and economic power. The fifth microculture to be discussed encompasses Arab Americans. For the first time in its history, in 2000, the U.S. Census Bureau classified persons in the United States with Arab ancestry. In 2009, more than one million people in the United States considered themselves as having Arab ancestry. Arab Americans represent a considerably diverse group of people about which generalizations are complicated. The sixth microculture to be discussed is lesbian, gay, bisexual, and transgendered (LGBT) persons. A debate continues over the rights of LGBT persons and whether they have a unique communication system.

Hispanics/Latinos

Hispanics/Latinos compose the largest microcultural group in the country. In 2008, there were nearly 47 million Hispanics in the United States. That is just over 15% of the population. Of these 47 million, 62% were born in the United States. Recall from Chapter 1 that the U.S. government distinguishes between race and Hispanic origin. The government considers the two to be separate and distinct. Hence, Hispanics are not considered a racial group. Specifically, the government defines Hispanic or Latino as "a person of Cuban, Mexican, Puerto Rican, South or Central American, or other Spanish culture or origin regardless of race." According to census data, nearly half of all Hispanics reported their race as White. From the other half, 6% reported they were of two or more races, 2% reported their race as Black or African American, while just over 1% indicated they were American Indian or Alaska native. The rest, 42% of Hispanics, indicated "some other race."[20]

So, Who Is Hispanic?

Given the above discussion, the term *Hispanic* is confusing to many. Crouch argues that the label is a cultural reference, a way of identifying people that is neither racial nor geographic. According to Crouch, persons who consider themselves Hispanic may be Black, as in the Dominican Republic; White, as in Argentina; or of mixed racial heritage, as in Mexico. Crouch argues that *Hispanic* is a cultural reference to people from any Spanish-speaking country except Spain (where people insist that they are Spanish, not Hispanic). In addition, Crouch argues that the term *Latino* is a cultural reference that is more or less interchangeable with *Hispanic*.[21]

Of the various groups represented under the Hispanic label, the Mexican population represents nearly 66%, Puerto Ricans compose just under 9%, and Cubans represent about 4%. The remaining Hispanics of "some other origin" include Central and South Americans (14%) and Dominicans (2%). The remaining approximately 16% are labeled "all other Hispanics." As a group, 56% of all Hispanics living in the United States were born in the United States. Hence, about 44% were foreign-born. For the total U.S. population, 88% of persons living in the United States were born in the United States and 12% were born outside the country.[22] See Table 3.2 for some facts about U.S. Hispanics/Latinos.

Like other microcultural groups, Hispanics are concentrated in certain geographical areas in the United States. In fact, nearly half of all Hispanics live in California and Texas. Other states with concentrated Hispanic populations include Arizona, Florida, Illinois, New Jersey, and New York. On the other hand, many states have very small Hispanic populations, such as Alabama, Kentucky, Maine, Mississippi, New Hampshire, North Dakota, South Dakota, Vermont, and West Virginia.[24] In addition to its overall population trends, the Hispanic population has unique demographics compared with the rest of the United States.

Cultural Values of Hispanics

Although very diverse, the Hispanic microculture is united by values, language, and religion. Consultants Anne Marie Pajewski and Luis Enriquez argue that, in Hispanic society, the family or group needs take precedence over individual needs. Hispanics seem collectivistic across a variety of contexts, including academics. According to Pajewski and Enriquez, in school settings, Hispanic students tend to be cooperative, whereas White students tend to be competitive and individualistic. When Hispanic students work in groups, not everyone is expected to do his or her equal share. A group member who does not work is not sanctioned, while in an Anglo group, each is expected to do his or her share.[25]

Table 3.2   Facts About U.S. Hispanics/Latinos[23]
More than one in eight people in the United States are of Hispanic origin.
Hispanics are more geographically concentrated than non-Hispanic Whites.
Hispanics tend to live inside the central cities of metropolitan areas.
Hispanics are more likely than Whites to be under the age of 18.
Three out of five Hispanics were born in the United States.
Hispanics tend to live in households that are larger than those of non-Hispanic Whites.
Nearly 40% of Hispanics over the age of 25 have not graduated from high school.
Hispanics are more likely than Whites to work in service occupations.
Hispanics are more likely than Whites to live in poverty.

Perhaps nowhere is the Hispanic group orientation more prevalent than in the family, or *familia*.[26] Commitment to the family is a dominant cultural value among virtually all Hispanics. Indeed, Crouch argues that

> the group bonding process begins the minute Mexican children are brought home from the hospital and put into the children's room—not their own, separate little pink or blue nursery. Their families tend to congregate in one large room. They are taught to play nicely with each other. Toys are toys and are played with by all the children. They are not owned by boy number one or girl number three. In Anglo culture, the more we misbehave with our siblings, the more attention we get . . . but beyond the conflicting pressures of adolescence, we seem to emerge as individualists . . . unlike the Mexicans, who believe that the more they conform, the more they will all prosper.[27]

In general, Hispanics are a very religious people, with as many as 90% of all Hispanics belonging to the Roman Catholic faith. Clutter and Nieto point out that the church is a strong influence on Hispanic family life. In addition, many Hispanic communities celebrate their patron saint's day with more importance and ceremony than individuals do for their own personal birthdays. Although Hispanics are generally very religious, they tend to believe in supernatural powers beyond their religious teachings. Many Hispanics believe in witchcraft and the *curadora* (i.e., healers), as well as the healing powers of women and certain herbs.[28]

Spanglish: The Language of Hispanic Americans

The communication style of most Hispanics is more formal than that of the dominant U.S. American culture. Hispanics are sensitive to rank and customarily make use of formal titles. Hispanics tend to demonstrate affection nonverbally through touching, hugging, pats on the back, and cheek kissing.[29] Verbally, many Hispanics speak **Spanglish**, a combination of Spanish and English. Linguists have noted that when groups of people from different cultures who speak different languages come together and live in the same society, a hybrid language sometimes evolves. This new language will take some of the phonological features (i.e., sounds) and syntactic structures (i.e., grammar) from each group's language and blend them, creating a hybrid language that serves as a vehicle for communication between the groups. This very phenomenon is happening in the United States.

According to Ilan Stavans, Spanglish is the intersection, perhaps the marriage (or divorce), of English and Spanish. Hispanics have taken English words and "Spanish-ized" them and have taken Spanish words and "English-ized" them. The result is what linguists call "Spanglish"— part Spanish and part English. Alfredo Ardila notes that Spanglish may be interpreted in different ways: as a pidgin, or Creole language; an interlanguage; or an Anglicized Spanish dialect. Although Spanglish appears to be a fairly recent phenomenon, Ardila argues that it has been around for more than 150 years and traces its origins to the U.S. annexation of Mexican territories in the early to mid-19th century. Ardila points out that in the mid-19th century, the Mexican–American war resulted in ceding about half of the Mexican territory to the United States, but millions of Spanish speakers remained in close contact with the American English speakers. During the late 19th century and early 20th century, an important amount of Latin Americans and Spaniards migrated to the United States.[30]

Scholars and laypeople alike agree that Spanglish unites the Hispanic community. Jane Rifkin of *Hispanic Times Magazine* points out that Spanglish is a widely accepted communication tool used by Spanish-speaking immigrants and native-born Americans. Although some reject Spanglish as intellectually unsophisticated, Rifkin believes that the hybrid language is an expression of friendship, acceptance, and approval. Rifkin refers to Spanglish as the new national slang and contends that Spanglish is "truly a form of communicating among people that has a warmth about it and an inviting expression meant to be non-threatening to people who come together in spite of language barriers."[31]

Stavans argues that there are many variations of Spanglish, depending on the nationality, age, and class of its users. He contends that the Spanglish spoken by Cuban Americans (i.e., Cubonics) is different from that spoken by Dominicans, which is different still from the Ganga Spanglish used by urban Hispanic gangs.[32]

Although there may be many variations of Spanglish in the United States, Bill Cruz and Bill Teck—editors of *Generation ñ,* a magazine primarily targeting Cuban American youths—argue that authentic Spanglish is heard when a speaker switches from English to Spanish, or from Spanish to English, within the same sentence. They argue that Spanglish is commonplace in the homes of Hispanics who, as children, were educated in American schools but spoke Spanish at home. In their defense of Spanglish as a legitimate language, Cruz and Teck maintain that often there are no words in English (or Spanish) that accurately express the speaker's intent. In such cases, the blending of the two languages allows the speaker to capture the essence of one culture in the language of the other. Cruz and Teck have compiled what they call *The Official Spanglish Dictionary.* Table 3.3 shows some examples of Spanglish, taken from their work.[33]

Chicano English

As immigrants from Mexico settled in California and other parts of the Southwest, they soon formed communities of people who spoke only Spanish. As usual, many of these people

Table 3.3   Examples of Spanglish

Spanglish	English Example
No creo que voy on the trip with you.	"I don't think I'm going on the trip with you."
lonchando (having lunch)	"I'm lonchando, I don't wanna talk to him now."
bacunclíner (vacuum cleaner)	"Aye! I think the bacunclíner just swallowed my earring!"
tiempo is money.	"Time is money."
frizando (to make frozen, or freezing)	"Turn up the heat, estoy frizando!"
el autopar	local auto parts store
guarejaus	a warehouse
Pisa Ho	Pizza Hut restaurant
Macdonal	McDonald's fast-food restaurant
Sebenileben	7–11 convenience store
Guendis	Wendy's fast food restaurant

began learning English. And, as is typical of immigrants, they took phonological and grammatical complexes from each language and combined them. But the children of these immigrants grew up using both Spanish and English, and as the communities began to grow, a new dialect of English, called Chicano English, evolved. Carmen Fought, a professor of linguistics, studies Chicano English. Fought maintains that Chicano English is neither Spanglish nor a version of nonstandard Spanish but, rather, is a unique dialect used by speakers who are typically not bilingual. In fact, Fought argues that most speakers of Chicano English do not know any Spanish at all.[34] Fought maintains that Chicano English is spoken only by native English speakers. She argues that the central myth about Chicano English is that it is spoken by people whose first language is Spanish and whose Spanish introduces mistakes into their English. Fought asserts that Chicano English

> is one of the English dialects available in the United States for native speakers to learn, like Appalachian English or AAE [African-American English] or the English spoken by professors at Harvard University, or by used car dealers in Houston. Chicano English cannot possibly be just a non-native variety spoken by second-language users of English if it is only spoken by people who *only* know English.[35]

Fought notes that because of its origins, Chicano English shares many of the phonological features of Spanish. But, she maintains, Chicano English is not Spanglish. For example, in endings for words such as *going* or *talking,* Chicano English speakers tend to have a higher vowel, more like the *i* of Spanish (as in *si*), so that the words sound like "goween" and "talkeen." According to Fought, people who hear Chicano English typically assume that they are hearing the "accent" of a native Spanish speaker. But Fought maintains that many speakers of Chicano English are not bilingual and may not know any Spanish at all. To be sure, notes Fought, these Mexican American speakers have learned English natively and fluently, like most children growing up in the United States. They just happen to have learned a nonstandard variety that retains indicators of contact with Spanish.[36]

Stereotypes of Hispanics

In most cultures, microcultural groups are often stereotyped by the dominant cultural group. In the United States, the Hispanic microculture has been the target of several unfortunate stereotypes. Perhaps the most common, and the most hotly debated, stereotype about Hispanics revolves around the construct of male gender identity called *machismo.* Machismo centers on the notion of Hispanic masculinity and male superiority and dominance in the traditional patriarchal Hispanic society. Stereotypical characteristics associated with macho males include aggressiveness, violence, dominance and supremacy over women, infidelity, and emotional insensitivity.[37]

Manuel Roman, a Puerto Rican psychiatrist, argues that the concept of machismo is power based. He says,

> Men are physically more powerful than women. And machismo is derived from the natural state of being bigger, more muscular. It has to do with dominance, autocracy, having power over others. A macho man is somebody who is expected to be sexually knowledgeable and aggressive with women, and to be fearless in his interactions with other males.[38]

To be sure, scholars disagree about the uniqueness of machismo in Hispanic culture. Counseling psychologist J. Manuel Casas and his associates argue that machismo has never been a uniquely Hispanic phenomenon. Instead, they argue that many of the traits associated with machismo can be found in virtually every culture. They note, however, that differences may exist in how the equivalent of the machismo construct is defined across cultures.[39] In other words, there may be many cultures in which the male gender identity is associated with aggressiveness, male supremacy, infidelity, and so on. Although there has not been a substantial amount of research conducted on the machismo identity, some data indicate that at least one characteristic associated with machismo, infidelity, is not unique to Hispanic males. University of Chicago sociologists Michael, Gagnon, Laumann, and Kolata—authors of the widely publicized "Sex in America" study—found that the infidelity rate among Hispanics in the United States is about the same as for the general U.S. population.[40]

U.S. media, especially advertisers, have been particularly culpable in the dissemination of Hispanic stereotypes. Octavio Nuiry points out that one of the earliest images of Hispanics, and particularly Mexicans, is that of the ruthless bandito. This image has been depicted in all sorts of media, from movie westerns to a famous advertising campaign for Frito corn chips. In 1967, Frito-Lay Corporation launched an advertising campaign for its brand of corn chips. The ads featured a cartoon character called the "Frito Bandito," whose persona was replete with a thick Spanish accent, a long handlebar mustache, a sombrero, and a pair of six-shooters. In the ads, the bandito was described as "cunning, clever, and sly." Contemporary ads, such as those for Taco Bell, encourage taco lovers to "Run for the Border!" in an apparent reference to the immigration issue. Interestingly, in what advertisers call crossover commercials, a Miller Lite beer advertisement features boxing champion Carlos Palomino encouraging viewers to "Drink Miller Lite, but don't drink the water."[41]

The influences of the Hispanic microculture in the United States are growing. Now more than ever, Hispanics are noticed by the dominant culture. We see images of Hispanics in television and movies. Hispanic cuisine is popular across the country. Although their unemployment rates are high and their incomes are low, as a microcultural group, Hispanics are increasing their political and economic power. Soon, their voices will not be muted.

African Americans

According to Richard Schaefer, the history of African Americans in the United States dates as far back as the history of Euro-Americans (persons of European descent). Blacks arrived in the new world with the first White explorers. Schaefer reports that in 1619, 20 Africans arrived in Jamestown as indentured servants. At that time, their children were born free people. By the 1660s, however, the British colonies passed laws making Africans slaves for life.[42]

According to Schaefer, the proportion of Blacks in the United States has varied over the centuries and actually declined until the 1940s, primarily because White immigration (mostly from Europe) far outdistanced population growth by Blacks. In 1790, Africans represented a little more than 19% of the total population of the United States. That percentage continued to decline to 9.7% in 1910.[43] Today, Blacks, or African Americans, represent about 12.5% of the population and are the second largest microcultural group in the United States. Currently, Blacks and Hispanics compose nearly 28% of the U.S. population. Unlike the rapid and disproportionate growth of the Hispanic population since 1990, the rate of Black population growth remains relatively stable.

African Americans made great progress in the 20th century due mostly to the civil rights movement. Although significant gaps remain between Blacks and Whites in such areas as income, education, employment, and housing, Blacks have come a long way in the past 65 years. For example, in 2005, nearly 30% of all Black families earned annual incomes of $50,000 or more. Politically, the number of Black elected officials has increased nearly 300% since 1972. Schaefer notes also that an interesting phenomenon is developing: an ever-growing proportion of the Black population consists of Blacks that are foreign-born. Since 1984, the percentage of Blacks in the United States born outside the United States (mostly in the Caribbean) has almost doubled.[44]

Black English, Dialect, and Ebonics

Some linguists maintain that 80% to 90% of African Americans engage in what is frequently labeled Ebonics.[45] To begin, it needs to be clear that both linguistically and functionally, Ebonics serves all communication functions. The term **Ebonics** (from the combination of the words *ebony* and *phonics*) was first coined in 1973 and refers to a grammatically complex African American speech pattern. Ebonics, or Black language, is uniquely derived from the language of descendents of slaves. Many linguists recognize Black language as a Creole that developed as a result of contact between Africans and Europeans; a new language was formed that was influenced by both languages and took on a variety of forms, depending on whether the influence was French, Portuguese, or English. According to Weber, there is evidence that these languages were spoken on the western coast of Africa as early as the 1500s. Some linguists believe that Africans responded to the English language as do all other nonnative speakers—that is, from the phonological and grammatical constructs of their native language.[46]

One of the primary ways in which members of cultural groups define themselves and establish in-group and out-group identities is through verbal and nonverbal language—that is, through conversation. Language is the foundation of individual and group construction. In a recent study, researchers at Stanford University explored the meanings of racial identity for African American students in a predominantly African American urban high school. The authors viewed racial identity as both related to membership in a racial group and as a fluid and dynamic disposition maintained by students in the local school context. After interviewing students in focus groups for 9 weeks, their findings showed that students had different meanings of African American racial identity and that these meanings were linked to academic achievement and engagement. Their findings also demonstrated that both high-achieving and low-achieving students considered language patterns to be important for their African American identity. The researchers noted that all the students they interviewed consistently used Ebonics and felt that its use was a part of African American racial identity.[47]

According to Ebonics scholar John Rickford, typical Ebonic pronunciations include the omission of the final consonant in words such as "pas" (i.e., *past*) or "han" (i.e., *hand*), the pronunciation of the "th" in *bath* as "t" (i.e., "bat"), and the pronunciation of the vowel in words such as *my* and *ride* as long "ah," as in "mah rahd." According to Rickford, Ebonics pronunciations are systematic and the result of regular rules and restrictions found in any and all languages. For instance, speakers regularly produce sentences without present tense *is* and *are,* as in "Joe trippin'" or "They all right." But they don't omit present tense *am.* Instead of the ungrammatical "Ah walkin,'" Ebonics speakers would say "Ahm walkin.'" Ebonics speakers use an invariant *be* in their speech (e.g., "They be goin' to school every day"); however, this *be* is not simply equivalent to *is* or *are*. Invariant *be* refers to actions that occur regularly or habitually rather than on just one occasion.[48]

In addition to its phonological and syntactic elements, Black language includes other communication dimensions that distinguish it from other languages and mark its speakers as members of a unique group (see Figure 3.1). Thomas Kochman argues that African American expression is characteristically "emotionally intense, dynamic, and demonstrative," whereas Euro-American expression is "more modest and emotionally restrained."[49]

In comparing African American and Euro-American modes of expression, Kochman asserts that when engaging an issue, Euro-Americans use a detached and unemotional form of "discussion," whereas African Americans use an intense and involving form of "argument." Kochman maintains that Euro-Americans tend to understate their talents, whereas African Americans tend to boast about theirs. In essence, African American speech acts and events are more animated, lively, and forceful than Euro-American speech acts. According to Kochman, the animation and vitality of Black communication is due to the emotional force and spiritual energy that Blacks invest in their public presentations and the functional role that emotions play in realizing the goals of Black interactions, activities, and events. For example, a common goal of many African American speech events is to energize the audience into an emotional and spiritual release. Such speech events require a strong speaker, a medium that facilitates the emotional and spiritual release, and active participation from the

Figure 3.1   Black language, including Ebonics, includes many different communication dimensions that distinguish it from other languages.

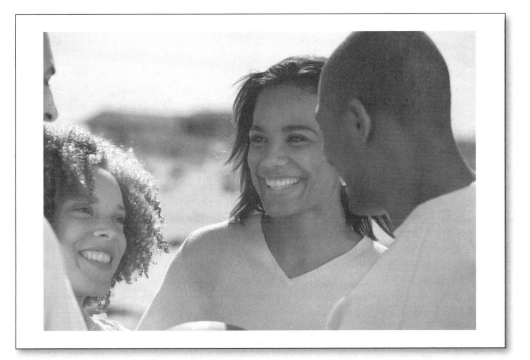

audience. One type of communication that captures the essence of such revitalization is the "call-and-response" pattern involving reciprocal speech acts between speaker and audience. In the typical call-and-response mode, a speaker begins by calling—that is, making some point or assertion to which the audience responds. African studies professor Shirley Weber describes an instance of call and response while teaching:

> During the lecture, one of my more vocal black students began to respond to the message with some encouraging remarks like "all right," "make it plain," "that all right," and "teach." She was soon joined by a few more black students who gave similar comments. I noticed that this surprised and confused some of the white students. When questioned later about this, their response was that they were not used to having more than one person talk at a time, and they really could not talk and listen at the same time. They found the comments annoying and disruptive. As the lecturer, I found the comments refreshing and inspiring.[50]

African Americans often engage in call-and-response modes in a variety of formalized settings, such as church meetings, and during informal, everyday gatherings.

Origins of Black Language

The origins of many of these African American communicative modes can be traced to ancient African philosophies about the relationship between humans, the spoken word, and the fostering of community. According to African scholar Janheinz Jahn, the traditional African view of the world is one of extraordinary harmony. All being, all essence, in whatever form it is conceived, is subsumed under one of four categories: (a) *muntu,* or human being; (b) *kintu,* or thing; (c) *hantu,* or place and time; and (d) *kuntu,* or modality. Everything that exists must necessarily belong to one of these four categories and is conceived of not as some tangible substance but as a force that affects and is affected by the other forces. All the forces are interrelated and work together to accomplish a common goal. For example, *scholar* belongs in the muntu category, *pen* in the kintu category, *university* in hantu, and *knowledge* in kuntu. Anything that exists has distinct characteristics that combine and relate with characteristics in the other categories. For example, the most distinguishing characteristic of muntu is the possession of *nommo*—that is, the magic power of the word. Through nommo, humans establish their mastery over the other things. According to Jahn, nommo is the

> life force, is the fluid as such, a unity of spiritual-physical fluidity, giving life to everything, penetrating everything, causing everything. . . . And since man has the power over the word, it is he who directs the life force. Through the word he receives it, shares it with other beings, and so fulfills the meaning of life.[51]

Nothing exists without nommo; it is the force that fosters the sense of community between speaker and audience wherein they become one as senders and receivers.

Shirley Weber argues that the philosophy of nommo has been carried into contemporary African American society, where the audience listening and responding to a message is equally as important as the speaker. One of the foremost goals within any African American communicative context is to bring speaker and audience together as one, hence the call-and-response mode. In contemporary and traditional African American speech contexts, the speaker and audience share the platform.[52]

The above discussion suggests that there are differences in the language use of African Americans and Euro-Americans and that the reason for such differences may lie in the language's purpose. African Americans tend to use language to establish and maintain a sense of community. The use of a language that expresses their unique history, bridges social and economic gaps, and helps build their future is a critical ingredient in African American communication and membership in their microcultural group.

Cultural Attitudes About Ebonics

Over the decades, numerous studies have shown that speakers using Ebonics are perceived as less credible than speakers using Standard American English (SAE). Consistent with the tenets of the muted group theory, members of the dominant cultural group prefer their language to that of microcultures. In a recent study, Andrew Billings sought to further test the hypothesis that speakers using Ebonics will be perceived as less competent and trustworthy than speakers using SAE. In his study, a total of nine video clips were produced. Three of the nine clips featured White people speaking SAE; three more featured Black people speaking SAE; the final three featured Black people (the same Black speakers as in the second group) speaking Ebonics. In essence, six speakers were used, with the three Black speakers appearing twice (once speaking SAE and once speaking Ebonics). After watching the videos, participants in the study completed scales that measured competence and trustworthiness. The results reveal that Black speakers of SAE were actually preferred to White speakers of SAE. Andrews maintains that these differences are the result of what he calls a novelty effect; that is, people expected that a Black speaker would use Ebonics, thus leading them to rate Blacks more favorably when they instead spoke SAE. Additional results showed clearly lower ratings of the Ebonics speakers in terms of intelligence, articulation, aggression, education, and qualification (all five measures of competence). Interestingly, the scales measuring trustworthiness—particularly honesty, likability, and attractiveness—did not differ between White and Black speakers. In addition to these results, Andrews reports that Whites preferred speakers of their own race in several measurements of character (e.g., likability, believability, honesty). Moreover, Blacks found White speakers of SAE to be more attractive, kind, and articulate. Finally, Andrews notes that Black participants were much harsher critics of Ebonics than were Whites. Thus, he concludes that within almost all variables, the dialect used and the race of the person who is speaking can significantly alter ratings of speaker perception.[53]

The Amish

One microcultural group that continues to fascinate much of America is the Amish. John Andrew Hostetler is a former Amish member who left his community and is considered the country's leading expert on Amish custom. Hostetler describes them as

> a church, a community, a spiritual union, a conservative branch of Christianity, a religion, a community whose members practice simple and austere living, a familistic entrepreneuring system, and an adaptive human community.[54]

The **Amish**, sometimes called "the Plain People" or "Old Order Amish," are an Anabaptist religious group that emigrated from Europe to the United States in the early 1700s. Currently, no Amish communities remain in Europe. Today, Amish groups have settled in about 22 states and Ontario, Canada. Historically, the Amish immigrated to the United States to escape religious persecution. Their name is derived from one of their earliest leaders, Jacob Amman, a young Alsatian bishop and farmer who held a strong Bible-centered faith and was staunchly conservative. To his followers, Amman advocated nonresistance, adult baptism, disciplinary dress standards, and separatism from worldly fashion and influence.

From 1730 through 1770, between 50 and 100 Amish families arrived in the United States and initially settled in Pennsylvania. Since then, several groups of Amish have moved farther west to settle in Ohio, Indiana, Illinois, Iowa, and Wisconsin, among other areas. The greatest concentration of Amish is in Holmes and adjoining counties in northeast Ohio. Next in size is a group of Amish people in Elkhart and surrounding counties in northeastern Indiana. Then comes the Amish settlement in Lancaster County, Pennsylvania. The Amish population in the United States numbers more than 150,000 and growing, due to large family size (seven children on average) and a church-member retention rate of approximately 80%.[55]

An Isolated Microculture

Perhaps more than any other microcultural group, the Amish have been relatively successful at isolating themselves from the influences of the dominant culture. The Amish follow five basic tenets: adult baptism; separation of church and state; excommunication from the church for those who break moral law; living life in accordance with the teachings of Christ; and refusal to bear arms, take oaths, or hold political office. Living what they call nonresistant lives, they do not serve in the U.S. military. According to Rich Huber, who was raised a Mennonite in Lancaster County, Pennsylvania, the Amish follow the Bible as literally as possible, citing "Be ye not conformed to the world" (Romans 12:2) as their fundamental principle. Based on their interpretation of this Biblical passage, the Amish believe that true followers of Christ are to be separate from the world. Hence, to evade worldliness and the corruption and sin associated with it, the Amish have drawn strict boundaries between themselves and the dominant cultural milieu.[56]

Although they are generally successful at avoiding contemporary American society, the Amish are considered American citizens and observe most U.S. laws. Hostetler notes that the Amish pay income, property, and sales taxes like everyone else. They do not pay Social Security taxes, nor do they receive Social Security benefits or any other type of government aid (e.g., food stamps, welfare). In addition, they avoid the courts in settlings of disputes, are forbidden to take oaths, do not serve on juries, and do not collect settlements from the courts.[57] Moreover, they take full responsibility for the education of their children and generally do not send them to public schools. In fact, in 1972, the Supreme Court heard the case of *Wisconsin v. Yoder* wherein the court exempted the various Amish sects from compulsory school attendance laws beyond eighth grade. *Wisconsin v. Yoder* represented the first time conflicts over education between the Amish and the government had been argued before the Supreme Court. This is significant because most Amish follow a "turn the other cheek" mentality and do not defend themselves. MacKaye notes that, when confronted, many Amish simply pack up their belongings and move somewhere else in order to be left alone.[58]

Today, most Amish children are taught in one-room schoolhouses by teachers with no more than an eighth-grade education. Amish children attend school until the eighth grade, after which they are educated at home and go to work on the family farms. The Amish consider their society as a form of schooling. The Amish train their children vocationally. Almost exclusively, Amish boys become farmers, carpenters, or tradesmen, and girls become homemakers. Beginning on their 16th birthdays, Amish youth enter a kind of decision-making phase, called a "simmie" period, wherein they are to contemplate whether or not they will maintain or renounce their Amish identity. During this time, they are exposed to deviant behaviors and attitudes. The Amish believe that exposing their youth to deviance sifts out those who might not be fit to be adult Amish. Professor Denise Reiling, of Eastern Michigan University, argues that many of the behaviors considered deviant among the Amish would be considered relatively harmless in many other cultural contexts. Such behaviors include being an annoyance, acting irresponsibly, hurting another person's feelings, telling lies, excluding another person from a group activity, or just acting in an unwise, reckless, or impractical fashion. Reiling reports that at the end of their simmie period, the teens announce their decision to either reject or adopt Amish identity. Approximately 20% of youths eventually defect from the Amish. Although the simmie period often results in depression and anxiety for the youth, Reiling notes that most youth remain in the simmie period for 2 to 3 years, whereas others take as long as 8 to 10 years to make a decision. Those that defect are immediately excommunicated, resulting in ostracism and physical separation from their families and from the entire Amish settlement.[59]

The Amish have virtually no unemployment.[60] As in other religiously oriented microcultural groups, the Amish believe that God is the absolute power in the universe. They believe that their life on earth is preparation for their afterlife in heaven. As a result, many of the values and behaviors of the Amish may be similar to mainstream America but for very different reasons. By the time they die, the Amish want their earthly sins settled; hence, every day is to be lived well so as to please God. The Amish do not believe that entrance to heaven is guaranteed, however.[61] As Hostetler notes, complete assurance of heaven is seen as obnoxious because it smacks of pride and boasting. Hence, humility, self-denial, and submissiveness are at the core of Amish values.[62]

Because the Amish want their group to remain much as it was in the 17th century, they are very slow to change. They choose to examine change very carefully before they accept it. If a new idea or change does not help them keep their lives simple and their families together, they will probably reject it. Hence, the Amish eschew most modern technologies such as electricity, automobiles, and other conveniences (see Figure 3.2).[63] Also, based on the Biblical passage "Thou shalt not make unto thee any graven image, or any likeness of anything that . . . is in the earth" (Exodus 20:4), the Amish do not allow anyone to photograph them.[64]

Unlike mainstream American society, the Amish are a collectivistic community—what they call *Gemeinde,* which translates to "redemptive community." From this perspective, individuals depend on their community for their identity. The Amish believe that a person's self-worth is defined by his or her role in the community. Individual achievement, self-ambition, power, and worldly acquisitions are not valued. Sharing, community effort, and trading are the core values of most Amish communities. The Amish believe that community service gains one access to God and eternal life.[65] Because of their collectivistic orientation, each member of the group has a well-defined role. For example, sex roles among Amish men and women

Figure 3.2 The Amish eschew many modern technologies.

are clearly prescribed. Patterns of dress and a strict division of labor separate men and women in Amish society. Exclusively, Amish women are homemakers and Amish men are farmers, with the exception of those men who join the ministry.[66]

Verbal Communication of the Amish

Most Amish are trilingual; that is, they speak three languages. They speak a dialect of German, called high German, during church services. At home or during informal gatherings, they speak low German, sometimes called Pennsylvania Dutch (the term derived from non-Amish mispronunciation of *Deutsche*). They also learn and speak English at school and use it when interacting with non-Amish persons. Like all other microcultures, the Amish frequently use phrases and sayings that carry meaning to them. In their study of Amish verbal phrases and colloquialisms, Moellendorf, Warsh, and Yoshimaru report that one traditional Amish saying in German is "Das alt Gebrauch ist besser," which translates to "The old way is the better way." According to Moellendorf and her colleagues, the Amish believe that past traditions and the old way of living are superior to the conveniences of modern life and its new technologies. Occasionally, outsiders look to the Amish as an idyllic community. They see the Amish lifestyle as free from the pressures of the modern world. To this, the

Amish say, "It's not all pies and cakes," meaning that the life of the Amish may appear simple and serene, but in reality, the life of an Amish person is hard, disciplined, and strenuous. Although it happens only infrequently, sometimes an individual will leave the Amish community and join a less demanding church, such as the Mennonites, or another community. About this, the Amish say, "He got his hair cut," as a polite way of communicating that the individual was unable to meet the rigorous standards of the Amish. The saying also suggests that the person has lost his masculine tie (i.e., his long hair) to the community. Another way of communicating a similar phenomenon is to say, "He went English," which is said when an Amish member has left the community to become a part of mainstream American culture.[67]

To enforce church order and discipline, the Amish engage in a form of excommunication called "the ban" or "shunning." Shunning includes prohibiting attendance at church and, in its most extreme form, most types of involvement with members of the community. The ban is particularly difficult for other members of a family who may have a member shunned. In such cases, they are expected to cut off all communication with that person.[68]

Nonverbal Communication of the Amish

Moellendorf and her colleagues also studied the nonverbal communication of the Amish and found that they have a distinct nonverbal communication system. According to Moellendorf, one's role in an Amish community is nonverbally communicated by his or her physical appearance and dress. For example, the style of hat worn by an Amish man communicates his age and marital status. A black hat with three or more inches of brim is given to Amish boys at about the age of 2. The larger brim communicates the young boy's innocence. A bridegroom's hat has a crease around the top and a wide seam along the brim signaling his marriage. Amish fathers wear hats with flat crowns. An Amish woman's bonnet is her way to communicate her marital status. All Amish women wear bonnets over the back part of their hair. Young girls wear colored bonnets and begin to wear black bonnets at about the age of 9. Married Amish women wear white bonnets.[69]

In addition to hats and bonnets, Amish hairstyles communicate status. Young girls wear braids that are fastened around their foreheads. At about the age of 10, their hair is arranged into a bun. Adult Amish women never cut their hair; they part it in the middle and wear a bun. Most Amish women do not shave their legs or trim their eyebrows, as such behavior is seen as interfering with God's work. Amish men shave until marriage, at which time they grow beards, which are analogous to wedding rings. If a single man reaches the age of 40, he may grow a beard. In all cases, married or not, the beard is left untrimmed, and mustaches are not allowed because of their long association with the military.[70]

To communicate submissiveness and pride, enhance group unity, and indicate the desire to be separate from the rest of the contemporary world, the Amish wear only plain clothing. To the Amish, dress is a statement of conformity to group values. A man's shirt is pocketless, and his trousers do not have hip pockets and are worn with suspenders so that they are not tight. For women, ribbons, bows, makeup, and jewelry are forbidden as they are seen as haughty and vain. The dresses of older Amish women close in front and have skirts that touch the tops of their shoes. Women are never allowed to wear pants and typically wear an apron over the dress. Generally, the colors of both men's and women's clothing are restricted to white, green, blue, or purple.[71]

Another nonverbal dimension to the Amish is the horse and buggy. Kraybill argues that the horse and buggy serve as the prime symbol of Amish life. To the Amish, the horse communicates tradition, time, and proof that the Amish have not succumbed to the conveniences of modern life. The buggy, which is typically gray, communicates *Gelassenheit,* which means a surrender to communal values and modesty. Moreover, because the buggies all look alike, they serve as a kind of equalizer among the Amish.[72]

Amidst incredible societal and technological change, the Amish have maintained their lifestyle for more than 200 years. Although they are generally a quiet and reserved microculture that prefers to be isolated from the dominant culture, some Amish recently have become the target of hate crimes. Ironically, their nonflamboyant appearance and subdued behavior, along with their horses and buggies and their refusal to adopt modern technologies, have rendered the Amish an easy target. In a recent example where a young man shot at an Amish buggy full of children and then raped a young Amish woman, the assailant was quoted as saying that he wanted the Amish to know that they do not own this world and that there are other people in the world.[73]

Father J. Mahoney, a priest who has studied various religious groups, argues that the Amish have tried to freeze their culture in the late 17th century. Throughout the centuries, as the mainstream culture of the United States progressed technologically, the Amish have tried to preserve their lifestyle, creating a disparity between them and the dominant culture. That disparity, and disagreements as to how far they should go in accommodating it, will remain the major challenge for the Amish in the coming decades.[74] As Hostetler notes:

> Over the past three centuries the Amish and other Anabaptist groups have been suspended between two opposing forces: the political forces that would eliminate ethnicity from the face of the earth and the human communities who regard ethnicity as a natural and necessary extension of the familial bonds that integrate human activities. Caught between these forces the "plain" people have sometimes prospered and sometimes suffered for their faith.[75]

The Hmong

While most students in the United States learn about America's involvement in the Vietnam War, some never learn of the "Secret War" fought on behalf of the United States during this time. This "Secret War" refers to the thousands of **Hmong** who were recruited by the U.S. military through the Central Intelligence Agency (CIA) to help fight the war against Communism in Southeast Asia. According to Daphne Winland, the Hmong belong to the Sino-Tibetan language family. They are culturally similar to the Chinese, and Hmong origins can be traced back to China, where they lived peacefully for hundreds of years. Approximately 150 years ago, Chinese rulers began a campaign of persecution to extinguish the Hmong language. The Hmong moved southward and westward out of China and organized communities in Burma, Thailand, North Vietnam, and the mountains of Laos. Winland points out that the Hmong, which means "free people" or "mountain people," were singled out by the CIA during the Vietnam War because of their geographically strategic location in the mountains of Laos.[76] In the 1960s, the CIA began secretly enlisting Hmong to prevent North Vietnamese troops from entering and moving supplies to South Vietnam through Laos.

The Hmong also set up navigational aids for American bombers and fought to protect them when they were attacked by the North Vietnamese. In addition, Hmong soldiers were highly skilled in the operations required to rescue American pilots shot down over Laos (the United States flew more tactical missions over Laos than it did over Vietnam).[77] The Hmong were fierce fighters yet suffered devastating losses estimated at more than 100 times greater (proportionately) than those of the United States. Although estimates vary, most experts agree that more than 25,000 Hmong lost their lives fighting for the United States during the Vietnam War.[78]

Due to intense political pressures at home, the United States had vowed not to escalate the war into Laos. Hence, the Hmong became known as the "Secret Army," and their participation in the war was called the "Secret War."[79] In 1975, the United States withdrew its forces from Vietnam. Concurrently, a Communist-backed government supported by the Vietnamese and Soviets, assumed power in Laos. One of the foremost goals of the new Laotian government was to annihilate the Hmong people because of their alliance with the United States. The Communists tortured, raped, and murdered thousands of Hmong. They napalmed their villages and slaughtered their cattle. There is evidence that the Communists used chemical and biological weapons in their attempt to wipe out the Hmong. With the United States having withdrawn from Vietnam, the Hmong were left without any allies in the midst of their enemies and a new war.[80]

More than 200,000 Hmong fled to Thailand, where they were housed in prison-like conditions in refugee camps. Many Hmong immigrated to the United States, Australia, and France. Approximately 100,000 made it to the United States. Today, about 150,000 Hmong reside in the United States, with large concentrations in California, Wisconsin, and Minnesota. Although they were hired and paid by the United States, Hmong soldiers have received little or no recognition for their efforts and do not receive veteran benefits. In May 1997, the United States finally acknowledged Hmong veterans with a granite marker in Arlington National Cemetery that reads, "The U.S. Secret Army in the Kingdom of Laos 1961–1973." In both the Laotian and Hmong languages, the marker also reads, "You will never be forgotten." In 1995, there were still as many as 40,000 Hmong residing in refugee camps in Thailand.[81]

Duffy alleges that life in the United States has been very difficult for many Hmong. For the most part, Hmong immigrants have not been welcomed. Unfortunately, many people inaccurately associate the Hmong with the "enemy" in the Vietnam War. To add to their arduous situation, many stereotypes preceded their immigration to the United States. News coverage of the Hmong often referred to them as a "pre-literate," "primitive," "hilltribe" group.[82] Moreover, writes Winland, during this time period just about anything associated with the Vietnam War was anathema. Hence, the Hmong entered the United States being doubted and distrusted by many and facing the straightforward bigotry of others. The Hmong find themselves in a situation of relative dependency on U.S. culture while simultaneously experiencing a real sense of cultural isolation.[83]

Unlike the African Americans or the Amish, who have been in the United States for centuries, the Hmong are unique in that they are first-generation immigrants. Their values, customs, and modes of communication have collided head-on with mainstream American culture. For example, the Hmong are traditionally a collectivistic culture. According to Katie Thao, a native Hmong who immigrated to the United States when she was a teenager, the most important group is the family clan. Hmong family clans are patrilineal. Hmong males are given two names—one in childhood and the other when they reach adulthood. When children are born, they are given their father's clan name. When women marry, they keep their father's clan name and do not adopt their husband's even though they become formal members of his clan. Conversely, Hmong women do not receive an adult name but become known by their husband's clan name. There are between 20 and 30 clan names. The most common clan names in the United States include Cha, Hang, Her, Kong, Kue, Moua, Lee, Lo or Lor, Thao or Thor, Vang, Vue, Xiong, and Yang.[84]

Role Relationships and Marriage

According to Ray Hutchison and Miles McNall, many of the Hmong customs associated with clan membership that have been imported to the United States include sex role relationships and marriage practices (see Figure 3.3). For the most part, these practices clash with American customs. For example, in traditional Hmong culture, women maintain clearly subordinate roles. Their role is to bear children, maintain the household, and be subservient to their husbands. One way Hmong women demonstrate their subordinate status is by walking directly behind their husbands when in public. Moreover, they have little or nothing to say in the decision making or political affairs of their clans. Some husbands refuse to allow their wives to learn English, hence keeping them muted and powerless in American culture. For the most part, first-generation Hmong women are not allowed an education and are expected to marry early, between the ages of 13 and 18 (whereas men marry between the ages of 18 and 30). Although the practices are gradually changing in the United States, many Hmong marriages are still arranged. Many communities report that a high percentage of Hmong girls drop out of high school to get married. Indeed, Hmong women have the youngest average marriage age of all Southeast Asian refugee groups. Moreover, Hmong fertility rates in the United States are much higher than those of any other refugee or immigrant group.[85]

Katie Thao participated in an arranged marriage. She did not meet her husband-to-be until the day of her wedding. To many Americans, an arranged marriage seems ridiculous and absurd. But Thao asserts that she was completely comfortable with the idea because she had confidence in her parents, especially her father, to negotiate a good husband for her. Thao contends that an arranged Hmong marriage is a matter of considerable maneuvering and bargaining. Typically, each family selects an elderly male spokesman. These spokesmen, usually the fathers, then negotiate and bargain a bride price that is to be paid to the bride's parents. The philosophy behind "buying a wife" is to ensure that she will be highly valued by her new family. In many cases, the bride's parents hold a feast of roasted pig in their home in celebration of the wedding. After the wedding ceremony, the souls and good fortune of the bride and groom are symbolically wrapped in an umbrella that is carried in procession to the groom's home, where another feast is held. If the bride is entering the groom's home for the first time (which is usually the case because the bride and groom are strangers), a rooster is waved over the bride to symbolize her membership in the groom's clan. In most cases, a Hmong marriage is seen not as a bonding of two people but as a union of two family clans. In some cases, if a married Hmong woman's husband dies, she automatically becomes the wife of his younger brother.[86]

Communication Patterns of the Hmong

Like most microcultural groups, the Hmong share some unique verbal and nonverbal communication patterns. The overwhelming majority of the first Hmong immigrants entering the

| Figure 3.3 | Many customs are imported to the United States, such as sex role relationships and marriage practices. |

United States did not speak English. Historically, because the Hmong migrated so often, their written language was eventually lost. Not until the 1950s were orthographies of the written language developed. Well over half of the Hmong who immigrated to the United States could not read or write. For the Hmong who immigrated to Laos, they were taught in Buddhist temples in the Lao language and Lao alphabet. In Laos today, there are two major dialects of Hmong language. One is *Hmoob Dawb,* meaning White Hmong, and the other is *Hmoob Ntsuab,* meaning Blue Hmong. Because the White Hmong are in the majority, Hmoob Dawb is spoken more frequently.[87]

According to Thao, the phrase "Playing a flute into a water buffalo's ear" is used by the Hmong when someone is trying, without success, to explain something to another who simply does not understand. Often, the Hmong will refer to someone who does not understand a message as some kind of animal, often a water buffalo. The idea of a flute is significant because in traditional Hmong culture, the flute communicates emotions, such as sorrow, love, and even anger or depression. Another phrase, "The grinder doesn't taste salty," is used to refer to a person who is bankrupt. Salt is a very valuable ingredient to the Hmong, and when there is no salt, it is an indication that the family is out of money.

The Hmong are animistic, meaning they believe that everything has a spirit. According to Thao, the supernatural is a very real part of Hmong life. Evil spirits are thought to exist in unpopulated areas; therefore, many Hmong are afraid to travel alone in uninhabited places. The phrase "The devil will not eat or chew anyone for it" is said when an act or crime is committed wherein no one will be caught or found guilty. The Hmong believe that evil spirits such as the devil are omnipresent and can hear and see everything. If the devil will not eat anyone, then the act will go unpunished. "Go check the mousetrap" is said in reference to a meal shared by an entire clan or village. The phrase is used to compare someone going to a meal to a mouse going to a trap in search of food. When a person goes to a meal, he or she gets trapped in the company of the clan or family. Many of the Hmong sayings and colloquialisms are indirect expressions. The Hmong believe that if the truth is spoken directly, evil spirits or unwanted guests can overhear it. Thao says that a Hmong farmer might call out to his family, "Come sharpen your knives," rather than calling out, "It's time to eat," because the latter might attract evil spirits or animals who will eat the meal.[88]

One of the most significant forms of nonverbal communication for the Hmong are their *paj ntaub,* pronounced "pandoa." Paj ntaub, meaning "flower cloth," are sophisticated stitched quilts embroidered with bright threads. They often feature picturesque geometric designs that occasionally feature animals or other creatures. Since their immigration to the United States, paj ntaub have evolved into "story cloths," often depicting the history and life experiences of the Hmong culture. Evolving from the Thai refugee camps, story cloths were a means to teach written language to Hmong children and others. Now they are treated as works of art and a vehicle for the Hmong to document their history and retain their cultural identity. Created exclusively by Hmong women, the cloths carry much significance. The quality of the needlework communicates the skill and creativity of the women who make them and may bring the women a higher bride price at the time of marriage bargaining.[89]

Other nonverbal gestures used in Hmong culture include twitching the eyes to communicate contempt to another. Twitching the eyes during a long stare is very offensive and may lead to a physical confrontation. Slapping oneself on the buttocks is a nonverbal way of saying "Kiss my ass" or "Lick my ass." Kneeling is done only by men when they want to express their thanks or to ask another for mercy and forgiveness. A woman's kneeling has little or no value because of her low rank and position in Hmong clans.[90]

Elliot Barkan writes that acculturation in the United States has been difficult for the Hmong. The first-generation Hmong, arriving in the United States in the mid-1970s, have tried hard to preserve their culture, whereas their children, exposed to the values and communication system of the dominant culture, are caught between two cultures. The older Hmong try to preserve the traditional ways while contemporary culture, including the educational system, encourages their assimilation. Acculturation for the elderly Hmong has been particularly difficult. The age and sex hierarchies that prescribed their superior status are gone. In Laos, women have few, if any, rights. In the United States, of course, women have equal rights. Language has played a key role as well. A Hmong child's quick acquisition of English almost reverses traditional family roles. Contrary to their traditional roles, the parents are now dependent on the child's communication skills to get along. Many parents feel that the learning of such skills undermines their authority; hence, some parents develop a sense of loss and worthlessness and fall into deep depressions.[91]

Arab Americans

Since the attacks on the World Trade Center towers in New York and the Pentagon in Washington, D.C., in September 2001, increased racial, ethnic, and religious hostility has left

Arab Americans, Middle Easterners, and those who bear physical likeness to members of these groups in a precarious state. Arab American groups (such as the American-Arab Anti-Discrimination Committee) report numerous attacks on people from these various cultural and ethnic groups since September 11, 2001. Hundreds of people have been beaten, killed, threatened, ridiculed, and harassed because they were thought to be Arabian and somehow associated with those who attacked the United States. But of all the microcultural groups discussed in this chapter thus far, these groups (i.e., Arab Americans, Middle Easterners) are perhaps the most ethnically, racially, and religiously diverse group in the country. In fact, to classify these people into one group is impossible.

The U.S. Census Bureau classifies Arabs as White. And for the first time in its history, in 2000, the U.S. Census Bureau officially classified persons in the United States who had Arab ancestry. According to the Census Bureau, people with ancestries originating from Arabic-speaking countries or areas of the world were classified as **Arab**. According to a 2008 report, the U.S. Census Bureau indicates that in 2003, 1.2 million people living in the United States consider themselves as having Arab ancestry, an increase of nearly 40% since 1990. However, the Arab American Institute believes that at least 3.5 million people in America have roots in the Arabic-speaking world. They maintain that Arab Americans are undercounted in the census because some Arab Americans do not understand the relevance of the census and its confidentiality or did not respond to the question that measures ethnic ancestry. Another problem with this classification is that a person is included in the Arab ancestry category if he or she reported being Arab, Egyptian, Iraqi, Jordanian, Lebanese, Middle Eastern, Moroccan, North African, Palestinian, Syrian, and so on. Yet many people from these countries do not consider themselves to be Arab, and conversely, some people who consider themselves Arab may not be included in this classification. For example, groups such as Kurds and Berbers, who are typically not considered Arab, were included in this definition for consistency with the 1990 and 2000 census. Moreover, some groups such as Mauritanians, Somalians, Djiboutians, Sudanese, and Comoros Islanders, who may consider themselves Arab, were not included. Arab Americans can be found in virtually every state in the United States, but more than 60% live in 10 states. Approximately 30% of all Arab Americans in the United States live in Los Angeles, Detroit, and New York. Moreover, the majority of Arab Americans were born in the United States, and more than 80% are citizens.[92]

To be sure, the Arab American population is misunderstood. For example, Arab Americans are often thought to be Muslim. But Helen Hatab Samhan, the executive director of the Arab American Institute, points out that Arab Americans are as diverse as any other microcultural group in the United States (see Figure 3.4). Moreover, she maintains that religious affiliation among Arab Americans is one of their most defining characteristics. Most people do not know, for example, that the majority of Arab Americans descend from mostly Christian immigrants. In fact, roughly two-thirds of the Arab population identifies with one or more Christian sects. To be sure, however, Samhan notes that since the 1950s, Arab **Muslims** have represented the fastest growing segment of the Arab American community. And Samhan recognizes that this creates some challenges for this group. For example, Muslim Arabs in America have religious traditions and practices that differ considerably from those of other religions in the United States. The beliefs of Islam emphasize the importance of modesty, reject interfaith marriage, and object to typical

Figure 3.4 In many cultures, tradition clashes with contemporary values.

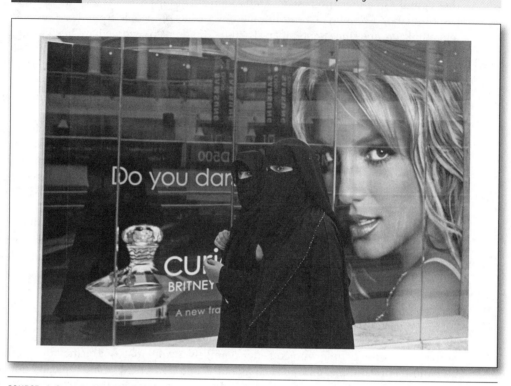

SOURCE: © Steve Raymer/Corbis.

standards of dating or gender integration. Other religious practices such as the five-times-daily prayers, the month-long fast at Ramadan, beards for men, and the wearing of the *hijab* (head cover) for women render Muslims more visible than other microcultural groups and, thus, open to stereotyping.

Despite the challenges, Samhan notes that Arab Americans continue to make significant contributions to U.S. culture. She points out that the Lebanese-born poet/artist Kahlil Gibran is widely read and appreciated by American readers, and author William Blatty (*The Exorcist*), children's author Naomi Shihab Nye, and Edward Said are also well known. White House press corps leader Helen Thomas and consumer advocate and former presidential candidate Ralph Nader are internationally known. In the field of entertainment, Arab Americans include the actor/comic Danny Thomas, actress Kathy Najimy, and actor Tony Shalhoub; singers Paul Anka and Paula Abdul; and Casey Kasem, "America's Top 40" disc jockey. Well-known sports figures include Doug Flutie and Jeff George of the National Football League. Such business stars as J. M. Haggar, the clothing manufacturer, and Paul Orfalea, founder of Kinko's photocopy stores, are among the many Arabs who have made significant contributions to American culture.[93]

Lesbian, Gay, Bisexual, and Transgendered Microcultural Groups

Of the six microcultural groups discussed in this chapter, the lesbian, gay, bisexual, and trans-gendered (LGBT) microcultural group is the most difficult to define and characterize. To be sure, LGBT issues are some of the most controversial and most politically contested areas of cultural diversity facing us today. Of the five characteristics that define microcultural groups presented at the beginning of this chapter, LGBT groups seem to meet all of them but not definitively. First, LGBT groups have a distinguishing cultural trait—that is, their sexual orientation. Beyond that, however, members of the LGBT microculture belong to myriad other demographic, educational, occupational, and social groups. Moreover, one's sexual orientation is not as overtly distinct as, say, skin color or style of dress. LGBT persons can be of any sex, race, ethnicity, nationality, occupation, or other demographic group.

Second, membership in this microculture appears to be involuntary, although some might disagree. In their recent book on LGBT studies, Meem, Gibson, and Alexander point out that, for more than a century, scientists and scholars have sought to identify the factors that make certain people feel sexual desire for someone of the same sex.[94] Meem and her colleagues chronicle decades of research that has tried to answer the question of whether one's sexual orientation is innate or learned. Some research suggests that it is learned, while other research points to an innate hypothesis. Meem points out that both sides have strengths and weaknesses in their arguments. Meem and her colleagues conclude:

> Methodological weaknesses have been perceived in both biological and psychological research, not the least of which is that both still assume heterosexuality as the default position. We can see heteronormativity at work in scientific inquiry; researchers look for a "gay gene," but why do they not attempt to isolate a "straight gene?" Presumably only the nonnormative—the queer—needs to be explained, while the normative goes unremarked as obviously and unquestionably natural.[95]

So while the question of whether one's sexuality is innate or learned goes unanswered, most members of the LGBT microculture maintain that their membership is involuntary. In a recent survey of sexual behavior in the United States, scholars at the Center for Sexual Health Promotion at Indiana University surveyed nearly 6,000 individuals ranging in age from 14 to 94 years old. They found that among adolescent males, 96% indicated they were heterosexual, and just under 4% indicated they were gay or lesbian, bisexual, or other. Among adolescent females, just over 90% indicated they were heterosexual, while just under 10% reported that they were gay or lesbian, bisexual, or other. Among adult males, just over 92% reported being heterosexual; thus, just under 8% indicated that they were gay or lesbian, bisexual, or other. Among adult women, 93% reported being heterosexual, while just under 7% indicated being gay or lesbian, bisexual, or other.[96]

Researchers note that estimating who is gay or lesbian, bisexual, or transgendered is fraught with difficulty. For example, does a person consider him/herself gay or lesbian after just one same-sex encounter? Two encounters? Three? Or what about the person who has had no same-sex encounters but considers him/herself gay? Like other microcultural groups, LGBT members tend to live in certain geographical regions of the United States, primarily large urban areas. For example, the top 10 U.S. cities with the largest percentage of LGBT inhabitants include the following:

City and Proportion of LGBT Inhabitants[97]

1. San Francisco   15.4%

2. Seattle   12.9%

3. Atlanta   12.8%

4. Minneapolis   12.5%

5. Boston   12.3%

6. Sacramento   9.8%

7. Portland   8.8%

8. Denver   8.2%

9. Washington, D.C.   8.1%

10. Orlando   7.7%

The third characteristic defining microcultural groups is endogamy. Addressing endogamy among LGBTs in the United States is impossible because in-group marriage between LGBT persons is illegal in 44 of 50 states. As of June 2011, same-sex marriage was legal in only five states: Massachusetts, Connecticut, Iowa, New Hampshire, Vermont, and New York. Same-sex marriage is also legal in Washington, D.C., as well as within the Coquille Indian Tribe in Oregon.

The fourth and fifth defining characteristics of microcultures are their awareness of their subordination and their unequal treatment by the larger dominant group. Clearly, the LGBT microculture is aware of its subordination and is treated unequally, even legally. For example, Title VII of the Civil Rights Act of 1964 was the landmark piece of legislation signed by President Johnson that legally banned discrimination against African Americans and women, including segregation based on race and/or sex. The Act banned racial segregation in schools, in the workplace, and by those facilities that served the general public. But as Julie Gedro points out in her review of the legal environment for LGBTs, noticeably absent from the Civil Rights Act is any mention of sexual orientation. Gedro points out that there are no federal prohibitions against employment discrimination for LGBT persons in the United States. Indeed, Gedro notes that currently, in 29 states, it is legal to discriminate in the workplace based on sexual orientation. More recent legislation, titled the Employment Non-Discrimination Act, would prohibit employment discrimination, preferential treatment, and retaliation on the basis of sexual orientation or gender identity by employers with 15 or more employees. The Act has been introduced to the U.S. Congress nine times—in 1994, 1995, 1996, 1997, 1998, 1999, 2002, 2003, and 2009—and has yet to pass. Yet Gedro identifies no fewer than 30 countries across the globe that prohibit discrimination on the basis of sexual orientation.[98]

In addition to the lack of federal prohibition against discrimination, there are a number of organizations across the United States that actively protest against the equal rights of LGBTs.

Not only do many of these groups actively try to subordinate LGBT groups, but they also advocate violence against LGBT persons and strive for their complete eradication. In 2010, the Southern Poverty Law Center asserted that LGBTs are the group of people most targeted by hate crimes. The Center profiled 18 organized groups, many of which are religiously oriented, whose primary goal was to thwart LGBT progress and equal rights. For example, Abiding Truth Ministries of Springfield, Massachusetts, sponsors an international anti-LGBT campaign. The founder, Scott Lively, coauthored the book *The Pink Swastika: Homosexuality in the Nazi Party,* which accuses homosexuals of running the Nazi Party and is widely cited by gay-bashers. Lively has taken his anti-LGBT rhetoric to Eastern Europe, Africa, and Russia. Americans for Truth About Homosexuality was formed in 1996 by Peter LaBarbera, who

STUDENT VOICES ACROSS CULTURES

Dr. Stephen Rupsch

Living as an openly gay man and working as a professor for a Catholic college has been an illuminating experience. Before I arrived here in the Midwest to take a teaching position, I lived most of my adult life on the West Coast and in larger cities, such as San Francisco. I also work in the theatre as a director and teacher. Within those geographic and social groups, the fact that I am gay was, for the most part, a non-issue. San Francisco has a large LGBT community, and the theatre world historically has been a refuge for all sorts of people from fringe groups. I am also 50 and have been out since I was 17. I know what direct silencing looks like and how it feels. What I was surprised with when I arrived for my new job was the amount of indirect silencing. This is what I now call *soft discrimination*.

Example 1: I am speaking with a colleague about minor personal matters. My colleague tells me all about his or her husband or wife, his or her kids, and his or her parents but never asks about my partner, Brett (whom he or she has met). I wouldn't use this as an example if it did not happen *frequently*.

Example 2: I meet a new colleague at a college social function. We have some polite conversation about general life on and off campus. As soon as that person realizes that I am gay, he or she says something like, "I have a friend who is gay," or "I love gay people." I know when people do this, they are trying to connect with me, but seriously, making a big deal about my gayness just makes me feel like they are *not* really OK with it. Again, this has happened several times.

Example 3: My partner Brett and I are grocery shopping. Brett loves big, beautiful rings and wears them often. I hear a man behind me make a strange "disgusting" sound and turn to look at him staring at Brett's ring, then at Brett, and then at me. I turn (probably rolling my eyes) and hear the sound of someone spitting and turn again to see the "loogie" at our feet and the man huffing away. And yes, this has happened a few times.

What is happening when one of your bosses speaks about diversity to a small group but doesn't look you in the eye? Am I imagining it? What is happening when you teach your class about a play with a gay character, but none of them can look at you when you are speaking about it?

I direct plays for a living and teach acting. I know that you can convey a lot of meaning with very subtle actions. Maybe it is involuntary, but maybe sometimes it's not. And sometimes it silences.

reorganized it in 2006 as a much more serious and influential, if often vicious, operation. The Christian Anti-Defamation Commission (CADC) is focused on the evils of homosexuality and has called the idea of allowing gays to serve openly in the military "evil." The CADC opposes hate crimes legislation and has written that "homosexuals have turned away from humbly worshipping the true and living God and his transcendent moral order in order to make an idol out of their sexual perversion and chaos."[99]

Gayspeak: Communication of the LGBT Microculture

In 1981, a book titled *Gayspeak: Gay Male/Lesbian Communication* was published. The book was the first scholarly volume devoted to gay and lesbian communication.[100] With a few exceptions, the book is a collection of essays articulating the thesis that the gay community uses language differently than does the heterosexual community. But the assertion that the LGBT microculture communicates in ways that distinguish it as a unique linguistic community is misleading because the LGBT community is so demographically diverse. For example, in one essay in *Gayspeak*, Joseph Hayes asserts that gayspeak serves three functions: (1) it is a language that protects against detection of one's homosexual status, (2) it facilitates the expression of gay and lesbian roles within gay culture, and (3) it is a vehicle for political identity and activism. While these claims seem reasonable and certainly may apply to LGBT communication, they are certainly not unique to this microculture. Any number of demographic, political, or social groups use language in this way.[101]

Unfortunate stereotypes abound that gay men speak like heterosexual women and lesbians sound like heterosexual men. The classic stereotype that gay men speak with overly careful pronunciation, a high and rapidly changing pitch, breathy tone, and use of sexual and erotic references and that lesbians use a lower pitch than heterosexual women is not supported by any sound empirical research. To be sure, virtually all legitimate scholarly research in this area rejects these stereotypes. Sims notes that a distinctive communication style unique to LGBT has not been identified because the LGBT microculture does not represent a single unified or delineable social or demographic group.[102]

On the other hand, some scholars have argued that members of the LGBT community may, at times, use a specialized vocabulary particularly when interacting among themselves. For example, in 1972, *The Queen's Vernacular: A Gay Lexicon* was published, and it is thought to be the first published dictionary of gay slang.[103] Examples from the book include the term *chicken,* referring to a young boy, or *package,* referring to a man's genitalia. Critics have maintained that many of the terms in the book are outdated and no longer used or recognized by LGBT groups. In his well-known book titled *Word's Out: Gay Men's English,* William Leap has argued that gay men's speech is a gendered approach to communication that may include a specialized vocabulary but may not. In fact, Leap has maintained that much gay communication is subtle due to the stigmatized nature of being gay. Leap describes openly gay communication as a language of risk. He also points to several functions of gay men's speech, including a language of desire, release of shame (from parents, society, religious institutions), cooperation, and a format for display (e.g., compliments, flirting, etc.).[104] So scholars from across a variety of academic disciplines disagree about whether the phenomenon of gayspeak exists. The communication patterns of the LGBT microculture are only beginning to be identified and understood. But, as Sims notes, the topic is a growing and promising area of research.[105]

CHAPTER SUMMARY

Within most cultures, there are groups of people who differ in some significant way from the general societal culture. In this book, the term *microculture* is used to refer to those identifiable groups of people who share a set of values, beliefs, and behaviors and who possess a common history and a verbal and nonverbal symbol system that is similar to the dominant culture but varies in some way, perhaps subtly. Microcultures can be different from the larger culture in a variety of ways, most often because of race, ethnicity, language, or behavior. But one's age group or occupation might also render one a member of a microcultural group. Perhaps every member of a culture is also a member of a microcultural group.

In this chapter, Hispanics, African Americans, Amish, Hmong, Arab Americans, and LGBT people were profiled as microcultural groups in the United States. Mostly because of immigration and high fertility rates, Hispanics are now the largest microcultural group in the United States. Like many microcultural groups, Hispanics experience lower incomes, higher poverty, and higher unemployment rates than do non-Hispanic White groups. The U.S. government estimates that the Hispanic population will continue to grow through the first half of the 21st century. By then, Hispanic economic influence will be significant. As an economic, political, and socially powerful group, African Americans have maintained an important part of their history—that is, their language. African American history is expressed in the language games that African Americans play and in their daily communication with others in the form of Ebonics. The Amish were also profiled in this chapter. More than any other microcultural group, the Amish have preserved their traditional culture while peacefully coexisting within the rule structure of the dominant cultural milieu. Unlike any other microcultural group, the Amish have successfully isolated themselves from most of mainstream American culture.

Possibly the newest microcultural group in the United States is the Hmong. The Hmong are a group of people who fought alongside American troops in the Vietnam War, only to be abandoned when the war was lost. The Hmong who have immigrated to the United States try desperately to adapt to U.S. culture while simultaneously maintaining some aspects of their traditional culture. Like African Americans, the Hmong face a great deal of racism and resentment. Arab Americans were also profiled in this chapter. Unfortunately, these people are now one of the most negatively stereotyped groups in the United States. Until we learn more about their complex culture, this trend will probably continue. Finally, the LGBT group was highlighted. This group is the most difficult to define and characterize. To be sure, LGBT issues are some of the most controversial and most politically contested areas of cultural diversity facing us today. Of the five characteristics that define microcultural groups presented at the beginning of this chapter, LGBT people seem to meet all of them but not definitively.

Although each of the microcultural groups portrayed in this chapter is obviously different from the others, they share at least one major feature—that is, language. Each group, while adapting and accommodating to the dominant cultural surroundings, has successfully preserved a part of its original culture through communication. The verbal and nonverbal language of its cultural group maintains its heritage and allows its people to pass along its ancestry for future generations.

Visit the student study site at www.sagepub.com/neuliep5e *for e-flashcards, web quizzes, web resources and more.*

DISCUSSION QUESTIONS

1. To what microcultural groups do you belong?

2. Who do you know who is a member of a microcultural group?

3. How are microcultural group members in your community treated differently than other members?

4. What are some of the common stereotypes in your community of microcultural group members?

5. How might members of your community assist microcultural groups in becoming fully engaged in the culture?

ETHICAL ISSUES AND MICROCULTURES

1. There has been considerable debate among Americans and even among members of the U.S. Congress and Senate that English should be the official language of the United States and that members of the above-profiled microcultures should be required to speak English, especially when engaged in civil and legal affairs. What do you think? Should English be the official language of the United States?

2. Some people argue that most members of the above microcultures are not doing enough to assimilate, take in, absorb, and become a part of American culture. Do you think microcultures should do more to assimilate to the dominant U.S. culture? Or should microcultures hold on to the traditions and customs of their native cultures?

KEY TERMS

African Americans   105

Amish   110

Arab   119

Ebonics   106

Hispanic   100

Hmong   114

LGBT   121

microculture   94

minority group   95

Muslim   119

muted groups   97

Spanglish   102

REFERENCES

1. Morris, R. (1997). Living in/between. In A. Gonzales, M. Houston, & V. Chen (Eds.), *Our Voices: Essays in Culture, Ethnicity, and Communication* (pp. 163–176). Los Angeles: Roxbury.

2. U.S. Census Bureau. (2009). *Statistical Abstract of the United States: 2010* (129th ed.). Washington, DC: Author. Retrieved from http://www.census.gov/statab/www/ and http://www.census.gov/compendia/statab/2010/tables/10s0043.pdf.

3. Schaefer, R. T. (2010). *Racial and Ethnic Groups* (12th ed.). New York: Prentice Hall.

4. This discussion of the defining characteristics of minority groups is based on the following sources: Meyers, B. (1984). Minority Group: An Ideological Formulation. *Social Problems, 32,* 1–15; Schaefer, *Racial and Ethnic Groups;* Wagley, C., & Harris, M. (1958). *Minorities in the New World: Six Cases.* New York: Columbia University Press.

5. Barrett, L. E. (1997). *The Rastafarians.* Boston: Beacon Press.

6. Laungani, P. D. (2007). *Understanding Cross-Cultural Psychology.* London: Sage; Schaefer, *Racial and Ethnic Groups.*

7. Ilcan, S. M. (1994). Marriage Regulation and the Rhetoric of Alliance in Northwestern Turkey. *Ethnology, 33,* 273–297.

8. Schaefer, *Racial and Ethnic Groups.*

9. Associated Press. (2008, January 22). Saudi Women Can Now Stay in Hotels Alone. Copyright © 2008 The Associated Press.

10. The muted group theory was first articulated by Shirley and Edwin Ardener. The sources used for this discussion are Ardener, S. (Ed.). (1975). *Perceiving Women.* London: Malaby; Kramarae, C. (1981). *Women and Men Speaking.* Rowley, MA: Newbury House.

11. Weber, S. N. (1991). The Need to Be: The Sociocultural Significance of Black Language. In L. A. Samovar & R. E. Porter (Eds.), *Intercultural Communication: A Reader* (6th ed., pp. 277–283). Belmont, CA: Wadsworth.

12. Tyson, C. (2001). Exploring the Generation Gap and Its Implications on African American Consciousness. *Doula: The Journal of Rap Music and Hip Hop Culture.* Available at www.urbanthinktank.org.

13. Adams, T. M., & Fuller, D. B. (2006). The Words Have Changed but the Ideology Remains the Same: Misogynistic Lyrics in Rap Music. *Journal of Black Studies, 36,* 938–957.

14. Tyson, Exploring the Generation Gap and Its Implications on African American Consciousness.

15. Konkka, A. (1998). *Power, Pride, and Politics in Rap Music.* Unpublished manuscript, Department of Translation Studies, University of Tampere, Finland. Retrieved from www.uta.fi/FAST/US8/PAPS/ak-rap.html.

16. Tyson, E. H. (2006). Rap-Music Attitude and Perception Scale: A Validation Study. *Research on Social Work Practice, 16,* 211–223.

17. Konkka, *Power, Pride, and Politics in Rap Music.*

18. Canadian Broadcasting Corporation. (2009, October). *Speaking Out: Quebec's Debate Over Language Laws.* Retrieved from http://www.cbc.ca/canada/story/2009/10/22/f-quebec-language-laws-bill-101.html.

19. Schaefer, *Racial and Ethnic Groups.*

20. Pew Hispanic Center. (2008). *Statistical Portrait of Hispanics in the United States, 2008: Pew Hispanic Center Tabulations of 2000 Census and 2008 American Community Survey.* Retrieved from http://pewhispanic.org; U.S. Census Bureau. (2008). *Monthly Resident Population Estimates by Age, Sex, Race, and Hispanic Origin for the United States: April 2000 to July 1, 2008.* Retrieved from www.census.gov/popest/national/asrh/2008-nat-res.html.

21. Crouch, N. (2004). *Mexicans and Americans: Cracking the Cultural Code.* Yarmouth, ME: Intercultural Press.

22. Pew Hispanic Center. (2008). *Statistical Portrait of Hispanics in the United States, 2008.* Retrieved from http://pewhispanic.org/factsheets/factsheet.php?FactsheetID=58.

23. Ibid.

24. Ibid.

25. Pajewski, A., & Enriquez, L. (1996). *Teaching From a Hispanic Perspective: A Handbook for Non-Hispanic Adult Educators.* Phoenix, AZ: The Arizona Adult Literacy and Technology Resource Center.

26. Crouch, *Mexicans and Americans.*

27. Crouch, *Mexicans and Americans,* p. 102.

28. Clutter, A. W., & Nieto, R. D. (2000). *Understanding Hispanic Culture: Ohio State University Fact Sheet.* Columbus: Ohio State University Extension.

29. Rodrigo Villalobos Arevalo, personal communication, January 20, 2010.

30. Ardila, A. (2005). Spanglish: An Anglicized Spanish Dialect. *Hispanic Journal of Behavioral Sciences, 27,* 60–81; Stavans, I. (2000, October 13). The Gravitas of Spanglish. *Chronicle of Higher Education, 47,* B7–B10; Stavans, I. (2003). *Spanglish: The Making of a New American Language.* New York: Rayo (HarperCollins).

31. Rifkin, J. M. (1990). No Problema—Spanglish Language Abounds. *Hispanic Times Magazine, 11,* 30–31.

32. Stavans, The Gravitas of Spanglish.

33. Cruz, B., & Teck, B. (1998). The Official Spanglish Dictionary. *Hispanic, 11,* 34–36; These examples of Spanglish can be found in Cruz, B., Teck, B., & the editors of *Generation ñ.* (1998). *The Official Spanglish Dictionary: Un User's Guia to More Than 300 Words and Phrases That Aren't Exactly Espanol or Ingles.* New York: Fireside.

34. Fought, C. (2001). Facts and Myths About Chicano Language. *Language Magazine, 1,* 3.

35. Fought, C. (2003). *Chicano English in Context.* Houndmills, Basingstoke, Hampshire, England: Palgrave MacMillan, p. 4.

36. Ibid.

37. Casas, J. M., Wagenheim, B. R., Banchero, R., & Mendoza-Romero, J. (1994). Hispanic Masculinity: Myth or Psychological Schema Meriting Clinical Consideration. *Hispanic Journal of Behavioral Sciences, 16,* 315–332; Mayo, Y. Q., & Resnick, R. P. (1996). The Impact of Machismo on Hispanic Women. *Journal of Women and Social Work, 11,* 257–278.

38. Anders, G. (1993). Machismo: Dead or Alive? *Hispanic, 6,* 14–18.

39. Casas et al., Hispanic Masculinity: Myth or Psychological Schema Meriting Clinical Consideration.

40. Michael, E. T., Gagnon, J. H., Laumann, E. O., & Kolata, G. (1995). *Sex in America: A Definitive Survey.* New York: Warner.

41. Nuiry, O. E. (1996). Ban the Bandito! *Hispanic, 9,* 26–31.

42. Schaefer, *Racial and Ethnic Groups.*

43. Ibid.

44. Ibid.

45. Smitherman, G., & Cunningham, S. (1997). Moving Beyond Resistance: Ebonics and African American Youth. *Journal of Black Psychology, 23,* 227–232.

46. Weber, S. N. (1994). The Need to Be: The Sociocultural Significance of Black Language. In L. A. Samovar & R. E. Porter (Eds.), *Intercultural Communication: A Reader* (7th ed., pp. 221–226). Belmont, CA: Wadsworth.

47. Nasir, N. S., McLaughlin, M. W., & Jones, A. (2009). What Does It Mean to Be African American? Constructions of Race and Academic Identity in an Urban Public High School. *American Educational Research Journal, 46*(1), 73–114.

48. Rickford, J. C. (2004). *What Is Ebonics (African-American Vernacular English)?* Washington, DC: Linguistic Society of America.

49. Kochman, T. (1990). Cultural Pluralism: Black and White Styles. In D. Carbaugh (Ed.), *Cultural Communication and Intercultural Context* (pp. 219–224). Hillsdale, NJ: Erlbaum.

50. Weber, The Need to Be: The Sociocultural Significance of Black Language, p. 279.

51. Jahn, J. (1961). *Muntu: An Outline of the New African Culture.* New York: Grove Press, p. 124.

52. Weber, The Need to Be: The Sociocultural Significance of Black Language.

53. Billings, A. (2005). Beyond the Ebonics Debate: Attitudes about Black and Standard American English. *Journal of Black Studies, 36,* 68–81.

54. Hostetler, J. A. (1993). *Amish Society.* Baltimore, MD: Johns Hopkins University Press. (Quote on p. 4)

55. Pennsylvania Dutch Country Welcome Center. (1998). *The Amish, the Mennonites, and "the Plain People."* Available from www.800padutch.com/amish.html; Powell, K., & Powell, A. (2008). *Amish 101: Amish Beliefs, Culture and Lifestyle: History of the Amish in America.* Available from http://pittsburgh.about.com/cs/pennsylvania/a/amish.htm; Schlabach, D. (1998). *An Amishman's Personal Expression.* Available from www.amish-heartland.com.

56. Huber, R. (1997). *Be Ye Not Conformed to This World.* Available from www.columbia.edu/cu/sipa/PUBS/SLANT/SPRING97/huber.html.

57. Hostetler, *Amish Society;* Pearce, S., Suminski, S., & Tschudy, K. (1996). *The Amish: Simple Values in a Complex World.* Unpublished manuscript, St. Norbert College, De Pere, WI.

58. MacKaye, W. R. (1971, December 9). High court hears Amish school case. *Washington Post.*

59. Reiling, D. M. (2002). The "Simmie" Side of Life: Old Order Amish Youths' Affective Response to Culturally Prescribed Deviance. *Youth and Society, 34,* 146–171.

60. *Origins of the Old Order Amish.* Available from http://holycrosslivonia.org/amish/origin.htm.

61. S. A. (1998). *Influences of World View on Individual Life and Culture.* Available from www.missouri.edu/~rsocjoel/rs150/papers/sall.html.

62. Hostetler, *Amish Society.*

63. Pennsylvania Dutch Country Welcome Center, *The Amish, the Mennonites, and "the Plain People."*

64. Huber, *Be Ye Not Conformed to This World.*

65. S. A., *Influences of World View on Individual Life and Culture.*

66. P. D. (1998). *Gender, Work, and Worldview: Reflections on Amish and American Society.* Available from www.missouri.edu/~rsocjoel/rs150/papers/pdun.html

67. Hostetler, *Amish Society;* Kraybill, D. B. (1989). *The Riddle of Amish Culture.* Baltimore, MD: Johns Hopkins University Press; Moellendorf, S., Warsh, H., & Yoshimaru, K. (1997). *The Amish Culture: A Closer Look at the People of Lancaster County.* Unpublished student manuscript, St. Norbert College, De Pere, WI.

68. Mahoney, J. (1998). *European Free-Church Family.* Available from www.jmahoney.com/european.htm; Ontario Consultants on Religious Tolerance. (1998). *The Amish.* Available from http://religioustolerance.org/amish.htm.

69. Buch, B. B. (1997). *The Nonverbal Cues of Amish Dress.* Unpublished manuscript, St. Norbert College, De Pere, WI; Hostetler, *Amish Society;* Kraybill, *The Riddle of Amish Culture;* Moellendorf, Warsh, & Yoshimaru, *The Amish Culture.*

70. Ibid.

71. Ibid.

72. Ibid.

73. P. D. (1998). *Amish and Mainstream Culture Clash.* Available from www.missouri.edu/~rsocjoel/rs150/papers/pd4.html.

74. Mahoney, *European Free-Church Family.*

75. Hostetler, J. A. (1992). An Amish Beginning. *American Scholar, 61,* 552–563. (Quote on p. 562)

76. Winland, D. N. (1992). The Role of Religious Affiliation in Refugee Resettlement: The Case of the Hmong. *Canadian Ethnic Studies, 24,* 96–120.

77. Tyson, J. L. (1994). Congress and State Department Ignore Persecution of Hmong. *Human Events, 50,* 12–14.

78. Honoring the Secret Warriors. (1997, May 26). *U.S. News and World Report, 122,* 13.

79. Duffy, J. (1996). *Who Are the Hmong? Legends of Literacy, History of Struggle.* Available from www.adone.com/ttj/news/050296/ent3.htm.

80. Thao, K. (1995). *The Hmong Culture.* Unpublished student manuscript, St. Norbert College, De Pere, WI.

81. Honoring the Secret Warriors.

82. Duffy, *Who Are the Hmong?*

83. Winland, The Role of Religious Affiliation in Refugee Resettlement.

84. Thao, *The Hmong Culture.*

85. Hutchison, R., & McNall, M. (1994). Early Marriage in a Hmong Cohort. *Journal of Marriage and the Family, 56,* 579–591.

86. Thao, *The Hmong Culture.*

87. Ibid.

88. Ibid.

89. Guensburg, C. (1996, June 16). The Fabric of Their Lives. *Milwaukee Journal Sentinel;* Lee, J. H. (1998). *Hmong Quilts—Pa Ndau—Reflect Hmong History.* Available from www.stolaf.edu/people/cdr/hmong/culture/ pandau2.html.

90. Thao, *The Hmong Culture.*

91. Barkan, E. R. (1995). Out of Carnage and Into the Crucible: Southeast Asian Refugees' Journey From Old Worlds to a New One. *Journal of American Ethnic History, 14,* 53–58.

92. Arab American Institute. (2008). *Arab Americans Demographics.* Retrieved January 30, 2008, from http://www.aaiusa.org/foundation/34/censusinfor mation; de la Cruz, G. P., & Brittingham, A. (2003). *The Arab Population: 2000.* Washington, DC: U.S. Department of Commerce, U.S. Census Bureau.

93. Samhan, H. H. (2001). *Who Are Arab Americans?* Groliers Multimedia Encyclopedia.

94. Meem, D. T., Gibson, M. A., & Alexander, J. F. (2010). *Finding Out: An Introduction to LGBT studies.* Los Angeles: Sage.

95. Ibid. (Quote on pp. 135–136)

96. Herbenick, D., Reece, M., Schick, V., Sanders, S. A., Dodge, B., & Fortenberry, J. D. (2010). Sexual Behavior in the United States: Results From a National Probability Sample of Men and Women Ages 14–94. *Journal of Sexual Medicine, 7*(5), 255–265.

97. Gates, G. J. (2006). *Same-Sex Couples and the Gay, Lesbian, Bisexual Population: New Estimates From the American Community Survey.* Los Angeles: Williams Institute on Sexual Orientation Law and Public Policy, UCLA School of Law.

98. Gedro, J. (2010). Understanding, Designing, and Teaching LGBT Issues. *Advances in Developing Human Resources, 12*(3), 352–366.

99. Schlatter, E. (2010, Winter). 18 Anti-Gay Groups and Their Propaganda. *Southern Poverty Law Center Intelligence Report,* (140).

100. Chesebro, J. (1981). *Gayspeak: Gay Male/Lesbian Communication.* New York: Pilgrim.

101. Cameron, D., & Kulick, D. (2003). *Language and Sexuality.* Cambridge, UK: Cambridge University Press.

102. Sims, A. (2004). Gayspeak. In C. J. Summers (Ed.), *glbtq: An Encyclopedia of Gay, Lesbian, Bisexual, Transgender, and Queer Culture.* Chicago: glbtq.

103. Rodgers, B. (1972). *The Queen's Vernacular: A Gay Lexicon.* San Francisco: Straight Arrow. (This book was later published in 1979 under the title *Gay Talk* by Paragon, New York.)

104. Leap, W. (1996). *Word's Out: Gay Men's English.* Minneapolis: University of Minnesota Press.

105. Sims, Gayspeak.

CHAPTER 4

The Environmental Context

After reading this chapter, you should be able to

1. compare and contrast high- and low-load environments;

2. discuss the relationship between culture and the natural environment;

3. recognize and discuss that natural disasters are cultural and social, as well as natural, events;

4. identify and describe fixed, semi-fixed, and informal built environments;

5. compare and contrast the housing patterns of Japanese, Navaho, and Marakwet cultures;

6. assess your orientation toward privacy; and

7. assess your monochronic/polychronic orientation.

Environment is heir to psyche.

—Howard F. Stein[1]

Consider the following two scenarios:[2]

Scenario #1: It is early evening, and you are alone in your dorm room. You're sitting on your bed reading a chapter in your intercultural communication textbook. You have some quiet music in the background that helps you concentrate. The room is quiet, as is the rest of the dormitory. Most of your friends are studying in their rooms as well.

Scenario #2: You are walking through the international terminal of a major airport. The terminal is crowded with people rushing to and from the various ticket counters. Announcements are coming in over the airport intercom system. The airport is very noisy, with people conversing, yelling, and laughing. You can hear the various jets landing and taking off as you rush to your gate. The lights are bright.

How would you compare these two environments? How might your verbal and nonverbal communication differ in each scenario? Would you feel and react the same in Scenario #1 as in Scenario #2?

All human communication occurs within a physical and perceptual environment. These environments have a pervasive influence on the nature of communication. The purpose of this chapter is to explore the environmental context of intercultural communication. In the contextual model of intercultural communication presented in Chapter 1, the environmental context is the third-largest circle surrounding the interactants. Recall that, in the model, the cultural and microcultural contexts encircle the environmental context. How humans perceive the physical environment is very much affected by their culture and microculture. Furthermore, like the cultural and microcultural contexts, the influence of the physical environment is generally outside our conscious awareness.

How we see the physical world around us is influenced by our individual psychological perceptions, which, in turn, are shaped by culture. People from all cultures project their mental perceptions onto the physical environment and act as though what is projected is, in fact, the true quality of the physical world. In other words, even the physical environment is subject to cultural interpretation. As Stein notes, far from being a passive component of culture, the environment is an active ingredient of the human experience.[3] In addition, the physical environment has a considerable impact on our communication. As we move from one physical location to another, our verbal and nonverbal messages adapt accordingly. The types of messages we send and receive in the classroom differ significantly from those we exchange in our dorm rooms or when we are shopping in the mall. As the environment changes, our messages change.

In this chapter, several aspects of the environment will be discussed, including the information load of an environment, the relationship between cultures and their natural environment, the *built* dimension of the physical environment, cross-cultural comparisons of housing, dimensions of privacy, and monochronic and polychronic time orientations. Each of these environmental dimensions affects how we communicate with others, and each varies considerably across cultures.

ENVIRONMENTS AND INFORMATION LOAD

Albert Mehrabian is well known for his work in environmental psychology. According to Mehrabian, there are a number of ways to compare one environment with another (e.g., Scenario #1 and Scenario #2 above). One way is to calculate the information rate—that is, the amount of information contained or perceived in the environment per some unit of time. According to Mehrabian, the more information available to process, the greater the information rate. An environment that has a high information rate has a high load, whereas one with a low information rate has a low load. Mehrabian and his colleagues developed a list of adjectives to describe the load of any given environment (see Table 4.1).[4]

An environment containing several of the left-hand adjectives has a high load, whereas one that can be described with the right-hand terms has a low load. Some environments might contain a blend of both the left- and right-hand terms. In comparing Scenario #1 with Scenario #2, many of the right-hand terms apply to Scenario #1, including *simple, small-scale, sparse, uncrowded, homogeneous, symmetrical, still, patterned,* and *probable.* On the other hand, Scenario #2 could be described using several of the left-hand terms, such as *varied, complex, large-scale, contrasting, dense, surprising, heterogeneous, crowded, asymmetrical, moving, random,* and *improbable.* Based on this comparison, Scenario #1 has a low information load and Scenario #2 has a high information load.[5]

Table 4.1   High Versus Low Load Descriptors

Environment Type	
High Load	**Low Load**
Uncertain	Certain
Varied	Redundant
Complex	Simple
Novel	Familiar
Large-scale	Small-scale
Contrasting	Similar
Dense	Sparse
Intermittent	Continuous
Surprising	Usual
Heterogeneous	Homogeneous
Crowded	Uncrowded
Asymmetrical	Symmetrical
Immediate	Distant
Moving	Still
Rare	Common
Random	Patterned
Improbable	Probable

Mehrabian argues that, to some extent, information load is equivalent to the level of uncertainty in a particular environment. The higher the information load, the higher the uncertainty, especially in novel and complex environments. The more familiar we are with a situation, the less uncertainty we experience. Of all the environmental factors, people are perhaps the greatest source of uncertainty. This is especially true of strangers, including people from different cultures. Hence, a crowded room of strangers contains high levels of uncertainty and a heavy information load. For this reason, when we are interacting with people from a different culture (especially in their environment), the information load probably will be high.[6]

Mehrabian contends that the information load of a particular environment can affect people's feelings in three ways: arousal–nonarousal, pleasure–displeasure, and dominance–submissiveness.[7] The arousal dimension refers to your level of stimulation and excitability. Pleasure refers to your degree of happiness and satisfaction. Dominance refers to your feelings of control or command of the situation. These emotional responses cause people to either approach or avoid the environment. Generally, lower load environments produce less negative arousal, are more pleasant, and are controllable. Hence, we're likely to approach these kinds of environments. Conversely, the heavily loaded environments produce anxiety (e.g., negative arousal), are unpleasant, and are less controllable. We may be more likely to avoid such situations.[8] Consider Scenario #1 and Scenario #2 from the beginning of this chapter. If you had the chance to choose one of the two scenarios, which would you choose? Of the two, which produces the most positive arousal, which is more pleasant, and which is more controllable? Likewise, how do you feel about approaching or avoiding communication situations with people from different cultures? Because such situations may be highly loaded, you may prefer to avoid them.

CULTURE AND THE NATURAL ENVIRONMENT

Jon T. Lang, Emeritus Professor of architecture at the University of New South Wales in Sydney, Australia, has written extensively about the relationship between people, their culture, and their environment. Lang explains that the natural, or terrestrial, environment includes the physical geography of the earth, its climate, and its natural processes. The **terrestrial environment** for every person is the planet Earth.[9] Environmental psychologist Richard Knopf maintains that the natural environment is valued differently by different people. A culture's relationship with nature is culture bound. According to Knopf, culture influences how much people value nature and the symbols they use to communicate about it. Aivilik Eskimos, notes Knopf, have more than a dozen different terms to describe the winds and various snow conditions. People perceive and create symbols of their environment based on their cultural experiences with it. Knopf argues that it is not the natural environment per se that generates affect but, rather, the verbal and nonverbal symbols that we use to communicate about nature. Moreover, how a culture values and treats the natural environment can change quickly, especially if that culture experiences shifts in religion or dramatic advances in science and technology.[10] The United States in the 20th century, for example, witnessed immense changes in how we treat the natural environment. Because of scientific and technological progress, we now see the environment as something we can control and dominate.

Although all cultures exist within specific terrestrial contexts, some aspects of the terrestrial environment exist in every culture, while others do not. Gravity, for example, exists everywhere on earth; however, oceans, lakes, streams, mountain ranges, deserts, valleys, trees, and forms of vegetation vary considerably across cultures. Indonesia, for example, is composed of more than 13,000 islands covering more than 700,000 square miles. The vegetation in Indonesia is diverse, with more than 40,000 species of flowering plants, including 5,000 species of orchids.[11] The country of Laos in Southeast Asia has a monsoonal climate wherein heavy rainfall sometimes averages 90 inches a year.[12] Conversely, in some areas of South Yemen, which lies in the southwest corner of the Arabian peninsula, only 4 inches of rain fall in a given year. Some northern and eastern sections of the country can go without rain for years.[13] Russia is the largest country in the world (i.e., geographically) with a land mass of more than 6.5 million square miles and dramatic climate extremes. Northern Siberia, for example, is covered with permafrost, where snow drifts can reach as high as 60 feet and little vegetation is found.[14] Norway's land mass is just more than 100,000 square miles—slightly larger than Arizona—and only 3% of the land is usable as farmland.[15] As the physical environment of a culture varies, so will the vocabulary of the culture. Cultures with different environments create verbal and nonverbal symbols that enable them to adapt to and communicate about their environment.

Lang asserts that the natural environment of any culture influences life in that culture. Physical and climatic aspects of the environment can restrict the kinds of activities that occur.[16] In many cultures, the pace of daily activities reflects the natural climate of the area. A quick example may help illuminate this point. In some southern European countries (e.g., Spain, southern Italy), during the warm-weather season, many shop owners close their stores from about midday until late afternoon. They do this to avoid working through the hottest part of the day, when the temperatures can rise above 100 degrees Fahrenheit, because most of the stores in these countries are not air-conditioned. Visitors from other countries, particularly the United States, may interpret this custom as laziness on the part of the shop owners, but in reality, the store owners are simply adjusting to the conditions of their natural climate.

Worldviews of the Natural Environment

Harvard University sociologist Florence Kluckhohn says that cultures can be described as having one of three orientations toward nature, depending on what their members believe: that people are subjugated to nature, that they are an inherent part of nature, or that they are dominant over nature.[17] A culture's orientation toward nature affects how people within that culture communicate about nature and organize their daily activities. Knowing and understanding a particular culture's orientation toward nature is a helpful step in becoming a competent intercultural communicator.

Irwin Altman and Martin Chemers argue that in cultures where nature is viewed as supreme, people believe they are at the mercy of an omnipotent nature. According to Altman and Chemers, in such cultures, nature is perceived as a dominant and unmanageable power. In Biblical times, and even more recently, the natural environment and nature were viewed as threatening and dangerous. Altman and Chemers note that Western fairy tales are replete with references to such environmental features as "dark forests," where danger is lurking around every corner.[18] In her research on East India, Rebecca Jo Bishop found that many East Indians believe that the elements of the natural environment dictate the health and well-being of the people. Indeed, astrologers play an important role in India, as the people believe that nothing in nature is accidental and the universe and all living components conform to a fundamental order over which they have no control.[19]

Kluckhohn claims that many cultures attempt a balancing act with nature and try to live in harmony with it. Indeed, argue Altman and Chemers, in these types of cultures, the natural environment is seen as orderly and cyclical. The days and seasons recur regularly, and natural events repeat themselves in consistent patterns. People and environment are viewed as one, changing together, in what Altman and Chemers describe as a timeless mutual relationship.[20] Reick and Ogura hold that in many Eastern societies, nature is perceived as an ally that people draw on for spiritual support. The people of the island nation of Sri Lanka, which sits 20 miles off the southern coast of India, attempt this alliance with nature. According to Reick and Ogura, the source of their belief has its roots in Buddhism, which professes equality among all living things.[21] The Japanese are well known for their attempts to harmonize with nature, which can be seen in Japanese art forms such as gardening and flower arrangements and Haiku poetry (which makes reference to the seasons). Altman and Chemers assert that the Pygmies of Zaire, Africa, view themselves as an intrinsic part of the rainforest where they dwell. To them, the forest is their mother and father, with whom they communicate on a personal basis.[22]

Kluckhohn's third orientation is seen in many Western societies, where people believe that nature is something to be controlled, domesticated, and subjugated.[23] According to Altman and Chemers, some scholars attribute this view to Judeo-Christian doctrine, in which God, who is seen as the creator of the universe, is said to have put humans on the Earth to do His will. People are not just part of the environment, like trees, plants, or animals, but are of divine origin. Such philosophies have led to a separation between humans and the environment. When the scientific revolution developed, nature was seen as mechanistic, further separating people from nature. Through technology, buildings, and modern agricultural methods, humans were able to dominate their natural setting to their liking. In the United States, people separate themselves from nature and believe they have the power, even the right, to dominate it in just about any way they can. Many of our proudest achievements (e.g., moon landings, dams, indoor sports facilities) are based on conquering or exploiting nature. As in other countries where European settlement has occurred, the environment is seen as an entity to be conquered. Much of Australia's economic activity is based on the extraction of natural resources such as timber, minerals, natural gas, and oil.[24]

CULTURE AND NATURAL DISASTERS

A culture's relationship with nature can be seen in how the culture deals with natural disasters. Whether they be drought, tornadoes, hurricanes, floods, or earthquakes, natural disasters occur in all cultures. How people manage such disaster is shaped by the culture and its view of nature. Moreover, many times when natural disasters strike, people from all over the world come together to help. Understanding the stricken culture's relationship with nature can facilitate communication among those directly affected and those offering aid and comfort. The Red Cross, for example, has people stationed around the world to help in times of need. Ironically, natural disasters provide an opportunity for intercultural communication.

One model of human responses to natural disasters, reviewed by Sorenson and White, segregates cultures into three types: folk or preindustrial, transitional, and industrial. Preindustrialized cultures such as Nigeria, Malawi, and rural China are characterized by primarily rural, agrarian land use and have low income and literacy levels, underdeveloped communication systems, and simple technology. In these cultures, land use is primarily for farming in small plots; housing is typically composed of adobe or mud. Many preindustrialized cultures believe in a harmonious relationship with nature. According to Sorenson and White, these societies have a low level of resource use, low material wealth, and less exposure to hazard risk; hence, they are the least vulnerable to catastrophic natural events. They display resonance with the environment and have great resilience to most natural hazards. Although most people in most cultures believe that natural disasters are random occurrences, individuals in preindustrial cultures are more likely to perceive environmental hazards as cyclical or clustered than are those in industrialized societies.[25]

According to Sorenson and White, transitional societies such as Sri Lanka, rural Turkey, and Brazil are characterized by rural-to-urban migration. These cultures may be investing in industry; see shifts from labor to capital-intensive land use; and have low to moderate income, basic-level literacy rates, developing communication systems, and some trade. Land use may be semimechanized, and housing is usually unreinforced concrete and frame. Many transitional societies view nature as dominating. They have more wealth and more people living in high-risk areas than do preindustrialized societies. Sorenson and White claim that because of their marginal economic status, which restricts their ability to prevent and recover from loss, these cultures are quite vulnerable to hazards, and their adaptability to disaster is low. As in preindustrialized cultures, people in transitional societies are more likely to perceive natural disasters as cyclical than are people in industrialized cultures.[26]

Industrial societies such as Great Britain, urban Japan, and Australia can be classified as primarily urban land use. According to Sorenson and White, these cultures are capital intensive and heavily mechanized, and they have high income and literacy levels, highly developed communication systems, and high trade. Land use is urban, suburban, residential, and industrial. Agriculture is highly mechanized with large corporate farming operations. Contemporary architecture and housing in many industrialized societies is earthquake resistant. These types of cultures believe that they are dominant over nature in a master/slave-like relationship. Although these societies have increased their exposure to natural disasters through intensive land use, their advanced technologies and greater wealth reduce the overall risk. Resilience is low but different from that of transitional societies because the vulnerability to disaster is decreased.[27]

Natural Disasters as Cultural and Social Events

Although natural disasters are triggered by natural events (e.g., tsunamis, earthquakes, floods, etc.), the effects of the disaster vary considerably across cultures because they take place within particular social and cultural systems of laws and values. Hence, an individual's vulnerability to the disaster is grounded in the social system and hierarchy within which that individual exists. In this sense, natural disasters are as much social phenomena as they are natural ones. In her extensive review of literature in this area, Sarah Fisher maintains that women are disproportionately affected by disasters because of the unequal power distance between men and women that is evident in many cultures.[28] To be sure, Fisher argues that other social factors also come into play, including one's age, ethnicity, social class standing, and disability. Even within sex groups, some women are disproportionately affected, such as widows, women of low income, and those belonging to marginalized groups. Fisher points out that in most cultures, women take on responsibilities—such as reproductive health needs and caring for children—for which the burden becomes heavier following a natural disaster. Of particular concern is violence against women following natural disasters. Fisher notes that there is considerable evidence that domestic and sexual violence against women increases in the wake of natural disasters. Much of this evidence is based on the reported increase of calls to violence intervention centers located in disaster-stricken areas. Fisher also notes that factors such as the considerable economic loss suffered by disaster-hit areas and the accompanying stress and trauma may account for the increase in violence against women in such situations.

Fisher points out the many factors that may increase violence against women, including the idea that the daily routines of families are upset and, thus, the responsibilities for income generation and the typical household jobs may shift across sexes. Most families will be faced with economic needs that create strain and stress in relationships. Extreme economic hardship may lead some women to sexual exploitation and prostitution, often with men in positions of authority, such as police officers, members of the military, and humanitarian workers. Moreover, Fisher maintains that men and women cope with the impacts of disasters differently. Women, she argues, are more likely to communicate grief with others and seek assistance from other women, whereas men are more likely to hold back their emotions and express anger and frustration through aggression, violence, and alcoholism. To make matters even worse, overcrowded disaster centers often leave women and children vulnerable to sexual violence. Fisher points to research that indicates women are often assaulted when using such facilities. To aid women in such hard times, Fisher calls for a gender-based violence prevention and response program to be implemented in government and humanitarian programs.[29]

THE BUILT ENVIRONMENT

Jon Lang explains that the **built environment** of any culture consists mainly of adaptations to the terrestrial environment, including architecture, housing, lighting, and landscaping (see Figure 4.1). The built environment artificially changes natural patterns of behavior, heat, light, sound, odor, and human communication. Hence, the built environment affects the interaction between people and the natural environment. Moreover, many of these changes are specifically designed to facilitate or restrict human interaction. The built environment is not random; it is an intentionally designed pattern of spatial relationships between objects and objects, objects and people, and people and people. The built environment organizes and manages human communication between people, and it varies considerably across cultures.[30]

Lang notes that, while sometimes designed for purely aesthetic reasons, the built environment is typically structured for specific activities. Classrooms, for example, are designed for a particular kind of communication. The size of the room, the positioning of the blackboards, and so on are all fashioned to facilitate interaction between the teacher and students. Culture affects how the built environment is designed. Amos Rapoport argues that the interior of any given built environment influences and directs the way activities are carried out, how the family is structured, how gender roles are played, attitudes toward privacy, and the overall process of social interaction. Moreover, says Rapoport, how the built environment is planned and constructed reflects the values, motivations, and resources of the culture wherein it exists. The overall economic, political, and legal system of a particular culture affects how that culture designs its built environment, including homes, schools, government, and private business buildings. As the built environments of cultures differ, so do communication patterns.[31]

Lang argues that the degree of ease or difficulty afforded by the built environment when moving from one place to another is a major predictor of human communication patterns. People are more likely to communicate with one another in those environments where access to others is facilitated by the built environment than in environments where access is restricted.[32] Anthropologist Edward Hall has identified three fundamental types of layout patterns in built environments: fixed-feature space, semifixed-feature space, and informal space. **Fixed-feature space** is defined by immoveable or permanent fixtures, such as walls,

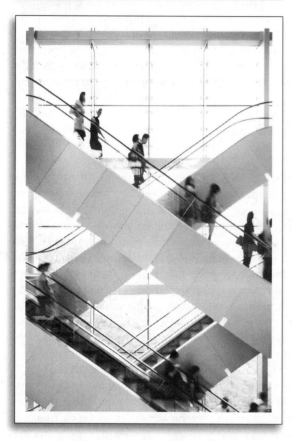

| Figure 4.1 | The architecture of different cultures affects the interaction between people and the natural environment. |

floors, windows, and so on. **Semifixed-feature space** includes that which is moveable (usually within fixed-feature space), such as furniture. **Informal space** is perceptual and varies according to the movement of the interactants. Informal space lasts only as long as the interactants communicate; it is not stated space and is usually outside the awareness of the people interacting.[33]

The variability of fixed, semifixed, or informal space influences human communication. Some environments must be restructured for certain kinds of activities, whereas others need not be adjusted at all. According to Lang, these kinds of environments are called *adaptable,* or *flexible*. For example, in an adaptable fixed-feature space such as a gymnasium, many kinds of activities—such as sporting events, gym classes, commencement ceremonies, dances, plays, speeches, and so on—can occur without any changes to the fixed features. In a flexible semifixed-feature space, changes are made to accommodate certain kinds of activities. Some schools and office buildings, for example, have portable walls. Informal (or dynamic) space between people is controlled, regulated, and managed by the nature of the relationship between the interactants.[34]

In addition to classifying fixed, semifixed, and informal space, Hall also developed a four-level classification of social distances. Hall argues that the physical environment guides behavior and the way that people define the space between themselves and others. Hall's classification scheme was modeled after the findings of ethologists (i.e., people who study animal behavior), who observed the various distances that animals maintain in their environments. Hall maintains that spatial distance between people is a vehicle for communication, much like sight, sound, smell, and touch. As distance decreases, people can see, hear, touch, and smell others differently than when distance increases. As the distance between interactants increases, the available visual, auditory, olfactic, thermal, and kinesthetic information decreases. As distance increases, the privacy of the person increases but the privacy of the interaction decreases.[35]

Hall's four-level classification specifies intimate, personal, social-consultative, and public distances. Intimate distance is reserved for close intimate contact, including touching. In this distance, there is much visual, auditory, and olfactic sensation. In the United States, intimate distance is 9 to 18 inches and is usually reserved for highly personal relationships.

The second type, personal distance, is 1.5 to 4 feet. This is sometimes called "arm's-length" distance because a comfortable distance between interactants is literally about one human arm's length. Social-consultative distance is the spacing people practice at casual gatherings and in working situations. In the United States, this distance is 4 to 12 feet. In social distance, there is a more formal atmosphere. Public distance is used for talking across a room and for public-speaking situations. In the United States, this distance extends from 12 feet and beyond. There is little olfactic sensation at this distance.[36]

To be sure, intimate, personal, social, and public distances vary by culture, and Hall's classifications may not be universal. Hall argues that other factors, such as the relationship between interactants or external environmental factors, may influence distances between people. In addition, the built environment plays a key role in how space is used. Smaller, more confined spaces, insists Hall, increase interaction distances, whereas larger environments motivate people to adopt smaller distances. Lustig and Koester note, for example, that people in so-called high-contact cultures (e.g., Arabs, Latin Americans, southern Europeans) tend to use closer interaction distances than do people from low-contact cultures. People in the United States, for example, prefer greater distances between themselves and others than do persons living in many Latin American cultures. People from colder climates have a tendency to use large physical distances when they communicate. Conversely, people from warm-weather climates tend to use small physical distances. Northern Europeans (e.g., England, Germany, Scandinavia) are said to have larger personal-space "bubbles" than do southern Europeans (e.g., Greece, Italy, Spain).[37] In some Middle Eastern cultures, people stand close enough to smell one another's breath.

Aiello has reviewed several studies and found that Indonesians used less space than did Australians and were more likely to initiate a conversation with a stranger. Other studies comparing Americans with other cultures have found no differences; that is, they have found common spatial behavior patterns. American, Australian, British, and South African young adults placed figures representing mental patients at approximately the same distances apart. In a similar study, American, British, Scottish, Swedish, and Pakistani subjects all rated different seating distances similarly for intimacy level. In an interesting study, it was found that when bilingual Japanese subjects spoke in their native tongue, they sat farther from a same-sex, same-nationality confederate than did both Americans and bilingual Venezuelans. But when all subjects spoke English, the three groups approximated the American seating pattern.[38]

CROSS-CULTURAL COMPARISONS OF HOUSING

The use of space is an integral part of every human being's communication. Decisions about where and when to perform our daily activities are based on spatial patterns that are learned culturally. We become so accustomed to our spatial definitions and boundaries that many of us experience anxiety when forced to interact in novel or unusual environments. Many people complain that they do not sleep well when outside their regular home environments. How we organize space within the built environment says much about our culture—its values and way of life. Perhaps more than any other aspect of the built environment, the home presents a particularly rich source of information about a culture's perception and use of space.

Japanese Housing

In the past 150 years, much has been written in the West about Japanese architecture, especially the Japanese home. Since World War II, great changes have occurred in Japanese housing. Many of the traditional Japanese homes, where most of the daily activities occurred in one room, have been replaced by Western-style homes and high-rises, where space is defined by walls.[39]

Houses of various types and styles can be found side by side in contemporary Japan. According to Kiyosi Sieke and Charles Terry, a fair number of homes still exist that reflect traditional Japanese architecture dating back to the 18th century. Other homes reveal clear European influences. Many others, perhaps the majority, have almost completely adopted a Western look. Sieke and Terry believe that the design of contemporary Japanese homes has been influenced by the breakdown of the traditional family system in Japan. Many young people are leaving the traditional multigeneration family home situation and moving to apartments or small houses of their own. In homes where two or three generations still live together, the main part of the house is intended for the second-generation husband and wife. A special section of the house might be designated for the family elders and another section especially for the children. In many homes like this, the elders' section is organized and decorated in traditional Japanese style, the children's section is completely Western, and the husband and wife's section is a combination of the two styles. This type of home was unheard of before the war.[40]

Although many contemporary Japanese houses reflect a Westernized design, the Japanese attitude about life has not changed. Charles Terry, past editor of *The Japan Architect,* asserts that an essential aspect of Japanese houses and Japanese culture is the gap between the public and private Japanese person. According to Terry, the impression that a Japanese person presents to society may be very different from how that person actually thinks or feels. In public settings, Japanese act according to clearly prescribed social rules. In private, they think and act as they please. This philosophy is reflected in the contemporary Japanese home and its Western influence. According to Terry, most Japanese who build Western-style homes do so because it is fashionable and expected of them. Terry alleges that most Japanese probably prefer the traditional style.[41] Atsushi Ueda, a Japanese author and scholar of traditional Japanese urban architecture, argues that the contemporary Japanese house is caught between tradition and modernism.[42]

Tetsuro Yoshida, one of Japan's leading contemporary architects, writes that because the Japanese believe in harmony with nature, the traditional Japanese home fits unobtrusively into the landscape, not appearing human-made. The traditional Japanese house is a detached house with a garden. Yoshida states that among traditional Japanese, there is an intimate relationship between the house and garden.[43]

Since ancient times, the Japanese garden has been considered more a work of art than a simple plot of land where flowers and vegetables are cultivated. The Japanese garden is treated as a painting or sculpture to be appreciated from some distance (see Figure 4.2). Yoshida describes the Japanese garden as a quiet monochrome compared with the colorful European or American garden.[44] In contrast, writes Ueda, one seldom encounters anything resembling a proper Japanese garden in contemporary Japanese homes. Instead, one of the most visible features of the modern Japanese home is a car or a garage.[45]

Figure 4.2 A traditional Japanese garden

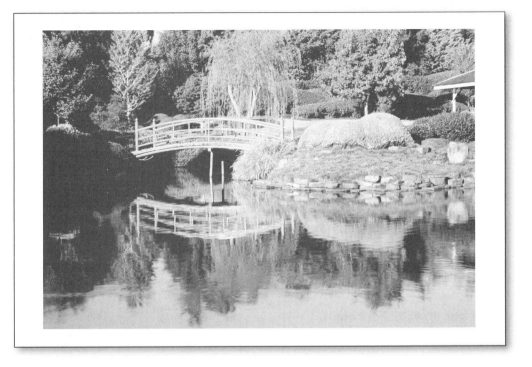

In traditional Japanese homes, writes Ueda, rooms are separated by *shoji* or *fusuma,* which are opaque sliding screens. A shoji panel is usually made of cedar lattice with translucent paper stretched over it. Shoji panels are lightweight and easy to slide open or closed with one finger. The purpose, and major advantage, of shoji is that they can be removed easily to convert the entire floor of a house into a single open room. The traditional Japanese house is fundamentally a one-room home partitioned by shoji. Because of the versatility of shoji, the plan of a house is flexible and the divisions of the rooms easily changed. According to Ueda, this is the major characteristic of space allocation in the Japanese home.[46]

Ueda alleges that, regardless of how Westernized they may have become, the Japanese have not abandoned the custom of taking off their shoes when entering a house and sitting on the floor. The Japanese *yuka* (i.e., floor) developed as a result of this custom. The yuka is actually a raised floor and was developed out of a need to maintain sanitary conditions. Even contemporary homes have a raised floor. According to Ueda, the size of a room in a Japanese home is measured by its number of *tatami mats.* The tatami mat is a modular floor mat made from straw that is used to cover the floor and on which one sits or sleeps. The principal room in a traditional Japanese home is the reception room, also called the sitting room. The average size of the room is 8 to 10 mats. The room usually faces the garden and incorporates an alcove, called the *tokonoma.* According to Ueda, the tokonoma is a recess arranged with staggered shelves, artistic ornaments, hanging scrolls, and perhaps a flower arrangement.

The tokonoma is the most sacred place in the home, holding a sort of spiritual or moral significance. The space immediately in front of the tokonoma is the most honored place in a traditional Japanese home.[47]

Two rooms that are not often discussed but are of primary importance in the Japanese home are the kitchen and bathroom. The kitchen, even in modern Japanese homes, is the domain of the wife. The kitchen is her place, not to be disturbed by other household members and not to be entered or even observed by guests. The kitchen is a private place. In both traditional and contemporary Japanese homes, the bath is of utmost importance and is thought of as a place of recuperation and solitude. The bathroom, which is in a separate room from the toilet, consists of two separate areas, one for bathing and the other for soaking. Initially, the Japanese will wash themselves with soap under a shower that is next to the bathtub. Following the shower, the Japanese will crouch in the tub, which is designed for sitting, not lying. The water is warmed and sometimes scented with flowers or lemons. The purpose of the tub is to relax and soothe the body. This water is kept for several days and used by all family members.

Japanese architect and author Atsushi Ueda maintains that the traditional Japanese house is a thing of the past. However, the contemporary Japanese house, he writes, is "nervously confessing its own insecurity."[48] Though dramatic changes have occurred in Japan in the past 50 years, much of the psychology driving the design of the traditional Japanese house still lives in the contemporary people.

American Navajo Housing

Susan Kent, an ethnoarchaeologist, has studied extensively the use of space in Native American Navajo housing. In her pioneering work, Kent compared the use of space across three American co-cultural groups: Native American Navajos, Spanish Americans, and Euro-Americans. Of particular interest is her work with Navajos. According to Kent's studies, many of the Navajos live in remote parts of reservations and have limited contact with White Americans. Traditional Navajo families speak mostly Navajo and live in aboriginal dwellings called hogans. Hogans typically consist of three large converging support posts that interlock at the top with smaller support posts. The hogan is covered with earth. In addition to the hogan, the Navajo camp may consist of a wooden ramada, a wood-chip storage area, a horse corral, and small fields of corn. The hogan is occupied in the winter, and the ramada is used in the summer (see Figure 4.3). The hogan is used for storage during the summer months. Water is hauled in from tribal wells. There is no outhouse. Some camps will have a sweat house.[49]

Navajo Hogan and Ramada

In her research, Kent discovered that the space inside the hogan was used differently by the occupants according to their sex. The men stayed almost exclusively in one half of the hogan, while the women and children used the other half. Food preparation always took place in the half occupied by the women and children, but the food was consumed in the half occupied by the men.[51]

Kent writes that in contrast to the sex-defined spaces inside the hogan, both sexes of all ages performed activities at the same locale out-of-doors and in the ramada. Not only did

Figure 4.3   Navajo Hogan and Ramada[50]

both sexes use the same activity area outside the hogan, but different types of activities were performed in the same location, including stripping hides, weaving, butchering, and washing. An individual's mood and the season seemed to be the only factors affecting the activity areas of the Navajo camp.[52]

Kent observed that the use of space within the ramada differed significantly from that in the hogan. The men were active in all parts of the ramada. The women and children also used most of the ramada without restriction. Chairs and beds were used by each family member regardless of sex or age. Kent also observed that the Navajos seemed to place little emphasis on the differences between the sexes and did not prescribe a traditional division of labor, as seen in many Euro-American homes. Moreover, asserts Kent, the Navajos had only a few sex-specific activities or sex-specific artifacts and very few single-function activity areas or artifacts. In fact, the only sex-specific activity areas used by the Navajos, observed Kent, were in the hogan, where traditional Navajos segregate space into sex-specific areas. In the ramada, there were no sex-specific areas, although identical activities of daily living occurred in both. Kent speculates that the reason for this is that the hogan is perceived as a sacred dwelling, whereas the ramada is not. According to Kent, the hogan is mentioned in important myths and prayers, and specific ceremonies must be conducted only in a hogan. Kent suggests that the circular hogan symbolizes the circular cosmos, whereas the rectangular ramada and out-of-doors do not. The round, sacred hogan is divided into the same male and female areas as is the round, sacred cosmos.[53]

Marakwet Housing

The Marakwet people are a part of the Kalenjin tribe, who live in western Kenya. Prior to 1900, very little had been written about this group. In 1986, Henrietta Moore published an extensive anthropological study of the Marakwet people focusing specifically on their use of space. The following discussion of the Marakwet is based on Moore's analysis.[54]

According to Moore, Marakwet country is one of the most secluded parts of Kenya. The Marakwet are divided into a number of villages called *kor*. The village is composed of family compounds consisting of a family house, store, and goat house. According to Moore, the Marakwet people are emotionally attached to the land and see themselves and the land they occupy as inseparable.[55]

Marakwet houses and their associated structures (i.e., stores and goat houses) are the only forms of built environment in the Marakwet village. There is no physically constructed space outside the family compound. According to Moore,

> The nature of village organisation is an interlocking set of social units which are also territorial units. At every moment, the life of the villages focuses down on the household, and that of the household expands out to meet the world of the village: a world where social relations are also spatial relations.[56]

The Marakwet insist that a house must never face out over the valley. In addition, the houses within a particular compound must always face one another. The majority of Marakwet houses are subcircular with a single entrance and a window and are made of wattle and daub. Wattle is a fabrication of poles interwoven with branches or reeds. Daub is a covering of some type, usually earth. The houses have thatched roofs. In the dry season, the houses are virtually indistinguishable from the natural terrain.

In her study, Moore observed that each house is divided into three areas, including the sleeping area, the cooking area, and the area beneath the roof store. The bed is typically placed behind the door and is considered the most private place in the house (see Figure 4.4). The fireplace/cooking area is just behind and to the side of the center post. The area beneath the roof store, then, is on the opposite side from the bed. Most family compounds within villages contain at least one house and a store or goat house. Like the houses, the stores are made of wattle and daub and are always elevated on stone stilts and have a thatched roof. Stores must always be placed to the back of the family compound. Every Marakwet man

| Figure 4.4 | The Interior of a Traditional Marakwet House in the Sibou Village[58] |

starts with one house. After he marries, he may build a second house. Ideally, the second house would be for his wife.[57]

Based on her observations, Moore concluded that the internal organization of the Marakwet houses is based on the social relationships between family members. In terms of the space, men and women are segregated. In Marakwet society, women are subordinate to men. Men spend the majority of their time away from the house, while women spend the majority of their time within the family house and compound. Men use the house primarily for sleeping and storage, while women use the house for cooking, child bearing and rearing, entertaining, and family maintenance. Men spend most of their time tending to the herds or attending meetings with the other men in the village. Moore notes that because the women spend most of their time in the house, they exert considerable control over its possessions. For example, fellow villagers must ask for and receive permission to enter a house or to remove something from it. Although Marakwet women are subordinate to Marakwet men, they wield a great deal of power within the boundaries of the household.[59]

Moore explains that of particular importance to the Marakwet is the organization and disposal of refuse, which she argues also reflects a clear male–female dichotomy. The majority of refuse for the Marakwet is made up of ash, animal dung, and chaff (i.e., seed coverings). The three types of refuse hold symbolic meaning and have distinct disposal locations. Ash is the result of cooking and burning—that is, a woman's job. Hence, ash is associated with womanness and female fertility. Ash, then, is always thrown behind the house. Chaff is placed in front of the compound, and dung is placed near the animal compound. Women are buried near the chaff because their work is to dig and remove chaff. Men are buried near the animal dung because their work is to herd the cattle. Goat dung is symbolic of male fertility. The Marakwet are adamant about not mixing the three types of refuse because of their relationship to burial locations and their symbolic meaning.[60]

PRIVACY

Most social scientists agree that human beings, regardless of culture, are a social species with an innate propensity to affiliate and communicate with other human beings. At the same time, however, human beings cannot tolerate extended physical contact with other humans and need privacy.[61] According to Alan Westin, these same competing needs are found in the animal kingdom. Westin maintains that virtually all animals sometimes desire the company of other animals and other times seek individual seclusion.[62]

Although the need for privacy is innate and universal, the degree to which an individual human feels the need for seclusion varies considerably across cultures. For example, Americans value privacy so much that they have made it law. Junior high school students learn that Article 4 of the Bill of Rights of the Constitution of the United States guarantees every citizen the right to be secure in their persons, houses, papers, and effects against unreasonable searches and seizures. Americans literally believe that they have *a right to privacy.* Anthropologists contend that individuals in virtually all cultures engage in a continuous process of seeking privacy at some times and companionship at others (see Figure 4.5). In this sense, privacy is culture bound and is considered a learned response to particular social situations. Irwin Altman argues that privacy is a "boundary control" process whereby people sometimes make themselves accessible to others and sometimes close themselves off from others. The behavioral and environmental strategies that people use to accomplish this process are defined by culture.[63]

Westin maintains that privacy is a necessary condition for acceptable social behavior. In some circumstances, privacy is literally required in order to not violate cultural norms. Most cultures specify (sometimes legally) that certain behaviors must be enacted in private. Such rules and norms vary from culture to culture.[64] Even within cultures, microcultural groups have different perceptions of privacy. In the United States, for example, African American opinions and policy preferences regarding privacy differ from those of the White majority. In comparison with Whites, African Americans are more concerned and believe others are more concerned with invasions of privacy.[65]

Jon Lang states that privacy is closely linked to the built environment because it can be designed or maneuvered in a number of ways to promote, encourage, or restrict communication with others.[66] In his seminal work on privacy, Alan Westin identified four types of privacy: (a) solitude, or the state of being free from observation of others; b) intimacy, or the state of being with another person but free from the outside world; (c) anonymity, or the state of being unknown even in a crowd; and (d) reserve, or the state in which a person employs psychological barriers to control unwanted intrusion.[67] These different forms of privacy serve different purposes, including personal autonomy, release of emotions, self-evaluation, and communication. Westin argues that the type and degree of privacy desired depends on the

Figure 4.5   People of all cultures seek privacy at some times and companionship at others.

SOURCE: © James W. Neuliep.

type of behavior in which one engages, the culture, and the individual's personality traits. The location of sexual intercourse, for example, may vary from culture to culture. In cultures such as the United States, where the nuclear family resides in a walled house that provides for privacy, sexual intercourse is likely to occur within the household. In cultures where the extended family lives together in a communal dwelling without clear spatial divisions, sexual intercourse probably occurs outside the built environment.[68]

Expanding on Westin's four categories of privacy, Darhl Pedersen identified six types of privacy: (a) reserve, (b) isolation, (c) solitude, (d), intimacy with family, (e) intimacy with friends, and (f) anonymity. Reserve indicates an *unwillingness* to be with others, especially strangers. Isolation is defined as total separation and detachment from others. Solitude implies an absence from others. Intimacy with family is being alone with members of one's own family. Intimacy with friends is being alone with friends. Anonymity is a desire to go unnoticed in a crowd. With the exception of isolation and solitude, these types of privacy are independent; that is, one type of privacy does not necessarily go with another. A privacy profile may be expected to be unique for a particular person or culture.[69]

Assessing Dimensions of Privacy

In his work on privacy, Darhl Pedersen developed a privacy questionnaire for measuring the types of privacy preferred by individuals. This questionnaire has been used in cross-cultural comparisons. The questionnaire contains 30 statements regarding the "privacy sphere" and is presented below.

Self-Assessment 4.1

Dimensions of Privacy Questionnaire[70]

Directions: To complete the questionnaire, indicate how often you engage in the activity or state represented in each statement by marking whether it (1) never, (2) rarely, (3) occasionally, (4) sometimes, (5) often, or (6) usually applies. Scoring procedures are outlined following the scale.

_____ 1. I sometimes need to be alone and away from anyone.

_____ 2. I would be reluctant to engage in a prolonged conversation with someone I had just met.

_____ 3. I like to go on vacation with just my family.

_____ 4. I like my friends to sympathize with me and to cheer me up when I am depressed.

_____ 5. I have to be encouraged to put on a stunt at a party even when others are doing the same sort of things.

_____ 6. I want my thoughts and ideas to be known by others.

_____ 7. I'd like to work on a farm all by myself for a summer.

_____ 8. I like to be the center of attention in my group.

_____ 9. I like living in an apartment house because it prevents me from being alone.

_____ 10. I do not like to be disturbed when I am at home engaged in a family activity.

_____ 11. It would be fun to be alone on a high mountain peak surveying the scene below.

_____ 12. I like to be alone at home where it is peaceful and quiet.

_____ 13. I like to be at home with nobody else around.

_____ 14. I have a special person that I can confide in.

_____ 15. I like to attend meetings if I do not know others.

_____ 16. At parties, I am more likely to sit by myself than to join the crowd.

_____ 17. I would like to have a mountain cabin where my family and I could be alone together.

_____ 18. I like my friends to fuss over me when I am sick.

_____ 19. I like other people to notice me when I am in public.

_____ 20. It pleases me when my accomplishments obtain recognition from my friends.

_____ 21. I reserve displays of physical affection for a select few friends and family.

_____ 22. I'd be happy living all alone in a cabin in the woods.

_____ 23. Sometimes I like to be alone where I cannot be observed by anyone.

_____ 24. I tell my problems only to my family.

_____ 25. My personal relations with people are cool and distant.

_____ 26. I think I'd like the kind of work a forest ranger does.

_____ 27. I prefer doing things with only my family.

_____ 28. I like to meet new people.

_____ 29. Whenever possible, I avoid being in a crowd.

_____ 30. I like being in a room by myself.

Scoring: Reverse your score for Items 6, 8, 9, 15, 19, and 28, and then follow the directions below.

Add your responses to Items 1, 12, 13, 23, and 30. This represents your "Solitude" score.

Add your responses to Items 4, 14, 18, 19, and 20. This represents your "Intimacy with Friends" score.

Add your responses to Items 2, 16, 25, 28, and 29. This represents your "Reserve" score.

Add your responses to Items 7, 9, 11, 22, and 26. This represents your "Isolation" score.

Add your responses to Items 3, 10, 17, 24, and 27. This represents your "Intimacy with Family" score.

Add your responses to Items 5, 6, 8, 15, and 21. This represents your "Anonymity" score.

Scores of 20 or higher on these subscales indicate a greater preference for the specific type of privacy.

SOURCE: Reprinted from Pedersen, D. M. (1979). Dimensions of Privacy. _Perceptual and Motor Skills, 48,_ 1291–1297. Used with permission.

Perceptions of Privacy in the United States

Although the United States literally legislates privacy, perceptions of privacy differ throughout the country and among microcultural groups. Moreover, attitudes about privacy have changed dramatically in the past decade or so. Clay Calvert, a professor who holds degrees in communication and law, argues that Americans live in a "voyeur nation." A voyeur is one who seeks sexual stimulation by visual means or is a prying observer of sordid or scandalous material. Calvert maintains that voyeurism has become a central theme of American entertainment and culture. Calvert argues that the American public has access to information not originally intended for public consumption, made available over television and the Internet in what he calls "mediated voyeurism." Calvert categorizes four types of mediated voyeurism. The first type is video vérité voyeurism—that is, unrehearsed and unscripted moments of actual events filmed by a video camera. The Rodney King beating and the television program *Cops* are examples of video vérité voyeurism. The second type is reconstruction voyeurism, where some actual event is dramatized for the benefit of the viewer. The television show *America's Most Wanted* is an example of reconstructed voyeurism. The third type, tell-all/show-all voyeurism, is typical of television shows such as *Jerry Springer*. Finally, the fourth type is sexual voyeurism, characterized by explicit Internet sites where hidden cameras are put into bathrooms, bedrooms, up women's skirts, and so on. Calvert maintains that the American voyeur mentality has serious implications for an individual's constitutional right to privacy. Frankly, Calvert is not particularly sanguine (optimistic) about the future of privacy rights in the United States.[71]

Sociologist Sherry Turkle argues that there is a tension in American culture between the individual's desire for and right to privacy and the invasion of personal privacy brought on by the computer age.[72] Because so much personal information about people is stored electronically, it is relatively easy to gain access to it, including virtually all of one's financial and medical data. According to Carole Lane, a paid Internet searcher,

> In a few hours, sitting at my computer, beginning with no more than your name and address, I can find out what you do for a living, the names and ages of your spouses and children, what kind of car you drive, the value of your house and how much taxes you pay on it.[73]

Different groups of people throughout the United States have different concerns about privacy. Many college students, for example, are concerned about what types of information, and how much, their college or university can disclose about them. The 1974 Family Educational Rights and Privacy Act, also known as the Buckley Amendment, forbids colleges from disclosing academic records without student approval. In October 1998, the U.S. Congress passed an amendment to the Family Educational Rights and Privacy Act that allows colleges and universities to inform parents any time a student under the age of 21 violates drug or alcohol laws. The privacy act still prohibits colleges and universities from releasing students' grades, but many colleges and universities are routinely calling parents and informing them of drug and alcohol policy violations. Moreover, colleges are not required to alert students when they have notified their parents. The new laws also allow colleges to disclose information regarding any violent crimes committed by students, and the new amendment now permits a college to release a student's grades to a court.[74]

African Americans seem to have different views on privacy compared with Whites. For example, Gandy reports that educated African Americans extend broad privacy rights to individuals and, unlike Whites, do not view information-gathering techniques used by businesses as invasions of privacy. In addition, when African Americans are concerned about privacy, it is because they sense that a loss of control over personal information renders them more susceptible to discrimination, especially in terms of employment, insurance, and credit. According to Gandy, African Americans are most concerned about privacy issues as they relate to relationships between individuals and the government, but not more so than other groups (e.g., Whites).[75]

Cross-Cultural Variations on Privacy

Pedersen's privacy questionnaire can be useful in determining the privacy preferences of a variety of cultural groups. Knowing a culture's preferences about privacy can help you determine when and where communication can and should take place. For example, if you knew when and how a culture desires privacy, you would know when to restrict communication with persons from that culture. Invasions of privacy are negatively perceived across cultures and will be interpreted as a sign of incompetent communication.

Pedersen and Frances found that within the United States, men tend to score higher on isolation, while women score higher on intimacy with family and intimacy with friends. They also found three consistent trends in the privacy choices of people across various regions of the United States. People from the mountain states tend to score higher than those on the West Coast in their preferences for isolation, anonymity, and solitude. People from the Southwest are like those on the West Coast in their low preference for isolation and like those in the mountain states in their high preference for anonymity. Those on the West Coast score lower than all others on solitude.[76]

A culture's definition and perception of privacy is often based on its history and dominant cultural values. China is a fascinating case study of how cultural values associated with privacy have changed over the years. In her studies of Chinese culture, Orna Naftali traces the history of privacy in China.[77] She notes that in traditional Chinese culture, the basic unit of privacy was not the individual but the extended family. An individual's privacy was held only within the social hierarchy of the family, where higher-ranked individuals enjoyed privacy from the lower ranked but not vice versa. Furthermore, children were seen as the private property of the higher-ranked family members. Naftali also notes that in traditional Chinese culture, the term *private* carried negative connotations and was associated with selfishness and immorality. During the socialist revolution in the mid-20th century, individual privacy was disdained. Private property was banned, and the desire for personal privacy, including one's own physical private space, was despised by the people.

But these cultural values have changed. Naftali argues that even though most Chinese do not benefit from the privacy that persons in Western cultures enjoy, for the past 30 years or so, the Chinese people have witnessed a return of a relative private and personal social life. Recall from Chapter 2 that in 1979 China imposed a one-child policy, which was established to limit that country's population explosion. Couples are allowed to have only one child each. That's quite an imposition of privacy. Naftali notes that with the recent reduction of socialist-era welfare policies and the introduction of market reforms, the Chinese government is shifting its focus from reliance on the state to a reliance on the self. Given the one-child policy, privacy has become a major focal point in child rearing. In fact, in 1992, China enacted the Law of Protection of Minors, which, among other things, legislated a child's right to privacy. This change in both attitude and policy has led to dramatic changes in education and housing. Urban Chinese houses now provide children with private spaces. In public areas, too, distinct areas are now partitioned for children. This is a dramatic change from when there were few or no doors between rooms in traditional Chinese homes and the parents had unconditional rights to enter the child's private space. In her study of urban Chinese homes, Naftali observed that most children had a room of their own.[78]

In a related study, Tang and Dong explored parents' and children's perceptions of privacy in China.[79] They maintain that unlike most Western cultures—where privacy is achieved primarily by means of space manipulation—in China, privacy is often defined in abstract ethical terms. But they agree that privacy issues have changed dramatically in China. In their study, Tang and Dong examined privacy in three areas: spatial, physical, and mental. Spatial privacy issues would include children being allowed to close the door when in a room with a group of friends. Physical privacy would include parents refraining from hugging or kissing their teenage children when in public if the children do not like it. Mental privacy is about parental access to what children watch on the Internet, their exam scores, e-mails to friends, etc. Tang and Dong surveyed both Chinese parents and children about these privacy areas. Their results showed that parents and children were consistent (with each other) in their ratings. Overall, both parents and children ranked spatial and physical privacy as important; that is, the children felt they deserved this privacy, and Chinese parents respected their children's privacy—although, interestingly, fathers rated these privacy areas higher than did mothers. The lowest-rated areas were those of mental privacy. Rated lowest were Internet, letter, and e-mail privacy. Tang and Dong note that this may be due to the Chinese government's strict control over the Internet. Based on their findings, Tang and Dong conclude that Chinese children have strong desires for privacy and that their parents generally respect those desires. They note that the concept of privacy that was once associated mainly with Western cultures seems to exist in China as well.[80]

Rustemli and Kokdemir administered Petersen's privacy questionnaire to Turkish students, and the results of their study are comparable to those for Americans. The overall preferences for solitude, isolation, anonymity, and intimacy are virtually the same for Americans and Turks. Preferences for reserve and intimacy with family differed across cultures, however. Unlike American subjects, the Turkish subjects demonstrated a lower preference for reserve and intimacy with family members. The Turkish subjects preferred intimacy with friends over intimacy with family. This may be due to the family structure in Turkish culture, where the family is an intact group with intense care for children. In the typical Turkish family, the children develop a very intimate and dependent, but restricted, relationship with their parents. The children become dependent on their parents but have limited intimate communication with them. Thus, issues of personal identity and intimacy are directed toward peers rather than parents.[81]

In referring to a paper delivered by Clifford Geertz, Westin describes the living arrangements of the people living in Java. According to Westin, the Javanese live in small, bamboo-walled houses that have no interior walls or doors. Except for the bathroom, there are no truly private areas. Westin claims that because the Javanese have no physical privacy, they have developed a kind of psychological privacy in their everyday behaviors and communication. They speak softly, conceal their feelings, are emotionally restrained, and are indirect in their verbal and nonverbal communication.[82]

Irwin Altman has reviewed the privacy behaviors of several groups, including the Mehinacu Indians, a tribal culture in central Brazil. According to Altman, the Mehinacu live in communal villages where there is virtually no privacy in their houses. Instead of achieving privacy within their homes, the Mehinacu create privacy by actually leaving the village for extended periods of time, even years. Newly born children and their parents are isolated from the village in their homes for several weeks or months. Young boys are required to stay within the home behind a wooden partition, where they have virtually no communication with anyone. Food and bathing materials are brought to them. Altman states that during their seclusion, the boys are taught to speak quietly, are not allowed to play, and must abstain from emotional displays. Young women also go through a similar seclusion after their initial menstruation. Other forms of seclusion occur after the death of a spouse. Altman notes that the typical Mehinacu Indian may spend as much as 7 to 8 years of his or her life in isolation from others.[83]

While the Javanese and Mehinacu cultures may be characterized by having minimal daily privacy, the Balinese and Tuareg cultures desire maximum privacy. According to Altman, the Balinese live in houses surrounded by high walls and narrow doorways. The Tuareg, a Moslem culture in North Africa, wear clothes that cover the entire body except for the eyes. In addition, they wear a sleeveless undergarment and a flowing outer garment that reaches from the shoulder to the ankle. A veil and headdress that cover the forehead and bridge over the nose are worn continuously throughout one's life. Altman suggests that the veil is not unlike a door that allows some to enter and keeps others out.[84]

Hesselink, Mullen, and Rouse have studied privacy in Moroccan culture. They claim that Moroccans value privacy as a way of protecting themselves from the external environment. Moroccans keep private the things they value most. The outside surface of Moroccan homes, for example, is very plain so as to expose little information about the people who live there. Hesselink notes that the walls of the homes are so tall that the only way to see into a home is to walk from the rooftop of one house to that of another. Moroccan women are also considered private and are hidden when males who are not a part of the immediate family enter a Moroccan home.[85]

The built environment is only one way a culture defines its communication with others. The way in which a particular culture achieves privacy involves a complex formula of environmental, verbal, nonverbal, and cultural factors. Focusing on only one of these dimensions provides a distorted view of the privacy regulation system of any culture.

Online Privacy Across Cultures

Recall from Chapter 1 the idea that technological advances in areas such as the Internet and cell phones have decentralized information across the globe—meaning that more people than ever before have access to more information. Recall that in India, more people have cell phones than there are people in the United States. Because so many people have access to information, information privacy is becoming a salient issue in our information-saturated global village. Recently, Cho, Rivera-Sanchez, and Lim conducted a multinational study of online privacy.[86] Cho and his colleagues argue that the overwhelming majority of consumers are concerned about their privacy and that such concerns limit online commerce. In their review of the research of online privacy issues, Cho, Rivera-Sanchez, and Lim point out that female Internet users are more concerned about their personal privacy than are male users.

Older and better-educated persons are also more concerned about privacy, presumably because they are more aware of privacy problems. Research is mixed regarding overall Internet usage and privacy concerns. Some studies show that as Internet usage increases, privacy concerns decrease; other research shows the opposite.

These authors hypothesize that two dimensions of cultural variability discussed in Chapter 2 may have implications for online privacy concerns. Specifically, they note that persons from individualistic cultures tend to place more value on private life, while those from collectivistic cultures more easily accept groups' and organizations' intrusion into their private lives. Power distance, too, may affect privacy concerns. Cho and his colleagues argue that persons from large power distance cultures tolerate power inequality but tend to mistrust those in power. Hence, they hypothesized that persons from individualistic cultures and those from large power distance cultures would exhibit higher concerns about online privacy. Five cities were selected for their study, including Seoul, Singapore, and Bangalore (India), which were selected because the authors assume that these are collectivistic and large power distance cultures. Sydney and New York were selected because they were assumed to be individualistic and small power distance. They also measured the age, sex, and education level of respondents in these cultures. Their results showed that older, female Internet users were more concerned with online privacy than were their younger male counterparts. More-educated persons were also more concerned with online privacy. Regarding the cultural variables of individualism and power distance, respondents from Sydney and New York—presumably individualistic—did report more concerns about online privacy than did respondents from Seoul, Singapore, and Bangalore. Power distance did not play a role, however. The authors reason that individualists desire a private life away from the collective, whereas collectivists (and those in high-context cultures) prefer indirect communication and, thus, do not seek explicit details about privacy protection.

MONOCHRONIC VERSUS POLYCHRONIC TIME ORIENTATION

In addition to its physical and spatial components, the built environment also contains a perceptual–temporal feature. Human communication occurs in a physical space and *perceptual time*. Edward Hall is well known for his discussion of time across cultures. As Hall asserts,

> Time talks. It speaks more plainly than words. The message it conveys comes through loud and clear. Because it is manipulated less consciously, it is subject to less distortion than the spoken language. It can shout truth where words lie.[87]

Like other components of the environment, the perception and use of time is cultural. Unlike other elements of the built environment, time is not physical or tangible; it is a *psychological* component of the environment. Regarding time, Hall categorizes cultures as either monochronic or polychronic. Monochronic- and polychronic-oriented cultures organize time and space differently. According to Hall, people with a **monochronic time** (or M-time) **orientation** emphasize schedules—the compartmentalization and segmentation of measurable units of time. Conversely, people with a **polychronic time** (or P-time) **orientation** see time as much less tangible and stress multiple activities with little emphasis on scheduling. P-time cultures stress involvement of people and the completion of tasks as opposed to a strict adherence to schedules. Hall maintains that the two orientations are incompatible.[88]

In M-time cultures, such as the United States, time is thought of as almost physical, like something you can touch and hold in your hand. Time is treated like money. We talk of saving, spending, wasting, and losing time. Hall argues that for M-time people, time is linear and compartmentalized into discrete units (e.g., minutes, hours, days). The schedule is paramount in M-time cultures. In M-time cultures, scheduling dictates just about every activity of every day. But in some ways, scheduling is like a computer program, specifying what actions will be performed while prohibiting others. Moreover, asserts Hall, scheduling allows only a limited number of activities to be performed in one place at one time. In M-time cultures, people are concerned with doing only one activity at a time. We often have said aloud, "I can do only one thing at a time!"[89]

Hall explains that by its very nature, scheduling segments people from one another and dictates how people conduct their relationships. Because time is viewed as so valuable, people with the most power and prestige are given the most time (and space) and are allowed more flexibility and less accountability with their time. Physicians, for example, are routinely late for appointments without sanction. Late or "no-show" patients, on the other hand, may pay heavily for their inconsideration of the physician's time.

Hall maintains that although an M-time orientation is learned and completely arbitrary, it becomes so ingrained in people that they have no other way of thinking about their world. At an early age, children are taught the importance of time, scheduling, and promptness. Moreover, they are often punished if they fail to adhere. A child learns when to eat, nap, and play. In schools, subjects are taught at certain times of the day for a specific duration. Through compartmentalizing and segmenting time, a person's day is completely planned and scheduled—including sleep, work, leisure, and even sex. Hall notes that tardiness and missed appointments are a source of extreme anxiety for many M-timers. Hall points out that perhaps the most important consequence of M-time is that it *denies the natural context and progression of human communication.* Rather than completing an assignment or finishing a conversation, scheduling forces people into an artificial pattern and sequence of behavior. Many M-time cultures are low context, including the United States, Germany, Scandinavia, Canada, France, and most of northern Europe.[90]

On the other hand, Hall argues that in P-time cultures, schedules are not important and are frequently broken. P-time people can do many things at once, and relationships take priority over schedules. P-timers are often distractible and tolerant of interruptions. In P-time cultures, time is not thought of as tangible, and a person may be engaged in several activities, in the same space with several people, simultaneously. P-time people are more interested in completing the task at hand than leaving it because of some predetermined schedule. Hall contends that people in P-time cultures are not slaves to schedules and are frequently late for appointments or may not show up at all. The guiding principle behind P-time cultures is that the natural context, *in the present,* guides behavior. Many P-time cultures are high context, including southern Europe, Latin America, and many African and Middle Eastern countries.[91]

Consequences of Monochronic and Polychronic Orientations

Monochronic people have a particularly difficult time adjusting to polychronic-oriented cultures. To an M-timer, people in P-time cultures may appear disorganized or even lazy. Harris and Moran warn American businesspersons traveling to Arab countries that they may find themselves waiting for days or even weeks to meet with their Middle Eastern affiliates. "Bukra insha Allah," meaning "Tomorrow if God wills," is a favorite expression of the traditional Arab. Unlike M-timers, Arabs believe that time is controlled by Allah. Hence, when trying to schedule an appointment, the Arab may respond, "Insha Allah"—or "If Allah wills"—and he means this quite literally. To the Arab, a person who tries to influence the future via scheduling is either insane or irreligious.[92]

M-time and P-time cultures organize their space in much the same way as their time. Hence, the M-timer has a specific space set aside for specific activities, and, generally, these are the only activities allowed in that space. In M-time office buildings, for example, people have their own private offices in which to conduct their business. Likewise, in P-time cultures, where multiple activities occur simultaneously, multiple activities are conducted in the same place. Keberlein describes the inside of the municipal building in a small Guatemalan town that has no interior walls to cordon off people from one another. Instead, the building is one large room where all the town's municipal needs are handled. There may be one desk surrounded by many people vying for the attention of the local mayor, who seems to be interacting with two or three people simultaneously. No lines are formed, and people compete for the mayor's attention. The mayor probably is a very important and informed person in this town.[93] Hall has observed that in many P-time cultures there is a defined centralization of bureaucratic control. This is because the leaders interact with many people, and the people are informed because they interact with one another. Polychronic people tend to be well informed of one another's business. Hall argues that their involvement with one another is the essence of their existence. Consequently, P-time bureaucracies can be slow and difficult to penetrate unless one knows an "insider."[94]

A similar contrast can be seen in the homes of M-time and P-time cultures. In most M-time cultures, the home is carefully planned and organized. The home is compartmentalized into individual rooms, each with its specific purpose (e.g., kitchen, dining room, bedroom, laundry room, bathroom). Many P-time homes, on the other hand, may be defined by one large living area. In traditional Japanese homes, for example, the main living area is a single room where the entire family eats, sleeps, and interacts as a group.

Some cultures possess elements of both M-time and P-time. Vandehey, Buerger, and Krueger explain that the Masai, a nomadic culture of Kenya, do not compartmentalize time into seconds, minutes, and hours but, instead, have specific periods of the day that are scheduled around the rising and setting sun and the feeding of their cattle. The typical Masai day begins just prior to sunrise when the cattle go to the river to drink. This period is called "the red blood period" because of the color of the sunrise. The afternoon consists of a period of time when "the shadows lower themselves." The evening begins when the cattle return from the river.[95]

According to Vandehey and her colleagues, the Masai have a unique way of classifying people by age. Rather than using a calendar of years, as most cultures do, the Masai belong to age sets. One's age set determines his or her privileges and responsibilities. Instead of a calendar, the Masai measure time periods by seasons and months, the duration of which is determined by rainfall. Although the Masai compartmentalize time into months, they are not restricted to any set time. For example, a particular month lasts as long as the rains continue. A new month does not begin until the rains have ceased.[96]

STUDENT VOICES ACROSS CULTURES

Monochronic Time in Germany

Being a German exchange student showed me how important it is to have an understanding of what different perceptions of time mean in nonverbal communication. I, for my part—like most people in Germany—feel strongly committed to a monochronic perception of time. Things such as always having to be on time, respecting deadlines, and doing one task after another are important to me and also affect my daily schedule, both at university and in my private life.

Apart from being overly punctual in private or business meetings, a good example to point out most Germans' perception of time is the public transportation system. Since many people commute to work, they count on the exact punctuality of the public transportation system. Thus, people usually get mad quickly if a train or bus is 5 minutes late because they see time as a precious resource.

Especially when dealing with members of different cultures, one should keep in mind that differences in the perception of time might predominate. While Germany and the United States share a more monochronic perception of time, I realized on a trip to Spain that the people there are committed to more polychronic time systems. Nobody really seems to care if the bus is on time or 20 minutes late, which is the result of a less formal perception of time.

Bio:

My name is Sebastian Friedemann. I'm from Düsseldorf, Germany, and I'm currently earning my master's degree in sports, media, and communication at the German Sports University in Cologne. Between 2008 and 2009, I was an exchange student at St. Norbert College in De Pere, WI.

AN INTERCULTURAL CONVERSATION: MONOCHRONIC AND POLYCHRONIC CULTURES

Mr. Paul Bersik is the international sales representative for his computer equipment company. His most recent trip takes him to Saudi Arabia, where he is scheduled to meet with his Saudi counterpart, Abdul Arami. In the following scenario, Mr. Bersik comes face to face with P-time. Mr. Bersik and his training team arrived in Saudi Arabia 3 days ago for a scheduled appointment with Mr. Arami. Mr. Arami has not yet met with Mr. Bersik or his team. Finally, a call to Mr. Bersik's hotel room indicates that Mr. Arami is prepared to meet with him. When he arrives at the location, Mr. Bersik is asked to wait outside Mr. Arami's office. As he waits, he notices many people entering and leaving Mr. Arami's office at a very quick pace. The hallways of this building are a hustle and bustle of activity, with people shuffling in and out of many rooms. Finally, after several hours, Mr. Bersik is called in to meet Mr. Arami.[97]

Mr. Bersik:	Ah, Mr. Arami, it's so good to finally see you. Gosh, I've been waiting for days. Did you forget our appointment?
Mr. Arami:	Hello, Mr. Bersik, please sit down. Everything is fine?
Mr. Bersik:	Actually no . . . (phone rings) . . . the problem is . . .
Mr. Arami:	Excuse me . . . (takes the phone call and speaks in Arabic. After several minutes, he concludes the phone conversation.) Yes, now . . . everything is fine?
Mr. Bersik:	Well, actually, I've got a small problem. You see, the computer equipment you ordered . . . (A staff person enters the room and hands Mr. Arami something to sign.)
Mr. Arami:	Oh, excuse me (signs the document). Yes, now, everything is fine?
Mr. Bersik:	As I was saying . . . all the computer equipment you ordered is just sitting on a ship in the dock. I need your help in getting it unloaded. I mean, it's been there for 2 weeks!
Mr. Arami:	Hmmm. I see . . . this is no problem.
Mr. Bersik:	Well, if it sits in the heat much longer it could be damaged. Could I get you to sign a work order to have it unloaded by Friday?
Mr. Arami:	There is no need for that. The job will get done, insha Allah.
Mr. Bersik:	Well, could we set up some kind of deadline? You see, I have a staff of people here waiting to train your people on the equipment. I need to let them know when it will be ready. How about this Friday? Could we do it then? My people are here now, and they're waiting to begin training.
Mr. Arami:	There is no great rush. We have lived for many generations without this equipment. We can wait a few more weeks, if necessary. This is not a problem. (Two men enter the room and begin a conversation with Mr. Arami.)

There is little chance that Mr. Arami will sign any kind of work order for Mr. Bersik. Within the context of the Saudi culture, Mr. Bersik's behavior is inappropriate. His emphasis on deadlines is perceived by Mr. Arami as either insane or irreligious. Mr. Bersik is also distressed by the constant interruptions. To Mr. Arami, Mr. Bersik is in too much of a hurry. When Mr. Arami says to Mr. Bersik that the job will get done "insha Allah," he means it quite literally. Unless God decrees it, a plan or schedule is useless. In the future, Mr. Bersik must learn that the Saudis' perception of time is very different from his own. Mr. Bersik is monochronic, whereas Mr. Arami is polychronic. When he does business in Saudi Arabia, Mr. Bersik must understand the temporal feature of the culture.

Self-Assessment 4.2

Assessing Time Orientation[98]

Directions: Below is a scale designed by Charles Phipps. The scale is designed to measure one's monochronic and/or polychronic time orientation. In the blank before each item, indicate the degree to which you (1) strongly agree, (2) agree, (3) are neutral, (4) disagree, or (5) strongly disagree with the statement. There are no right or wrong answers, and many of the statements are similar; this is by design. Work quickly and record your first impression.

_____ 1. I usually feel frustrated after I choose to do a number of tasks when I could have chosen to do one at a time.

_____ 2. When I talk with my friends in a group setting, I feel comfortable trying to hold two or three conversations at a time.

_____ 3. When I work on a project around the house, it doesn't bother me to stop in the middle of one job to pick up another job that needs to be done.

_____ 4. I like to finish one task before going on to another task.

_____ 5. At church, it wouldn't bother me to meet at the same time with several different people who all had different church matters to discuss.

_____ 6. I tend to concentrate on one job before moving on to another task.

_____ 7. The easiest way for me to function is to organize my day with activities with a schedule.

_____ 8. If I were a teacher and had several students wishing to talk with me about assigned homework, I would meet with the whole group rather than one student at a time.

_____ 9. I like doing several tasks at one time.

_____ 10. I am frustrated when I have to start on a task without first finishing a previous one.

_____ 11. In trying to solve problems, I find it stimulating to think about several different problems at the same time.

_____ 12. I am mildly irritated when someone in a meeting wants to bring up a personal topic that is unrelated to the purpose of the meeting.

_____ 13. In school, I prefer studying one subject to completion before going on to the next subject.

_____ 14. I'm hesitant to focus my attention on only one thing because I may miss something equally important.

_____ 15. I usually need to pay attention to only one task at a time to finish it.

(Continued)

(Continued)

Scoring: For Items 2, 3, 5, 8, 9, and 11, reverse your responses: (5 = 1), (4 = 2), (3 = 3), (2 = 4), and (1 = 5). For example, if your response to Item #2 was 5, reverse it to 1. If your response to Item #3 was 4, reverse it to 2. Once you have reversed your responses to those 6 items, sum the scores of all 15 items. Scores of approximately 30 and below indicate a monochronic orientation. Scores of approximately 42 and above indicate a polychronic orientation.

SOURCE: This scale was developed by Charles A. Phipps as a part of his senior honors thesis, titled *The Measurement of Monochronic and Polychronic Cognitions Among Hispanics and Anglos,* Abilene Christian University, 1987. Used with permission.

CHAPTER SUMMARY

The relationship between humans and their environment is complex. By its very nature, the environment, natural or built, is loaded with information. How that information is perceived and processed is strongly influenced by culture and can dramatically affect communication. In this chapter, we saw that cultures vary considerably in how they view the natural environment. Some see the environment as a dominating force, one that cannot be harnessed. Other cultures prefer a balancing act between the environment and their needs. These cultures try to coexist with nature peacefully. Still others see nature as a slave and try to control and rule it. Whether dominated by it, living in harmony with it, or treating it as a slave, humans are in constant interaction with their environment.

As the contextual model of intercultural communication shows, all human communication exists within some kind of environment. Most human communication occurs within a built environment. The built environment is specifically designed either to restrict or facilitate human interaction. How a culture designs its built environment says much about how it approaches communication, especially through its housing. Understanding how cultures manage the built and home environments leads one to a better understanding of cultures and to being a more competent intercultural communicator.

This chapter also discussed issues of privacy. People of all cultures have an innate inclination to affiliate and communicate with other human beings. At the same time, however, people cannot tolerate extended physical contact with others and have a need for privacy. The degree to which one senses privacy is learned and varies from culture to culture.

Finally, this chapter described two orientations toward the perceptual environmental variable of time: monochronic and polychronic. Monochronic time orientations emphasize schedules, the compartmentalization and segmentation of measurable units of time, and promptness. Conversely, polychronic time orientations see time as much less tangible and stress multiple activities at once with little emphasis on scheduling. Polychronic cultures stress involvement of people and the completion of tasks as opposed to a strict adherence to artificial schedules. The natural, built, and perceptual aspects of the environment are pervasive influences on how people communicate with one another. Moreover, our perceptions of the environment are largely molded by our culture.

 Visit the student study site at **www.sagepub.com/neuliep5e** *for e-flashcards, web quizzes, web resources and more.*

DISCUSSION QUESTIONS

1. How does the information load of your classrooms change throughout the semester?

2. How does your perception of time (i.e., monochronic or polychronic) affect your daily life? Your study schedule? Your free time?

3. How do you go about securing privacy when you need it? How does your culture facilitate or hinder privacy?

4. How does your physical environment restrict and enhance your sensation; that is, how does it affect what you see, hear, taste, touch, and smell? Give examples.

ETHICS AND THE ENVIRONMENTAL CONTEXT

1. Upon graduation, you've decided to spend a year in the Peace Corps. Your first assignment is to southern provinces of Sri Lanka, where a flood has left thousands homeless. Upon your arrival at the humanitarian aid station, you are stunned to find men routinely and openly sexually assaulting displaced women. No one seems to be helping. Do you intervene?

2. You've just finished a semester at college where your grades were not as good as you would have liked. When you arrive home for break, you learn that your college has mailed your grades to your parents and they have seen them. What do you do now? Was it fair of your college to mail your grades home?

3. You work for a nonprofit group that brings aid to underdeveloped counties across the world. Presently, you are in South America helping a small tribe build a water works station to bring much-needed fresh water to most of the townspeople. The station can be built at only one location, above a well, and this will require that your team cut down several trees. The locals ask that you not cut down the trees because they hold spiritual value for them. What will you do?

KEY TERMS

built environment   139

fixed-feature space   139

high load   133

informal space   140

information rate   133

low load   133

monochronic time orientation   156

polychronic time orientation   157

semifixed-feature space   140

terrestrial environment   135

REFERENCES

1. Stein, H. F. (1987). *Developmental Time, Cultural Space*. Norman: University of Oklahoma Press.

2. Although different, the idea to compare two scenarios is adapted from Mehrabian, A. (1976). *Public Places*

and Private Spaces: The Psychology of Work, Play, and Living Arrangements. New York: Basic.

3. Stein, *Developmental Time, Cultural Space.*

4. Mehrabian, *Public Places and Private Spaces.*

5. Ibid.

6. Ibid.

7. Ibid.

8. Ibid.

9. Lang, J. (1987). *Creating Architectural Theory: The Role of the Behavioral Sciences in Environmental Design.* New York: Van Nostrand Reinhold.

10. Knopf, R. C. (1987). Human Behavior, Cognitions, and Affect in the Natural Environment. In D. Stokols & I. Altman (Eds.), *Handbook of Environmental Psychology* (Vol. 1, pp. 783–826). New York: Wiley.

11. Safra, J. E. (1997). Indonesia. *The New Encyclopedia Britannica* (Vol. 6, pp. 298–299). Chicago: Encyclopedia Britannica; Wibisono, A. K., & Schultz, W. (1996). *Cultural Examination of Indonesia.* Unpublished student manuscript, St. Norbert College, De Pere, WI.

12. Thao, K. (1995). *The Hmong Culture.* Unpublished student manuscript, St. Norbert College, De Pere, WI; Yang, D. (1993). *Hmong at the Turning Point.* Minneapolis, MN: Worldbridge.

13. Bichler, S., Jaeger, R., & Schiefelbein, B. (1996). *Life and Culture in South Yemen.* Unpublished student manuscript, St. Norbert College, De Pere, WI; Nyrop, R. F. (Ed.). (1986). *The Yemens: Country Studies.* Washington, DC: U.S. Government Printing Office.

14. Shoemaker, M. W. (1996). *Russia, Eurasian States, and Eastern Europe: 1996.* Harpers Ferry, WV: Stryler-Post; Westfahl, G., Koltz, R., & Manders, A. (1996). *Ethnic Russian Culture and Society.* Unpublished student manuscript, St. Norbert College, De Pere, WI.

15. Central Intelligence Agency. (1995). *The World Fact Book.* Washington, DC: U.S. Government Printing Office; Yurkovich, D., Pliscott, K., & Halverson, R. (1996). *The Norwegian Culture.* Unpublished student manuscript, St. Norbert College, De Pere, WI.

16. Lang, *Creating Architectural Theory.*

17. Kluckhohn, F. R. (1953). Dominant and Variant Value Orientations. In C. Kluckhohn, H. A. Murray, & D. M. Schneider (Eds.), *Personality in Nature, Culture, and Society* (pp. 342–357). New York: Knopf.

18. Altman, I., & Chemers, N. M. (1980). Cultural Aspects of the Environment–Behavior Relationship. In H. C. Triandis & R. W. Brislin (Eds.), *Handbook of Cross-Cultural Psychology* (Vol. 5, pp. 335–394). Boston: Allyn & Bacon.

19. Bishop, R. J. (1995). *Cultural Profile, Examination of Value Orientations and Sociocultural Influences, and Verbal and Nonverbal Language Aspects of the East Indian Culture.* Unpublished manuscript, St. Norbert College, De Pere, WI; Harris, P. R., & Moran, R. T. (1996).

Managing Cultural Differences (4th ed.). Houston, TX: Gulf; Srinivasan, R. (1951). *India.* New York: Marshall Cavendish.

20. Altman & Chemers, Cultural Aspects of the Environment–Behavior Relationship.

21. Borden, G. A., Conaway, W. A., & Morrison, T. (1993). *Kiss, Bow, or Shake Hands.* Holbrook, MA: Bob Adams; Reick, S., & Ogura, M. (1996). *Sri Lanka: The Pearl of the Indian Ocean.* Unpublished student manuscript, St. Norbert College, De Pere, WI.

22. Altman & Chemers, Cultural Aspects of the Environment–Behavior Relationship.

23. Kluckhohn, Dominant and Variant Value Orientations.

24. Altman and Chemers, Cultural Aspects of the Environment–Behavior Relationship; Thorne, R., & Hall, R. (1987). Environmental Psychology in Australia. In D. Stokols & I. Altman (Eds.), *Handbook of Environmental Psychology* (Vol. 2, pp. 1137–1154). New York: Wiley.

25. Sorenson, J. H., & White, G. F. (1980). Natural Disasters: A Cross-Cultural Perspective. In I. Altman, A. Rapoport, & J. F. Wohlwill (Eds.), *Human Behavior and Environment: Advances in Theory and Research* (Vol. 4, pp. 279–318). New York: Plenum.

26. Ibid.

27. Ibid.

28. Fisher, S. (2010). Violence Against Women and Natural Disasters: Findings From Post-Tsunami Sri Lanka. *Violence Against Women, 16*(8), 902–918.

29. Ibid.

30. Lang, *Creating Architectural Theory;* Rapoport, A. (1980). Cross-Cultural Aspects of Environmental Design. In I. Altman, A. Rapoport, & J. F. Wohlwill (Eds.), *Human Behavior and Environment: Advances in Theory and Research* (pp. 7–46). New York: Plenum.

31. Rapoport, A. (1969). *House Form and Culture.* Englewood Cliffs, NJ: Prentice-Hall.

32. Lang, *Creating Architectural Theory.*

33. Hall, E. T. (1966). *The Hidden Dimension.* New York: Doubleday.

34. Lang, *Creating Architectural Theory.*

35. Altman, I., & Vinsel, A. M. (1977). Personal Space: An Analysis of E. T. Hall's Proxemics Framework. In I. Altman & J. F. Wohlwill (Eds.), *Human Behavior and Environment: Advances in Theory and Research* (Vol. 2, pp. 181–260). New York: Plenum; Hall, *The Hidden Dimension.*

36. Hall, *The Hidden Dimension.*

37. Lustig, M. W., & Koester, J. (1996). *Intercultural Competence: Interpersonal Communication Across Cultures* (2nd ed.). New York: HarperCollins.

38. For an excellent summary of research related to personal space across cultures, see Aiello, J. (1987). Human Spatial Behavior. In D. Stokols & I. Altman (Eds.), *Handbook of Environmental Psychology* (Vol. 1, pp. 389–504). New York: Wiley.

39. Hagino, G., Mochizuki, M., & Yamamoto, T. (1987). Environmental Psychology in Japan. In D. Stokols & I. Altman (Eds.), *Handbook of Environmental Psychology* (Vol. 2, pp. 1155–1170). New York: Wiley.

40. Sieke, K., & Terry, C. S. (1970). *Contemporary Japanese Houses*. Tokyo: Kodansha.

41. Ibid., pp. 11–12.

42. Ueda, A. (1990). *The Inner Harmony of the Japanese House*. Tokyo: Kodansha.

43. Yoshida, T. (1969). *The Japanese House and Garden*. London: Pall Mall.

44. Ibid.

45. Ueda, *The Inner Harmony of the Japanese House*.

46. Ibid.

47. Ueda, *The Inner Harmony of the Japanese House;* Yoshida, *The Japanese House and Garden*.

48. Ueda, *The Inner Harmony of the Japanese House*, p. 9.

49. Kent, S. (1984). *Analyzing Activity Areas: An Ethnoarchaeological Study of the Use of Space*. Albuquerque: University of New Mexico Press.

50. Though not an exact duplication, this graphic is based on those present in Kent's *Analyzing Activity Areas*.

51. Kent, *Analyzing Activity Areas*.

52. Ibid.

53. Ibid.

54. Moore, H. L. (1986). *Space, Text, and Gender: An Anthropological Study of the Marakwet of Kenya*. Cambridge, UK: Cambridge University Press.

55. Ibid.

56. Ibid., p. 45.

57. Ibid.

58. Though not an exact duplication, Figure 4.4 is based on Moore's.

59. Moore, *Space, Text, and Gender*.

60. Ibid.

61. Burgoon, J. K. (1978). A Communication Model of Personal Space Violations: Explication and an Initial Test. *Human Communication Research, 4*(2), 129–142.

62. Westin, A. F. (1967). *Privacy and Freedom*. New York: Atheneum.

63. Altman, I. (1977). Privacy Regulation: Culturally Universal or Culturally Specific? *Journal of Social Issues, 83*(3), 66–84.

64. Westin, *Privacy and Freedom*.

65. Gandy, O. H. (1993). African-Americans and Privacy: Understanding the Black Perspective in the Emerging Policy Debate. *Journal of Black Studies, 42*(2), 178–195.

66. Lang, *Creating Architectural Theory*.

67. Westin, *Privacy and Freedom*.

68. Ibid.

69. Pedersen, D. M. (1979). Dimensions of Privacy. *Perceptual and Motor Skills, 48*, 1291–1297.

70. Ibid. Reprinted by permission.

71. Calvert, C. (2000). *Voyeur Nation: Media, Privacy, and Peering in Modern Culture*. Boulder, CO: Westview; Stepp, C. S. (2001). Playing at Peeping Tom. *American Journalism Review, 23*, 58.

72. Quittner, J., & Dowell, W. (1997). Invasion of Privacy. *Time, 150*, 28–36.

73. Ibid.

74. Burd, S. (2000). Colleges Allowed to Tell Parents About Alcohol Use. *Chronicle of Higher Education, 46*, A31; Reisberg, L. (2001). 2 Years After Colleges Started Calling Home, Administrators Say Alcohol Policy Works. *Chronicle of Higher Education, 47*, A34.

75. Gandy, African-Americans and Privacy.

76. Pedersen, D. M., & Frances, S. (1990). Regional Differences in Privacy Preferences. *Psychological Reports, 66*, 731–736.

77. Naftali, O. (2010). Caged Golden Canaries: Childhood, Privacy, and the Subjectivity in Contemporary Urban China. *Childhood, 17*, 297–311.

78. Ibid.

79. Tang, S., & Dong, X. (2006). Parents' and Children's Perceptions of Privacy Rights in China. *Journal of Family Issues, 27*(3), 285–300.

80. Ibid.

81. Rustemli, A., & Kokdemir, D. (1993). Privacy Dimensions and Preferences Among Turkish Students. *Journal of Social Psychology, 133*(6), 807–814.

82. Westin, *Privacy and Freedom*.

83. Altman, Privacy Regulation, pp. 66–84; Roberts, J. M., & Gregor, T. A. (1971). Privacy: A Cultural View. In J. R. Pennock & J. W. Chapman (Eds.), *Privacy* (pp. 199–225). New York: Atherton.

84. Altman, Privacy Regulation.

85. Bowles, P. (1993). *Morocco*. New York: Abrams; Hesselink, R. C., Mullen, R. T., & Rouse, J. M. (1996). *Moroccan Culture: An In-Depth Study*. Unpublished manuscript, St. Norbert College, De Pere, WI; *Overview of Islamic Architecture*. Available from http://venture.cob.ohio-state.edu:1111/khalid/pages/archtcre/overview.htm; Seward, P. (1995). *Cultures of the World: Morocco*. New York: Marshall Cavendish.

86. Cho, M., Rivera-Sanchez, M., & Lim, S. S. (2009). A Multinational Study on Online Privacy: Global Concerns and Local Responses. *New Media and Society, 11*(3), 395–416.

87. Hall, E. T. (1959). *The Silent Language*. Greenwich, CT: Fawcett, p. 15.

88. Hall, *The Silent Language;* Hall, E. T. (1983). *The Dance of Life*. New York: Doubleday.

89. Ibid.

90. Ibid.

91. Ibid.

92. Harris and Moran, *Managing Cultural Differences*.

93. Keberlein, M. C. G. (1993). *A Cultural Profile of the Guatemalan Ladinos.* Unpublished manuscript, St. Norbert College, De Pere, WI.

94. Hall, *The Silent Language.*

95. Hollis, A. C. (1995). *The Masai: Their Language and Folklore* (Rev. ed.). New York: Clarendon; Vandehey, K., Buerger, C., & Krueger, K. (1996). *Traditional Aspects and Struggles of the Masai Culture.* Unpublished manuscript, St. Norbert College, De Pere, WI.

96. Ibid.

97. Although different, the model for the dialogue is adapted from Copeland, L. (Producer). (1982). *Managing the Overseas Assignment* [Motion picture]. San Francisco: Copeland Griggs.

98. This scale was developed by Charles A. Phipps as a part of his senior honors thesis, titled *The Measurement of Monochronic and Polychronic Cognitions Among Hispanics and Anglos,* Abilene Christian University, 1987.

C H A P T E R 5

The Perceptual Context

After reading this chapter, you should be able to

1. list and discuss the three stages of human information processing,

2. discuss cross-cultural differences in perception,

3. define and discuss short- and long-term memory,

4. discuss cross-cultural differences in memory and recall,

5. define and discuss at least four types of mental categories,

6. define and discuss racial and ethnic stereotypes,

7. identify and discuss at least two reasons why people stereotype,

8. define and discuss the nature of ethnocentrism, and

9. define and discuss the nature of racism.

It seems to me that we have sound reasons for thus considering theoretical knowledge as more objective than immediate experience.

—Michael Polyani[1]

———————

Think back to when you were in the second grade. You were about 7 years old then; it was quite a few years ago. Who was your second-grade teacher? Do you remember his/her name? You probably do. Now, think back to last week. What did you have for dinner on Tuesday night? Can't remember? After so many years, you can recall the name of your second-grade teacher almost immediately, but you can't remember what you had for dinner last Tuesday night. What's going on in your head that allows you to recall your second-grade teacher's name in a matter of seconds when you can't recall Tuesday night's dinner choice no matter how hard you try?

Consider the following interaction between Jim, an American college student, and Olga, a Ukrainian exchange student studying at the same college as Jim in the United States.

Whenever two people come together and interact, like Jim and Olga, they process great quantities of information. In addition to the cultural, microcultural, and environmental contexts influencing their interaction, Jim and Olga both bring with them their unique perceptual experiences, which affect their observations of the world around them. In this chapter, the perceptual context refers to how people take in, store, and recall information. In this brief conversation, Jim and Olga encode, decode, and interpret a vast amount of information about themselves, their cultures' histories, current events, their surroundings, and each other.

Jim: Ya know, Olga, I've been thinking about America's involvement in the war in Afghanistan. I see reports of people starving and dying, and it's just so depressing. I hope this is over soon.

Olga: Yes, I know, it's a terrible thing. My country has experienced a lot of starvation and war, too.

Jim: Really?

Olga: Oh, yes. My country has been fought over and suppressed for a long time. We gained our independence from Russia for a short time between 1917 and 1920, but that was followed by ruthless Soviet rule that was responsible for two famines in which over 8 million people died. Can you imagine that, Jim? And then World War II, where the German and Soviet armies killed some 7 million of my people. So in the 20th century alone, over 15 million people died, some say for no good reason.

Jim: I had no idea. I can't imagine how that makes you feel.

Olga: Right, I understand. Our history gives my people a whole different perspective on life and how we see and live our lives. It's almost impossible not to carry a little sadness in our hearts.

Jim: My generation has never experienced anything like that. This is brand new to us. It's very confusing.

Because they come from different cultures, they see the world differently. Their interpretations of world events differ dramatically.

Intercultural communication is a process of connecting perceptual contexts. Although the ability to process information is a universal phenomenon, it is influenced by culture. Our knowledge of the world is dependent on our senses. What we see, hear, smell, taste, and touch provides the data from which we construct our world. Yet what we see, hear, smell, taste, and touch is subjective and biased. You might enjoy the smell of hamburgers being grilled, but your Hindu friend from India is repulsed by that same smell. Our perception of the world is subjective and biased.

Dutch sociologist Geert Hofstede argues that culture is the software of the mind.[2] Think of the human mind as a computer where information is entered, stored, and recalled. As you sit at your computer, you type in information (i.e., data input). After a while, you decide to take a break from writing and you hit the save button, which stores the information in the computer's memory. Later, when you return to the computer, you recall the information (i.e., open the saved file) and continue writing. Analogously, the human mind works in the same way. Via our senses, we take in information (i.e., we see it, hear it, smell it, taste it, and feel it). We then store the information in memory, and we recall it later. All human brains, regardless of culture, take in, store, and recall information. Without the brain's ability to take in, store, and recall information, human communication would be impossible.

Following Hofstede's analogy, culture represents the computer's (i.e., the brain's) software. In other words, exactly how we take in information, how we store it, and how we recall it, is based on our culture—that is, our software. We are *born* human. All normal human brains are naturally equipped to take in, store, and retrieve information. But we *become* cultural.

Culture teaches and conditions the human brain exactly how to take in, store, and retrieve information. Culture is the software of the mind. And culture is not objective; it is biased. Some of our subjectivity is based on the simple physiological differences among humans. No two humans are biologically exactly alike, for example. Many people suffer from astigmatism, an eye disorder in which the cornea (the clear tissue covering the front of the eye) is abnormally curved, causing out-of-focus vision. People are born with astigmatism. Some of our subjectivity is based on culture. To a degree, culture teaches us what looks good and what looks bad and is not at all related to whether we have an astigmatism.

This chapter is about the higher mental activities of the individual that constitute the perceptual context of intercultural communication. In addition to the cultural, microcultural, and environmental contexts, the perceptual context affects how people interact. Every time we enter into a communicative exchange with someone, we bring with us a perceptual frame of reference through which all our messages are filtered. The cultural, microcultural, environmental, and perceptual contexts are interdependent influences that combine in a complex formula and that ultimately define our interactions with others.

The first part of this chapter introduces the idea of culture and cognition and outlines a model of human information processing. The second part of the chapter explains a common form of information processing called categorization. The third part of the chapter focuses on two attitudinal dimensions of information processing: stereotyping and ethnocentrism. The overall purpose of the chapter is to explain how the human mind processes information during communication, especially during intercultural communication.

CULTURE AND COGNITION

People from different cultures think about different things. The Aleutian Eskimos of western Alaska and the Marakwet tribe in western Kenya think about different things because of the extreme differences in their natural environments. Moreover, people from different cultures think differently about their life experiences. The life experiences of a Guatemalan Ladino are markedly different from those of a Ukrainian. Few people question that the content of thought for people in different cultures varies. What is open to speculation, however, is whether higher mental processes, such as perception and remembering, differ across cultures. How much do the cultural, microcultural, and environmental contexts affect how the human brain processes information?

The Geography of Thought

Richard Nisbett, a distinguished professor at the University of Michigan, has researched and written extensively about how humans process information. His central thesis is that geographical differences in culture have a dramatic influence on how humans in those distinct geographical areas perceive the world. Specifically, his focus is on how Asians (Eastern cultures) and Westerners think differently from each other and why. His argument is that peoples from the East and West think differently because of foundations of Eastern and Western philosophies that were professed 2,500 years ago by the ancient Greeks and Chinese.

Professor Nisbett compares the Confucian-influenced Chinese thinking of the collective against the Greek-Western orientation of the individual. The ancient Greeks focused on linear methods of understanding and seeing separate objects in isolation without much regard for the context in which they existed. Individuals are unique, with distinct attributes and goals. Confucian-driven Chinese philosophies emphasized fluctuation, holism, interdependence, and harmony. All things (e.g., people and objects) are to be understood in terms of their relationships with others, their groupness—including the environment in which they exist. Nisbett contrasts the Western tendency to classify objects into discrete categories based on their similarity with the Eastern preference to classify objects into categories based on their relationships.[3] Consider the photograph below:

Describe what you see in the above photo. When Nisbett asked American students to describe the photo, most of them referred to the fish. When Japanese students described it, they referred to the pond. How did you describe it?

Now, consider the three photos on page 172.

Your task is to group two of the three photos together. Which two photos do you think go together? Nisbett found that American children tend to group the cow and the chicken together, as animals. Chinese children tend to put the cow and grass together, as a relationship, because the cow eats the grass. Obviously, you can see that Nisbett is tapping into the individualism and collectivism dimension of cultural variability discussed in Chapter 2.

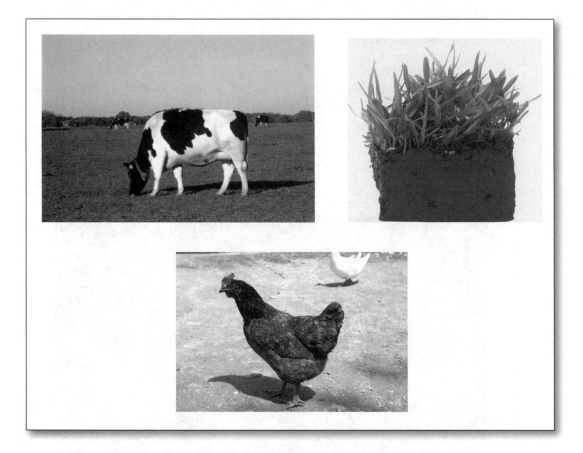

The essential point here is that these orientations affect the way humans process information. We are not objective processors; we are biased processors. One way is not necessarily better than the other, but it is important to understand that not all humans think the same way.

A Model of Human Information Processing

As mentioned above, the human mind is analogous to a computer. Information is entered, stored, and retrieved in a sequence of stages, where each stage performs a specific operation on the information.[4] During Stage 1, the input stage, information is taken in via the senses. In Stage 2, the storage stage, information is held in memory. During Stage 3, the retrieval stage, information is recalled. In order for people to communicate with one another, in any culture, they are required to take in, store, and recall information. Although these stages are probably universal, culture influences the specific strategies and styles of processing information in each stage.

Stage #1: Input/Sensation

The first stage of information processing is the input stage, where raw information is taken in through the senses. This is called **perception**. Margaret Matlin defines perception as the mental interpretation of external stimuli via **sensation**.[5] According to Matlin, at any given point in time, especially during human communication, human beings are bombarded with external stimuli. Humans take in visual stimuli with their eyes, auditory stimuli with their ears, olfactic stimuli with their noses, taste stimuli with their mouths, and tactile stimuli through the skin (see Figure 5.1).

During intercultural communication, many of the stimuli come from the cultural, micro-cultural, and environmental context. Once taken in through the senses and prior to being stored in memory, the stimuli are passed through at least three **perceptual filters**: physiological, sociological, and psychological (see Figure 5.2).[6]

Physiological filters include the natural or genetic differences in how one sees, hears, smells, tastes, or feels. For example, eyesight varies considerably from person to person. Many people are required to wear eyeglasses to accommodate their poor visual sensation. As most people age, they lose some of their hearing. Some research has shown that as people age, they also lose some of their sense of smell.

Figure 5.1 Human Information Processor

Figure 5.2 Sensation and Perceptual Filters

Sociological filters represent demographic data and one's membership in groups, including one's culture, microculture, and hometown, for example. The groups to which people belong influence how they perceive incoming stimuli. For example, many college-aged persons in the United States enjoy listening to rap music, a form of auditory stimuli. Few octogenarians (persons in their 80s) enjoy listening to such music, however.

Psychological filters include the attitudes, beliefs, and dispositions of the individual. A person's likes, dislikes, and beliefs about what is right or wrong filter the perception of incoming stimuli. If someone has a negative attitude about a professor, he or she may perceive that professor's class as especially boring or uninformative. If people believe that abortion is immoral, then they may perceive an abortion rights speaker as unattractive. Although all of us are bombarded with the same visual, auditory, tactile, olfactic, and taste stimuli, our sensations and perceptions of those stimuli will differ considerably, especially if we come from different cultures.

Cross-Cultural Differences in Sensation and Perception

In addition to the physiological, sociological, and psychological filters, culture affects one's ability to perceive incoming information. John Berry and his associates outline four explanations for cross-cultural differences in the perception of sensory stimuli: (a) conditions of the physical environment, (b) indirect environmental conditions, (c) genetic differences, and (d) cultural differences in how people interact with their environment.[7]

Regarding conditions in the physical environment, in the early 1970s, Reuning and Wortley conducted a cross-cultural study on auditory acuity (i.e., sharpness). In their comparison of Kalahari Bushmen, Danish, and American subjects, they found less hearing loss in the Kalahari sample than in the Danish or American samples, particularly among older subjects. Reuning and Wortley attributed their findings to low levels of ambient noise in the Kalahari Desert region. They also cited other studies that found a slower loss of hearing in nonindustrialized societies. This may suggest that environmental noise, such as that heard in industrialized societies, has a negative effect on hearing.[8]

In his study, Wyndham attributed an indirect environmental factor, specifically poor nutrition, as the reason for slower dark adaptation among Black South African miners than among Whites. Wyndham found that it took longer for the eyes of Black miners to adapt to the dark than it did for White miners. Wyndham suggests that many of the Black mine workers might suffer from forms of liver ailments, which in turn could be associated with nutritional deficiencies in early childhood.[9]

Berry and his associates argue that genetic factors seem to account for red–green colorblindness, taste blindness, and the "alcoholic flush" phenomenon. Many studies have demonstrated that the frequency of red–green colorblindness is much lower in non-Caucasian groups than among Caucasians. Approximately 30% of all Caucasians are taste blind to certain substances that taste bitter to Africans and Native American Indians. The alcoholic flush, a reddening of the face after consuming only a few alcoholic drinks, is much more common in Asian populations than in Caucasians.[10]

Socialization and enculturation with the environment play a role in sensory stimulation. Children are taught to pay attention to certain kinds of stimuli. Africans, for example, tend to excel in auditory tasks, whereas Europeans tend to excel in visual tasks. Cultural groups are taught to favor some **sensory receptors** over others. These people develop a sensotype—that is, the relative importance of one sensory modality over the others.[11]

An extensive body of cross-cultural research on perception has been conducted by Marshall Segall and his colleagues.[12] Segall believes that repeated experience with certain objects affects how those objects are perceived. His study involved the perception of optical illusions. Almost 2,000 subjects, from 14 non-Western cultures (mostly in Africa) and 3 Western cultures, participated in the study. Each participant was shown a series of optical illusions. Segall argued that optical illusions occur because previously learned interpretations of visual cues are misapplied due to unusual or misleading characteristics of stimuli. One hypothesis that explains vulnerability to illusions is called the carpentered-world hypothesis.

According to Segall and the **carpentered-world hypothesis**, there is a learned tendency among those raised in an environment shaped by carpenters (e.g., rectangular furniture, houses, right angles) to interpret nonrectangular figures as representations of rectangular figures seen *in perspective*. In most urbanized places, rooms and buildings are typically rectangular, with lots of right angles. Look around the room you are in right now. Look at all the right angles. They are everywhere! The windows, the corner of your desk, the doorway, and where the walls meet the ceiling all form right angles. Being surrounded by such an environment, we learn to depend on depth cues based on a linear perspective more than would people who live in less-carpentered (i.e., built) environments. For example, rural isolated Zulus live in a non-carpentered world, with round huts and round doors. They do not plow their land in straight rows as farmers in the United States would but, instead, tend to plow in curves.

Segall uses the Sander parallelogram to explain the carpentered-world hypothesis (see Figure 5.3). For people living in carpentered societies, the diagonal line bisecting the larger, left-hand parallelogram appears to be considerably longer than the diagonal line bisecting the smaller, right-hand parallelogram—but they are, in fact, the same length. In other words, the apparently longer portion of the figure may be interpreted as the corner of a room receding in depth, because the wings of the illusion act as linear perspective cues.[13]

Figure 5.3 Sander Parallelogram

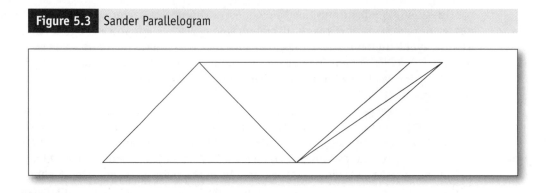

Stage #2: Storage/Memory

Once information has been sensed and passed through the perceptual filters, it is processed into memory. **Memory** involves maintaining information over time.[14] Memory is required for virtually all human communication. Without the ability to store information over time, we could not communicate with others. Imagine not being able to remember your own name or recognize your family members. Without memory, you could not read this book, nor would you be able to construct a single spoken sentence! The importance of memory is why many cultures regard it as the most crucial component of human intelligence. Generally, cognitive psychologists recognize two types of memory: working memory and long-term memory.[15]

According to Margaret Matlin, working memory, sometimes called **short-term memory**, is brief, immediate memory for information that you are processing at the current moment. Working memory coordinates ongoing mental activities, and information is constantly being handled, combined, and transformed. It holds both new and old information that has been retrieved from long-term memory. In some cases, the information is committed to long-term memory, and in many other cases, the information is simply lost.[16] The amount of information stored in short-term memory is quite limited. Although psychologists disagree, many concur with George Miller's conclusion that short-term memory is limited to seven items, plus or minus two. In what is now considered a classic article, Miller coined the phrase "The magical number seven, plus or minus two" in referring to the storage capacity of short-term memory.[17]

In her summary of research associated with working memory, Matlin notes that working memory is relatively fragile and that, unless rehearsed and repeated, information held in working memory is easily lost within about 30 seconds. Although working memory is temporary, limited, and fragile, it is essential for human communication. In any culture, most communicative tasks, such as reading, writing, listening, and speaking, are entirely dependent on the ability to maintain information for short periods of time. In any culture, the ability to finish a spoken or written sentence is contingent on remembering its first words.[18]

Individuals' working memory may be affected by differences in their writing systems, however. In his work, Tavassoli found that memory for the presentation order of written words was better for native English speakers than for native Chinese speakers. This may be because English words rely to a greater degree on sounds than on visual features, which are emphasized in written Chinese. For example, in English, the letters in the alphabet represent sounds. In contrast, Chinese characters represent meanings (what is called a logographic script). There appear to be fundamental processing differences between reading alphabetic and logographic scripts. Whereas reading alphabetic words, as English speakers do, is dominated by phonological cognitive processes, reading logographs, as Chinese speakers do, appears to rely to a greater degree on visual cognitive processes. Readers of Chinese logographs also appear to attend more to visual features of complete written words. For example, compared with readers of alphabetic English words, readers of Chinese logographs were more likely to remember the print color of words.[19]

In addition to working memory, humans possess **long-term memory**. The essential difference between working and long-term memory is the duration of storage. Unlike working memory, information in long-term memory may be held for a lifetime. People may be able to recall events that took place 40 or 50 years ago. A second major difference between the two stores is their capacity. Whereas the working short-term store may be limited to seven items, plus or minus two, the storage capacity in long-term memory is virtually unlimited. Another difference between the two memories is their method of forgetting. Information in working memory seems to be lost due to **decay**; that is, if the information is not used, it simply fades away. Although long-term memories also decay, the long-term store seems most disrupted by interference; that is, other information gets in the way of stored information.[20]

Many cognitive psychologists distinguish between three types of long-term memory: episodic or autobiographical memory, semantic memory, and procedural memory.[21] Although these three types of long-term memory appear to be different, they are also highly interconnected and probably operate interdependently. **Episodic long-term memory** refers to that type of stored information pertaining to the unique experiences of the individual. Episodic memory is autobiographical. One's birthday, first-grade teacher, first date, and so on are different for each person and are representative of the type of information stored in episodic long-term memory.

Wang and Brockmeier suggest that one's cultural background affects autobiographical memory. Remember from Chapter 2 that in individualistic cultures, such as that of the United States, an independent self is promoted. In many East Asian cultures, such as that of China, an interdependent self is advocated. Wang and Brockmeier point out that such differences affect the content of autobiographical memory because the relationship between memory and self is built into the culture.[22] In fact, Wang found that, compared with Caucasian Americans, who recalled their earliest autobiographical memories from as early as 3.5 years of age, Asians and Asian Americans reported memories dated more than 6 months later. In related research, Wang asked American and Chinese college students to report their earliest childhood memory. Wang found that the descriptions provided by Americans were mostly individual focused and self-assured, while the descriptions provided by Chinese tended to be group oriented and modest. Wang concluded that an independently oriented self is associated with the earlier establishment of an autobiographical history that is elaborate, specific, emotionally charged, and self-focused. On the other hand, a collectivistic self is associated with the later establishment of an autobiographical memory that is brief, general, emotionally unexpressive, and relationship centered.[23]

Semantic long-term memory preserves a person's general conceptual information, world knowledge, and language abilities unrelated to an individual's experiences. Semantic memory allows humans to communicate with language. How to spell words, count, and construct sentences would be information preserved in semantic long-term memory. In a very interesting study, Durga found that bilingual individuals take significantly more time to process verbal information than do monolingual individuals.[24]

Procedural memory refers to one's knowledge about how to do something manually. For example, remembering how to ride a bike and how to send an e-mail message to a friend are accomplished via procedural memory.[25] Although persons from different cultures certainly perform different manual tasks, very little research has investigated specific cross-cultural differences in procedural memory.

Stage #3: Recall/Retrieval

Once information has been stored, it is relatively useless unless it can be retrieved. The human information processor excels at retrieval. Information that has been stored for a lifetime yet is rarely used can be recalled in an instant. Other times, however, recently stored information seems very difficult to recall. Most adults can easily recall the name of their first-grade teacher but cannot remember what they had for dinner three nights ago. Moreover, the quality of human information retrieval is typically approximate rather than literate. People retain global memories of conversations or events rather than verbatim transcriptions. According to Lachman and his colleagues, forgetting is memory failure—the inability to recall or recognize stored information. Although most of us regret it when we forget something, cognitive psychologists now treat long-term memory forgetting as an asset rather than a liability because it is a useful way to prevent long-term memory from getting cluttered with information that is not being used. Forgetting often follows what is called a "negatively accelerated curve." Most forgetting occurs rapidly and then levels off over time. Other researchers contend that information is never really forgotten; people just lose access to it.[26]

Matlin points out that there are many reasons why we might forget something, including decay, interference, arousal, trauma, and depth of processing. Forgetting that is due to decay occurs when a memory is not rehearsed or used over time. Eventually, the information diminishes or fades from memory. **Interference** occurs when other information intrudes on stored information. Sometimes, forgetting occurs when old memories interfere with the storage of new information. Other times, forgetting occurs when new information disrupts previously stored "old" memories. Matlin devised a mini-experiment that demonstrates the effect of interference (see p. 179).

Negative arousal, or anxiety, is also thought to interfere with the retrieval of information from long-term memory.[28] Persons suffering from anxiety often report being unable to recall certain information. Students, for example, often complain that test anxiety prohibits them from performing well on exams. According to Matlin, another form of forgetting may be due to repression. This occurs when people actively, but unconsciously, forget unpleasant material. Similarly, pleasant material may be processed more easily than unpleasant. Refer back to the interference forgetting mini-experiment. After your friend completes the experiment, make a note of the first few and the last few vegetables on the list. Chances are that those vegetables listed first are the ones your friend enjoys while those listed toward the end are those that he or she dislikes.[29]

Matlin suggests that the effort required to gather and store information may also affect its retrieval. Meaningful information that requires deeper cognitive processing may be easier to recall than information that requires minimal effort to encode. Likewise, the context in which

Interference Forgetting Mini-Experiment[27]

Present the following word list to a friend or roommate:

River   Card

Door   Test

Cat   Tree

Plate   Ball

Book   Road

Allow a few moments for your friend to read the list. After he/she finishes, ask him/her to either write down or recite orally a list of 10 vegetables. When he/she has finished the list of vegetables, ask him/her to recall the words on the list he/she read. See how many he/she recalls and with what degree of accuracy. Repeat the experiment with another friend, but this time delete the vegetable list exercise. Compare their results. Theoretically, the vegetable word list exercise should interfere with your friend's ability to store the word list in memory.

the information is encoded may facilitate recall. In this situation, called *encoding specificity,* the contextual cues present during the gathering and storing of information may serve as cues for the recall of stored information.[30]

Cross-Cultural Differences in Memory and Retrieval

Several studies indicate that culture affects information retrieval. In addition to culture, age and education are two other variables strongly linked to recall. Age and recall are curvilinearly related (see Figure 5.4). Up to a point, one's age facilitates recall. When many people reach a certain age, however, their memory skills deteriorate. Likewise, educated persons seem to employ different kinds of memory strategies. Barbara Rogoff claims that to the extent that cultures have different educational systems and methods, their people may have different memory skills. Persons educated in industrialized cultures have been taught to remember disconnected bits of information, such as names and dates. These persons may be more likely than nonschooled individuals to use memory strategies that facilitate the organization of unrelated items. Moreover, Rogoff asserts that schooled individuals are more likely to classify similar objects together, whereas nonschooled persons classify objects based on their functional similarity. For example, in many memory tests, persons are presented with lists of unrelated pieces of information, not unlike the word list presented in the interference forgetting mini-experiment. This type of information may be remembered better if the person employs some sort of mnemonic (pronounced "neh-monic," meaning a

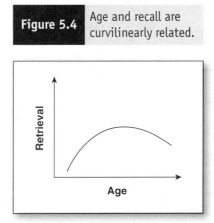

Figure 5.4   Age and recall are curvilinearly related.

technique for improving memory) device such as rehearsing or classifying. Nonschooled persons, including preschool children, generally do not employ mnemonic strategies and have difficulty with such tasks.[31]

With contextually organized information, however, fewer memory differences are observed between schooled and nonschooled persons. In one study reported by Rogoff, for example, Guatemalan Mayan and American 9-year-olds watched an experimenter place 20 miniature objects such as cars, animals, furniture, people, and household items into a panorama model of a town. The 20 items were then removed from the panorama and put into a pool of 80 other objects. The children were then asked to reconstruct the panorama using as many of the original 20 items as they could remember. The Mayan children performed slightly better than the American children. The performance of the Mayan children may have been due to the fact that about one third of the American children used rehearsal strategies, such as rehearsing the names of the objects, typical for remembering unrelated bits of information. This type of strategy may be inappropriate for remembering spatially oriented, contextual information.[32]

In related research, Yoshida, Fernandez, and Stigler explored Japanese and American students' recognition memory for statements made during a videotaped mathematics lesson. Japanese and American fourth- and sixth-graders watched either a Japanese or English version of the same lesson and then were tested for recognition of teacher statements that were relevant or irrelevant to the content of the lesson. The Japanese and American students were equally successful at recognizing relevant statements, but American students remembered more irrelevant statements than did the Japanese.[33]

Cole and Gay assert that a culture's language and literacy rate may affect recall. Some evidence indicates that nonliterate societies develop mnemonic skills different from those of literate societies. In nonliterate societies, there may be no written language to facilitate memory. Imagine studying for an examination for which you have no notes! Cole and Gay note that in nonliterate societies, people must store information in memory rather than on a piece of paper. Likewise, the histories of nonliterate societies must be stored in the memories of their people rather than on paper or in books.[34] In a study conducted by Ross and Millson, two groups of university students, one group from Ghana and the other from New York, were read several stories aloud and then asked to recall them. Generally, the Ghanaian students had better recall of the stories than did the American students. Researchers in a related study examined the effects of culturally based knowledge on memory for stories about people performing common activities.[35]

In a study by Harris, Schoen, and Hensley, college students from America and Mexico read three brief stories of everyday activities. There were two versions of the same story, consistent with either an American or a Mexican cultural script. The students read each version. Researchers then administered memory tests immediately after the students read the story, 30 minutes after they read the story, and 1 week after they read the story. After 1 week, both groups of students mistakenly recalled the stories from the other culture as being more like their own culture than they in fact were.[36]

Other memory research reviewed by Liu indicates that Chinese persons may have superior memory. For example, in word-pair association memory tasks, Chinese college students usually attain perfect recall within two or three trials compared with students from other cultures, whose accuracy is typically below 70%.[37] Until more is known, final conclusions about the relationship between culture and memory should be made with some degree of caution. Although several studies indicate a connection between culture and memory, these studies actually may be revealing differences in other factors that affect recall, such as socialization or education. Because cultures differ in so many ways, it is difficult to pinpoint culture as the sole mechanism for memory ability.

Categorization and Mental Economy

Humans are constantly bombarded by so many stimuli simultaneously that they cannot possibly process all of it. In order to manage the enormous quantities of information, humans tend to engage in mental economy strategies. One such strategy is called categorization. **Categorization** consists of grouping, sorting, or classifying objects, events, or living things into identifiable groups or compartments based on the belief that the category members share certain features or characteristics. Most cognitive psychologists argue that all people, regardless of culture, engage in categorization and that it is a necessary part of everyday life. Categorization is an essential cognitive mechanism by which humans organize and manage the natural and social world that surrounds them.[38] Eleanor Rosch is well known for her work on categorization. She has argued that

> the world consists of a virtually infinite number of discriminably different stimuli. Since no organism can cope with infinite diversity, one of the most basic functions of all organisms is the cutting up of the environment into classifications by which nonidentical stimuli can be treated as equivalent.[39]

Although people categorize just about everything (e.g., plants, cars, events), intercultural communication researchers are interested in the ways people categorize people. Gudykunst and Kim suggest that categories are useful because they help the information processor reduce uncertainty and increase the accuracy of predictions about others. Moreover, categories help us make attributions about the behavior of others and help us recall and recognize information. Understanding categorization is particularly important for intercultural communication because whenever we interact with someone from a different culture, we are faced with high levels of uncertainty and unfamiliar stimuli to process.[40]

According to Richard Brislin, people often form categories on the basis of perceived conspicuous differences. Conspicuous differences categories are based on easily seen similarities or differences. According to Brislin, these types of categories are formed quickly during initial interaction with someone from a different culture. Conspicuous differences may stem from skin color, dress, language, or occupation. These differences help classify others as members of in-groups and out-groups.[41] Unfortunately, there is evidence to suggest that in-group–out-group categorization is a principal category formed by people that often leads to intergroup discrimination and intergroup bias. David Wilder has argued that intergroup bias and prejudice are an unavoidable by-product of categorization. Moreover, Wilder maintains that such bias may have nothing to do with irrational thought processes but is a consequence of people's attempts to organize and simplify their environment (i.e., categorization).[42] Likewise, Park and Judd point out that it is probably impossible to eliminate in-group–out-group categorization and that it may not be possible for human beings to think of one another as "individuals" or as all one and the same. They maintain that most social categorization schemes are correlated with ethnicity and form the basis for intergroup hostilities.[43] To be sure, Ridley and Hill maintain that categorization is the primary cognitive process associated with racism.[44]

Although people in all cultures categorize, researchers have found that culture affects categorization. In their summary of this research, Unsworth, Sears, and Pexman found that people from Asian cultures, especially the Chinese, create holistic categories and that Westerners create analytic categories. Unsworth and her colleagues point out that holistic categories focus on context and environmental factors; relationships are explained with reference to how objects are related to their environment, and it is held that a part cannot be separated from the whole. Analytic categories, on the other hand, are characterized by the separation of an object from its context; similarity among objects or people is used to differentiate them into distinct groups, and predictions about people are made based on these categories.[45]

STEREOTYPING

By constructing categories, the human mind processes information more efficiently. Once created, categories are the basis of prejudgment, such as stereotyping. Considered a subset of categorization, stereotyping involves members of one group attributing characteristics to members of another group. These attributions typically carry a positive or negative evaluation. In this sense, stereotypes are categories with an attitude. **Stereotypes** typically refer to membership in social categories—such as sex, race, age, or profession—that are believed to be associated with certain traits and behaviors. In the United States, race and gender groups are often stereotyped. Richard Schaefer defines stereotypes as exaggerated images of the characteristics of a particular group held by prejudiced people who hold ill feelings toward that group. Gudykunst and Kim define stereotypes as cognitive representations of another group that influence one's feelings about the group. They argue that stereotypes provide the content of social categories.[46]

Although it is hard to admit it, we all stereotype. Stereotyping is a natural and universal information-processing strategy. Taylor and Porter maintain that stereotyping should be seen as a normal process that is a useful information-processing tool in diverse societies.[47] The difficulty arises when stereotypes carry a negative valence and are used to overgeneralize negative traits to an entire group of people when, in reality, few members of the group actually possess such traits. In this way, stereotyping can lead to ethnocentrism, prejudice, and discrimination (see Figures 5.5a and 5.5b).

Figure 5.5a What stereotype traits might be associated with these young women?

Figure 5.5b   What stereotype traits might be associated with these young men?

STUDENT VOICES ACROSS CULTURES

Amanda Garrity

Many are aware of the inescapable shadow of stereotypes that follows a pageant girl no matter what spotlight she stands in. Typical stereotypes of pageant girls are that we are blonde, unrealistically thin, vain, and remarkably unintelligent. As a blonde, slender young woman who wears a crown of my own, I am the target of these stereotypes. However, these misconceptions only give me the satisfying challenge of proving the true image and beauty of my pageant world.

Like most stereotypes, those surrounding women who participate in pageants are limiting and inaccurate, especially when those who hold the stereotypes use media outlets to spread their distorted perceptions. Often, pageants are seen as a pedestal for young women to display their sex appeal, where beauty is equated with vanity and shallowness. Those experienced in the world of pageantry could not disagree more.

I started entering pageants at the age of 13, not in hopes of having people dote on my prettiness but to gain confidence and to accept and express myself. However, after competing and winning my first title, these stereotypes began to loom over me and shook the very confidence I was seeking. When I would wear my crown to community events, to spread the news and information about my platform, people would glare negatively,

(Continued)

(Continued)

tell my parents that they should be ashamed of themselves, and avoid me. At school, false allegations were made that I had developed an eating disorder, and friends stopped sending me invitations to join them in my favorite activities: four-wheeling, soccer, etc. As fast as the crown was placed on my head, the perceptions of me changed. With these stereotypes weighing on me, there were times that I actually believed it would be easier to become the person they saw me as instead of spending all my time and energy defending myself.

There was a short time when I started to believe that these stereotypes may be true. Only when I realized where and how these stereotypes were developed, and that I would only be turning into another statistic if I gave in by becoming who they thought I was, did I begin to recognize and promote the positive effects pageant can have on young women and to debunk the distortions. Through my experiences with pageant organizations, I was able to attend the college of my choice, after receiving many academic scholarships, and graduate debt free.

By featuring stage competitions, such as evening gown, swimsuit, talent, and onstage questions, pageant organizations emphasize the importance of taking care of yourself, leading a healthy lifestyle, promoting and sharing your talents, and forming a strong personal opinion about world events. These are all qualities and standards that people should have in their lives in order to be accomplished and successful.

Because of pageants, I have the confidence to stay true to who I really am. Whether I'm camping with my family and not wearing any makeup for weeks at a time, leaving my heels in the closet to lace up my sneakers for a day full of dirty course, or standing on the grandest stage of all at Miss America, I can stand tall knowing that because of pageants, I am proud of who I have become.

Racial and Ethnic Stereotypes

Social scientists have long been interested in stereotypes and prejudice, two concepts that are often related. The systematic study of racial and ethnic stereotypes in the United States began in the 1930s with a classic study conducted by David Katz and Kenneth Braly. In their study, college students were presented with a list of 84 adjectives (e.g., lazy, ignorant, arrogant, intelligent) and were asked to indicate which traits were characteristic of 10 ethnic groups: Americans, Blacks, Chinese, English, Germans, Italians, Irish, Japanese, Jews, and Turks. The results of their study showed that the college students consistently agreed on which traits described which group. The results were particularly consistent for Blacks and Jews.

Traits Associated With Blacks (Katz & Braly, 1933)	*Traits Associated With Jews (Katz & Braly, 1933)*
Superstitious	Shrewd
Lazy	Mercenary (selfish)
Happy-go-lucky	Sly
Ignorant	Aggressive
Stupid	Industrious
Dirty (physically)	Intelligent
Musical	Ambitious
Religious	

In their original study, Katz and Braly found a high level of consistency in the adjectives respondents associated with the Black stereotype. Moreover, the adjectives selected were generally negative. Since their original work, several other researchers have replicated Katz and Braly's stereotype checklist method using the same 84 adjectives as in the original study—Gilbert in 1950 and Gordon in 1969 and 1982. Patricia Devine and Andrew Elliot replicated the research in 1995. In their work, however, Devine and Elliot added 9 new characteristics to the original 84-item adjective checklist.[48]

Devine and Elliot argue that despite a shift in social norms discouraging the overt expression of prejudice and discrimination, stereotypical images of Blacks remain salient in U.S. culture. Devine and Elliot conclude,

> Although efforts such as affirmative action and increased sensitivity to media portrayals of Blacks may ultimately have positive effects and facilitate the fading of cultural racial stereotypes, it is likely that such changes will take place over a protracted period of time.[49]

American Stereotypes

Canadian psychologists Donald Taylor and Lana Porter examined some of the socially desirable aspects of stereotyping and allege that the negative connotation associated with stereotyping may be uniquely American. They argue that, historically, the study of stereotypes in the United States mainly has focused on White stereotypes of African Americans, which have been particularly brutal and negative (see Figure 5.6). Second, Taylor and Porter suggest that the essence of the political doctrine in the United States is modeled after the "melting-pot" metaphor, wherein the peoples of all the different cultures immigrating to the United States get "stirred up in the great pot until cultural differences are boiled away and a single culture remains—American." Because stereotyping, by definition, recognizes and highlights differences among groups, it directly conflicts with the melting-pot image. Third, Taylor and Porter suggest that psychologists studying interpersonal attraction have long understood that perceived similarity is a major determinant in how much people are attracted to and like others. The more we perceive people to be similar to us, the more likely we are to be attracted to and like them. Hence, stereotypes that emphasize group differences essentially block the potential for intergroup friendships. Given these trends, Taylor and Porter assert that there are compelling reasons why Americans view stereotyping as a destructive social force. This, they argue, has led to an enormous investment in human and financial resources to rid people of their stereotypes.[50]

Traits Associated With Blacks (Devine & Elliot, 1995)

Lazy	Rhythmic
Ignorant	Unintelligent
Dirty (physically)	Poor
Loud	Criminal
Athletic	Hostile

STUDENT VOICES ACROSS CULTURES

Stereotypes

Morgan Johnson

 Whether the purpose is academic, service, or leisure oriented, I have always eagerly sought travel to Spanish-speaking locations to help master my second language. In the past few years, I have been fortunate enough to travel to Puerto Rico, Mexico, Costa Rica, Ecuador, and Spain. With each new place comes a unique community that, like any other, internalizes various beliefs, values, attitudes, and ways of life. Naturally, as a stranger entering their environment, members of each community immediately stereotype me. Most frequently, I am categorized as a young, White, American female. By young, they mean I am naïve with little work ethic; by White, affluent; by American, culturally ignorant, demanding, and more focused on financial gain than family tradition; by female, dainty and in need of male assistance. Generally speaking, I am not offended by the stereotypes assigned to me, as our conversations ultimately refute many of them. For example, although young, I have faced many life obstacles, including domestic violence, divorce, poverty, the death of a parent, and health challenges, all of which taught me a great deal about life. I understand the usefulness of stereotypes to provide comfort in an unfamiliar situation; however, if we overlook the time to teach others about who we are as individuals, life-changing experiences will be lost and negative stereotypes will persist.

One specific instance of stereotyping, among many, happened to me while in Ecuador for an internship. I was at a family reunion of the hostess with whom I was living, and throughout the day I found myself isolated; everyone in the family interacted among themselves, not with me. I felt like a child looking in on a perfectly choreographed ballet—wanting to join but fearing I did not possess sufficient skills. At the time, I did not realize that I was being stereotyped by her extended family. Based on their observations that I was young and American, they deduced that I was not family oriented and thus not worth getting to know.

Twenty of us ate dinner that evening, and the topic of my impending return home surfaced. Someone asked me what I loved most about Ecuador. I replied that it was the strength and importance of family and went on to relate characteristics about their family to mine. As soon as my desire to see my family again became apparent, the discussion shifted to their notions about the values and traditions of the American family: how kids get "kicked out" at 18 years of age, how families move very far away from one another and never see one another, and how we never help one another. I told them quite a different story of family: that I live at home when I am not away at college, how my extended family lives within 30 miles of everyone, and how my mom helped me prepare for my trip. Throughout the night, we dispelled stereotypes by participating in mutual self-disclosure. For example, an aunt brought out a personalized calendar with pictures of her family and shared stories about each member with me as we flipped through the months. I truly felt like part of their family, and I still consider them part of mine.

Taylor and Porter recognize that people in countries different from the United States are brought up in entirely different cultural contexts where it is perfectly acceptable to categorize people into groups. In Europe and Canada, for example, people presume that

Figure 5.6 Often, White stereotypes of African Americans have been brutal and negative.

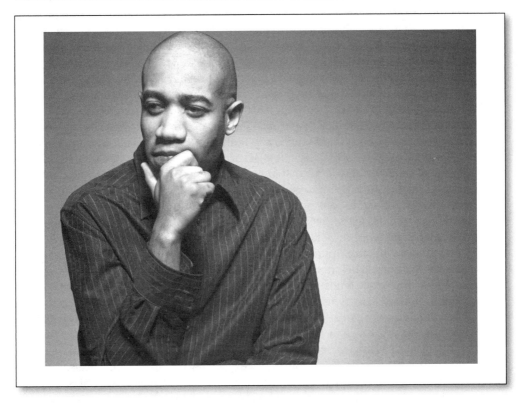

society is culturally diverse and are proud of their various group memberships. Taylor and Porter suggest that this philosophy contrasts sharply with the American melting-pot metaphor, which emphasizes cultural homogeneity. In other countries, the significance of cultural diversity is symbolized through metaphors that are very different from the melting pot, such as a mosaic or montage—that is, an assortment of people in the same place but not necessarily blending together.

Taylor and Porter claim that a fundamental feature of any pluralistic society is that ethnic attitudes exist between different groups, particularly in-groups and out-groups. Ethnic attitudes and stereotypes are a part of all cultures, and no one can avoid learning them.[51] In fact, research conducted by Trice and Rush indicates that stereotypes are well established in children's memories long before they acquire the intellectual ability to question or evaluate them. In their study of American 4-year-olds, Trice and Rush found that boys were significantly more likely to accept male-stereotyped occupations (e.g., police officer, truck driver, house builder) than female-stereotyped occupations (e.g., teacher, nurse, secretary). Likewise, girls were significantly more likely to accept female-stereotyped occupations than male-stereotyped occupations.[52]

STEREOTYPE CONTENT MODEL

For the past 10 years, professors Amy Cuddy and Susan Fiske have embarked on an extensive and extremely productive program of theory and research on stereotypes. They have created a model, called the **Stereotype Content Model** (SCM), that explains how and why people stereotype and the essential content of those stereotypes. Cuddy and Fiske maintain that the model is applicable across cultures and have presented convincing data to support their claims.[53]

At the core of the SCM is the thesis that individuals' social perceptions (i.e., stereotypes) about others are based on two judgments: (a) warmth and (b) competence. The model posits that people ask two questions upon encountering out-group members: *Do they intend to harm me?* and *Are they capable of harming me?* In the SCM, judgments of warmth and competence stem from two appraisals: (a) the potential harm or benefit of the target's intent and (b) whether the target can effectively enact that intent. Judgments of warmth are based on social perceptions of honesty, trustworthiness, friendliness, sincerity, etc. Judgments of competence are based on social perceptions of skillfulness, knowledge, intelligence, confidence, etc. When stereotyping, competitors lack warmth, while noncompetitors are warm; high-status people are competent, while low-status people are incompetent. While both warmth and competence are core dimensions in all stereotypes, judgments of warmth seem to be primary; that is, warmth is judged before competence, probably because judgments of warmth determine approach–avoidance tendencies (e.g., Is this person safe?). However, according to the SCM, when a person stereotypes someone, that stereotype is based on a combination of both warmth and competence. The stereotyped person could be judged as either high or low on warmth and either high or low on competence.

Cuddy and Fiske agree that some stereotypes may have some idiosyncratic content but that warmth and competence constitute the core of all stereotypes and are universal across cultures. The SCM model posits that some groups, perhaps many, will receive ambivalent judgments—that is, positive on one dimension and negative on another. Some groups may be perceived as warm but not competent, while others may be perceived as competent but not warm. To be sure, some groups may be perceived as warm and competent, while others are perceived as not warm (i.e., cold) and not competent. The SCM model proposes that warmth and competence judgments elicit one of four unique emotional responses: admiration, envy, contempt, or pity.

Judgment	Emotion
Low Competence–Low Warmth	Contempt (out-groups)
Low Competence–High Warmth	Pity (paternalistic stereotype)
High Competence–Low Warmth	Admiration (envious stereotype)
High Competence–High Warmth	Pride (in-groups)

In addition to these four emotional responses, judgments of warmth and competence elicit active and passive behavioral responses. Perceived warmth predicts active behaviors, while perceived competence predicts passive behaviors.

For example, admired groups (i.e., competent and warm) elicit both active and passive facilitation—that is, both helping and associating. Envied groups (i.e., low competent and cold)

Judgment	Behavior
High Warmth	Active Facilitation (e.g., help)
Low Warmth	Active Harm (e.g., attack/discriminate)
High Competence	Passive Facilitation (e.g., obligatory association)
Low Competence	Passive Harm (e.g., neglect, ignoring)

elicit both kinds of harm—active attack and passive neglect. The ambivalent combinations are more unpredictable. For example, pitied groups elicit both active helping and passive neglect. Cuddy and Fiske point to the patronizing behavior toward older and disabled people, who are sometimes over-helped yet at other times neglected. On the other hand, envied groups elicit both passive association and active harm—for example, when people shop at the stores of the out-group but then, during social or economic duress, attack and loot those same stores.

According to the SCM, the origins of perceived warmth and competence stem from larger social structures seen in all cultures, specifically competition and status. In all cultures, groups compete with one another for resources (e.g., jobs, schools, housing). In all cultures, groups are ranked within some social hierarchy (e.g., microcultures). Noncompetitive groups are seen as warm, while competitive groups are seen as cold. High-status groups are seen as competent, while low-status groups are seen as incompetent. SCM posits a direct link between the larger social structures, stereotypes, prejudice, and discrimination:

In testing the SCM, Cuddy and Fiske and their associates have surveyed diverse samples of people from across the United States. Participants in their studies were asked to rate a variety of social groups on both perceptions of warmth and competence. The rated groups included occupational groups, nationality, race, ethnicity, socioeconomic status, religion, and gender groups. Participants were not asked to rate the groups according to their own perceptions but, rather, according to how they believed others see these groups. Some of the results are presented below.

Low Competence–Low Warmth	Low Competence–High Warmth	High Competence–High Warmth	High Competence–Low Warmth
Welfare recipients	Elderly	Americans	Asians
Arabs	Disabled	Christians	Jews
Poor	Retarded	Irish	Rich
Feminists	Black professionals	Whites	
Turks	Middle class	British	
Drug addicts	Housewives		

The authors of the SCM claim its universality across cultures and have tested the model in several cross-cultural studies. In one study, respondents from 17 European countries completed a survey similar to the one completed by U.S. respondents reported above. The respondents completed survey items measuring warmth and competence of the various cultural groups (all the surveys were translated into the appropriate languages). The results were as follows:

Low Competence–High Warmth	High Competence–Low Warmth	Extreme High Competence–Extreme Low Warmth
Spain	Belgium	Germany
Ireland	Finland	United Kingdom
Italy	Sweden	
Greece	Denmark	
Portugal	Netherlands	
Austria		

Cuddy and Fiske also conducted a study including East Asian samples, arguing that Asian cultures tend to differ from Western cultures on dimensions of cultural variability such as individualism and collectivism. Specifically, they asked Chinese students in Hong Kong to complete surveys similar to the ones described above to rate social groups in Hong Kong.

Low Competence–Low Warmth	Low Competence–High Warmth	Mod Competence–Mod Warmth	High Competence–Low Warmth
Mainlanders	Children	Students	Rich
Filipino maids	Christians	Chinese	Professionals
Unemployed	Mentally ill	Blue-collar	
Immigrants	Elderly	Women	
Pakistanis	Foreigners		
Asians			
Singles			
College grads			
Hong Kong locals			

These researchers recognize that there may be any number of cultural differences that could challenge their claim of the universal principles of stereotyping. For example, as we have seen in this chapter, culture affects basic cognitive processes, especially categorization. Culture shapes the ideologies that seem to justify prejudice and discrimination against some groups (e.g., microcultures). As we saw in Chapter 2, cultural values vary considerably. Cuddy points out that some societies might not value competence and warmth as strongly as do other cultures. Finally, a culture's political climate influences how people perceive out-groups. In the United States, for example, Cuddy notes that political correctness might lead some to grant out-groups a positive stereotype.

To be sure, Cuddy and Fiske and their colleagues continue their program research on the SCM. They have produced considerable evidence that social perceptions of warmth and competence, driven by the social structures of competition and status, operate as universal dimensions of stereotypes. Targets perceived as warm and competent elicit uniformly positive emotions. Those lacking both warmth and competence are stereotyped negatively.[54]

Why Stereotype?

In addition to the logic provided by the SCM discussed above, there are other explanations as to why stereotyping is so common and universal, none of which relate to prejudice. One explanation is called the **out-group homogeneity effect**. The out-group homogeneity effect is the tendency for people to see members of an out-group as less diverse and more stereotypic than the members of that group see themselves. We have a tendency to see out-group members as highly similar (i.e., homogeneous) yet view ourselves and our in-group members as unique and individual. For example, students may think that all professors are the same. Likewise, professors may think that all students are alike. Yet neither professors nor students see themselves as "just like" all the others. The out-group homogeneity effect has been observed across a wide variety of different kinds of groups, including national, religious, political, and age groups. The effect is a theoretically important one because differences in the perceived variability of groups can cause differences in the stereotyping of those groups. Taylor and Porter contend that because in-groups and out-groups do not interact much, they may be unable to develop accurate representations of each other.[55]

A second plausible explanation for stereotyping, originally proposed by Hamilton and Gifford, is called the **illusory correlation principle**. Hamilton and Gifford argued that negative behaviors are numerically rare and when performed by microcultural group members—who, by definition, are also numerically rare—these behaviors become disproportionately memorable, leading to later impressions that microcultural group members are responsible for more than their fair share of undesirable behavior. Hamilton and Gifford point out that no prior expectation regarding the rare groups is necessary to produce the effects, just the unique memorability of rare-group/rare-behavior pairings due to their relative infrequency. Recently, Risen, Gilovich, and Dunning of Cornell University found evidence of one-shot illusory correlations—in which a single instance of unusual behavior by a member of a rare group is sufficient to create an association between group and behavior. As Taylor and Porter explain, when two objects that are unfamiliar or unusual in some way are observed to be connected on some occasion, we have the tendency to believe that they are always connected. For example, if we observe an out-group member participating in some atypical incident or behavior, such as a felony, then out-group members and felonies become associated in our minds. Then, the next time we see a member of the same out-group, we will stereotype him or her as a felon. The correlation between the out-group members and felonies is illusory or unreal because the out-group is now linked to felonies on account of only one, or relatively few, observed occurrences.[56]

Neither the out-group homogeneity effect nor the illusory correlation principle is necessarily wrong or socially "bad." Both are naturally occurring information-processing strategies that are a part of everyone's normal cognitive repertoire. The problem is that they may lead to negative attitudes and subsequent prejudice. If people understand their information-processing functions and are informed of these kinds of strategies, then they can become mindful of the process and ward off any potentially harmful negative consequences that may result.

Richard Schaefer offers two other reasons why stereotypes are so widely held by groups of people. First, he argues that stereotypes may arise out of real conditions. For example, a disproportionate number of people from a particular racial or ethnic group may live in poverty, so members of other groups stereotype all of them as poor or even lazy. A second explanation of stereotypes is their role in self-fulfilling prophecies. The dominant group in a particular culture may construct social or legal obstacles, making it hard for members of the stereotyped group to act differently from the stereotype. Hence, conformity to the stereotype, although forced, validates the stereotype in the minds of the dominant group. For example, members of a subordinate stereotyped group may have difficulty obtaining high-paying, prestigious employment because members of the dominant group refuse to hire them. Hence, they accept low-paying, less prestigious jobs and reinforce the stereotype.[57]

Henri Tajfel contends that another reason why people retain stereotypes is that they help us develop and maintain a positive self-esteem. Our memberships in various groups constitute a major aspect of our self-concept. Our social identities essentially are made up of our group memberships (e.g., husband, professor, colleague, friend, counsel). Tajfel asserts that our sense of esteem is nourished when we differentiate our in-groups from out-groups, usually by assigning traits (i.e., stereotypes) that are favorable to the in-group and negative for the out-group. Typically, we differentiate our in-groups on the basis of power, ancestry, religion, language, culture, race, or a whole host of other variables.[58]

According to Steele and Aronson, some members of stereotyped groups actually start to believe the stereotype. They call this phenomenon stereotype threat. **Stereotype threat** occurs when we sense that some aspect of our self (e.g., our behavior, physical characteristics, or social condition) seems to match the stereotype, making it appear valid. Steele and Aronson believe that stereotype threat is experienced essentially as a self-evaluative threat.

In related research, Steele, Spencer, and Aronson assert that whenever there is a negative group stereotype, along with a person to whom the stereotype can be applied and a performance that might confirm the applicability of the stereotype to the person, stereotype threat can emerge. Specifically, stereotype threat is the fear or anxiety people feel when performing in some area in which their group is stereotyped to lack ability—as in test taking, for example. Stereotype threat occurs because individuals are afraid of the implications of confirming the stereotype held by others.

In their research on stereotype threat, Steele and Aronson varied the stereotype vulnerability of African Americans taking a difficult verbal test. In one condition, the African Americans were told that the test was a valid measure of intellectual ability. In a second condition, they were told that the test was simply a problem-solving activity that was not designed to measure ability. Their results showed that African Americans performed worse than Whites when the test was presented as a measure of their intellectual ability but improved dramatically, matching the performance of Whites, when the test was presented as less reflective of ability. Steele and Aronson theorize that stereotype threat inhibits efficient information processing such as that caused by other evaluative pressures. Stereotype-threatened persons alternate their attention between trying to accomplish the task at hand and trying to assess their self-significance. This leads to reduced speed and accuracy.

Other studies have shown a stereotype threat effect on a wide variety of stigmatized groups, including women performing poorly on math exams, elderly people on cognitive tests, and people from low socioeconomic backgrounds on measures of intelligence. Stereotype threat is not limited to stigmatized groups, however. In recent related research, Frantz and her colleagues demonstrated that the threat of appearing racist led White students to perform poorly on a test that measures racism; that is, they received scores indicating that they were racist.[59]

In their recent research, Shapiro and Neuberg claim that stereotype threat can occur in a variety of ways, including as a threat to one's personal self ("What if this stereotype is true of me?"), one's group membership ("What if this stereotype is true of my group?"), one's standing as perceived by out-group members ("What if out-groups see me as stereotypic?"), one's in-group's standing as perceived by out-group members ("What if out-groups see my group as stereotypic?"), one's own reputation as perceived by in-group members ("What if my in-group sees me as stereotypic?"), and one's in-group's standing as perceived by in-group members ("What if my in-group sees our group as stereotypic?").[60]

In their summary of research related to stereotype, Shapiro and Neuberg note that women have been observed to underperform on quantitative tasks, in comparison with men, when stereotypes about women's math abilities are made explicit but not when these stereotypes are presented as irrelevant to the task. Similarly, Latinos performed less well on tests labeled as predictive of intelligence. But Shapiro and Neuberg maintain that stereotype threat is situational and can emerge in any situation in which negative stereotypes about one's group membership are perceived to apply. They point out that membership in a group with relatively low status (e.g., microcultural groups) is not a prerequisite for the experience of stereotype threat. For example, White men may experience stereotype threat in math performance when Asians' superior mathematical ability is made salient.[61]

Stereotypes and Expectations

Although evidence suggests that stereotyping may be independent of one's attitudes about others, some studies have demonstrated that stereotypes distort social perception of others. Human perception is not necessarily accurate and honest. Perception is influenced by one's needs, wishes, and expectations. In many cases, people perceive what they expect to perceive, regardless of reality. Figure 5.7 is a popular illustration of how expectations affect perception. Most read the words in the triangle as "Paris in the spring," failing to notice the duplication of the word *the*. By definition, stereotyping

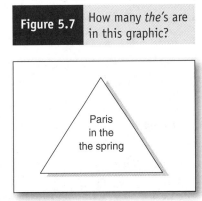

Figure 5.7 How many *the*'s are in this graphic?

Paris
in the
the spring

is categorizing people according to some easily identifiable characteristic and then attributing to them qualities or behaviors believed to be typical of members of that classification. In this sense, stereotyping leads to expectations that, in turn, affect our social perception of others. In what is now considered a classic experiment, Bruner and Goodman found that persons of lower socioeconomic status tended to accentuate the size of coins.[62]

In related research, Duncan found that perceptions of an ambiguously aggressive act are strongly influenced by racial stereotypes. In his study, White male college students coded the behaviors observed in what they thought was a live conversation displayed on a television monitor. The conversation ended with an ambiguous shove. Approximately half of the students witnessed a Black actor shove another person, whereas the other half observed the identical act by a White actor. Of the 48 observers, 35 coded the shove as violent behavior when it was performed by a Black actor, yet only 6 of the 48 observers coded the identical act as violent behavior when it was performed by a White actor. Duncan argued that because of stereotypes associating Blacks with violence, the violent behavior category is cognitively more accessible to observers viewing a Black perpetrator than to those viewing a White one.[63]

The results of Duncan's study were replicated by Sagar and Schofield, who studied Black and White sixth-graders. The students were shown a variety of ambiguously aggressive acts performed by Black and White actors. Both Black and White students rated the behaviors of Black actors as more mean and threatening than when the identical acts were performed by White actors. Sagar and Schofield argue that stereotypes create expectations and conclude that "in the existing social order, the stereotype is all too real. To activate it, the person engaging in an ambiguous behavior need only be black."[64]

AN INTERCULTURAL CONVERSATION: STEREOTYPING

Akira is an exchange student from Japan who is spending a semester at an American university. Jim is a student at the same university. Jim was born and raised in Milwaukee. Jim and Akira are meeting for the first time. Below is an excerpt from their initial interaction.

Jim: Hi. (Thinks to himself—"Man, he's so short, he's just like all the other Asians I've seen.")

Akira: Hi. I'm Akira. (Thinks to himself—"Wow, he's pretty tall.")

Jim: I'm Jim, are you a student here? (Thinks to himself—"He's probably a math major.")

Akira: Yes. (Thinks to himself—"He probably thinks I'm Chinese.")

Jim: Are you from Japan? (Thinks to himself—"He probably wonders if I drive a Honda. I wonder if he realizes how many Americans are unemployed because of all the imported Japanese cars.")

Akira: Yes, I am. (Thinks to himself—"What will he ask me now? These Americans are so impolite.")

Jim: Yeah? That's cool. How do you like it here in the United States? Have you been here before? (Thinks to himself—"He must love it here . . . it's got to be better than his country.")

Akira: I like it here a lot. (Thinks to himself—"I'd better not tell him that the food here is horrible. It might upset him.")

In this brief exchange, both Jim and Akira engage in categorization and stereotyping. Initially, Jim categorizes Akira based on conspicuous differences ("Man, he's short"). Jim seems to experience the out-group homogeneity effect ("He's just like all the other Asians I've seen") and the illusory correlation principle ("He's probably a math major"), and he tries to enhance his in-group's self-esteem ("I wonder if he realizes how many Americans are unemployed because of all the imported Japanese cars"). Akira categorizes and stereotypes Jim in much the same way.

ETHNOCENTRISM

One of the central concepts in understanding out-group attitudes and intergroup relations is ethnocentrism. Sumner originally defined ethnocentrism as "the technical name for this view of things in which one's own group is the center of everything, and all others are scaled and rated with reference to it."[65] Many scholars maintain that ethnocentricity is a natural condition and that most peoples of the world do not like foreigners and openly display feelings of hostility and fear toward them.[66] At the core of **ethnocentrism**, asserts Segall, is the tendency for any people to put their own group in a position of centrality and worth while creating and reinforcing negative attitudes and behaviors toward out-groups.[67] As Dutch sociologist Geert Hofstede argues, ethnocentrism is to a people what egocentrism is to an individual.[68] The term comes from the Greek words *ethnos,* which refers to nation, and *kentron,* which refers to center.[69] Neuliep and McCroskey assert, however, that the term can also be applied to an ethnic or microcultural group within a country. Similar views can be held based on religion (e.g., Judaism is the only true religion) or a region of origin (e.g., Texans are the only real Americans).[70]

Ethnocentric persons hold attitudes and behaviors toward in-groups that are different from their attitudes and behaviors toward out-groups. Specifically, the attitudes and behaviors of ethnocentric persons are biased in favor of the in-group, often at the expense of the out-group. Although ethnocentrism is generally thought to be a negative trait, it fosters in-group survival, solidarity, conformity, cooperation, loyalty, and effectiveness. In his seminal work, Levinson argued that ethnocentrism is

> based on a pervasive and rigid in-group–out-group distinction; it involves
> stereotyped, negative imagery and hostile attitudes regarding out-groups,
> stereotyped positive imagery and submissive attitudes regarding in-groups, and a
> hierarchical, authoritarian view of group interaction in which in-groups are rightly
> dominant, out-groups subordinate.[71]

In related research, Taylor and Jaggi introduced a phenomenon called **ethnocentric attributional bias**. In his research, Pettigrew referred to this phenomenon as the *ultimate attribution error.* Both labels refer to the idea that when people perceive what they regard as some negative act performed by a member of an out-group, they attribute such behavior to some internal disposition possessed by the out-group member (e.g., he's lazy, he's a thief). Yet when people perceive what they regard as a positive act performed by members of an out-group, they attribute such behavior to situational factors (e.g., she got lucky). Conversely, when people perceive what they regard as some negative act performed by a member of an in-group, they attribute such behavior to situational factors (e.g., it's not his fault). And when people perceive what they regard as a positive act performed by members of an in-group, they attribute such behavior to dispositional factors (e.g., she's so smart).[72]

A Contemporary Conceptualization of Ethnocentrism

Neuliep and McCroskey have offered a contemporary conceptualization of ethnocentrism. We argue that ethnocentrism should be viewed along a continuum—that everyone is, to some extent, ethnocentric. As newborns, humans are entirely, and naturally, egocentric. Eventually, we develop an awareness of others around us. By age 2 or 3, we engage in social perspective taking of those most central to us. These people, our biological or adopted families, are the center of our universe. As we become socialized, we observe that our families coexist with other families and that this culmination of people constitutes some form of neighborhood, clan, tribe, community, city, society, and finally culture. By the time we realize that we are a part of some much larger whole, we are officially enculturated and ethnocentric.[73]

Ethnocentrism is essentially descriptive, not necessarily pejorative. On one end of the continuum, ethnocentrism may serve a valuable function when one's central group is under actual attack or threat of attack. Ethnocentrism forms the basis for patriotism and the willingness to sacrifice for one's central group. On the other end of the continuum, the tendency for people to see their own way as the only right way can be dangerous and lead to pathological forms of ethnocentrism that result in prejudice, discrimination, and even ethnic cleansing (see Figure 5.8).[74]

To the extent that humans are ethnocentric, we tend to view other cultures (and microcultures) from our own cultural vantage point. That is, our culture is the standard by which we evaluate other cultures and the people from those cultures. Most deviations from that standard are viewed negatively and will be used as evidence of the inferiority of people from the other culture.

Ethnocentrism, Intercultural Communication, and Interpersonal Perception

Ethnocentrism negatively influences intercultural communication. Gudykunst points out that one's cultural orientation acts as a filter for processing incoming and outgoing verbal and nonverbal messages. To this extent, all intercultural exchanges are necessarily, to a greater or lesser degree, charged with ethnocentrism.[75] Indeed, most cross-cultural researchers recognize that human communication is replete with cultural noise that interferes with the transmission of information. Guan points out that ethnocentrism leads to "self-centered dialogue" where interactants use their own cultural standards to evaluate and communicate with others.[76]

Figure 5.8 Ethnocentrism Continuum

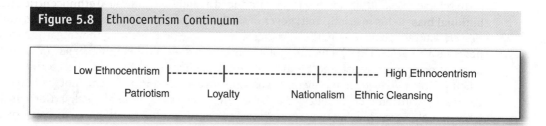

Gudykunst and Kim assert that high levels of ethnocentrism are dysfunctional with respect to intercultural communication and expand on Peng's concept of communicative distance and Lukens's concept of ethnocentric speech.[77] Peng alleges that ethnocentric attitudes are reflected in linguistic diversity and create communicative distance between interactants that manifests itself in the expressions, idioms, and words of the speakers.[78] Lukens claims that ethnocentric speech results in three types of communicative distance: indifference, avoidance, and disparagement.[79] The distance of indifference is communicated in speech patterns such as talking loudly and slowly to a nonnative speaker of the language, including exaggerated pronunciation and simplification. The communicative distance of indifference is also communicated in such expressions as "Jew them down," "top of the totem pole," and "the blind leading the blind." The distance of avoidance communicates that the speaker prefers to minimize or avoid contact with persons from other cultures through the use of in-group jargon or slang that members of other cultures or out-groups do not understand. The distance of disparagement is meant to openly express contempt for persons of different cultures and is communicated through ethnophaulisms such as "nigger," "nip," "chink," and so on.[80]

Neuliep and McCroskey contend that ethnocentrism acts as a perceptual filter that affects not only the perceptions of verbal and nonverbal messages but also perceptions of their source. For the most part, we tend to initiate and maintain communication with those to whom we are attracted. When we interact with someone from another culture, however, our perception of the other's attractiveness is affected by our degree of ethnocentrism.

Moreover, many studies indicate that perceived similarity is related to attraction. Thus, if we perceive someone as similar to ourselves, we are more likely to be attracted to that person. But, by definition, ethnocentrics perceive themselves as dissimilar to out-groups. Specifically, ethnocentrics perceive themselves as superior to out-groups (e.g., ethnic/racial groups). Hence, when interacting with people from a different culture or ethnicity, high ethnocentrics are likely to perceive out-group members as less attractive than in-group members. Judgment of another's credibility is also affected by ethnocentrism. Persons are thought to be credible to the degree that they are perceived to be informed, qualified, trained, intelligent, trustworthy, and so on. However, because they see themselves as superior, ethnocentrics tend to judge out-group members as less competent, less honest, less trustworthy, and so on.[81]

Ethnocentrism and Communication in the Workplace

The effects of ethnocentrism are manifest in any social context, including organizational environments where persons of different cultural backgrounds interact in the workplace. In their research, Neuliep, Hintz, and McCroskey investigated the effects of ethnocentrism in an employment interview. In their study, U.S. students watched a videotape of a Korean national student being interviewed for a job in the financial aid office of her U.S. college. The students then completed measures of ethnocentrism, interpersonal attraction, and credibility, and they were asked to give a hiring recommendation. Their results showed that ethnocentrism was negatively and significantly correlated with perceptions of social attraction, competence, character, and hiring recommendations.[82] Their results are consistent with House, who reports that cultural or ethnic similarity, or both, between interviewee and interviewer may play a role in hiring decisions. House maintains that interviewers are more likely to hire people with whom they feel they have the most in common (e.g., culture or ethnicity). This effect may be enhanced by ethnocentrism.[83]

In additional research, Neuliep, Hintz, and McCroskey investigated the effects of ethnocentrism on manager–subordinate communication. In this study, participants watched a video of an Asian student manager reprimanding a White student worker. A different group of participants watched a nearly identical video of a White student manager reprimanding the same White student worker (the same scripts were used for both videos). After watching the video, each group of participants completed measures of ethnocentrism, interpersonal attraction, credibility, attitudes about the manager, and managerial effectiveness. For the group of participants who watched the Asian student manager reprimanding the White student worker, ethnocentrism was negatively and significantly correlated with perceptions of the manager's physical, social, and task attraction and competence as well as general attitudes about the manager. For the group of participants who watched the White student manager, there were no significant correlations between ethnocentrism and any of the other variables.[84]

The implications of these results are significant. In an increasingly diverse workplace, managers and subordinates of different cultures and ethnicities are likely to find themselves interacting together. To the extent that such interactants are ethnocentric, interpersonal perceptions and communication will be influenced negatively. In addition to providing leadership functions, one of the primary functions of management, in any organization, is performance appraisal of subordinates. The results of this study suggest that in cases where managers and subordinates are of different cultures or ethnicities, subordinate ethnocentrism may interfere with the interpretation of managerial appraisals. If ethnocentric subordinates perceive managers of different cultures/ethnicities to be less attractive, less competent, and less credible, they may be less likely to accept their appraisal and any of the recommendations contained therein. Moreover, the position of an effective manager is one that fosters a certain level of obedience and compliance by subordinates. To the extent that managers are perceived as credible, subordinates are more likely to comply with them. As Neuliep, Hintz, and McCroskey found, in manager–subordinate transactions, ethnocentrism interferes with perceptions; that is, ethnocentric managers perceive out-group subordinates as less attractive or credible. Similarly, ethnocentric subordinates may perceive out-group managers as less credible or attractive.

Other research has found that the consequences of racial or ethnic differences between managers and subordinates are most clearly evident in performance appraisals. For example, Landy and Farr, and Kraiger and Ford found that African American and White managers consistently gave more positive appraisals to members of their own race. Manager or subordinate ethnocentrism may amplify this effect.[85]

Ethnocentrism and Racism

Although the terms *racism* and *ethnocentrism* are not synonymous, they are related. Ethnocentrism refers to the degree to which one sees his or her culture as superior and the standard by which other cultures should be judged. Racism refers to a belief that one racial group is superior to others and that other racial groups are necessarily inferior. To be ethnocentric but not racist is possible. To be racist and not ethnocentric is unlikely. In other words, you may believe your culture is superior to other cultures but not necessarily believe that your race is superior. However, if you believe that your race is superior, chances are good that you also believe your culture is superior. There is a biological component at the core of racist ideology that does not exist in the concept of ethnocentrism. Racist ideology is a belief in the moral or intellectual superiority of one race over the others. This superiority is biologically based. Because such superiority is biological, rather than social, it cannot be conditioned by culture or education. However, racist ideology asserts that racial–biological superiority does, in fact, translate into cultural or social superiority. Hence, a superior race produces a superior culture. Whereas racism refers to the hierarchical ranking of one race above the others, ethnocentrism refers to the strong preference for one's own culture over other cultures. Just as racism is rooted in biology, ethnocentrism is rooted in ethnicity and culture.

Racial groups are biological. Ethnic groups can be based on blood, common history, nationality, religion, or even geographic region.[86] In addition to their conceptual differences, racism and ethnocentrism have different origins. As mentioned previously, many scholars believe that ethnocentrism is a universal phenomenon that reflects a biologically rooted survival instinct experienced, to some degree, by all people in all cultures. Hence, it is thought that ethnocentrism is innately human; that is, we are born ethnocentric. Racism, on the other hand, is not universal and is thought to be learned. This begs the question, Why would anyone teach others to be racist? One argument, espoused by scholars from across a wide variety of disciplines, is that racism is the by-product of ignorance, fear, and hate.

Although slavery is not unique to the United States, in American history, racism is often associated with the forced immigration and enslavement of Africans. Because the U.S. Constitution was predicated on the tenet that all men are created equal, slavery presented a moral dilemma for the country. The enslavement and brutal treatment of Africans was a blatant violation of any sort of equality creed. But if Whites could define Blacks as biologically inferior, then they could justify slavery and practice it with a clear conscience.[87] Hence, the institutionalization of a flagrantly racist system of unequal treatment was established. Many political scientists offer a socioeconomic-political explanation of the causes of racism, frequently called the frustration–aggression hypothesis. During times of social, economic, or political stress (e.g., depressed economy, mass immigration), the dominant cultural group often will place blame on subordinate racial groups. Racism becomes a way of releasing the stress and frustration associated with difficult social, economic, or political times. In these situations, the dominant group often will act out its frustration against the subordinate racial group via prejudice and discrimination.[88] Racism, stereotyping, prejudice, and discrimination are often linked. When a racial group is labeled inferior, stereotypes emerge, such as those presented earlier in this chapter. Because racial stereotypes are often negative, people become prejudiced toward the racial group and discriminate against it. Prejudice determines how people feel or think about a particular group, and discrimination is the behavioral outcome—that is, action against that group.

CHAPTER SUMMARY

The purpose of this chapter was to describe and explain the psychological context of intercultural communication. Whenever two people come together and interact, they process immense amounts of information. Some communicative situations, especially intercultural communication contexts, have higher information rates than others and require the interactants to reduce more uncertainty than usual. Another important point of this chapter is that regardless of culture, human beings, for the most part, process information similarly. Although culture affects the types of information we process, all humans take in, store, and recall information in much the same way. Culture's role in this process leads us to make different kinds of interpretations about the information we process. All persons categorize, stereotype, and to some extent are ethnocentric with the information they process.

 Visit the student study site at **www.sagepub.com/neuliep5e** *for e-flashcards, web quizzes, web resources and more.*

DISCUSSION QUESTIONS

1. What are your initial impressions when you think about people from different cultures?

2. When you actually meet someone from a different culture, what do you remember about him or her?

3. Although difficult to admit, what are some of the stereotypes you hold about people from other cultures?

4. What are some of the stereotypes others hold about you and your cultural group?

5. Go back to Chapter 1 and review your score on the GENE Scale. Are you ethnocentric? Why or why not?

ETHICS AND THE PERCEPTUAL CONTEXT

1. You are having a party at your dorm/apartment tonight. What groups of people will you not invite because of the stereotypes you hold regarding these groups? Be honest.

2. The author of this book was once at a restaurant in France and asked the waiter how an item on the menu was prepared. The waiter responded in a gruff tone, "Well, you're an American. You know everything, how would you like it prepared?" How would you explain the waiter's response?

KEY TERMS

carpentered-world hypothesis   175

categorization   181

episodic long-term memory   177

ethnocentric attributional bias   195

ethnocentrism   195

illusory correlation principle   191

interference   178

long-term memory   177

memory   176

out-group homogeneity effect   191

perception   173

perceptual filters   173

semantic long-term memory   177

sensation   173

sensory receptors   175

short-term memory   176

stereotype   182

Stereotype Content Model   188

stereotype threat   192

REFERENCES

1. Polyani, M. (1958). *Personal Knowledge: Towards a Post-Critical Philosophy.* Chicago: University of Chicago Press.

2. Hofstede, G., Hofstede, G.-J. & Minkov, M. (2010). *Cultures and Organizations: Software of the Mind.* New York: McGraw-Hill.

3. Nisbett, R. E. (2003). *The Geography of Thought: How Asians and Westerners Think Differently and Why.* New York: Free Press.

4. This discussion of information processing is based on Lachman, R., Lachman, J. L., & Butterfield, E. C. (1979). *Cognitive Psychology and Information Processing: An Introduction.* Hillsdale, NJ: Erlbaum; see also Stillings, N. A., Weisler, S. E., Chase, C. H., Feinstein, M. H., Garfield, J. L., & Rissland, E. L. (1995). *Cognitive Science: An Introduction.* Cambridge: MIT Press.

5. Matlin, M. (2005). *Cognition* (6th ed.). Hoboken, NJ: Wiley.

6. Goss, B. (1989). *The Psychology of Human Communication.* Prospect Heights, IL: Waveland.

7. Berry, J. W., Poortinga, Y. H., Segall, M. H., & Dasen, P. R. (2002). *Cross-Cultural Psychology: Research and Applications* (2nd ed.). Cambridge, UK: Cambridge University Press.

8. Reuning, H., & Wortley, W. (1973). Psychological Studies of the Bushmen. *Psychologia Africana (Monograph Supplement #7);* cited in Berry et al., *Cross-Cultural Psychology.*

9. Wyndham, C. H. (1975). Ergonomic Problems in the Transition From Peasant to Industrial Life in South Africa. In A. Chapanis (Ed.), *Ethnic Variables in Human Factor Engineering* (pp. 115–134). Baltimore: Johns Hopkins University Press; see also Berry et al., *Cross-Cultural Psychology.*

10. Berry et al., *Cross-Cultural Psychology.*

11. Ibid.

12. Segall, M. H. (1994). A Cross-Cultural Research Contribution to Unraveling the Nativist–Empiricist Controversy. In W. J. Lonner & R. Malpass (Eds.), *Psychology and Culture* (pp. 135–138). Boston: Allyn & Bacon.

13. Ibid. See also Coren, S., Ward, L. M., & Enns, J. T. (2004). *Sensation and Perception* (6th ed.). Hoboken, NJ: Wiley.

14. Lachman, Lachman, & Butterfield, *Cognitive Psychology and Information Processing.*

15. Matlin, *Cognition.*

16. Ibid.

17. Miller, G. A. (1956). The Magical Number Seven, Plus or Minus Two: Some Limits on Our Capacity for Processing Information. *Psychological Review, 63,* 81–97.

18. Matlin, *Cognition.*

19. Tavassoli, N. T. (2002). Spatial Memory for Chinese and English. *Journal of Cross-Cultural Psychology, 33,* 415–431.

20. Howard, R. W. (1995). *Learning and Memory: Major Ideas, Principles, Issues, and Applications.* Westport, CT: Praeger.

21. Matlin, *Cognition.*

22. Wang, Q., & Brockmeier, J. (2002). Autobiographical Remembering as Cultural Practice: Understanding the Interplay Between Memory, Self, and Culture. *Culture and Psychology, 8,* 45–64.

23. Wang, Q. (2001). Cultural Effects on Adults' Earliest Childhood Recollection and Self-Description: Implications for the Relation Between Memory and the Self. *Journal of Personality and Social Psychology, 81*(2), 220–233.

24. Durga, R. (1978). Bilingualism and Interlingual Interference. *Journal of Cross-Cultural Psychology, 9,* 401–415.

25. Matlin, *Cognition.*

26. Howard, *Learning and Memory;* Lachman, Lachman, & Butterfield, *Cognitive Psychology and Information Processing.*

27. Matlin, *Cognition.*

28. Goss, B., Neuliep, J. W., & O'Hair, D. (1985). Reduced Conversational Recall as a Function of Negative Arousal: A Preliminary Analysis. *Communication Research Reports, 2,* 202–205.

29. Matlin, *Cognition.*

30. Ibid.

31. Rogoff, B. (1990). *Apprenticeship in Thinking: Cognitive Development in Social Context.* New York: Oxford University Press.

32. Ibid.

33. Yoshida, M., Fernandez, C., & Stigler, J. W. (1993). Japanese and American Students' Differential Recognition Memory for Teachers' Statements During a Mathematics Lesson. *Journal of Educational Psychology, 85,* 610–617.

34. Cole, M., & Gay, J. (1972). Culture and Memory. *American Anthropologist, 74,* 1066–1084.

35. Ross, B. M., & Millson, C. (1970). Repeated Memory of Oral Prose in Ghana and New York. *International Journal of Psychology, 5,* 173–181.

36. Harris, R. J., Schoen, L. M., & Hensley, D. I. (1992). A Cross-Cultural Study of Story Memory. *Journal of Cross-Cultural Psychology, 23,* 133–147.

37. Liu, I. (1986). Chinese Cognition. In M. H. Bond (Ed.), *The Psychology of the Chinese People* (pp. 73–105). Hong Kong: Oxford University Press.

38. Park, B., & Judd, C. M. (2005). Rethinking the Link Between Categorization and Prejudice Within the Social Cognition Perspective. *Personality and Social Psychology Review, 9,* 108–130; Ridley, C. R., & Hill, C. L. (1999). Categorization as a Primary-Process Cognition in Racism: Implications for Counseling. *The Counseling Psychologist, 27,* 245–255.

39. Rosch, E. (1977). Human Categorization. In N. Warren (Ed.), *Studies in Cross-Cultural Psychology* (Vol. 1, pp. 1–49). New York: Academic. (Quote on pp. 1–2.)

40. Gudykunst, W. B., & Kim, Y. Y. (1997). *Communicating With Strangers: An Approach to Intercultural Communication.* New York: McGraw-Hill.

41. Brislin, R. (1981). *Cross-Cultural Encounters.* Elmsford, NY: Pergamon.

42. Wilder, D. A. (1981). Perceiving Persons as a Group: Categorization and Intergroup Relations. In D. L. Hamilton

(Ed.), *Cognitive Processes in Stereotyping and Intergroup Behavior* (pp. 213–257). Hillsdale, NJ: Erlbaum.

43. Park & Judd, Rethinking the Link Between Categorization and Prejudice Within the Social Cognition Perspective.

44. Ridley & Hill, Categorization as a Primary-Process Cognition in Racism: Implications for Counseling.

45. Unsworth, S. J., Sears, C. R., & Pexman, P. M. (2005). Cultural Influences on Categorization Processes. *Journal of Cross-Cultural Psychology, 36,* 662–688.

46. Gudykunst & Kim, *Communicating With Strangers;* Schaefer, R. T. (2007). *Racial and Ethnic Groups* (11th ed.). New York: Prentice Hall.

47. Berry et al., *Cross-Cultural Psychology;* Taylor, D. M., & Porter, L. E. (1994). A Multicultural View of Stereotyping. In W. J. Lonner & R. Malpass (Eds.), Psychology and Culture (pp. 85–90). Boston: Allyn & Bacon.

48. Devine, P. G., & Elliot, A. J. (1995). Are Racial Stereotypes Really Fading? The Princeton Trilogy Revisited. *Personality and Social Psychology Bulletin, 21,* 1139–1150; Gilbert, G. (1951). Stereotype Persistence and Change Among College Students. *Journal of Abnormal and Social Psychology, 46,* 245–254; Gordon, L. (1973). The Fragmentation of Literary Stereotypes of Jews and Negroes Among College Students. *Pacific Sociological Review, 16,* 411–425; Gordon, L. (1986). College Student Stereotypes of Blacks and Jews on Two Campuses: Four Studies Spanning 50 Years. *Sociology and Social Research, 70,* 200–201; Katz, D., & Braly, K. W. (1933). Racial Stereotypes of One Hundred College Students. *Journal of Abnormal Sociology and Psychology, 28,* 280–290.

49. Devine & Elliot, Are Racial Stereotypes Really Fading? p. 1149.

50. Taylor & Porter, A Multicultural View of Stereotyping.

51. Ibid.

52. Trice, A. D., & Rush, K. (1995). Sex-Stereotyping in Four-Year-Olds' Occupational Aspirations. *Perceptual and Motor Skills, 81,* 701–702.

53. This discussion of the Stereotype Content Model is based on a number of sources, including the following: Caprariello, P. A., Cuddy, A. J. C., & Fiske, S. T. (2009). Social Structure Shapes Cultural Stereotypes and Emotions: A Causal Test of the Stereotype Content Model. *Group Processes and Intergroup Relations, 12*(2), 147–155; Cuddy, A. J. C., & Fiske, S. T. (2002). Doddering, But Dear: Process, Content, and Function in Stereotyping of Older Persons. In T. D. Nelson (Ed.), *Ageism* (pp. 3–26). Cambridge: MIT Press; Cuddy, A. J. C., Fiske, S. T., & Glick, P. (2004). When Professionals Become Mothers, Warmth Doesn't Cut the Ice. *Journal of Social Issues, 60,* 701–718; Cuddy, A. J. C., Fiske, S. T., & Glick, P. (2007). The BIAS Map: Behaviors from Intergroup Affect and Stereotypes. *Journal of Personality and Social Psychology, 92,* 631–648; Cuddy, A. J. C., Fiske, S. T., & Glick, P. (2008). Warmth and Competence as Universal Dimensions of Social Perception: The Stereotype Content Model and the BIAS Map. In M. P. Zanna (Ed.), *Advances in Experimental Social Psychology* (Vol. 40, pp. 62–150). San Diego: Academic Press; Cuddy, A. J. C., Fiske, S. T., Kwan, V. S. Y., Glick, P., Demoulin, S., Leyens, J.-Ph., et al. (2009). Is the Stereotype Content Model Culture-Bound? A Cross-Cultural Comparison Reveals Systematic Similarities and Differences. *British Journal of Social Psychology, 48,* 1–33; Cuddy, A. J. C., Norton, M. I., & Fiske, S. T. (2005). This Old Stereotype: The Pervasiveness and Persistence of the Elderly Stereotype. *Journal of Social Issues, 61,* 265–283; Fiske, S. T., & Cuddy, A. J. C. (2006). Stereotype Content Across Cultures as a Function of Group Status. In S. Guimond (Ed.), *Social Comparison Processes and Levels of Analysis.* New York: Cambridge University Press; Fiske, S. T., Cuddy, A. J., & Glick, P. (2002). Emotions Up and Down: Intergroup Emotions Result From Perceived Status and Competition. In D. M. Mackie & E. R. Smith (Eds.), *From Prejudice to Intergroup Emotions: Differentiated Reactions to Social Groups* (pp. 247–264). Philadelphia: Psychology Press; Fiske, S. T., Cuddy, A. J. C., & Glick, P. (2007). Universal Dimensions of Social Cognition: Warmth and Competence. *Trends in Cognitive Science*s, *11,* 77–83; Fiske, S. T., Cuddy, A. J. C., Glick, P., & Xu, J. (2002). A Model of (Often Mixed) Stereotype Content: Competence and Warmth Respectively Follow From Perceived Status and Competition. *Journal of Personality and Social Psychology, 82,* 878–902.

54. Ibid.

55. Judd, C. M., & Park, B. (1988). Outgroup Homogeneity: Judgments of Variability at the Individual and Group Levels. *Journal of Personality and Social Psychology, 54,* 778–788; Park, B., & Judd, C. M. (1990). Measures and Models of Perceived Outgroup Variability. *Journal of Personality and Social Psychology, 59,* 173–191; Rubin, M., & Badea, C. (2007). Why Do People Perceive Ingroup Homogeneity on Ingroup Traits and Outgroup Homogeneity on Outgroup Traits? *Personality and Social Psychology Bulletin, 33,* 31–42; Taylor & Porter, A Multicultural View of Stereotyping.

56. Hamilton, D. L., & Gifford, R. K. (1976). Illusory Correlation in Interpersonal Perception: A Cognitive Basis of Stereotypic Judgments. *Journal of Experimental Social Psychology, 12,* 392–407; Risen, J. L., Gilovich, T., & Dunning, D. (2007). One-Shot Illusory Correlations and Stereotype Formation. *Personality and Social Psychology Bulletin, 33,* 1492–1502; Taylor & Porter, A Multicultural View of Stereotyping.

57. Schaefer, *Racial and Ethnic Groups.*

58. Tajfel, H. (1978). *Differentiating Between Social Groups: Studies in Intergroup Behavior.* London: Academic Press.

59. Croizet, J. C., & Claire, T. (1998). Extending the Concept of Stereotype Threat to Social Class: The Intellectual Underperformance of Students From Low Socioeconomic Backgrounds. *Personality and Social Psychology*

Bulletin, 24, 588–594; Frantz, C. M., Cuddy, A. J. C., Burnett, M., Ray, H., & Hart, A. (2004). A Threat in the Computer: The Race Implicit Association Test as a Stereotype Threat Experience. *Personality and Social Psychology Bulletin, 30,* 1611–1624; Hess, T. M., Auman, C., Colcombe, S. J., & Rahhal, T. A. (2003). The Impact of Stereotype Threat on Age Differences in Memory Performance. *Journals of Gerontology: Series B: Psychological Sciences and Social Sciences, 58B,* 3–11; Spencer, S. J., Steele, C. M., & Quinn, D. M. (1999). Stereotype Threat and Women's Math Performance. *Journal of Experimental Social Psychology, 35,* 4–28; Steele, C. M., & Aronson, J. (1995). Stereotype Threat and the Intellectual Performance of African Americans. *Journal of Personality and Social Psychology, 69,* 797–811; Steele, C. M., Spencer, S. J., & Aronson, J. (2002). Contending With Group Image: The Psychology of Stereotype and Social Identity Threat. In M. P. Zanna (Ed.), *Advances in Experimental Social Psychology* (Vol. 34, pp. 379–440). San Diego, CA: Academic Press.

60. Shapiro, J. R., & Neuberg, S. L. (2007). From Stereotype Threat to Stereotype Threats: Implications of a Multi-Threat Framework for Causes, Moderators, Mediators, Consequences, and Interventions. *Personality and Social Psychology Review, 11,* 107–130.

61. Ibid.

62. Bruner, J. S., & Goodman, C. C. (1947). Value and Need as Organizing Factors in Perception. *Journal of Abnormal Social Psychology, 42,* 33–44.

63. Duncan, B. L. (1976). Differential Social Perception and Attribution of Intergroup Violence: Testing the Lower Limits of Stereotyping of Blacks. *Journal of Personality and Social Psychology, 34,* 590–598.

64. Sagar, A. H., & Schofield, J. W. (1980). Racial and Behavioral Cues in Black and White Children's Perceptions of Ambiguously Aggressive Acts. *Journal of Personality and Social Psychology, 39,* 590–598.

65. Sumner, W. G. (1906). *Folkways.* Boston: Ginn.

66. Lewis, I. M. (1985). *Social Anthropology in Perspective.* Cambridge, UK: Cambridge University Press; Lynn, R. (1976, July). The Sociobiology of Nationalism. *New Society,* pp. 11–14; Rushton, J. P. (1984). Genetic Similarity, Human Altruism, and Group Selection. *Behavioral and Brain Sciences, 12,* 503–559.

67. Segall, *Cross-Cultural Psychology.*

68. Hofstede, G. (1991). *Cultures and Organizations: Software of the Mind.* London: McGraw-Hill.

69. Klopf, D. W. (1995). *Intercultural Encounters: The Fundamentals of Intercultural Communication.* Englewood, CO: Morton.

70. Neuliep, J. W., & McCroskey, J. C. (1997). The Development of a U.S. and Generalized Ethnocentrism Scale. *Communication Research Reports, 14,* 385–398.

71. Levinson, D. J. (1950). Politico-Economic Ideology and Group Memberships in Relation to Ethnocentrism. In T. W. Adorno, E. Frenkel-Brunswik, D. J. Levinson, & R. N. Sanford (Eds.), *The Authoritarian Personality* (pp. 151–221). New York: Harper & Brothers. (Quote on p. 151)

72. Pettigrew, T. F. (1979). The Ultimate Attribution Error: Extending Allport's Cognitive Analysis of Prejudice. *Personality and Social Psychology Bulletin, 5*(4), 461–476; Taylor, D. M., & Jaggi, V. (1974). Ethnocentrism and Causal Attribution in a South Indian Context. *Journal of Cross-Cultural Psychology, 5,* 162–171.

73. Neuliep & McCroskey, The Development of a U.S. and Generalized Ethnocentrism Scale.

74. Ibid.

75. Gudykunst & Kim, *Communicating With Strangers.*

76. Guan, S. J. (1995). *Intercultural Communication.* Beijing: Peking University Press.

77. Gudykunst & Kim, *Communicating With Strangers.*

78. Peng, F. (1974). Communicative Distance. *Language Science, 31,* 32–38.

79. Lukens, J. (1978). Ethnocentric Speech. *Ethnic Groups, 2,* 35–53.

80. Gudykunst & Kim, *Communicating With Strangers;* Lukens, Ethnocentric Speech; Peng, Communicative Distance.

81. Neuliep & McCroskey, The Development of a U.S. and Generalized Ethnocentrism Scale.

82. Neuliep, J. W., Hintz, S. M., & McCroskey, J. C. (2005). The Influence of Ethnocentrism in Organizational Contexts: Perceptions of Interviewee and Managerial Attractiveness, Credibility, and Effectiveness. *Communication Quarterly, 53*(1), 41–56.

83. House, T. (2001). Equal Hiring a Must. *Computerworld, 35,* 32–34.

84. Neuliep et al., The Influence of Ethnocentrism in Organizational Contexts.

85. Kraiger, K., & Ford, J. K. (1985). A Meta-Analysis of Ratee Race Effects in Performance Ratings. *Journal of Applied Psychology, 70,* 56–65; Landy, F., & Farr, J. (1980). Performance Rating. *Psychological Bulletin, 87,* 72–107.

86. This discussion of racism is based on de Benoist, A. (1999). What Is Racism? *Telos, 114,* 11–49; D'Souza, D. (1995). *The End of Racism: Principles for a Multiracial Society.* New York: Free Press.

87. This slavery argument is found in a variety of sources. The sources used here are A Learned Behaviour. (1996). *Canada and the World Backgrounder, 61,* 4–10; M. T. Briggs (Director & Producer). (1987). *Ethnic Notions* [Motion picture]. Available from California Newsreel, Berkeley, CA.

88. Castle, S. (1993). Explaining Racism in the New Germany. *Social Alternatives, 12,* 9–13; Wolfe, C. T., & Spencer, S. J. (1996). Stereotypes and Prejudice. *American Behavioral Scientist, 40,* 177–187.

C H A P T E R 6

The Sociorelational Context

After reading this chapter, you should be able to

1. compare and contrast membership and nonmembership groups,

2. compare and contrast voluntary and involuntary groups,

3. define and discuss the significance of reference groups,

4. define and discuss the concept of group roles,

5. compare and contrast formal and informal roles across cultures,

6. compare and contrast sex roles across cultures, and

7. compare and contrast family roles across cultures.

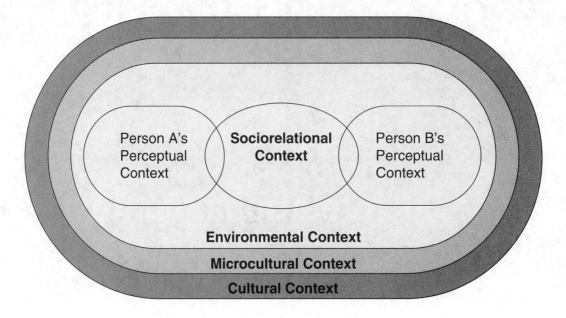

All human beings, regardless of culture, belong to groups. Although some cultures (such as that of the United States) promote individuality and independence, our survival depends on our interdependency and cooperation with other humans. This, of course, requires human communication. Historians believe that it was social cooperation, social organization, the initiation of group hunting methods, a system of distributing work, and our ability to share knowledge that empowered our human ancestors to survive when other related species, such as Neanderthals, became extinct.[2]

In many ways, intercultural communication is a group phenomenon experienced by individuals. In other words, when people from different cultures come together to interact, they typically view one another not as unique individuals but as members of a different cultural *group*. Think about your own communication experiences with strangers from different cultures. When you meet a stranger from a different culture, do you see that person as an individual or as a member of a cultural group that is different from your own? Even intraculturally—that is, within our own culture—when we meet strangers, we typically see them in terms of the groups to which they belong (e.g., sex, race, age). In fact, there is no other way to describe a stranger than by the groups to which he or she belongs.[3]

The **sociorelational context**, then, refers to how group memberships affect communication. Whenever people from different cultures come together to interact, their verbal and nonverbal messages are defined by, and filtered through, their group memberships. The social relationship they develop is significantly influenced by the groups to which they belong, hence the term *sociorelational context*. Although all people belong to groups, the nature of group membership and group behavior, especially group communication, differs considerably across cultures. The number of social groups to which a person belongs, the length of association with those groups, whether group membership is determined by birth or eligibility, and the purpose of the groups vary from one culture to the next. Our membership in groups represents the sociorelational context of intercultural communication.

The purpose of this chapter is to explore the idea of groupness and how social groups vary across cultures. The first part of this chapter focuses on definitional aspects of group memberships and categories of groups. The second part of the chapter discusses role relationships, social hierarchies, and stratification across cultures. The third part of the chapter looks at family groups, and the final part of the chapter examines gender groups.

DIMENSIONS OF GROUP VARIABILITY

Membership and Nonmembership Groups

Much of what makes each of us human is our membership in social groups. Regardless of our culture, we all belong to groups. For individuals in any culture, there are those groups to which they belong, called **membership groups**, and those groups to which they do not belong, called **nonmembership groups**. There are two classes of membership groups: voluntary and involuntary. **Involuntary membership groups** are those groups to which people have no choice but to belong. Examples of involuntary membership groups include one's age, race, sex, and biological family group. Obviously, we cannot choose our age, race, or sex. Although we may choose to interact or not with our biological family group, we cannot choose our biological father, mother, brother, or sister. **Voluntary membership groups** are those to which people consciously choose to belong. Examples of voluntary groups include one's political affiliation, religion, occupation, and to some extent, economic status, among others.[4]

Whether group membership is voluntary or involuntary varies according to culture. In some cultures, such as that of China, people may have little choice but to belong to a particular religion or political party. In fact, there may be strong sanctions for not belonging to a group. For example, Islam is the official religion of the Kingdom of Saudi Arabia. According to Saudi law, the public practice of any religion other than Islam is illegal. Hence, essentially 100% of the native population publicly practices some form of Islam. Christian worship services are sometimes broken up by police, and those responsible for hosting the services are often punished by lashing. Conversion by a Muslim to another religion is considered apostasy. Public apostasy (i.e., abandonment or renunciation of one's religion) is a crime under Saudi law and punishable by death, although such punishment is rare.[5] In stark contrast to Saudi Arabia, more than 130 organized religions exist in the United States, and a person can choose to belong to any one of them. As we all know, the U.S. Constitution guarantees freedom of religion.

Voluntary and **involuntary nonmembership groups** are those groups to which people do not belong. Some people may want to belong to a group but are ineligible to join because they do not possess the needed qualifications (e.g., age, education). In other cases, people might be eligible for membership in a group but choose not to join. The distinction is important because people who are eligible to join a group but choose not to belong may be more likely than ineligible nonmembers to accept and embrace the norms and behaviors of the group. Nonmembers may also differ regarding their ability and motivation to become members. For example, some nonmembers may aspire to membership, some may be indifferent, and others may be motivated to remain unaffiliated.

In India, people are divided into social classes called castes. There are dramatic social disparities between the different levels of the caste system. Laungani notes that since one is born into a given caste, it is virtually impossible to move from one caste to another. Usually, members of the lower levels are exploited and treated harshly. The four main castes, from highest to lowest, are Brahmans, Kshatriyas, Vaisyas, and Sudras. As mentioned, a native person is born into a caste and cannot leave it until the beginning of the next lifetime. Hence, one's caste level is an involuntary membership group, and a person is ineligible for membership in any other caste.[6]

In-Groups and Out-Groups

In 1906, sociologist William Graham Sumner introduced the concepts of in-group and out-group when he wrote,

> A differentiation arises between ourselves, the we-group, or in-group, and everybody else, or the others-group, out-group. The insiders in a we-group are in a relation of peace, order, law, government and industry, to each other. Their relation to all outsiders, or others-group, is one of war and plunder, except as agreements have modified it. . . . The relation of comradeship and peace in the we-group and that of hostility and war towards the others-group are correlative to each other.[7]

Figure 6.1 In the United States, racist groups such as the Ku Klux Klan are characterized by potent internal cohesiveness among their members and an intense hostility toward out-groups.

Based on Sumner's thesis, an in-group represents a special class of membership group characterized by a potent internal cohesiveness among its members and a sometimes intense hostility toward out-groups (see Figure 6.1). To be sure, however, earnest loyalty to one's membership group does not necessarily mean that you will feel hostility toward nonmembership groups or out-groups. Sumner's dichotomy of in-group–out-group animosity can be seen in cases of extreme nationalism. Nationalists are members of a group, usually ethnic or religious, who believe that their group should dominate and rule a political entity such as a state or nation. A nationalist state, then, is dominated by an ethnic or religious group. The symbols and laws of a nationalist state are reflective of the particular ethnic or religious group. Nationalist groups believe that political organizations within the state or nation should be ethnic or religious in character and may take extreme measures to see that they are.[8]

Harry Triandis defines an **in-group** as a group whose norms, aspirations, and values shape the behavior of its members. An **out-group**, on the other hand, is a group whose attributes are dissimilar from those of the in-group, or that opposes the accomplishment of the in-group's goals. Triandis maintains that in order to be classified as an out-group, the group must be perceived as threatening in some way to the in-group and be relatively stable, impenetrable, and dissimilar. An important point articulated by Triandis is that persons can be perceived as in-group members in one context and out-group members in another.[9] For example, a White American might view a Black American as a member of an out-group within the boundaries of the United States but see the same person as an in-group member while visiting a foreign country. Furthermore, definitions of in-groups and out-groups differ widely across cultures. In Greece, for example, family and close friends are considered in-group members, whereas other Greeks are out-group members.

Brewer and Campbell assert that the tendency to distinguish between in-groups and out-groups is universal.[10] As mentioned in Chapter 5, when we meet someone from a different culture for the first time, we immediately categorize him or her as an in-group or out-group member. Attributions about in-group and out-group members are typically biased in favor of the in-group at the expense of the out-group. Some theorists argue that in-group biases function to promote, enhance, protect, and maintain the in-group's self-esteem.

Others maintain that in-group biases function to preserve in-group solidarity and justify the exploitation of out-groups. Tajfel and Turner argue that the mere presence of an out-group is sufficient to provoke intergroup competition or discriminatory responses from the in-group. Moreover, the magnitude of in-group and out-group dissimilarity tends to intensify in-group biases. That is, the more different the groups appear (e.g., sex, race, religion, status), the greater the extent of in-group bias.[11]

Richard Schaefer points out that in-group bias can manifest itself in what he calls in-group virtues and out-group vices. The behaviors and practices of the in-group often are perceived by the in-group as virtuous (i.e., in-group virtues), yet when the very same behaviors are practiced by the out-group, they are seen as unacceptable (i.e., out-group vices).[12] For example, Christians may view the fervor with which they practice their religion as commendable yet think of Islamic or Jewish fundamentalism as unprogressive and backward. White students on some college campuses complain that formation of Black student unions and Black fraternities and sororities constitutes a kind of "self-segregation" of Blacks. Blacks, however, may label their behavior as "self-affirmation."[13]

Reference Groups

Another type of group that affects our communication and our relationships with others is the reference group. A **reference group** is a group to which we may or may not belong but with which we identify in some important way. A reference group possesses some quality to which we aspire and, hence, serves as a "reference" for our decisions or behavior. From time to time, we are faced with decisions about matters of which we know very little or for which we need direction. We may not know how to feel about a particular political issue or which way to vote in an upcoming referendum. In these kinds of situations, we often look to others whose opinion we value and trust to help us make our decision. For example, students often look to teachers for guidance. In this way, teachers are a reference group for students. Attorneys may be a reference group for law students. We use the group's position on an issue as a reference, standard, or barometer in developing our own attitudes. Reference groups can be membership or nonmembership and positive or negative. For example, in deciding for which political candidate to cast your vote, you may look to your political party (i.e., a membership group) for guidance. A law student, for example, might view lawyers or judges as a reference group but does not yet belong to the group. Usually, though not necessarily, voluntary membership in-groups serve as positive reference groups, whereas voluntary nonmembership out-groups are seen as negative reference groups.

Napier and Gershenfeld point out that reference groups serve two functions—a comparative function and a normative function.[14] We often compare ourselves against reference groups in making judgments and evaluations. For example, when professors return examinations, students try to see the grades of their peers in an effort to determine their own relative standing. If a student fails an examination but learns that most of the class failed, then she or he does not feel so bad. A failing grade has less impact if several other students failed as well. Individuals also use reference groups to establish the norms and standards to which they conform. For example, many students on college campuses dress according to how other students dress. Our reference groups influence our self-concept, our self-esteem, and our relationships with others. For example, in most cultures, children look to their elders as a positive reference group. The elders of the Masai culture of southern Kenya are an important reference group. Social power in Masai culture is based on age; this is called a gerontocracy. In the Masai gerontocracy, wisdom, insight, and sound judgment stem from age and are highly respected. The elders have moral and political authority, and the younger Masai age groups look to them for advice and direction. Through their age-based level in the hierarchy, the elders are the central reference group of their culture.[15]

ROLE RELATIONSHIPS

Whenever we join a group, voluntarily or involuntarily, we assume a role. A **role** is one's relative position in a group—that is, one's rank. Any group role exists in relation to some other role in that group. In fact, roles cannot exist in isolation; they are always related to some other role. You cannot be a son without a father. You cannot be a student without a teacher. Leaders cannot lead without followers.

With all roles, in all groups, certain behaviors are expected. A role, then, can be defined as one's relative position in a group with an expected set of verbal and nonverbal behaviors. By virtue of our membership in groups, even family groups, we are expected to behave in certain ways, usually according to some set of standards or norms established by the group. In your role as student, for example, you are expected to attend class, write papers, and complete examinations, among other behaviors. Within groups, roles are hierarchically organized, where some roles have more influence and prestige than others. In this sense, our role in a group represents our relative position or rank in the group.[16]

There are two types of roles in most cultures: formal and informal.[17] Formal roles have well-defined, and often contractual, behavioral expectations associated with them. The chief executive officer of a corporation, the president of your college or university, and the president of the United States have a clearly prescribed set of behaviors that they are expected to enact by virtue of their roles. Most fraternities, sororities, and academic organizations have constitutions or charters that specifically spell out the roles of their officers and members. In many cases, the person assuming a formal role takes an oath declaring his or her allegiance to the group and pledging a faithful effort to follow the expectations prescribed. Violations of such prescriptions are often subject to negative evaluation and even removal from the role. An important point about formal roles is that regardless of who assumes the role, the behavioral expectations remain the same. Formal roles and their prescriptions vary across cultures.

Informal roles are learned informally and are much less explicit than formal roles. Unlike formal roles, the behavioral expectations associated with informal roles must be mastered by experience and vary considerably from person to person and group to group. Your role as son or daughter, brother or sister, or even boyfriend or girlfriend, for example, is learned through experience. What it means to be a son or daughter in your family may be quite different from what it means to be a son or daughter in the family of your next-door neighbor. Informal roles and their prescriptions vary across and within cultures.

Roles and communication are integrally linked. Roles prescribe (1) with whom, (2) about what, and (3) how to communicate.[18] Because you are assuming the role of student, most of the people with whom you communicate include teachers, students, resident hall assistants, librarians, and so on. If not for your role as college student, you probably would not have communicated with any of the people with whom you have already communicated today. In addition to prescribing with whom you communicate, your role prescribes the topic of your communication. With teachers, for example, much of your interaction is about class-related topics and assignments. Finally, your role defines how you communicate, or your style of communication (see Figure 6.2). When you are interacting with your professors about class-related topics, you probably engage in a more formal communication pattern than when you interact with other students. You probably use less slang and perhaps speak more politely with professors than with other students. Although your role as a student is probably your most defining role now, the total combination of all your roles (e.g., brother, sister, boyfriend, girlfriend, coworker, son, daughter) defines your **social identity**. Your social identity is how the society around you sees you and hierarchically ranks you.

Because the nature and prevalence of formal and informal roles varies so much across cultures, the roles we assume in our native culture may not be practiced or valued similarly in another culture. This would include the roles we assume in our cultural, national, ethnic, demographic, and various other in-groups. Because roles and communication are so closely related, they must be considered cross-cultural; that is, roles vary significantly across cultures. For example, although there are probably teachers and students in every culture, what it means to be a teacher or student in the United States might differ remarkably from what it means in China or Japan.

Gudykunst and Kim argue that there are at least four dimensions on which roles vary across cultures: the degree of personalness, formality, hierarchy, and deviation from the ideal

| **Figure 6.2** | How does your communication style shift when interacting with persons in different roles? |

role enactment.[19] According to Gudykunst and Kim, roles can vary from personal to impersonal. Some role relationships are quite close and perhaps intimate, whereas others are distant. The degree of formality between roles varies from formal to informal. In some cases, our role relationships are prim and proper, whereas others are casual and relaxed. The degree of hierarchy refers to how strictly roles are ranked. In some cultures, there may be a very rigid hierarchical distinction between student and teacher, whereas in others, the difference is quite loose and flexible. The degree of deviation allowed refers to how much a person is permitted to deviate from the prescribed role expectation without significant negative sanction.

The roles of teacher and student in the United States and Korea illustrate how Gudykunst and Kim's four dimensions can be applied. In Korea, an old adage states, "One should not step even on the shadow of one's teacher." This expression, emphasizing the degree of respect accorded teachers, has been a guiding tenet in Korean education for years. Social order in Korea is based on Confucianism, whose central axiom is obedience to superiors. At just about any type of social gathering, who greets whom first, who sits where, who sits first, who speaks first, and so on are of utmost importance. In Korea, special care must be taken not to upset the social order, for to do so is interpreted as uncouth and lacking in social decorum. In Korea, the recognition of one's place in the social hierarchy is communicated via special vocabularies. These vocabularies consist of particular terms and phrases for addressing one who is superior, equal, or of lower status.[20]

In the United States, most students respect their teachers but do not recognize strict adherence to formality and hierarchy to the degree seen in Korea. In Korea, the student/teacher role relationship is quite proper and formal and the communication is scripted. Similarly, the difference in rank between Korean student and teacher is strict and recognized. On the other hand, the student/teacher role relationship in the United States is more personal and usually allows for more deviation from the ideal role prescription. Students and teacher can interact informally and may even engage in activities outside the formal classroom. On the four role dimensions outlined by Gudykunst and Kim, we can see where the student/teacher role relationship might fall in both cultures (see Figure 6.3). In most cases, the student/teacher relationship in Korea is less personal, more formal, and more hierarchical, with less room for deviation from the ideal role enactment than in the United States.

| Figure 6.3 | Four Dimensions of Cross-Cultural Role Variation |

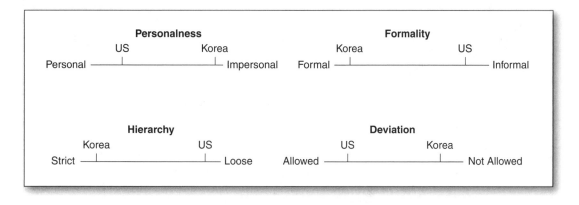

AN INTERCULTURAL CONVERSATION:
STUDENT/TEACHER ROLE POSITIONS

Because roles prescribe with whom, about what, and how people communicate, differences in the four role dimensions manifest themselves in communication. On page 214 there are two cross-cultural interactions between a student and a teacher. Scenario A is between a student and a teacher in the United States. Scenario B is between a student and a teacher in Korea. Note the differences in formality and personalness and the degree to which the students recognize the hierarchical difference between themselves and the teacher. In each case, the student wishes to speak to the teacher about an assignment.

The conversation between Jeff and Dr. Neuliep is generally smooth and coordinated. The situation is informal enough that Jeff shows up unannounced, without an appointment. Jeff uses informal dialect (e.g., "havin,'" "ya") and refers to Dr. Neuliep as "Dr. N.," demonstrating a degree of personalness. Dr. Neuliep invites Jeff to sit down, reducing the hierarchical distance between them. Generally, their conversation, though perfectly respectful, is informal. In Scenario B, Mino has set up an appointment with Dr. Choi prior to the meeting, shows up at the appointed time, and asks permission to enter the office. The conversation is rather formal and impersonal. Mino does not engage in any slang or informal vocabulary, does not sit down, and keeps the conversation as short as possible. Unlike Jeff, Mino is prepared to state his choice of subject. To ask the professor for a suggestion, as Jeff did in Scenario A, would be impertinent in Korean culture, where responsibility rests entirely on the student.

Role Differentiation and Stratification

As mentioned earlier, whenever we assume a role in a group, that role represents our rank or relative position within the group. On a much larger scale, our roles are ranked by our culture as well. Some roles are at the top of the hierarchy, while others are at the bottom. In the United States, for example, physicians and attorneys are high-ranked roles, whereas used-car

Scenario A:

Jeff: (Approaches Dr. Neuliep's office unannounced) Hey, Dr. N., how's it goin'?

Dr. Neuliep: Hey, Jeff, what's up?

Jeff: (Steps into the office) I thought I would stop by an' see if I could talk to ya about my paper assignment.

Dr. Neuliep: Sure, c'mon in, have a seat. What are you thinking about?

Jeff: Well . . . I'm kinda havin' some trouble coming up with a topic. Do you have any ideas?

Dr. Neuliep: I suggest doing something that's interesting to you; otherwise, the assignment might bore you to death. Stay away from topics that have very little research associated with them. Also . . . you might try doing a search on the Internet. Sometimes you'll find topics that you might not ever have thought of yourself.

Jeff: Yeah . . . that's a good idea. If I find somethin', can I stop by and show it to you before I get started?

Dr. Neuliep: Sure, just stop by or leave a message on my voice mail.

Jeff: OK, yeah. OK, well . . . thanks a lot.

Dr. Neuliep: Sure.

Scenario B:

Mino: (Approaches Dr. Choi's office and knocks on the door) Good morning, Professor Choi.

Dr. Choi: Hello, Mino.

Mino: I am here for my appointment.

Dr. Choi: Yes.

Mino: May I come in?

Dr. Choi: Yes.

Mino: Thank you (enters Dr. Choi's office). I am here to approve my topic for the research paper assignment, as you requested.

Dr. Choi: Yes, what have you decided?

Mino: I would like to research the natural resources of northern India, if that is acceptable.

Dr. Choi: Yes, that topic is fine.

Mino: Thank you. Thank you for seeing me this morning.

Dr. Choi: Yes, you are welcome. Good day.

salespeople are low-ranked occupational roles. The rank ordering of roles within a culture is called **social stratification**.

Social stratification varies across cultures, and not all roles are valued the same across cultures. The complexity of the role hierarchy varies from culture to culture, too. Some cultures make relatively few distinctions, whereas others make many; this is called role differentiation. For example, a relatively undifferentiated culture might distinguish among only a few roles, such as family, social, and occupational roles. A highly differentiated culture may make numerous role distinctions, such as corporate roles (e.g., owner, vice president, manager, worker, retiree), religious roles (e.g., pope, cardinal, bishop, priest, parishioner), educational roles (e.g., superintendent, principal, teacher, senior, junior, sophomore, freshman), and military roles (e.g., general, colonel, major, captain, lieutenant), among others.

According to cross-cultural researcher John Berry and his colleagues, social stratification exists in a culture with a highly differentiated role hierarchy that is organized in a vertical status structure. As mentioned above, most cultures have some form of role hierarchy that distinguishes among high- and low-ranking roles. Berry maintains that cultural role differentiation and stratification appear to be related to the ecological systems among cultures. For example, nomadic hunter–gatherer cultures tend to have less role differentiation and stratification, whereas industrialized urban cultures are typically quite differentiated and stratified. Sedentary agricultural societies fall somewhere in the middle.[21]

Although it is impossible to generalize across every culture, many collectivistic, high-context, and large power distance cultures possess a relatively strict hierarchical role stratification compared with low-context, individualistic, small power distance cultures. Recall from Chapter 2 that, generally, individualistic, small power distance cultures believe that people are created equal and have inalienable rights. Collectivistic cultures, on the other hand, see people not as individuals but as members of groups. In these cultures, one's level in the role stratification hierarchy often is based on one's membership in sex, age, family, and occupation groups. In such cultures, one person is almost always more powerful than another.

Mike Keberlien points out that the Guatemalan Ladino stratification is vertically shaped, like a pyramid, with the wealthy on top and the poor on the bottom. Belonging to an upper class means owning a home and having land to work and rent. Members of the upper class have their own social in-groups, such as the International Rotary Club, to which only they are accepted for membership. Lower-class Ladinos are left to work the land. They are also the ones who attend church most often. The upper class, however, establishes the rules for what is considered socially acceptable. Interestingly, according to Keberlien, the lower-class Ladinos practice the values of the culture more than any other social class.

As mentioned earlier, the most notorious system of social stratification is the caste system of India. The caste system—whose origins date back more than 3,500 years—prescribes a strict and practiced code of conduct. A person's social status depends on the caste to which he or she belongs. Although deemed illegal 50 years ago, the caste system still operates in many parts of India today, especially in rural areas. Although the system contains literally thousands of subcastes, there are four or five generally recognized levels. At the top of the castes are the Brahmins. These are priests or seers who possess spiritual power. Next are the Kshatriyas—that is, warriors and rulers. The third level is the Vaishyas, or merchants. The fourth level is the Sudras, whose main function is to serve the needs of the upper three levels.

The Sudras are further subdivided into touchables and untouchables. The touchable Sudras engage in occupations that are considered by the upper three to be demeaning, such as barber, hairdresser, cleaner, water carrier, and so on. The untouchables—or as Gandhi termed them, the Harijan, meaning "children of God"—are workers who take on the lowest of jobs, which are considered to be spiritually polluting, such as sweepers, butchers, potters, and so on. Also outside the system are tribal groups (called *adivasis*) with unique ethnic, linguistic, and cultural histories.[22]

Because roles prescribe with whom, about what, and how to communicate with others, communication in cultures with a rigid social stratification system is very predictable. Verbal and nonverbal messages are prescribed according to one's role and rank in the social hierarchy. Accepted forms of address, vocabulary, nonverbal behavior such as eye contact, and social manners are defined for practically every social situation. When two strangers interact for the first time, much uncertainty is reduced simply by recognizing role differences. They need only to know each other's role in order to communicate appropriately. Although not exclusively, many of these cultures can be found in the East (e.g., China, Japan, India, Korea).

Many individualistic, low-context, small power distance cultures profess equality and minimize role stratification. In the United States, for example, children are taught that they are equal to everyone else. In fact, in many of these cultures, equality is legislated. Although role differences are recognized and respected, these cultures believe that a person occupying a role is a unique individual. In this sense, knowing someone's role provides only minimal information about the person. Hence, knowing one's role does not reduce as much uncertainty as it would in a high-context, large power distance culture. Many of these cultures can be found in the West, but there are certainly exceptions (e.g., Australia, New Zealand).

Understanding a culture's role differentiation and stratification is important for communication because special vocabularies exist for different roles. Klopf and McCroskey note, for example, that in Korea, the terms a husband will use to refer to his wife vary depending on with whom he is interacting. She is his *cho* when he is speaking to someone of higher rank, his *chip saram* when speaking to an equal, or his *ago omoni* when speaking to a person of lower rank or status.[23]

Communication problems often result when persons from different cultures do not understand or recognize the role differences between cultures. Many international exchange students may find American teachers rather informal and personal compared with their teachers back home. Students from Eastern cultures, for example, find an American teacher's use of humor quite strange, because teachers in their cultures would never act in such a way.

AN INTERCULTURAL CONVERSATION: CROSS-CULTURAL ROLE POSITIONS

In cultures such as the United States, Canada, and Australia, among others, people are accustomed to treating everyone else as equal regardless of sex, age, occupation, and so on. This can lead to misunderstandings when interacting with people who, in their culture's role hierarchy, are accorded special privileges. In the following cross-cultural interaction, Mr. Mammen, an East Indian living in the United States, has taken his wife and family to a nice restaurant.

When he arrives at the restaurant, he expects to be seated even though he has not made dinner reservations. Because of his social standing, he assumes that he will be accommodated.[24]

Because of his cultural role position, in Mr. Mammen's native culture, he probably would have been seated in the restaurant even though he did not have a reservation. In the United States, however, one's occupational role will not ensure any special favors outside that occupation. The host of this restaurant is simply following his culture's way of treating everyone—that is, equally. As shown in the illustration below, this has led to conflict and misunderstanding.

Mr. Mammen:	(Approaches the host)
Host:	Good evening, may I help you?
Mr. Mammen:	Yes, my wife and family are here for dinner.
Host:	Certainly, your name please?
Mr. Mammen:	I am Mr. Mammen.
Host:	I'm sorry, I don't see your name on our reservation listing.
Mr. Mammen:	I don't have reservations, but I can make them now.
Host:	I'm sorry, but this evening's dinner reservation list is completely full.
Mr. Mammen:	No . . . I disagree. This restaurant is not full. I see empty tables.
Host:	Yes, but these tables are reserved for those people who have reservations for this evening.
Mr. Mammen:	I will make a reservation right now.
Host:	I'm sorry, but the evening is completely full.
Mr. Mammen:	I can see that it is not full. I want to see a manager right now! I am here to have dinner!

Family Groups

All human beings, regardless of culture, belong to a family. One's biological or adoptive family is the first and probably most significant socialization influence on a child. The structure of the family and the degree of influence a family has on its children differ notably across cultures. The nuclear family consists of the father, mother, and children. The extended family consists of the nuclear family plus other relatives, such as grandparents, uncles, aunts, cousins, and in-laws. As a unit, the nuclear family is prevalent in most low-context, individualistic, small power distance cultures such as the United States, Canada, and northern European cultures such as England, Ireland, Germany, and France. Extended families are common in Central and South America, Africa, the Middle East, and throughout Asia, although trends are changing even in these countries. There are clearly exceptions to the above list, such as African American families in the United States, who have a cultural pattern of a strong extended family interaction and kinship network.

In collectivistic cultures, families are generally cohesive and well integrated. Familial relations are caring and warm but also hierarchical. The decision-making process typically is not democratic. The interests of the family group take precedence over individual family members. Familial role prescriptions are clearly defined not only within the family but also in the larger cultural context. In individualistic cultures, on the other hand, there is less emphasis on hierarchy and more emphasis on individual development. Family decisions may be more participative than in collectivistic cultures. Familial role prescriptions are open and may vary considerably across the cultural context.[25]

In the Hmong culture of Laos, the most important sociocultural groups are the family and the clan, both of which are headed by men. According to Katie Thao, the Hmong clan system combines social, political, economic, and religious dimensions and is the primary guide for Hmong behavior. Within a clan, each person has certain obligations to others. When one shares with fellow clan members, the act is returned. Clan members of the same generation (but of different biological families) will call one another "brothers" and "sisters." Although the bond is not biological, it is so close that marriages between members of the same clan are seen as almost incestuous, leading to the Hmong practice of clan exogamy.[26] In most cultures, the family group is the most valued society structure.

Familial role prescriptions, however, differ widely across cultures. For example, two important variables in understanding Korean family structure are family surname and Confucianism. According to Sungjong Paik, there are only about 250 family names in South and North Korea. In fact, more than half of the population uses one of five family names: Kim, Yi, Pak, Ch'oe, and Chong. One in five family names in Korea is Kim. Of all Koreans, 15% use Yi, 9% use Pak, 5% use Ch'oe, and 4% use Chong. In comparison, in many other countries, such as the United States, literally hundreds of thousands of family names are used.[27] Many Koreans believe that because of their common family names, they are descended from a common ancestor. Hence, many Koreans belong to formal family name organizations, called *taejong-hoe*. According to Paik, taejonghoe are rather formal organizations with head offices in Seoul and hundreds of branch offices throughout the country. Taejonghoe publish newsletters, award scholarships, and sponsor sporting events. Paik argues that taejonghoe exercise great influence on Korean social life. For example, one's social status is often determined by membership in a specific family name lineage. Moreover, Paik asserts that many politicians try to use their family names to gain political influence.[28]

As in many cultures, the family is the foundation of Korean society. Historically, and in traditional Korean society, family roles and social interaction were governed by patriarchal Confucianism. Kyung-Sup Chang asserts that patriarchal Confucianism prescribes a social structure of *authoritarian collectivism*. According to Chang, traditional Korean patriarchal Confucianism imposes a rigid hierarchy and inequality between different age groups and between men and women. Males dominate females, and elders dominate the young. In traditional Confucian families, children are socialized to conform to traditional gender stereotypes and are segregated by sex. Following the father, the eldest son has the highest social status in the family.[29]

Kim notes that in traditional Korean families, certain rooms in the home are reserved for communication. Men interact only with men in the outer room (*sarangbang*), and women interact only with women in the inner room (*anbang*).[30] Communication in Confucian familial relationships would require the use of a restricted code. In the United States, when speaking to a brother or sister, or an aunt or uncle, English speakers use the generic terms *brother, sister, aunt,* or *uncle.* Linguistically, one's age or status is irrelevant. In Korean language (i.e., Hangul), the relationship term used to refer to a familial relative changes based on the sender's and receiver's familial rank, which is based on his or her age and sex.

As in many cultures, family life in Korea is changing. Levande, Herrick, and Sung maintain that while filial piety (i.e., loyalty and obedience to parents, the elderly) remains a central value among Koreans, familial relationships between parents and children are changing from one of duty and obligation to intergenerational affection. Levande, Herrick, and Sung argue that Korean families are moving away from the authoritarian and patriarchal norms of the past to more egalitarian and reciprocal patterns of mutual support between generations. For example, younger Koreans, in pursuit of educational and occupational opportunities, are increasingly moving to urban areas. The effect has been a decrease in the number of multigenerational, co-residing nuclear families. For example, in 1975, more than 90% of elderly Koreans lived with their children. That number has decreased significantly to less than 50% in 2008. Such trends are observed mostly in rural areas, where elderly people constitute the majority of the population. In urban areas, such as Seoul, the capital of South Korea, 65% of persons 60 or older live with their children. The majority of these persons live with their married sons.[31] Kim argues that living apart does not necessarily translate into autonomy from parents. Korean sons are still responsible for the parents' well-being and are expected to provide emotional and material support for them. Kim maintains that, in contemporary Korean society, nuclear families are faced with the social dilemma of having to appear autonomous yet interdependent and private yet communal simultaneously. Chun and MacDermid agree and assert that contemporary Korean families still value connectedness over separateness. They maintain that in contemporary Korean families, children associate strict parental control with warmth rather than hostility.[32]

According to Tehmina Basit, the family group represents the foundation of Islamic society. Basit argues that obedience and respect for parents are repeatedly stressed in Islamic teachings. Mohammed Haroun maintains that, in Islam, the individual is not allowed to be just an individual who is free to do whatever he or she desires. Haroun alleges that any political or social system that makes the individual the basic unit of society does not take into account the natural bonds and needs of family. He says that the most *natural* unit of society is the family, and that in Islam, three factors keep the family together: kinship or blood ties, marital commitments, and faith. The traditional Muslim household is multigenerational and typically includes grandparents; parents; married sons, their wives, and children; unmarried sons and daughters; and sometimes an unmarried, widowed, or divorced uncle or aunt. Although Islamic teachings stipulate that men and women are equal, within the context of marriage, the man is endowed with authority over the woman and the family setting. Pels maintains that the role of the eldest male is that of patriarch; therefore, his authority is undisputed and paramount.[33]

Sex and Gender Groups

One group to which every human being belongs, regardless of culture, is determined by biological sex. Biological differences between males and females are universally recognized.

But like any other group, to be a member of a sex group is to assume a role—in this case, a sex role. And like any other role, one's **sex role**, or gender, is a set of expectations about how one should behave.

The terms *sex* and *gender* often are used interchangeably, but as Sandra Bem notes, the terms are not synonymous. Bem has done considerable research on sex roles. Like others, Bem recognizes that **sex** refers to the biological and anatomical classifications of males and females. **Gender**, on the other hand, is a social and symbolic creation that we learn through enculturation and socialization. Whereas sex is innate, gender is learned. In most cultures, however, there is a close association between sex and gender. That is, most cultures establish norms and expectations that they assign people on the basis of their biological sex. According to Bem, our sex role orientation (i.e., gender) is based on the extent to which we internalize our culture's sex type expectations of desirable behavior for men and women.

In most cases, there is a high correlation between biological sex and sex role orientation. In other words, most people assume the gender roles that their culture prescribes. We are taught by our parents, teachers, and peers how we should behave based on our culture's standards. Boys are taught to be masculine (however the culture defines it), and girls are expected to act feminine (however the culture defines it). Thus, when cultures recognize some behaviors as masculine and others as feminine, they are saying that the majority of people taking on this role should be male (for the former) and female (for the latter). Gender, then, can be defined as the behavioral, cultural, and psychological traits typically associated with one's sex. To be sure, as Bem notes, this is not to say that a person of a certain sex cannot fulfill the other role but, rather, that the characteristics of the person assuming the role are associated with that sex. Indeed, some people possess both feminine and masculine traits. These persons may be classified as androgynous, a term that combines *andro,* meaning male/masculine, and *gyne,* meaning woman.[34]

The value associated with masculinity and femininity seems to vary across cultures (see Table 6.1). In his seminal cross-cultural survey of more than 50 countries, Dutch sociologist Geert Hofstede asked participants to rate the value of masculinity. According to Hofstede, masculinity stands for a society in which social gender roles are clearly distinct. In masculine cultures, men are conditioned to be assertive, tough, and focused on material success. In these same cultures, women are conditioned to be modest, tender, and concerned with the quality of life. Hofstede argues that feminine-oriented cultures see sex roles as overlapping in some cases.[35]

The expectations and behaviors associated with masculinity and femininity can vary remarkably across cultures. In his study of the Sambian society of Papua, New Guinea, anthropologist Gilbert Herdt found that adolescent boys are required to perform fellatio (oral sex) on older men as a part of the initiation into manhood. Their culture believes that a Sambian boy cannot mature physically or emotionally unless he ingests another man's semen over a period of several years. In Sambian culture, such behavior is considered masculine.[36]

When people deviate from their cultural sex role expectations, they are often negatively sanctioned. Some researchers have argued that collectivistic cultures are more traditional than individualistic cultures and are more likely to punish persons who violate cultural sex role expectations. Recall from Chapter 2 that collectivistic cultures stress interdependence, prescribe clear role expectations, and value conforming to the needs of the group. Violating one's

Table 6.1 Countries and Masculinity Scores

Countries With High Masculinity Scores	Countries With Low Masculinity Scores
Japan	South Korea
Austria	Uruguay
Venezuela	Guatemala
Italy	Thailand
Switzerland	Portugal
Mexico	Chile
Ireland	Finland
Jamaica	Yugoslavia
Great Britain	Costa Rica
Germany (FR)	Denmark
Philippines	Netherlands
Colombia	Norway
South Africa	Sweden
Ecuador	
USA	

role prescription (including sex role) disrupts the harmony of the group. Individualistic cultures, on the other hand, value independence, self-expression, and the pursuit of individual goals over group goals. Promotion of an individual's uniqueness is common in individualistic cultures. Therefore, when an individual violates a cultural sex role expectation, it is likely to be tolerated more in an individualistic culture than in a collectivistic culture.[37]

Gender Stereotypes

In most cultures, men and women carry out different sex roles, yet there is remarkable consistency in how cultures view the roles of men and women. Beginning in 1990, John Williams and Deborah Best, professors of psychology at Wake Forest University, conducted a series of cross-cultural studies investigating gender stereotypes. Williams and Best asked university students in more than 30 countries to consider a list of 300 adjectives and to indicate whether in their culture the adjectives are more frequently associated with men, with women, or equally with both. The responses of the participants in each country were tallied to determine the frequency with which each adjective was associated with men and with women. A surprising degree of cross-cultural agreement was found among 100 of the 300 adjectives. The 100 adjectives are presented in Table 6.2. The countries surveyed included Canada, Finland, England, Italy, Pakistan, Malaysia, Nigeria, Singapore, India, Japan, the Netherlands, Venezuela, Germany, the United States, New Zealand, Peru, Australia, South Africa, and Brazil. Williams

Table 6.2   Adjectives Associated With Sex Stereotypes

Male Associated		Female Associated	
Active	Loud	Affected	Modest
Adventurous	Obnoxious	Affectionate	Nervous
Aggressive	Opinionated	Appreciative	Patient
Arrogant	Opportunistic	Cautious	Pleasant
Autocratic	Pleasure-seeking	Changeable	Prudish
Bossy	Precise	Charming	Self-pitying
Capable	Progressive	Complaining	Sensitive
Coarse	Quick	Complicated	Sentimental
Conceited	Rational	Confused	Sexy
Confident	Realistic	Curious	Shy
Courageous	Reckless	Dependent	Softhearted
Cruel	Resourceful	Dreamy	Sophisticated
Cynical	Rigid	Emotional	Submissive
Determined	Robust	Excitable	Suggestible
Disorderly	Serious	Fault-finding	Talkative
Enterprising	Sharp-witted	Fearful	Timid
Greedy	Show-off	Fickle	Touchy
Hardheaded	Steady	Foolish	Unambitious
Humorous	Stern	Forgiving	Unintelligent
Indifferent	Stingy	Frivolous	Unstable
Individualistic	Stolid (detached)	Fussy	Warm
Initiative	Tough	Gentle	Weak
Interests wide	Unfriendly	Imaginative	Worrying
Inventive	Unscrupulous	Kind	Understanding
Lazy	Witty	Mild	Superstitious

and Best also scored each of the adjectives in terms of its affective meaning (i.e., its favorability, strength, and activity). They found that the characteristics associated with men were generally stronger (e.g., *Tough*) and more active (e.g., *Robust*) than those associated with women but that the adjectives were equally favorable for both men and women. Williams and Best also concluded that the male stereotypes were more favorable than the female stereotypes in certain countries such as Japan, South Africa, and Nigeria, whereas the female stereotypes were more favorable in countries such as Italy, Peru, and Australia. They also found that gender stereotypes were more differentiated in Protestant countries than in Catholic countries.[38]

In a related study, Williams and Best surveyed 5- and 8-year-old children in 25 countries. In this study, the children were shown silhouettes of a man and a woman and were asked to select between the silhouettes which ones were described in brief stories. The stories were written to reflect the more important features of the adult sex stereotype characteristics. For example, children were asked to select "the person who gets into the most fights" or "the person who cries a lot." Their results indicate that the children in each culture showed at least a beginning knowledge of the adult stereotypes. The stories most frequently associated with the male figures were those involving the strong, aggressive, and cruel characteristics, whereas the stories associated with women were emotional, weak, and soft-hearted. Pakistani children seemed to show the most developed gender stereotypes, and the Brazilian children showed the least. In each country, there was a significant increase in stereotype knowledge when moving from the 5- to the 8-year-old children.[39]

SEX AND GENDER ROLES ACROSS CULTURES

The variability of sex roles across cultures is dramatic. But many anthropologists and some feminist writers contend that although the customs and practices with which women's subordination is expressed differ from culture to culture, the secondary status of women across the globe is one of the few universal cross-cultural truisms. No book or chapter could possibly describe all the sex role differences between males and females across all cultures. Discussed below is a selection of cultures and their sex roles, with special attention given to women's roles.

Morocco

Leila Hessini has written about women's roles in Moroccan culture and points out that Moroccan society defines physical space according to male and female roles. Private space within the home is for family and is considered female space. Public space, on the other hand, is male space. Women are to fulfill their roles inside the female space—that is, the interior of the home. Men fulfill their roles in public spaces—that is, almost anywhere outside the home. Men are free to sit in public spaces where women are not welcome.[40]

Both men's and women's rights in Morocco are codified in the *Moudawana*—that is, the personal status code, also known as the family code, in Moroccan law. The Moudawana spells out in no fewer than 400 articles the regulations of marriage, polygamy, divorce, inheritance, and child custody. The most recent revision of the code was passed by the Moroccan parliament in 2004. Moreover, this version allows women far more rights than ever before. For example, the preamble of the revised version of the Moudawana states:

One: Adopt a modern form of wording and remove degrading and debasing terms for women.

Place the family under the joint responsibility of both spouses, given that "women are men's sisters before the law" in keeping with the words of my ancestor the Chosen Prophet Sidna Mohammed, Peace Be Upon Him, as reported, "Only an honourable person dignifies women, and only a villainous one degrades them."

Two: Entitle the woman who has come of age to tutelage as a right, and she may exercise it according to her choice and interests, on the basis of an interpretation of a holy verse stipulating that a woman cannot be compelled to marry against her will: " . . . place not difficulties in the way of their marrying their husbands, if it is agreed between them in kindness." A woman may of her own free will delegate tutelage to her father or a male relative.

Three: Equality between women and men with respect to the minimum age for marriage, which is now fixed at eighteen years for both, in accordance with certain provisions of the Malekite School, and authorize the judge to reduce this age only in justified cases, and further, equality between girls and boys under custody who may choose their custodian at the age of fifteen.[41]

Among myriad other provisions, the revised Moudawana stipulates that marriage is a legal contract by which a man and a woman mutually consent and that the purpose of marriage is fidelity, virtue, and the creation of a stable family, under the supervision of both spouses. These changes are seen as revolutionary.

Dowries are still a part of Moroccan marriages. In Article 26, the Moudawana stipulates that a dowry is the responsibility of the husband. He presents the woman a dowry as an expression of his desire to marry her and begin a stable family. The dowry is to carry moral and symbolic value rather than material value. The dowry is the woman's property to use as she wishes, and the Moudawana prescribes that the husband has no right to ask her for furniture or anything else in exchange for the dowry. Moreover, the wife may ask for the payment of the dowry before starting conjugal (i.e., married) life. All possessions the wife brings with her to the marriage, including furniture and other items, are her property. However, if there is a dispute about ownership of possessions, the matter is decided according to general rules of evidence. If neither the husband nor the wife presents any evidence, the husband is allowed ownership of those possessions that men habitually use and the wife claims those possessions that women habitually use.[42]

Japan

Sumiko Iwao has written a fascinating book portraying the role of women in contemporary Japan. Iwao notes that the "kimono clad, bamboo parasol–toting, bowing female walking three paces behind her husband" is still seen in some parts of Japan. But she contends that the lives and attitudes of many younger contemporary Japanese women have undergone dramatic changes in the past 25 years. The postwar Japanese Constitution stipulates that all Japanese are equal under the law and outlaws discrimination on the basis of sex. To be sure, however, most private and political organizations that compose the dominant Japanese culture are controlled by men. But Japanese women enjoy more freedom today than perhaps ever in their history (see Figure 6.4).

Yet, as Ui and Matsui note in their recent survey of Japanese adults' sex role attitudes, a close look at Japanese society shows very few women in parliament or in corporate management positions. Ui and Matsui note that many women, much more so than men, are burdened by household duties and child rearing. In their survey of Japanese adults, Ui and Matsui

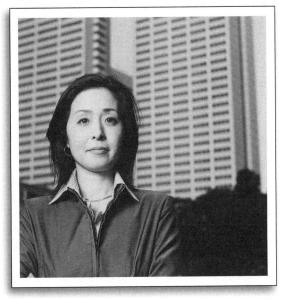

Figure 6.4 Japanese women enjoy more freedom today than perhaps ever in their history.

found that more women than men have egalitarian (i.e., democratic or classless) attitudes toward sex roles, and more men than women have sexist attitudes. Ui and Matsui also point out that such attitudes are linked to the age group being surveyed. Younger Japanese have egalitarian attitudes toward sex roles, whereas older age groups prefer more traditional (i.e., male dominance) sex roles.

To be sure, Iwao remarks that although today's Japanese women are much more outspoken and direct than their mothers, even modern Japanese women recognize their secondary status and have not completely discarded their earmark passivity. Moreover, when asked, many Japanese women acknowledge their fate as a subordinate group. Even the modern Japanese woman's happiness remains tied to her family, so much so that she will repress her personal feelings to an extent that many American women would find unendurable. Following their collectivistic histories, most Japanese women continue to sacrifice personal goals for the sake of the harmony of the family. Because they have fewer opportunities than men, maintaining interpersonal harmony is of the utmost concern for Japanese women.[43]

India

In his extensive writing on his native India, Pittu Laungani indicates that there are significant differences in the socialization processes of boys and girls in India. To be sure, writes Laungani, boys are privileged—so much so that in impoverished homes, of which there are many, a larger share of food is given to the male children, and they are also fed first by the family members. Laungani notes that the birth of a male child is considered a blessing because it ensures the continuation of the family name. Male children are seen as an economic asset and, when married, bring to their family a nice dowry (i.e., obligatory gift from the bride's family, usually money). The birth of a daughter, on the other hand, is seen as a burden. She is seen as an economic liability, and she never really possesses an identity of her own. Laungani has observed that while boys are pampered and accorded privileges, girls are raised on a strict regime. Girls are made aware of the role they are to play, where "verily is virtue and virginity venerated."[44]

Margot Duley has written about women in India also. According to Duley, the Preamble of the Indian Constitution guarantees all citizens "equality of status." Unfortunately, writes Duley, legal equality remains elusive for most Indian women. She argues that the subordination of women in India is primarily economically based. Most women work in agricultural jobs, but in the past few decades, India has developed a commercial market economy with capital-intensive production. Although laws favoring women's rights have been passed, they have not had much impact. For example, there are no uniform statutes governing marriage and inheritance laws. In most areas, there is a strong emphasis on purity and chastity of women. Most young women marry by the age of 17. The Dowry Prohibition Act of 1961 is largely ignored. The practice of giving a dowry has actually spread in recent years because of the overwhelming pressure on girls to marry. Women also have less access to education than do men, and women's literacy rate (25%) is less than half the rate among men. Only 13% of women enroll in high school. Duley writes that because of the large dowries required at marriage, daughters receive poor nutrition and healthcare and less love and nurturance than their brothers. Essentially, women are seen as an economic liability.[45] In some areas, female infanticide is still practiced.[46]

Saudi Arabia

Most Arab states (e.g., Saudi Arabia, Iraq) and Arab societies adhere to a patriarchal (i.e., male-ruled) social and political system in which a woman's position within and duties toward the family precede her rights as an individual. In September 2000, Amnesty International released a report that denounced Saudi Arabia for its treatment of women. According to the report, the situation for Saudi women is "untenable" by any legal or moral standard. The report contends that female domestic workers are often locked inside homes, beaten, and raped by their Saudi employers.[47]

Saudi women are not allowed to vote, drive a car, sail a boat, or fly a plane. They cannot check into a hotel without a male family member. They cannot appear outdoors with hair, wrists, or ankles exposed. They cannot marry, work, study, travel, or obtain identification papers without the permission of a male guardian. If a Saudi woman does work, with the permission of her husband or a male guardian, she may not work alongside males. Although many women pursue university degrees, Saudi women make up just 5% of the private work-force (most women are teachers). Moreover, women and/or their guardians are not allowed to postpone marriages for the purpose of continuing education.[48]

In 2004, Saudi's reform-minded Crown Prince Abdullah initiated a series of forums on women's rights in Saudi Arabia. Saudis are now actively debating the pros and cons of women driving, how the court system and divorce laws favor men, the high unemployment rate among women, and whether desegregated workplaces violate Islamic law. To be sure, many outsiders assume that Islam is the source of discrimination against women, but this is not entirely accurate. Some scholars argue, for example, that religious texts are often distorted to fit existing traditions. The ban on women driving, for example, is unique to Saudi law; that is, other Islamic countries allow women to drive. The Saudi custom of *ikhtilat* (i.e., the mixing of men and women socially) also has no religious justification.[49]

Egypt

According to the 1971 constitution, all Egyptian citizens enjoy a constitutional right to public posts without discrimination between males and females. In addition, the constitution guarantees the protection of motherhood, childhood, and the existence of a harmony between the duties of a woman toward her family and her role in society. Even with such constitutional rights, gender segregation is an integral part of social etiquette and class structure in Egypt.

STUDENT VOICES ACROSS CULTURES

Ala Aldahneem

When I arrived in the United States from Saudi Arabia, I was the first Saudi female at my college. The students, faculty, and staff welcomed me and took into consideration our cultural differences. At the same time, most of the people who first met me would ask questions about a woman's role in Saudi Arabia. They were mostly curious if it was true that women have no voice or opinions. Others would ask if it is hard to move to the United Sates due to the cultures being so different. As the conversations continued, people frequently asked if I wanted to go back to Saudi Arabia or stay in the United States. I saw many surprised faces when they learned that I wanted to finish schooling first and then go back to Saudi Arabia. I chose that because, in my country, I have respect and my needs will be guaranteed.

Unlike the stereotype that women are not respected and cannot make any choices for themselves in Saudi Arabia, I feel I have more respect than what many Westerners think—just like any mother, wife, or daughter in other families. Take the example of my moving to the United States. My family respects that I am a grown adult, and when I decided to study in the United States, they considered my choice and let me come alone.

These stereotypes are probably the result of some of Saudi's laws. It is true that many laws are restrictive toward women, such as driving or checking into a hotel without a male guardian. I cannot travel without permission. That is, I can travel without a man, but I must have the proper papers/permission to travel out of Saudi Arabia. I traveled with my dad the week I got married, but they did not let me go without his permission. However, it is not how it seems. Regarding driving, most families in Saudi Arabia have drivers who drive women wherever they want to go. Otherwise, the father or brothers are more than happy to give rides.

Another example would be checking into a hotel. I still remember the day when I traveled to Medina in the western part of Saudi Arabia. The receptionist told me that I could not check in without a male family member and that he was sorry for that. Because of the law, I was informed I had to wait for my family to arrive before I could check in and get comfortable in the hotel after a long day of travel.

Even though there are some restrictions on women, my life is guaranteed. I have a place to live regardless of whether I am working or not. My father or husband is responsible for my housing and other personal needs. It doesn't matter if women are rich, working, or poor. Therefore, in any case, I have someone who will be responsible for me with love and a family orientation.

Nemat Guenena and Nadia Wassef have written extensively about the changing role of women in Egyptian society. Egyptian women, together with children, represent about 70% of the population. According to Guenena and Wassef, Egyptian women have struggled for more than a century to establish their rights as equal partners with men. Their progress for equality has advanced as a result of numerous factors, including education, economic necessity, and significant political changes. Guenena and Wassef note, however, that the many advances women have made are contradicted by high rates of illiteracy, minimal political participation, declining representation in parliament, and the return to requiring of modest dress.

Regarding education, a significantly greater proportion of women over men are illiterate. Nearly 62% of females as opposed to 38% of males are illiterate. In addition, Guenena and Wassef note that boys and girls receive different kinds of education. Girls are taught home economics, whereas boys are taught agricultural economics—topics that are considered gender appropriate. Guenena and Wassef have observed that Egyptian media portray women and men in very different ways. Women are seen as mothers, wives, and daughters who are in need of protection by their fathers, husbands, and brothers. In exchange for such protection, women are required to submit to male authority. On the other hand, men are portrayed as wise, compassionate, generous, and knowledgeable about what is best for their women.

Finally, Guenena and Wassef note that women are not treated equally under Egyptian law. For example, the penalty for murdering one's spouse (upon discovery of adultery) is much harsher for the wife than the husband. Typically, men are given a prison sentence of not more than 3 years. Women are often sentenced to death or hard labor for life. Guenena and Wassef contend that this difference stems from the Egyptian attitude that a man's reputation is dependent on his wife's high merit. Consequently, murdering one's adulterous wife is excusable, especially if committed in the heat of the moment.[50]

Although rape in Egypt is penalized, forced or nonconsensual marital intercourse is not considered a criminal offense. One study found that 46% of Egyptian men believe they are entitled to force their wives into intercourse. Egyptian law also stipulates that husbands, but not wives, may physically punish their spouses in case of disobedience so long as no permanent damage is inflicted. In a recent study of how Egyptian women respond to physical violence in their intimate relationships, Kathryn Yount interviewed a number of Egyptian women. Her results are disturbing. She found that most of the women she interviewed blamed the wife for physical abuse, and most women recommended actually modifying her (i.e., the wife's) behavior to end it. Tolerance of abuse was the next most common reaction. Moreover, Yount notes, when tolerance fails to end the abuse, a woman might ask a male relative to mediate. Yount notes that most women felt that seeking legal action was shameful and would jeopardize the woman's marriage.[51]

China

In X. M. Wang's 1993 monograph, "The Storm of a Divorce," the husband of a female student in China says to his wife, "You're such a good person. You'd be an excellent wife if you weren't studying for your doctorate."[52] In a survey of 10,000 Chinese urban men and women, 92% of the men indicated that they wanted a wife who would be aggressive in her career, yet 96% of men desired a virtuous wife who would do most of the household chores. Nearly half the Chinese women surveyed, however, wanted men to share chores more and considered an equal division of labor as important for the development of equality between men and women.[53]

The husbands' sentiments are typical of China's long history of women having little freedom and few rights. According to Gracie Ming Zhao, for most of its history, China has been a feudal society in which the Chinese were under the dictatorial rule of an emperor. About 100 years ago, the Chinese overthrew that system, and about 60 years ago, they established the People's Republic. Since then, the Chinese women's liberation movement has made significant advances toward women's rights. Zhao notes, for example, that the 1954 Constitution stipulated the freedom of marriage and stated that every individual has the right to decide his or her own marriage. Moreover, asserts Zhao, the 1950 Marriage Law abolished all feudal forms of marriage, such as concubines (i.e., where a young woman is in a quasi-matrimonial relationship with a man of higher social status), polygamy, and arranged marriages. Zhao laments, however, that while the Chinese government has enacted several laws and policies that equate women and men legally and socially, they are of little use in abolishing the long-standing preference of males over females.[54]

In her research, Davin notes that Chinese are generally expected to live with their family circle unless there is reason to do otherwise and that such expectations are greater for women than for men. Chinese women, especially single women, are considered more vulnerable and less capable of dealing with the outside world than are men. Davin reports that women are seen as needing the protection and supervision of their families in order to preserve their virginity and marriageability.[55]

Within marriages, Pimentel points out, the division of household chores has changed in contemporary Chinese culture. According to Pimentel, fewer young women, compared with older women, take on the entire load of domestic work. Ironically, these same Chinese women are increasingly dissatisfied with the division of labor and less happy in their marriages. Pimentel suggests that the push for women's equality in the family has produced a backlash among men, such that younger Chinese men are actually far less democratic than their older counterparts. Chinese men and women seem to be growing further apart. Because marriage quality is linked to separation and divorce, the communication that Chinese men and women have within their homes is extremely important. Moreover, notes Pimentel, the road to women's liberation in China remains a long one. Asking women to achieve their own equality in a male-defined and -centered world has negative implications for men and women and the relations between them.[56]

Mexico

Celina Melgoza Marquez was born in a small town in Guanajuato, Mexico. In addition to her parents, she has four sisters and five brothers. Recently, Marquez published a book about the role of women in Mexico.[57] In it, she profiles the status of women and the advances they have made in contemporary Mexico. In terms of population, Mexico has approximately 110 million people, of which women hold a slight majority. Marquez maintains that the marital status of Mexican people represents the rights and responsibilities of men and women because it reflects the population's social levels.

More Mexican women than men are divorced, possibly because Mexican men tend to emigrate once they are divorced. Historically, the average marrying age of the population was 16 years old. However, by 1995, both sexes started marrying later, with the national average marrying age being 20 years old for women and a little more than 23 years old for men. The increase in age results from Mexicans pursuing higher education. Marquez says that a Mexican woman's childbearing rate is related to her educational, social, and economic conditions. For example, Marquez notes that in 1976, 5.7 children were born per woman. In 1986, the rate decreased to 3.8; in 1995, to 2.8; and in 2007, to 2.4 children. Today, Mexican women are more educated than ever. In the past 25 years, the literacy rate of the Mexican population has increased noticeably. In 2004, the literacy rate among men was 92%, and among women it was 89%. Marquez maintains that males and females used to have specific and separate roles. Traditionally, men were the providers and women did the domestic work. During the past few years, however, the roles of men and women have changed noticeably. For example, 35 years ago, 17% of women age 12 years and older worked outside the home. By 1995, that number increased to 35%. Today, about 42% of Mexican women are in the labor force.[58]

Although women now contribute much in the work world, they also contribute at home with the family. Nearly 93% of women age 12 years and older do domestic work. But, Marquez argues, men and women often work together to maintain the family. As a result, some men do domestic activities while some women work outside the home. Marquez notes that in Mexico, authority and responsibility are given to the father or to the oldest male, or *jefe*, of the household. Few women hold this position. Authority in Mexican society has been held by the men. Men are in charge of the family direction, and women take this responsibility only when the men have left home.

CHAPTER SUMMARY

Our lives are inextricably tied to our group memberships and the roles we play. How we see ourselves and how our culture treats us is based on the total accumulation of roles we assume. They represent our social standing in our culture. This chapter has focused on the sociorelational context of intercultural communication—that is, the group memberships we assume. All of us belong to any number of groups. Groups to which we belong are called membership groups. Some of these are voluntary, whereas others are involuntary. Voluntary in-groups often serve as reference groups, which help us make decisions about significant issues in our lives. The reference group serves as a standard by which we judge ourselves. As group members, we assume roles that define with whom, about what, and how we communicate with others. Some of our roles are formal, whereas others are informal. Regardless, roles prescribe how we should communicate with others. Roles are a set of expectations that, if violated, are subject to negative sanctions. Roles vary considerably across cultures, especially family and sex roles. In order for us to be competent communicators across cultures, we must understand the expectations of the roles we assume. We must also understand and appreciate that the roles we assume in our native culture may be quite different in other cultures.

 Visit the student study site at **www.sagepub.com/neuliep5e** *for e-flashcards, web quizzes, web resources and more.*

DISCUSSION QUESTIONS

1. List the number of groups to which you now belong. Include both voluntary and involuntary groups.

2. How do the groups you have listed above affect the way you think, feel, and act in your society?

3. What is your role within these groups?

4. How does society perceive the groups to which you belong? Favorably or unfavorably? In other words, by virtue of your membership in these groups, how are you treated by others?

5. What are some of the groups to which you would like to belong but do not?

ETHICS AND THE SOCIORELATIONAL CONTEXT

1. You are a member of a sales team that is opening accounts in Egypt and Saudi Arabia. You are to send a representative from your company to Egypt and Saudi Arabia to meet with the Egyptian and Saudi company counterparts and begin a marketing campaign. Your top salesperson is

Susan Que. She's young and motivated and knows and understands the company products well. Should you send her or Tom Smith, the salesperson who has been with the company for 18 years but isn't exactly the best salesperson? Being male, he would probably have better success in both of these countries. Sending Susan might insult your new partners. What will you do?

2. Mino Choi is a friend of yours from South Korea. He's an international student at your college/university. He's a senior and will graduate with you this year. In a recent conversation, you asked Mino what he's going to do after he graduates and returns to Korea. You are curious as to what kind of job and career he will pursue. When you ask him, he answers that his father will make that decision for him. What do you think of that idea? Would you be comfortable having your father make such decisions about your life?

KEY TERMS

gender   220

in-group   209

involuntary membership group   207

involuntary nonmembership group   207

membership group   207

nonmembership group   207

out-group   209

reference group   209

role   210

sex   220

sex role   220

social identity   211

social stratification   215

sociorelational context   206

voluntary membership group   207

voluntary nonmembership group   207

REFERENCES

1. de Tocqueville, A. (1900). *Democracy in America* (translated by Henry Reeve, Vol. 2). New York: P. F. Collier (Copyright 1900 by the Colonial Press), p. 114.

2. Johnson, D. W., & Johnson, F. P. (2009). *Joining Together: Group Theory and Group Skills* (10th ed.). Needham Heights, MA: Allyn & Bacon.

3. Gudykunst, W. B., & Kim, Y. Y. (2003). *Communicating With Strangers: An Approach to Intercultural Communication* (4th ed.). New York: McGraw-Hill.

4. This discussion of membership, nonmembership, and voluntary and involuntary groups can be found in a number of textbooks. The source used here is Merton, R. K. (1959). *Social Theory and Social Structure.* Glencoe, IL: Free Press.

5. Ahmed I. Alshaya, personal communication, January 29, 2011. Mr. Alshaya is a native Saudi studying in the United States.

6. Laungani, P. D. (2007). *Understanding Cross-Cultural Psychology.* London: Sage.

7. Sumner, W. G. (1906). *Folkways.* Boston: Ginn (pp. 12–13).

8. Merton, *Social Theory and Social Structure.*

9. Triandis, H. (1990). Cross-Cultural Studies in Individualism and Collectivism. In J. J. Berman (Ed.), *Nebraska Symposium on Motivation, 1989* (pp. 41–133). Lincoln: University of Nebraska Press.

10. Brewer, M. B., & Campbell, D. T. (1976). *Ethnocentrism and Intergroup Attitudes.* New York: Wiley.

11. Brewer, M. B. (1979). Ingroup Bias in the Minimal Intergroup Situation: A Cognitive Motivational Analysis. *Psychological Bulletin, 86,* 307–324; Tajfel, H., & Turner, J. (1979). An Integrative Theory of Intergroup Conflict. In W. Austin & S. Worchel (Eds.), *The Social Psychology of Intergroup Conflict.* Monterey, CA: Brooks/Cole; Weber, J. (1994).

The Nature of Ethnocentric Attribution Bias: Ingroup Projection or Enhancement? *Journal of Experimental Social Psychology, 30,* 482–504.

12. Schaefer, R. T. (2010). *Racial and Ethnic Groups* (12th ed.). New York: Pearson.

13. These examples of Christians and Jews are adapted from Schaefer, *Racial and Ethnic Groups.*

14. Napier, R. W., & Gershenfeld, M. K. (2003). *Groups: Theory and Experience* (7th ed.). Boston: Houghton Mifflin.

15. Spear, T., & Waller, R. (Eds.). (1993). *Being Masai.* London: James Currey; Vandehey, K., Buerger, C. M., & Krueger, K. (1996). *Traditional Aspects and Struggles of the Masai Culture.* Unpublished manuscript, St. Norbert College, De Pere, WI.

16. The discussion of roles can be found in any number of group textbooks. The particular one used here is Fisher, B. A., & Ellis, D. G. (1990). *Small Group Decision Making* (3rd ed.). New York: McGraw-Hill.

17. This discussion of formal and informal roles was based on Galanes, G. J., & Adams, K. (2010). *Effective Group Discussion: Theory and Practice* (13th ed.). Boston: McGraw-Hill.

18. Adler, R. B., & Proctor, R. F. (2010). *Looking Out Looking In* (13th ed.). Belmont, CA: Wadsworth.

19. Gudykunst & Kim, *Communicating With Strangers.*

20. This information about Korea was found on the following webpage: *Customs and Traditions in Korea.* (1997). Available from www.emb.washington.dc.us/Korea/Scustoms.html.

21. Berry, J. W., Poortinga, Y. H., Segall, M. H., & Dasen, P. R. (1992). *Cross-Cultural Psychology: Research and Applications.* Cambridge, UK: Cambridge University Press.

22. Keberlein, M. (1993). *A Cultural Profile of the Guatemalan Ladinos.* Unpublished manuscript, St. Norbert College, De Pere, WI; Laungani, *Understanding Cross-Cultural Psychology.*

23. Klopf, D. W., & McCroskey, J. C. (2006). *Intercultural Encounters: The Fundamentals of Intercultural Communication.* Boston: Allyn & Bacon.

24. Although different, this dialogue is adapted from a scene in Copeland, L. (Producer). (1982). *Managing the Overseas Assignment* [Motion picture]. San Francisco: Copeland Griggs.

25. Condon, J. C., & Yousef, F. (1975). *An Introduction to Intercultural Communication.* Indianapolis, IN: Bobbs-Merrill.

26. Chan, S. (1984). *Hmong Means Free.* Philadelphia: Temple University Press; Thao, K. (1995). *The Hmong Culture.* Unpublished manuscript, St. Norbert College, De Pere, WI.

27. Paik, S. (2000). The Formation of the United Lineage in Korea. *History of the Family, 5,* 75–90.

28. Ibid.

29. Chang, K. S. (1997). Modernity Through the Family: Familial Foundations of Korean Society. *International Review of Sociology, 7,* 51–64.

30. Kim, M. (1993). Transformation of Family Ideology in Upper-Middle-Class Families in Urban South Korea. *Ethnology, 32,* 69–86.

31. Levande, D., Herrick, J., & Sung, K. (2000). Eldercare in the United States and South Korea. *Journal of Family Issues, 21,* 632–652.

32. Chun, Y., & MacDermid, S. M. (1997). Perceptions of Family Differentiation, Individuation, and Self-Esteem Among Korean Adolescents. *Journal of Marriage and the Family, 59,* 451–463; Kim, Transformation of Family Ideology in Upper-Middle-Class Families in Urban South Korea.

33. Basit, T. (1997). "I Want More Freedom, But Not Too Much": British Muslim Girls and the Dynamism of Family Values. *Gender and Education, 9,* 425–440; Haroun, M. (1999, January 16). *Family Life in Islam.* The Lahore Ahmadiyya Movement for the Propagation of Islam. Available from www.aaiil.org/text/articles/others/family lifeinislam.shtml; Pels, T. (2000). Muslim Families From Morocco in the Netherlands: Gender Dynamics and Fathers' Roles in a Context of Change. *Current Sociology, 48,* 75–94.

34. Bem, S. L. (1974). The Measurement of Psychological Androgyny. *Journal of Consulting and Clinical Psychology, 81,* 506–520; Wood, J. (2000). Gender, Communication, and Culture. In L. A. Samovar & R. E. Porter (Eds.), *Intercultural Communication: A Reader* (9th ed., pp. 170–179). Belmont, CA: Wadsworth.

35. Hofstede, G. (1991). *Cultures and Organization: Software of the Mind.* New York: McGraw-Hill.

36. Herdt, G. H. (Ed.). (1984). *Ritualized Homosexuality in Melanesia.* Berkeley and Los Angeles: University of California Press.

37. Lobel, T. E., Mashraki-Redhatzur, S., Mantzur, A., & Libby, S. (2000). Gender Discrimination as a Function of Stereotypic and Counterstereotypic Behavior: A Cross-Cultural Study. *Sex Roles, 43,* 395–406.

38. Williams, J. E., & Best, D. L. (1990). *Measuring Sex Stereotypes Across Cultures: A Multi-Nation Study.* Newbury Park, CA: Sage.

39. Williams, J. E., & Best, D. L. (1994). Cross-Cultural Views of Women and Men. In W. J. Lonner & R. Malpass (Eds.), *Psychology and Culture* (pp. 191–196). Boston: Allyn & Bacon.

40. Hessini, L. (1994). Wearing the Hijab in Contemporary Morocco: Choice and Identity. In F. M. Gogek & S. Balaghi (Eds.), *Reconstructing Gender in the Middle East* (pp. 40–56). New York: Columbia University Press.

41. *The Moroccan Family Code: Human Rights Education Association.* Translation copyright 2005 by Global Rights.

42. Ibid.

43. Iwao, S. (1993). *The Japanese Woman: Traditional Image and Changing Reality.* Cambridge, MA: Harvard University Press; Sugihara, Y., & Katsurada, E. (1999). Masculinity and Femininity in Japanese Culture: A Pilot Study. *Sex Roles, 40,* 635–646; Ui, M., & Matsui, Y. (2008). Japanese Adults' Sex Role Attitudes and Judgment Criteria Concerning Gender Equality: The Diversity of Gender Egalitarianism. *Sex Roles, 58,* 412–422.

44. Laungani, P. D. (2007). *Understanding Cross-Cultural Psychology.* London: Sage.

45. Duley, M. I. (1986). Women in India. In M. I. Duley & M. I. Edwards (Eds.), *The Cross-Cultural Study of Women* (pp. 127–236). New York: Feminist Press; India: Dowry Deaths Still Increasing. (1996). *Women's International Network News, 22,* 67; Mandelbaum, P. (1999). Dowry Deaths in India. *Commonweal, 126,* 18–21.

46. India: Actions to Stop Feticide. (2000). *Women's International Network News, 26,* 47.

47. Ahmad, K. (2000). Amnesty International Denounces Treatment of Women. *The Lancet, 356,* 1252.

48. Ambah, F. S. (2004). In Rare Public Dialogue, Saudi Women Talk Rights. *Christian Science Monitor, 96,* 1; Out of the Shadows, Into the World. (2004). *The Economist, 371,* 26–28.

49. Ibid.

50. Guenena, N., & Wassef, N. (1999). *Unfulfilled Promises: Women's Rights in Egypt.* Cairo: Population Council of West Asia and North Africa.

51. Yount, K. (2011). Women's Conformity as Resistance to Intimate Partner Violence in Assiut, Egypt. *Sex Roles, 64*(1/2), 43–58.

52. Wang, X. M. (1993). The Storm of a Divorce. *Chinese Education and Society, 26,* 48.

53. Pimentel, E. E. (2006). Gender Ideology, Household Behavior, and Backlash in Urban China. *Journal of Family Issues, 27,* 341–365.

54. Zhao, G. M. (2003). Trafficking of Women for Marriage in China: Policy and Practice. *Criminal Justice, 3,* 83–102.

55. Davin, D. (2005). Women and Migration in Contemporary China. *China Report, 41,* 29–38.

56. Pimentel, Gender Ideology, Household Behavior, and Backlash in Urban China.

57. Marquez, C. M. *An Introduction to Mexico and the Role of Women.* West Virginia University Extension Service. WP513. (No date on the publication)

58. McCaa, R., Esteve, A., Gutierrez, R., & Vasquez, G. (2004, January). *Women in the Workforce: Calibrating Census Microdata Against Gold Standards Mexico, 1990–2000.* University of Minnesota Population Center.

CHAPTER 7

The Verbal Code

Human Language

CHAPTER OBJECTIVES

After reading this chapter, you should be able to

1. explain the relationship between language and culture,

2. explain the principles of linguistic relativity and linguistic determinism,

3. define the three levels of language,

4. explain the principle of universal grammar,

5. list and define three universals of language,

6. compare and contrast elaborated and restricted codes, and

7. compare and contrast U.S. American dialects.

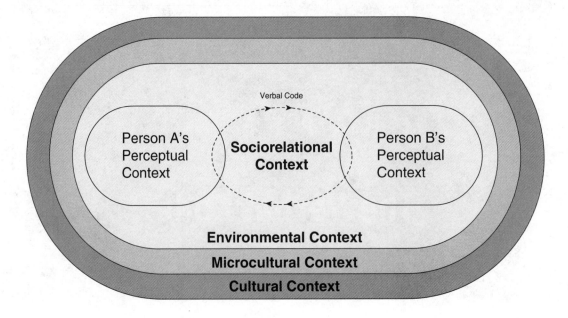

The language faculty is a system, a subsystem of the brain. . . . Its major elements don't appear to exist in other similar organisms. . . . To a large extent it appears to be determined by our biological endowment and is essentially invariant across the species.

—Noam Chomsky[1]

The capacity of the human brain to acquire language may be the distinguishing feature that separates humans from the rest of the living beings on the planet. Our ability to put thoughts into a code in order to communicate with someone else empowers us beyond imagination. Other living beings are larger, stronger, faster, and smaller, but no other living being has the capacity for language. Language has put humans on top of the evolutionary ladder. Because of their capacity for language, humans have become the most powerful living beings on Earth. The purpose of this chapter is to explore the idea of language and how it varies across cultures. This chapter will outline the relationship between language and culture by first exploring the Sapir-Whorf hypothesis. The second part of this chapter will outline the fundamental structure of language, including a discussion of the concept of a universal grammar that applies to all languages. The third part of this chapter will look at universals of language that are shared across cultures. The fourth part of the chapter focuses on how the use of language differs across cultures, including a look at elaborate and restricted codes and cross-cultural comparisons of language style.

THE RELATIONSHIP BETWEEN LANGUAGE AND CULTURE

Linguist and cultural anthropologist Zdenek Salzmann points out that, historically, anthropologists and linguists often grouped language, culture, and race together as though any one of them automatically implied the other two. Contemporary linguistic anthropologists generally agree, however, that culture, race, and language are historically distinct. In other words, a person's race does not determine what language he or she will speak. As we saw in Chapter 5, however, the language of a particular culture and the thought processes of its people are related.[2]

Sapir-Whorf Hypothesis

In 1928, anthropologist and linguist Edward Sapir published a paper in the journal *Language* that changed the face of the study of language and culture. Sapir's thesis was that the language of a particular culture directly influences how people think. In the paper he wrote,

> The network of cultural patterns of a civilization is indexed in the language which expresses that civilization. . . . Language is a guide to "social reality." . . . Human beings do not live in the objective world alone . . . but are very much at the mercy of the particular language which has become the medium of expression for their society.[3]

Sapir continued to argue that the ways in which people perceive the world around them, including their natural and social environments, are essentially dictated by their language. In fact, Sapir argued that the speakers of different languages see different worlds. Strongly influenced by Sapir was one of his students, Benjamin Whorf.[4] Whorf was persuaded by Sapir's writings and further developed this line of thought. In 1940, Whorf wrote,

> The background linguistic system (in other words the grammar) of each language is not merely a reproducing instrument for voicing ideas but rather is itself the shaper of ideas. . . . We dissect nature along lines laid down by our native languages.[5]

Like Sapir, Whorf believed the people who speak different languages are directed to different types of observations; therefore, they are not equivalent as observers and must arrive at somewhat different views of the world.[6] Sapir and Whorf's ideas received a great deal of attention and have become well known as the Sapir-Whorf hypothesis. Salzmann contends that the Sapir-Whorf hypothesis delineates two principles. One is the principle of linguistic determinism, which says that the way one thinks is determined by the language one speaks. Taken at its extreme, this principle means that if we don't have a word for it, then we can't think about it. The second is the principle of linguistic relativity, which says that the differences among languages must be reflected in the differences in the worldviews of their speakers.[7]

These principles raise some important issues for cross-cultural communication. If how we think is a reflection of the language we speak, then the speakers of two very different languages must think very differently. This could render effective and successful intercultural communication extremely difficult, if not impossible. The well-known linguist Steven Pinker maintains that the Sapir-Whorf hypothesis is unfounded and that if the principle of linguistic determinism were valid, speakers of one language would find it impossible, or at least extremely difficult, to think in a particular way that comes naturally to speakers of another language. Another reason why Pinker believes that language does not determine thought is because people consistently create new language forms, a topic we will review in this chapter.[8]

Today, most linguists, like Pinker, believe that the reason the vocabulary and grammar of a particular language differ from others is because languages reflect nonverbal elements of culture. In other words, the geographic, climatic, kinesic, spatial, and proxemic aspects of a culture are emphasized and accented in a culture's language. Salzmann notes, for example, that in Pintupi (one of the aboriginal languages of Australia), there are at least 10 words designating various kinds of holes. *Mutara* is a special hole in a spear, *pulpa* refers to a rabbit burrow, *makarnpa* is the burrow of a monitor lizard, and *katarta* is the hole left by a monitor lizard after it has broken the surface after hibernation.

Moreover, linguists believe that the syntactic features of a language influence how speakers of that language categorize and mentally organize their worlds. For example, speakers of English use the personal pronoun *you* whether they are addressing one or several children, adults, old persons, subordinates, or individuals much superior in rank to themselves. Other languages operate differently. When addressing someone, speakers of Dutch, French, German, Italian, Russian, and Spanish must choose between the "familiar" personal pronoun and the "polite" personal pronoun and/or the corresponding verb form. In English, the word *teacher* refers to a person who teaches, whether it is a man or a woman. In German, *Lehrer* is the masculine form of teacher and *Lehrerin* is the feminine form. In this way, speakers of Dutch, French, German, and Italian may be more conscious of the status differences between them and another person because their language requires them to use words designating the power differential.[9] Therefore, most linguists now believe that the users of a particular language may overlook or ignore objects or events that speakers of another language may emphasize.

THE STRUCTURE OF HUMAN LANGUAGE

All **languages** consist of a systematic set of sounds, combined with a set of rules, for the sole purpose of creating meaning and communicating.[10] Any and all human languages are made up of a set of sounds. These sounds are represented symbolically in the language's alphabet. In English, for example, there are approximately 40 sounds represented in an alphabet of 26 letters. The Korean script, called Hangul, consists of 16 consonants—of which there are five basic forms—and 10 vowels. The Hebrew alphabet of 22 letters (5 of which have a different form when they appear at the end of a word) consists entirely of consonants. The language is written from right to left without vowels. Thus, the word *kelev* (i.e., dog) appears as the Hebrew equivalents of, from right to left, *k, l,* and *v.* If you are not familiar with Hebrew, it is impossible to know how to pronounce a word from the way it is written.[11]

Figure 7.1 Kanji Examples

hito: human being, man, person

otona: adult (big + person)

The written form of Japanese consists of three major alphabets. A fourth alphabet, called *romaji,* is a Romanization using English letters. All four alphabets are used simultaneously in any given piece of writing. The first alphabet, called *kanji,* consists of more than 5,000 borrowed characters from Chinese. The word *kanji* means "Chinese character." Kanji are the Chinese characters used in written Japanese. Each kanji character represents an idea or concept, rather than a simple sound. The meaning of the character changes when the combination of characters varies. For an example, see Figure 7.1. To be able to read a Japanese newspaper, you would need to know and understand at least 2,000 basic characters. Moreover, you would have to learn the different readings or compounds of two or more kanji. There are more than 4,000 kanji compounds. The Japanese also have two phonetic alphabets, called *hiragana* and *katakana.* Hiragani consists of 46 characters. These are phonetic sounds that make up the kanji and are used to change verb tenses. The katakana also consists of 46 sounds. The katakana sounds coincide with the hiragana, but the characters are different. Katakana is used for many foreign words coming from outside Japan.[12]

Sounds and Symbols

The letters of a language's alphabet are symbols representing sounds, called **phonemes**. Phonemes are the smallest unit of sound in a language. For example, in English, the letter *c* represents the sound "see" or "ka," the letter *a* represents the sound "ah," and the letter *t* represents the sound "tee." When combined, phonemes become words—what linguists call **morphemes**, the smallest unit of sound that has meaning. When coarticulated, the sounds "ka," "ah," and "tee" create the word/morpheme *cat.*

There is no natural or inherent relationship between the sounds and their accompanying alphabet. That is, there is no intrinsic or immanent relationship between the symbol *c* and the "see" sound, the *a* and the "ah" sound, or the *t* and the "tee" sound. That *c* represents the "see" sound is completely random and arbitrary. Likewise, there is no natural relationship between any word and its referent. In other words, there is no natural or necessary relationship between the word *cat* and that fuzzy little animal walking across the room. In Spanish, for example, the fuzzy little animal walking across the floor is called *gato;* in Japanese, *neko;* and in French, *chat.* Each of the different languages uses a different set of sounds to refer to the same referent. Although the letters and the sound systems of any two languages may be different, the function of an alphabet is the same across languages—to symbolize sound. A **symbol**, then, is an arbitrarily selected and learned stimulus representing something else.[13] The ability to represent sounds with symbols seems to be limited to humans. To be sure, animals can learn to associate sounds with behaviors, as in teaching a dog to sit when you say "sit." But they can do so only at a very rudimentary level. Animals do not understand the concept of democracy or freedom, for example.

STUDENT VOICES ACROSS CULTURES

Chen Chen

Chinese is a tonal language. There are four basic tones in common speech. Different tones convey different meanings.

The four tones are represented by the following tone marks:

" ˉ " is the first tone.

" ´ " is the second tone.

" ˇ " is the third tone.

" ` " is the fourth tone.

Besides these four basic tones, there are some variations of the tones, such as third-tone sandhi and neutral tone.

Here are examples of the four tones:

(Chinese character, tone, and English translation)

妈 (mā) mother

麻 (má) hemp

马 (mǎ) horse

骂 (mà) to curse somebody

Syntax and Universal Grammar

Along with a system of sounds, all languages have a set of rules for combining the sounds to create meaning. The set of rules, or grammar, is called syntax. Through syntax, sentences are generated. Through syntax, sound and meaning are connected. Noam Chomsky is perhaps the most recognized linguist in the world. Over the past 50 years, Chomsky has developed a fascinating theory about syntax.[14] Chomsky contends that although the 5,000 or so languages that are spoken in the world today appear to be very different, they are, in fact, remarkably similar. Moreover, Chomsky asserts that the differences among languages are actually quite trivial. Chomsky maintains that the languages spoken on the planet today are all dialects of one common language—human language.[15]

Chomsky argues that all human languages share a **universal grammar** that is innate in the human species and culturally invariant. Chomsky and other linguists claim that every normal child is genetically programmed for human language. Just as humans are programmed to walk upright, so are humans programmed with universal grammar (see Figure 7.2). In this sense, language is as much a part of the human brain as the thumb is a part of the human hand. Hence, just as humans do not learn how to see, they do not learn language. They come into the world already equipped with it. But Chomsky points out that humans are not born knowing any specific language, such as English or Spanish. They are born with universal grammar—that is, a deep-seated set of rules (i.e., syntax) that all the languages of the world follow in some way or another.

Figure 7.2 Humans have a need to communicate.

Humans do, however, learn a specific language. The acquisition of a particular language (e.g., English, Japanese) is influenced by the specific cultural environment in which a child is born.[16] In other words, no individual language is universal to human beings. Children learn their specific language by being exposed to it in their cultural environment. Children born and raised in China learn to speak Chinese, whereas children born and raised in Norway learn to speak Norwegian—not because of their race or ethnicity but because of their cultural environment.

The commonalities between the different languages (e.g., Chinese and Norwegian) are so striking that Chomsky and other linguists are convinced that the fundamental syntax for all languages is universal and that the particular languages of any given culture are simply dialects or subsets of the universal grammar. For example, all languages, the world over, rely on word order or inflections to convey meaning. English, for example, relies heavily on word order. The phrase "The man is in the car" means something very different from "The car is in the man." English also uses inflection to carry meaning. Inflections are changes to words to indicate grammatical relationships such as number, case, gender, tense, and so on. For example, to indicate the plural of something in English, we add the letter *s* to the end of a word. A single fuzzy little animal is called a "cat," and two fuzzy little animals are called "cats." The language of the Warlpiri people of Australia relies almost exclusively on inflection rather than on word order. Latin also relies heavily on inflection. The point is that word order and inflection are a part of all languages, as are many other grammatical rules. As linguist Dan Slobin asserts,

> In a way [language is] like the human face. A human face is very simple—two eyes, a nose, and a mouth. You can draw a simple sketch of it. But look at the incredible diversity. Each one of us has a uniquely different face. Yet each face is obviously a human face. Languages are the same. Each one is obviously a different language, but they're clearly examples of the same kind of system.[17]

Lila Gleitman puts forward two additional arguments in favor of the universality of language.[18] The first is that language learning proceeds uniformly among children within and across cultures. Chinese children and Norwegian children learn language at the same time in their development. All normal children begin to use language at about the same time, across cultures. Pinker has observed that sometime around their first birthday, all babies start to understand and use words. At about 18 months, children's vocabulary, across all cultures, increases at a rate of about one word every 2 hours and continues to grow through adolescence. Also at about 18 months, two-word strings appear. These two-word combinations are highly similar across cultures. Children announce when objects appear, disappear, and move about. According to Pinker, by the age of 3 years, a child's vocabulary grows dramatically, and he or she can produce fluent grammatical conversation. Such sentences, though quite short, illustrate the child's knowledge and competence of the basic structure of language (e.g., appropriate word order). For example, even though he or she has never had a lesson on English grammar, an English-speaking child might say, "I want cookie," but would never say, "Want I cookie." By the age of 5 or so, children in normal learning settings begin to use complex sentences.[19]

Gleitman argues that even in cases where the learning environment changes, children learn language at essentially the same rate. For example, studies indicate that a child's language learning rate is basically unaffected by differences in mothers' speech. Furthermore, deaf and blind children learn language at the same time and rate as children with normal hearing and sight. Gleitman points out that the vocabulary and syntax of sign languages are essentially the same as those of spoken languages. At about the age of 2, deaf children start to put gestures together into elementary two- and three-gesture sentences. By 5 years of age, they are constructing complex, multigesture sentences. In addition, blind children have little trouble acquiring terms that describe visual experiences. Gleitman suggests that because blind children are unable to see, phrases referring to sight (e.g., "Look at that!") might be absent from their speech. Yet such terms are some of the first to appear in blind children's vocabulary. For example, in response to the command

Figure 7.3   Deaf and blind children learn language at the same time and rate as children with normal hearing and sight.

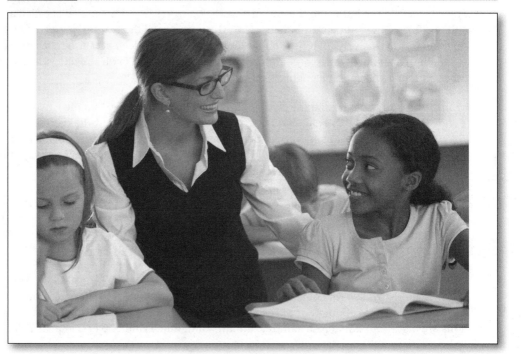

"look up," blind children raise their hands instead of their heads. When they are told that they can "look but not touch," blind children very slowly stretch out their hands and cautiously touch the object. When told "go ahead and look," they handle the object with enthusiasm (see Figure 7.3).[20]

The second point supporting the universality of language argument is that children across cultures acquire many linguistic generalizations that experience alone could not have given them. Children of all cultures say things that no one could have taught them. Chomsky argues that in advance of experience, children of all cultures are already equipped with an understanding of the basic structure of any human language. Like walking or growing hair, language is encoded into the genetic makeup of normal functioning human beings. By the age of 3, for example, there are any number of things children cannot do, such as tie their own shoes, perform mathematical computations, or spell most words, but they can, however, construct meaningful sentences in ways that no one has ever taught them.[21]

Moreover, as Pinker notes, the sentences they create are grammatically correct. Indeed, asserts Pinker, children never make certain mistakes. For example, a child might ask, "What did you eat your eggs with?" but would never say, "What did you eat your eggs and?" which seems to be a straightforward extension of the statement "I ate ham and eggs." The interesting point here is that no one has ever taught the child not to end sentences with the word *and.* Pinker and Chomsky argue that children never make such errors because to do so would violate some principle of universal grammar. Below is another example provided by Pinker. In this example, a language learner who hears the (a) and (b) sentences could quite sensibly extract a general rule that, when applied to the (c) sentence, would yield sentence (d). But the resulting sentence (d) is something no one would say.

(a) We expect the bird to fly.

(b) We expect the bird will fly.

(c) The bird is expected to fly.

(d) The bird is expected will fly.[22]

The proposition that all languages share a universal grammar that is innate to humans is widely accepted among contemporary linguists. But these linguists also recognize that all human languages are somewhat different. For example, although virtually all languages rely on some form of word order to construct sentences, the word order may vary across languages. For example, the word order for a sentence in most European languages is subject–verb–object, as in the sentence "I watch television." In Japanese, however, the order is subject–object–verb, as in the sentence "I television watch." In addition, Japanese, like other Asian languages, does not contain a grammatical equivalent to plurality, as found in English.[23]

The Swahili alphabet lacks the letters *c, q,* and *x* but contains a number of its own. The letter *dh* is pronounced like the "th" of *this,* and *gh* like the German *ch.* Whereas English grammatical inflections occur at the end of a word, in Swahili everything is done at the beginning. *Kitabu* is the Swahili word for "book," but the word for "books" is *vitabu.* This word falls into the so-called Ki Mi class, one of eight in the Swahili language. Others include the M Mi class (e.g., *mkono* = "hand," *mikono* = "hands"; *mji* = "town," *miji* = "towns") and the M Wa class, used mainly to refer to people (e.g., *mtu* = "man," *watu* = "men"; *mjinga* = "fool," *wajinga* = "fools"). Thus, "one big book" in Swahili is *kitabu kikubwa kimoja,* which translates as "book–big–one," but "two big books" is *vitabi vikubwa viwili.* Many languages are read from left to right, as in English. Most languages of the Middle East, however, including Arabic, Hebrew, and Persian, are read from right to left. Korean writing differs considerably from most other languages in that the letters of each syllable are grouped together into clusters, as if the English word *seldom* were written in one of the following ways:

S D		S E L
E O	or	D O M
L M		

The point here is that although human languages across the globe have much in common, each is unique in some way.[24]

All human languages have a set of rules that is used to combine the language's sounds into meaningful units. Complex languages exist even in remote parts of the world, where people have yet to be exposed to modern technology and media. Papua, New Guinea, for example, is where some of the most isolated people on earth live, and yet it is probably the most linguistically diverse country. Among the population of three million people, more than 750 languages are spoken—about one fifth of the total number of languages on Earth. Some of the languages are spoken by fewer than 1,000 people. In his longitudinal work with the Menya people of Papua, New Guinea, Carl Whitehead has found that the Menya use a language as complex as any other language. He argues that one of the most remarkable features of the Menya language is its verb system. Some Menya verbs, according to Whitehead, can have as many as 2,000 to 3,000 different forms as compared with English, where a verb can have up to five forms. Languages such as Menya are as highly rule governed as any other language. In this sense, there is no such thing as a primitive language.[25]

Universals of Language

Another reason why so many linguists believe that all languages evolved from a universal grammar is their numerous commonalities. All languages are remarkably similar. For example, all languages have some way of labeling objects, places, or things (like the English noun). All languages have a way of naming action (like the English verb). All human languages have some way of stating the negative (e.g., "It is *not* raining out"), a way to construct interrogatives, and a way of differentiating between singular and plural.[26]

According to Salzmann, the uniquely human way of communicating via speech shares several other universal features, regardless of culture, race, and particular lexicon. First, Salzmann notes that all human speech is transmitted via a vocal–auditory channel. Conversely, some sounds produced by animals are not vocal or are not received auditorily (e.g., bees have no ears). An important advantage of the vocal–auditory channel for humans is that the rest of the body is left free to carry on other activities. Second, speech sounds are emitted from their source of origin in all directions, making it possible to determine the location of the source. Functionally, this is important because the sender and the receiver do not have to see each other to communicate. This is also important because it enables speakers to communicate without necessarily being face to face—for example, from around corners, or in the dark.

Third, speech sounds are heard within a limited range and only during production. Soon after, they are lost. In this sense, speech is transitory. Fourth, speech is also interchangeable. We are capable of repeating what others say. This is not true of many animal species. Fifth, human speakers are equipped with complete intrapersonal feedback. As speakers, we can hear ourselves and are capable of monitoring our own messages. Sixth, speech is specialized. Human speech has only a single function—that is, to communicate. Seventh, speech can be displaced from time and space. We can talk about something that happened 1,000 years ago or project what we think will happen 1,000 years from now. Eighth, what a person may say can be completely false. Ninth, speech is reflexive. We use language to talk about language. Finally, tenth, the speakers of any language can learn a second language or even several languages in addition to their native tongue.[27]

Generative Grammar

Recall that according to the Sapir-Whorf hypothesis, human thought is restricted by the vocabulary of one's language. Yet one of the most remarkable features of any language's rule structure (i.e., syntax) is that it allows the speakers to generate sentences that have never before been spoken. Chomsky refers to this aspect of language as its **generative grammar**. From a finite set of sounds and a finite set of rules, speakers of any language can create an infinite number of sentences, many of which have never before been uttered yet are easily comprehended by other speakers of the same language.[28]

Most of the sentences you have produced today have never before been spoken by anyone on the planet, and yet everyone understood them. Linguist George A. Miller contends that any sentence more than 20 words in length has probably never before been spoken. Miller demonstrates this through an example. According to Miller, suppose it is possible for someone to choose the next word that he or she is going to say from a list of 10 possible words. Continuing on, assume that the second word someone is going to speak is also one of 10 possible words. At this point, the total number of possible combinations of two-word sentences is 10 times 10, or 100 possible two-word sentences. Now assume that the person is to select a third word out of a possible 10 words. The number of possible three-word sentences is 10 to the third power, or 1,000 possible sentences (see Figure 7.4).

Moving on to a fourth possible word, out of a list of 10 possible words, the number of potential four-word sentences is 10 to the fourth power, or 10,000 possible sentences. The number of possible messages increases rapidly as the length of the message increases. Following this example, the number of possible 20-word sentences is 10 to the 20th power, or 100,000,000,000,000,000,000 possible sentences. Based on this example, Miller alleges that the number of possible sentences in any language is essentially infinite.[29]

In addition to creating new sentences, people routinely create new words to refer to people, places, and events in their world. The academic journal *American Speech,* which is

Figure 7.4	Number of Possible Two- and Three-Word Sentences

First Word Options	Second Word Options	
Blue	Dog	
Green	Cat	
Yellow	Bird	
Red	Pig	Number of possible two-word
Black	Cow	sentences is 10 × 10 = 100
Brown	Horse	
Orange	Chicken	
Grey	Rat	
White	Mouse	
Violet	Fish	

First Word Options	Second Word Options	Third Word Options	
Stephanie	Ran	Fast	
Jim	Walked	Slow	
Gary	Jumped	Quickly	
Karen	Limped	Rapidly	Number of possible three-word
Kevin	Opened	Leisurely	sentences is 10 × 10 × 10 = 1,000
Donna	Cried	Gradually	
Jeff	Laughed	Briefly	
Judy	Rode	Promptly	
Steve	Drove	Swiftly	
Noreen	Flew	Fashionably	

SOURCE: © James W. Neuliep.

published quarterly, devotes to each issue a section titled "Among the New Words," where the journal's editors highlight new words in the American English lexicon. Consider some of the following entries:[30]

bodysnarking: *n* Among women, belittling or criticizing the appearance of another woman

bromance: *n* Strong (platonic) relationship between two men

-cation: *suffix* Combining form connoting and derived from *vacation*

-break-cation: *n* Taken over short period, not far from home, and with short notice

-daycation: *n* Overnight holiday or trip

-edu-cation: *n* A vacation taken for the purpose of learning

-faux-cation: *n* Vacation during which a person works

-mancation: *n* Trip or vacation taken together by men without the company of women

-paycation: *n* Discounted vacation offered to travel agents for training as a reward

DWT: *n* Driving While Texting

First Dude, first dude: *n* Male spouse of a female president or governor

Game-Changer: *n* In sports and competitive contests, something or someone that could potentially change, or has changed, the outcome of a match or contest

Hockey-mom: *n* Mother, often portrayed as resilient and capable, who is heavily involved with her child's participation in hockey

Obamamania: *n* Enthusiasm for, or obsession over, Barack Obama or his policies

Obamanomics: *n* Economic policies of the U.S. government during the Obama administration

Obamaniac: *n* Fervent admirer or supporter of Barack Obama

Thought-shower: *n* Moment or session of creative thinking; brainstorm

So, as you can see, not only does language not limit or curb our thinking, as the principle of linguistic determinism posits, but its syntax actually frees the mind to create new words and sentences never before heard or spoken yet readily understood.

ELABORATED AND RESTRICTED CODES

Although the world's 5,000 or so languages have much in common, the style or fashion in which they are used by the people who speak them differs considerably from culture to culture. In fact, speakers of the same language often use it differently. Some of these differences may be explained by Hall's concept of high- and low-context cultures. Persons in high-context cultures generally rely more on their nonverbal code than on their verbal code to communicate, whereas members of low-context cultures rely extensively on the verbal code during communication. Basil Bernstein argues that the use of linguistic codes is closely related to the social structure of a particular culture. First, Bernstein differentiates between language and speech. As it is described above, Bernstein agrees that language is a system of sounds and syntax that allows speakers to represent their reality and generate an infinite number of sentences. In fact, he argues that all languages are equal in terms of their ability to represent reality. Speech, on the other hand, is at the mercy of the social circumstances wherein it is employed. Bernstein maintains that whereas language symbolizes what is *possible* to do, speech symbolizes what is actually occurring. The social context of communication sets up the boundaries for the type of speech that is preferred, obligated, or prohibited. As the social context varies, the speakers of the language will generate different kinds of speech, even if they speak the same language. The social system delimits the speaker's options in terms of language use. The speech codes, then, are not defined in terms of lexicon or syntax but by the social structure of the culture.[31]

Broadly speaking, Bernstein identifies two types of linguistic/speech codes: elaborated and restricted. A **restricted code** is one wherein the options (not necessarily the vocabulary) are limited as to what the speakers can say or do verbally. A restricted code is considered a status-oriented speech system. The code reinforces the social system by restricting or limiting its speakers to a limited number of linguistic options during communication. Restricted codes are most often seen in high-context cultures wherein the status of the interactants dictates who says what to whom and how it is said. When interactants of a high-context, collectivistic culture communicate, their words and phrases are strictly prescribed, leaving them little choice about what to say or how to say it. In this way, their code is "restricted" and is highly predictable.

Bernstein points out that the Chinese, for example, operate with a restricted code yet have one of the most complex languages on earth. Chinese people need to learn several thousand characters in order to read and write, but they speak with a restricted code because the social system (highly status and group oriented) dictates what can be said to whom in a given social circumstance. Restricted codes also emerge in individualistic cultures as interactants develop close relationships. Restricted codes can be found in what Bernstein calls "closed" communities, such as prison camps and criminal subgroups, but can develop within any social structure where the individuals share social identifications (e.g., spouses, coworkers). In this way, restricted codes show up in both high- and low-context cultures, although they tend to be more salient across the entire culture in a high- rather than low-context culture.[32]

With an **elaborated code**, speakers can choose from among a variety of linguistic options to communicate. Bernstein argues that speakers using an elaborated code are able, via the social system, to put their thoughts, intents, and goals into an explicit verbal message. Bernstein argues that elaborated codes develop in circumstances where the speakers' intents are unknown or vary widely, as in individualistic cultures. Because the individual speaker's intent is unclear, the speaker has a variety of linguistic options available from which to choose. The speaker must expand and elaborate so that his or her intentions are clearly communicated. Any language will allow the speaker to do that, but the social system regulates it. The social structure of an elaborated code user is such that considerable flexibility exists in one's role prescription. To communicate his or her intent, the speaker must be given much linguistic latitude. In this way, it is difficult to predict the vocabulary and syntax of a speaker using an elaborated code. Students in the United States, for example, may have no idea what kinds of things a new professor will say on the first day of class. Students in China, on the other hand, can probably predict quite accurately the kinds of messages their professor will send. In the United States, the culture generally uses an elaborated code, whereas in China, it is restricted.[33]

CROSS-CULTURAL COMMUNICATION STYLES

Although the capacity for language is universal, the language of a particular culture must be learned by its members. Moreover, cultures seem to have a predominant manner, fashion, or style in which they use their language. Communication theorists William Gudykunst and Stella Ting-Toomey argue that at different language acquisition stages, children learn not only the structure and lexicon of their culture's language but also the various styles of language interaction unique to their culture. Such language style reflects the affective, moral, and aesthetic patterns of a culture. Gudykunst and Ting-Toomey describe a culture's verbal style as its tonal coloring of a message that is communicated through shades of tonal qualities. Gudykunst and Ting-Toomey describe four verbal communication styles that have been identified by intercultural theorists. The styles are direct–indirect, elaborate–succinct, personal–contextual, and instrumental–affective. Variations of these styles may exist in any culture, but one style tends to dominate within a culture.[34]

Direct and Indirect Styles

According to Gudykunst and Ting-Toomey, cultures differ in the degree to which speakers disclose their intentions through precise and candid verbal communication. Persons using a **direct style** employ overt expressions of intention. In using a direct style, interactants assert self-face needs. Such messages clearly articulate the speaker's desires and needs. Direct styles are often used in low-context, individualistic cultures. Conversely, an **indirect style**, which is often seen in high-context and collectivistic cultures, is one where the speaker's intentions are hidden or only hinted at during interaction. The use of ambiguity and vagueness is characteristic of an indirect style. In high-context cultures, there is no need to articulate every message. True understanding is implicit, coming not from words but from actions in the environment. Moreover, indirect communication prevents potentially embarrassing moments that might threaten the face of either speaker.[35]

The direct style is preferred in cultures such as the United States, England, Australia, Germany, and Israel, among others. In the United States, we frequently use such phrases as "for sure," "no question," and "without a doubt." We value verbal precision and self-expression. Americans are encouraged to "speak their minds." We are so direct and candid that we will even announce to an entire room when we are going to use the bathroom, as in "I'll be right back; I have to use the restroom." Gudykunst and Ting-Toomey allege that Israel is also considered a direct culture, perhaps even more so than the United States. Fedarko points out that many Israelis use the direct style of *dugri* (straight talk) that is quintessentially Israeli. Israelis value communication that is simple, direct, and honest. A speaker displaying dugri places substance before style and makes no attempt at pretense or deception. Some have referred to Israel as having an "in-your-face" culture when it comes to interacting.[36] Germans, too, value frankness and directness in their interaction with others and are especially fond of the use of examples. Along with their direct style is an absence of small talk. Hall and Hall maintain that in their quest for direct and candid talk, Germans despise social chitchat. Sometimes, Germans are perceived by their European counterparts as brutally frank.[37]

The use of an indirect style of language is seen in many Asian cultures. Indirectness is valued in these cultures because saving face and maintaining harmony in social relationships are highly valued. Directness threatens both of these goals. According to Gudykunst and Ting-Toomey, Japanese speakers, for example, limit themselves to implicit and even ambiguous use of words such as *maybe* and *perhaps*. Children in Japan are taught not to be self-centered, and those who take the initiative are generally not rewarded. Japanese mothers typically use rhetorical questions and tone of voice and context to express disapproval.

Sumiko Iwao argues that there is an unspoken belief among Japanese that verbalizing deep feelings spoils their value. To the Japanese, being understood without words is far more cherished than precise articulation. Iwao asserts that in Japan, interpersonal communication is based on a great deal of guessing and reading between the lines. Directness is disagreeable and repugnant. The ability to correctly grasp what a person thinks and feels without verbal expression is considered a sign of closeness between two persons. In marital relationships, verbal communication is thought to be unnecessary. Iwao calls Japan "a culture of no words." She alleges that this may be due to the high value placed on masculinity. According to Japanese ideals, the most masculine of men is one of few words who does not disclose personal weakness by complaining or expose his innermost thoughts and feelings, especially to his wife.[38]

To a certain degree, the French are indirect. Hall and Hall argue that the French often indulge in small talk and prefer some mystery in their interaction with others. They maintain that the French will often talk around the point they wish to make.[39]

AN INTERCULTURAL CONVERSATION: DIRECT AND INDIRECT SPEAKING

To some extent, direct and indirect modes of communication are universal. Indirect modes, for example, are often used out of simple politeness. But direct modes of communication are seen most often in cultures such as that of the United States, whereas indirect modes are seen in many Asian cultures, such as those of Japan, Korea, and China. The following dialogue takes place between a young couple who have been dating for a short time. The man is a U.S. student, and the woman is from an Asian culture. Note the misunderstanding that results as a consequence of the use of direct and indirect modes of communication.[40]

In all likelihood, Jim is not going to get much of a direct answer from Michiko. She continues throughout the dialogue to use rather general answers to Jim's very specific and direct questions about her feelings toward the United States. Michiko might believe that Jim is being far too direct and invading her privacy. Besides, the fact that she has traveled halfway around

Jim:	Ya know, Michiko, I really enjoy the time we spend together. I really like you. I've been so happy since we met.
Michiko:	Hmmm, thank you.
Jim:	I mean, I feel like I've learned so much about you and your culture.
Michiko:	Yeah . . .
Jim:	I'm so glad you came to the United States. Do you like it here? What is your favorite thing about us?
Michiko:	Well, it's pretty big. It's nice here.
Jim:	What do you think about Americans?
Michiko:	I don't know. Maybe I haven't been here long enough to know.
Jim:	You must think something!
Michiko:	Well, I'd probably have to think about it.
Jim:	I mean, do you like us?
Michiko:	Well, I don't really know that many Americans yet.

the world should be indicative of her desire to be here, right? There must be something about the United States that attracted her. Michiko cannot possibly say something critical about the United States because she would lose face, as would Jim, being a native. She relies on imprecise and indefinite answers.

Elaborate, Exacting, and Succinct Styles

According to Gudykunst and Ting-Toomey, the elaborate, exacting, or succinct communication style deals with the quantity or volume of talk that is preferred across cultural groups. There are three levels: an **elaborate style**, which emphasizes flashy and embellished language; an **exacting style**, where persons say no more or less than is needed; and a **succinct style** characterized by the use of concise statements, understatements, and even silence.[41] An elaborate style of communication can be seen in many Arab, Middle Eastern, and Afro-American cultures. Many Middle Easterners tend to use metaphors, similes, and adjectives in everyday conversation. African Americans, too, prefer personalized, often exaggerated, spontaneous styles of interaction. Kochman writes,

> Stylistic self-expression within Black culture is characterized by dramatic self-conscious flair. . . . Black stylistic self-expression is also characterized by inventive (humorously ironic) exaggeration as in the self-promotion of demonstrably capable aspects of self ("If you've got it, flaunt it") or even by less demonstrably positive capabilities ("If you don't have it, flaunt it anyway"), which is all part of Afro-American boasting: the "making of one's noise." As Hollywood Henderson said, "I put a lot of pressure on myself to see if I can play up to my mouth." But exaggeration also serves to characterize (and neutralize the impact of) negative situations, such as poverty ("The soles on my shoes are so thin, I can step on a dime and tell you whether it's heads or tails").[42]

Generally, European Americans prefer an exacting style of interaction consistent with a "just-the-facts" mentality, popularized by the 1960s television series *Dragnet*. A succinct style can be found in Japan, China, and some Native American (e.g., Apache, Navajo) cultures. These cultures value the use of concise talk and silence. To the Chinese, silence is a means to maintain social control in a situation. Stowell points out that the Chinese, as a rule, do not value verbal skills. In fact, speaking skills in general are considered immoral. The skilled speaker may be labeled as "having a flattering mouth," "an oil mouth," or a "honey mouth." Chinese children are taught to be cautious about the use of words. The Chinese say, "One should use the eyes and ears, not the mouth" and "Disaster emanates from careless talk." The Chinese consider the wisest and most trustworthy person to be the one who talks the least but listens, watches, and restricts his or her verbal communication.[43]

The American Indian tribes of the Navajo and Apache also value the use of silence as a way to deal with ambiguity. Steven Pratt, an actively participating member of the Osage tribe, and Lawrence Weider, a professor of communication, argue,

> To the real Indian, it appears that White Americans who are strangers to each other may freely engage in conversation in such places as the supermarket check-out line. Commercial airlines provide an even more intense opportunity for easy conversation

between strangers. Seatmates often disclose their life histories to each other. In the culture of real Indians, these are extraordinary and improper ways to behave, especially when both parties are real Indians. When real Indians who are strangers to one another pass each other in a public space, wait in line, occupy adjoining seats, and so forth, they take it that it is proper to remain silent and to not initiate conversation. Being silent at this point is a constituent part of the real Indian's mode of communicating with others, especially other Indians.[44]

The use of an elaborated, exacting, or succinct style is closely related to Hall's high- and low-context communication and Bernstein's classification of restricted and elaborated codes. Gudykunst and Kim contend that restricted codes resemble jargon or shorthand speech in which speakers are almost telegraphic. This seems to correlate with a succinct style. Conversely, Bernstein asserts that elaborated codes rely heavily on verbal amplification for message transmission, with much less emphasis on the nonverbal code or environmental cues. This seems to correspond with the elaborate style.[45]

Personal and Contextual Styles

Gudykunst and Ting-Toomey define the **personal style** of communication as one that amplifies the individual identity of the speaker. Such a style stresses and underscores "personhood." This style is often seen in individualistic cultures. A personal style relies on the use of first-person pronouns in sentence construction. Person-oriented language stresses informality and symmetrical power relationships. For example, English has only one form for the second person—that is, *you*. Regardless of whether they are speaking to someone of higher, equal, or lower status, English speakers use the same form for the second person. For example, if we were to meet the president of the United States, we might say, "It's nice to meet you." If we were to meet a new colleague or neighbor, we could say, "It's nice to meet you." If we were to meet our new colleague's first-grade daughter, we might say, "It's nice to meet you." The personal nature of our language does not distinguish status or rank via pronoun usage.

Moreover, in the United States, we tend to treat one another with informality and forgo the use of formal titles and strict manners. These cultural attitudes are reflected in our personal verbal style. As Condon notes, two of the most frequently used words in English are *I* and *you*. He points out that for many Americans, it is difficult to talk for any length of time without using pronouns. In Japan, however, there are at least 10 words that might be equivalent to the English *I*.[46] In addition, Storti notes that the Thai language has 12 forms of the pronoun *you*.[47]

On the other hand, assert Gudykunst and Ting-Toomey, a **contextual style** accentuates and highlights one's role identity and status. In cultures that employ a contextual style, the social context dictates word choice, especially personal pronouns. For example, when using the Thai language, one must look carefully at the situation, including the status and intimacy levels among the interactants, in order to decide what form of pronoun to use. Unlike a personal style, where pronoun usage is consistent across situations, contextual-style language varies across situations. The correct pronoun form is contingent on the context.

Storti notes that German and French, for example, have familiar and formal forms of the pronoun *you*. The decision to use one form over another is based on the context of the interactants.[48] To use the familiar form with an unfamiliar interactant would be inappropriate. Germans are well known for their formality and strict use of titles, even among friends. German neighbors who have known each other for years still use the title "Herr" when addressing each other.

June Ock Yum maintains that a fundamental function of many East Asian languages is to recognize the social status, degree of intimacy, age, and sex of the interactants. These types of demographics will influence the degree of formality and the use of honorifics in the language code. Many Asian languages highlight status differences and asymmetrical power relationships. According to Samuel Martin, Korean and Japanese have what he calls two "axes of distinction"—the axis of address and the axis of reference. In the axis of address, the speaker carefully chooses language based on the status role of the other speaker. With the axis of reference, the speaker chooses language based on the other speaker's attitude about the subject of communication. Yum provides the example of the phrase "to eat." In English, "to eat" is "to eat" regardless of with whom one is eating (e.g., a friend, a parent, or the president of the United States). In Korean, however, there are at least three different ways to say "to eat" depending on the role of the speakers: *muka-da* (plain), *du-shin-da* (polite), and *chap-soo-shin-da* (honorific).[49]

The Japanese use a contextual style, and their language includes an elaborate system of honorifics. Honorifics are linguistic forms that communicate respect according to one's rank and the rank of those to whom one is speaking. Honorifics take the form of suffixes to nouns, adjectives, and verbs. For example, the informal form of the verb "to go," *iku,* is used when speaking to someone with whom one is intimate. If the person with whom one is interacting is a stranger or is older, then the politeness marker, *-masu,* appears, as in *iki-masu.* If the person with whom one is interacting is socially superior, then the honorific form of the verb "to go," *irassyaru,* is used.[50] Hooker notes that one cannot learn to speak Japanese without learning the honorific language forms, including syntax and grammar, for defining one's social status. According to Hooker, through most of Japanese history, learning the language meant experiencing and reinforcing the social differences that ordered society. He points out that there was a time in Japanese history when one literally could not construct a sentence without defining one's own social class and the social class of the person to whom one was speaking. In addition, Hooker notes, Japanese honorifics are a gendered system. Women's speech tends to be filled with honorifics and a sense of deference (i.e., honor, regard) to males.[51]

AN INTERCULTURAL CONVERSATION: PERSONAL AND CONTEXTUAL SPEAKING

In the following interaction, Jim is a student at a local university. He was born and raised in the United States. Akira is an exchange student from Japan. Jim and Akira are eating dinner together in a local restaurant. They have known each other for only a short time. Not only is Jim's style of communication overtly personal, but he's also quite direct.

Jim:	Hey, buddy, what do you think of this American restaurant? I really like it.
Akira:	Yes, Mr. Jim. This is very nice.
Jim:	I always prefer restaurants like this, kinda casual but good food. I come here a lot. Do you go out to eat much in Japan?
Akira:	Japanese restaurants are nice, too.
Jim:	Yeah, but do you go out to eat much?
Akira:	Sure, Japanese people like restaurants.
Jim:	Whenever I come here, I usually order the same thing. It's kinda funny, but since I like it, I figure I may as well eat it. I have a lot of friends that do that.
Akira:	Sure.
Jim:	Yeah, I was thinking the other day that since the dorm food sucks so bad, I should go out to eat more often.
Akira:	Yes, that's a good idea.

Jim is trying to involve Akira in the conversation by relating to him his personal experiences and preferences. Jim uses the first person "I" no fewer than 11 times and even refers to Akira as "buddy." Akira never refers to himself in the first person. Akira generally defers to Jim and says little, even addressing him as "Mr. Jim." As a foreigner, Akira probably sees Jim as socially superior and uses a formal title. Moreover, rather than talking about his personal preferences, Akira mentions that Japanese people enjoy restaurants.

Instrumental and Affective Styles

Gudykunst and Ting-Toomey define an **instrumental style** as sender based and goal–outcome based. The instrumental speaker uses communication to achieve some goal or outcome. Instrumental messages often are constructed to persuade and influence others and to maintain one's face. Yum says that instrumental-style users believe that communication should end after some goal has been attained and outcomes can be assessed, such as friends gained, opponents defeated, or some form of self-fulfillment reached.[52] Julia Wood reports that men in the United States engage in an instrumental style more often than do U.S. women. U.S. women, on the other hand, use collaborative and cooperative talk.[53]

An **affective style** of communication is receiver and process oriented. The affective speaker is concerned not so much with the outcome of the communication but with the process. In cultures where an instrumental style predominates, the burden of understanding often rests with the speaker. The speaker carefully chooses and organizes his or her messages in order to be understood by the audience. In cultures where an affective style is used, the responsibility of understanding rests with both parties—that is, the speaker and the listener. Affective speakers carefully watch for the reactions of their listeners. Verbal expressions are insinuated and quite subtle. Affective speakers often operate on an intuitive sense and are nonverbally expressive. Hall and Hall assert that before getting down to business, the French prefer to establish a mood or a feeling, and a certain amount of intuition is required on the part of the listener in order to discover the meaning.[54] Condon argues that where Americans like to talk about themselves, Japanese talk about each other. The Japanese are very conscious of the other person with whom they are interacting; it is an interdependent concern, unlike the American concern for independence. Condon notes,

> The difference in orientations is apparent when friends who have not seen each other for a while happen to meet. Americans are likely to ask about each other and tell each other about where they have been or what they have been doing. Who speaks first does not seem to matter very much. When Japanese friends meet, one is likely to begin by thanking the other for some previous favor or gift or letter that was sent. Most often, a reference to the last time they were together is part of this greeting. Thus, they re-establish a particular continuing relationship.[55]

Samuel Martin contends that the Japanese language has a complex array of polite formulas, or stock phrases, that have a leveling effect in just about any social situation. Martin argues that foreigners traveling in Japan can increase their effectiveness if they memorize these 20 or 30 polite formulas. Martin states that, to some extent, Japanese conversation is all formula and no content.[56] The affective style of the Japanese is perhaps best reflected in Haiku poetry. Haiku is a short form of poetry popular in Japan. Haiku poems always deal with some aspect of the seasons. Japanese Haiku poets are required to communicate a vivid impression using only 17 Japanese characters. The Haiku poem is concise while simultaneously communicating a deep spiritual understanding. From the reader of Haiku, much effort is required. One of the most popular Haiku poets was Basho, who lived some 300 years ago but whose poetry is still used as the definitive model for contemporary Haiku poets.

Waterjar cracks:

I lie awake

This icy night.

Lightning:

Heron's cry

Stabs the darkness

Sick on a journey:

Over parched fields

Dreams wander on.[57]

Chinese communication is also said to be more affective than instrumental. Becker argues that Chinese people reject debate and argumentation during the process of communication.[58] June Ock Yum believes that Confucianism has a large impact on Chinese communication and asserts that the Chinese emphasize a process and receiver orientation. According to Confucian philosophy, the primary function of communication is to initiate, develop, and maintain social relationships. Yum states that in China, it is important to engage in small talk before initiating business and to communicate personalized information. The Chinese view communication as a never-ending interpretive process. During a conversation, Chinese do not calculate what they give or receive. To do so, states Yum, would be to think about immediate personal profits, which conflicts with the Confucian notion of mutual faithfulness. The Chinese are disgusted by purely businesslike transactions that are carefully planned and orchestrated.[59] Echoing Yum's seminal work, Stowell contends that Chinese is a listener-responsible language rather than a speaker-responsible language, as is English. In a listener-responsible language, the listener is required to construct the meaning based on his or her relationship with the speaker. The Chinese view communication as an interdependent process whereby both speaker and listener are active participants who, together, create meaning.[60]

AN INTERCULTURAL CONVERSATION: INSTRUMENTAL AND AFFECTIVE SPEAKING

In the following dialogue, Mr. Benton has traveled to China to introduce Mr. Yeh-Ching to a new operating system. Mr. Benton is coming from a culture that values an instrumental style of speaking, so he wants to get right down to business. Mr. Yeh-Ching, on the other hand, wants to establish a relationship before discussing any business possibilities. Mr. Benton and Mr. Yeh-Ching are meeting at a local restaurant in Beijing.[61]

Mr. Benton:	Ah, Mr. Yeh-Ching. I've been waiting awhile. Had you forgotten about our meeting?
Mr. Yeh-Ching:	Good morning, Jerry, it is so nice to see you.
Mr. Benton:	Well . . . I'm glad you're finally here. I have all the material you need to see about the new computers we're installing. Here's our plan . . .
Mr. Yeh-Ching:	Jerry, have you seen much of our city?
Mr. Benton:	Well . . . I really don't have much time for sightseeing. This isn't a vacation, ya know. Business, business, business. My boss expects me to close this deal today and be back in New York by the weekend. So, here's my idea for installation.
Mr. Yeh-Ching:	Our city is so beautiful and full of history. Please allow me to arrange a tour for you. We can go together.
Mr. Benton:	I'd love to, but ya know . . . business is business.
Mr. Yeh-Ching:	Can I arrange a tour for you? My staff would be delighted to get to meet you.
Mr. Benton:	No thanks, but I'd like to show you something. Look at these new configurations for the computers we're installing. Now . . . notice that—
Mr. Yeh-Ching:	Here is a menu. This restaurant has some very interesting Chinese dishes that I would like for you to try.
Mr. Benton:	Oh, I grabbed a bite to eat at the Hilton. Go ahead and eat, though. I can show you the production schedule.

Chances are pretty good that Mr. Yeh-Ching will not buy Mr. Benton's new computer system. To an affective speaker such as Mr. Yeh-Ching, Mr. Benton is too concerned about his business and not concerned enough about the personal side of business—that is, relationships. Affective speakers are sometimes suspicious of people who refuse to get to know each other before striking a deal.

LANGUAGE AND ETHNIC IDENTITY

As we saw in Chapter 6, a fundamental way in which groups distinguish themselves from other groups, and thereby maintain their group identity, is through the language they speak. Within groups, status and hierarchy are recognized primarily through the use of language. Often, immigrant groups maintain their cultural heritage and identity by using their native language in their host culture and by teaching it to their children. Other immigrant groups may discourage the use of their native tongue so as to establish themselves as legitimate members of their new culture. McNamara argues that immigrants entering a new culture may have to redefine their former social identity. In a study of Hebrew-speaking Israeli immigrants in Australia, McNamara found that as the Israeli immigrants changed their social identities, there was a corresponding change in their attitudes favoring English over Hebrew. The subjects in McNamara's study were considered *yordin,* a term with negative connotations referring to Israelis living abroad. Among other things, language identified the yordin as an outgroup in Australia. As with most migrant languages used in Australia, Hebrew had low status. By learning and speaking English and teaching it to their children, the yordin were able, to some extent, to manage their negative social identities in their new host culture.[62]

Patricia SanAntonio conducted research on the language practices of an American computer company based in Japan. This particular company required its employees to speak English. Because they wanted to hire native Japanese persons with business expertise and English skills, however, they had trouble attracting high-quality candidates. In order to compete with other Japanese companies, they hired new college graduates who lacked proficient English skills. The result was that they had a workforce with a great deal of English-speaking variety; that is, some were quite competent, whereas others struggled considerably. Because English was so important to the company, the ability to speak English and to interact with American managers became a real source of power within the company. SanAntonio argued that within the Japanese context, language and identity are inextricably linked and that the ability and willingness of Japanese employees to use English identified them and their desire to integrate into the organization. SanAntonio concluded that the English-only policy created a boundary between the Japanese and Americans such that Japanese input was reduced. The policy essentially circumvented the Japanese hierarchy and allowed the Americans to maintain control within the organization.[63]

Intraculturally, the use of language can mark a person as a member of a particular group. In their analysis, Weider and Pratt argue that among some Native Americans, being silent is fundamental in the real Indian's mode of communicating. Moreover, the topic of one's "Indianness" is forbidden; "real" Indians do not discuss it. Real Indians do not engage in casual conversation or idle chitchat with other Indians. Weider and Pratt note that individuals who initiate small talk or openly discuss their Indianness are disqualified from the group of "real" Indians.[64]

Gerry Philipsen, in his research on speaking "like a man in Teamsterville," argued that to present oneself as a man requires an implicit understanding of the communication rules of the particular speech community of real men. "Real" men in Teamsterville engage in a variety of communicative strategies that signal their membership in the group. Real men do not rely on speech as their primary mode of self-expression. Only in situations where the interactants are equal (e.g., two "men") is speaking allowed. Here, speaking serves as a means for solidarity.

Speaking is restricted when the communicants are unequal, as in cases where a man is interacting with someone of higher status, such as a boss, or of lower status, such as a wife/ girlfriend or children. Moreover, speaking is discouraged when a man must assert his power or influence over others, as in cases where he is responding to an insult to himself or his wife/ girlfriend, in cases of disciplining children, and in asserting himself in political or economic discussions. In these types of contexts, nonverbal communication is preferred. In some cases, men may be silent, but in others, they may react physically, as in the case of responding to an insult. As Philipsen argues,

> In critical symbolic ways, as protector and as master of a house, . . . the Teamsterville man disvalues speech as a resource for male role enactment. . . . Speech is not an integral part of earning a living or other aspects of economic life. . . . For the Teamsterville man, minimal emphasis of talk in work settings is one part of a pattern of minimal talk with outsiders to the neighborhood, with persons in positions of authority who are not long-time associates, and with white collar persons, with whom there is a perceived status difference.[65]

Like any other group in the United States, African Americans are identified by their use of language, specifically Ebonics. Moreover, Blacks clearly identify themselves in terms of their use of Ebonics. Smitherman estimates that 80% to 90% of all African Americans use some form of Ebonics in some situations. Weber asserts that Ebonics is critical in fostering Black identity in the United States for at least three reasons. First, Weber maintains that because Blacks experience life differently from other groups, they need a language to express their unique experience. Second, Black language bridges the economic, educational, and social gap among Blacks. Weber states that Ebonics "is the language that binds, that creates community for blacks, so that the brother in the three-piece Brooks Brothers suit can go to the local corner where folks 'hang out' and say, 'hey blood, what it is?' and be one with them." Finally, Ebonics expresses a political statement that Blacks have not relinquished a vital part of themselves—that is, language—and that they can maintain control over at least one part of their lives.[66]

The controversy over Ebonics is both political and linguistic. Linguists disagree about whether Ebonics is a dialect (of English) or a language by itself. If a language is defined as a set of sounds combined with a set of rules for the purpose of communicating, then Ebonics should be considered a language. A **dialect** is typically thought of as a regional variety, or subset, of a language. Dialects are distinguished from other regional varieties by their variations in vocabulary, grammar, and pronunciation. As Smitherman notes, the labels "language" and "dialect" are equally respectable among linguists. The term *dialect* has, however, taken on negative connotations among the public.[67] Politically, the debate centers on the appropriateness of Ebonics in various social settings, such as schools. Politically, some factions argue that Ebonics is appropriate and should be taught in schools. For example, in December 1996, the Oakland, California School Board wrote,

> BE IT RESOLVED that the Board of Education officially recognizes the existence, and the cultural and historic bases of West and Niger-Congo African Language Systems, and each language as the predominantly primary language of African-American students. . . . BE IT FURTHER RESOLVED that the Superintendent in conjunction with her staff shall immediately devise and implement the best possible academic program for imparting instruction to African-American students in their primary language for the combined purposes of maintaining the legitimacy and richness of . . ."Ebonics" . . . and to facilitate their acquisition and mastery of English language skills.[68]

The resolution prompted an anti-Ebonics movement spearheaded by Peter King (New York), member of the U.S. House of Representatives. On January 9, 1997, King introduced House Resolution 28, which read, in part, that no federal funds should be used to pay for or support any program that is based on the premise that Ebonics is a legitimate language.[69] Linguistic and political arguments notwithstanding, Ebonics is clearly a medium of expression for many African Americans. Ebonics not only serves as a vehicle for communication but also fosters a sense of identity and community among those who speak it.

Do You Speak American?

In 2004, celebrated award-winning author and journalist Robert MacNeil traveled across the United States exploring how the English language is used throughout the various regions of the country. MacNeil wanted to answer the question, What does it mean to "speak American"? Throughout his travels, MacNeil discovered that the English used in the United States differs considerably from region to region, among ethnic and social groups, and by age and gender. In addition, MacNeil found that many people shift from one version of English to another depending on the person with whom they are speaking (see Figures 7.5a and 7.5b).[70]

Linguists often argue over the term **Standard English**—that is, the variety of English spoken in the United States that is considered correct. Some linguists argue that there is a right and a wrong way to speak English and that certain correct forms should always be used. But most linguists also recognize that different varieties of English exist in different geographical areas. As we move from region to region across the country, we can hear differences in pronunciation, grammatical structures, vocabulary, and pitch. Most people think of such differences as *accents;* hence, "Southern accent" is used to describe the speech of people who live in the southern United States. Another term often used by sociolinguists (scholars who study language as it is used in various social contexts) is **dialect**—that is, a language variety associated with a particular region or social group. An accent or dialect should not be confused with *slang* or *jargon*. Slang refers to words or expressions typically used in informal communication. Slang words often do not last long, and other slang replaces them. Jargon refers to the specialized or technical vocabulary used by persons in the same group, such as doctors, lawyers, computer specialists, and so on. Many sociolinguists now use the term **language variety** to refer to the way a particular group of people uses language.[71]

Figure 7.5a & b American dialects can be found in many different areas of pop culture. The movie *Clueless* focused on a group of rich kids in Los Angeles who speak in the "Valley Girl" dialect. The Car Talk guys (from an NPR radio show) speak in a distinct "R-less" dialect (you can hear a portion of their show at http://cartalk.com).

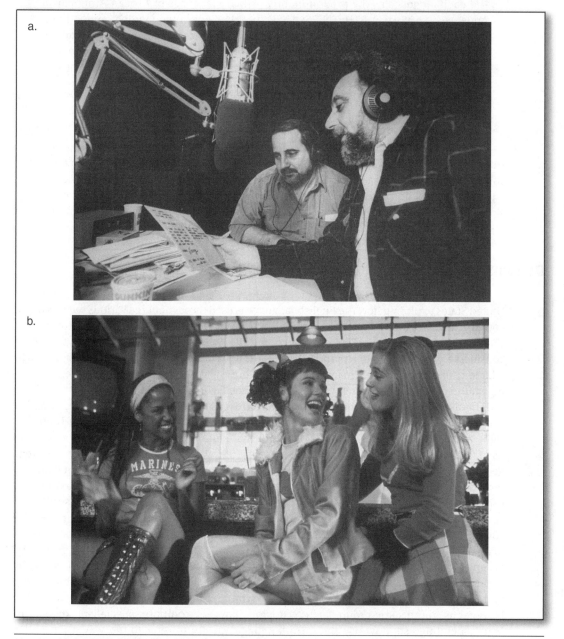

a.

b.

SOURCES: (a) © CORBIS SYGMA. (b) © Richard Howard/Getty Images.

Speakers of a particular dialect often believe that their language variety is the best, correct, and standard way to speak. They may even believe that their language variety is so standard that it is not even considered a dialect. Noted sociolinguist Walt Wolfram argues that everyone speaks some form of dialect. Wolfram maintains that it is not possible to speak a language without speaking a dialect of that language. Moreover, he dispels the myth that dialects result from unsuccessful attempts of people to speak the correct form of a language. Instead, Wolfram contends that speakers acquire their dialect by adopting the speech features of those around them, not by failing in their attempts to adopt standard language features. Dialects, like all language systems, are systematic and regular, and they function as any standard language variety.[72]

Estimating the number of dialects in the United States is difficult. Some linguists argue that there may be as few as three, whereas others contend that there are as many as 25 dialects in the United States (which would include Ebonics, Spanglish, and Chicano English, discussed in Chapter 3). Still others maintain that it is impossible to count the possible language varieties in the United States. A few U.S. dialects are discussed below.

Appalachian English

Appalachian English is spoken by people in the Appalachian Mountains from eastern Pennsylvania to North Carolina. Perhaps the most distinctive feature of this dialect is *a-prefixing*—that is, putting an *a* sound before words that end in *-ing,* as in "I was a-slippin' and a-slidin' on the ice" or "What are you a-doin' here so early?" The a-prefix can occur only with verb complements, not with *-ing* participles that function as nouns. Thus, the sentence "The man went a-sailin'" is appropriate, but the sentence "The man likes a-sailin'" is not.[73]

Cajun English

Cajun English, sometimes called Linguistic Gumbo, is the term that describes the variety of French spoken in South Louisiana. It originates from the language spoken by the French and Acadian people who settled in Louisiana in the 17th century. Five features distinguish Cajun English: vowel pronunciation, stress changes, the lack of the /th/ phonemes, non-aspiration of /p/, /t/, and /k/, and lexical differences. Cajuns talk extremely fast, their vowels are clipped, and French terms abound in their speech.[74]

R-Less or R-Dropping Dialects

Regional differences in how the *r* sound is pronounced distinguish one dialect from another. The *r* sound before a vowel (e.g., *red, bread*) is pronounced much the same way across the United States. But in many dialects of the East Coast (e.g., Boston, New York), the *r* sound before a consonant is dropped and speakers of such dialects lengthen the preceding vowel sound, as in "paahk the caah."[75]

California English

In recent years, much attention has focused on the Valley Girl dialect phenomenon (e.g., "Gag me with a spoon!"). But California is very diverse ethnically, with substantial Black and Hispanic populations; thus, the stereotypic Valley Girl dialect is spoken mostly by the White population. In such speech, the vowels of *hock* and *hawk, cot* and *caught,* are pronounced the same—so *awesome* rhymes with *possum.* Also, the vowels in *boot* and *boat* (called back vowels because they are pronounced in the back of the mouth) all have a tendency to move forward in the mouth; so the vowel in *dude* or *spoon* (as in "gag me with a . . .") sounds a little like the word *you,* or the vowel in *pure* or *cute.* Also, *boat* and *loan* often sound like *bewt* and *lewn—*or *eeeeuuw.*[76]

Texas English

Pamela Colloff reports on how linguistics professor Guy Bailey studies the regional dialects of Texas. According to Bailey, the Texas dialect began when two populations merged in Texas in the 1850s. Those who migrated from Louisiana, Alabama, and Mississippi brought with them their Lower South Dialect (i.e., drawl), while those from Tennessee and Kentucky brought with them the South Midland Dialect (i.e., twang). Bailey notes that many Texans use a flattened vowel sound that makes the word *night* sound like "naht," an indicator of the Texas twang. In an interesting observation, Bailey maintains that the Texas twang is actually expanding across many socioeconomic groups, particularly among young Texans. Bailey notes that phrases such as "y'all" and "fixin' to" are becoming trendy among young Texans. Another characteristic is that where a Southerner might say "muthuh an' fathuh," a Texan would say "muther an' father." Bailey also identifies the monophthong as the key indicator of a Texas accent. Merging the words *fire* and *far,* the vowel in both becomes a monophthong, as in "The house is on fahr" and "How fahr is it to the next town?" Another characteristic is the vowel merger. The vowel merger is a blending of vowel sounds so that words like *win* and *when* sound alike, as do *cot* and *caught, feel* and *fill.*[77]

The Midwest Accent?

Many Midwesterners are under the illusion that they speak without an accent. They may even believe that they speak Standard American English. But most linguists understand that there is not a single, correct way to speak English. So, yes, even Midwesterners speak with an accent. Professor of English Matthew Gordon has written about the Midwestern accent. Many Midwesterners, he maintains, mispronounce words and fall victim to a phenomenon known as the "lower back vowel merger," or what many linguists call the *cot/caught* merger. Many Midwesterners pronounce the words *cot* and *caught* the same way, as they would pronounce the words *don* and *dawn* the same way. The vowel sound in *cot* and *don* is supposed to be pronounced with the tongue low and back in the mouth and with the lips spread open. The vowel sound in *caught* and *dawn* is suppose to involve a higher tongue position and a rounding of the lips. But many Midwesterners pronounce the words the same way.

Professor Gordan cites a personal experience with the *don/dawn* merger. He recalls a time when an acquaintance was speaking about a friend named Dawn. The friend's grandmother was confused, asking why Dawn's parents had given her a boy's name (i.e., Don). Gordan also reports that a colleague from Michigan is sometimes asked why his son, Ian, has a girl's name. Apparently, some of his fellow Michiganders hear the name Ann, which they pronounce as "eeyan."[78]

Language has an immense impact on how individuals see themselves and others within any cultural milieu. Language is perhaps the major marker that people use to categorize and group others.

CHAPTER SUMMARY

All human languages are made up of a system of sounds, syntax, and semantics. The sole purpose of language is to communicate. Historically, linguists believed that language was tied to race and culture. Contemporary linguists have discounted that notion in favor of the idea that languages are essentially human and are not unique to any particular race or culture. As humans, regardless of culture, we are born with a universal grammar that allows us to learn the particular language of our culture. Any individual language is simply a subset of the universal grammar that is embedded in our brains. Considerable evidence shows that children (even deaf and blind children) acquire language in the same way at about the same time. Moreover, children are able to construct grammatically correct sentences without ever having been formally taught. Language is a guide to social reality, helping people observe events around them and organize their thoughts. Moreover, language is so powerful that speakers can generate an infinite number of never-before-spoken sentences that are completely comprehensible by speakers of the same language. Although the universal grammar of all languages is similar, persons from different cultures use different styles of language, ranging from direct to indirect, personal to contextual, instrumental to affective, and elaborate to succinct. Direct–indirect style refers to how speakers reveal their intentions. The personal–contextual style refers to the degree to which speakers focus on themselves or on their partner during communication. Instrumental styles are goal oriented, whereas affective styles are process oriented. Elaborate and succinct styles refer to the actual quantity or volume of talk that is preferred. These different styles probably reflect cultural values and beliefs.

Visit the student study site at **www.sagepub.com/neuliep5e** *for e-flashcards, web quizzes, web resources and more.*

DISCUSSION QUESTIONS

1. How does your language affect the way you think?
2. When you hear people speak a dialect of English that is different from yours, how do you feel about them?
3. Do you think your brand of English is better than others? Why or why not?
4. List five words that you and your friends use that few other people would recognize.
5. List five of your favorite phrases that you use repeatedly every day. How do these phrases define you?
6. What is your least favorite U.S. dialect? Why?

ETHICS AND THE VERBAL CODE

1. In the United States, there is an English-only movement, also known as the Official English movement. Members of this organization advocate that only the English language should be used in official government operations and that English should be the official language in the United

States. What do you think? Should English be the official language of the Unites States? Or should people be allowed to speak any language they wish? Some store owners across the country have signs in their store windows that read: "Only English spoken here." Does the linguistic variation we hear across the United States erode our country's identity?

2. There is a debate across the country as to whether Ebonics and/or Spanglish are valid languages. Some argue that they are legitimate languages. Others argue that they are slang or jargon used by groups too lazy to speak Standard English. What do you think?

KEY TERMS

affective style   254

contextual style   252

dialect   258

direct style   249

elaborated code   248

elaborate style   251

exacting style   251

generative grammar   245

indirect style   249

instrumental style   254

language   238

language variety   259

morpheme   239

personal style   252

phoneme   239

restricted code   247

Standard English   259

succinct style   251

symbol   239

universal grammar   240

REFERENCES

1. Searchinger, G. (Director & Producer). (1996). *The Human Language Series: Part I: Colorless Green Ideas* [Motion picture]. Available from Ways of Knowing, Inc., 200 West 72nd Street, New York, NY 10023.

2. Salzmann, Z. (1993). *Language, Culture, and Society.* Boulder, CO: Westview.

3. Sapir, E. (1929). The Status of Linguistics as a Science. *Language, 5,* 207–214.

4. Salzmann, *Language, Culture, and Society.*

5. Whorf, B. (1940). Science and Linguistics. *Technology Review, 42,* 229–231, 247–248.

6. Whorf, B. (1940). Linguistics as an Exact Science. *Technology Review, 43,* 61–63, 80–83.

7. Salzmann, *Language, Culture, and Society.*

8. Pinker, S. (2007). *The Stuff of Thought: Language as a Window Into Human Nature.* New York: Viking.

9. Salzmann, *Language, Culture, and Society.*

10. Chomsky, N. (1965). *Aspects of the Theory of Syntax.* Cambridge: MIT Press; Goss, B., & O'Hair, D. (1988). *Communicating in Interpersonal Relationships.* New York: Macmillan.

11. Katzner, K. (1975). *Languages of the World.* New York: Funk & Wagnalls.

12. Tohsaku, C. K. (1997). *Japanese "Kanji."* Available from http://edweb.sdsu.edu/courses/edtec670/cardboard/card/k/kanji.html.

13. Goss & O'Hair, *Communicating in Interpersonal Relationships.*

14. Chomsky, N. (1957). *Syntactic Structures.* The Hague, Netherlands: Mouton.

15. Much of this discussion of language is based on interviews with Chomsky and other linguists in Searchinger, *The Human Language Series.*

16. Searchinger, *The Human Language Series.*

17. Ibid.

18. Gleitman, L. R. (1993). A Human Universal: The Capacity to Learn Language. *Modern Philology, 90,* s13–s33.

19. Pinker, S. (1995). Language Acquisition. In L. R. Gleitman & M. Liberman (Eds.), *An Invitation to Cognitive Science: Vol. 1: Language* (2nd ed.). Cambridge: MIT Press.

20. Gleitman, A Human Universal.

21. Searchinger, *The Human Language Series.*

22. Pinker, Language Acquisition. Some of these examples are from an interview with Pinker in Searchinger, *The Human Language Series.*

23. Heath, J. (1997). *Super-Quick Overview of Characteristics of the Japanese Language.* Available from http://stripe.colorado.edu/-jheath/faq4.html.

24. Katzner, *Languages of the World.*

25. Kulick, D. (1992). *Language Shift and Cultural Reproduction: Socialization, Self, and Syncretism in a Papua New Guinean Village.* Cambridge, UK: Cambridge University Press; Searchinger, *The Human Language Series.*

26. Ibid.

27. Salzmann, *Language, Culture, and Society.*

28. Searchinger, *The Human Language Series.*

29. Ibid.

30. All these entries are from Barrett, G. (2009). Among the New Words. *American Speech, 84*(2), 192–210.

31. Bernstein, B. (1966). Elaborated and Restricted Codes: Their Social Origins and Some Consequences. In A. G. Smith (Ed.), *Communication and Culture* (pp. 427–441). New York: Holt, Rinehart & Winston.

32. Ibid.

33. Ibid.

34. Gudykunst, W. B., & Ting-Toomey, S. (1988). Verbal Communication Styles. In W. B. Gudykunst & S. Ting-Toomey (Eds.), *Culture and Interpersonal Communication* (pp. 99–115). Newbury Park, CA: Sage.

35. Ibid.

36. Fedarko, K. (1995). Man of Israel: Rabin's Stirring Life Story Marks Out the Mileposts in the History of His Nation. *Time, 146*(20), 68–72.

37. Hall, E. T., & Hall, M. R. (1990). *Understanding Cultural Differences: Germans, French, and Americans.* Yarmouth, ME: Intercultural Press.

38. Iwao, S. (1993). *The Japanese Woman: Traditional Image and Changing Reality.* Cambridge, MA: Harvard University Press.

39. Hall & Hall, *Understanding Cultural Differences.*

40. This dialogue is loosely adapted from Storti, C. (1994). *Cross-Cultural Dialogues: 74 Brief Encounters With Cultural Difference.* Yarmouth, ME: Intercultural Press.

41. Gudykunst & Ting-Toomey, Verbal Communication Styles.

42. Kochman, T. (1990). Cultural Pluralism: Black and White Styles. In D. Carbaugh (Ed.), *Cultural Communication and Intercultural Contact* (pp. 219–224). Hillsdale, NJ: Erlbaum.

43. Stowell, J. (1996). *The Changing Face of Chinese Communication: A Synthesis of Interpersonal Communication Concepts.* Paper presented at the annual convention of the Speech Communication Association, San Diego, CA.

44. Weider, D. L., & Pratt, S. (1990). On Being a Recognizable Indian Among Indians. In D. Carbaugh (Ed.), *Cultural Communication and Intercultural Contact* (pp. 45–64). Hillsdale, NJ: Erlbaum.

45. Bernstein, Elaborated and Restricted Codes; Gudykunst, W. B., & Kim, Y. Y. (1997). *Communicating With Strangers: An Approach to Intercultural Communication.* New York: McGraw-Hill.

46. Condon, J. C. (1984). *With Respect to the Japanese: A Guide for Americans.* Yarmouth, ME: Intercultural Press; Gudykunst & Ting-Toomey, *Culture and Interpersonal Communication.*

47. Storti, *Cross-Cultural Dialogues.*

48. Ibid.

49. Martin, S. E. (1964). Speech Levels in Japan and Korea. In D. Hymes (Ed.), *Language in Culture and Society* (pp. 407–415). New York: Harper & Row; Yum, J. O. (1997). The Impact of Confucianism on Interpersonal Relationships and Communication Patterns in East Asia. In L. A. Samovar & R. E. Porter (Eds.), *Intercultural Communication: A Reader* (pp. 78–88). Belmont, CA: Wadsworth.

50. Miyagawa, S. (1995). *The Japanese Language.* Massachusetts Institute of Technology. Available from www.japan.mit.edu/articles/JapaneseLanguage.html.

51. Hooker, R. (1999). *The Japanese Language.* Available from www.wsu.edu:8080/ ~ dee/ANCJAPAN/language.htm.

52. Gudykunst & Ting-Toomey, *Verbal Communication Styles;* Yum, The Impact of Confucianism on Interpersonal Relationships and Communication Patterns in East Asia.

53. Wood, J. T. (1997). *Gendered Lives: Communication, Gender, and Culture.* Belmont, CA: Wadsworth.

54. Hall & Hall, *Understanding Cultural Differences.*

55. Condon, *With Respect to the Japanese,* p. 50.

56. Martin, Speech Levels in Japan and Korea.

57. *A Haiku Homepage.* Available from http://www.dmu.ac.uk/-pkal/haiku.html; *The Shiki Internet Salon.* Available from http://mikan.cc.matsuyama.u.acjp/-shiki/.

58. Becker, C. B. (1986). Reasons for the Lack of Argumentation and Debate in the Far East. *International Journal of Intercultural Relations, 10,* 75–92.

59. Yum, The Impact of Confucianism on Interpersonal Relationships and Communication Patterns in East Asia.

60. Lustig, M. W., & Koester, J. (1996). *Intercultural Competence: Interpersonal Communication Across Cultures.*

New York: HarperCollins; Stowell, *The Changing Face of Chinese Communication*.

61. This dialogue is adapted from Copeland, L. (Producer). (1983). *Managing the Overseas Assignment* [Motion picture]. San Francisco: Copeland Griggs Productions.

62. McNamara, T. F. (1988). Language and Social Identity: Israelis Abroad. In W. B. Gudykunst (Ed.), *Language and Ethnic Identity* (pp. 59–72). Clevedon, UK: Multilingual Matters.

63. SanAntonio, P. M. (1988). Social Mobility and Language Use in an American Company in Japan. In W. B. Gudykunst (Ed.), *Language and Ethnic Identity* (pp. 35–44). Clevedon, UK: Multilingual Matters.

64. Weider & Pratt, On Being a Recognizable Indian Among Indians.

65. Philipsen, G. (1990). Speaking "Like a Man" in Teamsterville: Culture Patterns of Role Enactment in an Urban Neighborhood. In D. Carbaugh (Ed.), *Cultural Communication and Intercultural Contact* (pp. 11–20). Hillsdale, NJ: Erlbaum, p. 17.

66. Smitherman, G. (2000). *Talkin That Talk: Language, Culture, and Education in African America.* New York: Routledge; Weber, S. (1994). The Need to Be: The Socio-Cultural Significance of Black Language. In L. A. Samovar & R. E. Porter (Eds.), *Intercultural Communication: A Reader* (pp. 221–226). Belmont, CA: Wadsworth.

67. Smitherman, *Talkin That Talk*.

68. Excerpt taken from Smitherman, *Talkin That Talk*, p. xi.

69. Richardson, E. (1998). The Anti-Ebonics Movement: "Standard" English Only. *Journal of English Linguistics, 26,* 156–170.

70. MacNeil, R., & Cran, W. (2005). *Do You Speak American?* New York: Random House. Available from www.pbs.org/speak.

71. MacNeil & Cran, *Do You Speak American?;* Wolfram, W., & Schilling-Estes, N. (2006). *American English: Dialects and Variation* (2nd ed.). Malden, MA: Blackwell.

72. Wolfram & Schilling-Estes, *American English*.

73. A-Prefixing in Appalachian English: Archaism or Innovation? *Do You Speak American?* Available from www.pbs.org/speak/seatosea/americanvarieties/a-prefixing/background.

74. Stirring the Linguistic Gumbo. *Do You Speak American?* Available from www.pbs.org/speak/seatosea/americanvarieties/cajun/.

75. Fought, J. (2004). *Starting With the Coast*. Available from http://www.pbs.org/speak/seatosea/americanvarieties/southern/.

76. Eckert, P., & Mendoza-Denton, N. (2002). Getting Real in the Golden State. *Language Magazine, 1*(7), 29–30, 33–34.

77. MacNeil & Cran, *Do You Speak American?;* see also Colloff, P. (2003, June 1). Drawl or Nothin': Did You Think Our Beloved Texas Accent Was Disappearing? Not so Fast, Y'all. Turns Out It's Hotter Than a Two-Dollar Pistol. *Texas Monthly.*

78. Gordon, M. J. (2002). Straight Talking From the Heartland. *Language Magazine 1*(5), 35–38.

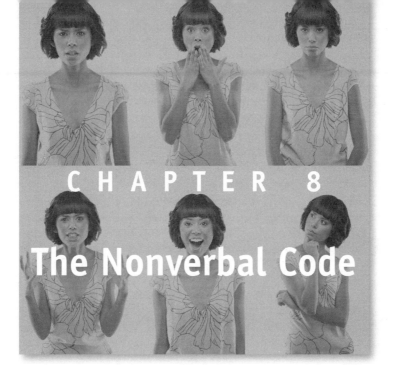

CHAPTER 8

The Nonverbal Code

After reading this chapter, you should be able to

1. define nonverbal communication,

2. compare and contrast verbal and nonverbal codes,

3. define kinesics and provide examples of kinesic behavior across cultures,

4. define paralanguage and provide cross-cultural examples of paralinguistic differences,

5. define proxemics and provide cross-cultural examples of proxemic differences,

6. define haptics and provide cross-cultural examples of haptic differences,

7. define olfactics and discuss how smell is perceived across cultures,

8. define chronemics and discuss how time is perceived across cultures, and

9. recount the fundamental assumptions of the nonverbal expectancy violations theory.

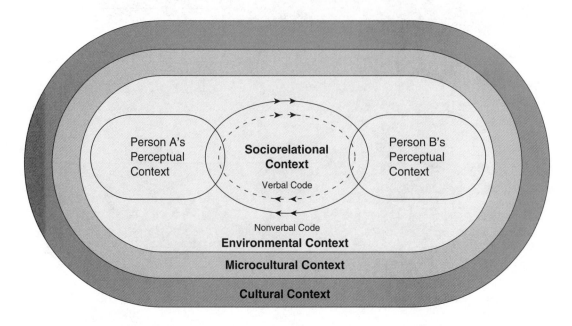

Speakers of every language accompany their words with nonverbal signals that serve to mark the structure of their utterances.

—Peter Farb[1]

Try to imagine what it would be like to be unable to comprehend the meaning of a nonverbal gesture. Imagine that you have traveled to Japan for a study abroad semester. You have been in Japan for only a short period of time. Today, you have gone shopping with a Japanese acquaintance in downtown Tokyo. While looking over some expensive designer clothing items, you notice that your Japanese friend takes the index and middle fingers of his right hand, pretends to lick them, and then wipes his eyebrows. He does this several times. Although you suspect this is meaningful in some way, you have no idea what it means. Your uncertainty level skyrockets. Are you doing something wrong? Is he trying to tell you something? Is your acquaintance just weird? A native Japanese would not be anxious about this at all, because he or she would understand that your friend is simply trying to tell you that the expensive designer clothing items you are considering are fakes. Do not be too alarmed by what has just happened to you. Research shows that the longer you stay in Japan, or any other culture, the more your ability to recognize gestures—and, hence, your intercultural communication competence—will increase.[2]

When you interact with someone from a different culture, a challenge you will face is learning the implicit rules of interpersonal communication. Becoming interculturally competent requires that you have some understanding of the verbal language of the new culture, but even more important is that you become proficient in your host culture's nonverbal system of communication.

Many linguists, psychologists, and sociologists believe that human language evolved from a system of nonlinguistic (nonverbal) communication. To these scholars, language and communication are not the same. As humans, we possess a host of nonlinguistic ways to communicate with one another through the use of our hands, arms, faces, and personal space. When we combine verbal and nonverbal language, we create an intricate communication system through which humans come to know and understand one another.[3] All animals interact nonlinguistically—that is, nonverbally—through sight, sound, smell, or touch. Moths, for example, communicate by smell and color. Through smell, some species of male moths can detect female moths miles away. Elephants communicate with low-frequency sound waves undetectable by humans. Felines are well known for rubbing their scent on (marking) people and objects to communicate their ownership of them. This kind of animal or nonlinguistic communication is probably innate and invariant within a particular species. Most scholars also recognize that a significant portion of our nonverbal behavior, such as the facial expression of certain emotions, is innate and varies little across cultures. Like verbal language, however, much of our nonverbal communication is learned and varies across cultures.

This chapter investigates nonverbal communication and how it differs across cultures. It begins with some definitions of nonverbal communication and a discussion of how verbal and nonverbal codes differ. The chapter then outlines the various channels of nonverbal communication and how cultures differ regarding their use. These channels are kinesics, paralanguage, proxemics, haptics, olfactics, physical appearance and dress, and chronemics. The chapter closes with a discussion of nonverbal expectancy violations theory.

DEFINITIONS OF NONVERBAL COMMUNICATION

The study of nonverbal communication focuses on the messages people send to one another that do not contain words, such as messages sent through body motions; vocal qualities; and the use of time, space, artifacts, dress, and even smell. Communication with the body, called kinesics, consists of the use of the hands, arms, legs, and face to send messages. Paralanguage, or the use of the voice, refers to vocal characteristics such as volume, pitch, rate, and so forth. Through paralanguage, people communicate their emotional state, veracity, and sincerity. Most of us can identify when speakers are confident or nervous through their vocal pitch, rate, and pace. Through chronemics, the use of time, people can communicate status and punctuality. We saw in Chapter 3 that cultures differ widely in their monochronic or polychronic orientation. By studying space, or proxemics, we can learn how people express intimacy and power. In the United States, for example, people tend to prefer an "arm's-length" distance from others during communication. Through smell, called olfactics, a person's ethnicity, social class, and status are communicated. Many cultures establish norms for acceptable and unacceptable scents associated with the human body. To other cultures, for example, people raised in the United States seem obsessed with deodorants, perfumes, soaps, and shampoos that mask natural body odors.

As stated in Chapter 1, intercultural communication is primarily a nonverbal act between people. During intercultural communication, verbal and nonverbal messages are sent simultaneously. Verbal communication represents the literal content of a message, whereas the nonverbal component communicates the style or how the message is to be interpreted. Hence, the nonverbal code often *complements, accents, substitutes, repeats,* or even *contradicts* the verbal message.[4] For example, a speaker might complement the verbal message "This dinner is delicious!" with a smile and increased vocal volume. Politicians often accent their speeches by pounding their fists on podiums. When asked how many minutes are left to complete an exam, the professor might simply raise five fingers to substitute for the words "5 minutes." Persons often repeat their verbal message "Yes" with affirmative head nodding.

Sometimes, however, a person's verbal and nonverbal messages contradict each other. When this happens, we usually believe the nonverbal message. For example, your roommate has been quiet and reserved for a couple of days. Finally, you ask what is wrong. Your roommate replies with a long sigh and says, "Oh . . . nothing." Which do you believe, the verbal or the nonverbal message? Most people believe the nonverbal message because, unlike the verbal message, which requires conscious effort to encode, nonverbal messages are often less conscious and therefore are perceived as more honest. Psychologist David McNeill argues that our nonverbal behavior is partly unconscious and represents a sort of visual metaphor or analogue of conscious thought. He states that gestures and other body motions are primitive forms of speech. Whereas verbal language takes thought and puts it into linear digital form—that is, a sentence—gestures and body movements show the instantaneous thought itself as an analogue of the thought.[5] This is why verbal communication is often called **digital communication** and nonverbal communication is called **analogic communication.** Because we have less control over our nonverbal behavior, it tends to be perceived as more honest than our verbal behavior.

In addition to complementing, accenting, substituting, repeating, and contradicting verbal communication, nonverbal communication also regulates and manages our conversations with others. Professors delivering lectures can monitor the reactions of their students through their eye contact, body posture, and other nonverbal behaviors (e.g., yawning) and adapt their lectures accordingly. Students who raise their hands are signaling the professor that they have questions or comments. Such behavior manages the flow of communication in the classroom. Individually, we can regulate the flow and pace of a conversation by engaging in direct eye contact, affirmative head nodding, and stance, thus signaling our conversational partner to continue or stop the communication.

THE RELATIONSHIP BETWEEN VERBAL AND NONVERBAL CODES

By comparing and contrasting the human verbal and nonverbal codes, many linguists have concluded that verbal language evolved from its nonlinguistic predecessor. Noam Chomsky argues that verbal language is an advanced and refined form of an inherited nonlinguistic (nonverbal) system.[6] A key distinction between the two is that the verbal language system is based primarily on symbols, whereas the nonverbal system is signal based. The difference between a symbol and a signal is that a *symbol* is an arbitrarily selected and *learned* stimulus representing something else. A *sign,* or *signal,* however, is a natural and constituent part of that which it represents. For example, when we hear thunder in the distance, it signals us that a storm is approaching. The thunder is a sign of a storm. But the thunder is also an intrinsic part of the storm. Sweating, for example, signals that one may be hot, but sweating is a natural part of being hot, as shivering is a natural part of being cold. Humans do not learn to sweat or shiver. Unlike signals, symbols have no natural relationship with that which they represent; therefore, they are arbitrary abstractions and must be learned. For example, the symbols *c a t* have no intrinsic connection with a feline animal. Speakers of any language learn to associate symbols with referents.

Another difference between the verbal and nonverbal code is that the nonverbal signal system is much more restrictive in sending capacity than the verbal code. For example, it is virtually impossible to communicate about the past or future through nonverbal communication. You might be able to signal a friend of impending danger by waving your hands, but you cannot warn your friend of danger that might occur tomorrow or recall danger that occurred yesterday with nonverbal signals. In addition, communication of negation is practically impossible with the nonverbal code system. Try communicating to a friend nonverbally that you are not going to the grocery store tomorrow. The same task is relatively easy through the linguistic system, however.[7]

Formal Versus Informal Code Systems

In Chapter 7, verbal language was defined as a systematic set of sounds combined with a set of rules for the sole purpose of communication. All verbal languages have a formal set of sounds, syntax, and semantics. The degree of formality of verbal language is not found in the nonverbal code, however. The alphabets of most verbal languages in the world represent about 40 sounds. No such formalized alphabet exists for nonverbal codes.

Different types of nonverbal behavior can be categorized, but these categories are much more loosely defined than in the verbal code. All verbal languages have a set of rules, called grammar or syntax, that prescribes how to combine the various sounds of the language into meaningful units, such as words and sentences. Although there are rules governing the use of nonverbal communication, a formal grammar or syntax does not exist. Nowhere is there a book or guide prescribing exactly what nonverbal behavior should be used when and where. There is no doubt that certain social contexts prescribe certain nonverbal behaviors, such as a handshake when greeting someone in the United States, but no systematic rule book on the same level of formality as an English grammar book exists for nonverbal communication. The rules for nonverbal communication are learned informally through socialization and vary considerably, even intraculturally.

Finally, the verbal code, when used with the correct syntax, takes on **denotative meaning.** When using verbal language, if we hear a word that we do not understand, we can quickly go to a dictionary that will define the word for us. The dictionary tells us what the language means. No such device exists for our nonverbal communication. If someone touches us, or stands too close, or engages in prolonged eye contact, we can only surmise its meaning. Popular psychology notwithstanding, we have no dictionary for nonverbal communication. To be sure, nonverbal communication is meaningful—perhaps even more meaningful than verbal communication—but the denotative meaning of the nonverbal act must be inferred.[8]

CHANNELS OF NONVERBAL COMMUNICATION

The closest thing the nonverbal code has to an alphabet is a gross classification system of the various channels though which nonverbal communication is sent. These channels are kinesics, paralanguage, proxemics, haptics, olfactics, physical appearance and dress, and chronemics. As we will see later in this chapter, some nonverbal expressions, particularly some facial expressions of emotion, seem to be universal, but much of our nonverbal behavior is learned and is therefore culturally unique.

Kinesics

Kinesic behavior, or body movement, includes gestures, hand and arm movements, leg movements, facial expressions, eye gaze and blinking, and stance or posture. Although just about any part of the body can be used for communicating nonverbally, the face, hands, and arms are the primary kinesic channels through which nonverbal messages are sent. Relative to other body parts, they have a high sending capacity, especially the face. The most widely recognized system for classifying kinesic channels was developed by Paul Ekman and Wallace Friesen. Together, they organized kinesic behavior into five broad categories: (1) *emblems,* (2) *illustrators,* (3) *affect displays,* (4) *regulators,* and (5) *adaptors.* The meaning behind most of these kinesic behaviors varies across cultures.[9]

Emblems and Illustrators

Emblems are primarily (though not exclusively) hand gestures that have a direct literal verbal translation. **Illustrators** are typically hand and arm movements that accompany speech or function to accent or complement what is being said. In the United States, the hand gesture used to represent "peace" is an example of a widely recognized emblem. Emblems vary considerably across cultures. Pounding your fist on the podium during a speech is an example of an illustrator. Illustrators serve a *metacommunicative function*—that is, they are messages about messages. They are nonverbal messages that tell us how to interpret verbal messages. For example, shaking your fist at someone while expressing anger is an illustrator. For the most part, emblems and illustrators are not taught in school but are learned informally through a child's socialization in his or her culture. There is growing evidence that emblems and illustrators play an important role in language, cognitive development, and communicative development.

Guidetti and Nicoladis assert that children use such gestures earlier in their communication development than words. While words eventually replace gestures as a child's preferred method of communication, children continue to gesture to reinforce and expand their verbal messages and even to replace them. They maintain that gestures also offer insight into children's unspoken thoughts.[10] Related research indicates that by 6 months of age, babies in all cultures begin to use gestures to communicate to their parents. Joanna Blake and her colleagues point out that the change in a child's inventory of gestures, from 9 to 14 months of age, may provide the foundation for verbal language acquisition. Specifically, across cultures, there is a shift in the types of gestures used by children at 1 year of age toward gestural sharing of objects and information. The development of these communicative gestures supports the idea of the universality of language and may form a base for language acquisition across cultures.[11]

Dane Archer maintains that emblems and illustrators are at least 2,500 years old and can be seen in the ancient artwork of various cultures. Archer asserts that the systematic study of gestures began about 400 years ago, during Shakespeare's time. Although cultures differ widely in their use of emblems and illustrators, people in most cultures tend to use them for the same kinds of communication situations. For example, most cultures use emblems and illustrators during greetings and departures, to insult or to communicate obscenities to others, to indicate fight or flight, and to designate friendly or romantic relationships.[12]

Understanding the meanings of nonverbal gestures, especially emblems and illustrators, is a prerequisite to becoming a competent intercultural communicator. Gestures are a part of the lexicon of every culture. The well-known, oft-cited anthropologist Edward Sapir noted that gestures are a part of the secret code of all cultures that is "written nowhere, known by none, and understood by all."[13] In their recent research, Molinsky, Krabbenhoft, Ambady, and Choi argue that in order for individuals to function effectively across cultures, gestures, such as emblems, are a critical feature of interpersonal communication and the navigation of intercultural situations. Indeed, they write that natives of a particular culture have the ability to seamlessly pilot through the maze of the secret code of gestures. Yet nonnatives do not share this same luxury. In their study of native and nonnative members of U.S. culture, Molinsky and his colleagues found that an individual's length of stay in the culture is directly linked to gesture recognition accuracy and perceptions of intercultural communication accuracy. Specifically, nonnative persons in the United States were able to correctly recognize both valid and invalid (i.e., fake) gestures based on their length of stay in the United States. These same persons were perceived by others (i.e., U.S. natives) as more interculturally competent than nonnatives with shorter lengths of stay.[14]

Greeting rituals are an important component in any person's communicative repertoire. Knowing the greetings of different cultures when interacting outside your own culture is a first step toward developing intercultural communication competence. In high-context and collectivistic cultures, greeting rituals often differ according to one's social status. Moreover, in some cultures, men and women have different rules for how to greet someone. Bowing is the customary greeting in Korea and other Asian cultures, such as Japan and Vietnam. When Koreans greet elders, professors, persons of power, and persons of higher status than themselves, they bow lower and longer and divert eye contact. When businesspeople or friends meet, the bow is generally shorter and quicker.[15] In Japan, the appropriate bow is made with the hands sliding down toward the knees, back and neck stiff, and eyes averted (see Figure 8.1). As in other Asian cultures, bowing recognizes social stratification. Social subordinates should bow lower and longer than their superiors. Persons of equal status match bows unless one is younger, in which case the younger person should bow a shade lower and longer. The eyes should always be lowered.[16]

In addition to bowing as a greeting, Japanese businesspeople typically exchange business cards. Double-sided business cards in Japanese and English are important because they demonstrate to your Japanese partners that you are serious and respect their culture. Typically, business cards are exchanged at the beginning of a meeting while standing. During the exchange, face your counterpart, bow slightly, and offer your card with the Japanese side pointing up, either with your right hand or both hands. The same procedures apply when

Figure 8.1 Bowing is the customary greeting in Japan.

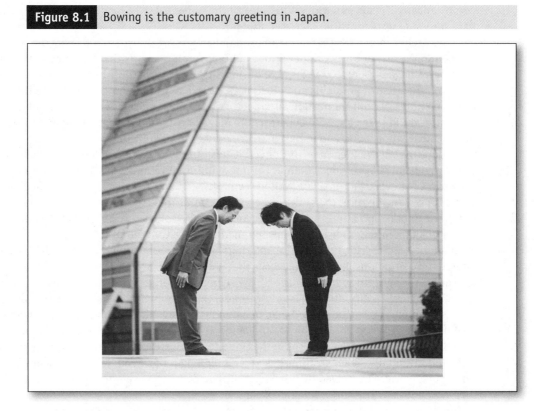

receiving a card. Do not immediately put the card away; take the time to review it. Japanese tend to exchange business cards routinely.[17]

Microcultural groups in the United States have unique greetings as well. Moellendorf notes that although most Amish generally will not initiate greetings with strangers or non-Amish persons, many Amish will respond to an outsider's wave by pointing their index finger toward the sky. The raised finger points to heaven and shows respect to the non-Amish while revealing the Amish people's strong religious beliefs.[18]

As in the United States, the handshake is a common gesture/illustrator during a greeting in most parts of developed Kenya. In this case, however, when greeting a person of higher status, such as a teacher, the person of lower status should take the left hand (the hand not being used in the handshake) and grasp his or her own right arm somewhere in the proximity of the forearm during the shake.

According to Axtell, the handshake is a common greeting in China as well. The traditional Chinese greeting is to cup one's hands (left over right), place them about chest high, and raise them while bowing.[19] According to Bishop, when greeting a holy man or priest, East Indians bow slightly or kneel with their hands pressed together palm to palm in front of their chests. This shows ultimate respect for the higher castes.[20]

Harris, Moran, and Moran report that when greeting male friends in Saudi Arabia, Saudi men kiss one another on both cheeks. They prefer to get very close during the greeting.

The cheek-kissing ritual is practiced in other Middle Eastern cultures as well. The Arab handshake feels loose compared with the firm handshake practiced in many Western cultures.[21] In traditional Sri Lankan greetings, the hands are placed together, palms touching at the chin level, and the person bows slightly and says "*Namaste,*" which means "I salute the Godlike qualities in you."[22]

Archer has observed that many cultures have emblems and illustrators for insulting others and for communicating obscenities. According to Archer, some cultures may have as many as six or seven obscene gestures, whereas some northern European cultures, such as the Netherlands and Norway, do not have any native obscene gestures.[23] Giving someone "the finger" (making a fist with the hand and extending the middle finger upward) is a widely recognized obscene gesture in many parts of the world, including the United States, Mexico, and much of Europe. Forming a "V" with the index and middle fingers with the palm facing in is vulgar in Australia and England, communicating the same intent as "the finger." Creating the very same gesture with the palm facing out is completely acceptable, however, and represents "V for victory."

In the Ladino culture of Guatemala, a hand gesture called *la mano caliente* ("the hot hand") is equivalent to "the finger" and is created by placing the thumb between the first and middle fingers, then squeezing the hand to make a fist (see Figure 8.2). This gesture is considered obscene in other Central and South American cultures as well. In the Ladino culture, however, this gesture is very offensive, and anyone using it should be prepared to fight. If a person were to direct *la mano caliente* toward a military or police officer, the offender could expect to spend time in jail or do hard labor in the army.[24] The same hand gesture is used in Hmong culture to belittle or

| **Figure 8.2** | In the Ladino culture of Guatemala, this gesture, called *la mano caliente*, is considered offensive. |

insult someone. In the Hmong culture, only males use this gesture.[25] In Jamaica, this gesture is called "the fig," and it is considered obscene there also.[26]

In Peru, making a pistol gesture with each hand and then pointing the "pistols" at someone from about waist level is considered obscene and may provoke a fight (see Figure 8.3). In Iran, putting an open hand directly in front of and horizontal to one's face with the palm facing in and rubbing the hand down over the face from about the eyes to the chin, almost as if stroking a beard, is considered obscene and is equivalent to saying "Fuck you" (see Figure 8.4). An obscene gesture recognized in many European cultures, especially France, is taking either hand and putting it palm down on the biceps of the opposite arm while quickly raising the opposite arm and making a fist, all in one fluid motion (see Figure 8.5). This gesture is basically equivalent to "the finger" and to the verbal designate "Up yours" or "Fuck you."[27]

Archer points out that in addition to obscene emblems and illustrators, many cultures have gestures indicating that someone is homosexual or an adulterer. These gestures are strongly linked to one's sex role. Gestures indicating that someone is a homosexual almost always apply to men, whereas gestures indicating that someone is unfaithful usually apply to women. In Japan, putting the hand, palm out, against the cheek while turning the face away—almost as if pretending to tell a secret—is a sign that someone is homosexual. In Colombia, making a circle with the index finger and thumb (like the "OK" gesture in the United States) and then placing the circle around the nose is a sign for homosexual. The limp-wrist gesture, or slight variations of it, for homosexual is recognized in the United States, China, Mexico, and

Figure 8.3 This hand gesture is highly offensive in Peru and could provoke a fight.

SOURCE: © James W. Neuliep.

Figure 8.4   This is the Iranian equivalent of "the finger."

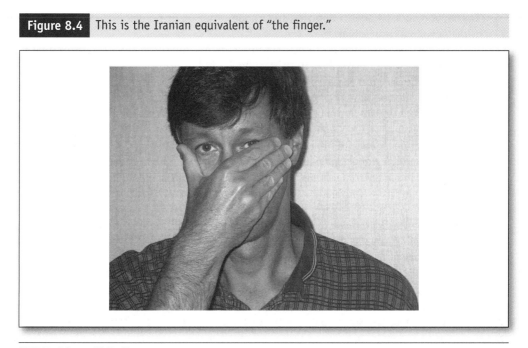

SOURCE: © James W. Neuliep.

Figure 8.5   In European cultures, this gesture is similar to "the finger."

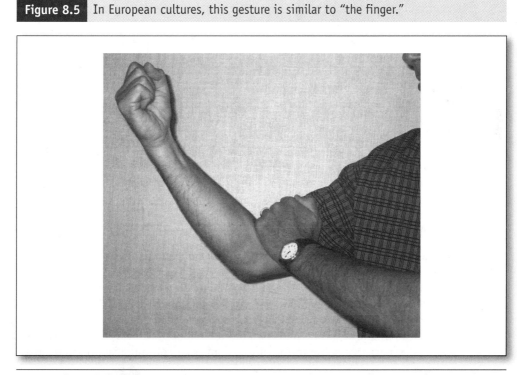

SOURCE: © James W. Neuliep.

Thailand, among other countries. In Uruguay, four or five quick claps of the hands indicate that a woman is a lesbian.[28]

Archer contends that gestures communicating "I am afraid" or "I want to fight you" (i.e., fight or flight) are uncommon in the United States but occur with some regularity across cultures. In Mexico and Nepal, placing a hand with the palm up and fingers extended upward while moving the fingers in and out, touching the thumb, is an invitation to fight. In Japan, putting the index fingers on the temples of the head, as if making horns, is a sign that one is angry. In China, pretending to pull up one's sleeve with the hand of the opposite arm designates that one is ready to fight.[29] In Hmong culture, clapping one's hands during an argument is a signal to the opponent that it is time to fight. The gesture is usually reserved for intense situations in which someone intends to physically harm someone else.[30]

Most cultures use emblems and illustrators to designate friendly or romantic relationships. In the United States, for example, crossing the index and middle fingers of the same hand designates closeness and communicates, "We're close" or "We're tight." In China, clasping the index fingers from each hand together signals love or romance. In Thailand, pressing the palms of both hands together and placing them against a cheek (as in a "Sleeping Beauty" gesture) is indicative of romance. Tapping the tips of the index fingers together in Japan or extending both index fingers parallel at waist level in Mexico communicates that someone is in love.[31]

Abigail Marsh and her colleagues point out that, as with their verbal code, people have nonverbal accents. Nonverbal accents are tendencies to display nonverbal behaviors in a certain manner, style, or fashion independent of the context. These styles are distinctions or variations in the degree to which the nonverbal gesture is expressed. Think, for example, about the number of different ways people walk or sit. Marsh notes that given all the possible combinations of all the gradations of all the muscle movements that can contribute to the expression of a gesture, there are probably myriad accents. Specifically, Marsh describes nonverbal accents as the tendency for the people of one culture to express a nonverbal gesture in a way that is more similar to others' within the culture than to expressions of the same gesture in another culture. This is comparable to the way a given word is pronounced more similarly among members of a given culture than between members of different cultures. All sorts of nonverbal expressions may be accented, such as laughing, shrugging the shoulders, giving the finger, waving, saluting, and one's gait or style of walking. In their research, Marsh and her colleagues found that nonverbal accents helped people distinguish the nationality of other persons displaying the expression. Specifically, American participants accurately determined the nationality of Australian and American adults when observing their emotional expressions but not neutral expressions. In another study, American participants accurately determined the nationality of Australians and Americans seen walking or waving in greeting.[32]

Affect Displays: Facial Expressions of Emotion

Knapp and Hall point out that perhaps more than any other part of the body, the face has the highest nonverbal sending capacity. Through facial expressions, we can communicate our personality, open and close channels of communication, complement or qualify other nonverbal behavior, and perhaps more than anything, communicate emotional states.[33]

Many linguists believe that our verbal language evolved from a system of nonlinguistic communication that was inherited from our animal past. If this is a valid assumption, then we should expect that some forms of our nonverbal communication are invariant across cultures. Current evidence suggests that some facial expressions of emotion, called **affect displays,** are universal. Paul Ekman alleges that humans can make more than 10,000 facial expressions and that 2,000 to 3,000 of them have to do with emotion. Ekman is careful to point out that by studying faces, we cannot tell what people are thinking, only what they are feeling about what they are thinking.[34] Initially, Ekman believed that affect displays, like so many other forms of communication, were the result of learning and were culturally unique. He originally agreed with sociologist Ray Birdwhistell, who wrote,

> Just as there are no universal words, no sound complexes, which carry the same meaning the world over, there are no body movements, facial expressions, or gestures which provoke identical responses the world over.[35]

In contrast to Birdwhistell, other scholars have hypothesized that because they were inherited, human nonverbal expressions should be similar, if not universal, the world over. The basis of this argument can be found in the writings of evolutionary scholar Charles Darwin, who wrote,

> We can thus also understand the fact that the young and the old of widely different races, both with man and animals, express the same state of mind by the same movements. . . . I have endeavoured to show in considerable detail that all the chief expressions exhibited by man are the same throughout the world. This fact is interesting, as it affords a new argument in favour of the several races being descended from a single parent-stock, which must have been almost completely human in structure, and to a large extent in mind, before the period at which the races diverged from each other.[36]

The late Harvard University professor Stephen Jay Gould, well known for his stance on evolution, agrees with Darwin and argues that although universal facial expressions may have been functional for the animals from whom we inherited them, they are not functional for us today. Take, for example, a facial expression of anger, in which a person snarls, grits his or her teeth, and displays the canine teeth (see Figure 8.6a). This facial expression is remarkably similar to expressions of anger in several animal species (see Figure 8.6b). The fact that there is no need for us to display our teeth in order to express anger (we can simply say how angry we are) suggests that such a gesture must have been inherited.[37]

Ekman was determined to find whether certain elements of facial behavior are universal or culturally specific. He and his colleagues believed that there may be distinctive movements of the face for the primary emotions of surprise, fear, anger, disgust, happiness, and sadness that are probably universal. They further argued that while people from divergent cultures may express emotions similarly, what stimulates the emotion and the intensity with which it is expressed is probably culturally specific. In other words, although Germans and Japanese may express fear, surprise, anger, happiness, disgust, and sadness similarly in terms of muscular facial expressions, what *elicits* fear in Germans may be different from what elicits fear in Japanese. Moreover, cultures may differ in how they manage and regulate facial expressions of emotion, particularly in the presence of others. Ekman and Friesen (among others) have conducted numerous studies testing their hypotheses.[38]

Figure 8.6	Some human facial expressions of emotion are innate and remarkably similar to those seen among animals.

a   b

In one study, Ekman, Friesen, and a number of their associates had more than 500 participants from 10 different countries look at slides of people expressing the six emotions of fear, anger, happiness, disgust, sadness, and surprise. The participants in the study came from a variety of cultures the world over: Estonia, Italy, Germany, Japan, Hong Kong, Scotland, Sumatra, Turkey, Greece, and the United States. Participants were shown photographs of Caucasians in posed facial expressions of the six different emotions, one at a time for 10 seconds each, and were instructed to indicate which of the six emotions was presented. The participants were also asked to rate the intensity of the presented emotion on a scale of 1 to 8.

The results showed that in an overwhelming number of trials, the emotion rated strongest by the largest number of observers in each culture was the predicted emotion. Where cultures differed was in their ratings of intensity of the emotion. Ekman reasoned that perhaps people judge a foreigner's expressions to be less intense than expressions shown by members of their own culture or that attributions of less intense emotions to foreigners might be due more to uncertainty about the emotional state of a person from an unfamiliar culture.

In interpreting these results, Izard claims that there appears to be an evolutionary and biological relationship between facial expressions and certain emotional states but that this connection can be uncoupled by the human capacity to exercise voluntary control over innate emotional expressions.[39] Although Ekman's studies provide evidence that facial expressions of primary emotions appear to be universal, other data suggest that cultural influences, such as individualism and collectivism, play a role in the expression of emotion. Stephan, Stephan, and De Vargas found that persons from individualistic cultures express emotions affirming independent self-conceptions, such as self-actualized, capable, self-satisfied, and proud of oneself. They also found that persons from collectivistic cultures were less comfortable expressing negative emotions (e.g., indignant, annoyed, distrustful) than were persons from individualistic cultures.[40]

In related research, Schimmack found that persons from individualistic cultures are better able to recognize happiness than are collectivists and that persons from high uncertainty avoidance cultures were less accurate in the recognition of facial expressions of fear and sadness than were persons with low uncertainty avoidance.[41] Matsumoto alleges that high uncertainty avoidance cultures create social institutions to deal with fear and, therefore, recognize this emotion less well.[42] Along similar lines, Pittam, Kroonenberg, Gallois, and Iwawaki found that Australians were rated as more expressive by Japanese and that Japanese may conceptualize emotions as less intense.[43]

In her ongoing research with nonverbal accents—that is, subtle differences in the appearance of facial expressions of emotion across cultures—Marsh argues that while some facial expressions of emotion seem to be universal, it is reasonable to expect that there will be some "local" (i.e., regional or cultural) variations across cultures. She notes that while Ekman's research is convincing, there is still room for fine distinctions. In one study, Marsh and her colleagues had students judge photographs of Japanese nationals and Japanese Americans posing with emotional facial expressions and neutral facial expressions. With the emotional expressions, the posers' muscle movements were standardized to eliminate differences in expressions. Yet they found that participants were able to guess the nationality of the posers at above-chance levels and with greater accuracy than they judged the nationality of the same posers displaying neutral facial expressions. Marsh argues that these findings demonstrate that facial expressions of emotion include nonverbal accents that identify the expresser's nationality or culture. She maintains that cultural differences are intensified during emotional expressions. Finally, she maintains that her evidence suggests that extreme positions regarding the universality of emotional expressions are incomplete and need further investigation.[44]

Cross-Racial Recognition of Faces

Most of us have heard statements such as "I can't tell one Japanese from another . . . they all look alike!" Although this statement smacks of racism and ignorance, scientific evidence indicates that own-race identifications tend to be more accurate, by as much as 10% to 15%, than cross-race identifications. Own-race identifications are those in which we identify someone of the same race as our own. Cross-race identifications are those in which we identify people from a race different from our own.[45] Legal scholars have expressed a concern over an own-race recognition bias in eyewitness identification for some time. In fact, Feingold argued nearly 90 years ago that it is well known that, other things being equal, individuals of a given race are distinguishable from one another in proportion to our familiarity and our contact with the race as a whole. Thus, to the uninitiated American, all Asiatics look alike, whereas to the Asiatic, all White people look alike.[46]

Experts in the field of eyewitness memory and about half of potential jurors endorse the belief that cross-racial identifications are less reliable than same-race identifications. This presumption is based on the belief in the existence of an own-race bias—that is, that people recognize people of their own race better than they do people of another race. Brigham and Malpass note that the own-race recognition bias has been demonstrated among Whites, Blacks, Asians, Latinos, and Hispanics. Explanations for this phenomenon vary. Some evidence shows that persons who have close friends of the other race show less of an own-race recognition bias.[47]

Moreover, Ferman and Entwistle found that children living in mixed-race environments show less of an own-race recognition bias than do children living in a segregated environment.[48] Conversely, other research indicates that the own-race recognition bias is not reduced by frequent contact with the other race and that prejudiced persons are no more likely to exhibit an own-race recognition bias than are nonprejudiced persons.[49] There is some evidence indicating that persons who view other-race faces tend to focus on the constituent (individual) features of the face, whereas observers of same-race faces focus on configural features of the face.[50]

Recent research conducted at the University of Miami offers an alternative explanation for the own-race recognition bias. Researchers there maintain that environmental or contextual cues, such as one's socioeconomic status, bring out a recategorization of same-race individuals as out-group members and thus reduce same-race face recognition but not other-race recognition. Shriver and his colleagues found that to middle-class White perceivers, presenting White faces on impoverished backgrounds led to significantly worse same-race recognition than presenting those same faces on wealthy backgrounds. Thus, a social context implying that an individual is a poor rather than middle-class White is enough to reduce the recognition advantage of same-race faces. In addition, for White faces on impoverished backgrounds, same-race recognition is approximately equal to other-race recognition, regardless of whether impoverished White faces are compared with impoverished Black faces or wealthy Black faces. However, the economic status shown by the background had no effect on the other-race recognition of Black faces, regardless of wealthy or impoverished contexts. Thus, when same-race faces were seen on backgrounds that indicated they were out-group members, the accuracy of same-race face recognition was reduced.[51]

Regulators

Nonverbal **regulators** are those behaviors and actions that govern, direct, or manage conversation. During conversations in the United States, for example, direct eye contact and affirmative head nodding typically communicate agreement or that a conversant understands what is being communicated. How close one stands to another during a conversation can also signal to the conversant whether to continue the communication. Rules for direct eye contact and distance during communication vary considerably across cultures. In many Asian cultures, such as South Korea, Vietnam, and Japan, direct eye contact is prohibited between persons of differing status. In these cultures, the person of lower status avoids making direct eye contact with his or her superior as a sign of respect. Direct eye contact in these cultures can communicate insolence or signal a challenge to the person of higher status. In South Korea, when people of higher status hand something to a person of lower status (e.g., a professor handing something to a student), the person of lower status accepts whatever is offered with both hands, gives a slight nod of the head, and averts his or her eyes during the act, all as a sign of recognizing the status differential.

Communicator distance during conversation can also govern the flow of communication (see Figure 8.7). According to Almaney and Alwan, in some Middle Eastern cultures, people stand close together during interaction to smell one another's breath. To smell one another is considered desirable. In fact, to deny someone your breath communicates shame.[52] Harris, Moran, and Moran point out that in many Arab cultures, men hold hands as they converse to demonstrate their trust in each other. During conversation, a raising of the eyebrows or a clicking of the tongue signifies a negative response and a disruption in the flow of communication.[53]

Adaptors

Adaptors are kinesic actions that satisfy physiological or psychological needs. Scratching an itch satisfies a physiological need, whereas tapping the tip of your pen on the desk while waiting for the professor to deliver a final exam satisfies a psychological need. Very little, if any, cross-cultural research on adaptors has been conducted. For the most part, adaptors are not learned and probably do not vary much across cultures.

Paralanguage

Paralanguage refers to vocal qualities that usually, though not necessarily, accompany speech. Knapp and Hall divide paralanguage into two broad categories: voice qualities and vocalizations. Paralinguistic voice qualities include pitch, rhythm, tempo, articulation, and resonance of the voice. Paralinguistic vocalizations include laughing, crying, sighing,

| Figure 8.7 | Communicator distance during conversation often governs the flow of communication and provides cues as to the nature of the relationship. |

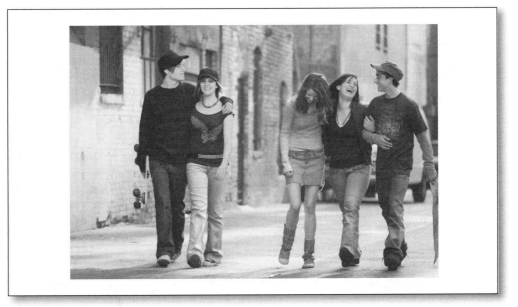

belching, swallowing, clearing the throat, snoring, and so forth. Other paralinguistic vocalizations are intensity and *nonfluencies,* such as "um," "ah," and "uh."

Silence is also considered within the domain of paralanguage.[54] Often, paralinguistic qualities, vocalizations, and nonfluencies reveal a speaker's emotional state or veracity. Audiences can discern when speakers are nervous or confident by listening to their tone of voice, rhythm, pace, and the number of nonfluencies they utter. Parents often detect a child's deception not so much by what the child says but by how it is said. Through paralanguage, we can tell whether speakers are being genuine, cynical, or sarcastic. Moreover, a person's geographical origin can be determined by listening closely to his or her paralanguage.[55]

In all spoken languages, vocal sounds are carried by vowels; it is impossible to speak words without them. Consonants, on the other hand, function to stop and start sound. Linguist Peter Ladefoged has observed that although there are perhaps as many as 900 consonants and 200 vowels in all the world's languages, many languages tend to use only five vowel sounds. In fact, one in five languages use the same vowel sounds as are used in Spanish and English—*a, e, i, o,* and *u*—although there are variations on their pronunciation. According to Ladefoged, although there are literally thousands of speech sounds that any human is capable of making, only a few hundred sounds have ever been observed among the world's spoken languages. The average language uses only about 40 sounds, and all babies are capable of making all of them.

All babies, the world over, make the same sounds during infancy. Linguists believe that these sounds are the building blocks by which infants construct mature sounds. Although infants have not yet learned the specific language of their culture and have not yet spoken a single word, they practice the sounds of all human languages. All babies regularly produce a small subset of universal syllable types that occur in all the world's languages. This is strong evidence that human language was not invented by humans but, rather, evolved. To be sure, unusual sounds show up in some languages. Clicking sounds, for example, can be heard in South Africa's Zulu and Xhosa languages, and nasal sounds are heard in Eskimo languages. Although these sounds may be unique components of these languages, all human babies, regardless of culture, can be heard making them at some time prior to learning their culture's formal verbal language.[56]

Some languages, called tonal languages, rely on vocalized tones to communicate meaning. In these languages, a rising or falling tone changes the meaning of a word. Thai is a pentatonal language that uses five tones: monotone, low, falling, high, and rising. Modern Vietnamese is a monosyllabic language, meaning that all words are only one syllable long. Like the Thai language, Vietnamese is tonal, and the meaning of the syllable changes with tone. The Chinese language is tonal also. Mandarin Chinese, the most common language in China, is based on four or five tones. Every syllable in Mandarin has its definite tone. The first tone, called *yinping,* is a high-pitched tone without variation from beginning to end. The syllable is spoken with an even tone, using the highest pitch of the speaker's voice. The second tone, *yangping,* starts from a lower pitch and ends high. The syllable is spoken with a rising tone, not unlike the one used by speakers of English asking a question. The third tone, *shangsheng,* is perhaps the most difficult to master. It begins as a middle-level tone, goes down, bounds up, and ends with a relatively higher pitch. The fourth tone, *chyusheng,* is a falling tone that starts high and ends at the lowest range of the speaker's voice. The fifth tone, *chingsheng,* is often left out of descriptions of Mandarin. This tone is spoken quickly and lightly, as if it has no tone. *Chingsheng* is often called the neutral tone.[57]

To be sure, English and other languages have inflections—that is, a change in pitch on certain words and sentences. English speakers can communicate anger or sadness by changing the pitch of their voice. Without the appropriate inflection, the meaning of an English speaker's sentence can be misinterpreted. In Chinese, however, tones completely change the meaning of a word. Take, for example, the word *ma*. In the first tone, *ma* is "mother." In the second tone, *ma* becomes "hemp" or "grass." In the third tone, *ma* becomes "horse," and in the fourth tone, *ma* becomes "to scold" or "to nag." In Mandarin Chinese, the meanings of words are strictly based on the tones, which remain constant in whispering, yelling, or even singing. Mandarin tones are relative to the natural pitch of the speaker. A deep-voiced man's high note may be much lower than the high note of a woman.[58]

As with any other form of communication, some paralinguistic devices are learned and vary across cultures. South Koreans are taught to avoid talking or laughing loudly in any situation; such behavior is seen as rude and unbecoming since it tends to draw attention. Many Koreans, especially women, cover their mouths when laughing.[59] In their study of paralanguage, Zukerman and Miyake introduce the idea of a vocal attractiveness stereotype. They contend that, like one's physical attractiveness, individuals perceived to be vocally attractive elicit more favorable impressions than those not perceived to be vocally attractive. The results of their study indicate that attractive voices are those that are relatively loud, resonant, and articulate. Unattractive voices are squeaky, nasal, monotone, and off pitch. Zukerman and Miyake found some sex differences in vocal attractiveness. For example, throatiness was perceived more negatively among female voices than among male voices.[60]

Perhaps in any culture, as we move from region to region, we can hear differences in paralanguage; that is, we hear differences in the pronunciation and vocal pitch of the people. Most people think of such differences as *accents*. But accents have both a verbal and nonverbal (i.e., paralinguistic) component. As we saw in Chapter 7, a person with a particular regional or cultural accent may use different words than someone from another region or culture, but they also *sound* different. In this way, an accent refers to one's manner of pronunciation. To be sure, the mode in which one speaks does include the words one uses, but it also includes the sounds of those words, which are nonverbal—specifically, paralinguistic. And our perceptions of people are often based not so much on *what* they say but *how* they say it.

A substantial body of research has emerged in the social sciences that focuses on native and nonnative paralinguistic accents. Much of this research indicates that persons with nonnative accents are perceived much differently, and usually more negatively, than those with native accents. One's accent is a considerable social force and carries with it a significant amount of information. In their review of some of the research in this area, Kinzler and her associates point out that perceived accent is an initial indicator of in-group–out-group distinctions and that children as young as 5 months old, who have virtually no verbal competence, can discriminate between two languages or dialects, provided that one of the languages/dialects is their own. They also suggest that 5-month-old infants display social preferences based on paralanguage. In their own studies, Kinzler and her colleagues presented 5-year-olds with photographs and voice recordings of children they did not know. The children chose to be friends with native speakers of their native language rather than children with foreign accents. Kinzler notes that these preferences were not due to the verbal intelligibility of the foreign speakers' speech, as children found the accented speech to be comprehensible; the preferences were based on paralinguistic cues. In addition, they found that children chose same-race children as friends when the target children were silent, but they chose other-race children with a native accent as friends over same-race children with accents. In other words, children use accent more than race as a criterion in choosing friends.[61]

In their recent review of literature on nonnative accents, Agata Gluszek and John Dovidio of Yale University assert that a nonnative accent is one of the most salient characteristics of a person that identifies him/her as an out-group member and that a nonnative accent almost always stigmatizes that person. Gluszek and Dovidio emphasize that a nonnative accent is distinct from verbal language competency. That is, people who are perfectly verbally fluent in a second language may still carry a nonnative accent after many years in a host country because they retain the paralinguistic phonology (i.e., the sounds) of their native tongue. These people, they argue, are usually stereotyped negatively, which carries serious social, professional, and economic consequences. Gluszek and Dovidio stress that nonnative accents are associated with a wide range of negative stereotypes, including perceptions that the people who speak them are less intelligent, less loyal, less competent, and lower in social status. But Gluszek and Dovidio also point out that in some cases, a nonnative accent is associated with positive traits. For example, in the United States, a British accent is often perceived as prestigious. Generally, in the United States, Western European accents are perceived more favorably than Asian or Hispanic accents. So, this idea, and the finding that children as young as 5 months old recognize accents as markers during person perception, suggests that there is nothing inherent to accents that renders some more aesthetically pleasing than others. Instead, accents serve as social identity cues, which, in turn, trigger negative or positive perceptions.[62]

In addition to being negatively stereotyped, persons with nonnative accents may face prejudice and discrimination and are unprotected by the courts. Nonnative accent discrimination differs from ethnic or racial discrimination in that the United States Civil Rights Act of 1964 prohibits discrimination on the basis of race or national origin, but it does not specifically mention accent. Gluszek and Dovidio point to research that has found that nonnative speakers of English face discrimination in housing and employment. They are more likely to be assigned lower-status positions within organizations and receive lower pay increments. In fact, according to Gluszek and Dovidio, many employers who have been sued by nonnative speakers for discrimination have actually won their cases, especially when they could demonstrate that the nonnative speaker's accent impaired his or her job performance.

Even in the college classroom, perceptions of nonnative accents affect student comprehension. In one study, two groups of students listened to the very same lecture while seeing a photo of either a Japanese or White instructor. The students who saw the Japanese photo actually believed they heard an accent and performed worse on a lecture comprehension test than those who were exposed to the White instructor's photograph. In another study, conducted in England, researchers manipulated the accent of a British male criminal suspect. They found that when participants listened to a recorded conversation between the British male criminal suspect and a male policeman, they rated the suspect as significantly more guilty when he employed a Birmingham accent rather than a standard British accent.[63]

While one's accent is something that is heard, silence is also a part of the paralinguistic channel. Hasegawa and Gudykunst maintain that silence is the lack of verbal communication or the absence of sound. Hasegawa and Gudykunst assert that culture influences the meaning and use of silence. In their research, they compared the use of silence among Japanese and Americans and found that, in the United States, silence is defined as a pause, break, empty space, or lack of verbal communication. Hasegawa and Gudykunst maintain that silence generally is not a part of Americans' everyday communication routines. They argue that although silence is acceptable among intimate others, when meeting strangers, Americans are conscious of silence and find it quite awkward. In Japan, however, silence is a space or pause during verbal communication that has important meaning. Pauses, or silence, are to be interpreted carefully. Stylistically, Japanese are taught to be indirect and sometimes ambiguous to maintain harmony. Silence, then, can be used to avoid directness, such as bluntly saying "no" to a request.[64]

Charles Braithwaite has studied silence across cultures and argues that silence is a central nonverbal component of any speech community. He argues that some communicative functions of silence may be universal and do not vary across cultures. For example, Braithwaite maintains that among Native American groups, Japanese, Japanese Americans in Hawaii, and people in rural Appalachia, the use of silence as a communicative act is associated with communication situations where the status of the interactants is uncertain, unpredictable, or ambiguous. In addition, Braithwaite argues that silence as a communicative act is associated with communication situations where there is a known and unequal distribution of power among interactants. In other words, when interactants consciously recognize their differential status, they consciously use silence. Braithwaite cites evidence of this in many cultures, including the Anang of southwestern Nigeria, the Wolof of Senegal, the Maori of New Zealand, the Malagasy in Madagascar, urban African American women, and some working-class White Americans.[65]

Proxemics

Proxemics refers to the perception and use of space, including territoriality and personal space. Territoriality refers to physical geographical space; personal space refers to perceptual or psychological space—sometimes thought of as the "bubble" of space that humans carry with them in their day-to-day activities. College students who live in the very close quarters of a dorm are usually quite sensitive to proxemics and territoriality. Dorm rooms do not allow for much personal space or territoriality. In their comparison of territoriality among Turkish and American students, Kaya and Weber found that in both cultures, men tended to demonstrate more nonsharing behavior and less personalization of their space than did women. The authors also report that students in both cultures who knew their roommates tended to share their personal belongings and other dimensions of the dorm room more than students who did not know their roommates previously. Interestingly, American students experienced their rooms as more personal and expressive of the self than did Turkish students. Americans are generally very protective of their space.[66]

In Nigeria, the student population in residence halls at colleges and universities has tripled over the past 20 years. In her research, Architect Dalapo Amole focused on the coping strategies used by Nigerian college students, gender differences in those coping styles, and the influence of the length of stay. Her results showed that men and women differed in many of the coping strategies. These included (a) rearranging the furniture, used more by males than females; (b) decorating personal place, used more by females than males; (c) generally segregating space in the bedroom, used more by females than males; (d) entertaining and meeting friends elsewhere, used more by males than females; and (e) coming to the room only to sleep, used more by males than females. Staying away from the room, storing some personal items elsewhere, and sleeping elsewhere were strategies used equally by both men and women. Length of stay in the dorm did not appear to be important except with respect to studying and entertaining friends.[67]

In cultures whose population density is high, personal space and territoriality are highly valued. Privacy in densely populated locations is often accomplished psychologically rather than physiologically. In Calcutta, India, for example, there are nearly 80,000 persons per square mile. There is literally not enough room in the city to claim any personal space. Touching and bumping into others while walking through the streets of Calcutta is quite common and to be expected.[68]

Socioeconomic factors can also affect a culture's perception of space. Cramped and insufficient housing is common in much of Sri Lanka. In the 1980s, most housing units were quite small. Of all the homes, 33% had only one room, another 33% had two rooms, and only 20% had three rooms. Moreover, the average number of persons per home was five. (Overcrowding in Sri Lanka is declining, however, since the government initiated intensive housing programs in the 1990s.)[69] The Moroccan perception of space reflects the culture's valuing of community. Personal space during a conversation is typically less than an arm's length. In mosques, worshipers line up shoulder to shoulder to pray. Houses typically have very little space between them as well.[70] Because Kenyan culture values harmony and sharing, Kenyans tend to be less aware of personal territory than are people in the United States. For example, many Kenyans do not designate specific rooms in the home for specific activities, such as a living room or a dining room. In addition, the personal space distance between interactants is much closer than in the United States.[71]

Saudi Arabians, too, are known to favor closer personal proximity than do Americans. Saudis typically enjoy getting very close, face to face, and engaging in direct eye contact.[72] Many other studies support the link between culture and proxemic behavior in comparing Americans with Arabs, Latin Americans, Pakistanis, Germans, Italians, Japanese, and Venezuelans. These examples suggest that culture plays a decisive role in how spatial distances are maintained during communication. Other variables besides culture can affect proxemic distances, however, such as the age and sex of the interactants, the nature of the relationship, the environment, and ethnicity. Several studies have documented that in most cultures, the need for personal space increases with age. In addition, the use of space as influenced by sex seems to vary significantly by culture.[73]

Haptics

Haptics, or tactile communication, refers to the use of touch. Knapp and Hall argue that touch may be the most primitive form of communication. In the United States, much research has been conducted to examine the impact of touching during the first few years of life.[74] Haptic communication varies widely across cultures, and the amount and kind of touch varies with the age, sex, situation, and relationship of the people involved. In his theorizing about culture and nonverbal communication, Edward Hall distinguishes between contact and noncontact cultures.[75] Contact cultures are those that tend to encourage touching and engage in touching more frequently than do either moderate-contact or noncontact cultures, in which touching occurs less frequently and is generally discouraged. Many South and Central American cultures are considered contact countries, as are many southern European countries. The United States is regarded as a moderate-contact culture, whereas many Asian countries are considered noncontact. Many Asian cultures have established norms that forbid public displays of affection and intimacy that involve touch. One of the five central tenets of Confucian philosophy is the division between the sexes. Because Confucianism is so central to many Asian cultures, engaging in touch with the opposite sex is considered uncivil.[76]

In their field study of touch patterns among cross-sex couples, McDaniel and Andersen observed the touch behavior of couples in airports. They found that couples from the United States touched most, followed by (in order of most to least touching) couples from Northern Europe, the Caribbean/Latin America, Southeast Asia, and Northeast Asia.[77] Psychologist Sidney Jourard conducted a study that counted the frequency of body contact between couples as they sat in cafés in different cities and countries. He found that the average number of touches per hour in San Juan, Puerto Rico, was 180; in Paris, 110; in Gainesville, Florida, 2; and in London, 0.[78]

Because we are often taught not to touch others, some people develop touch avoidance. These people feel uncomfortable in situations requiring touch and generally avoid touching when possible. In her study of Americans, Japanese, Puerto Ricans, and Koreans, Beth Casteel found no touch avoidance differences in same-sex dyads for the Japanese and Americans, in that both were significantly more touch avoidant than were same-sex dyads in Puerto Rico and Korea. In opposite-sex dyads, however, Japanese and Koreans showed much higher levels of touch avoidance than did Americans and Puerto Ricans. Casteel concluded that the Japanese and Americans allow women to touch other women, but men should not touch men. Koreans and Puerto Ricans are just the reverse.[79] In their comparison of high-contact cultures of southern Europe and low-contact cultures of northern Europe, psychologists Remland, Jones, and Brinkman found that more touch was observed among Italian and Greek dyads than among English, French, and Dutch dyads.[80] The people of northern Italy have few inhibitions about personal space and touch. Heterosexual men are often seen kissing each other on both cheeks and walking together arm in arm, as are women. East Indians are very expressive with touch. To touch the feet of elders is a sign of respect. Indians demonstrate their trust for one another by holding hands briefly during a conversation or religious activity. When a Hindu priest blesses others at religious gatherings, he gently touches the palms of their outstretched hands.[81] Saudi Arabians tend to value touching also. Saudi businessmen often hold hands as a sign of trust, a form of touch behavior that some Americans often misunderstand. Saudi women, however, are never to be touched in public.[82]

Most cultures prohibit some forms of touch. Harris, Moran, and Moran observe that in Thailand, Sri Lanka, and some other cultures, the head is considered sacred and should not be touched by others. Americans sometimes make the mistake of patting children of other cultures on the top of the head as a sign of affection or endearment. In some cultures, this is seen as a serious breach of etiquette.[83] In many African and Middle Eastern cultures, the use of the left hand is forbidden in certain social situations. In Kenya, Indonesia, and Pakistan, for example, the left hand should not be used in eating or serving food. Harris, Moran, and Moran report that in Kenya, the left hand is considered weak and unimportant. Sometimes, Kenyans intentionally use the left hand when serving food to someone they disrespect. In other cultures, such as Iraq and Iran, the left hand is used for cleaning oneself following bodily functions and should never be used to give or receive gifts or other objects.[84] Like proxemics, the nature of touch is often mediated by more than culture. The relationship between the interactants, the location and duration of touch, the relative pressure of the touch, the environment in which the touch occurs (public or private), and whether the touch is intentional or accidental influence touch across cultures.

STUDENT VOICES ACROSS CULTURES

Lindsey Novitzke

I'm a 20-year-old college student from New Richmond, Wisconsin. In May of 2010, I visited Zambia, Africa, with an organization called The Zambia Project, which works throughout the year doing various fundraising events for Zambian Open Community Schools, a nonprofit that exists to provide education to orphans in Zambia. I had the adventure of a lifetime visiting schools, distributing school supplies, interacting with the people, and experiencing Zambian culture.

Nonverbal communication played a crucial role in my interactions with the people from Zambia. Although the official language is English, many of the people of Zambia speak primarily their own native and cultural languages, in addition to a different kind of English than what we speak in the United States. Oftentimes, the younger children did not know any English; therefore, much of our communication was nonverbal. Most specifically, touch played a considerable role in all our interactions with the Zambian people, and even more so with the children. Zambian culture is a high-contact culture, where even the handshake they use as a greeting involves more touch than a handshake in the United States.

I would often see male and female children of all ages holding hands as they walked to and from school. Zambian social structure, such as schools and homes, promotes a heavy amount of touch, requiring people to sit and work closely with one another. Young girls and women carry their children or siblings in a sling that hangs off their shoulder, where the baby is constantly touching them—teaching them, from an early age, that touch is essential. Since my verbal communication with the younger children was minimal, I often held their hands or let them sit in my lap as a way to demonstrate my friendship.

For adults to touch one another as they interacted was not uncommon. Their personal space "bubbles" were small, almost nonexistent. Being from a low-contact culture, I felt bombarded by the amount of touch occurring during interactions. Many of the children loved to rub my skin and touch my hair, since many of them had never before seen blond hair or a Caucasian person up close. Ironically, after returning to the United States, I actually craved touch and felt that people in the United States were unusually distant. Touch played a major role in my visit to Zambia.

Olfactics

Probably the least understood, yet most fascinating, of all human sensations is **olfactics**—that is, our sense of smell. Our lack of understanding is certainly not because we lack a sense of smell. According to Gibbons, humans can detect as many as 10,000 different compounds by smell. Moreover, approximately 1 % of our genes are devoted to detecting odors. Although this may not seem like much, humans have more olfactory genes than any other type of gene identified in human and mammalian DNA. Gibbons suggests that our lack of understanding may be because we lack a vocabulary for smell and are discouraged from talking about smell. Particularly in the United States, we have become obsessed with masking certain smells, especially those of the human body. According to Gibbons, the biggest users of fragrance in the world are U.S.-based companies such as Procter & Gamble, Lever Bros., and Colgate. Some brands of soap use more than two million pounds of fragrance a year. In many Western cultures, body odor is regarded as unpleasant and distasteful, and we go to great efforts to mask or remove it.[85]

David Stoddart asserts that in addition to their ability to detect odors, humans are even more adept at producing odors. According to Stoddart, evidence from anatomy, chemistry, and psychology indicates that humans are the most highly scented of all the apes. Human scent comes from two types of glands that lie beneath the skin, the sebaceous glands and the apocrine glands. Sebaceous glands are all over the body, wherever there are hair follicles. They produce an odorous, oily fluid whose original purpose was to protect hair. The apocrine glands are a type of sweat gland. They are most dense in our armpits but are also found in the pubic and anal regions, the face, the scalp, and the umbilical region of the abdomen (the belly button). Women appear to have more apocrine glands than do men, but some evidence suggests that their glands are less active than those in men. The most distasteful odors come from the apocrine glands, which are activated when we are frightened, excited, or aroused. Human saliva and urine also produce human scent.[86]

According to Kohl and Francoeur, research has repeatedly shown that women perceive odors differently at various phases of their menstrual cycles. They tend to be the most sensitive to odors during ovulation. Other studies indicate that when in close proximity to one another over time, as in dormitory living, women synchronize their menstrual cycles. Scientists believe that axillary organ secretions function as odor cues to stimulate their cycles. On a related note, studies have shown that vaginal secretions during ovulation are minimally unpleasant, whereas such secretions before and after ovulation are described as distinctly unpleasant.[87]

Kohl and Francoeur suggest that although preferences for certain smells seem to vary across cultures, there appears to be a universal preference for some kinds of scents that may have biological and evolutionary roots. These preferences are probably mediated by culture to some extent, however. For example, the finest perfumes in the world contain olfactory hints of urine. Scientists allege that these scents function as sex attractants. We know, for example, that sex-attractant pheromones are expelled from the body in urine. These two kinds of smell may mirror those of our humanoid ancestors and unconsciously stimulate the deepest parts of the brain.[88]

In addition to functioning as a sex attractant, smell is also used politically for marking social class distinctions. Classen, Howes, and Synnott contend that smell plays a significant role in the construction of power relations in many societies.[89] Le Guerer comments, for example, that idiomatic expressions often employ smell-related terms to voice antagonism and repugnance toward others. People refer to persons they dislike as "stinkers." When we are suspicious of someone, we say we "smell a rat." When something seems wrong or amiss, we comment that "it doesn't smell right" or "smells fishy." Dishonest politicians may "reek of hypocrisy."[90]

Anthony Synnott claims that odor is often used to categorize groups of people into status, power, and moral classes. To be sure, the smells themselves are not intrinsically moral or immoral, but the qualities or thoughts attributed to the specific scents are what give them their moral significance. Synott argues that a person's scent is not only an individual emission and a moral statement but also a perceived social attribute that is especially significant for members of subordinate groups, who are often labeled "smelly." Such labels often foster racial, ethnic, and religious prejudice and hatred. Subordinate and microcultural groups are often described as possessing negative olfactory characteristics. In fact, Synnott argues that perceived foul odors legitimize inequalities and are one of the criteria by which a negative identity is imposed on a particular class or race.[91]

Many cultures establish norms for acceptable and unacceptable scents associated with the human body. When individuals or groups of people fail to fit into the realm of acceptability, their odor signals that something is "wrong" with them, either physically or mentally. Kohl and Francoeur note that the American Puritan tradition of "cleanliness is next to godliness" may explain the American obsession with deodorants, perfumes, soaps, and shampoos.[92] Muslims believe that cleanliness of the body and purity of the soul are related. Muslim women are told to purify themselves after menstruation, and cleanliness for all is prescribed before and after meals. The Koran specifies that all five daily prayers must be preceded by washing of the hands, arms, and feet.[93]

Social class distinctions based on smells are the cultural product of education, religion, parenting, and social pressure from peers. With the exception of those scents that appeal to everyone, people are conditioned to find certain scents attractive and others dirty or foul. Moreover, such distinctions sustain social barriers between groups and even justify a dominant group's persecution of subordinate groups.[94] In the Middle Ages, wealthy people bought perfumes to diminish the scent of the lower classes. Nineteenth-century Japanese described European traders with the term *bata-kusai*—"stinks of butter."[95] Adolf Hitler's hatred of Jews was based partially on olfactics; he claimed that their foul odor was representative of their "moral mildew" and reflected their outer and inner foulness and, therefore, their immorality.[96]

Gibbons reports that during World Wars I and II, German and English soldiers claimed they could identify the enemy by their smell. Similar claims have been made by North Vietnamese and U.S. troops.[97] Baker reports that in U.S. history, Thomas Jefferson is purported to have said that Blacks have "a very strong and disagreeable odour."[98] Dollard claims that many White racists used the "disagreeable scent" of Blacks as a final proof of the impossibility of close association between the races.[99] In 1912, sociologist Georg Simmel wrote, "It would appear impossible for the Negro ever to be accepted into high society in North America because of his bodily odor."[100] Indeed, Simmel concluded that "the moral ideal of harmony and equality between the different classes and races runs up against the brick wall of an invincible disgust inspired by the sense of smell."[101]

Classen, Howes, and Synnott maintain that more than any other group, women are stereotyped and classified by their scent. Historically, in many cultures, women were considered the fragrant sex, unless they were prostitutes or suffragettes or challenged the male-dominated social order. The role of fragrance was primarily to entice men. In general, the Western cultural axiom has been that, unless perfumed, women stink. Jonathan Swift's poem *The Lady's Dressing Room* expresses this belief:

> *His foul imagination links*
>
> *Each Dame he sees with all her Stinks:*
>
> *And, if unsav'ry Odours fly,*
>
> *Conceives a Lady standing by.[102]*

Although it may be the least studied of all the senses, social scientists are discovering that olfactory sensation is a potent influence on social interaction. Survey data indicate that a significant percentage of adults are conscious of and influenced by smells in their environment.

In their poll of more than 350 American adults, the Olfactory Research Fund found that 64% of respondents indicated that smell greatly influenced the quality of their lives. Specifically, 76% of the respondents reported that the sense of smell was "very important" in their daily relationships with persons of the opposite sex, and 20% indicated that it was "somewhat important." As related to their relationships with their spouses, 74% indicated that smell was "very important," and 22% said that it was "somewhat important." Although the percentages dropped somewhat, 36% of the respondents indicated that smell was "important" in their relationships with friends, and 40% agreed that smell was "very important" in their relationships with coworkers. Of all respondents, 80% reported using environmental fragrances, such as potpourri, room sprays, and scented candles. Well over 60% of respondents believed that particular aromas enhance the quality of life, relieve stress, and help retrieve memories. Of those respondents who used cologne, perfume, or aftershave, 83% said they did so because they liked the scent, 68% said it made them feel better about themselves, 56% said it enhanced their sense of well-being, 51% said they used fragrances to make themselves more romantically attractive to others, and 46% said they used fragrances to make a fashion statement.[103]

This emphasis on smell is often motivated by the pivotal role olfactics play in the maintenance of social relationships. Todrank, Byrnes, Wrzesniewski, and Rozin assert that most cultures assign meaning to odors that is often displaced onto the people wearing them.[104] This is especially evident in relationships with members of the opposite sex. Although it is widely recognized that odors play a determinant role in the mating practices of many animal species, Kohl and Francoeur argue that odors are also an important ingredient in human mating and bonding and cite empirical evidence showing that odors hasten puberty, mediate women's menstrual cycles, and even influence sexual orientation.[105] Extant research indicates that odors help people identify their family members, facilitate the bond between parents and children, and influence how often and with whom individuals mate.

Kate Fox is a social anthropologist and the director of the Social Issues Research Center in Oxford, England. Fox has studied cultural differences in olfactics, with a special emphasis on non-Western cultures. Fox maintains that, unlike in most Western cultures, smell is "the emperor of the senses" in many cultures. For example, Fox describes the importance of smell among the Ongee people of the Andaman Islands, a group of islands off the southeast coast of India. According to Fox, much of Ongee cultural life revolves around smell. For example, their calendar is based on the smell of flowers that bloom at different times of the year. One's personal identity is defined by smell. Fox writes that to refer to oneself, an Ongee touches the tip of his or her nose, which is a gesture meaning both "me" and "my smell." Fox also reports that during greetings, Ongee routinely ask, "How is your nose?" rather than "How are you?" Ongee etiquette prescribes that if a person responds that he or she feels "heavy with smell," the greeter should inhale deeply to remove the excess smell. Conversely, if the greeted person indicates that he or she is short on smell energy, Ongee etiquette prescribes that the greeter contribute some extra scent by blowing on him or her.[106]

Fox also describes smell rituals among the Bororo peoples of Brazil and the Serer Ndut of Senegal (western Africa). Among the Bororo, personal body smell indicates the life force of the individual, whereas one's breath odor indicates the state of one's soul. The Ndut believe that individuals possess a physical smell, defined by one's body and breath odor, and a spiritual smell. The spiritual smell is thought to be a reincarnated smell. For example, the Ndut can tell which ancestor has been reincarnated by associating the smell of a child with that of a deceased person.[107]

Self-Assessment 8.1

Personal Report of Olfactory Perception and Sensitivity (PROPS)

Directions: The following instrument is designed to assess your level of olfactory perception and sensitivity. On a scale of 1 to 7, indicate the degree to which each statement applies to you.

1 = strongly disagree, 2 = disagree, 3 = slightly disagree, 4 = undecided, 5 =slightly agree, 6 = agree, and 7 = strongly agree.

_____ 1. When interacting with a stranger of the opposite sex, I am typically conscious of the scent of his or her breath.

_____ 2. When interacting with a stranger of the opposite sex, I am typically conscious of the scent of his or her body.

_____ 3. When interacting with a stranger of the opposite sex, I am typically conscious of the scent of his or her cologne or perfume.

_____ 4. When interacting with a stranger of the same sex, I am typically conscious of the scent of his or her breath.

_____ 5. When interacting with a stranger of the same sex, I am typically conscious of the scent of his or her body.

_____ 6. When interacting with a stranger of the same sex, I am typically conscious of the scent of his or her cologne or perfume.

_____ 7. When interacting with a close friend of the opposite sex, I am typically conscious of the scent of his or her breath.

_____ 8. When interacting with a close friend of the opposite sex, I am typically conscious of the scent of his or her body.

_____ 9. When interacting with a close friend of the opposite sex, I am typically conscious of the scent of his or her cologne or perfume.

_____ 10. When interacting with a close friend of the same sex, I am typically conscious of the scent of his or her breath.

_____ 11. When interacting with a close friend of the same sex, I am typically conscious of the scent of his or her body.

_____ 12. When interacting with a close friend of the same sex, I am typically conscious of the scent of his or her cologne or perfume.

_____ 13. When interacting with a stranger of the opposite sex, I am typically conscious of the scent of my breath.

_____ 14. When interacting with a stranger of the opposite sex, I am typically conscious of the scent of my body.

_____ 15. When interacting with a stranger of the opposite sex, I am typically conscious of the scent of my cologne or perfume.

_____ 16. When interacting with a stranger of the same sex, I am typically conscious of the scent of my breath.

_____ 17. When interacting with a stranger of the same sex, I am typically conscious of the scent of my body.

_____ 18. When interacting with a stranger of the same sex, I am typically conscious of the scent of my cologne or perfume.

_____ 19. When interacting with a close friend of the opposite sex, I am typically conscious of the scent of my breath.

_____ 20. When interacting with a close friend of the opposite sex, I am typically conscious of the scent of my body.

_____ 21. When interacting with a close friend of the opposite sex, I am typically conscious of the scent of my cologne or perfume.

_____ 22. When interacting with a close friend of the same sex, I am typically conscious of the scent of my breath.

_____ 23. When interacting with a close friend of the same sex, I am typically conscious of the scent of my body.

_____ 24. When interacting with a close friend of the same sex, I am typically conscious of the scent of my cologne or perfume.

_____ 25. When interacting with someone from a different culture or ethnicity, I am typically conscious of the scent of his or her breath.

_____ 26. When interacting with someone from a different culture or ethnicity, I am typically conscious of the scent of his or her cologne or perfume.

_____ 27. When interacting with someone from a different culture or ethnicity, I am typically conscious of the scent of his or her body.

_____ 28. When interacting with someone in a private environment, I am typically conscious of the scent of the immediate surroundings.

_____ 29. When interacting with someone in a private environment, I am typically conscious of the scent of the furniture.

_____ 30. When interacting with someone in a public environment, I am typically conscious of the scent of the immediate surroundings.

Scoring: To calculate your PROPS score, sum your responses as follows:

1. Perception and sensitivity to others: add Items 1–12 (range = 12–84).

2. Perception and sensitivity to self: add Items 13–24 (range = 12–84).

3. Perception and sensitivity to different cultures: add Items 25–27 (range = 3–21).

4. Perception and sensitivity to environment: add Items 28–30 (range = 3–21).

Higher scores indicate more sensitivity to the particular contexts. For example, scores above 50 for perception and sensitivity to others and/or self would be high, whereas scores below 30 would be considered low sensitivity. Scores above 15 for perception and sensitivity to persons from different cultures would be considered high, whereas scores below 7 would be considered low sensitivity.

SOURCE: J. W. Neuliep and E. L. Groshkopf, *Toward a Communication Theory of Olfactics: Explication, Development of the Personal Report of Olfactic Perception and Sensation and Some Initial Tests.* Paper presented at the 2001 annual convention of the National Communication Association, Atlanta, GA.

In her olfactic research, Fox has discovered that among those cultures where smell is closely associated with one's personal identity, the exchange or mixing of odors among people is carefully prescribed. For example, among the Amazonian Desana, members of a particular tribal group are thought to share a similar odor. Marriage is allowed only between people of different odors; that is, between members of different tribal groups. Similarly, among the Batek Negrito of the Malay Peninsula, people of similar odor groups are prohibited from engaging in sexual intercourse and even sitting too close to one another. The Batek Negrito believe that the prolonged mixing of similar odors causes illness in the people themselves and any children they may conceive.[108]

Fox also writes that Western smell preferences are not universal. For example, the Dassanetch, a tribal cattle-raising group in Ethiopia, believe that the smell of cows is the most pleasing of all smells. Dassanetch men routinely wash their hands in cattle urine and smear their bodies with cattle manure. Such smells are associated with status and fertility. The Dogon people of Mali find the scent of onions attractive, especially for young men and women, who rub fried onions all over their bodies.[109]

Physical Appearance and Dress

Often, we can identify a person's culture by his or her physical appearance and dress. Communication with another is often preceded by visual observations of the other's physical appearance. Moreover, in most cultures, people consciously manipulate their physical appearance to communicate their identity. Most cultures have strict rules for how their members should present themselves. Violating a culture's prescriptions for appearance may result in negative sanctions. In many cultures, a person's physical appearance and dress communicate the person's age, sex, and status within the culture.

In virtually every culture, men and women dress differently, and in many cultures, the differences begin at birth. In the United States, for example, male infants are traditionally dressed in blue and female infants in pink. In the Masai culture of Kenya, the distinction between young girls and women is communicated through body artifacts. According to Vandehey, Buerger, and Krueger, Masai women wear specific necklaces and earrings to designate their marital status. For a married woman to be seen without her earrings may bring harsh physical punishment from her husband. Masai men wear earrings and arm rings that designate social status. The specific earring distinguishes the man as an elder or warrior. Other body ornaments communicate whether a Masai (male or female) has been circumcised.[110]

In most Islamic cultures, Muslim women are easily recognized by their headscarves, or turbans, which are important symbols of religious faith among Muslims. Smucker maintains that the scarves are often perceived by Westerners as a sign of male subjugation of women. In Turkey, however, many young Muslim women believe that rather than being a symbol of subservience to men, the headscarf, or veil, serves as a guard against the eyes of men and as a symbol of women's allegiance to God, rather than to their husbands or fathers.[111] Harris, Moran, and Moran note that in many Middle Eastern cultures, such as Saudi Arabia, Islamic law decrees that women dress conservatively and cover their hair in public. Although women are not required to wear the traditional full-length *abaya* (black cloak) over their clothing, they are encouraged to wear a knee-length tunic/dress over slacks and a scarf on their heads. Moreover, they should avoid explicit makeup in the presence of Saudi men. The idea behind these dictates is to avoid sexually arousing men. Saudi men may wear either Saudi dress or their normal Western dress but should not wear shorts or open shirts. Long hair for men is discouraged.[112]

Harris, Moran, and Moran observe that in India, businessmen wear a *dhoti,* a single piece of white cloth about 5 yards long and 3 feet wide that wraps around their lower body. Long shirts are worn on the upper part of the body. Most Indian women wear a sari and blouse. A sari consists of several yards of lightweight cloth draped so that one end forms a skirt and the other a head and shoulder covering. It is not acceptable for women to show skin above the knees or a large portion of the back. Wearing clothes that are in any way revealing is discouraged because it may unintentionally communicate that one is "a loose woman."[113] In Japan, the kimono—a long robe with wide sleeves—is the traditional clothing for both men and women; it is traditionally worn with a broad sash, or *obi,* as an outer garment. The specific design of the kimono varies according to one's sex, age, and marital status, the time of year, and the occasion. In the ancient past, there was no distinction between a man's and a woman's kimono. Today, there are several types of kimonos worn by men, women, and children. Men typically wear kimonos of blue, black, brown, gray, or white. Women's kimonos are the most elaborate and varied in style and design. The fabric, cut, color, sleeve length, and details of the obi vary according to a woman's age, social status, and marital status, as well as the season. During the summer months, women wear *yukatas,* or lightweight cotton kimonos. Many Japanese hotels provide yukatas for guests to wear in their rooms. In Japan, on "7–5–3 Day" (November 15), boys who are 3 or 5 years old and girls who are 3 or 7 years old dress in kimonos to pray at the temples. There is also a special day for all girls and all boys to go to the temple: March 3 is Girls' Day and May 5 is Boys' Day. Kimonos are worn on those days as well.[114]

Chronemics

Chronemics refers to the nonverbal channel of time. Recall (from Chapter 4) Hall's description of monochronic and polychronic time-oriented cultures. According to Hall, monochronic (M-time) orientations emphasize schedules and the compartmentalization and segmentation of measurable units of time. Many M-time cultures are low context, including the United States, Germany, Scandinavia, Canada, France, and most of northern Europe. Conversely, polychronic (P-time) orientations see time as much less tangible and stress multiple activities with little emphasis on scheduling. P-time cultures stress involvement of people and the completion of tasks as opposed to a strict adherence to schedules. Many P-time cultures are high context, including southern Europe, Latin America, and many African and Middle Eastern countries.[115]

The primary system for organizing time, in just about every culture, is the calendar. According to L. E. Doggett, one of the world's leading authorities on calendars, cultures create and use calendars as a way of organizing units of time to satisfy the needs of the society. Doggett maintains that calendars give people a sense that they can control time. Calendars also provide a link between people and the cosmos, or the supernatural. Doggett asserts that, in many cultures, calendars are considered nearly sacred and serve as a source of social order and cultural identity. In many ways, calendars dictate human communication patterns. When people eat, work, celebrate, worship, engage in leisure, attend school, hunt, rest, and fight wars is often prescribed by the calendar. Social contracts of just about every kind are typically determined by calendars. For example, marriages are deemed successful by the number of years they have lasted. Prison terms are defined in terms of months or years. In most cultures, an individual's age, which is measured by a calendar, is the primary criterion for social and cultural privileges and responsibilities.[116]

According to Doggett, there are about 40 calendars used in the world today. Most of these calendars are astronomically based. The primary astronomical cycles include the day, month, and year. Days are defined by the rotation of the Earth on its axis. The month is based on the revolution of the moon around the Earth. The year is based on the revolution of the Earth around the sun. Most cultures use either a solar, lunar, or lunisolar calendar. Many Western cultures, such as the United States, use a solar calendar. Islamic cultures use a lunar calendar. The Hebrew and Chinese use a lunisolar calendar.[117]

Doggett points out that the Gregorian calendar (a solar calendar) serves as the international standard. The United States functions under the Gregorian calendar. A common year is 365 days, with leap years of 366 days. Months are either 30 or 31 days, except for February, which has 28 or 29 days depending on whether or not the year is a leap year. The Hebrew calendar is lunisolar and is the official calendar of Israel. Each year consists of either 12 or 13 months. Months consist of either 29 or 30 days. The beginning of each month is determined by a new moon. Traditionally, days of the week are designated by number, except for the seventh day, the Sabbath. Days begin and end at sunset. In the Islamic calendar, months correspond to the lunar cycle. Based on religious principles, each month begins upon the first visibility of the moon's crescent. Like the Hebrew calendar, days begin at sunset. In China, the Gregorian calendar is used for governmental purposes, but the traditional Chinese calendar is used for scheduling cultural festivals and for timing agricultural activities. The Chinese calendar is lunisolar, where months are either 29 or 30 days.[118]

Hall has pointed out that perceptions of time differ considerably across cultures. In the United States, for example, time is tangible (i.e., concrete, perceptible). Hall notes that to Americans, time can be bought, sold, saved, spent, wasted, lost, made up, and measured. Americans are also future oriented in that we take great efforts to plan and schedule what we expect (or want) to happen. Conversely, to many Arabs, a person who tries to look into the future is regarded as either irreligious or insane. To many Arabs, only God can decree what will or will not occur. Hall also notes that duration is an important component to one's perception of time. According to Hall, duration is what happens between two points. Most Americans view time in this manner and carefully schedule and evaluate cultural events according to their duration (e.g., minutes, hours, days), as in "Oh, that movie was way too long," "This won't take but a minute," and "When will you get here?" To some Native American groups, time is not thought of as measurable; time is a sequence of events that differs for each set of circumstances.[119]

NONVERBAL COMMUNICATION AND DIMENSIONS OF CULTURAL VARIABILITY

Throughout this book, several dimensions of cultural variability have been discussed, including individualism–collectivism, power distance, and high–low context. Each of these dimensions can help explain cultural differences in nonverbal communication across cultures.

Individualism–Collectivism

In Chapter 2, individualism was defined as a cultural orientation where individuals precede groups in importance. In individualistic cultures, emphasis is placed on individual goals over group goals, and social behavior is guided by personal goals, perhaps at the expense of other types of goals. Individualistic cultures stress values that benefit the individual person. The self is promoted because each person is viewed as uniquely endowed and possessing distinctive talent and potential.

In collectivistic cultures, on the other hand, group goals have precedence over individual goals. Collectivistic cultures stress values that serve the in-group by subordinating personal goals for the sake of preserving the in-group. Collectivistic societies are characterized by extended primary groups such as the family, neighborhood, or occupational group, in which members have diffuse mutual obligations and expectations based on their status or rank. In collectivistic cultures, people are not seen as isolated individuals but as *interdependent* with others (e.g., their in-group), where responsibility is shared and accountability is collective. A person is seen not as an individual but as a member of a group.

In their review of nonverbal communication in individualistic and collectivistic cultures, Andersen, Hecht, Hoobler, and Smallwood note that persons in individualistic cultures tend to be distant proximally, whereas persons in collectivistic cultures tend to work, play, live, and sleep in close proximity. In addition, body movements tend to be more synchronized in collectivistic cultures than in individualistic cultures. Facial behaviors (i.e., affect displays) differ as well. Persons in individualistic cultures tend to smile more than persons in collectivistic cultures. Andersen and his colleagues reason that people in collectivistic cultures are more likely to suppress their emotional displays because maintaining group harmony is primary. Finally, individualistic cultures are more nonverbally affiliative (i.e., enlisting nonverbal behaviors that bring people closer together physically and psychologically) than collectivistic cultures.[120]

Power Distance

A culture's power distance (i.e., large vs. small) may account for nonverbal differences across cultures. Power distance refers to the extent to which less powerful members of a culture expect and accept that power is distributed unequally. Cultures with a smaller power distance emphasize that inequalities among people should be minimized and that there should be interdependence between less and more powerful people. In cultures with a larger power distance, inequalities among people are both expected and desired. Less powerful people should be dependent on more powerful people. In high power distance cultures, interaction between persons of low and high power may be restricted, thus limiting the amount of nonverbal interaction. Andersen and his colleagues point out that in large power distance cultures, people without power are expected to express only positive emotional displays when interacting with those of higher power (e.g., smile more).[121]

Power distance also affects paralinguistic cues. Persons in small power distance cultures are generally less aware of their vocalics (e.g., volume, intensity) than are persons in large power distance cultures. Andersen and his colleagues mention that North Americans (small power distance) are often perceived as noisy, exaggerated, and childlike.[122]

Occulesics, the ways the eyes are used during communication, are also affected by power distance. In large power distance cultures, subordinates are taught to avert direct eye contact, often as a sign of respect for those in superior roles. For example, in large power distance cultures, students rarely give teachers direct eye contact. Direct eye gaze can be interpreted as a threat or a challenge to the person of higher power.

High and Low Context

Recall from Chapter 2 that high and low context refers to the degree to which interactants focus on the physical, social, and psychological (i.e., the nonverbal) context for information. Persons in high-context cultures are especially sensitive to the nonverbal context. Persons in low-context cultures focus less on the social or physical context and more on the explicit verbal code. Persons from low-context cultures are perceived as direct and talkative, whereas persons from high-context cultures are perceived as quiet, shy, and perhaps even sneaky.

Persons in high-context cultures tend to pay a great deal of attention to nonverbal behavior during interaction. Thus, facial expressions, touch, distance, and eye contact serve as important cues. Subtle body movements that may be missed by a low-context person may take on special meaning to the high-context person.

Nonverbal Expectancy Violations Theory

Judee Burgoon has formalized a theory of nonverbal communication called the **nonverbal expectancy violations theory** (NEV).[123] The basic premise of the theory is that people hold expectancies about the appropriateness of the nonverbal behaviors of others. These expectations are learned and culturally driven. For example, in the United States, people expect to shake hands when they are introduced to someone. Burgoon posits that, occasionally, people violate nonverbal expectations. When this happens, the violation produces arousal, which can be physiological or cognitive and positive or negative.

Burgoon maintains that once a violation has been committed and arousal is triggered, the recipient evaluates the violation and the violator. Violations initiated by highly attractive sources may be evaluated positively, whereas those initiated by unattractive sources may be evaluated negatively.[124] The same violation may produce very different evaluations, depending on who committed it. The evaluation of the violation depends on (a) the evaluation of the communicator, (b) implicit messages associated with the violation, and (c) evaluations of the act itself. In presenting the theory, Burgoon outlines several key assumptions (see Table 8.1).

Burgoon bases Assumption 1 on literature from anthropology, sociology, and psychology, indicating that humans are a social species with a biological/survival instinct to be with other humans. Conversely, humans cannot tolerate extended physical contact, or excessive closeness, with others; that is, humans have a basic need to insulate themselves from others and a need for privacy. Although this first assumption appears to be universal, the degree to which a person feels the need to be with others or insulated from them is probably culturally driven. Individualists may be more comfortable alone in the same situations in which a collectivist feels uncomfortable. Moreover, the way in which a person satisfies the need for privacy or affiliation certainly varies across cultures. In the United States and Germany, for example, privacy is often satisfied by physical separation from others (e.g., closed doors), whereas in densely populated cultures such as India, privacy may be fulfilled psychologically.

Table 8.1 Fundamental Assumptions of the Nonverbal Expectancy Violations Theory

Assumption 1: Humans have two competing needs, a need for affiliation and a need for personal space (or distance). These two needs cannot be satisfied at once.

Assumption 2: The desire for affiliation may be elicited or magnified by the presence of rewards in the communication context. The rewards may be biological or social.

Assumption 3: The greater the degree to which a person or situation is defined as rewarding, the greater the tendency for others to approach that person or situation; the greater the degree to which a person or situation is defined as punishing, the greater the tendency for others to avoid that person or situation.

Assumption 4: Humans are able to perceive gradations in distance.

Assumption 5: Human interaction patterns, including personal space or distance patterns, are normative.

Assumption 6: Humans may develop idiosyncratic behavior patterns that differ from the social norms.

Assumption 7: In any communication context, the norms are a function of three classes of factors: (a) characteristics of the interactants, (b) features of the interaction itself, and (c) features of the immediate physical environment.

Assumption 8: Interactants develop expectations about the communication behavior of others. Consequently, they are able to recognize or at least respond differently to normative versus deviant behaviors on the part of others.

Assumption 9: Deviations from expectations have arousal value.

Assumption 10: Interactants make evaluations of others.

Assumption 11: Evaluations are influenced by the degree to which the other is perceived as rewarding, such that a positively valued message is only rewarding if the source is highly regarded and a negatively valued message is only punishing if the source is not highly regarded.

SOURCE: Reprinted from Burgoon, J. K. (1978). A Communication Model of Personal Space Violations: Explication and an Initial Test. In *Human Communication Research, 4,* 129–142.

Assumption 2 indicates that affiliation with others is triggered by rewards within the communicative context. These rewards may be biological (e.g., food, sex, safety) or social (e.g., belonging, esteem, status). Biological needs are no doubt universal, but social needs are often learned and vary across cultures. Belonging needs are felt much more strongly in collectivistic cultures than in individualistic ones. Conversely, esteem needs are more strongly felt in individualistic cultures than in collectivistic ones. Assumption 3 extends Assumption 2 by stating that humans are attracted to rewarding situations and repelled by punishing situations. This phenomenon is probably universal, but it should be noted that what people deem rewarding and punishing varies across cultures.

Assumption 4 asserts that humans have the perceptual ability to discern differences in spatial relationships. We can tell when someone is standing close to us or far away from us. Assumption 5 deals with the establishment of normative nonverbal behaviors. Normative behavior is that which is usual or typical, or that follows a regular pattern. For example, the lecture style of your professor is probably consistent day after day. The professor has established a normative way of delivering his or her material. Many normative behaviors are established by society and culture. In the United States, for example, saying "good-bye" is a normative way of terminating a telephone conversation.

Assumption 6 recognizes that even though most of us follow similar normative rules and regulations for our verbal and nonverbal behavior, we also develop our own personal style of interaction that is unique in some way. Assumption 7 states that norms operate as a function of the interactants, the interaction, and the environment. Characteristics of the interactants might include their sex, age, personality, and race. Characteristics of the interaction itself might include status differences or degree of intimacy between the interactants. Finally, characteristics of the environment may include the physical features of the setting, such as furniture arrangement, lighting, or even temperature.

Assumption 8 deals with the notion of expectancies, a key element of the theory. Burgoon argues that during interaction, interactants develop expectancies and preferences about the behaviors of others. These expectancies are anticipations of others' behavior that are perceived to be appropriate for the situation. Typically, expectancies are based on a combination of societal and cultural norms. For example, students expect that their professors will behave in an appropriate and consistent manner. In certain cases, however, students might expect idiosyncratic deviations from the norms for particular professors (e.g., a certain professor frequently tells jokes in class).

Assumption 9 focuses on two other key ingredients in the theory: violation of expectancies and arousal. Burgoon subscribes to the notion that when a person's nonverbal expectancies are violated, the person becomes aroused. The violation tends to stimulate the receiver/communicator's attention and to arouse either adaptive or defensive reactions. For example, we learned earlier in this chapter that in some cultures (e.g., Korea), touching the top of a child's head is prohibited. Doing so would be a violation of expectancy, and the child or the parents might respond negatively or defensively. In some situations, however, some violations are perceived positively. A shaman may be allowed to touch the top of a child's head, and such behavior may be perceived positively. Assumption 10 states that people make value judgments about others. Assumption 11 extends this notion by specifying how evaluations are made.

Burgoon contends that the first factor influencing the positive or negative evaluation of a violation is the communicator reward valence—that is, how much the violator is perceived as someone with whom it is desirable to interact. Thus, communicator reward valence is based on communicator and relationship characteristics (e.g., age, sex, personality, status, reputation, anticipated future interaction) and interactional behaviors (e.g., style, positive feedback). Communicator reward valence influences how one will evaluate the violation of expectancies. Burgoon's theory holds that more favorable evaluations will be given when the violation is committed by a high-reward person than when it is committed by a low-reward person. If someone to whom you are attracted stands close to you at a party, much closer than is normative, you may interpret this violation positively as a sign of mutual attraction or affiliation. Conversely, if someone by whom you are repulsed stands too close to you at a party, you may evaluate this violation quite negatively. Burgoon asserts that positively evaluated violations produce favorable communication patterns and consequences, whereas negatively evaluated violations produce unfavorable communication patterns. In addition, Burgoon contends that even extreme violations, if committed by a high-reward person, can be evaluated positively and produce reciprocal communication patterns. Although a significant number of studies support the assumptions of Burgoon's theory, very few, if any, have investigated its cross-cultural applicability.

Cultural Contexts and Nonverbal Expectancies

As we have seen throughout this book, the cultures of Japan and the United States differ significantly. Japan is a collectivistic, high-context culture, whereas the United States is an individualistic, low-context culture. Individualistic cultures stress the importance of an individual's unique identity. Emphasis is placed on individual goals over group goals. In contrast, American children are taught from an early age that they are individuals with unique abilities and talents. People are rewarded for being "the best," "the one and only," and "number one" in whatever they do. The goal of Americans is to be the best that they can be and to strive for the top. A well-known cliché in the United States notes that "the squeaky wheel gets the grease," meaning that in order to get attention or to have one's needs met, one must draw attention to oneself. In contrast, collectivistic cultures place precedence on group goals over individual goals. Collectivistic cultures emphasize values that serve the in-group by subordinating personal goals for the sake of the in-group. Group activities are dominant and pervasive. Responsibility is shared, and accountability is collective.[125] Japan has an unofficial motto that reads, *"Deru kugi wa utareru,"* or "The tallest nail gets hammered down." Children are taught at a young age that their identity is based on their relationship within the group (family or business). Group leadership, rather than individual initiative, is valued. However, especially among Japanese youth, a new sense of individualism is growing in Japan.[126]

A high-context culture, such as Japan, is one whose members are highly sensitive to the perceptual, sociorelational, and environmental contexts for information. High-context cultures have a restricted code system (i.e., language). Members do not rely on verbal communication as their main source of information. Silence and nonverbal behavior are most informative. Statements or actions of affection are rare. Members are quite adept at decoding nonverbal behavior. Japanese, for example, expect others (i.e., other Japanese) to understand their unarticulated communication. Cultural members are expected to know how to perform in various situations where the guidelines are implicit.[127]

Members of a low-context culture, such as the United States, are less sensitive to the perceptual, sociorelational, and environmental contexts. That is not to say that they ignore the environment—they are simply less aware of it than are members of a high-context culture. A low-context communication is one in which the mass of information is found in the explicit code. Hence, low-context cultures have an elaborated code system. Verbal messages are extremely important when information to be shared with others is coded in the verbal message. Members of low-context cultures do not perceive the environment as a source of information. Guidelines and expectations are frequently explained explicitly.[128]

In addition to high-context/low-context distinctions between the two countries, Japan is considered a low-contact culture, whereas the United States is considered a moderate-contact culture. Many of the communicative behaviors of high/low-context, individualistic/collectivistic, and high/low-contact cultures are different, and the interactants will inevitably violate one another's expectations regarding appropriate nonverbal behavior.

AN INTERCULTURAL CONVERSATION: VIOLATION OF NONVERBAL EXPECTANCIES

In the following two scenarios, Jim, Akira, and Mitsuko interact. Akira and Mitsuko are exchange students from Japan who are spending a semester studying at an American college. Jim is an American student at the same college. Notice how each violates the other's expectations without realizing it.

When reading the scenes, keep in mind the different cultural orientations and the assumptions of nonverbal expectancy violations theory.

Jim and Akira are at a party.

1. *Jim:* (Nudges Akira and says loudly) This is a great party, eh?

2. *Akira:* (Is startled—stands back—tries to put some distance between himself and Jim) Yes, thank you.

3. *Jim:* (Leaning forward toward Akira, with direct eye contact) If you want to meet some girls, I could introduce you.

4. *Akira:* (Shocked by such an offer, he backs away) But I don't know them. They might be upset.

5. *Jim:* Well, how else are you going to meet them?

6. *Akira:* (Uncomfortable) Maybe during a class or something.

Mitsuko, another Japanese exchange student, approaches Jim and Akira. She knows Akira but not Jim.

7. *Mitsuko:* Hello, Akira. (Bows slightly and looks down)

8. *Akira:* Ah, Mitsuko, this is my friend Jim.

9. *Jim:* Hi! (Forward leaning into her space)

10. *Mitsuko:* Hi, Jim. (Bows slightly and does not make direct eye contact)

11. *Jim:* Are you two friends? (Wonders why she won't look at him, thinks to himself, "Well, I'm not one of them. She probably thinks I'm ugly.")

12. *Akira:* Yes, we know each other.

A long pause ensues.

13. *Jim:* (Thinks to himself, "This is going nowhere—I've got to think of something to say." He speaks rather loudly) Great party, hey guys?

Akira and Mitsuko both jump back.

14. *Akira:* (Thinks to himself, "This guy is too weird.") Yeah, this is fun.

During this scenario, Jim violates Akira's kinesic, proxemic, paralinguistic, and haptic expectations. Several of the axioms and propositions from Burgoon's NEV theory can be applied to this interaction. Notice in Lines 1 through 4 that Akira perceives that Jim is standing too close and talking too loudly and, thus, backs away. From Akira's point of view, Jim violated his proxemic and paralinguistic expectations. In Line 1, Jim touches Akira, which probably violates Akira's nonverbal expectations regarding haptics. From Jim's vantage point, Akira violates his expectations as well, by not looking at him and not responding to his offer to introduce him to women. According to NEV theory, violations have arousal value (Assumption 9).

Throughout the dialogue, we can see how Akira and Jim become aroused (e.g., shocked, uncomfortable, startled, annoyed) by each other's violations. Both Mitsuko and Akira jump when Jim yells, "Great party, hey guys?" In Lines 13 and 14, we can see how Burgoon's Assumption 10 applies in that the arousal leads to evaluations (e.g., "This is going nowhere," "This guy is too weird."). In this case, the evaluations are negative.

According to the theory, the greater the degree to which a person is perceived as rewarding, the greater the tendency for others to approach that person. Likewise, the greater the degree to which a person is perceived as punishing, the greater the tendency for others to avoid that person. Unfortunately for Akira, because he is in a "foreign" country, he will be the more likely of the two to change his behavior to conform to the expectations of others.

CHAPTER SUMMARY

Many social scientists believe that our verbal language evolved from a system of nonlinguistic communication that we inherited from our animal predecessors. As humans, we possess a host of nonlinguistic ways to communicate with one another through the use of kinesics, proxemics, paralanguage, haptics, olfactics, and physical appearance. Our nonverbal communication, when combined with verbal language, creates a complicated communication system through which humans come to know and understand one another.

Our nonverbal behavior is innate and learned. Many of our unconscious behaviors, such as the expression of emotions, are universal. People from all cultures express anger, happiness, and sadness the very same way. Yet other forms of nonverbal communication, such as gestures, are unique manifestations of our culture's distinctive cosmos. We learn how to communicate with our bodies (kinesics), through the use of space (proxemics), by touching others (haptics), with our voices (paralanguage), with smell (olfactics), and through the way we dress and present ourselves. Sometimes, our nonverbal behaviors violate the expectations of others. Sometimes, we stand too close or touch too much. When this happens, the other person evaluates the violation as positive or negative depending on whether we are perceived as attractive or unattractive. If we are thought of as attractive, our violation may be welcome. If we are perceived as unattractive, the same violation may be evaluated quite negatively.

Visit the student study site at **www.sagepub.com/neuliep5e** *for e-flashcards, web quizzes, web resources and more.*

DISCUSSION QUESTIONS

1. When you observe the nonverbal behavior of others, what do you notice first?

2. How does your style of dress identify you as a member of a particular culture?

3. What types of gestures have you used today to communicate without words?

4. How do you communicate intimacy nonverbally?

5. Without using words, how do you communicate to someone that you do not understand what he or she is saying?

6. How do you try to manipulate your unique smell?

ETHICS AND THE NONVERBAL CODE

1. Recently, the author of this excellently written text had a female student from Saudi Arabia enrolled in his class. At one of their first meetings, the author extended his hand to her as a greeting. She refused to shake his hand and said it was against her culture's rules to shake the hand of a male. What do you think? As a visiting international exchange student, should she have shook hands with the author?

2. Recently, the author of this excellently written text had several male students from Saudi Arabia enrolled in his class. Oftentimes in his class, the author distributes handouts to the students. The Saudi students asked that he not use his left hand to pass them the handouts. What do you think? Is their request unreasonable? Should the author comply?

3. A student recently complained that his roommate, who is an international exchange student, bathes only occasionally and smells bad. What do you think? Should the student say something to his roommate? Perhaps the roommate is comfortable with the natural scent of the human body.

KEY TERMS

adaptors   283

affect displays   279

analogic communication   270

chronemics   297

denotative meaning   271

digital communication   270

emblems   272

haptics   288

illustrators   272

kinesics   272

nonverbal expectancy violations theory   300

olfactics   290

paralanguage   283

proxemics   287

regulators   282

REFERENCES

1.   Farb, P. (1973). *Word Play: What Happens When People Talk*. New York: Bantam, p. 234.

2.   Molinsky, A. L., Krabbenhoft, M. A., Ambady, N., & Choi, Y. S. (2005). Cracking the Nonverbal Code: Intercultural Competence and Gesture Recognition Across Cultures. *Journal of Cross-Cultural Psychology, 36,* 380–395.

3.   Searchinger, G. (Director & Producer). (1996). *The Human Language Series: Part III: With and Without*

Words [Motion picture]. Available from Ways of Knowing, Inc., 200 West 72nd Street, New York, NY 10023.

4.   Knapp, M. L., & Hall, J. A. (2005). *Nonverbal Communication in Human Interaction* (6th ed.). Belmont, CA: Wadsworth (Thomson Learning).

5.   Searchinger, *The Human Language Series.*

6.   Ibid.

7.   Ibid.

8.   Condon, J. C., & Yousef, F. (1975). *An Approach to Intercultural Communication.* Indianapolis, IN: Bobbs-Merrill; Littlejohn, S. W. (1996). *Theories of Human Communication* (5th ed.). Belmont, CA: Wadsworth.

9.   Ekman, P., & Friesen, W. V. (1969). The Repertoire of Nonverbal Behavior: Categories, Origins, Usage, and Coding. *Semiotica, 1,* 49–98.

10.   Guidetti, M., & Nicoladis, E. (2006). Gestures and Communicative Development. *First Language, 26,* 346.

11.   Blake, J., Osborne, P., Cabral, M., & Gluck, P. (2003). The Development of Communicative Gestures in Japanese Infants. *First Language, 23,* 3–20.

12.   Archer, D. (Producer), & Silver, J. (Director). (1991). *A World of Gestures: Culture and Nonverbal Communication* [Motion picture]. Available from University of California Extension, Center for Media and Independent Learning, 2000 Center Street, Fourth Floor, Berkeley, CA 94704.

13.   Sapir, E. (1949). The Unconscious Patterning of Behaviour in Society. In D. G. Mendelbaum (Ed.), *Selected Writings of Edward Sapir* (pp. 544–559). Berkeley: University of California Press. (Quote on p. 554)

14.   Molinsky, A. L., Krabbenhoft, M. A., Ambady, N., & Choi, Y. S. (2005). Cracking the Nonverbal Code: Intercultural Competence and Gesture Recognition Across Cultures. *Journal of Cross-Cultural Psychology, 36,* 380–395.

15.   Choi, M. (1995). *Cultural Profile of South Korea.* Unpublished student manuscript, St. Norbert College, De Pere, WI.

16.   Harris, P. R., Moran, R. T., & Moran, S. V. (2004). *Managing Cultural Differences: Global Leadership Strategies for the 21st Century* (6th ed.). Burlington, MA: Elsevier, Butterworth-Heineman.

17.   *Visiting Cards in Japan.* Retrieved February 24, 2008, from http://www.japan-guide.com/e/e2227.html.

18.   Moellendorf, S., Warsh, H., & Yoshimaru, K. (1996). *The Amish Culture: A Closer Look at the People of Lancaster County.* Unpublished manuscript, St. Norbert College, De Pere, WI.

19.   Axtell, R. E. (1991). *Gestures: The Do's and Taboos of Gestures and Body Language Around the World.* New York: Wiley.

20.   Bishop, R. J. (1995). *Cultural Profile, Examination of Value Orientations and Sociocultural Influences, and Verbal and Nonverbal Language Aspects of the East Indian Culture.* Unpublished student manuscript, St. Norbert College, De Pere, WI.

21.   Harris et al., *Managing Cultural Differences;* Wolter, A. (1994). *Saudi Arabia and Its Culture.* Unpublished manuscript, St. Norbert College, De Pere, WI.

22.   Rieck, S., & Ogura, M. (1996). *Sri Lanka: The Pearl of the Indian Ocean.* Unpublished manuscript, St. Norbert College, De Pere, WI.

23.   Archer & Silver, *A World of Gestures.*

24.   Keberlein, M. C. (1993). *A Cultural Profile of the Guatemalan Ladinos.* Unpublished manuscript, St. Norbert College, De Pere, WI.

25.   Thao, K. (1995). *The Hmong Culture.* Unpublished student manuscript, St. Norbert College, De Pere, WI.

26.   Penasa, A. G., Peters, M., & Smits, S. (1996). *Jamaica: Out of Many, One People.* Unpublished manuscript, St. Norbert College, De Pere, WI.

27.   These examples are shown in Archer & Silver, *A World of Gestures.*

28.   Ibid.

29.   Ibid.

30.   Thao, *The Hmong Culture.*

31.   Archer & Silver, *A World of Gestures.*

32.   Marsh, A. A., Anger-Elfenbein, H., & Ambady, N. (2007). Separated by a Common Language: Nonverbal Accents and Cultural Stereotypes About Americans and Australians. *Journal of Cross-Cultural Psychology, 38,* 284–301.

33.   Knapp & Hall, *Nonverbal Communication in Human Interaction.*

34.   Searchinger, *The Human Language Series.*

35.   Birdwhistell, R. L. (1970). *Kinesics and Context: Essays on Body Motion Communication.* New York: Ballantine, p. 42.

36.   Darwin, C. (1872). *The Expression of the Emotions in Man and Animals.* London: J. Murray, p. 361.

37.   Searchinger, *The Human Language Series.*

38.   Ekman, P., Friesen, W., O'Sullivan, M., Chan, A., Diacoyanni-Tarlatzis, I., Heider, K., et al. (1987). Universals and Cultural Differences in the Judgment of Facial Expressions of Emotions. *Journal of Personality and Social Psychology, 53,* 712–717.

39.   Izard, C. E. (1994). Innate and Universal Facial Expressions: Evidence From Developmental and Cross-Cultural Research. *Psychological Bulletin, 115,* 288–299.

40.   Stephan, W. G., Stephan, C. W., & De Vargas, M. C. (1996). Emotional Expressions in Costa Rica and the United States. *Journal of Cross-Cultural Psychology, 27,* 147–160.

41.   Schimmack, U. (1996). Cultural Influences on the Recognition of Emotion by Facial Expressions. *Journal of Cross-Cultural Psychology, 27,* 37–51.

42.   Matsumoto, D. (1989). Cultural Influences on the Perception of Emotion. *Journal of Cross-Cultural Psychology, 20,* 92–105.

43.   Pittam, J., Kroonenberg, P., Gallois, C., & Iwawaki, S. (1995). Australian and Japanese Concepts of

Expressive Behavior. *Journal of Cross-Cultural Psychology, 26,* 451–464.

44. Marsh, A., Elfenbein, H. A, & Ambady, N. (2003). Nonverbal "Accents": Cultural Differences in Facial Expressions of Emotion. *Psychological Science, 14,* 373–376.

45. Bothwell, R. K., Brigham, J. C., & Malpass, R. S. (1989). Cross-Racial Identification. *Personality and Psychology Bulletin, 15,* 19–25; Malpass, R. S., & Kravitz, J. (1969). Recognition for Faces of Own and Other Race. *Journal of Personality and Social Psychology, 13,* 330–354.

46. Feingold, C. A. (1914). The Influence of Environment on Identification of Persons and Things. *Journal of Criminal Law and Police Science, 5,* 50.

47. Brigham, J. C., & Malpass, R. S. (1985). The Role of Experience and Contact in the Recognition of Faces of Own- and Other-Race Persons. *Journal of Social Issues, 41,* 139–155.

48. Ferman, S., & Entwistle, D. R. (1976). Children's Ability to Recognize Other Children's Faces. *Child Development, 47,* 506–510.

49. Brigham, J. C., & Barkowitz, P. (1978). Do They All Look Alike? The Effect of Race, Sex, Experience, and Attitudes on the Ability to Recognize Faces. *Journal of Applied Social Psychology, 8,* 306–318; Malpass & Kravitz, Recognition for Faces of Own and Other Race; Ng, W. J., & Lindsay, R. C. L. (1994). Cross-Race Facial Recognition: Failure of the Contact Hypothesis. *Journal of Cross-Cultural Psychology, 25,* 217–232; Teitelbaum, S., & Geiselman, R. E. (1997). Observer Mood and Cross-Racial Recognition of Faces. *Journal of Cross-Cultural Psychology, 28,* 93–106.

50. Rhodes, G., Tan, S., Brake, S., & Taylor, K. (1989). Expertise and Configural Coding in Face Recognition. *British Journal of Psychology, 80,* 313–331.

51. Shriver, E. R., Young, S. G., Hugenberg, K., Bernstein, M. J., & Lanter, J. R. (2008). Class, Race, and the Face: Social Context Modulates the Cross-Race Effect in Face Recognition. *Personality and Social Psychology Bulletin, 34,* 260–274.

52. Almaney, A., & Alwan, A. (1982). *Communicating With the Arabs.* Prospect Heights, IL: Waveland.

53. Harris et al., *Managing Cultural Differences.*

54. Knapp & Hall, *Nonverbal Communication in Human Interaction.*

55. Ibid.

56. Searchinger, *The Human Language Series.*

57. Hsin-Yun, Y. (1998). *The Four Tones in Mandarin Chinese.* Available from www.wellgot.ca/english-fm .html; Mandarin Tones. *Qi: The Journal of Traditional Eastern Health and Fitness.* Available from www.qi-journal .com/tones.html.

58. Ibid.

59. Choi, *Cultural Profile of South Korea.*

60. Zuckerman, M., & Miyake, K. (1993). The Attractive Voice: What Makes It So? *Journal of Nonverbal Behavior, 17,* 119–135.

61. Kinzler, K. D., Shutts, K., DeJesus, J., & Spelke, E. S. (2009). Accent trumps race in guiding children's social preferences. *Social Cognition, 27,* 623–634.

62. Gluszek, A., & Dovidio, J. F. (2010). The Way They Speak: A Social Psychological Perspective on the Social Stigma of Nonnative Accents in Communication. *Personality and Social Psychology Review, 14*(2), 214–237.

63. Dixon, J. A., Mahoney, B., & Cocks, R. (2002). Accents of Guilt? Effects of Regional Accents, Race, and Crime Type on Attributions of Guilt. *Journal of Language and Social Psychology, 21*(2), 162–168; Gluszek & Dovidio, The Way *They* Speak; Rubin, D. L. (1992). Nonlanguage Factors Affecting Undergraduates' Judgments of Nonnative English-Speaking Teaching Assistants. *Research in Higher Education, 33,* 511–531.

64. Hasegawa, T., & Gudykunst, W. B. (1998). Silence in Japan and the United States. *Journal of Cross-Cultural Psychology, 29,* 668–684.

65. Braithwaite, C. A. (1999). Cultural Uses and Interpretations of Silence. In L. K. Guerrero, J. A. DeVito, & M. L. Hecht (Eds.), *The Nonverbal Communication Reader* (2nd ed., pp. 163–172). Prospect Heights, IL: Waveland.

66. Kaya, N., & Weber, M. J. (2003). Territorial Behavior in Residence Halls: A Cross-Cultural Study. *Environment and Behavior, 35,* 400–415.

67. Amole, D. (2005). Coping Strategies for Living in Student Residential Facilities in Nigeria. *Environment and Behavior, 37,* 201–219.

68. Bishop, *Cultural Profile, Examination of Value Orientations and Sociocultural Influences, and Verbal and Nonverbal Language Aspects of the East Indian Culture.*

69. Rieck & Ogura, *Sri Lanka: The Pearl of the Indian Ocean.*

70. Hesselink, R. C., Mullen, R. T., & Rouse, J. M. (1996). *Moroccan Culture: An In-Depth Study.* Unpublished manuscript, St. Norbert College, De Pere, WI.

71. Ishikawa, Y., & Hashimoto, M. (1996). *The Kenyan Culture.* Unpublished student manuscript, St. Norbert College, De Pere, WI.

72. Argyle, M. (1975). *Bodily Communication.* New York: International Universities Press; Wolter, *Saudi Arabia and Its Culture.*

73. Dolphin, C. Z. (1997). Variables in the Use of Personal Space in Intercultural Transactions. In L. A. Samovar & R. E. Porter (Eds.), *Intercultural Communication: A Reader* (8th ed., pp. 266–276). Belmont, CA: Wadsworth, 1997.

74. Knapp & Hall, *Nonverbal Communication in Human Interaction.*

75. Hall, E. T. (1963). A System for the Notation of Proxemic Behavior. *American Anthropologist, 65,* 1003–1026.

76. Kim, M. S. (1998). A Comparative Analysis of Nonverbal Expressions as Portrayed by Korean and American Print-Media Advertising. In J. N. Martin, T. K. Nakayama, & L. A. Flores (Eds.), *Readings in Cultural Contexts* (pp. 206–216). Mountain View, CA: Mayfield.

77. McDaniel, E., & Andersen, P. A. (1998). International Patterns of Interpersonal Tactile Communication: A Field Study. *Journal of Nonverbal Behavior, 22,* 59–76.

78. Jourard, S. M. (1966). An Exploratory Study of Body Accessibility. *British Journal of Social and Clinical Psychology, 5,* 221–231.

79. Casteel, B. (1995). *A Cross-Cultural Study of Touch Avoidance.* Unpublished master's thesis, West Virginia University. Cited in D. W. Klopf (1995), *Intercultural Encounters: The Fundamentals of Intercultural Communication.* Englewood, CO: Morton.

80. Remland, M. S., Jones, T. S., & Brinkman, H. (1995). Interpersonal Distance, Body Orientation, and Touch: Effects of Culture, Gender, and Age. *Journal of Social Psychology, 135,* 281–298.

81. Bishop, *Cultural Profile, Examination of Value Orientations and Sociocultural Influences, and Verbal and Nonverbal Language Aspects of the East Indian Culture.*

82. Wolter, *Saudi Arabia and Its Culture.*

83. Harris et al., *Managing Cultural Differences.*

84. Ibid.

85. Gibbons, B. (1987). The Intimate Sense of Smell. *National Geographic, 170,* 324–361.

86. Stoddart, D. M. (1990). *The Scented Ape: The Biology and Culture of Human Odour.* Cambridge, UK: Cambridge University Press.

87. Kohl, J. V., & Francoeur, R. T. (1995). *The Scent of Eros.* New York: Continuum.

88. Ibid.

89. Classen, C., Howes, D., & Synnott, A. (1994). *Aroma: The Cultural History of Smell.* New York: Routledge.

90. Le Guerer, A. (1992). *Scent: The Mysterious and Essential Powers of Smell.* New York: Turtle Bay Books.

91. Howes, D., Synnott, A., & Classen, C. (1995). The Anthropology of Odour. In A. N. Gilbert (Ed.), *Compendium of Olfactory Research* (pp. 111–116). Dubuque, Iowa: Kendall-Hunt; Synnott, A. (1996). A Sociology of Smell. *Canadian Review of Sociology and Anthropology, 28*(4), 437–460.

92. Kohl & Francoeur, *The Scent of Eros.*

93. Fernea, E., & Fernea, R. (1994). Cleanliness and Culture. In W. J. Lonner & R. Malpass (Eds.), *Psychology and Culture* (pp. 65–70). Boston: Allyn & Bacon.

94. Classen et al., *Aroma: The Cultural History of Smell.*

95. Gibbons, The Intimate Sense of Smell.

96. Synnott, A Sociology of Smell.

97. Gibbons, The Intimate Sense of Smell.

98. Baker, R. L. (1974). *Race.* New York: Oxford University Press.

99. Classen et al., *Aroma: The Cultural History of Smell;* Dollard, J. (1957). *Caste and Class in a Southern Town.* New York: Doubleday.

100. Classen et al., *Aroma: The Cultural History of Smell;* Le Guerer, *Scent: The Mysterious and Essential Powers of Smell;* Simmel, G. (1912). *Mélanges de Philosophie Relativiste.* Paris: F. Alcon, p. 12.

101. Classen et al., *Aroma: The Cultural History of Smell;* Le Guerer, *Scent: The Mysterious and Essential Powers of Smell;* Simmel, *Mélanges de Philosophie Relativiste,* p. 34.

102. This poem was cited in Classen et al., *Aroma: The Cultural History of Smell.* The original source is H. Williams (1937), *The Poems of Jonathan Swift* (Vol. 2). Oxford, UK: Clarendon, p. 529.

103. Olfactory Research Fund. *Enthusiastic Response to Website Sense of Smell Survey (1996–1997).* Available from www.olfactory.org/response.html

104. Todrank, J., Byrnes, D., Wrzesniewski, A., & Rozin, P. (1995). Odors Can Change Preferences for People in Photographs: A Cross-Modal Evaluative Conditioning Study With Olfactory USs and Visual CSs. *Learning and Motivation, 26,* 116–140.

105. Kohl & Francoeur, *The Scent of Eros.*

106. Fox, K. (2001). *The Smell Report.* Oxford, UK: Social Issues Research Centre.

107. Ibid.

108. Ibid.

109. Ibid.

110. Vandehey, K., Buerger, C., & Krueger, K. (1996). *Traditional Aspects and Struggles of the Masai Culture.* Unpublished manuscript, St. Norbert College, De Pere, WI.

111. Smucker, P. G. (1998, March 16). The Meaning of a Scarf: Turkish Students Fight to Wear Islamic Head Coverings. *US News & World Report,* pp. 31–33.

112. Batarfi, K. M. (1998). *Welcome to Saudi Arabia: The Land of Islam.* Available from http://darkwing.uoregon.edu/~kbatarfi/saudi.html; Harris et al., *Managing Cultural Differences.*

113. Harris et al., *Managing Cultural Differences; Recreational Travel Guide to India.* (1993). Available from www.solutions.mb.ca/rec-traqvel/asia/india/india-guide.html.

114. *A History of Kimono.* Available from www.japan.mit.edu/kimono/intro.html. This site is a part of the Japanese Language and Culture Network.

115. Hall, E. T. (1959). *The Silent Language.* New York: Doubleday.

116. Doggett, L. E. (1992). Calendars. In P. K. Seidelmann (Ed.), *Explanatory Supplement to the Astronomical Almanac* (p. 579). Sausalito, CA: University Science Books.

117. Ibid.

118. Ibid.

119. Hall, *The Silent Language.*

120.   Andersen, P. A., Hecht, M. L., Hoobler, G. D., & Smallwood, M. (2003). Nonverbal Communication Across Cultures. In W. B. Gudykunst (Ed.), *Cross-Cultural and Intercultural Communication* (pp. 73–90). Thousand Oaks, CA: Sage.

121.   Ibid.

122.   Ibid.

123.   Burgoon, J. K. (1978). A Communication Model of Personal Space Violations: Explication and an Initial Test. *Human Communication Research, 4,* 129–142; Burgoon, J. K., & Jones, S. B. (1976). Toward a Theory of Personal Space Expectations and Their Violations. *Human Communication Research, 2,* 131–146.

124.   An excellent review of research associated with NEV can be found in Burgoon, J. K., & Hale, J. L. (1988). Nonverbal Expectancy Violations: Model Elaboration and Application to Immediacy Behaviors. *Communication Monographs, 55,* 58–79.

125.   Schwartz, S. H. (1990). Individualism–Collectivism: Critique and Proposed Refinements. *Journal of Cross-Cultural Psychology, 21,* 139–157.

126.   Harris et al., *Managing Cultural Differences.*

127.   Schwartz, Individualism–Collectivism.

128.   Gudykunst, W. B. (Ed.). (1983). *Intercultural Communication Theory: Current Perspectives.* Beverly Hills, CA: Sage.

CHAPTER 9

Developing Intercultural Relationships

After reading this chapter, you should be able to

1. recount the fundamental assumptions of the uncertainty reduction theory,

2. discuss the relationship between uncertainty reduction and intercultural communication apprehension,

3. cogently discuss the fundamental assumptions of anxiety uncertainty management theory,

4. identify assertive and responsive sociocommunicative styles,

5. define relational empathy and third-culture building,

6. compare ratings of relational intimacy across cultures,

7. describe differences in relationships between Eastern and Western cultures,

8. compare marital types across cultures, and

9. compare divorce rates across cultures.

Without others, there is no self.

—Kenneth J. Gergen[1]

———

Before reading this chapter any further, take a moment and think about you. Yes, think about yourself. If someone were to ask you to describe yourself, what would you say? Now, in the space below, write three terms that describe you. Use whatever terms you want.

_____

_____

_____

Next question: How do you know that the terms you wrote above are accurate? Perhaps you wrote that you are a *good student,* a *loyal friend, honest,* or a *fast runner.* How do you know that these descriptors are accurate? The only reason you know that these terms are correct is because of *others* around you. Yes, other people (i.e., your relationships) help you define yourself. For example, if you describe yourself as a good student, the only reason you know that is because of your relationships with teachers who have provided you with feedback. If you describe yourself as a fast runner, the only way you know that is by comparing your running with that of other runners. You can describe yourself only in relation to others. You cannot be tall unless someone else is short. As the quote at the beginning of the chapter states, without others, there is no self.

Initiating and maintaining relationships with others is one of the most necessary and challenging functions of human survival. Our self-concept and self-esteem are sustained largely by the substance of our relationships with others. From our relational partners, we receive feedback that we use to assess ourselves. In essence, the only way we know ourselves is through our relationships with others. Our existence is relative to other people. Regardless of one's cultural origins, relationships provide the substance of life. Several variables affect the initiation and maintenance of personal relationships. Much of our communication behavior during the first stage of a relationship is designed to reduce uncertainty about our relational partner. One factor that affects our ability to do that is the degree to which we experience intercultural communication apprehension. Another variable that affects the uncertainty process is our **sociocommunicative style**—that is, the extent to which we are assertive and responsive with our relational partners.

Two other variables that affect our relations with others are the degree to which we can empathize with others and how similar we perceive ourselves to be to others. Uncertainty reduction, intercultural communication apprehension, sociocommunicative style, empathy, and similarity are experienced differently by each interactant in a relationship. The relationship established by any two people is the result of a complex combination of these factors, as depicted in Figure 9.1.

Figure 9.1   Factors That Affect Intercultural Relationships

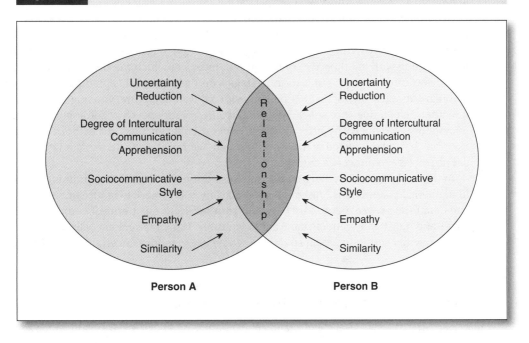

This chapter explores a variety of topics associated with relationships. The first section deals with uncertainty reduction and factors that affect how people go about reducing uncertainty, including intercultural communication apprehension and sociocommunicative style. The next part of the chapter focuses on empathy, third-culture building, and similarity. The third part of the chapter examines how perceptions about relationships vary across cultures, with particular emphasis on how relationships are perceived in Eastern and Western cultures. The final part of the chapter looks at intercultural, interracial, and lesbian/gay relationships, along with mate selection across cultures, arranged marriages, and divorce.

COMMUNICATION AND UNCERTAINTY

All relationships must begin somewhere. The people with whom we are now intimate were at one time strangers. Think about your closest friends. At some point, they were strangers. Can you remember the first time you interacted with them? Communication with a stranger, particularly a person from a different culture, can be frightening and full of uncertainty. **Uncertainty** refers to the amount of predictability in a communication situation. Many people experience anxiety when interacting with others for the first time. Moreover, interacting with a person from a different culture may be even more anxiety producing. In an attempt to explain our communication behavior during initial communication encounters with others, Charles Berger and Richard Calabrese developed a communication theory called **uncertainty reduction theory** (URT). The major premise of this theory is that when strangers first meet, their primary goal is to reduce uncertainty and increase predictability in their own and the other person's behavior.[2] In order to accomplish this, they use specific communication strategies.

According to URT, uncertainty can be both a proactive and a retroactive process. That is, we can experience and reduce uncertainty both before and after interacting with someone. We can proactively reduce uncertainty when we weigh alternative behavioral options prior to interacting with another. We try to figure out ways in which the other might interact and then select our own communication strategies on the basis of this prediction. For example, if you are about to interact with a person from a different culture, you might anticipate that the other person does not speak English and adjust your speech accordingly. Retroactively, uncertainty is reduced by attempting to explain behavior after it has been enacted. For example, having interacted with a South Korean, we may be able to explain why the person did not engage in direct eye contact.

In their original theory, Berger and Calabrese posited seven axioms outlining the theory's fundamental assumptions.[3] Although people in any culture seek to reduce uncertainty, Berger and Calabrese's seven axioms are based on communication patterns of people in the United States and may not be generalizable across cultures. Many researchers believe that the verbal and nonverbal communication strategies people use to reduce uncertainty vary from culture

The Seven Axioms of Uncertainty Reduction Theory

Axiom 1: Given the high level of uncertainty present at the onset of the entry phase, as the amount of verbal communication between strangers increases, the level of uncertainty for each interactant in the relationship will decrease. As uncertainty is further reduced, the amount of verbal communication will increase.

Axiom 2: As nonverbal affiliative expressiveness increases, uncertainty levels will decrease in an initial interaction situation. In addition, decreases in uncertainty level will cause increases in nonverbal affiliative expressiveness.

Axiom 3: High levels of uncertainty cause increases in information-seeking behavior. As uncertainty levels decline, information-seeking behavior decreases.

Axiom 4: High levels of uncertainty in a relationship cause decreases in the intimacy level of communication content. Low levels of uncertainty produce high levels of intimacy.

Axiom 5: High levels of uncertainty produce high rates of reciprocity. Low levels of uncertainty produce low reciprocity rates.

Axiom 6: Similarities between persons reduce uncertainty, whereas dissimilarities produce increases in uncertainty.

Axiom 7: Increases in uncertainty level produce decreases in liking; decreases in uncertainty level produce increases in liking.

SOURCE: C. R. Berger and R. J. Calabrese, "Some Explorations in Initial Interaction and Beyond: Toward a Developmental Theory of Interpersonal Communication," *Human Communication Research, 1* (1975), 99–112. Used by permission of International Communication Association and Charles R. Berger.

to culture. For example, William Gudykunst and his associates have begun a research program investigating cross-cultural differences in uncertainty-reduction communication.

Gudykunst and Kim maintain that people may be more motivated to reduce uncertainty during initial intercultural communication than during communication with someone who is familiar.[4] Gudykunst argues that several factors may influence the amount of uncertainty experienced by people during an intercultural encounter, including the interactants' expectations about communicating, individual social identities, the degree of similarity between interactants, shared communication networks, and the interpersonal salience of the contact with strangers. For example, Gudykunst points out that, like others, people from high-context cultures try to reduce uncertainty in initial encounters, but the nature of the information they seek seems to be different from that sought by persons from low-context cultures. Because much of the information resides in the context as opposed to the individual, persons from high-context cultures are more cautious concerning what they talk about with strangers. In addition, certain types of information are more important sources of uncertainty to persons in high-context cultures than to people in low-context cultures, including the others' social background, knowing whether others will behave in a socially appropriate manner, knowing that others understand individuals' feelings, knowing what others mean when they communicate, and knowing whether others will make allowances for individuals when they communicate.[5] So when interacting together for the first time, people from high- and low-context cultures are each trying to reduce uncertainty, but they use different kinds of communication. The low-context person asks a lot of questions, whereas the high-context person focuses on nonverbal aspects.

Axioms 1 and 2 deal with the quantity of verbal and nonverbal communication and its effect on uncertainty—that is, as communication increases, uncertainty decreases. Gudykunst and Nishida found that the frequency of communication predicts uncertainty reduction in individualistic, low-context cultures but not in collectivistic, high-context cultures.[6] In Axiom 2, "nonverbal affiliative expressiveness" refers to nonverbal behaviors that reduce the physiological and psychological distance between interactants. In the United States, direct eye contact, pleasantness of vocal expressions, affirmative head nods, number of head and arm gestures per minute, and closer physical distance between interactants are considered affiliative. In other cultures, these same behaviors may actually increase uncertainty and anxiety. In cultures such as South Korea and Guatemala, for example, persons of lower status do not engage in direct eye contact with parents or people of higher status because doing so communicates a challenge. Sanders and Wiseman found that positive nonverbal expressiveness predicts uncertainty reduction for Whites, Hispanics, and Asian Americans, but not for African Americans.[7] These studies indicate that the specific nonverbal behaviors that constitute affiliative expressiveness may vary across cultures.

Axiom 3 is closely related to the first two insofar as information-seeking behavior is defined as the number of questions asked by each interactant. In the United States, people seek information from others by asking questions. In other cultures, particularly high-context cultures, people may seek information through nonverbal means, perhaps through silence or by observing the other's cultural and sociorelational background. In fact, Gudykunst, Sodetani, and Sonoda suggest that question asking as a form of uncertainty reduction may be limited to Whites.[8]

Axiom 4 refers not to the quantity of communication, as do the preceding axioms, but to the quality of communication. In this case, the lower the level of uncertainty, the higher the level of intimacy in the communication. Intimate communication may be defined as interaction based on issues related to the interactants' attitudes, beliefs, motivations, and dispositions. There is limited cross-cultural research in this area.

Axiom 5 deals with the concept of communication reciprocity, or the mutual exchange of information between interactants. Berger and Calabrese contend that at early stages in a relationship, the interactants are compelled to ask for and give the same kinds of information at the same rate so that neither person gains information power over the other. As the relationship develops, and uncertainty is reduced, there is less felt need to reciprocate because the interactants are more comfortable with the relationship.[9] To date, little or no cross-cultural research has examined this hypothesis outside the United States.

Axiom 6 centers on the notion of similarity. Berger and Calabrese argue that as similarity between interactants increases, uncertainty decreases. Likewise, the more dissimilarity present, the more uncertainty. Berger and Calabrese assert that knowledge of dissimilar attitudes leads to a greater number of attributions about why another may hold such attitudes, thus increasing uncertainty about the other.[10] Cross-cultural research on Germany, Norway, Canada, and Japan seems to validate this axiom. People can be similar to one another in a number of ways. Two people may share race, language, age, sex, or occupation. Linguistic similarity is of particular importance here. Uncertainty can be difficult to reduce if two people speak different languages and have little knowledge of the other's linguistic code.[11]

Finally, Axiom 7 focuses on the concept of liking. Unless we know something about other people, it is difficult to like them. Thus, liking other people is somewhat contingent on knowing something about them. The research on this axiom, even within the United States, is mixed. In some cases, the more we know about another, the less we may like that person.

ANXIETY UNCERTAINTY MANAGEMENT THEORY OF EFFECTIVE COMMUNICATION

Noted intercultural communication scholar William Gudykunst developed a theory, called anxiety uncertainty management theory (AUM), to explain the interrelationships among uncertainty, anxiety, mindfulness, and communication effectiveness.[12] According to AUM, the general processes underlying communication between people from different cultures or ethnicities are the same processes underlying communication between people from the same culture. Gudykunst refers to these common properties as *communicating with strangers*. According to AUM, a stranger is someone who is physically near and conceptually distant simultaneously. Thus, interacting with strangers is replete with uncertainty and anxiety. AUM and URT are similar in that each theory focuses on the effects of uncertainty and anxiety on communication.

But AUM is different from URT because it shifts the focus from uncertainty and anxiety reduction to uncertainty and anxiety *management*. AUM also incorporates the concepts of mindfulness and communication effectiveness. Gudykunst maintains that the focus of AUM is toward effective communication; that is, to the extent that interactants can manage uncertainty and anxiety, and be mindful, effective communication can be achieved.[13] According to AUM, uncertainty is a cognitive phenomenon. Uncertainty affects the way people *think* about communication and involves our ability, or inability, to predict a stranger's attitudes, beliefs,

STUDENT VOICES ACROSS CULTURES

Establishing Relationships: Colombia

My name is Karen Margarita Henao Carbonell, and I am 21 years old. I was born and raised in Bogota, Colombia, a city with a population of about seven million people. I graduated from high school in Colombia and decided to come to the United States in 2006 to learn English. After I attended high school in Madison, Wisconsin, for a year, I decided to stay and further my education at St. Norbert College.

I'll never forget my first day in an American high school. I was nervous and excited, especially because I wanted to make friends. Of course, everyone was staring at me, trying to figure out who I was, but people were friendly overall. As a couple of girls approached me and said: "Hey, you're the new girl from Colombia, right?" I leaned toward them, kissed each one of them on the cheek, and said: "Yes, my name is Karen, nice to meet you!" They were extremely shocked after that, and they could not believe I had just greeted them by kissing their cheeks, especially since we had met only a minute before.

It seems as though establishing relationships in Latin American countries, particularly in Colombia, is a whole lot easier than here in the United States. When you meet someone for the first time in Colombia, not only do you kiss each others' cheeks, but you jump right into talking about your life, what you do for a living, what neighborhood you live in, and even where you purchased the shoes you are wearing. Once you have become acquainted with someone, it is socially acceptable to allow physical contact and "burst the invisible bubble."

After living in the United States for more than 5 years, I have realized that establishing relationships with people in this country is more difficult. Americans believe that it takes a lot of time for a person to begin trusting and revealing personal information; they are friendly and willing to help, but trust needs to be built before they open the doors into their lives. When such relationships have been established, people confide in each other, but the physical aspect is not an important factor.

---

values, and behaviors. People experience more uncertainty when interacting with strangers. Anxiety is the affective equivalent of uncertainty. Anxiety affects the way people *feel* about interacting with someone else and includes a sense of uneasiness, apprehensiveness, worry, and so on. Uncertainty and anxiety are related in that as uncertainty increases, people experience anxiety. Anxiety affects one's motivation to approach or avoid communication.[14]

AUM stipulates that people have minimum and maximum thresholds for uncertainty and anxiety. The maximum threshold is the highest amount of uncertainty or anxiety individuals can experience and still believe they can predict a stranger's attitudes, beliefs, values, and so on, and remain comfortable communicating. An individual's minimum threshold of uncertainty or anxiety is the lowest amount of uncertainty a person can experience before becoming unmotivated or overconfident about predicting the stranger's behavior when interacting. If our uncertainty is above the maximum or below the minimum thresholds, we cannot communicate effectively; thus, communicating effectively requires that uncertainty and anxiety be between the minimum and maximum thresholds. Gudykunst also points out that minimum and maximum thresholds vary considerably across cultures.[15]

In addition to uncertainty and anxiety, AUM incorporates the concepts of mindfulness and communication effectiveness. Mindfulness refers to the idea that most of the time, people are not acutely aware of their behavior and operate on a kind of automatic pilot. To be sure, many communicative acts are routine or habitual and do not require intense cognitive attention. For example, the automatic cognitive process of categorizing and stereotyping strangers was discussed in Chapter 5. Mindfulness, on the other hand, refers to a person's conscious attention to incoming information. A mindful communicator is open to new information and the processing of new categories. Mindful communicators perceive aspects of the self and others that mindless communicators miss. Gudykunst points out that to be mindful, people must recognize that strangers may use different perspectives to understand or explain interaction. When we are mindless, we tend to assume that strangers interpret our messages the same way we do. Mindfulness, on the other hand, means *negotiating* meaning with strangers. Communication effectiveness refers to the idea that a person receiving and interpreting a message attaches a meaning to the message that is relatively similar to what was intended by the person transmitting it. The result of communication effectiveness is maximum understanding among communicators. Gudykunst maintains that the majority of the time, when people are not mindful, communication is ineffective.[16]

In his theory of AUM, Gudykunst identifies seven superficial causes that mediate one's ability to manage uncertainty and anxiety. To the extent that one can mediate uncertainty and anxiety, and be mindful, communication effectiveness can be achieved. Gudykunst's schematic of AUM appears in Figure 9.2.[17]

According to the schematic, the degree of communication effectiveness achieved is based on the degree to which uncertainty and anxiety are managed, plus one's degree of mindfulness. Mindfulness can either increase or decrease uncertainty and anxiety during interaction. Mindfulness decreases uncertainty and anxiety in cases where we try to understand the perspectives of strangers. But mindfulness can sometimes increase uncertainty and anxiety because it heightens our awareness of the differences between us and strangers.

In the model, the seven superficial causes are those factors that can either facilitate or hinder the management of uncertainty and anxiety. For example, regarding the self-concept, Gudykunst maintains that an increase in the degree to which our social identities, personal identities, and self-esteem guide our interactions with strangers will produce a decrease in uncertainty and anxiety and increase our ability to predict their behavior, but *only when we are not mindful;* when we are mindful, we choose how to communicate and our behavior is not determined by such internal characteristics as social or personal identities. Our self-concept also affects our motivation to interact with strangers. An increase in our need for group inclusion and our need to sustain our self-concept increases our anxiety when interacting with strangers, but only when we are not mindful. Yet an increase in the degree to which strangers confirm our self-concept produces a decrease in our anxiety. How we react to strangers also affects our communication effectiveness. To the extent that we can empathize and are tolerant of ambiguity, our uncertainty and anxiety will decrease. Moreover, if we maintain rigid and inflexible social categories and stereotypes of strangers, our uncertainty and anxiety will increase. The context (i.e., situational processes) in which we interact and our connection with strangers also affect our levels of uncertainty and anxiety. If we are engaged in cooperative work tasks that require interdependence with strangers (i.e., team efforts where everyone has a specific but related role to play), our levels of uncertainty and anxiety will decrease. In such tasks, as the quality and quantity of interaction with strangers increases, our levels of uncertainty and anxiety will

| Figure 9.2 | Model of Anxiety Uncertainty Management |

Self-Concept
Social identities
Personal identities
Collective self-esteem

Motivation to Interaction
Need for predictability
Need for group inclusion
Need to sustain self-concept

Reactions to Strangers
Empathy
Tolerance for ambiguity
Rigid intergroup attitudes

Social Categorization of Strangers
Positive expectations
Perceived similarities
Understanding group differences

Situational Processes
In-group power
Cooperative tasks
Presence of in-group members

Connection With Strangers
Attraction to strangers
Interdependence with strangers
Quality and quantity of contact

Ethical Interactions
Maintaining dignity
Moral inclusiveness
Respect for strangers

Uncertainty Management

Anxiety Management

Mindfulness

Communication Effectiveness

Superficial Causes   **Basic Causes**   **Moderating Processes**   **Outcomes**

decrease. Finally, if we can maintain our own self-dignity and respect strangers' differences, our uncertainty and anxiety will decrease.[18]

Two additional concepts also have relevance regarding uncertainty and anxiety management and mindfulness during intercultural communication: ethnocentrism and intercultural communication apprehension. As mentioned in Chapters 1 and 5, ethnocentrism refers to the degree to which persons believe that the attitudes and behaviors of their in-group should serve as the standard by which other groups are judged. To the extent that people are ethnocentric, they tend to view other cultures (and microcultures) from their own cultural vantage point. That is, one's own culture is the standard by which other cultures and the people from those cultures are evaluated. Deviations from that standard are viewed negatively. Moreover, because highly ethnocentric persons see themselves as superior to persons from different cultures, they sense little or no motivation to communicate effectively with them, are generally not mindful, and have little or no motivation to reduce uncertainty.

Ethnocentrism acts as a perceptual filter that affects not only the perceptions of verbal and nonverbal messages but also perceptions of their source. Thus, when highly ethnocentric persons enter into an intercultural communicative exchange, few positive outcomes can be expected, including lowering uncertainty to manageable levels. Ethnocentrics prefer *intra*cultural interaction and avoid communicating with persons from other cultures. Such avoidance tendencies inhibit the reduction or management of uncertainty and anxiety and, thus, impede mindfulness.

Recall also from Chapter 1 that intercultural communication apprehension (ICA) is the fear or anxiety associated with either real or anticipated communication with people from different cultural or ethnic groups. ICA also inhibits uncertainty reduction and management and hinders mindfulness. Conceptually, like ethnocentrism, ICA interferes with effective intercultural communication. ICA also interferes with the reduction of uncertainty associated with the future behavior of a fellow interactant, the other's behavior, and the participant's feelings about the interaction. Furthermore, other studies claim that ICA and ethnocentrism are negatively related to intercultural willingness to communicate and intentions to engage in intercultural interactions (i.e., affective-approach tendencies). Like high ethnocentrics, individuals with high ICA prefer intracultural interaction and are less likely to approach intercultural strangers, thus inhibiting their reduction and management of uncertainty and anxiety.

UNCERTAINTY REDUCTION AND INTERCULTURAL COMMUNICATION APPREHENSION

Communication researchers Jim Neuliep and Dan Ryan investigated the relationship between ICA and uncertainty reduction during initial intercultural interaction. Imagine that you have just been introduced to someone from a different culture. You have never met this person before and know very little about his or her culture. Chances are good that you will experience a bit of anxiety and apprehension. This is a common response, and you need not feel bad about yourself for having felt it. Neuliep and Ryan argue that because intercultural communication is loaded with novelty and dissimilarity, people may experience inordinate amounts of anxiety, which inhibit the ability to reduce uncertainty.[19]

Many people, regardless of culture, experience anxiety when communicating, or when anticipating communicating, with persons from different cultures or ethnic groups. Often, we tend to avoid those situations that make us feel anxious. In this case, if intercultural communication causes us to feel anxious, we may avoid initiating interaction with people from different cultures. However, unless we interact, we cannot reduce much uncertainty, and, therefore, our anxiety levels remain high. In their theory of uncertainty reduction, Berger and

Calabrese maintain that the principal way people reduce uncertainty during initial interaction is through verbal and nonverbal communication.[20]

To the extent that people can reduce uncertainty and anxiety during communication, they can increase their communication effectiveness. In their study, Neuliep and Ryan found a direct relationship between ICA and uncertainty reduction. Specifically, they found that during initial intercultural communication, people who experienced high ICA also experienced high uncertainty. Neuliep and Ryan reasoned that because persons with high ICA may avoid or withdraw from communication with persons from different cultures, they are less likely to engage in communication tactics that reduce uncertainty. Persons who generally do not experience apprehension interacting with persons from other cultures communicate comfortably, thereby facilitating uncertainty reduction. A lesson here is that by increasing our interaction with persons from different cultures, we can reduce our uncertainty about them and reduce our anxiety.[21]

In fact, in related research, Neuliep and Grohskopf found that as individuals reduce uncertainty, their satisfaction with communication increases. Hence, by engaging in intercultural communication, we can reduce uncertainty, which will reduce anxiety and result in more satisfying communication with others. It is a "win–win" situation![22]

Although an individual may be faced with large amounts of uncertainty and anxiety during initial intercultural communication, Neuliep and Ryan reasoned that the person's communication style may enable him or her to effectively reduce uncertainty. Jim McCroskey and Virginia Richmond have outlined two types of communication style—what they call *socio-communicative orientation*—that affect how one communicates in different situations. These types of communication include assertiveness and responsiveness.[23] **Assertiveness** refers to one's ability to make requests; actively disagree; express positive or negative personal rights and feelings; initiate, sustain, and terminate conversations; and defend oneself without attacking others. **Responsiveness** refers to one's ability to be sensitive to the communication of others, be a good listener, engage in comforting communication, and recognize the needs and wants of relevant others.

McCroskey and Richmond note that assertiveness and responsiveness are inversely related to communication apprehension. In other words, persons high in communication apprehension are not likely to engage in assertive or responsive communication behaviors. Because apprehensive persons tend to avoid communication, they are not likely to initiate conversation or advance their position on a topic of communication during a conversation.[24] Likewise, a responsive communicator is one who invites others to engage in conversation. In their research, Neuliep and Ryan argued that these tendencies may be highlighted during initial intercultural interaction, in which situational novelty, unfamiliarity, and dissimilarity are prominent. Indeed, in their study, Neuliep and Ryan found that people who were assertive and responsive reported experiencing less ICA.[25]

Neuliep and Ryan contend that the fundamental components of assertiveness and responsiveness are consistent with those behaviors associated with reduced uncertainty. For example, a characteristic of assertiveness is the ability to make requests. In Axiom 3 of URT, Berger and Calabrese point out that as information-seeking behavior (question asking) increases, uncertainty decreases. In addition, assertiveness is associated with initiation and maintenance of conversations. In Axiom 1 of URT, Berger and Calabrese maintain that as verbal communication increases, uncertainty decreases. Responsive communicators invite others to interact, thus increasing verbal communication. Likewise, responsive communicators are nonverbally sensitive to others. Responsiveness is communicated through eye contact, smiling, forward leaning, and touching. Axiom 2 states that as nonverbal affiliative expressiveness increases, uncertainty decreases. From the association of assertiveness and responsiveness with behaviors designed to reduce uncertainty, Neuliep and Ryan predicted that assertive and responsive communicators may be better able to reduce uncertainty. Their results supported their prediction. Persons scoring high on assertiveness and responsiveness instruments reported experiencing less uncertainty during initial cross-cultural interaction.[26]

AN INTERCULTURAL CONVERSATION: UNCERTAINTY REDUCTION AND SOCIOCOMMUNICATIVE STYLE

In the following intercultural conversations, we see how an individual's sociocommunicative style affects uncertainty reduction during initial intercultural communication. In the first conversation, we see Dan, who is from the United States, interacting with Natasha, who is from Ukraine. Dan seems unassertive and unresponsive. In the second conversation, we see Jim, who is from the United States, interacting with Foday, who is from Sierra Leone. In comparison with Dan, Jim seems assertive and responsive. Jim's assertiveness and responsiveness help him reduce uncertainty about Foday and Sierra Leone.

Natasha:	Hi, I'm Natasha.
Dan:	Oh, hi.
Natasha:	What's your name?
Dan:	Dan.
Natasha:	Hi, Dan.
Dan:	Hi.
Natasha:	I'm not from here. I'm from Ukraine.
Dan:	Oh.
Natasha:	You've heard of it?
Dan:	Ah, yeah, I think so.
Natasha:	Ukraine is in Eastern Europe, between Poland and Russia.
Dan:	Oh.
Natasha:	Yeah. Have you ever been to Europe?
Dan:	Yeah, but I was pretty young.
Natasha:	It must have been quite an experience, though.

Dan:	Ah . . . do you know what time it is?
Natasha:	It's about 3 o'clock.
Dan:	I have to go now. Bye.
Natasha:	Bye, Dan, nice meeting you.
Jim:	Hi, I'm Jim. I don't believe we've met.
Foday:	Hello, Jim, I'm Foday.
Jim:	Hi, Foday, where are you from?
Foday:	I'm from Sierra Leone.
Jim:	Oh really? Where is Sierra Leone? I know it's on the African continent, but I'm not sure where.
Foday:	It's on the western coast between Guinea and Liberia.
Jim:	Oh, toward the north? How big is it?
Foday:	Yes, that's right. We're about the size of your South Carolina.
Jim:	That's interesting. What kind of government do you have in Sierra Leone?
Foday:	We have a constitutional democracy.
Jim:	Is that based on English law?
Foday:	Yes.
Jim:	By the way, you speak English very well. Is that your official language?
Foday:	English is the official language of my country, but it is spoken only by a literate minority of about 20% of the population.
Jim:	Really? What language does the other 80% speak?
Foday:	People in the north speak a vernacular language called Temme, whereas those in the south speak Mende.
Jim:	That's fascinating. I suspect that most citizens are Muslim?
Foday:	About 60% are Muslim, with about 20% Christian. The other 20% or so vary.
Jim:	I understand that mining is a major industry in Sierra Leone. I hear you mine diamonds.
Foday:	Yes, they are a big export. But many people live by simple subsistence farming, like my father.
Jim:	Foday, it has been really nice meeting you. I'd like to introduce you to my girlfriend. She's over there.
Foday:	Thank you, I'd like to meet her.

In comparing the two conversations, notice how much more uncertainty Jim reduces in his short conversation with Foday than Dan does with Natasha. Jim is assertive in initiating conversation with Foday and asking him questions about his country. Jim also appears responsive to Foday, using such comments as "That's interesting." Dan, on the other hand, says very little, even when prompted by Natasha. Natasha is probably more uncertain about Dan after the conversation than before. His lack of assertiveness and responsiveness probably leaves a negative impression with her.

Assessing Sociocommunicative Orientation/Style

In their study of uncertainty reduction during initial intercultural communication, Neuliep and Ryan measured assertiveness and responsiveness using an instrument developed by McCroskey and Richmond. These scales have been used successfully in other cultures, including those of China, Finland, Japan, Korea, and Russia. Note, however, that these scales were designed to measure assertiveness and responsiveness as defined in the United States and may not be generalizable across all cultures. In fact, studies examining assertiveness and responsiveness across cultures have reported differences. American men and women, for example, score higher on the assertiveness dimension than do Finnish and Japanese men and women. Generally, American women score higher on the responsiveness scale than do men and women from other cultures. Within most cultures, however, men generally score higher on the assertiveness scale, whereas women score higher on the responsiveness scale.[27]

EMPATHY AND SIMILARITY IN RELATIONSHIP DEVELOPMENT

The majority of uncertainty reduction occurs during the initial stages of a relationship. To the extent that relational partners are able to reduce uncertainty, they learn more about each other and can further develop their relationship. Two factors (among others) that have a significant influence on communication and relational development are empathy and similarity. Empathy and similarity are important in any relationship, but they take on added importance in intercultural relationships. Due to their cultural differences, persons in intercultural relationships may find it difficult to empathize with their relational partners because they are dissimilar.

Empathy

As uncertainty is reduced, people get to know each other more and can work on developing their relationship. The ability to empathize with someone is a crucial ingredient in any relationship. Empathy takes on added importance in intercultural relationships, however. Because persons from other cultures are different from us, it may be difficult for us to empathize with them, their ideas, and their style of communication. In these types of relationships, reducing uncertainty becomes essential. In fact, some communication scholars maintain that empathy may be impossible in intercultural communication. However, in general, communication scholars believe that because empathy motivates communication behavior, it is an essential ingredient in effective interpersonal communication. Empathy is often defined as the degree to which we can accurately infer another's thoughts or feelings. Benjamin Broome contends

Self-Assessment 9.1

The Sociocommunicative Orientation/Style Instrument[28]

Directions: The following questionnaire lists 20 personality traits. Indicate the degree to which you believe each of these characteristics applies to you, as you normally communicate with others, by marking whether you (5) strongly agree that it applies, (4) agree that it applies, (3) are undecided, (2) disagree that it applies, or (1) strongly disagree that it applies. There are no right or wrong answers. Work quickly; record your first impression.

_____ 1. Helpful

_____ 2. Defends own beliefs

_____ 3. Independent

_____ 4. Responsive to others

_____ 5. Forceful

_____ 6. Has strong personality

_____ 7. Sympathetic

_____ 8. Compassionate

_____ 9. Assertive

_____ 10. Sensitive to the needs of others

_____ 11. Dominant

_____ 12. Sincere

_____ 13. Gentle

_____ 14. Willing to take a stand

_____ 15. Warm

_____ 16. Tender

_____ 17. Friendly

_____ 18. Acts as a leader

_____ 19. Aggressive

_____ 20. Competitive

Scoring: Items 2, 3, 5, 6, 9, 11, 14, 18, 19, and 20 measure assertiveness. Add the scores on these items to get your assertiveness score. Scores above 40 indicate that you see yourself as assertive. Items 1, 4, 7, 8, 10, 12, 13, 15, 16, and 17 measure responsiveness. Add the scores on these items to get your responsiveness score. Scores above 40 suggest that you see yourself as responsive. Being assertive and responsive is not necessarily "good" or "bad." Your sociocommunicative style is a barometer of how you interact with others, not whether you are a good or bad person.

that this definition is inadequate for the study of intercultural communication and offers what he calls a model of **relational empathy** (see Figure 9.3). Broome argues that because our thoughts and perceptions are based on our unique personal, cultural, sociocultural, and individual past experiences, we can never completely comprehend or directly know what another is thinking or feeling. Broome argues, "While we can never become another person, it is possible to erect a structure within the framework of which the other's interpretation of the world or us takes shape or assumes meaning."[29]

The model of relational empathy is based on the idea that whenever two people come together and interact, they create a **third culture** of shared meaning and relational empathy.[30] Broome argues that mutual understanding and shared meaning are a product of the meeting between individuals. Relational empathy is conceptualized not as the ability to accurately reproduce another's perceptions or emotions but, rather, as the perceptions or emotions that are created by two people interacting. This third culture of relational empathy and shared meaning is the outcome or harmonization of communication in which unique values, beliefs, norms, and symbols are shared by the interactants. Broome asserts that the third culture emerges when the interactants are open and willing to communicate with others and expose themselves to new meanings. According to the model, persons cannot possess direct, first-hand knowledge of the emotional states or cognitive processes of another person. Instead, people possess objective and subjective meanings. Objective meaning, according to Broome, is one's interpretation of one's own personal experiences to oneself. For example, your interpretation of what it meant to grow up in your hometown with your family is a part of your own objective meaning. Subjective meaning, on the other hand, is one's interpretation of the other person's experiences in relation to one's own. For example, a friend's description of

Figure 9.3 Model of Relational Empathy

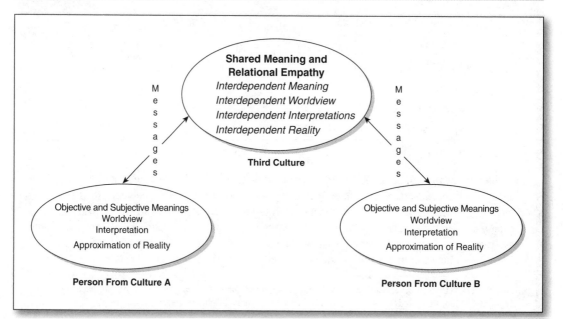

what it meant to grow up in his or her hometown and of his or her family experiences would be a part of your subjective meaning.

When two people come together and interact, a product of the third culture is interdependent meaning—that is, new meaning based on the combining of each individual's objective and subjective meanings. People also bring with them a personal worldview largely based on cultural orientation. Hence, a Japanese person brings a collectivistic, high-context worldview, and an American brings an individualistic, low-context worldview. In a relationship, these two different worldviews merge into an interdependent worldview. Because of the individuals' objective and subjective knowledge and worldviews, they have different interpretations of what is real. Through the establishment of relational empathy, an interdependent interpretation and approximation of reality materializes.

Broome asserts that similarity among individuals is not necessary to achieve relational empathy and shared meaning. Instead, Broome's model assumes that the emergence of a third culture creates a medium in which the interactants can relate and in which similarity becomes moot. Because a third culture has evolved through the verbal and nonverbal messages of the interactants, each is an active participant in its creation. Hence, neither person has to re-create anything, because each is an integral part of its existence.[31]

Intercultural researcher Donald Klopf maintains that we can approach empathy with others by developing empathic listening skills. Empathic listening means listening more to the meanings than to the words of another person. According to Klopf, empathic listening involves (a) *paraphrasing,* rewording what the other person has said; (b) *reflecting feelings,* relating back to the other the feelings we believe the other is experiencing; (c) *reflecting meanings,* restating what we heard to confirm its meaning; and (d) *summarizing,* briefly restating the major topics the other has communicated.[32]

Although no one can experience complete empathy, taking Broome's model of relational empathy and Klopf's prescription for empathic listening into account and practice, we can develop and enhance our relationships with persons from cultures different from our own.

Similarity

Although Broome's model of relational empathy discounts the importance of similarity, a great deal of research (mostly conducted in the United States) has demonstrated that similarity plays a key role in the establishment and development of relationships. As communication researcher Steve Duck states, "All communication and all relationships are likewise founded on a necessary base of similarity of understanding or similarity of meaning that facilitates the development of each."[33] This topic is important for communication researchers because of the belief that we are attracted to those people we perceive as similar to ourselves. Intercultural researchers have found that the more we perceive another as similar to ourselves, the more we are able to reduce uncertainty about the person and to form accurate categories of him or her. Thus, similarity may be particularly important during initial encounters with another person. Similarity, then, is a powerful force for attraction and approach tendencies. That is, we are attracted to those we perceive as similar, and we are likely to approach them.

One of the pioneers in the study of similarity is Donn Byrne. Although similarity may come in many forms, Byrne's efforts have focused mainly on attitude similarity and attraction. Byrne's fundamental postulate is that attitude similarity between persons leads to positive affect, which in turn leads to attraction (see Figure 9.4).[34] Byrne has become well known

Figure 9.4 Relationship Between Similarity and Attraction

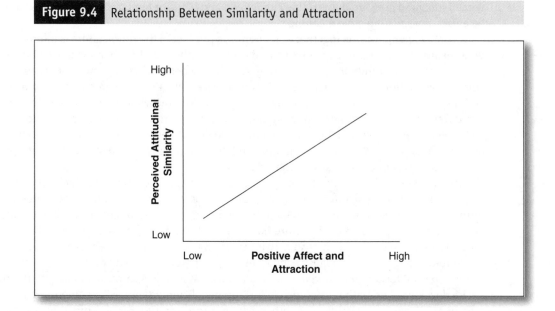

for his "bogus stranger" experiments, which have relevance for intercultural communication. In these experiments, Byrne asks research participants to indicate their attitudes on a variety of topics and issues. The participants are then paired with a "stranger," who is portrayed as a research participant whose attitudes on the same topics and issues were assessed at an earlier time. Prior to the pairing of the research participants and the stranger, the research participants are shown the stranger's attitude responses. In actuality, however, the stranger is "bogus" because his or her attitude responses are manufactured to either match or conflict with the research participants' attitude responses. After interacting with the stranger, the research participants then rate the stranger's level of attractiveness. Consistently, those research participants paired with an attitudinally similar stranger provide higher attractiveness ratings than those paired with an attitudinally dissimilar stranger. Yet in each case, the stranger is the same person.[35]

Attitude similarity is only one way in which people label themselves as like or unlike others. A White student once commented that similarity was not a factor in her relationship with her boyfriend, explaining that he was Black. Upon further questioning, it was discovered that she and her boyfriend were the same age, were studying at the same college, were pursuing the same major, enjoyed similar tastes in music and food, and had similar attitudes on a variety of topics. The point here is that although we may have dissimilarities with others, the people with whom we develop and maintain interpersonal relationships are typically very much like ourselves. Perceived similarity, sometimes called perceived homophily, is perhaps the most dominant force in our motivations to interact with others. But similarity can come in many shapes and sizes. We can be similar to others culturally, attitudinally, linguistically, racially, behaviorally, affectively, or physically. The more we find ourselves like someone else, the more likely we are to initiate and sustain communication with that person. Although it facilitates interaction and attraction, cultural similarity (which is only one kind of similarity) may not be a necessary ingredient in forming meaningful and lasting relationships. Two persons from radically different cultures may find a great deal of similarity with each other.

PERCEPTIONS OF RELATIONAL INTIMACY ACROSS CULTURES

Although the same types of relationships exist across cultures, the level of intimacy varies considerably. In other words, what it means to be a student in your culture is probably not the same as what it means to be a student in another culture. Moreover, the relationship between student and teacher varies widely across cultures. In the United States, for example, student–teacher relationships at the college level might be perceived as relatively informal and personal compared with student–teacher relationships in China or Korea. William Gudykunst and Tsukasa Nishida studied the influence of culture on perceptions of intimacy and communication behavior in the United States and Japan.[36] In each culture, students were asked to rate the level of intimacy (on a scale of 1 to 9, where 1 = intimate, 9 = nonintimate) for 30 different relationships. Gudykunst and Nishida reasoned that because of their collectivistic tendencies, the Japanese students would perceive in-group relationships as more intimate than would the American students, who are individualistic. Gudykunst and Nishida also maintained that because Japan is considered a masculine-oriented culture in which sex roles are clearly differentiated, male–female relationships (e.g., lover, spouse, boy/girlfriend) would be perceived as less intimate than in the United States. Gudykunst and Nishida argued that in cultures such as Japan, where sex roles are strictly distinguished, there is not much informal interaction between males and females. Moreover, when interaction does occur, the content of it is relatively superficial. The results of their survey are shown in Table 9.1.

When comparing the ratings, American students are often surprised to see that Japanese students rate *close friend* and *best friend* as the most intimate of their relationships. In Japan, even classmates are rated as more intimate than spouses. These results confirm the notion that when you travel to a land with a culture different from your own, your relationships in that culture (as student, friend, employee) could be perceived very differently from when you occupy the same roles in the United States.

Eastern and Western Cultures and Relationships

As demonstrated by Gudykunst and Nishida, perceptions of relationships differ widely across cultures. In individualistic cultures such as the United States, relationships are typically viewed from the perspective of the self. As June Ock Yum asserts, individualists see themselves as distinct individuals who participate in relationships to maximize their own self-interests.[37] In many collectivistic cultures, such as that of China, relationships are guided by Confucianism. According to Yum, the fundamental theme of Confucianism is that proper relationships form the cornerstone of society. Moreover, an individual's conduct in society should be guided by four principles: (a) *humanism,* treating others as one wishes to be treated; (b) *faithfulness,* loyalty rather than personal interest or profit; (c) *propriety,* social decorum and etiquette; and (d) *wisdom.*[38]

Table 9.1   Relationship Terms and Intimacy Ratings

Relationship Type	U.S.*	Japan*
Family		
Spouse (*haigusha*)	1.33	4.32
Father (*chichioya*)	2.75	2.57
Mother (*hahaoya*)	2.35	2.06
Son (*musuko*)	2.59	4.76
Daughter (*musume*)	2.55	4.87
Brother (*kyodai*)	3.12	3.51
Sister (*shimai*)	2.88	3.78
Aunt (*oba*)	4.53	4.99
Cousin (*itoko*)	4.67	4.66
Grandparent (*sofubo*)	3.75	4.15
Uncle (*oji*)	4.55	5.21
Social		
Fiancé (*konyakusha*)	1.29	4.32
Lover (*koibito*)	1.25	2.81
Boy/girlfriend (*otoko/onna tomodachi*)	1.70	3.32
Best friend (*ichiban no shinyu*)	2.51	1.73
Mate (*tsureai*)	1.75	4.45
Steady (*kosai shiteiru hito*)	2.27	2.92
Close friend (*shinyu*)	2.85	1.83
Friend (*tomo*)	3.67	3.42
Date (*detonoaite*)	4.02	3.48
Companion (*tomodachi*)	3.08	3.05
Neighbor (*kinjo no hito*)	5.72	5.92
Acquaintance (*chijin*)	6.79	4.95
Professional/Work		
Cohort (*nakama*)	5.40	2.85
Coworker (*shigato-makama*)	5.76	5.27
Employer (*koyosha*)	6.39	6.86
Colleague (*doryo*)	5.33	4.76

Relationship Type	U.S.*	Japan*
Roommate (*doshukusha*)	3.85	4.88
Classmate (*dokyusei*)	5.72	3.84
Other		
Stranger (*shiranai hito*)	8.35	7.99

SOURCE: W. B. Gudykunst and T. Nishida. (1986). The Influence of Cultural Variability on Perceptions of Communication Behavior Associated With Relationship Terms. *Human Communication Research, 13,* 147–166. Reprinted by permission of Sage Publications.

*In each culture, students were asked to rate the level of intimacy for 30 different relationships on a scale of 1 to 9 (1 = intimate; 9 = nonintimate). Lower scores represent more perceived intimacy.

Yum points out that three of these four principles have direct implications for how relationships are perceived in East Asian cultures such as that of China, as compared with Western cultures such as that of the United States. First, in contrasting Eastern and Western relationships, Yum alleges that many East Asian cultures practice *particularism*—that is, the belief that there are particular or unique rules and guidelines that apply to each individual relationship. Relational partners are to be sensitive to differences in such things as status when interacting with others. Most East Asian cultures believe in strict and well-defined social hierarchies in which people are perceived as higher or lower. In contrast, persons in Western cultures practice what Yum calls a *universalistic orientation* to relationships. Yum alleges that most Westerners try to treat others as equally as possible, regardless of status or intimacy level of the partners.[39]

Yum also contends that relational partners in Eastern cultures engage in *long-term* and *asymmetrical reciprocity*. You may recall from Chapter 3 that reciprocity refers to the give-and-take, or mutual exchange, in interpersonal encounters. According to Yum, in Confucian philosophy, dependency on others is an inevitable and accepted part of relations with others. People will always be indebted to others who help or assist them in some way. Yum states that

> under this system of reciprocity, the individual does not calculate what he or she gives and receives. To calculate would be to think about immediate personal profits, which is the opposite of the principle of faithfulness.[40]

Western relationships, on the other hand, are characterized by short-term and symmetrical reciprocity or even contractual reciprocity. In the United States, for example, some marital relationships begin with premarital legal agreements that carefully spell out expectations, possessions, and obligations that are to be followed.

Another difference between Eastern and Western relationships is that in many Eastern cultures, there is a clear difference between who is and is not a member of the in-group or the out-group. Yum maintains that Confucian philosophy prescribes that people associate and identify with relatively few, yet very cohesive, groups. Moreover, one's affiliation with in-groups is long-lived, perhaps even lifelong. Group associations in most Western cultures are, for the most part, optional and voluntary. Many of the groups with whom one associates in the United States, for example, are designed to somehow facilitate one's individual development (e.g., "self-help" groups), and one's association with such a group lasts only as long as one benefits from membership.[41]

A fourth difference between relationships in Eastern and Western cultures is the use of intermediaries (go-betweens). For the most part, persons in Western cultures prefer direct, face-to-face contact in interpersonal relationships, including those with business associates. In the United States, for example, the use of intermediaries is typically reserved for formal or legal situations and is usually contractual (as with lawyers or realtors). Yum points out that in Eastern cultures, because the distinctions between in-groups and out-groups are so well defined, intermediaries are essential and are used even in informal situations—such as introductions, dating, and marital arrangements—and in relatively small business transactions. The principle behind the use of intermediaries is to save face.[42]

A fifth difference in interpersonal relations in Eastern and Western cultures, according to Yum, is that Confucianism's emphasis on faithfulness and loyalty in relationships leads to blending of personal and public relationships. In the United States, people can maintain "strictly business" relationships, whereas many Eastern cultures prefer to do business with trusted associates with whom they have established a strong interpersonal bond. Many U.S. businesses would be well served by initiating frequent contact, establishing mutual interests, and developing shared experiences with their Eastern-culture counterparts.[43]

Intercultural and Interracial Relationships and Marriages

Marital relationships exist in virtually every culture. According to anthropologist Michael Howard, the most common type of marriage practice in the United States and most Western industrialized nations is monogamy—that is, marriage between one man and one woman. In most cases, monogamy is prescribed legally, and acquiring multiple spouses is illegal. In cultures in which marriage is governed legally, people are allowed, by law, to enter into and leave marriages—that is, people can marry, divorce, and marry again. This is called *serial monogamy*. Howard asserts that most cultures prefer not to limit the number of spouses available to a person. These cultures practice **polygamy**—that is, marriage to more than one spouse. Contrary to popular belief, polygamy is not the practice of a husband's having multiple wives. Actually, there are two types of polygamy: **polygyny**, in which a man has multiple wives, and **polyandry**, in which a woman has more than one husband. According to Howard, polygyny is permitted in the majority of societies.[44] Indeed, in their study of cross-cultural differences in family and sexual life among 68 cultures, Becker and Posner report that only 2 of those cultures did not practice polygyny.[45]

Although the number of intercultural and interracial marriages is growing, according to the U.S. Census Bureau, in 2006, 97 % of married couples in the United States were of the same race. Nearly 95 % of unmarried couples living together were of the same race. Interracial couples accounted for only 2 % of the population of married couples and just over 4 % of unmarried couples living together.[46] It is important to note, however, that these percentages take into account only interracial marriages and couples living together. The number of intercultural marriages may be much higher. To be sure, societal and attitudinal changes about intercultural marriages and relationships take time. There remain social sanctions discouraging them. In fact, legislation banning interracial marriages still existed in the United States as recently as the year 2000, when Alabama was the last state to remove such laws.

A common assumption is that intercultural and interracial relationships experience more difficulties than intracultural relationships because of the cultural or ethnic differences. And there is evidence that interracial marriages are more likely to end in divorce than intraracial marriages. Approximately two thirds of interracial marriages end in divorce, compared with 40% to 50% for all marriages. In their literature review, Troy, Lewis-Smith, and Laurenceau point to research that shows that interracial partners may face obstacles that intraracial partners do not. For example, interracial couples are often stared at in public; are negatively stereotyped; face social-network opposition, including pressure not to marry; are discriminated against by restaurant staff, real-estate agents, hotel managers, and retail clerks; and receive obscene phone calls, hate mail, and vandalized property.

Regarding intercultural relationships, Sullivan and Cottone point out that specific cultural differences affect couples, such as religious practices, differing cultural expectations and coping strategies, communication and mood expression styles, sex roles, social network preferences, migration histories, and acculturation issues.

Troy and his associates also maintain that ethnic and or racial differences might intensify conflict management differences. So Troy and his colleagues conducted a study comparing intra- and interracial couples to test the assumption that the relationship quality of interracial couples is lower compared with that of intraracial relationships. In their study, they surveyed more than 100 heterosexual couples, of which 32 were interracial and 86 were intraracial. Surprisingly, their results showed that partners in interracial relationships reported significantly higher relational satisfaction compared with those in intraracial relationships, and no differences were found for conflict or attachment style. That is, interracial couples do not engage in or use conflict techniques differently than intraracial couples and they report being equally as attached to their partners, despite the racial differences. Troy and his colleagues assert that their results contradict the notion that interracial relationships are more dysfunctional than intraracial ones. Their results shed light on the similarity research reported above. That is, while similarity plays an important role in attraction and approach tendencies, some types of similarity (e.g., attitude similarity) may play a larger role than other types of similarity—in this case, racial similarity.[47]

In addition to the growing number of interracial marriages, American attitudes about these relationships are changing. A 2001 survey conducted by *The Washington Post,* the Henry J. Kaiser Family Foundation, and Harvard University found that 86% of Black respondents said their families would welcome a White, Asian, or Hispanic person into their family. Among Whites, 66% would accept Hispanics or Asians, but only 55% would accept a Black person. Among Hispanics, 86% would accept Whites, 79% would accept Asians, and 74% would accept Blacks. Among Asians, 77% would accept Whites, 71% would accept Hispanics, and 66% would accept Blacks. Although the percentage of interracial marriages is growing and the attitudes about such relationships are improving, cross-cultural (i.e., racial or ethnic) relationships are susceptible to pressures and strains not experienced in same-race or same-ethnicity marriages or relationships. For example, results from the same survey reported above show that 65% of White–Black couples said they experienced problems within their families at the start of their relationship, and 24% of White–Asian or White–Hispanic couples reported problems.[48]

Intercultural Relational Maintenance

In the past several decades, a substantial body of literature in the social sciences has emerged focusing on *relational maintenance,* which centers on how relational partners uphold and sustain their established relationships. Many studies in relational maintenance investigate how relational partners keep the relationship in satisfactory condition and/or how they repair relationships that need mending, including use of conflict management. Laura Stafford of the University of Kentucky has worked extensively in this area. In some of her most recent research, Stafford proposes a typology of seven relational maintenance behaviors that couples use to sustain their relationships: (a) self-disclosure, where relational partners reveal aspects of themselves to their partners; (b) relationship talk, where couples communicate about the status of the relationship; (c) positivity, interacting with the partner in a cheerful, optimistic, and uncritical manner; (d) understanding, feeling understood by the partner; (e) assurances, messages that stress one's continuation in the relationship; (f) networks, use of social networks, including interacting with or relying on common affiliations and relatives; and (g) tasks, attempts to maintain the relationship by performing one's responsibilities, such as household chores.

Relational maintenance researchers generally agree that these seven behaviors are representative of the types of behaviors couples use to sustain their relationships, but little work has been done to identify the types of relational maintenance behaviors employed by partners in intercultural relationships. Michael Reiter and Christina Gee sought to find out if two additional relational maintenance behaviors might affect intercultural relationships. These include open communication and support. Open communication is a maintenance behavior that includes self-disclosure (as defined by Stafford above) but here includes a lack of topic avoidance, meaning that individuals who engage in more open communication tend not to avoid topics. Reiter and Gee believe this is an important issue for intercultural dyads, especially if they tend to avoid communication about cultural differences. Support involves giving advice, offering comfort, and providing reassurance, which appear to overlap with Stafford's maintenance behaviors of assurances and advice. But here, Reiter and Gee extend this to mean relationship-specific support, which likely plays a particularly important role in relational maintenance for intercultural relationships given the types of societal obstacles these couples face.

Here, Reiter and Gee extend the construct of the relationship-specific support to include support for culture. In their study, Reiter and Gee asked nearly 400 participants to complete measures of open communication and support regarding their romantic relationships. The majority of participants identified their relationships as intracultural, and approximately one third categorized their relationships as intercultural. The findings of their study indicated that, when compared with intracultural relationships, individuals in intercultural relationships were more likely to report conflict related to cultural differences. However, individuals in intercultural relationships were also more likely to indicate that discussion of these differences facilitated relationship maintenance. Additional results showed that in intercultural relationships, higher levels of open communication about culture and higher levels of cultural support were related to lower levels of relationship distress. Reiter and Gee point out that when compared with intracultural partners, intercultural partners were more likely to report that exchange of cultural values with their partner helped their relationship grow.

Here, Reiter and Gee argue that if partners are able to understand, appreciate, and integrate each other's similarities and differences, they will be able to use these differences to maintain their relationship quality. In addition, this result also demonstrates the overall benefit of open communication about culture between partners as a relational maintenance strategy. Finally, for individuals in intercultural relationships, higher levels of open communication about culture and cultural support predicted higher levels of relationship satisfaction.[49]

Stafford has extended her research on relational maintenance to gay and lesbian relationships, arguing that because gay and lesbian couples are not fully accepted in most societies, they may rely on unique maintenance behaviors to sustain their relationships. After surveying a number of gay men and lesbian women, Stafford found that, overall, the maintenance behaviors reported by gay and lesbian couples are quite similar to those reported by heterosexual couples. In addition, Stafford found that gay and lesbian couples also utilize particular relationship maintenance behaviors, including (a) gay/lesbian supportive environments and (b) being the same as heterosexual couples. Supportive environments refer to the choice to live, work, or socialize in places that are supportive of gay and lesbian relationships. The second new maintenance behavior, being the same as heterosexual couples, included references to how gay and lesbian couples did not see themselves as different from heterosexual couples. Stafford also noted that gay and lesbian couples use a third type of maintenance behavior that has been reported in previous research—that is, social support—but that they use it in a unique way, such that references to support meant being openly gay/lesbian with family, friends, and coworkers in public places.[50]

As we can see from the research reported above, communication plays a principal role in marriage. Depending on the type of marriage, however, communication within marriages can vary considerably. For example, Howard notes that jealousy and rivalry among wives is common in cultures that practice polygyny. Sororal polygyny, in which a man marries sisters, is one way of getting around the interpersonal problems associated with polygyny. Another is restricting the communication among wives—for example, housing each wife in a separate dwelling, as is practiced by the Plauteau Tonga. Rationing communication is another strategy: the Tanala people of Madagascar require that a husband must spend one day with each of his wives in succession. In the Lacandon culture of southern Mexico, wives are assigned hierarchical positions in which senior-ranking wives have more privileges than junior-ranking wives.[51]

Australian researchers Halford, Hahlweg, and Dunne argue that communication skills consistently differentiate distressed from nondistressed marital couples across countries. They note, however, that specific types of communication skills may vary across cultures. In their research, they coded the communication behaviors of happy and unhappy German and Australian couples. Their results showed that, across both cultures, unhappy couples engaged in higher rates of negative verbal and nonverbal behaviors and were more likely to engage in coercive escalation—that is, a sequence of negative responses that increase as the length of interaction increases. They also observed cultural differences in couples' reactions to negative responses. Happy Australian couples typically accepted or agreed with negative responses, whereas unhappy and happy German couples and unhappy Australian couples typically counterrefused.[52]

Although the Koran permits polygyny, it is not widely practiced in Muslim countries, contrary to popular belief. The Koran permits polygyny only under certain circumstances. For example, a Muslim man may have up to four wives, but he must be "perfectly equitable" with each wife. If married to more than one wife, he must spend absolutely the same amount of time with each of his wives and treat each wife exactly the same. He is not allowed the slightest preference for one wife over another. Most Muslims believe that no man can fulfill the Koran's requirement of complete and total impartiality, so most do not engage in the practice of multiple wives.[53]

In a recent article, Cynthia Cook argues that polygyny has a positive effect on population growth and fertility but can be harmful to the physical and psychological health of women and children. Cook has observed that some single African American women engage in a kind of polygyny she calls *man-sharing*. According to Cook, the lack of eligible or employable African American men is a key reason for the high incidence of single-parent households among African Americans. Many of these women, she argues, may engage in man-sharing—that is, having a relationship with a man who already has a wife and a job. Cook argues that man-sharing may be an adaptive cultural practice for the African American community in that it stabilizes its birth rate. Ironically, writes Cook, African American women are typically horrified when they learn about African polygamy, since they have been socialized to look forward to a monogamous relationship. Yet many unmarried African American mothers are actually participating in polygyny/man-sharing without the social and cultural recognition as the second or third wife.[54]

Polyandry, the practice of having multiple husbands, is observed less frequently than polygyny. Howard reports that polyandry is practiced on a regular basis in Tibet and in some parts of India, Nepal, and Sri Lanka. Howard also reports that the most common form of polyandry is fraternal polyandry—that is, a woman who marries brothers.[55]

What are some of the factors that may lead someone to initiate an intercultural relationship? Shana Levin and her colleagues sought to answer this question. Like others, Levin and her associates recognize the importance of perceived similarity in establishing a relationship. But if intercultural or interracial dating or marriage was solely influenced by similarity, then there would be far fewer intercultural couples than what we see today. In her study, Levin collected data from more than 2,000 students attending a large multiethnic university. Her sample included a sizeable number of White, Asian American, Latino, and African American students. The students completed a number of questionnaires that asked about their demographics, social class, in-group friendships, college dating patterns, in-group bias, intergroup anxiety, and in-group identification. The results show some interesting patterns.

First, consistent with the theory that perceived similarity is a dominant factor in initiating a relationship (i.e., approach tendencies), an overwhelming number of students from all four groups dated members of their own group more than they dated members of other groups. Whites dated Whites, Asian Americans dated Asian Americans, Latinos dated Latinos, and African Americans dated African Americans. Levin also found, however, that many students dated at least one member of another group during their college years. In these cases, Whites were more likely to have dated Latinos and Asian Americans than to have dated African Americans; Asian Americans were more likely to have dated Whites, followed by Latinos, and then African Americans; Latinos were more likely to have dated Whites than to have dated Asian Americans and African Americans; and African Americans were more likely to have dated Latinos and Whites than to have dated Asian Americans.

Availability also plays a role in who dates whom—that is, what options are available to someone when choosing to date someone else. In this study, Asian Americans represented the largest group, followed closely by Whites. Latinos and African Americans were the smallest groups, with half as many Latinos and one sixth as many African Americans. Levin reasoned that if partner availability were a significant factor in intergroup dating choice, Whites and Asian Americans would date one another with much greater frequency than they date Latinos and African Americans. The results showed that only Asian Americans choose intergroup dating partners consistent with availability. In this study, when they date outside their group, Asian American students date Whites over Latinos and African Americans. Factors other than availability seem to be influencing the intergroup dating choices of Whites, Latinos, and African Americans. One demographic variable also played a role in intergroup dating, where men were more likely to intergroup date than were women.

Regarding group attitudes, results indicated that students who exhibited more in-group bias, were more anxious about interacting with members of other groups, and had higher levels of group identification before college were less likely to intergroup date. Yet pressure from in-group members not to socialize with or date out-group members before college was not significantly associated with college intergroup dating. Results also indicated that students who engaged in more intergroup dating in college reported less in-group bias at the end of college. Students who dated more outside their group during college also felt less anxious interacting with people of different groups at the end of their fourth year in college. Group identification at the end of college was not significantly associated with college intergroup dating. Students with more college intergroup dating experience did, however, feel significantly more pressure from in-group members not to socialize with or date out-group members at the end of their fourth year in college. Interestingly, Asian Americans with more college intergroup dating experience felt significantly more pressure from in-group members not to socialize with or date out-group members at the end of college. However, this relationship was not seen among either Whites or Latinos.

Overall, Levin concludes that these results demonstrate the generally positive nature of intergroup dating during the college years for Whites, Asian Americans, and Latinos. Specifically, the more they dated members of other groups during college, the less in-group bias students from all three groups showed and the less intergroup anxiety Asian American and Latino students expressed at the end of college. However, Asian American students who dated outside their group more during college also felt more pressure from members of their own group not to socialize with or date members of other groups at the end of college.[56]

The Internet as Relational Maintenance

Without a doubt, the Internet has profoundly changed the way humans communicate. Estimates vary, but we can rest assured knowing that millions of people use the Internet to connect with others. Correa and her colleagues report that more than 75% of U.S. adults have been online and that even more teenagers have been online—approximately 95%. Correa notes that, initially, people went online because it offered a unique form of anonymity. But now people use it to socialize with and expand their social networks. Two of the primary Internet tools for initiating and maintaining relationships are social networking sites (SNSs), such as Facebook, and instant messaging. Although the body of research on social networking is developing and growing, we do not know much about who uses SNSs and how they may affect intercultural communication. Studies have shown that while SNSs are beginning to attract older Americans, an overwhelming number of SNS users are young people.

Correa and her associates found that the personality traits of extraversion and openness to experiences were positively related to social media use and that emotional stability (i.e., neuroticism) was not. They also note that these results were moderated by sex; that is, only men with greater degrees of emotional instability were more regular users. Professor Wang and her colleagues at the University of Buffalo found that both males and females were more likely to initiate friendships on Facebook with opposite-sex profile owners who had attractive photos than with those who had unattractive photos. Interestingly, they also found that Facebook users were more likely to initiate friendships with other Facebook users who did not include visual cues than with those who revealed an unattractive photo. Tiffany Pempek and her colleagues at Georgetown University found that students use Facebook for approximately 30 minutes throughout the day and that they spend more time observing content than actually posting it.

One study in particular investigated the role of culture in self-expression on Facebook pages. This study compared the Facebook profiles of U.S. Caucasians, African Americans, and Asians attending a Midwestern university. The results indicate that African American profiles contained more descriptive statements that expressed their internal attitudes, beliefs, and values—including the use of personal pronouns—than did those of Caucasian or Asian students. Asian students had more statements reflecting their social affiliations (i.e., group memberships) than did Caucasians or African Americans. Regarding the total amount of self-descriptive statements, African Americans had the most, followed by Caucasians and Asians. The authors of this study contend that these results are reflective of individualism and collectivism; that is, as the authors state, African Americans are "the most individualistic individuals" compared with Caucasians and then Asians, who are more collectivistic than either of the other two groups.[57]

A general conclusion that most research has supported is that SNSs are used primarily for social interaction with friends with whom users have a preestablished relationship offline and that they serve mostly to support preexisting social relations within geographically bound communities. That is, as far as we can tell, most SNS users are not using social media to initiate new relationships outside their geographical areas. In fact, one study showed that only 15% of Facebook networks were composed of people who had never actually met. Although we are in the early stages of this research, it appears that currently, SNSs such as Facebook are not the primary means by which people meet and initiate relationships with others from different cultures.[58]

Mate Selection and Desirability Across Cultures

When you think about getting married or finding a romantic partner, what are the characteristics you imagine? Are you looking for someone who is good-looking? Educated? In possession of a good sense of humor? Wealthy? The famed evolutionary psychologist David Buss has been interested in the answers to these questions and has investigated mate preferences and opposite-sex desirability across cultures for decades. Before looking at his findings, take a moment to complete the following survey.

Self-Assessment 9.2

Selecting a Mate: Factors in Choosing a Mate

Directions: Below are 18 characteristics of people that you may find either desirable or undesirable. On a scale of 0 to 3, rate each of the characteristics on how important or desirable it is in choosing a mate.

A score of 0 = irrelevant or unimportant, 1 = somewhat important, 2 = important, and 3 = indispensable.

_____ 1. Sociability

_____ 2. Similar education

_____ 3. Pleasing disposition

_____ 4. Refinement, neatness

_____ 5. Similar religious background

_____ 6. Good looks

_____ 7. Education and intelligence

_____ 8. Mutual attraction—love

_____ 9. Good cook and housekeeper

_____ 10. Good financial prospect

_____ 11. Desire for home and children

_____ 12. Chastity (no previous experience in sexual intercourse)

_____ 13. Dependable character

_____ 14. Good health

_____ 15. Favorable social status or rating

_____ 16. Similar political background

_____ 17. Emotional stability and maturity

_____ 18. Ambitious and industrious

Preferences Concerning Potential Mates

Directions: Below is a set of 13 characteristics. Please rank them on their desirability in someone you might marry. Give a 1 to the most desirable characteristic in a potential mate, a 2 to the second most desirable characteristic in a potential mate, a 3 to the third most desirable characteristic in a potential mate, and so on until you have ranked all 13 characteristics. No characteristic can receive the same ranking as another.

_____ 1. Easygoing

_____ 2. Healthy

(Continued)

(Continued)

_____   3. Physically attractive

_____   4. Good heredity

_____   5. College graduate

_____   6. Exciting personality

_____   7. Intelligent

_____   8. Creative and artistic

_____   9. Good housekeeper

_____   10. Good earning capacity

_____   11. Religious

_____   12. Wants children

_____   13. Kind and understanding

SOURCES: Buss, D. M. (1994). Mate Preferences in Thirty-Seven Cultures. In W. J. Lonner & R. Malpass (Eds.), *Psychology and Culture* (pp. 197–202). Boston: Allyn & Bacon; Buss, D. M. (1989). Sex Differences in Human Mate Preference: Evolutionary Hypotheses Tested in Thirty-Seven Cultures. *Behavioral and Brain Sciences, 12,* 1–49.

In some of his most recent research, Buss and his colleague Susan Hill argue that a man's and a woman's mate preferences have evolved in response to recurring and different adaptive problems that each sex has had to solve when judging the desirability of someone else. These different mate preferences present men and women with a different set of assessment problems when evaluating the desirability of members of the opposite sex. One source of information about the desirability of another as a romantic partner is how that person is perceived when interacting with same-sex others. Buss and Hill found that women rate men more desirable when the men are shown surrounded by women than when they are shown alone or with other men. They label this the desirability enhancement effect. In contrast, men rate women less desirable when they are shown surrounded by men than when they are shown alone or with women. Buss and Hill call this the desirability diminution effect. The authors maintain that both effects are reflected in men's and women's judgments of intrasexual rivals, such that women will judge other women depicted with men as being less desirable to men than the same women depicted alone or with other women. Moreover, men will judge other men depicted with women as being more desirable to women than the same men depicted alone or with other men.[59]

In his earlier research, Buss initiated the International Mate Selection Project, consisting of 49 research collaborators from 33 countries located on six continents and five islands.[60] The focus of the project has been to identify people's preferences in choosing a mate. According to Buss, scholars from myriad academic fields are interested in mating practices and mate selection. Evolutionary biologists, for example, believe that mate preference is a central evolutionary force. Sociologists study mating practices because they affect the distribution of wealth in society (e.g., when the rich prefer to mate with the rich). Geneticists understand that mate preferences can affect genetic inheritability estimates. Social psychologists see mate preference as a psychological phenomenon related to interpersonal attraction. Yet despite all the interest, Buss alleges that very little is known about the types of characteristics people value in potential mates and how these values might vary across cultures. Hence, Buss initiated the International Mate Selection Project.

The purpose of his research was to identify (a) which characteristics individuals value in potential mates, (b) similarities and differences among countries in their values, (c) clusters of countries that are similar to one another, and (d) sex differences in the degree of variation in mate selection within each country. Buss and his research collaborators surveyed more than 10,000 people from 33 different countries. In Africa, subjects were from Nigeria, South Africa, and Zambia. Asian countries sampled were China, India, Japan, and Taiwan. In the Middle East, Jewish and Palestinian Israel and Iran were surveyed. European countries studied were Belgium, Bulgaria, Estonia, Finland, France, Germany, Great Britain, Greece, Ireland, Italy, the Netherlands, Norway, Poland, Spain, Sweden, and the former Yugoslavia. In North America, the United States (including Hawaii) and Canada were sampled. South American countries surveyed were Brazil, Colombia, and Venezuela. Oceanic countries were Australia and New Zealand. Participants from Indonesia were also sampled.[61]

In the study, individuals were asked to complete the "Factors in Choosing a Mate" and the "Preferences Concerning Potential Mates" instruments (see Self-Assessment 9.2). After analyzing the completed surveys, Buss found that in spite of the unique cultural variability associated with each sample, there were substantial commonalities among all the samples. Table 9.2 outlines the four top-rated variables. Some of the least preferred characteristics from the rating instruments were "chastity," "similar religious background," "similar political background," and "favorable social status." The lowest-ranked characteristics were "college graduate," "good earning capacity," and "religion."

Table 9.2   Universally Preferred Characteristics

Universally Preferred Characteristics: Ranking Instrument = Preferences Concerning Potential Mates

1. Kind and understanding
2. Intelligent
3. Exciting personality
4. Healthy

Universally Preferred Characteristics: Rating Instrument = Factors in Choosing a Mate

1. Mutual attraction–love
2. Emotional stability and maturity
3. Good health
4. Pleasing disposition

SOURCES: Buss, D. M. (1994). Mate Preferences in Thirty-Seven Cultures. In W. J. Lonner & R. Malpass (Eds.), *Psychology and Culture* (pp. 197–202). Boston: Allyn & Bacon; Buss, D. M. (1989). Sex Differences in Human Mate Preference: Evolutionary Hypotheses Tested in Thirty-Seven Cultures. *Behavioral and Brain Sciences, 12,* 1–49.

Buss noted that although there were some overall commonalities among the cultures, each country displayed some unique mate preferences. For example, the highest-rated characteristic for Iranian men and women was "refinement and neatness." On the other hand, Chinese men rated "good health" as most important. Chinese women chose "emotional stability" as their top-rated characteristic. Nigerian men rated "good health" the highest, whereas Nigerian women rated "emotional stability" the highest. Buss reported that the largest effect of culture was seen in the variable of "chastity." China, India, Indonesia, Iran, Taiwan, and Palestinian Israel placed the most importance on this characteristic, whereas Sweden, Finland, Norway, the Netherlands, and West Germany ranked it the least important.

Probably the greatest difference among cultures occurred between men and women. In some countries, the sexes differed little in their rankings, whereas in others, they differed greatly. The two countries with the highest degree of sexual dimorphism, Nigeria and Zambia, were also the two that practice polygyny. Moreover, there was more similarity between men and women from the same culture than between men and men or women and women from different cultures. The largest sex difference occurred for the variables of "good financial prospect" and "good earning capacity." Women generally valued these traits more than did men. Men across the globe valued physical attractiveness in marriage partners more than did women. Buss states,

> The importance of good looks is not limited to Western Europe or North America; nor is it limited to cultures saturated with visual media such as television, movies, and videos; nor is it limited to particular racial, ethnic, religious, or political groups. In all known cultures worldwide, from the inner-continental tribal societies of Africa and South America to the big cities of Madrid, London, and Paris, men place a premium on the physical appearance of a potential mate.[62]

Women, on the other hand, place somewhat greater value than do men on "emotional stability and maturity," "favorable social status," "education and intelligence," and "college graduate." In another sex difference, men worldwide prefer wives who are younger than themselves. In polygynic cultures such as Zambia and Nigeria, where men may have multiple wives, men prefer brides who are much younger than themselves. Conversely, women prefer men who are older. In his conclusion, Buss notes that culture appears to exert substantial effects on mate preferences and that, in general, the effects of sex on mate preferences are small compared with those of culture (see Figure 9.5).[63]

Buss's research above shows us that mutual attraction and love are nearly universal factors in choosing a mate. But how people from different cultures define love may differ. In their review of some of the research on love across cultures, Todd Jackson and his colleagues contend that love is conceived differently across cultures. They point to research that has found that students of Asian descent score higher on measures of companionate and pragmatic love styles and lower on erotic love styles compared with their European-descended counterparts.

In related research, Rothbaum and Tsang found that, in comparison with U.S. love songs, Chinese love songs focus on love in the natural world and love as a value of Confucianism, Buddhism, and Taoism, with an emphasis on interdependence. U.S. love songs focus on the love partner without regard to context. Other studies have found that Chinese concepts of love typically stress love as related to sadness, jealousy, and betrayal, while U.S. concepts of love equate it with happiness.

| Figure 9.5 | Although commonalities can be found across cultures, culture is thought to exert great influence over individuals' mate preferences. |

To extend this research, Jackson and his colleagues asked American and Chinese couples to complete the Love Stories Scale, an instrument designed to assess preferences for 25 metaphors for love. Examples of love metaphors include *history,* love forms an indelible record where partners keep a mental and physical record of their relationship; *war,* love is a series of battles in a continuing war; *mystery,* love is a mystery where partners do not let themselves be known; *pornography,* love is dirty and partners are objectified; *fantasy,* love results in couples living happily ever after; *democracy,* love is two partners equally sharing power; and so on. Their results showed that fantasy emerged as a prototypical theme for Americans that was missing from the Chinese responses. For the Chinese, democracy and history emerged as themes, where the sharing of power and history between partners was an important ingredient of love. Pornography emerged in both Chinese and American themes.[64]

Shuangyue Zhang and Susan Kline have also studied mate selection across cultures. Their study examined the influence of one's social network on intention to marry and relational commitment to another in both China and the United States. Zhang and Kline point out that the familial network of a potential mate is highly valued in East Asian cultures, particularly in China. To be sure, however, social network support is positively related to relationship development and stability in the United States as well. But Zhang and Kline were interested in finely tuning how and to what extent family and friend networks affect one's decision in the process of mate selection in both China and the United

States. Zhang and Kline point to research that has documented that one's social networks significantly influence the initiation, development, maintenance, and dissolution of any given relationship. Noting that personal relationships do not exist in isolation from one another, Zhang and Kline assert that social networks are important because relational partners need validation of their own perspectives regarding their relationship from members of their close networks. In fact, some interesting research shows that one's social network is often better at predicting his/her relationship outcome than are the individuals involved in the relationship!

Also, other studies have demonstrated that perceived support from one's network positively affects relationship development and stability. For example, Zhang and Kline point to research that shows that romantic partners experience less uncertainty and are less likely to terminate their relationship when they communicate frequently with their partners' social network. In their own study, Zhang and Kline examined the role of social networks in mate selection between China and the United States. They suspected that the cultural orientations of individualism and collectivism may play a role in the impact of social networks and mate selection across these two cultures. Recall from Chapter 2 that filial piety is one of the most salient values in Chinese culture. In China, the family is seen as the basic unit of society. In their study, Chinese and American students completed surveys that measure the role of social networks in mate preferences. Zhang and Kline predicted that (a) family-oriented beliefs would be considered more important for Chinese than for Americans, (b) Chinese would be more likely to comply with their network members regarding their marriage decisions than would Americans, (c) Chinese would be more likely to indicate network disapproval as an obstacle to marrying their dating partners than would Americans, and (d) the influence of family and friends would be a better predictor of one's marriage intentions and relational commitment for Chinese than for Americans. All their predictions were confirmed. In their discussion of the results, Zhang and Kline point to China's collectivistic orientation, and especially filial piety, as accountable for the emphasis on social networks.[65]

Arranged Marriages

In some cultures, an individual's preference in selecting a mate is moot because marriage is arranged by parents or a trusted family friend or mediator. In many instances, the bride and groom of an **arranged marriage** do not even meet until the day of the wedding. A bride price, similar to a dowry, is an essential ingredient of the arranged marriage in many cultures. Although not as common as they once were, arranged marriages are still practiced in a variety of cultures and within some microcultural groups in the United States, such as the Hmong. Many young persons in the United States find the prospect of an arranged marriage quite frightening and unnerving. Yet Katie Thao, a Hmong woman who emigrated from Laos to the United States when she was young, indicates that the arranged marriage in which she participated was one of the most satisfying events of her life.[66] To Katie, the time and effort associated with searching for a mate represented considerable uncertainty and anxiety. In traditional Hmong culture, arranged marriages are negotiated by the parents. Because Katie had faith and trust in her parents to select for her the ideal spouse, she had little to worry about and very little uncertainty. Although she admits to being nervous on her wedding day,

Thao says she loves the man she married very much, and they have three children. Although it happens infrequently, the woman can reject the match. As Lor notes, however, there are certain situations in which the match cannot be refused. According to Lor, if the groom's family clan has high status, is unusually wealthy, or is related to the bride's family in some way, the match is essentially permanent.[67]

Jill Hoffman estimates that as many as 95% of marriages in India are arranged. As in other cultures with arranged marriages, in India, a certain amount of bargaining and negotiation is involved. Hoffman notes that family status and wealth play key roles in the process. Although it is illegal, in southern India, according to Hoffman, the groom's family often pays a bride price, especially if the bride is exceptionally beautiful or if the groom himself is flawed or impaired in some way. In most cases, the bride and groom do not meet before the wedding.[68]

In her analysis of marriage in Iran, Kelly Pretty found that in traditional Iranian families, a marriage is arranged by the parents and a bride price is negotiated. In some instances, arranged marriages are between cousins, although this trend is changing.[69] In traditional Pakistani families, marriages are arranged by the fathers. According to Rebecca Sinnen, Pakistanis place a great deal of importance on status and wealth and are careful to arrange marriages between a bride and groom of the same caste. Typically, the fathers negotiate through intermediaries. Sinnen notes that parents consider this the most important of all parental duties.[70] In Japan, as many as one in five marriages are arranged through an intermediary called a *pro nakodo*. The pro nakodo serves as a kind of dating service in that he interacts with other nakodos in order to find an appropriate match. Prospective brides and grooms begin the procedure by completing a lengthy registration process. Their applications are then kept on file and can be reviewed by other pro nakodos looking for a match. When a possible match is made, the clients meet to become acquainted. If the match is successful, the pro nakodo receives a substantial payment for his services. Another payment is then made to the bride's family. For the groom's family, the process can be expensive. Renkens notes that the success rate is rather low, at about 20%.[71]

In China, a grotesque form of arranged marriage has been rekindled: bride trafficking. *Newsweek* correspondent Dorinda Elliot reports that in many of the rural communities of China, crooked marriage brokers offer kidnapped women and girls for sale to prospective buyers. According to Elliot, in recent years, Chinese authorities freed almost 100,000 kidnapped women and children and arrested almost 150,000 bride traffickers for participating in what she calls a virtual slave trade. Ironically, writes Elliot, local Chinese peasants sympathize with men who buy their wives, believing that if a woman takes the bride price and sends it to her parents, the man deserves to have her as his wife.[72]

Marital Dissolution and Divorce Across Cultures

A fact of life for all of us is that some of our relationships will end. Like marriage practices, divorce customs vary across cultures. Although it is relatively easy to calculate the divorce rate in any given culture, to understand why people divorce is a much more difficult task. In many cultures, social and economic issues often play a role in divorce decisions. Factors such as income, sexual dissatisfaction, childlessness, women's equality issues, religion, and the ease with which one can obtain a divorce all vary across cultures.

STUDENT VOICES ACROSS CULTURES

Marriage

 My name is Mohammad I. Alshaya, and I am from Riyadh, Saudi Arabia. I graduated from St. Norbert College with a major in business administration. Since Saudi Arabia is heavily influenced by the religion of Islam, marriage is considered holy. This is because Islam encourages its followers to get married and multiply. However, these days, there are concerns among people who are getting married. There are, of course, some burdens on both the bride and the groom. The most difficult part of marriage, for example, is the bride wealth (dowry).

The point of marriage is to bring two individuals together. However, there are more important aspects associated with marriage than uniting two people. For example, marriage in Saudi could bring two families together; this is essential in all marriages because those two families could become one family. Another vital reason for marriage is the importance of forming a family that contributes well to society.

Mothers from both the groom's and the bride's sides play a major part in matching two individuals as a wife and a husband. Arranged marriages are very common where I am from. The mother of the groom usually plays the role of matchmaker, for which she will be given the descriptive qualities that the man is looking for in a woman. What most men seek in a wife is not quite the same as in other cultures. Qualities are similar, but the order is different. For Saudi men, reputation is probably ranked first, followed by social status. Attractiveness is very important, but it will never be as crucial as reputation and social status.

In general, monogamy is correlated with lower divorce rates than polygyny.[73] Although the reasons for divorce vary, one trend that seems to be consistent across most cultures is that the overall divorce rate is on the rise. In Japan, the divorce rate doubled from 1990 to 2004. In India, however, the divorce rate remains low, where only 1 in 100 marriages end in divorce. Laungani notes that there is a strong stigma against divorce in India, especially on women. Indian women should not even think of divorce, asserts Laungani, lest they face the loss of status, removal of custody of their children, and threat of poverty. So strong are the social consequences of divorce that most married Indian women endure the most appalling domestic conditions to remain married.[74]

In China, the divorce rate is increasing. Since the passage of legislative reforms in the early 1980s and then more reform in 2003, divorce has become much simpler in China, and divorce rates are soaring. In urban areas, such as Beijing, the divorce rate increased from 2% in 1981 to almost 20% in 1992.[75] Compared with 2003, nearly 300,000 more couples divorced in 2004—an increase of 21.2%. Approximately 48% of Canadian marriages now end in divorce.[76] Citing increased opportunities for women, the *Women's International Network News* reports that the divorce rate in Russia is rising quickly.

Because they are able to find new apartments and support themselves financially, more and more Russian women are seeking divorce. The divorce rate in Russia has plateaued at about 40%.[77]

CHAPTER SUMMARY

People across the world, in all cultures, initiate, maintain, and dissolve relationships. Reducing uncertainty is a major part of initiating relationships, and one's level of intercultural communication apprehension and one's sociocommunicative style affect this process. Empathy and similarity are important in maintaining relationships. Perceptions of relationships differ significantly across cultures, particularly between Eastern and Western cultures. Perhaps the most important of all relationships, marriage, varies across cultures in terms of the different types of marriage, mate selection, arranged marriage, and marital dissolution.

 Visit the student study site at **www.sagepub.com/neuliep5e** *for e-flashcards, web quizzes, web resources and more.*

DISCUSSION QUESTIONS

1. In thinking about the quote at the beginning of the chapter, "Without others, there is no self," how do your family, friends, and professors define who you are?

2. What are the communication strategies you use to reduce uncertainty when interacting with others?

3. After completing the Sociocommunicative Orientation/Style Instrument in this chapter, how does your level of assertiveness and responsiveness affect your relationships?

4. In what ways are you similar to your closest friends?

5. What are the primary characteristics you look for in a potential relational partner?

6. Why would you or would you not consider a person from a different culture as a potential mate?

KEY TERMS

arranged marriage   344

assertiveness   321

polyandry   332

polygamy   332

polygyny   332

relational empathy   326

responsiveness   321

sociocommunicative style   312

third culture   326

uncertainty   313

uncertainty reduction theory   313

REFERENCES

1. Gergen, K. J. (1991). *The Saturated Self: Dilemmas of Identity in Contemporary Life.* New York: Basic. (Quote on p. 178)

2. Berger, C. R., & Calabrese, R. J. (1975). Some Explorations in Initial Interaction and Beyond: Toward a Developmental Theory of Interpersonal Communication. *Human Communication Research, 1,* 99–112.

3. Berger & Calabrese, Some Explorations in Initial Interaction and Beyond. Reproduced with permission of Oxford University Press, Inc. via Copyright Clearance Center.

4. Gudykunst, W. B., & Kim, Y. Y. (1997). *Communicating With Strangers: An Approach to Intercultural Communication.* New York: McGraw-Hill.

5. Gudykunst, W. B. (1983). Uncertainty Reduction and Predictability of Behavior in Low- and High-Context Cultures. *Communication Quarterly, 31,* 49–55; Gudykunst, W. B. (1988). Uncertainty and Anxiety. In Y. Y. Kim & W. B. Gudykunst (Eds.), *Theories of Intercultural Communication* (pp. 123–156). Newbury Park, CA: Sage; Gudykunst, W. B. (1995). Anxiety/Uncertainty Management (AUM) Theory. In R. Wiseman (Ed.), *Intercultural Communication Theory* (pp. 8–58). Thousand Oaks, CA: Sage.

6. Gudykunst, W. B., & Nishida, T. (1984). Individual and Cultural Influences on Uncertainty Reduction. *Communication Monographs, 51,* 23–36.

7. Sanders, J., & Wiseman, R. (1991). *Uncertainty Reduction Among Ethnicities in the United States.* Paper presented at the annual convention of the International Communication Association, Chicago, IL.

8. Gudykunst, W. B., Sodetani, L. L., & Sonoda, K. T. (1987). Uncertainty Reduction in Japanese-American-Caucasian Relationships in Hawaii. *Western Journal of Speech Communication, 51,* 256–278.

9. Berger & Calabrese, Some Explorations in Initial Interaction and Beyond, pp. 99–112.

10. Ibid.

11. Gudykunst & Kim, *Communicating With Strangers.*

12. Gudykunst, W. B. (2005). An Anxiety/Uncertainty Management (AUM) Theory of Effective Communication: Making the Mesh of the Net Finer. In W. B. Gudykunst (Ed.), *Theorizing About Intercultural Communication* (pp. 281–322). Thousand Oaks, CA: Sage.

13. Ibid.

14. Ibid.

15. Ibid.

16. Ibid.

17. Ibid.

18. Ibid.

19. Neuliep, J. W., & Ryan, D. J. (1998). The Influence of Intercultural Communication Apprehension and Socio-Communicative Orientation on Uncertainty Reduction During Initial Cross-Cultural Interaction. *Communication Quarterly, 46,* 88–99.

20. Berger & Calabrese, Some Explorations in Initial Interaction and Beyond.

21. Neuliep & Ryan, The Influence of Intercultural Communication Apprehension and Socio-Communicative Orientation on Uncertainty Reduction During Initial Cross-Cultural Interaction.

22. Neuliep, J. W., & Grohskopf, E. L. (2000). Uncertainty Reduction and Communication Satisfaction During Initial Interaction: An Initial Test and Replication of a New Axiom. *Communication Reports, 13,* 67–78.

23. McCroskey, J. C., & Richmond, V. P. (1996). *Fundamentals of Human Communication.* Prospect Heights, IL: Waveland.

24. Ibid.

25. Neuliep & Ryan, The Influence of Intercultural Communication Apprehension and Socio-Communicative Orientation on Uncertainty Reduction During Initial Cross-Cultural Interaction.

26. Ibid.; Berger & Calabrese, Some Explorations in Initial Interaction and Beyond.

27. Anderson, C. M., Martin, M. M., Zhong, M., & West, D. (1997). *Reliability, Separation of Factors, and Sex Difference on the Assertiveness–Responsiveness Measure: A Chinese Sample.* Paper presented at the annual convention of the International Communication Association, Montreal, Quebec, Canada; Thompson, C. A., Ishii, S., & Klopf, D. W. (1990). Japanese and Americans Compared on Assertiveness/Responsiveness. *Psychological Reports, 66,* 829–830; Thompson, C. A., & Klopf, D. W. (1991). An Analysis of Social Style Among Disparate Cultures. *Communication Research Reports, 8,* 65–72.

28. McCroskey, J. C., & Richmond, V. P. (1996). *Fundamentals of Human Communication: An Interpersonal Perspective.* Prospect Heights, IL: Waveland.

29. Broome, B. J. (1991). Building Shared Meaning: Implications of a Relational Approach to Empathy for Teaching Intercultural Communication. *Communication Education, 40,* 235–249. (Quote on p. 240)

30. The concept of third-culture building was initially articulated by Fred Casmir. Broome's approach is based on Casmir's work in this area.

31. Broome, Building Shared Meaning.

32. Klopf, D. W. (1998). *Intercultural Encounters: The Fundamentals of Intercultural Communication.* Englewood, CO: Morton.

33. Duck, S., & Barnes, M. K. (1992). Disagreeing About Agreement: Reconciling Differences About Similarity. *Communication Monographs, 59,* 199–208.

34. Byrne, D. (1992). The Transition From Controlled Laboratory Experimentation to Less Controlled Settings: Surprise! Additional Variables Are Operative. *Communication Monographs, 59,* 190–198.

35. Ibid.

36. Gudykunst, W. B., & Nishida, T. (1986). The Influence of Cultural Variability on Perceptions of Communication Behavior Associated With Relationship Terms. *Human Communication Research, 13,* 147–166.

37. Yum, J. O. (1997). The Impact of Confucianism on Interpersonal Relationships and Communication Patterns in East Asia. In L. A. Samovar & R. E. Porter (Eds.), *Intercultural Communication: A Reader* (8th ed., pp. 78–88). Belmont, CA: Wadsworth.

38. Ibid.

39. Ibid.

40. Ibid., p. 81.

41. Ibid.

42. Ibid.

43. Ibid.

44. Howard, M. C. (1989). *Contemporary Cultural Anthropology.* Glenview, IL: Scott, Foresman.

45. Becker, G. S., & Posner, R. A. (1993). Cross-Cultural Differences in Family and Sexual Life. *Rationality and Society, 5,* 421–432.

46. *American Families and Living Arrangements: 2006 Current Population Survey Reports.* Washington, DC: U.S. Census Bureau. Available from http://www.census .gov/population/www/socdemo/hh-fam.html.

47. Sullivan, C., & Cottone, R. R. (2006). Culturally Based Couple Therapy and Intercultural Relationships: A Review of the Literature. *Family Journal, 14,* 221–225; Troy, A. B., Lewis-Smith, J., & Laurenceau, J.-P. (2006). Interracial and Intraracial Romantic Relationships: The Search for Differences in Satisfaction, Conflict, and Attachment Style. *Journal of Social and Personal Relationships, 23,* 65–80.

48. *Race and Ethnicity in 2001: Attitudes, Perceptions, and Experience.* Menlo Park, CA: The Henry J. Kaiser Foundation. Available from www.kff.org.

49. Reiter, M. J., & Gee, C. B. (2008). Open Communication and Partner Support in Intercultural and Interfaith Romantic Relationships: A Relational Maintenance Approach. *Journal of Social and Personal Relationships, 25,* 539–559; Stafford, L. (2011). Measuring Relationship Maintenance Behaviors: Critique and Development of the Revised Relationship Maintenance Behavior Scale. *Journal of Social and Personal Relationships, 28,* 278–303.

50. Haas, S., & Stafford, L. (1998). An Initial Examination of Maintenance Behaviors in Gay and Lesbian Relationships. *Journal of Social and Personal Relationships, 15,* 846–855.

51. Howard, *Contemporary Cultural Anthropology.*

52. Halford, W. K., Hahlweg, K., & Dunne, M. (1990). The Cross-Cultural Consistency of Marital Communication Associated With Marital Distress. *Journal of Marriage and the Family, 52,* 487–501.

53. Armstrong, K. (1998). *Polygamy in Islam.* Available from twf.org/Library/Polygamy.html; *Polygamy: The Truth.* Available from www.moslem.org/polygamy/htm.

54. Cook, C. T. (2007). Polygyny: Did the Africans Get It Right? *Journal of Black Studies, 38,* 232–250.

55. Howard, *Contemporary Cultural Anthropology.*

56. Levin, S., Taylor, P. L., & Caudle, E. (2007). Interethnic and Interracial Dating in College: A Longitudinal Study. *Journal of Social and Personal Relationships, 24,* 323–341.

57. Correa, T., Hinsley, A. W., & Gil de Zuniga, H. (2010). Who Interacts on the Web? The Intersection of Users' Personality and Social Media Use. *Computers in Human Behavior, 26,* 247–253; DeAndrea, D. C., Shaw, A. S., & Levine, T. R. (2010). Online Language: The Roles of Culture in Self-Expression and Self-Construal on Facebook. *Journal of Language and Social Psychology, 29,* 425–442; Pempek, T. A., Yermolayeva, Y. A., & Calvert, S. L. (2009). College Students' Social Networking Experiences on Facebook. *Journal of Applied Developmental Psychology, 30,* 227–238; Wang, S. S., Moon, S., Kwon, K. H., Evans, C. A., & Stefanone, M. A. (2010). Face Off: Implications of Visual Cues on Initiating Friendship on Facebook. *Computers in Human Behavior, 26,* 226–234.

58. Ibid.

59. Hill, S. E., & Buss, D. M. (2008). The Mere Presence of Opposite-Sex Others on Judgments of Sexual and Romantic Desirability: Opposite Effects for Men and Women. *Personality and Social Psychology Bulletin, 34(5),* 635–647. (Published online first, February 26, 2008)

60. Buss, D. M. (1989). Sex Differences in Human Mate Preference: Evolutionary Hypotheses Tested in Thirty-Seven Cultures. *Behavioral and Brain Sciences, 12,* 1–49; Buss, D. M. (1994). Mate Preferences in Thirty-Seven Cultures. In W. J. Lonner & R. Malpass (Eds.), *Psychology and Culture* (pp. 197–202). Boston: Allyn & Bacon.

61. Ibid.

62. Ibid., p. 200.

63. Ibid.

64. Jackson, T., Chen, H., Guo, C., & Gao, X. (2006). Stories We Love by: Conceptions of Love Among Couples from the People's Republic of China and the United States. *Journal of Cross-Cultural Psychology, 37,* 446–464; Rothbaum, F., & Tsang, B. (1998). Love Songs in the United

States and China. *Journal of Cross-Cultural Psychology, 26,* 306–319.

65. Zhang, S., & Kline, S. (2009). Can I Make My Own Decision? A Cross-Cultural Study of Perceived Social Network Influence in Mate Selection. *Journal of Cross-Cultural Psychology, 40,* 3–23.

66. The account was provided by Katie Thao in a personal communication in the summer of 1995.

67. Lor, H. (1997). *The Hmong.* Unpublished student manuscript, St. Norbert College, De Pere, WI.

68. Hoffman, J. (1997). *Arranged Marriage in India: Rules Governing the Process.* Unpublished student manuscript, St. Norbert College, De Pere, WI; Laungani, P. D. (2007). *Understanding Cross-Cultural Psychology.* London: Sage.

69. Pretty, K. (1997). *Marriage in Iran: A Changing Way of Life.* Unpublished student manuscript, St. Norbert College, De Pere, WI.

70. Sinnen, R. (1997). *Arranged Marriages in Traditional Pakistani Culture.* Unpublished student manuscript, St. Norbert College, De Pere, WI.

71. Renkens, S. (1997). *Pro Nakodo Arranged Marriages.* Unpublished student manuscript, St. Norbert College, De Pere, WI.

72. Elliot, D. (1998). Trying to Stand on Two Feet. *Newsweek, 313,* 48–50.

73. Gage-Brandon, A. J. (1992). The Polygyny-Divorce Relationship: A Case Study of Nigeria. *Journal of Marriage and the Family, 54,* 285–293.

74. Laungani, *Understanding Cross-Cultural Psychology.*

75. China: Divorce Increase and Change Affect Women. (1994). *Women's International Network News, 20,* 59; *China's Divorce Rate up 21.2 Percent in 2004.* (2005). *China Daily.* Available from http://www.china daily.com.cn/english/doc/2005–03/01/content_420456.htm.

76. *Divorce Rate in Canada.* Retrieved February 28, 2008, from http://www.divorcerate.org/divorce-rates-in-canada.html.

77. Russian Business Women Are Moving Up Slowly. (1998). *Women's International Network News, 24,* 75.

Intercultural Conflict

After reading this chapter, you should be able to

1. define intercultural conflict;

2. list and explain the three levels of conflict;

3. assess your self-face, other-face, and mutual-face concerns;

4. define facework and identify three primary facework strategies;

5. list and define the 11 subcategories of facework;

6. list and define the five primary styles of conflict communication;

7. list and define the three secondary styles of conflict communication;

8. identify and discuss the conflict styles preferred by individualistic and collectivistic cultures; and

9. identify and discuss the conflict styles preferred by high- versus low-context cultures.

Honest disagreement is often a good sign of progress.

—Mahatma Gandhi

Imagine yourself in the following situation:

> Akira Abe is an international exchange student from Japan who lives down the hall from you in your dorm. You have interacted with Akira only occasionally and do not know him very well. This morning, Akira approached you to complain that you frequently play your music so loudly that he is unable to study or sleep. Akira then asked if you would please stop playing your music so loudly.

What would you do in this situation? How would you resolve this conflict? Would you comply with Akira's request? Would you argue with Akira?

Conflict, such as the one depicted above, is an inevitable part of living in a society with others. All types of human relationships, from strangers to acquaintances to intimates, experience conflict. Communication plays a paradoxical role in most conflicts because communication is required both to instigate conflict and to resolve conflict. Unfortunately, conflict is the source of much relational stress and dissolution.

Fortunately, the successful resolution of conflict is one of the strongest and most consistent predictors of relational satisfaction. Hence, an understanding of conflict and how to resolve it is an essential part of becoming a competent communicator, especially in your relationships with persons from other cultures.

DEFINITION OF INTERCULTURAL CONFLICT

In the past 20 years, a growing body of theory and research has emerged in the intercultural communication literature regarding the nature of intercultural conflict. Much of this research is based on the work of Stella Ting-Toomey and John Oetzel.[1] Ting-Toomey and Oetzel define intercultural conflict as the experience of emotional frustration or mismatched expectations between individuals from different cultures who perceive an incompatibility between their values, norms, goals, scarce resources, or outcomes during an intercultural exchange. Ting-Toomey and Oetzel assert that intercultural conflict occurs when cultural group membership factors influence how individuals approach, avoid, and manage conflict.[2]

Recall from Chapter 1 that a fundamental assumption of intercultural communication is that it is a group phenomenon experienced by individuals. Likewise, during intercultural conflict, one's group membership (i.e., culture) becomes a factor in how conflict is perceived, managed, and resolved. Some of these cultural factors may be unconscious, such as one's degree of individualism or collectivism. Other factors are probably very conscious. Recall your conflict with Akira. The two of you have incompatible goals and desire different outcomes. You choose to play your music loudly. Akira prefers that you not play your music loudly. You may wonder if all Japanese are quiet and dislike loud music. Perhaps Akira questions if all Americans are rude and insensitive to the wishes of others. Although the conflict between you and Akira could just as easily have been between two American students or two Japanese students, the fact that it occurred between an American and a Japanese complicates the issue.

Ting-Toomey and Oetzel maintain that intercultural conflict involves a certain degree of ethnocentric perceptions and judgments. Recall from Chapter 1 and Chapter 5 that ethnocentric persons hold attitudes and behaviors about their in-group that are biased in favor of the in-group, often at the expense of the out-group. Ethnocentric persons foster cooperative relations with in-group members while competing with, and perhaps even battling, out-group members.[3] Hence, by virtue of our cultural upbringing, we think we are correct (i.e., loud music is great vs. loud music is disrespectful).

A Model of Intercultural Conflict

The well-known intercultural communication scholar Young Yum Kim has developed a model of intercultural conflict. Kim argues that intercultural conflict occurs at three interdependent and interrelated levels, including a micro, or individual level; an intermediary level; and a macro, or societal level (see Figure 10.1).[4]

The micro, or *individual,* level of intercultural conflict refers to each individual's unique attitudes, dispositions, and beliefs that he or she brings to the conflict. According to Kim's model, cognitive simplicity/rigidity refers to the degree of inflexibility in the way the individuals think about people from different cultures. Rigid, simplistic thinking would include gross

Figure 10.1   Kim's Model of Intercultural Conflict

Macro Level
- History of subjugation
- Ideological or structural inequalities
- Minority group strength

Intermediary Level
- Segregation/contact
- Intergroup salience
- Status discrepancy

Micro Level
- Cognitive simplicity/rigidity
- In-group bias
- Insecurity/frustration
- Divergent behaviors

Macro Level
Intermediary Level
Micro Level

categorization and stereotyping (e.g., all Americans are rude, all Japanese are quiet). In-group bias refers to the degree to which the individual is ethnocentric. Recall from Chapter 1 that ethnocentrism is defined as viewing one's own group as being at the center of everything and using the standards of one's own group to measure or gauge the worth of all other groups. Insecurity/frustration refers to the degree to which the individual has a high level of uncertainty about, and fear of, out-group members (e.g., they will steal our jobs). Divergent behavior refers to the behavioral patterns of the individual that clearly *differentiate* and distance him or her from out-group members. For example, obviously different speech patterns or accents may ostensibly separate groups from one another. During conflict, people will often exaggerate their mannerisms and speech to accentuate their differences compared with out-groups. Because you are upset about Akira's complaint, you intentionally turn up the volume on your music. Imagine two employees working together, each from a different culture, who have gross stereotypes of each other, are both ethnocentric, fear each other, and have highly divergent behavioral patterns. The model predicts that such a situation is likely to engender conflict.[5]

The *intermediary* level of intercultural conflict refers to the actual location and context of the conflict. Some environments (e.g., neighborhoods, school, work) may be more likely than others to facilitate conflict. Segregation and contact refer to the extent to which the cultural groups of the individuals interact on a daily basis. Perhaps the most basic condition for intercultural conflict is contact between diverse cultures or ethnicities on a day-to-day basis. Segregated workplaces or schools do not allow for much interaction, and components at the individual level (e.g., cognitive rigidity, in-group bias) tend to escalate to intolerable levels that facilitate intercultural conflict. Intergroup salience refers to the observable physical and social differences between the conflicting individuals. Such cultural markers include distinct physical and behavioral differences, such as race, language, and speech patterns. As Kim notes, to the extent that the groups are culturally distinct, the communicative skills of the less powerful cultural group will clash with those of the majority group members. The majority group's symbol system is dominant. Status discrepancy refers to the degree to which conflicting parties differ in status along cultural lines. For example, Blacks often argue that American culture practices an asymmetrical power structure. Blacks may feel that the American corporate culture reflects the same asymmetry. On the job, managers and supervisors have more power than workers. If all the managers in a business are White and all the workers are Black (or Hispanic, etc.), then the status discrepancy is heightened.[6]

The macro, or *societal,* level of intercultural conflict includes factors that probably are out of the control of the interactants. These conditions include any history of subjugation, ideological/structural inequality, and minority group strength. The history of subjugation of one group by another is a key environmental factor in many intercultural conflicts. For example, Blacks have long been subjugated by Whites in America. Historically, African Americans were slaves. Even upon emancipation, they were not allowed to vote. As late as the 1960s, restaurants in the South had separate bathrooms, seating areas, and drinking fountains for Blacks and Whites (see Figure 10.2).

Often, the tensions expressed today are rooted in the history of the subjugation of one group over another. Ideological and structural inequity refers to societal differences regarding power, prestige, and economic reward. Historically, in the United States, Whites have held most of the power positions and gained most of the economic reward. Hence, there is a vast ideological and structural difference between Whites and other groups. Blacks and Hispanics

Figure 10.2   Segregated drinking fountain in use in the American South

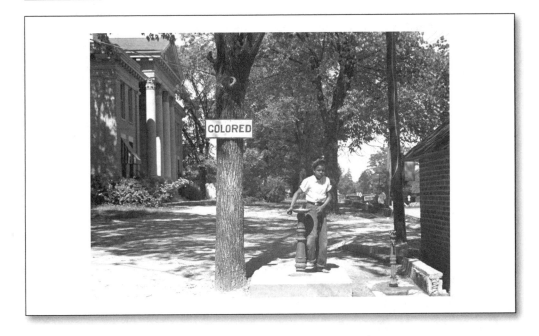

have much higher levels of unemployment, for example. Minority (i.e., microcultural) group strength refers to the amount of power (e.g., legal, political, economic) a particular group possesses. Microcultural groups vary in their ability to rally their members against structural inequalities. Minority group strength varies as a function of the status of the group's language within the society, the sheer number of members in the group, and forms of societal support (e.g., governmental services designed specifically for the group). Relative to other microcultural groups, Blacks, for example, are economically and politically quite powerful. Political scientists argue, for instance, that presidential elections are swung by the African American voting block. According to Kim, the greater the ethnic group's strength, the more likely that an individual in that group will take action in intercultural conflict situations.[7]

Taken together, these three levels of conflict merge during any intercultural conflict. To the extent that these individual, intermediary, and societal factors are present, intercultural conflict will likely ignite.

AN INTERCULTURAL CONVERSATION: KIM'S MODEL OF INTERCULTURAL CONFLICT

Mike Romney is the supervising director of Acme Marketing Firm. Acme is a direct marketing firm for insurance agencies. Mike, 42 years old, is White. He was born and raised in Kenilworth, Illinois, a wealthy Chicago suburb. Mike has six directors under him in Acme's organizational hierarchy. These six directors each manage and supervise about seven employees. Thus, Mike supervises more than 50 employees. Once a year, Mike has one-on-one meetings with each employee. These annual meetings are a part of each employee's annual evaluation. Today, Mike is meeting with Nicole Norton. Nicole is a relatively new employee and has worked for Acme for just over a year. This will be her first annual evaluation meeting. She was hired as a telemarketer and hopes to move up in the organization soon. She is Black and 33 years old. She was raised in the city of Chicago, in the Robert Taylor public housing district, a notoriously impoverished and violent area. Their meeting takes place in Mike's office.

Mike:	Good morning, Nicole, come in and have a seat.
Nicole:	Hi, Mike.
Mike:	Actually, until I get to know my employees, I prefer to be called Mr. Romney.
Nicole:	Oh, OK, Mister Romney. (placing an accent on the "Mister")
Mike:	(Noticing her tone of voice) So, where are you from?
Nicole:	I grew up on the south side.
Mike:	(Thinks to himself, "Probably in the projects. She and I have nothing in common.") Oh, I'm from Kenilworth.
Nicole:	Yeah, I've heard of that.
Mike:	Yes, well . . . I've been reading the monthly assessments completed by your manager about your performance. I can see you need improvement in several areas, including customer service and attitude.
Nicole:	Hmmm, I thought I was doing fine.
Mike:	Well, your manager says you are too informal with customers, which leaves a bad impression. (Thinks to himself, "She's probably not had much formal education.")
Nicole:	Really? I think they like it. I think it's OK to be a little relaxed once in a while.
Mike:	Well, maybe at home you can do that, but not here. (Thinks to himself, "I can't imagine what her home must be like.")
Nicole:	(Thinks to herself, "What does this have to do with my home?") Hmm, well, have any of my customers complained?
Mike:	Not directly, no.
Nicole:	So, then, what's the problem? (Thinks to herself, "What's his problem? He thinks he's pretty special.")
Mike:	Look, Nicole, I'm not going to argue with you. I'm telling you to improve your attitude and stop being so informal with the customers.
Nicole:	Whatever you say, Mister Romney.

Several of the factors outlined in the Kim model can be applied to this brief conflict exchange between Mike and Nicole. In terms of the micro-individual level, Mike's cognitive rigidity and simplicity is reflected in his comments to himself about Nicole's home and education. Mike also shows some signs of in-group bias in thinking that he and Nicole have nothing in common. Regarding the intermediary level, that Mike prefers for Nicole to call him "Mr. Romney" highlights the status discrepancy between them. That Mike meets with his employees only once a year shows that he has little contact with (i.e., is segregated from) them. Moreover, persons in Kenilworth probably rarely interact with persons in the inner city. Finally, at a societal-macro level, there is a history of subjugation between their groups, and Nicole's group has demonstrable minority group strength.

THE CONCEPT OF FACE, FACEWORK, AND COMMUNICATION CONFLICT STYLES

Face

In an effort to explain intercultural conflict, a number of researchers apply a theory called *face negotiation theory.*[8] According to this view, the concept of *face* explains how people of different cultures manage conflict. Face refers to a person's sense of favorable self-worth or self-image experienced during communicative situations. Face is an emotional extension of the self-concept. It is considered a universal concept; that is, people in all cultures have a sense of face, but the specific meanings of face may vary across cultures. Ting-Toomey and her associates differentiate among three types of face: self-face, other-face, and mutual-face. Self-face is the concern for one's own image, other-face is the concern for another's image, and mutual-face is the concern for both parties' images or the image of the relationship. Ting-Toomey maintains that one's face can be threatened, enhanced, undermined, and bargained over both emotionally and cognitively. According to face negotiation theory, people in all cultures try to maintain and negotiate face in virtually all communication situations. Generally, however, persons of individualistic cultures have a greater concern for self-face and a lesser concern for other-face than do members of collectivistic cultures.[9] The concept of face becomes particularly significant in situations where uncertainty is high, as in conflict situations where the character of the communicators might be called into question.

Facework

In most conflict situations, interactants are required to defend or save their face when it is threatened or attacked. The various ways one might deal with conflict and face are called *facework*. Specifically, facework refers to the communicative strategies employed to manage one's own face or to support or challenge another's face. Facework can be employed to initiate, manage, or terminate conflict.[11] John Oetzel and his colleagues classify three general types of facework strategies used in intercultural conflict: dominating, avoiding, and integrating facework (see Table 10.1). Dominating facework behaviors are characterized by an individual's need to control the conflict situation and defend his or her self-face. Avoiding facework behaviors focus on an attempt to save the face of the other person. Integrating facework allows for the shared concern for self- and other-face and strives for closure in the conflict.[12]

Self-Assessment 10.1[10]

Self-Face, Other-Face, and Mutual-Face Concerns

Remember your conflict with Akira Abe at the opening of this chapter? Now, try to imagine yourself in a different situation.

You loaned your car, with a full tank of gas, to Akira. Recall that he is an international exchange student from Japan, whom you do not know well. After he returned your car, you noticed that half of the gas had been used.

Directions: Take a moment and imagine yourself in the above conflict. What would you do? How would you handle this situation? For the following items, please indicate the degree to which you (5) strongly agree, (4) agree, (3) are neutral, (2) disagree, or (1) strongly disagree in terms of the conflict situation presented above.

_____ 1. I am concerned with respectful treatment for both of us.

_____ 2. My primary concern is saving my own face.

_____ 3. Relationship harmony is important to me.

_____ 4. I am concerned with maintaining the poise of the other person.

_____ 5. Maintaining humbleness to preserve the relationship is important to me.

_____ 6. Helping maintain the other person's pride is important to me.

_____ 7. I am concerned with protecting my self-image.

_____ 8. My concern is to act humble in order to make the other person feel good.

_____ 9. My concern is to help the other person maintain his or her dignity.

_____ 10. I don't want to embarrass myself in front of the other person.

Scoring:

1. Sum your responses to Items 2, 7, and 10. Scores must range from 3 to 15. This is your self-face score. Higher scores, above 12, indicate a high self-face concern.

2. Sum your responses to Items 4, 6, 8, and 9. Scores must range from 4 to 20. This is your other-face score. Higher scores, above 16, indicate a high other-face concern.

3. Sum your responses to Items 1, 3, and 5. Scores must range from 3 to 15. This is your mutual-face score. Higher scores, above 12, indicate a high mutual-face concern.

Cross-cultural research has shown that individualists, such as U.S. Americans, tend to prefer facework behaviors that defend the self-face or confront the other (i.e., aggression). Collectivists, such as Taiwanese and Chinese, tend to prefer other-face strategies such as avoiding the conflict, seeking a third party, or giving in to the other. Collectivists also prefer mutual-face facework such as attempting to solve the problem through a third party, having a private discussion, or apologizing.[14]

Table 10.1   Facework Behaviors[13]

Dominating Facework Behaviors

1. Aggression: verbally assault the other person

   "I would say nasty things about the other person."

   "I would ridicule the other person."

2. Defend self: reply to a threat

   "I would be firm in my demands and not give in."

   "I would insist my position be accepted."

Avoiding Facework Behaviors

1. Avoidance/pretend: dismissal of the conflict that does not threaten the other's face

   "I would act as though I wasn't upset at all."

   "I would try to ignore it and behave as if nothing happened."

2. Give in: succumb and/or yield to the other

   "I would give in to the other person's wishes."

   "I would let the other person win."

3. Involve a third party: reliance on an outside party to help manage the conflict

   "I would ask another friend to help us negotiate a solution."

   "I would talk with the other person through an outside party."

Integrating Facework Behaviors

1. Apologize: offer an apology for the conflict

   "I would offer an apology even though I didn't do anything wrong."

   "I would say I'm sorry and act as though it didn't happen."

2. Compromise: utilize direct discussion to resolve the conflict

   "I would try to find some middle ground to solve the problem."

   "I would try to combine both our viewpoints."

3. Consider the other: show concern for the other

   "I would listen to the other person and show respect."

   "I would tell the other person I'm aware of their position."

4. Private discussion: engage in relational talk about the conflict in a private setting

   "I would keep our discussions private."

   "I would wait until we were by ourselves to talk about it."

5. Remain calm: stay quiet and unruffled

   "I would try to remain calm."

   "I would try to listen well."

6. Express emotions: communicate feelings about the conflict

   "I would express my feelings in a straightforward manner."

   "I would be direct in expressing my feelings."

Conflict Communication Styles

In addition to the facework strategies one might use to manage face during conflict, researchers have studied conflict interaction styles. Whereas facework is employed to manage and uphold face during conflict, conflict interaction styles refer to the ways individuals manage the actual conflict. How people manage communication during conflict differs considerably across cultures.[15]

One's conflict interaction style is based on two communication dimensions. The first is the degree to which a person asserts a *self-face need*—that is, seeks to satisfy his or her own interests during conflict. The second is the degree to which a person is cooperative (i.e., observes an *other-face need*) and seeks to incorporate the interests of the other.[16] The combination of assertiveness, or self-face need, and cooperativeness, or other-face need, defines five primary communication styles of managing conflict and three secondary styles. The five primary styles are dominating, integrating, obliging, avoiding, and compromising.[17] The three secondary styles include emotional expression, third-party help, and neglect (see Figure 10.3).[18]

The degree to which a person asserts a high self-face need while simultaneously discounting the other-face need defines the dominating communication style. A person exercising a dominating approach might use his or her authority, expertise, or rank to try to win the conflict. The person who assumes a high self-face need while also attending to the needs of the other-face takes on an integrating style. This person might try to collaborate with the opponent or try to find an agreeable solution that fully satisfies both parties. The person who tries

Figure 10.3 Self-Face Concern, Other-Face Concern, and Communication Styles of Managing Conflict

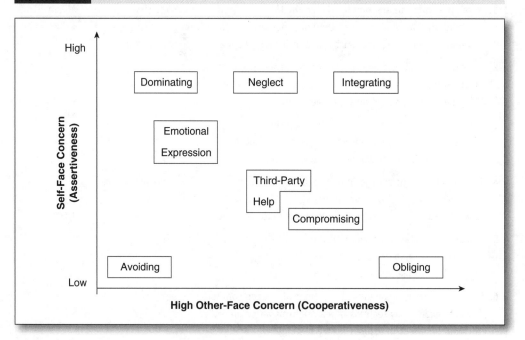

to balance both self-face and other-face needs takes on a compromising style. This person would probably use a "give-and-take" approach and might propose some middle ground for resolving the conflict, understanding that each party may have to give up something in order to gain. The person using an avoiding style ignores both self-face need and other-face need. This person might keep the conflict to him- or herself and not discuss it. The person who puts the other-face need ahead of self-face need assumes an obliging style. This person will try to accommodate the opponent or try to satisfy the needs of the other before satisfying his or her own needs.

Ting-Toomey and Oetzel maintain that the five primary conflict styles overlook some of the subtle fine distinctions of conflict behavior used across cultures, and they have added three secondary styles. Emotional expression refers to how one might use his or her emotions to guide conflict. This is demonstrated by the type of person who listens to his or her base feelings and proceeds accordingly. Third-party help is the extent to which a person would engage an outsider to act as a go-between in the conflict. Neglect is the use of a passive-aggressive approach where one might ignore the conflict but attempt to elicit a response from the other via aggressive acts. For example, this person might insult the other or say things that might damage the other's reputation (e.g., "I would say nasty things about the person to others").[19]

Research in this area has shown that, in general, individualists tend to use more dominating styles during conflict than do collectivists. Collectivists tend to use more integrative, obliging, and avoiding styles during conflict. Such generalizations do not hold for all cultures considered collectivistic, however. For example, in a study comparing five cultures, Ting-Toomey and her colleagues found that Korean, Japanese, and American college students used fewer avoidance-type conflict styles than did Chinese and Taiwanese students. They also found that Korean and American students were less likely to engage in obliging styles than were Chinese, Japanese, and Taiwanese students.[20] In their study, Lee and Rogan found that Americans were actually less confrontational during conflict than were Koreans, a culture considered to be collectivistic.[21]

AN INTERCULTURAL CONVERSATION: DOMINATING AND THIRD-PARTY CONFLICT STYLES

Kevin, who grew up in Madison, Wisconsin, is a student at the University of Wisconsin. Kevin is enrolled in an introductory communication course. The professor has assigned Kevin and Kokkeong, an international exchange student from Malaysia, to work on a project together. The professor has given them the option of either submitting a paper or giving a presentation. Kevin and Kokkeong disagree on which option to pursue. Kevin prefers the presentation option, while Kokkeong prefers the paper option.

In the following conversation, Kevin asserts himself forcefully. He stresses his experience and expertise on the matter of presentations versus papers. His approach is typical of a dominating conflict style. Kokkeong, on the other hand, tries to convince Kevin that they should seek the advice of some third party, either other students or the professor. Kevin simply refuses.

Kevin:	Well, Kokkeong, I think we should do a presentation. I hate writing papers.
Kokkeong:	Well, what have other students done?
Kevin:	Who cares?
Kokkeong:	Well, maybe they might have some advice.
Kevin:	Advice about what?
Kokkeong:	About which assignment is preferred.
Kevin:	Look, I already know what assignment I prefer.
Kokkeong:	I wonder if we should ask the professor for his advice.
Kevin:	Why? He's already given us the option. Look, I've been a student here for 2 years. I know how these things work. Let's just do the presentation.
Kokkeong:	I think I'll ask some others what they think.
Kevin:	Go ahead and do what you want, but I'm not budging. We're doing a presentation. I know what I'm talking about.

THE INTERCULTURAL CONFLICT STYLE INVENTORY

Mitchell Hammer has developed a model of intercultural conflict based on his Intercultural Conflict Style (ICS) Inventory. Hammer is the founder of several organizations that focus on intercultural communication. He has applied his conflict model with the NASA Johnson Space Center, the Federal Bureau of Investigation, and the National Institutes of Health. Hammer's ICS Inventory is a theoretical model and assessment tool used by professional mediators and trainers to diagnose and manage intercultural conflicts. Hammer contends that the dynamics of conflict revolve around two fundamental features of all conflict: disagreement and emotional reaction. Like others, Hammer maintains that a central characteristic of conflict is disagreement. This is consistent with Ting-Toomey and Oetzel's definition, presented earlier in this chapter, where conflict was defined as mismatched expectations between individuals from different cultures who perceive an incompatibility between their values, norms, goals, scarce resources, or outcomes. Disagreement would be considered the cognitive component of conflict. A second fundamental feature of conflict is the affective or emotional response to the disagreement. According to Hammer, conflicting parties experience an antagonistic emotional reaction toward each other based on their disagreement and the perception of threat associated with it. So Hammer's conflict model is based on a cognitive and affective component—that is, disagreement and the negative emotional reaction to it.[22]

The focus of Hammer's model is on intercultural conflict style. Like others, Hammer contends that people respond in patterned ways to conflict and that their communication styles are predictable. Conflict style, then, is the behavioral component of conflict that follows from the cognitive (i.e., disagreement) and affective (i.e., negative emotional reaction) dimensions of conflict. Echoing the work of Ting-Toomey and others, Hammer maintains that one's conflict style is learned culturally. But Hammer argues that the five conflict styles based on an individual's concern for self- or other-face have been developed within individualistic Western cultural concepts and that these models may not adequately reflect intercultural conflict styles. Take, for example, the avoiding style, where the person ignores both self-face need and other-face need. Consistent with Ting-Toomey's research, Hammer notes that in collectivistic cultures, an avoiding style is used to maintain relational harmony and actually reflects a high concern for self and others. Following his contention that conflicts evolve from disagreement and its resulting negative emotional reactions, Hammer proposes that people, regardless of culture, deal with disagreement either directly or indirectly and that they either openly express or restrain their emotional reactions to conflict. Thus, one's intercultural conflict style is defined by one's direct or indirect communication about disagreements and his or her emotionally expressive or emotionally restrained behaviors.

Recall from Chapter 7 that direct communication includes the use of precise language, where one's intentions are explicitly stated and the sender is responsible for making his or her case known. Indirect communication includes the use of ambiguous language, or hinting, and the burden of understanding rests with both the sender and receiver. Ting-Toomey's research has indicated that a direct style is often associated with individualisic and low-context cultures, while an indirect style is associated with collectivistic and high-context cultures. Emotionally expressive individuals overtly and visibly (i.e., nonverbally) communicate their feelings through intense facial expressions, frequent gesturing, body posture, and overall active involvement. Emotionally restrained individuals minimize gesturing, mask their emotions both verbally and nonverbally, hold back their sentiments, and control their feelings. Extant research suggests that individualistic and low-context cultures are often emotionally expressive, while collectivistic, high-context cultures are often emotionally restrained.[23]

According to Hammer's model, during conflict, the extent to which an individual is either direct or indirect and emotionally expressive or emotionally restrained defines his or her intercultural conflict syle, of which there are four types. Hammer maintains that these styles are independent of culture. The four styles are (a) discussion, (b) engagement, (c) accommodation, and (d) dynamic.[24]

	Emotionally Restrained	Emotionally Expressive
Directness	Discussion Style	Engagement Style
Indirectness	Accommodation Style	Dynamic Style

As the graphic shows, an individual who approaches conflict directly but is emotionally restrained takes on a discussion conflict style. This person emphasizes precise language and straightforward communication about the disagreement while withholding his or her emotions. This person is typically comfortable addressing conflict and is calm and collected emotionally. The person who is direct in his or her communication and is also emotionally expressive takes on an engagement style. This person is confrontational about the disagreement and forthright with his or her emotions. This is the type of style that "pulls no punches." When one communicates about conflict indirectly and without emotion, he or she takes on an accommodation style. This is the type of person who only hints at the nature of the disagreement and may prefer an intermediary to address the conflict. This person sees emotional outbursts as potentially dangerous. Finally, the person who communicates indirectly about the disagreement but is emotionally expressive takes on a dynamic style. Verbally, this person may use exaggeration and repetition of his or her messages while also employing a nonverbal emotionally confrontational form of expression.

Hammer has developed an instrument that measures these four styles. He maintains that the ICS Inventory is useful in applied settings, such as in organizations and even within families. Hammer asserts that after the conflicting parties recognize their own style and that of their counterpart, conflict is better managed. For example, Hammer cites a case in which one of the conflicting parties used an engagement style while the other's style was accommodation. Hammer points out that a large part of the conflict between the two was the misperceptions each party held about the other. The accommodation-style individual felt that the engagement-style person was rude and aggressive, while the engagement-style party felt that the accommodating-style individual was deceptive and lacking in commitment.

Hammer also notes that, particularly in the United States, many people believe that their conflict style is discussion and that this is the most appropriate style. But after completing his scales, these people see that they actually approach conflict with an accommodation, engagement, or dynamic style. Hammer concludes by saying that when persons try to implement a discussion style, thinking it is the most appropriate and having little awareness of the other three styles—and particularly of the cultural roots in these styles—they tend to see the engagement style as callous, the accommodation style as lacking sincerity, and the dynamic style as unstable and disorganized. Knowledge of these various styles is the first step toward successful conflict management and resolution.[25]

A CULTURE-BASED SITUATIONAL MODEL OF CONFLICT

Taking into consideration many of the features of conflict discussed above, Ting-Toomey and Oetzel have developed what they call a culture-based situational model of conflict.[26] In their model, Ting-Toomey and Oetzel highlight four main factors that come into play during an intercultural conflict episode: individual factors, conflict process factors, situational features, and conflict outcomes. During intercultural conflict, these four factors come together in a complex formula that defines the specific conflict episode.

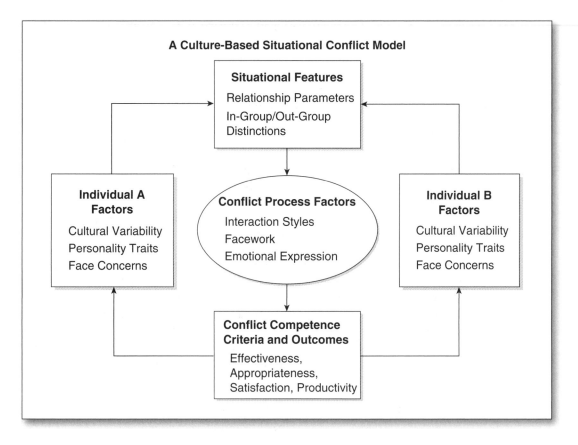

The individual factors are similar to the microlevel factors of the Kim model of conflict. Here, the individual factors include such variables as the person's degree of individualism or collectivism. Ting-Toomey and Oetzel point out that individualists tend to express conflict through assertiveness, express their emotions, and value personal accountability. Collectivists restrain their emotions and protect the in-group. The individual factors also include large and small power distance. Persons from large and small power distance cultures manage conflict differently. For example, children in small power distance cultures may challenge their parents, as in the United States, whereas children in China, a large power distance culture where filial piety is highly valued, would not challenge their parents. An individual's personality traits would include those characteristics that may or may not be directly linked to culture. For example, in any culture, people experience anxiety. This could lead to one's approach–avoidance tendencies during conflict. Face concerns also contribute to conflict, as we have seen in the paragraphs above. A person's self-, other-, or mutual-face concern affects how he or she approaches and manages conflict.[27]

Unique situational features also affect the conflict episode. Relationship parameters include the specific relational dynamics of the parties involved. Ting-Toomey and Oetzel point to three specific relational parameters that affect conflict: whether the parties see themselves as competitive or cooperative, whether they trust or distrust each other, and the degree to which they see themselves as intimate and close (i.e., affiliative) or experience issues related to control and dominance. In-group–out-group distinctions refer to the degree to which the parties involved are members of the same in-groups or whether there are clear group differences between them, including race, ethnicity, and or sex differences.

The conflict process factors include those factors that emerge from the conflict interaction itself. For example, during conflict, the two individuals' conflict interaction styles come into play interdependently. So how does Individual A's competitive style combine with Individual B's avoidance style? Likewise, what type of facework do the individuals engage in? (Refer back to Table 10.1 for the list of facework behaviors.) Finally, how do the individuals manage their emotions? Are they expressive or restrained?

Last, the model includes conflict competence criteria and outcomes, which include effectiveness, appropriateness, satisfaction, and productivity. Conflict competence refers to the application of intercultural conflict knowledge. In other words, are we to use what we know about conflict to act competently and produce an effective, appropriate resolution? Appropriateness refers to the degree to which the individuals' behaviors are suitable for the cultural context in which they occur. Effectiveness refers to the degree to which the individuals achieve mutually shared meaning, which leads to intercultural understanding. Satisfaction refers to the degree to which the individuals are able to create the desired images of themselves, and to what extent those images are accepted by the opposing party. Finally, productivity refers to the perception by both parties that a successful resolution was reached. Ting-Toomey and Oetzel refer to productive resolution as a "win–win" conflict orientation and to unproductive resolution as a "win–lose" conflict orientation. A comparison of the two orientations is presented below.[28]

Win–Lose Conflict Orientation	*Win–Win Conflict Orientation*
Ignoring cultural differences	Respecting cultural differences
Insensitivity to conflict context	Sensitivity to conflict context
Arguing and defending self-interest	Uncovering deeper conflict needs
Conflict mode	Compromising mode
Engaging in mindless behaviors	Practicing mindful conflict skills
Rigidity of conflict posture	Willingness to change

INDIVIDUALISTIC AND COLLECTIVISTIC APPROACHES TO CONFLICT

A central theme articulated throughout this book is that whenever individuals from different cultures come together and interact, they bring with them a whole host of different value orientations, cultural expectations, verbal and nonverbal routines, perceptual experiences (e.g., ethnocentrism), and divergent group memberships (e.g., ethnicity) that often lead to communication problems and conflict. A source of intercultural conflict is often a felt need to protect one's group—that is, one's culture. This need may be felt passionately.

In her work, Ting-Toomey maintains that persons from individualistic cultures approach conflict differently than do persons from collectivistic cultures.[29] According to Ting-Toomey, individualists tend to follow an outcome-oriented approach to intercultural conflict. Collectivists, on the other hand, tend to follow a process-oriented approach. The outcome-oriented approach preferred by individualists emphasizes the importance of asserting their self-identity in the conflict and the accomplishment of perceived tangible outcomes or goals. The process-oriented approach preferred by collectivists focuses on mutual-face or group-face interests. These interests are sought prior to, or in lieu of, any tangible outcomes or goals.[30] The specific characteristics of the outcome-oriented approach are summarized below.[31]

1. To the individualist, conflict is closely related to the goals or outcomes. Conflict is "end" oriented, in that the individualist seeks to achieve something.

2. Individualists become frustrated during conflict when their counterparts are unwilling to address the conflict openly and honestly.

3. Individualists see conflict as satisfying when their counterparts are willing to confront the conflict openly and assert their feelings honestly.

4. Conflict is seen as unproductive when no tangible outcomes are negotiated and no plan of action is executed.

5. Conflict is seen as productive when tangible resolutions are reached.

6. Successful management of conflict is defined as when individual goals and the differences between the parties are addressed openly and honestly.

The specific characteristics of the process-oriented approach are summarized below.[32]

1. The significance of the conflict is assessed against any face threat incurred in the conflict; it is also evaluated in terms of in-group versus out-group.

2. Conflict is seen as threatening when the parties move forward on substantive issues before proper facework management.

3. Conflict is seen as satisfying when the parties engage in mutual face-saving and face-giving behavior and attend to verbal and nonverbal communication.

4. Conflict is seen as unproductive when face issues and relational/group feelings are not addressed properly.

5. Conflict is defined as productive when both parties can declare win–win results on facework in addition to substantive agreement.

6. Successful management of conflict means that the faces of both conflict parties are saved or upgraded and each person has dealt with the conflict strategically in conjunction with substantive gains or losses.

Ting-Toomey maintains that the outcome-oriented model preferred by individualists encourages an effective finish to the conflict over the appropriate treatment of the parties involved. The collectivist-preferred process-oriented model emphasizes the appropriate treatment of the parties involved over an effective solution. Moreover, asserts Ting-Toomey, the accomplishment of one criterion may help accomplish the other. For example, as individualists successfully address the core issues in the conflict, appropriate and genial interaction between the parties can follow naturally—that is, face saving. On the other hand, from the collectivist's perspective, acting appropriately in the conflict by engaging in necessary facework eventually brings about effective outcomes. For collectivists, strategic facework is more important than winning or losing a conflict. In fact, collectivists often see losing a given conflict for the moment as gaining key advantages in the long term. In the end, the key to competent intercultural conflict management is *mindfulness,* where each person is mindful of cultural differences, mindful of the different goals, and willing to experiment with different conflict management styles.[33]

CONFLICT RESOLUTION IN HIGH- VERSUS LOW-CONTEXT CULTURES

Human communication is dependent on the context in which it occurs. In addition to the verbal and nonverbal codes exchanged between interactants, the salient features of a communicative context include the cultural, physical, sociorelational, and perceptual environments. Recall from Chapter 2 that the degree to which interactants focus on these contexts while communicating varies considerably from culture to culture. In some cultures, persons choose to focus more on the verbal codes than on the nonverbal elements, while in other cultures, people will actively monitor the nonverbal elements of the context. Hall describes the former as low context and the latter as high context.

According to Hall, a high-context culture is one in which most of the information during communication is found in the physical context internalized in the person, while very little is found in the explicit code (see Figure 10.4). A low-context culture is one in which the mass of information is in the explicit code (i.e., the verbal code). Elizabeth Chua and William Gudykunst have compared conflict resolution styles between high- and low-context cultures.[34] They argue that in low-context cultures, such as that of the United States, individuals are more likely to separate the conflict issue from the persons involved. In high-context cultures, such as that of China, the conflict issue and the persons involved are typically connected. For example, directly disagreeing with someone may be seen as losing face and is perceived as insulting. Moreover, Chua and Gudykunst assert that persons in low-context cultures tend to be more direct and explicit in their dealings with conflict, whereas persons in high-context cultures prefer implicit communication. In their study of nearly

Figure 10.4 What type of facework might be at play here?

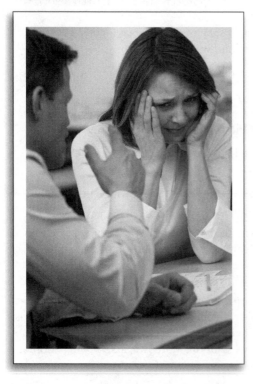

400 persons from both high- and low-context cultures, Chua and Gudykunst found that persons from low-context cultures preferred solution-oriented conflict resolution styles, whereas persons from high-context cultures preferred nonconfrontational styles.[35]

Solution-Oriented Conflict Styles Preferred by Low-Context Cultures

1. Direct communication about the conflict
2. Collaborating behaviors that aim to find a solution for both parties
3. Giving in or compromising
4. Accommodating the other
5. Confronting the issue

Nonconfrontational Styles Preferred by High-Context Cultures

1. Indirect communication
2. Avoiding or withdrawing from the issue
3. Using silence
4. Glossing over differences
5. Concealing ill feelings

Chua and Gudykunst conclude that their results are consistent with other research that has found a similar pattern between high- and low-context cultures. Specifically, research has revealed that Mexicans (i.e., a high-context culture) prefer to deny that conflict exists or avoid instigating conflict, while U.S. Americans (i.e., a low-context culture) are more direct in their dealings with conflict.

STUDENT VOICES ACROSS CULTURES

Rodrigo Villalobos

I am from Leon, Guanajuato, Mexico, but now reside in the United States. I am a graphic design major.

I do not believe that people from Mexico deal with trouble or stressful situations in the same way as others do. To generalize on a particular set of characteristics that define how a person of Mexican nationality resolves his or her own problems would be almost impossible. The social and economic surroundings of every individual in Mexico are usually completely different, which makes their problem-solving processes much different as well.

However, there are a certain number of behaviors or attitudes that one can expect to see from a Mexican when that person is in a stressful or uncomfortable situation.

(Continued)

(Continued)

As Mexicans are Latinos, our character and personalities are rather warm and heartfelt. We express our feelings, to a certain extent, more than people from other races or ethnicities do. For example, when a situation makes a Mexican person happy, he or she will express it more boldly than someone from Sweden would. In the same manner, when a Mexican person feels uncomfortable, upset, or mad about a specific problem or situation, this person's reaction will be quite volatile (e.g., yelling, screaming, lack of verbal communication, trying to avoid the problem, etc.).

We all know that the shortest way to solve problems is through communication and an open-minded understanding of the situation. Perhaps the slower pace of life in Mexico affects how Mexicans approach their problems (e.g., postponing dealing with problems). Also, pride and lack of will to reconcile might be obstacles that a Mexican must confront when it's necessary to admit his or her problems before a possible solution can be considered.

Since friendships have a lot of value to persons from Latin America (not saying they don't to people from other places), friends will ask for advice and talk to one another for insight into a problem.

CHAPTER SUMMARY

This chapter began by asking you to imagine yourself in a conflict. All types of human relationships, from strangers to acquaintances to intimates, experience conflict. We cannot avoid or eliminate conflict, but we can manage and reduce it. Communication plays a paradoxical role in most conflicts because communication is required both to instigate conflict and to resolve it. Unfortunately, conflict is the source of much relational stress and dissolution. In this chapter, we have seen that a variety of factors play a role in triggering and escalating conflict. In addition to the Kim model of intercultural conflict, we have seen how the concept of face and facework contributes to intercultural conflict. Finally, the chapter ends with a model of conflict styles and a discussion of how persons from different cultures manage conflict.

Visit the student study site at **www.sagepub.com/neuliep5e** *for e-flashcards, web quizzes, web resources and more.*

DISCUSSION QUESTIONS

1. Recall a conflict that you have experienced. How did your cultural background affect how you handled it?

2. What types of intercultural conflicts occur on your college or university campus? What groups or cultures have frequent conflicts?

3. Regarding Question #2 above, how do these groups manage and address the conflict?

4. Do you prefer to handle conflict directly or to avoid it altogether?

5. What irritates you the most about how others handle conflict? Why?

ETHICS AND INTERCULTURAL CONFLICT

1. Your roommate is friends with an international exchange student from China. Recently, your roommate and his Chinese friend have been disagreeing about several issues. Your roommate discloses to you that his Chinese friend typically avoids conflict and uses avoidance facework and conflict styles. Your roommate thinks that this will give him a unique advantage and decides to assertively approach his Chinese friend and engage in dominating facework and a competitive conflict style in order to win the conflict. Is your roommate's strategy a good one?

REFERENCES

1. Oetzel, J. G., & Ting-Toomey, S. (2003). Face Concerns in Interpersonal Conflict: A Cross-Cultural Empirical Test of the Face Negotiation Theory. *Communication Research, 30,* 599–624; Ting-Toomey, S., & Oetzel, J. G. (2001). *Managing Intercultural Conflict Effectively.* Thousand Oaks, CA: Sage; Ting-Toomey, S. (1994). Managing Conflict in Intimate Intercultural Relationships. In D. Cahn (Ed.), *Intimate Conflict in Personal Relationships* (pp. 47–77). Hillsdale, NJ: Erlbaum; Ting-Toomey, S. (1994). Managing Intercultural Conflict Effectively. In L. Samovar & R. Porter (Eds.), *Intercultural Communication: A Reader* (7th ed., pp. 360–372). Belmont, CA: Wadsworth.

2. Ting-Toomey & Oetzel, Managing Intercultural Conflict Effectively.

3. Ibid.

4. Kim, Y. Y. (1989). Interethnic Conflict: An Interdisciplinary Overview. In J. B. Gittler (Ed.), *Annual Review of Conflict Knowledge and Conflict Resolution* (Vol. 1). New York: Garland; Kim, Y. Y. (1990). *Explaining Interethnic Conflict: An Interdisciplinary Overview.* Paper presented at the annual convention of the Speech Communication Association, Chicago, IL.

5. Ibid.

6. Ibid.

7. Ibid.

8. This discussion of face negotiation theory is based on the following sources: Oetzel, J. G., & Ting-Toomey, S. (2003). Face Concerns in Interpersonal Conflict: A Cross-Cultural Empirical Test of the Face Negotiation Theory. *Communication Research, 30,* 599–624; Ting-Toomey, S. (1988). Intercultural Conflict Styles: A Face-Negotiation Theory. In Y. Kim & W. Gudykunst (Eds.), *Theories in Intercultural Communication.* Newbury Park, CA: Sage; Ting-Toomey, S. (2005). The Matrix of Face: An Updated Face-Negotiation Theory. In W. B. Gudykunst (Ed.), *Theorizing About Intercultural Communication.* Thousand Oaks, CA: Sage; Ting-Toomey, S., & Kurogi, A. (1998). Facework Competence in Intercultural Conflict: An Updated Face-Negotiation Theory. *International Journal of Intercultural Relations, 22,* 187–225.

9. Ting-Toomey & Kurogi, Facework Competence in Intercultural Conflict.

10. This scale is an adaptation of the Face Concern Scale used in Oetzel, J. G., Ting-Toomey, S., Masumoto, T., Yokochi, Y., Pan, X., Takai, J., et al. (2001). Face and Facework in Conflict: A Cross-Cultural Comparison of China, Germany, Japan, and the United States. *Communication Monographs, 68,* 235–258, and Ting-Toomey, S., & Oetzel, J. G. (2001). *Managing Intercultural Conflict Effectively.* Thousand Oaks, CA: Sage.

11. Oetzel, J. G., Ting-Toomey, S., Masumoto, T., Yokochi, Y., & Takai, J. (2000). A Typology of Facework Behaviors in Conflicts With Best Friends and Relative Strangers. *Communication Quarterly, 48,* 397–419.

12. Ibid.

13. Ibid.

14. Cocroft, B., & Ting-Toomey, S. (1994). Facework in Japan and the United States. *International Journal of Intercultural Relations, 18,* 469–506; Oetzel et al., A Typology of Facework Behaviors in Conflicts With Best Friends and Relative Strangers.

15. Ting-Toomey, S., & Oetzel, J. G. (2003). Cross-Cultural Face Concerns and Conflict Styles. In W. B. Gudykunst (Ed.), *Cross-Cultural and Intercultural Communication* (pp. 127–147). Thousand Oaks, CA: Sage.

16. The concepts of assertiveness and cooperativeness are found in a number of sources, including Rahim, M. A. (1983). A Measure of Styles of Handling Interpersonal Conflict. *Academy of Management Journal, 26,* 368–376; Thomas, K. W., & Kilmann, R. H. (1974). *Thomas-Kilmann Conflict MODE Instrument.* New York: XICOM, Tuxedo; Ting-Toomey, S. (1988). Intercultural Conflict Styles: A Face-Negotiation Theory. In Y. Y. Kim & W. B. Gudykunst (Eds.), *Theories of Intercultural Communication* (pp. 213–235). Newbury Park, CA: Sage.

17. Rahim, A Measure of Styles of Handling Interpersonal Conflict.

18. Ting-Toomey & Oetzel, *Managing Intercultural Conflict Effectively.*

19. Ting-Toomey & Oetzel, *Managing Intercultural Conflict Effectively;* Ting-Toomey, S., Yee-Jung, K. K., Shapiro, R. B., Garcia, W., Wright, T. J., et al. (2000). Ethnic/Cultural Identity Salience and Conflict Styles in Four U.S. Ethnic Groups. *International Journal of Intercultural Relations, 24,* 47–81.

20. Ting-Toomey, S., Gao, G., Trubisky, P., Yang, Z., Kim, H. S., Lin, S. L., et al. (1991). Culture, Face Maintenance, and Styles of Handling Interpersonal Conflict: A Study in Five Cultures. *International Journal of Conflict Management, 2,* 275–296.

21. Lee, H. O., & Rogan, R. G. (1991). A Cross-Cultural Comparison of Organizational Conflict Management Behaviors. *International Journal of Conflict Management, 2,* 181–199.

22. Hammer, M. R. (2005). The Intercultural Conflict Style Inventory: A Conceptual Framework and Measure of Intercultural Conflict Resolution Approaches. *International Journal of Intercultural Relations, 29,* 675–695.

23. Ibid.; Ting-Toomey et al., Ethnic/Cultural Identity Salience and Conflict Styles in Four U.S. Groups; Ting-Toomey, S. (1994). Managing Intercultural Conflicts Effectively. In L. Samovar & R. E. Porter (Eds.), *Intercultural Communication: A Reader* (pp. 360–372). Belmont, CA: Wadsworth; Ting-Toomey, S. (1999). *Communicating Across Cultures.* New York; Guilford.

24. Hammer, The Intercultural Conflict Style Inventory.

25. Ibid.

26. Ting-Toomey & Oetzel, *Managing Intercultural Conflict Effectively.*

27. Ibid.

28. Ibid.

29. Ting-Toomey, *Communicating Across Cultures.*

30. Ting-Toomey, *Communicating Across Cultures;* see also Ting-Toomey & Oetzel, *Managing Intercultural Conflict Effectively.*

31. Ibid.

32. Ibid.

33. Ibid.

34. Chua, E. G., & Gudykunst, W. B. (1987). Conflict Resolution Styles in Low- and High-Context Cultures. *Communication Research Reports, 4,* 32–37.

35. Ibid.

CHAPTER 11

Intercultural Communication in Organizations

CHAPTER OBJECTIVES

After reading this chapter, you should be able to

1. discuss how dimensions of the cultural context affect organizations across cultures;

2. identify how the environmental context affects doing business in other cultures;

3. identify variables in the perceptual context and how they influence business with other cultures;

4. compare and contrast sociorelational contexts on the job across cultures;

5. discuss some verbal and nonverbal differences across cultures;

6. compare managerial styles of Japanese, Germans, Mexicans, Chinese, and Arabs; and

7. describe differences in manager–subordinate relationships in Japan, Germany, Mexico, China, and Arab countries.

However objective and uniform we try to make organizations, they will not have the same meaning for individuals from different cultures.

—Fons Trompenaars[1]

———

Imagine the following scenario:

You have just graduated from college and accepted a management job with Acme Corporation. Acme has placed you in one of its Mexican offices. During your first week in your new job, you decide to schedule a meeting with your Mexican employees. The meeting is scheduled for 9:00 a.m. on Wednesday. On Wednesday morning, you show up a bit early to prepare for your meeting. By 9:00 a.m., not a single employee has arrived for the meeting. By 9:20 a.m., two people finally show up. Not until 9:45 a.m. are all the members of the team in attendance. What has happened? You are confused, frustrated, and feeling a bit angry.

Doing business in Mexico (and in many other countries) is different from doing business in the United States. Mexican cultural values, such as collectivism and large power distance; Mexican social expectations; and Mexican workplace practices of workers and managers are different from those of U.S. workers and managers. To be sure, they are so different that U.S. managers working in Mexico often find themselves ineffective. The U.S. manager who does not take the effort to learn about these differences and adjust his or her managerial style accordingly will end up just as you did in the above scenario—frustrated and disillusioned.

Wal-Mart has more than 4,000 stores in the United States. Of all Americans, 90% live within 15 miles of a Wal-Mart. On average, every American household spends just more than $2,000 each year at Wal-Mart. In the United States, every seven days, 100 million people shop at a Wal-Mart. Wal-Mart is also successful internationally. It is the largest retailer in both Canada and Mexico, and the second largest in Britain. Worldwide, more than seven billion people shop at Wal-Mart. That's more than the world's population. So, this year, the statistical equivalent of every person on the planet will shop at a Wal-Mart.[2]

Wal-Mart is clearly a financial success, both nationally and internationally. But as Landler and Barbaro note in 2006 Wal-Mart closed its stores in Germany. The chain has had difficulty breaking into the Korean and Japanese markets as well. Something was not working in Germany, and many believe that some of Wal-Mart's international problems stem from the company's arrogance and overestimation of its competence. For a company that boasts seven billion customers a year, a certain degree of confidence is understandable. But in some places, Wal-Mart's attempts to impose its values on the market just do not work—at least not in places such as Germany, Korea, and Japan.

Referring to its failure in Germany, a Wal-Mart international spokesperson commented that it was a good lesson for the company and that they have learned to be more sensitive to cultural differences. For example, many Germans found the idea of a smiling greeter at the door of every Wal-Mart off-putting. In fact, many male shoppers interpreted it as flirting. The company also failed to foster good relations with German labor unions (Wal-Marts in the United States are not union). At one point during its tenure in Germany, Wal-Mart closed the headquarters of one of its chains and moved it to another geographic location—a common occurrence in the United States, usually accompanied by employees packing up and moving with the company. But in Germany, most of the employees quit rather than moving. A major problem was that the American managers in Germany just did not understand the German market or customers.

Landler and Barbaro point out that the conglomerate also has made cultural gaffes in Brazil and Mexico. In Brazil, the company focused a campaign on golf clubs, in a country where many do not play golf. In Mexico, it emphasized ice skates! In Korea, the Wal-Mart product shelves were so tall that customers had to use ladders to reach the products! The point of this account is that the management and sales tactics of one country, no matter how successful they may be in that country, probably are not suitable for another country. Even if you can boast seven billion shoppers, you still need to be perceptive of cultural differences.[3]

Coordinating and managing people from different cultures within an organizational context represents one of the greatest challenges for the corporate world in the new millennium. Few managers will survive and function effectively without an understanding of the subtleties and complexities of managing others in a multicultural and multinational business environment. Businesses and organizations from virtually every culture have entered into the global marketplace. The top 10 countries with which the United States trades, in terms of both imports and exports, are, in order, Canada, China, Mexico, Japan, Germany, the United Kingdom, South Korea, France, Taiwan, and Brazil. In 2010, U.S. trade with these 10 countries accounted for nearly $3 trillion (i.e., $3,000,000,000,000).[4]

Within U.S. borders as well, the face of business is becoming more and more intercultural. In 2007, Hispanics owned 2.3 million businesses in the United States, an increase of 44% from 2002. These firms accounted for 1.6% of total U.S. employment. That same year, African Americans owned nearly two million U.S. businesses, an increase of 60.5% from 2002. These businesses employed nearly one million people and generated $140 billion of business. Asians owned 1.6 million U.S. businesses in 2007, an increase of 40% from 2002. These firms accounted for 6% of all nonfarm businesses in the United States, 2.4% of total employment, and 2% of total receipts. The government defines Asian-owned businesses as firms in which Asian Indians, Chinese, Filipinos, Japanese, Koreans, Vietnamese, and other Asians own 51% or more of the stock or equity of the business.[5]

Given the dramatic cultural transformation in today's marketplace, the relevance of intercultural communication competence cannot be overstated. To compete in the global and U.S. markets, today's managers must possess the skills to interact with people who are different from themselves.

INTERCULTURAL MANAGEMENT

The purpose of this chapter is to introduce some of the salient issues affecting intercultural management. This chapter will take the components of the model of intercultural communication introduced in Chapter 1 and apply them to intercultural management. First, the cultural context within organizations will be explored prior to a discussion of the environmental context. Next, the chapter will identify the variables in the perceptual context and how they affect business in other cultures. The chapter will then compare and contrast sociorelational job contexts across cultures, along with discussing some verbal and nonverbal differences. Finally, the chapter will examine managerial practices among Japanese, German, Mexican, Chinese, and Arab managers.

There is no culture-free theory of management. Managing other people is the responsibility of people who, like everyone else, have been enculturated and socialized into a cultural set of values and beliefs that governs their thinking, emotions, and behaviors. Like communication, management is culture bound. Moreover, managerial perceptions regarding the factors that lead to organizational success vary across cultures. Unfortunately, many U.S. managers are ill equipped to handle overseas assignments. In fact, roughly 40% to 50% of all U.S. managers sent abroad receive no formal cross-cultural training.[6] As a result, up to 40% of overseas assignments are unsuccessful.[7] Although fostering competent intercultural managerial skills represents an enormous challenge, the rewards of successful international commerce are extraordinary.

Professor Philip Rosenzweig of Harvard University argues that successful cross-cultural management depends on the abilities of managers to communicate effectively. Rosenzweig points out that communication is especially important during the initial stages of a business relationship. Depending on the culture, the process of building trust among business partners may take days, weeks, or even months. Moreover, Rosenzweig asserts, this process cannot be accelerated. Rosenzweig recognizes that many American managers prefer to "get down to business" without spending much time getting to know their business partners. In fact, according to Rosenzweig, many American managers view such relationship building as a waste of valuable time. Rosenzweig argues that investing time and energy into building trust and developing relationships may earn huge benefits in terms of confidence and trust.[8]

Perceptions of time and timing are also important considerations in cross-cultural business exchanges. Rosenzweig recommends that American managers allow the pace of negotiations to develop on its own. He cautions managers not to impose artificial deadlines for the sake of efficiency. How agreement and disagreement are communicated is another important factor during cross-cultural negotiations. Rosenzweig points out that American managers tend to favor forthrightness during negotiations. In many other cultures, such directness may be seen as rude and discourteous. Finally, Rosenzweig points out that the specificity with which a contract is written may vary considerably across cultures. In the United States, we tend to favor explicit contracts that include a great deal of precise wording covering all aspects of the agreement. In some cultures, this may be interpreted as a sign of distrust. Many cultures prefer general contracts, and such cultures place significance on trust and mutual obligation rather than on formalized agreement.[9]

Most of what you have been exposed to in this textbook can be applied to your role in organizational settings across cultures. The topics and issues discussed in each chapter can guide you in becoming a successful intercultural manager. Most businesses and organizations can be thought of as mini-cultures, each representing a pattern of values held by a recognizable group of people with a common goal that is pursued by means of a collective verbal and nonverbal symbol system (Figure 11.1). Like cultures themselves, organizations

Figure 11.1 The values of an organization often mirror those of its culture.

possess value systems, exist in some environmental context, process information with a unique perceptual perspective, develop sociorelations with others, and communicate using distinctive verbal and nonverbal codes. As you prepare to conduct business with persons in organizations from different cultures or microcultures, you cannot assume that your business practices will be understood or accepted by your counterparts. Figure 11.2 outlines some of the more salient issues that affect the development of organizational culture in any country culture.

Prior to entering into a business transaction with an organization from a different culture or microculture, you should conduct an extensive organizational analysis. This model can help. In your analysis, take into account your foreign partner's cultural, environmental, perceptual, and sociorelational contexts, as well as the verbal and nonverbal code system and the nature of the relationships you are about to initiate.

The Cultural Context

First, consider the **cultural context** of an organization. **Organizational culture** often parallels country culture. Hence, if values differ significantly across cultures, then the management practices of those cultures are also likely to differ. When managing people from other cultures, try to ascertain where on the individualism–collectivism continuum an organization

Figure 11.2 Dimensions of Culture and the Organizational Culture

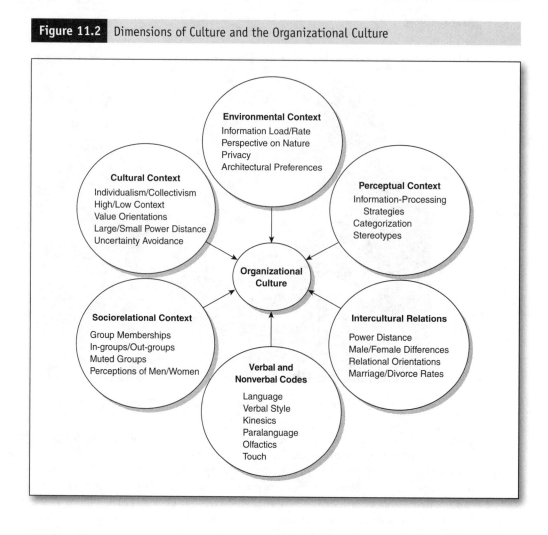

falls. Organizations in collectivistic cultures are more likely to emphasize group harmony and teamwork. In this way, the organization may be more like a community than like an entity. Individualistic corporations emphasize personal goals and within-organization promotion. Employees often compete for organizational resources and promotions, and the organization is seen more as an entity than as a community.

AN INTERCULTURAL CONVERSATION: CLASHING CULTURAL CONCEPTS ON THE JOB

In the following conversation, American businessman Jim Neumouth is applying for a job in Japanese businessman Kietaro Matsumoto's corporation, located in Kyoto, Japan.

Kietaro:	So, Mr. Neumouth, why would you like to work for our corporation?
Jim:	I believe I have the necessary skills and experience for this position. I'm very independent, I set very high goals for myself, and I believe your company will allow me to pursue them.
Kietaro:	What do you mean by "goals"?
Jim:	I have very high sales objectives. I try to reach the top in whatever I do. One of my goals is to become your leading salesperson. For example, I had the highest percentage of sales of anyone in the company I worked for in the United States. I was named salesperson of the year in 2008.
Kietaro:	I see, that's very impressive.
Jim:	Thanks. Now, I'd like to expand into an international market, and I'd like to bring my experience and motivation to your company. I think I can be the best here, too.

In the above conversation, Mr. Neumouth does a good job of expressing his talents and experience. In the United States, he might appear to be the ideal candidate; however, to Mr. Matsumoto, he does not appear to be a team player because he may disrupt the harmony of the sales teams. Therefore, when doing business with companies in collective cultures, it may be wise to formulate strategies that are consistent with group unity. Strategies that are perceived to promote the individual within the organization may be frowned on. Also, keep in mind that reaching a decision in collectivistic organizations sometimes takes much longer than in individualistic organizations. Often, collectivists go to great pains to win everyone over in order to achieve consensus.

Power distance is another important cultural influence to assess when dealing with organizations across cultures. Organizations in large power distance cultures will be status conscious (e.g., a person's position, degree), will employ top-down communication, and will be mindful of employee welfare. Formality between employer and employee will be the rule. Employees will not be expected to participate in management's decision making. In small power distance cultures, such as that of the United States, employees are routinely asked for their opinion on work-related issues. This style of management is labeled "participatory." The thought is that if workers are allowed to participate in decision making, they will be more committed to the decision. Uncertainty avoidance is another important consideration. Because the United States is a low uncertainty avoidance culture, the U.S. marketplace is associated with a great deal of risk. Risky business propositions are likely to be rejected by cultures high in uncertainty avoidance, however.

Detelin Elenkov has investigated cultural differences between Russia and the United States. He argues that Russia is more collectivistic and exhibits larger power distance and higher uncertainty avoidance than does the United States. In his comparison of managers and business students from Russia and the United States, Elenkov found that the Russians scored higher than did the persons from the United States on measures of collectivism, power distance, and uncertainty avoidance. In discussing his research, Elenkov argues that the results of his study support the contention that managerial values closely parallel cultural values.[10]

The Environmental Context

Consider the following scenario:

You have traveled to Korea to meet with your Korean counterpart, whom you have never met in person but with whom you have communicated through letters, e-mail, and so forth. You arrive at his office building at the appointed time. The weather in Seoul today is incredibly hot and humid. As you enter the floor of your partner's office, you notice that there are no walls separating the various desks. The scene appears relaxed to you. Most of the men are sitting around in their undershirts. When you locate your partner, you find him sitting with his feet up on the desk, in his undershirt, fanning himself. When you introduce yourself, your Korean partner acts as if nothing has happened and puts on a shirt, tie, and jacket in a very matter-of-fact way. Your meeting then begins.[11]

In addition to assessing an organization's cultural context, it is important to assess its **environmental context**—that is, its perspective on the environment, including such issues as information load, privacy, and the company's overall orientation to nature. Recall from Chapter 4 that some cultures believe they can master nature, whereas others attempt to live in harmony with it, and still others believe they are subjugated by it. International business expert Fons Trompenaars suggests that a culture's perspective on nature often translates into its organizational practices. Paralleling their culture's attitude toward nature, some organizations believe they can control market forces and create new markets where none exist. Others attempt a balancing act with the market, sometimes trying to influence it and at other times adjusting to its fluctuations. Still others believe that the market is in control and that they simply react to it. Trompenaars points to Indonesia as a culture that sees itself as controlled by external forces (e.g., nature, the marketplace). In Indonesia, incentive programs designed to motivate employees may fail because they consider market changes to be natural and arbitrary. To them, it makes no sense to attribute blame or lack of incentive to those who are caught in a market downturn. Moreover, it makes even less sense to reward those who have the fortune of being in a market upturn. As Trompenaars notes, to either blame or reward may deplete the morale of the team by simply adding to the randomness of events.[12]

Assumptions about privacy are also important to take into account. In collectivistic cultures, for example, in which group harmony is paramount, employees may prefer to work together in the same physical location, not isolated by office walls and doors. Many U.S. corporations have borrowed the Japanese model of an open working environment devoid of private offices. Imagine what the reaction might be if a U.S. corporation hired a group of Japanese managers and put each in his or her own private office, or if a U.S. manager in Japan requested a private space. The scenario presented at the beginning of this section is based on a fascinating discussion of privacy in Korea by Philip Harris and Robert Moran. They report that in Korea, privacy is a luxury that few possess or can afford. Because privacy may be impossible to obtain physically, Koreans build imaginary or psychological walls around themselves. A client calling on a Korean on a typically hot and humid day may actually find this person in his undershirt with his feet on his desk, fanning himself. Because there are no physical walls, the informed visitor coughs to announce his arrival. Harris and Moran allege that although the person he has come to visit is in clear view, the visitor pretends not to "see" him. Moreover, the Korean does not "see" the visitor. Only after he has risen, put on his shirt, coat, and tie, and adjusted himself do they "see" each other and introduce themselves. According to Harris and Moran, in order to secure some level of privacy, Koreans retreat behind a psychological curtain and do what they have to do, not being seen by those who are in plain view. To violate the screen of privacy once it has been created is rude and discourteous.[13]

The Perceptual Context

The **perceptual context** of the individual, learned through enculturation, is often manifest in the organization. Understanding how the organization processes information is crucial to establishing and maintaining effective communication. One information-processing strategy in which people from all cultures engage is categorizing and stereotyping. Before embarking on a business venture with people from a foreign culture, it may be useful to know of the culture's perceptions of Americans and their business practices. In 2005, the Pew Research Center conducted its Pew Global Attitudes Project, a 16-nation attitude survey conducted among nearly 17,000 people in the United States and 15 other countries. The results show that the United States remains disliked in most of the countries surveyed, particularly in Muslim countries. Ironically, opinions of the United States are the most unfavorable among America's traditional allies, such as Canada. Even more ironically, in Russia, against whom America fought the Cold War, favorable opinion of the United States has increased from 36% in 2002 to 52% in 2005. America's image is strongest in India, where 71% of those polled expressed a positive opinion of the United States.[14]

As mentioned earlier, Canada is the United States' largest trading partner, yet Canadians hold some of the most negative views of the American people. In most of the Western countries surveyed, perceptions of Americans are positive. Characteristics such as "honest," "inventive," and "hardworking" are typical. But they also associate Americans with negative traits such as "greedy" and "violent." Canadians, in particular, do not view Americans as honest, and Canada is the only Western nation in which the majority regard Americans as rude.[15]

According to the survey, Muslim countries are much more likely than others to view the American people as immoral. Yet Muslim countries also see Americans as hardworking and inventive. The Chinese are critical of Americans. They are the least likely of the 16 countries surveyed to consider Americans hardworking, and just more than 35% of the Chinese surveyed view Americans as honest. A majority of Chinese associate Americans with being violent and greedy. The one positive trait most Chinese associate with Americans is inventiveness.[16] To be sure, these perceptions of Americans are unpleasant; moreover, they will be reflected in the workplace as U.S. managers relocate abroad and attempt to supervise people in other cultures.

The Sociorelational Context

An organization's emphasis on group membership is clearly something that U.S. managers should know about their foreign counterparts. As mentioned in Chapter 6, all people of all cultures belong to groups. One of the primary groups to which all people belong is the family. Recall that Chapter 6 profiled family life across a variety of cultures. Trompenaars employs a family metaphor in describing a particular type of ideal corporate culture seen often in Turkey,

Venezuela, Hong Kong, Malaysia, India, Singapore, and Spain. This does not mean that all corporations in these countries are family-like; it simply means that this prototype is seen more frequently in these cultures than in others. According to Trompenaars, the family corporation culture is simultaneously personal, with close face-to-face relationships, and hierarchical, in the sense that everyone knows his or her place in the rank order. At the top of the hierarchy are the parents (i.e., the chief executives), who are regarded as caring and as knowing better than the children (i.e., the subordinates). The power at the top is perceived not as threatening but as intimate and benign. The philosophy of the employees is to do more than is required contractually to please the older brother or father (i.e., the person of higher rank).

Trompenaars notes that the primary reason for working hard and performing well in this type of corporate culture is the pleasure derived from familial relations. To please one's elders is a reward in itself. The main sanction for poor performance is loss of affection and place in the family. In the family corporate culture, pressures to perform are moral and social rather than financial or legal. Trompenaars argues that family corporate cultures sometimes experience difficulty with project–group organization, in which authority is divided. Moreover, U.S. businesses dealing with family-oriented cultures often see them as nepotistic (i.e., as practicing favoritism or patronage, usually with family members). In many instances, such corporations literally hire and promote bona fide family members over other candidates who may be more qualified. Trompenaars notes that the strict hierarchy in family corporations is akin (metaphorically) to the gradient angle of a triangle. The steeper the angle, the stricter the hierarchy. The hierarchy in the family-oriented corporation is analogous to the steep triangles depicted in Figure 11.3.[17]

Verbal and Nonverbal Codes

Obviously, understanding the verbal and nonverbal codes of your foreign counterparts is an essential part of a successful business venture. Although it is true that most of your foreign business partners will speak some English, your knowledge and use of their language

| Figure 11.3 | Organizational Hierarchies in Various Cultures |

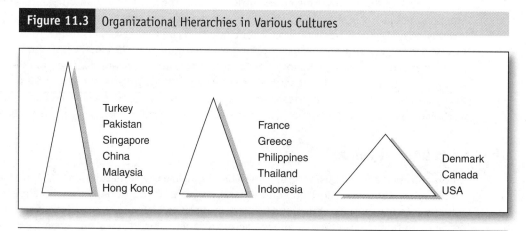

Turkey
Pakistan
Singapore
China
Malaysia
Hong Kong

France
Greece
Philippines
Thailand
Indonesia

Denmark
Canada
USA

SOURCE: Adapted from Trompenaars, F. (1994). *Riding the Waves of Culture: Understanding Diversity in Global Business.* Burr Ridge, IL: Irwin.

demonstrates your willingness to meet them halfway and will be much appreciated. International business expert Roger Axtell argues that although most of the representatives of international corporations speak English, the English spoken in the United States is of such a type that it is not understood by foreigners. In a survey of persons doing business overseas with a foreign corporation, Axtell found that 80% had difficulties interacting with foreigners because of the latter's misunderstanding of American English. However, the same respondents reported that the problem lay with them, not with their foreign counterparts. The type of English spoken in the United States is so laden with jargon, colloquialisms, and slang that English-speaking foreigners have a difficult time understanding us. Most foreigners learn standard English and are unfamiliar with how Americans actually use the language. As Axtell notes, American business is perhaps the worst offender in language proliferation. Axtell points out what he calls the "seven deadliest sins" of international misunderstanding: local color, jargon, slang, officialese, humor, vocabulary, and grammar.[18]

When conducting business with your foreign counterparts, be conscious of terms and phrases that may be well understood within your corporation but misunderstood by an outsider. At St. Norbert College, for example, women's groups such as sororities annually select an "Ugly Man" to represent their group in homecoming activities. An "Ugly Man" is analogous to a homecoming king. Imagine how a foreigner might respond to seeing "Ugly Man" on a potential client's resume! Axtell recalls a U.S. firm that lost an international client by using the phrase "This is a whole new ballgame" during sensitive renegotiations of a contract. Apparently, the client did not consider the negotiations a "game" and terminated their relationship. Consider the slang, jargon, and colloquialisms listed in the next section and how they might be misinterpreted across cultures. Axtell recommends that when verbally communicating with your foreign host, you should not speak too quickly or too slowly. Fast speech is difficult to comprehend, whereas slow is offensive and condescending. Finally, Axtell remembers a piece of advice given to him by a well-traveled vice president, who recommended talking with your foreign host as if answering a somewhat hard-of-hearing, wealthy old aunt who just asked you how much money to leave you in her will.[19]

Another important consideration here is the use of a mediator. Unlike U.S. businesspeople, who enjoy face-to-face encounters and direct bargaining, some Asian cultures, such as that of China, save face by negotiating through the use of a mediator. In addition, because of their emphasis on the group in such cultures, the overuse of personal pronouns, for example, is perceived negatively.

AN INTERCULTURAL CONVERSATION: MISINTERPRETATION OF COMMON U.S. PHRASES

One's verbal style is of utmost importance in situations where managers need to resolve conflicts with coworkers from different cultures. For example, American managers often misinterpret silence used by their Asian (e.g., Chinese, Japanese, Korean) coworkers. Asians characteristically express objection with silence. U.S. managers often interpret the silence as an expression of consent. Similarly, many Asian managers misread U.S. managers' directness in communication. Asians often see directness as unreasonable and disrespectful. Morris and his colleagues point out that Asian managers typically use an avoiding style of conflict resolution characterized by low levels of assertiveness and cooperativeness. The avoiding manager tends to evade conflict. Conversely, U.S. managers favor a competing style of conflict resolution, characterized by high levels of assertiveness and low levels of cooperativeness. The competing manager confronts conflict directly and forcefully.[20]

Although knowing your foreign partner's language (and he or she knowing yours) is certainly an advantage, there are other communication considerations, independent of verbal language, that can affect your business propositions—most notably, nonverbal communication. As discussed in Chapter 8, nonverbal communication varies a great deal across cultures. One's kinesic, paralinguistic, olfactory, haptic, and proxemic behaviors can be interpreted differently depending on with whom one is interacting. For example, greetings occur in all cultures and are typically ritualized within a particular culture. In the United States, businesspersons typically greet each other with a firm handshake and direct eye contact. In the Middle East, however, a limp handshake is preferred. Moreover, many Middle Eastern men will hold hands with their male counterparts as a display of trust in the business deal. Most U.S. businessmen would find such behavior disquieting, to say the least. Direct eye contact should also be avoided during greetings in many Asian cultures, where it is interpreted as a challenge or as an instigation of conflict. In what may seem like unusual rituals, some East African tribesmen greet each other by spitting at each other's feet, and Tibetan men greet each other by sticking out their tongues.[21]

American Phrase	Foreign Interpretation
"See ya later."	To schedule a definite future contact
"Y'all come for another visit."	Bring more people next time; "y'all" interpreted to mean "more"
"You're on a roll."	I look like a hot dog or hamburger?
"Let's use a shotgun approach."	Shoot our competition?
"Let's organize this like a Chinese menu."	Offensive to Chinese counterparts
"Send me your response ASAP."	Have no idea what you're talking about
"I have to find a bathroom."	You're going to take a bath now?
"It'll take me the better part of the day to finish this report."	Which is the better part? Morning, midday, or evening?
"We need to cover all the bases."	Do we need a blanket?

In addition to kinesics, Trompenaars notes that one's tone of voice may prove crucial during cross-cultural business transactions. Tone of voice can communicate much about the person speaking. Figure 11.4 shows characteristic paralinguistic patterns for Anglo, Latin, and Asian cultures. Trompenaars suggests that fluctuations and variations in vocal pitch carry different meanings across cultures. For example, in Latin American cultures, exaggerated ups and downs in pitch communicate that the individual is actively involved in what is being said.

| **Figure 11.4** | Characteristic Paralinguistic Patterns for Anglo, Latin, and Asian Cultures |

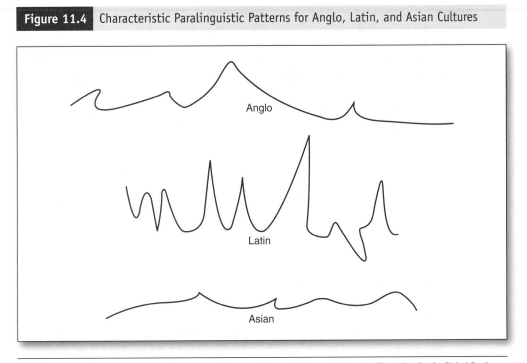

SOURCE: Adapted from Trompenaars, F. (1994). *Riding the Waves of Culture: Understanding Diversity in Global Business.* Burr Ridge, IL: Irwin.

Many Asian cultures, however, prefer a more monotonous style, which communicates self-control and respect for the person with whom one is communicating. Most Anglo speakers are in between the Latin and Asian models. Trompenaars recalls the story of a British manager in Nigeria who raised his voice during meetings and presentations. The Nigerians perceived his way of speaking as positive and as demonstrative of his concern for the issues. The same manager was relocated to Malaysia, where he employed the same vocal style, but in Malaysia he was perceived negatively and was quickly transferred out.[22]

Other channels of nonverbal communication are equally important in the cross-cultural business exchange but are often overlooked—for example, olfactics, or smell. Most Americans are taught to bathe frequently and to mask as much of the natural odor of the human body as possible. To other cultures, we smell antiseptic. Koreans, for example, have been known to call American businesspersons "butter-breath." Apparently, our use of dairy products is evident in our breath.

INTERCULTURAL RELATIONS

As mentioned throughout this textbook, especially in Chapters 6 and 9, perceptions of relationships vary dramatically across cultures. Especially important are male–female relations within corporations. Although women have made great strides in the U.S. corporate world, in many cultures, women still occupy a subordinate role and are treated as second-class citizens. Because of this situation, more than half (54%) of multinational corporations in North America say they are hesitant to send female managers abroad for fear that the host culture's perspective on women will have a negative impact on their effectiveness. According to Nancy Adler, many countries simply do not promote women into management positions. In Japan, reports Adler, women are encouraged to obtain the level of education that will enable them to *marry* managers rather than attain management positions for themselves. In fact, according to Adler, many large Japanese corporations encourage female employees to marry male employees and then use the company's anti-nepotism policies to force those women to retire.

Moreover, one third of Japanese companies indicate that they will not promote female college graduates even if they are as qualified as their male counterparts. Even in Europe, reports Adler, opposition to women in high-level management is quite strong. In one survey, nearly 70% of British managers said they preferred male applicants for executive positions. Likewise, two thirds of Italian managers said they did not want to receive orders from female managers. In Germany, nearly 95% of job advertisements for top executives use the masculine noun form, thereby discouraging women from even applying for the position. There are encouraging signs, however, especially for American women entering the international market. According to Adler, in many cultures, foreign women (e.g., Americans) are much better received in management positions than are local women. Moreover, many women managing abroad have achieved excellent results, thereby encouraging U.S. corporations to continue sending women abroad. In addition, the success of U.S. women abroad encourages the local community to hire more of their own women into management positions.[23]

As more and more U.S. businesses enter the intensely competitive global marketplace, they will be confronted with myriad management styles, especially within those cultures with whom we do much business. As mentioned at the beginning of this chapter, in 2008, four of the United States' top five trading partners were Japan, Mexico, the Federal Republic of Germany, and China. Because Japan, Mexico, Germany, and China represent such important trading partners, their cultures and management practices will be profiled next. Then, discussions about doing business in the Middle East will follow.

Japanese Management Practices

Japan is a country of nearly 130 million people, including a workforce of 67 million. According to the U.S. Department of State, per capita income is just more than $34,000 a year. Japan is considered an urban culture because only about 7% of the workforce is engaged in agriculture. Japan's $4.9 trillion economy is the third largest in the world. After maintaining one of the highest economic growth rates in the world from the 1960s through the 1980s, the Japanese economy slowed significantly in the 1990s. According to the U.S. State Department, the economic relationship between Japan and the United States is quite healthy. Although it has taken time and patience, American businesses are competing successfully in Japanese markets.[24]

Grainger and Miyamoto argue that Japanese organizations are essentially social organizations, of which two key features are lifetime employment (*shushin koyo*) and seniority grading (*nenko joretsu*). Based on these principles, the Japanese company is seen as a custodian of employee security and welfare. The lifetime employment system is based on a psychological contract between the employees and the company about the employee's lifetime dedication to the company in exchange for lifetime job security from the organization. Japanese organizations also practice a seniority-based wage and promotion arrangement where employees are promoted and compensated based on the number of years they have served the organization. The system rewards older and longer-serving employees. Conversely, employees who change their employers are penalized. Grainger and Miyamoto maintain that under these arrangements, employees willingly sacrifice their short-term losses for long-term company success. Hence, employees maintain high morale and loyalty to the company, which enables the company to invest more resources in employee career development.[25]

Ronald Dore is a British sociologist specializing in Japanese economy and society. Dore argues that the nature of the firm in Japan is much more like a community than in other countries. This is probably reflective of Japan's traditional collectivistic orientation. Dore also maintains that the lifetime employment system has survived to a remarkable degree. To be sure, Dore notes, there is a degree of career mobility for young Japanese. But, Dore points out, the proportion of young Japanese workers between the ages of 30 and 34 who have been working for their particular company for less than 1 year was 4% in 1985, rose to 5% in 1990, and was back to 3% in 2002. Hence, career mobility among young Japanese remains restricted. The same is true for the Japanese who are moving up by changing firms, which is still quite rare.

Dore notes that one aspect of Japanese business has changed. The majority of Japanese firms now have a kind of performance-based pay, replacing the seniority-based merit system discussed above. But Dore is cautious about whether this change will endure. Many of the Japanese firms that introduced the new system in the mid-1990s have backtracked because of the heavy administration costs and dramatic effects on the morale of the workers. Also, objectively measuring differences in performance was seen as counterproductive by many Japanese.[26]

Many Japanese work groups begin their day by exercising together, an activity called *taiso*. Interestingly, the primary purpose of taiso is not for physical benefits but to engage the group members in coordinated activity. After the day's work is finished, businesses encourage their employees to eat and drink together to maintain harmonious group relationships. Though it may appear that such activity is for purely social reasons, the underlying motivation is to continue work. According to Brown, Lubove, and Kwalwasser, the typical Japanese worker spends more than 2,500 hours on the job every year, compared with about 1,900 hours for the typical U.S. worker. In their interviews of Japanese managers, Brown, Lubove, and Kwalwasser found that because many Japanese workers spend their entire working careers with one company, maintaining harmony with their colleagues is considered a prime motive. Brown and his colleagues also found that, on average, Japanese managers are less than satisfied with their jobs, perhaps because of the stress of long hours.[27]

Robert Bolda of the University of Michigan asked Japanese and American managers to list the skills, behaviors, traits, or other attributes that they thought were characteristic of productive supervisors. Although there was a broad range of agreement between the Japanese and American managers, there were some interesting disagreements.

Traits Characteristic of Productive Supervisors

Traits Endorsed by Japanese and American Managers	*Traits Endorsed by American Managers*	*Traits Endorsed by Japanese Managers*
Prioritizes tasks	Works well with people	Is open to innovation
Motivates employees	Delegates	Is a good listener
Communicates clearly	Considers alternatives	Puts right person in right job
Has leadership skills	States expectations	Thinks in future tense
Makes good use of resources	Is a good speaker	Thinks about the "big picture"
Has decision-making ability	Can shift attention	Helps other departments get job done
	Is knowledgeable of company	Monitors employee progress

Traits Where Japanese and American Managers Differed the Most

Believes in his or her ability to get job done (Americans agreed/Japanese disagreed)

Helps other departments get their job done (Americans disagreed/Japanese agreed)

Delegates (Americans agreed/Japanese disagreed)

Reprimands and disciplines employees (Americans agreed/Japanese disagreed)

Monitors employees (Americans disagreed/Japanese agreed)

SOURCE: Data from Bolda, R. A. (1990). Correlates of Personal Productivity of Supervisors: Perceptions of American and Japanese Managers. *Current Psychology, 9,* 339–346.

In reviewing the results of this survey, Bolda concluded that Japanese managers endorsed behaviors that were other oriented and principle oriented. For example, Japanese managers preferred traits that dealt with innovations, employee selection, and performance monitoring. The American managers, on the other hand, supported behaviors that were more instrumental—that is, goal oriented—such as individual supervisory skills, belief in one's own ability, and decision-making skills.[28]

Although the Japanese and American managers in Bolda's survey agreed on many of the traits that constitute good management, the differences expressed by the two groups of managers may lead to communication problems on the job. Neil Abramson and his colleagues maintain that contract negotiations between Japanese and American firms are often difficult and frustrating. Abramson points out that the American preference for individualistic, rational decision making often clashes with the Japanese tendency toward relationships and group harmony. Moreover, Abramson points out that American and Japanese managers may require different kinds of information to solve problems or negotiate contracts. Americans, for example, tend to negotiate by exchanging information with the expectation that the other side will reciprocate. Furthermore, Americans have a tendency to focus on efficiency and quick closure to negotiations by pinpointing disagreements and attempting to resolve them promptly. Additionally, Americans do not highly value interpersonal relationships with their negotiation partners, instead allowing legal contracts to define future alliances. On the other hand, contends Abramson, Japanese negotiate by trying to foster steady relationships with their partners with the ultimate goal of consensus. Whereas Americans negotiate a contractual agreement, Japanese think of it as negotiating a relationship. During initial stages of a negotiation, Japanese are more interested in interpersonal attraction and deference toward their partner (as opposed to clearly identifying any disagreements). Instead of quickly reaching closure, Japanese prefer to take their time in order to establish relationships built on trust and deliberate negotiations.

In their comparison of North American and Japanese management students, Abramson and his colleagues found that the North Americans preferred a thinking-based cognitive style that is logical, impersonal, and objective. Abramson claims that such a style may lead to quick, impersonal, and analytically based decisions. In such cases, there may be a tendency to subordinate human relationships by discounting some kinds of information (e.g., affiliation with a partner) in favor of theoretically based models of decision making. The Japanese management students, on the other hand, preferred a feeling-based cognitive style that emphasizes the human element in decision making. Such a style, according to Abramson, expresses a concern for group harmony and a preference for friendly relations with one's partner. In decision making and in contract negotiations, Japanese may resist fast decisions and remain open to new information.[29]

Negotiating With the Japanese

The *Manager's Intelligence Report* listed several recommendations for negotiating with the Japanese. The recommendations are based on case study analyses of a variety of U.S. firms doing business in Japan.

1. *Stay in the game.* Be prepared for long negotiations. The Japanese take their time to get to know you and your business. They want to establish a relationship before signing any deal.

2. *Understand the "need" principle.* The Japanese will try to create and count on the idea that you "need" their deal. Once you start believing that you might lose the much-needed deal, you lose face to them.

3. *Communicate with their top decision makers.* Too much time is wasted interacting with people who can't and won't make decisions.

4. *Suspend assumptions and expectations.* The deal isn't done until it's done. Do not assume that once you have an agreement, it's a done deal.

5. *Focus on the Japanese rather than yourself.* Attend to what the Japanese need from you and demonstrate how you can accommodate them.

6. *Instead of telling them, let the Japanese discover what you want.* Negotiations in the United States are often characterized by one side explicitly telling the other side what it wants and needs. But to the Japanese, the skill of negotiating is to allow your position to surface on its own.

SOURCE: What You Can Learn From Japanese Negotiation. (1996). *Manager's Intelligence Report*, pp. 8–10.

In related research, Brett and Okumura studied the negotiation styles of U.S. and Japanese managers. They reasoned that because U.S. culture is individualistic and egalitarian and Japanese culture is collectivistic and hierarchical, managers from the two cultures would exercise different styles of negotiation. Their results showed that Japanese negotiators paid significantly more attention to power during negotiations than did U.S. negotiators. Brett and Okumura also found a difference in the two cultures' focus on self-interest during negotiations. The American negotiators were much more focused on self-interest than were the Japanese. The two researchers also found that joint gains in negotiations were significantly higher in intracultural negotiations than in intercultural ones. In other words, when U.S. managers negotiated with other U.S. managers, there were higher gains than when U.S. managers negotiated with Japanese managers. The same result was found among Japanese managers.[30]

In most organizations across cultures, managers are in positions of power and influence. As such, managers engage in a variety of behavioral strategies to influence the attitudes and behaviors of their subordinates. In a recent study, Rao, Hashimoto, and Rao surveyed Japanese managers regarding their preferences for a variety of influence strategies. Although some of the Japanese managers preferred influence tactics similar to those preferred by U.S. managers, Rao, Hashimoto, and Rao identified several strategies that appear to be unique to the Japanese. One strategy is labeled firm's authority. In contrast to American managers, who may appeal to "higher-ups" to influence their employees, Japanese managers do not appeal to a specific person in the organizational hierarchy but, rather, to the entire organization itself, independent of their superiors. This strategy is probably linked to the Japanese concept of business organization as a family.

A second type of strategy, called personal development, occurs when a Japanese manager convinces his (most managers are men) employees to comply with a request to enhance their careers within the organization. This tactic may be effective because many Japanese remain with a single company for their entire lives. American managers, on the other hand, convince employees that by complying with a request, the employees will develop skills they can take with them when they leave the organization.

Another strategy is labeled "socializing." With this strategy, Japanese managers ask to spend time with their employees after hours. According to Rao, Hashimoto, and Rao, such a strategy allows for informal interaction between managers and subordinates that is impossible in the context of the formal work environment. Interestingly, they also report that Japanese managers in Canada were disappointed when their subordinates rejected their requests to socialize after work. The Japanese managers felt that this severely limited their influence potential, and they had to resort to using assertive tactics on the job.

Rao, Hashimoto, and Rao report that Japanese managers use a variety of tactics outside the work environment to influence their subordinates. In general, compared with American managers, Japanese managers use influence tactics that are subtle and indirect. For example, if a Japanese manager wants a subordinate to focus on the Canadian market for a specific product, the manager, rather than telling him or her directly, might funnel information about that market to the employee, hoping that the employee will sense his intent. In addition, Japanese managers use strategies that rely on the influence of the organization and group harmony.[31]

According to William Drake and Associates, work attitudes within an organization evolve from the senior members of the organization, who are ensured promotion and lifetime employment. One reason the older employees are so satisfied with their jobs is that they know they are secure; they do not have to worry about the younger, more energetic employees jeopardizing their jobs.

While interacting with Japanese businesspersons, Americans often notice behaviors that are widely misunderstood by non-Japanese (see Table 11.1). To be sure, the Japanese businessperson has perceptions of American behavior that may be misinterpreted as well. For example, Japanese are astonished by the typical American's informality and spontaneity. The quick pace of conversation and what are perceived to be ostentatious—that is, flashy or showy—nonverbal mannerisms are off-putting to most Japanese. In fact, many Japanese believe that Americans are inclined to make mistakes because of the fast pace with which they conduct business dealings. The "don't take it personally—it's just business" attitude portrayed by most American businesspersons intimidates Japanese because, to them, it disrupts the harmony of the business relationship. The Japanese tend to view conversations and negotiations as formalized rituals rather than as a meeting of minds.[32]

German Management Practices

Although there have been fluctuations in the German economy since reunification, in 2010, the German economy was growing at a rate of about 3.3%; it is now the fifth largest economy in the world. The average income per capita in U.S. dollars is $36,000. The U.S. Department of State maintains that the German market, the largest in Europe, is attractive to many

Table 11.1 American Perceptions and Japanese Realities

American Perception	Japanese Reality
The Japanese are really shy.	As a high-context culture, the Japanese do not feel a need to talk. They are comfortable with silence.
Japanese fall asleep a lot during class or presentations.	Many Japanese close their eyes when they are deeply concentrating.
Japanese say yes even when they mean no. Why can't they just say what they mean?	To save face (yours and theirs), Japanese will agree with you in principle.
It takes Japanese forever to make decisions or even to respond to a fax or written correspondence.	Japanese will not make a decision without first consulting relevant others to reach a consensus.
Japanese will never look you in the eye.	Indirect eye contact is a sign of deference in Japan.
When Japanese talk, they seem so ambiguous. I never know what they're trying to say or what they really mean.	Japanese language is vague. But even more than that, to the Japanese, communication is a two-way process. The burden of understanding rests with the speaker and the listener. Often, the speaker will only hint at what is meant. The listener must be an active participant.

SOURCE: Table adapted from pages 410–412 of *When Cultures Collide,* by R. D. Lewis. Copyright © 2000 Nicholas Brealey.

U.S. businesses. Germans are attracted to innovative products that display high quality and contemporary styling. They are especially interested in high-tech products, particularly those that assist them in entering the age of the Internet.[33]

Like the United States and Europe in general, Germany is a decentralized collection of states and regions. Many are quite diverse, with unique customs and conventions. The northern and southern regions are particularly different, so generalizing about Germany is difficult and should be approached with some degree of caution. According to intercultural consultants William Drake and Associates, most Germans believe that people are controlled by their own actions, that facts are more important than face (in sharp contrast to the Japanese), and that factual honesty is more important than politeness (again, clashing with Japanese conventions). According to Drake, German children are taught that useless people amount to nothing and that children are to be quiet and respectful. They are also taught to "save for a rainy day."[34]

Glunk, Wilderom, and Ogilvie point out that a unique feature of Germany's economic structure is a state-regulated apprentice system where young German adults learn a well-defined skill, for which they receive a state diploma. According to Glunk and her colleagues, the learning is both on-the-job and theoretical. The curriculum is determined by the government, an employers' association, and German trade unions. During their apprenticeship, the students are supervised by local chambers of commerce. This system leads to a remarkably well-trained workforce. According to Glunk, approximately 70% of German workers have been through this system. Glunk also notes that technical knowledge and engineering skills are highly valued in Germany. She maintains that German employees are continuously challenged with new procedures, tools, and techniques.

In addition, German managers are known to be specialists for which a technical background is more typical than a formal education. German foremen, supervisors, and managers typically have professional rather than academic degrees. Hence, quality of skill and amount of experience are the most important promotion considerations in German firms. Finally, Glunk and her colleagues note that many German organizations implement a shadow-worker program where managers choose and train their own replacements. Germans believe that this kind of program reduces the politics of promotion ploys and insecurity around who is succeeding whom. In this type of program, vacations, illness, and other periods of absence are covered by the designated replacement. Thus, the successor can temporarily experience his or her future position. Glunk maintains that this policy preserves smooth organizational functioning.[35]

Focusing their analysis primarily on West Germans, anthropologists Edward and Mildred Hall contend that compartmentalization is the most prominent structural feature of German culture—that is, that Germans have a tendency to isolate and divide many aspects of their lives into discrete, independent units. Germans are known to compartmentalize their daily schedules, educational system, office buildings, corporations, homes, and even lines of communication. In fact, Hall and Hall argue that on the job, Germans will not share information with others except within their own working groups. Hall and Hall maintain that such a restricted flow of information may be the biggest obstacle in doing business with the Germans. One result of German compartmentalization is a culture in which significant events and changes can take place without people knowing about them. Even informal information networks that connect public and private organizational boundaries are rare in Germany.[36] Given this condition, U.S. companies wishing to do business in Germany would be wise to understand that they may not be able to operate out of a centralized location. Instead, they may have to set up multiple sites from which to conduct commerce. German emphasis on compartmentalization manifests itself in many areas of German life and business, particularly with respect to privacy and specialization. Germans are a private (and formal) people. Most German managers isolate themselves in their offices behind closed doors, contrasting sharply with open-door policies exercised by American managers.

Doors are an important cultural symbol to the Germans. According to Hall and Hall, doors provide a protective shield between the individual and outsiders. Upon encountering a closed door in German businesses or homes, an "intruder" should always knock. As Hall and Hall note, closed doors uphold the honor of the space, afford a boundary between people, and eliminate the possibility of eavesdropping, interruptions, and accidental intrusions. Moreover, according to Hall and Hall, within corporations, the closed door indicates that a manager respects the privacy of subordinates and is not looking over their shoulders.[37]

German compartmentalization can also be seen in the overall market strategy of many successful German corporations. Unlike many U.S. or Japanese corporate conglomerates whose global market success is attributable to diversification, many German firms concentrate on specialization—that is, doing one thing and doing it right. German corporations with large shares of specialized markets can focus on design, quality, and service rather than on competitive pricing. Such corporations manufacture a smaller and narrower class of products, sell to fewer consumers, and contract with fewer suppliers than do their less successful competitors. To be sure, many of these exclusive products are expensive, but the Germans believe that specialization leads to quality and profit. German products are known worldwide for their high caliber and quality workmanship (e.g., Mercedes, BMW). Steiner Optik maintains 80% of the global market for military field glasses. Krones manufactures more than 70% of the world's bottle-labeling machines. The Germans seem to be teaching the rest of the world that, at least for them, specialization works.[38]

Like the United States, Germany is considered a low-context, monochrome culture, except even more so. According to Hall and Hall, the German language is quite literal, with individual German words having exact and precise meaning. For example, the Germans have no fewer than eight words for "comfort," each reflecting a slightly different type of comfort. Having been conditioned by their language, Germans are fairly formal, nitpicky about precision, punctual, and fanatic about facts. All these characteristics carry over into their business relations. On the job and in business dealings, Germans are absolutely obsessed with facts and precision. Lines of authority are carefully observed. Interactions between business partners and friends are reserved and formalized. Germans are conscious of rank and will always refer to someone by the person's appropriate title. Even neighbors who may have lived next door to each other for years address each other with their last names, as in "Herr (Mr.) Schmidt." If a person also carries a degree, such as a PhD or an MD, he will be called "Herr Doktor Neulieb," and so forth.[39] Women, however, are typically addressed with their first names, as in "Frau Batina Neulieb."

Even in social situations, Germans often appear unfriendly. They generally will not smile during a greeting and are intolerant of small talk. On the job, German workers expect that their managers will respect their privacy and that procedures will be executed precisely. Table 11.2 outlines some features of doing business with Germans that may help Americans transacting business in Germany.

Table 11.2	Interacting Effectively With Germans

1. Be prepared. In business, the Germans will be informed and will expect that you are, too.

2. Engage in only minimal small talk.

3. Be informed about, and use, appropriate titles.

4. Avoid emotional appeals. Emphasize facts and figures. Germans respect quantitative reports.

5. Observe hierarchical seating and order of speaking.

6. Organize your presentation in compartments, and have your specialists present their own areas separately and as distinct parts of the presentation.

7. Be punctual; start and stop as you planned. Follow your agenda closely.

8. Avoid humor. Be frank, direct, and honest. Demonstrate that you have done your homework.

SOURCES: Based on William Drake and Associates. (1997). Managing Business Relationships in Germany (www.culturebank.com/demo/demogermany/sld001.htm); E. T. Hall and M. R. Hall. (1990). *Understanding Cultural Differences.* Yarmouth, ME: Intercultural Press; P. R. Harris and R. T. Moran. (1996). *Managing Cultural Differences* (4th ed.). Houston: Gulf; R. D. Lewis. (1997). *When Cultures Collide.* London: Nicholas Brealey.

Although to many Americans, the outward appearance and demeanor of the typical German is aloof, intense, humorless, and quite formal and rigid, on the inside, Germans desire meaningful interpersonal relationships. As intercultural expert Richard Lewis asserts,

> Anglo-Saxons do not always see the way towards making quick friends with them, but when they succeed in entering into the somewhat complicated structure of a German friendship, they find rich rewards. A German is generally a loyal and true friend of incredible durability. Outwardly glum and cautious, they are inwardly desperate for affection and popularity. They want to be cherished just as the rest of us do. . . . A German friendship is indeed a very worthwhile investment.[40]

Mexican Management Practices

Mexico has a free-market economy, with a gross domestic product in 2010 of $1.3 trillion and a growth rate of 5%. The Mexican per capita income is $14,000, one third that of the United States. Income distribution remains highly unequal, with more than 45% of the population living in moderate poverty and 18% in extreme poverty. Trade with the United States and Canada has tripled since the implementation of NAFTA in 1994. As mentioned earlier, in 2010, Mexico was the United States' third most important trading partner, following Canada and China.[41]

As noted previously, a country's cultural orientation and values are typically reflected in the business practices of that culture. Three dimensions of cultural variability discussed in Chapter 2 are closely associated with Mexican business practices: individualism–collectivism, power distance, and uncertainty avoidance. Generally, in comparison with the United States, Mexico is more collectivistic and is considered a large power distance and high uncertainty avoidance culture.[42] Crouch points out that Mexicans are unusually group oriented. He maintains that Mexicans are exceptionally concerned about any behavior that would upset the harmony of their household, church, or workplace. In fact, Crouch argues that on a scale of individual- versus group-oriented work styles, Mexicans and Americans would fall at opposite ends of the continuum.

Mexican workers assume that working together is the ideal, because people who work better in solidarity with others, valuing loyalty to the group above individual effort, will prosper in a group-oriented work environment. Generally, Mexican organizations do not emphasize self-determination on the job. Unlike workers in the United States, Mexicans usually are not rewarded for initiative. Pelled and Xin point out that Mexicans see work as a "necessary evil." To many Mexicans, work is required to appreciate the more important things in life, such as family and friends.

Crouch cautions American managers working in Mexico not to reward individuals within work groups. Generally, Mexican workers do not wish to call attention to themselves for outperforming coworkers and may be ashamed and embarrassed if recognized above others. In Mexico, individual effort and self-starting are met with suspicion. Even arriving early to work requires an explanation to coworkers, because they will think that person is trying to get ahead by showing off. Crouch points out that for a worker to leave his or her workstation to talk to the supervisor about mundane, work-related issues is disquieting to others in the group, unless the employee has explained his or her need to communicate with the supervisor beforehand. Moreover, Crouch asserts that the Mexican worker's attitude toward the boss is virtually never confrontational. Mexican workers value harmony above all else. A manager expressing favoritism to an individual Mexican worker will upset the harmony and shatter the team spirit.[43]

In the United States, people often change jobs and switch organizations in order to get ahead and be promoted. U.S. workers are generally in charge of their own careers and strive to succeed individually. Schuler and his colleagues argue that under Mexican law, Mexican organizations are responsible for the life, health, and dignity of their workers. In this way, Mexican organizations are considered paternalistic. Consistent with a collectivistic orientation, Mexican workers value harmonious relations between union and management. Conversely, in the United States, union and management interactions are often antagonistic. De Forest points out that traditional Mexican ideals stress employee–employer interdependence, mutual responsibilities, loyalty between superiors and subordinates, belongingness, cooperation (rather than competition), and not exceeding boundaries. According to De Forest, Mexican employers rebuff employees who criticize others to higher authorities and are competitive on the job, because such behaviors disrupt the harmony of the organization.[44]

Mexico is considered a large power distance culture. Recall that in large power distance cultures, people expect and accept that the power within the culture and its institutions will be distributed unequally. De Forest contends that Mexico's large power distance can be seen in the government, in the church, and throughout Mexican society. According to De Forest, most Mexican businesses have a rigid hierarchy where the power is centralized in the person or people at the top. Often, the top positions are not gained through hard work and initiative but are inherited or acquired through friendships or mutual favors. De Forest has observed that Mexican managers reward submission, taking direction, and loyalty to the person with power. Crouch explains that, historically, Mexicans have never known a world without hierarchy. For example, the Spanish had kings and queens, and the Aztecs had powerful *caciques* (warrior chiefs). To be sure, the Spanish language is replete with words and phrases that communicate hierarchy (e.g., proper titles, salutations, and honorifics) and emphasize the idea that some people hold superior positions over others. Crouch asserts that Mexicans hold to traditional hierarchical roles based on family, education, age, and position. According to Crouch, Mexicans are puzzled and offended by Americans' casual and informal communication style. He maintains that Mexicans find the relaxed and easy communication between people of different hierarchical levels off-putting. The Mexican distinction between superior and subordinate is part of a deeply rooted pattern dating back to Aztec divisions among priest, prince, and peasant, and among the Spanish queen, soldier, and citizen. For the small power distance Americans, the implications of superior and inferior status that accompany this pattern are unacceptable.[45]

Relationships between Mexican managers and their subordinates are generally distant, and communication is rather formal. For example, managers and subordinates are usually not on a first-name basis. Unlike U.S. manager–subordinate communication, interactive strategies that promote equality, participative decision making, open communication, and employee ownership are not considered necessary—or even desirable—in Mexican organizations. When interacting with Mexican employees, managers need not explain the reasoning behind a decision, because employees may perceive this as a sign of weakness. In fact, Mexican workers expect to be given orders. They accept their unequal status and prefer that those in power protect their interests, give clear direction, and treat them with civility. Communication channels should follow the hierarchical structure of the business.[46]

In low (or weak) uncertainty avoidance cultures such as the United States, employees are encouraged to innovate and take risks. In high (or strong) uncertainty avoidance cultures such as Mexico, innovative or risk-taking behavior is inappropriate. Mexican workers generally prefer close supervision. Likewise, compensation based on incentive is eschewed. Mexican workers prefer to know exactly what they are supposed to do, and they want to be rewarded for doing it.

De Forest maintains that one of the most frustrating aspects for Americans doing business in Mexico is the Mexican perception of time. American managers should be advised to be patient. According to De Forest, life is simply slower in Mexico than in the United States. She points out that in Mexico, time does not advance; it tends to be either right now or some other time. American managers should be prepared for delays. De Forest says that phone service may take months to be installed or repaired; obtaining a post office box can take weeks or months; people frequently show up late for meetings; businesses and government offices open and close at all hours, as if at random; and electricity shuts down for no apparent reason and may remain off for days.[47] Since the start of NAFTA, the United States and Mexico have been active trading partners. If American managers can adjust to the culturally influenced business environment in Mexico, they can make great strides. The key to being successful in Mexico is adjusting and adapting to the cultural environment.

Chinese Management Practices

In 2010, the People's Republic of China surpassed Japan as the world's second largest economy (following the United States), with a gross domestic product worth an estimated $1.4 trillion. China's economy is also the world's fastest-growing major economy, with average growth rates of 10% over the past three decades. Much of this economic power is the result of free-market reforms that were instituted in 1978. China is the largest exporter and second largest importer of goods in the world. For example, China overtook the United States last year as the biggest automobile market in the world. Indeed, China has now surpassed Germany as the largest exporter of automobiles. Moreover, China is the world's biggest buyer of iron ore and copper and the second biggest importer of crude oil.[48] Out of 183 world economies, the World Bank rates China 79th in terms of ease of doing business. China ranks 151st in terms of starting a business, 65th in terms of getting credit, and 15th in terms of trading across borders.[49]

Several times throughout this book, China has been described as a collectivistic, large power distance culture. China's large power distance can be attributed to its Confucian heritage, which results in a hierarchical society. As we saw in Chapter 2, modesty, obedience, and respect for seniors are deeply rooted Chinese values. Confucian ideals are at the base of Chinese management. China is also considered a high-context culture. As such, China's Confucianism, collectivism, power distance, and high context are ingrained in Chinese management practices. Because of the culture's high-context orientation, the environment in which business is conducted is important. Where the meeting takes place, who is invited, and who is presenting all are critical ingredients in a successful business meeting.

China's Confucian heritage affects how Chinese will approach their business relationships. Recall from Chapter 6 that in Confucian-based societies, great emphasis is placed on harmonious relationships and knowing one's proper place in the social hierarchy. All relationships are seen as unequal, and one's ethics are directed toward observing these inequalities. Contrary to the United States, where business is business and not to be taken personally, the Chinese will go to great lengths to establish trust and a social bond in their international business relationships. When doing business in China, you can expect your Chinese counterpart to invite you to informal gatherings and to discuss factors unrelated to the business at hand, such as politics, the arts, information about your family, etc. The Chinese want to see you as a member of the business family—that is, the group.[50]

Decision making is an important part of management. In the United States, management decision making is often a collaboration between workers and managers where debate is encouraged (and sometimes legislated via union agreements). Tang and Ward point out that in Chinese management, the manager is expected to make decisions on behalf of the entire group. This is expected and desired among both the managers and workers. The idea of open communication between managers and workers is not only unheard of but thought of as odd and peculiar. Tang and Ward hypothesize that this style is probably reflective of collectivistic thinking, where workers are a part of one group and managers a part of another. In-group–out-group distinctions are a part of collectivistic thinking. These distinctions are also Confucianistic. Tang and Ward note that this can be an effective and efficient decision-making process on the one hand, but it can also be time-consuming when a particular question is not asked to the right person and must make its way to the top of the hierarchy before it can be answered.[51]

Communication between managers and workers is restricted. Tang and Ward note that workers are on a need-to-know basis, and the flow of job-related information is limited. Likewise, and consistent with the collectivistic, large power distance, and high-context nature, Chinese workers will probably not initiate communication with a manager, even if they have concerns about the way in which a job is being handled. While they may discuss it with another worker, they will not address the manager, probably due to the workers' desire not to stand out and be thought of as confrontational. Recall from Chapter 2 that modesty and finding the middle ground are valued in China. In addition, recall from Chapter 10 that collectivists, and particularly Chinese, do not approach conflict but, rather, avoid it in an effort to maintain harmony. Plus, in an effort to save everyone's face—both that of managers and workers—on-the-job conflict is resolved via mediation and compromise.[52]

To make one final point about doing business in China, gift giving was once an important part of Chinese culture. But today, Chinese business culture prohibits giving gifts. In fact, gift giving is actually considered bribery and is technically illegal. But, depending on the specific case, attitudes about giving gifts are relaxing. If you wish to give a gift to an individual, do it privately—in the context of friendship, not business. Your Chinese counterpart will probably decline the gift two or three times before accepting it. Once the gift is accepted, express gratitude. Giving a gift to the entire company, rather than to an individual, can be an acceptable alternative. But make sure you give the gift to the appropriate team leader.[53]

Commerce in the Middle East

To many Americans, the Middle East is a place of great mystery, riddled with intrigue, hostility, and contradiction. Most Americans are uninformed of the history, geography, and culture of the Middle East. After World War II, many Arab countries, which had been subjected to European colonial rule, won independence. Along with independence came many new challenges. Unfortunately, few Arab countries had experienced leaders able to cope with their novel circumstances. Of the many tests facing the Arab world, national development is in the vanguard. Many Arab countries have spent immense amounts of financial and human resources in an attempt to improve the capabilities and performance of their national economies and generate change in their political systems and innovations in technology. Today, however, most Arab states are ruled by authoritarian political regimes that do not encourage, or allow, public participation in decision making. The determination of war, investment strategies, military armaments, and national budgetary allocations is ultimately decreed by one person. There is virtually no free press or free expression, and the citizenry is essentially insulated from any governmental practices. To make matters worse, corruption is so prevalent that most public officials deem it a natural part of doing business.[54]

Members of the Arab League

Algeria	Egypt	Lebanon
Bahrain	Iraq	Libya
Comoros	Jordan	Mauritania
Djibouti	Kuwait	Morocco

The Arab world's population is projected to increase to more than 400 million in 2020. Egypt, for example, is expected to double its population in the next 20 years. The U.S. Arab population totaled 1.19 million people in 2000—up from 610,000 in 1980 and 860,000 in 1990—and made up about 0.42% of the country's 281.4 million people. In addition, the Arab world has a youthful population, with high levels of poverty and unemployment. In the Arab world as a whole, 40% of the population is under the age of 14. In 2005, more than 60% of the Arab population earned less than US$1,000 annually. Illiteracy is also problematic. In Egypt, nearly half of the people are illiterate.[55]

National development seems to be the top priority among most Middle Eastern Arab countries. Following their independence, Arab governments became the instant owners and operators of public utilities, banks, railways, airlines, mass transit systems, and telephone systems, and providers of water, gas, and electricity. Most of the governments simply lacked the technological and human resources to manage. Coupled with national development, a push toward industrialization has generated immense pressures in many Arab countries. Ali contends that the existing infrastructures (e.g., roads, ports, distribution centers) have been unable to keep pace with the rapid growth of most Arab countries. Moreover, asserts Ali, a severe shortage of skilled managers in the new government and private institutions has forced many organizations to hire foreign experts and workers. Finally, writes Ali, most Arab countries suffer from "cultural discontinuity." For more than 500 years, the Arab world has been under the influence of numerous foreign powers. Generations of Arabs have lost their attachments to their cultural roots and values. In fact, explains Ali, formal education systems did not exist in Arabia until the beginning of this century.[56]

Although faced with problems, the growth of many Arab economies has been rapid, and the United States has played an active role. For example, according to the U.S. Department of State, the United States is Saudi Arabia's leading trade and joint venture partner. In 2007, U.S. exports to Saudi Arabia increased to $10 billion, whereas Saudi exports to the United States increased to $35 billion. There are more than 200 U.S. companies in Saudi Arabia. Economic relations between the United States and Saudi Arabia, its main trade partner in the Middle East, have been greatly damaged in the period following the attacks of September 11, 2001, against the United States. In Kuwait, the United States is the largest supplier of goods and services. U.S. corporations are the source of nearly 40% of Kuwait's import market. Moreover, U.S. exports to Kuwait in 2007 totaled about $2.5 billion. Qatar, one of the smallest yet wealthiest Arab countries, has become an active trading partner with the United States. In 2007, U.S. exports to Qatar amounted to more than $2 billion, while Qatari exports to the United States reached nearly $500 million.[57]

Because of their lack of knowledge and sensitivity, many American managers are unable to conduct business successfully in Arabia. Even Arab names, for example, are so confusing to most Americans that they give up trying to understand. An Arab man's name could be Ali bin Ahmed bin Saleh Al-Fulani. His first name is Ali, and he is probably called that by his friends. His family name is Al-Fulani. The word *bin* means "son of." So Ali bin Ahmed bin Saleh means that he is the son of Ahmed, who is the son of Saleh. Many Arabs give their ancestors' names to their children for at least five or six generations. Women's names are handled a bit differently. From the example above, say Ali has a sister. Her name might be Nura bint Ahmed bin Saleh Al-Fulani. *Bint* means "daughter of." She is

Nura, the daughter of Ahmed, who is the son of Saleh. Her family name is Al-Fulani. When an Arab woman marries, she does not change her name, although her children take their father's name.[58]

AN INTERCULTURAL CONVERSATION:
BUSINESS COMMUNICATION IN THE MIDDLE EAST

Names notwithstanding, many Americans are completely ignorant of subtle Arab conventions that can define the success or failure of a business deal. Consider the following exchange between Arab businessman Hashim Abdu Hashim and his American counterpart, Steve Jones.[59]

The scene: Mr. Jones is sitting (on the floor) in the hallway of a building in Saudi Arabia, waiting to meet with his Saudi counterpart, Hashim Abdu Hashim. The hallway is noisy, cluttered with people moving quickly from room to room. Mr. Jones arrived in Saudi Arabia two days earlier for a scheduled meeting. Since then, his meeting has been postponed and rescheduled several times. After several hours of waiting in the hallway, Mr. Jones is called into Hashim's office. The office has no chairs but, instead, elaborate and ornate pillows on the floor. The walls are draped with embellished afghans. Mr. Jones enters.

Jones:	Hello, Hashim. Gosh, I finally get to see you. I've been waiting for two days!
Hashim:	Ah, hello, Mr. Jones. It is good to see you.
Jones:	Thanks. It's good to see you also. How's Mrs. Hashim?
Hashim:	Was your trip to our country all right?
Jones:	Yes, everything is fine. (At this point, the two are interrupted by a servant pouring tea. Jones refuses.) No . . . no . . . thanks, I've had enough tea. So . . . Hashim. I came all the way over here to see if I could get you to speed things up with our order. See, our supplies have been sitting in some dock along the coast for two weeks. I was wondering if you could sign this petition (hands it to Hashim using his left hand) to hurry up the process.
Hashim:	Hmmm . . . this is a problem?
Jones:	Yes, gosh, Hashim, I understand that sometimes supplies sit on ships for weeks at a time! Your people could really use these computers you've ordered. I need to have them released to your custody as soon as possible.
Hashim:	I see. Well . . . we have been without computers for thousands of years. Waiting is no problem.

Mr. Jones commits five cultural blunders that severely jeopardize any possible future contract with Hashim. First, he mentions that he's been waiting for two days to see Hashim. Jones has not recognized the polychronic nature of Saudi Arabia. Business gets done on its own time. Second, he refuses the tea that has been offered to him in hospitality. Then, in a gross error of etiquette, he inquires about Hashim's wife. In Saudi Arabia, a man's wife is for his eyes only. Continuing on his blundering way, Jones hands Hashim the contract with his left hand. In many Muslim cultures, the left hand is the "dirty" hand; that is, it is used for cleaning the body, handling waste, and so on. Finally, Jones demonstrates the urgency of his mission and getting the computers off the supply ship. His emphasis on schedules and deadlines communicates to Hashim that he is either insane or irreligious. Many Arabs believe literally in the phrase "Insha Allah," meaning "God willing." To them, the nature of things, especially time, is controlled by God. Events, meetings, and happenings are completed only if God wills them.

According to Ali, one of the problems facing expatriates in the Middle East is the lack of any coherent Arab management profession or theory. Ali contends that Arab societies moved too rapidly toward industrialization without establishing the foundations necessary for dealing with the challenges of modern institutions. This, according to Ali, has led to inefficient operations, lack of clear direction, displacement of the traditional labor force, and dramatic shifts in social structures. Specifically, asserts Ali, Arab management reflects the political and social instability of the region, which serves only the powerful political elites.[60]

In the absence of an Arab management theory, Ali points to several societal qualities in Arab cultures that have management implications in Arab organizations. Arab idealism and hopefulness are necessary elements in Arab society. Hence, organizational development can be introduced without resentment as long as the changes conform to the ideal. Arab infatuation with ideal forms means that new and modern management practices can be used. Unlike the Germans, who are persuaded only by facts and figures, the typical Arab resorts to personal relationships, emotional appeals, and intuitiveness in decision making. Ali labels this phenomenon "non–decision making." Yet Arab reliance on intuition can speed up the decision-making process through flexibility and tolerance for ambiguity.

Arabs also tend to avoid public conflict and criticism. Hence, mediation is sometimes necessary in conducting business. Dimensions of Islamic teaching also enter into the management picture. Hard work is a virtue to Muslims; thus, commitment to organizational goals can be sustained. Islam also preaches that one should deal with other people as equals. Within the organization, equity issues are salient where a horizontal (rather than vertical) line of authority is preferred. In fact, directives from the top are often received negatively. In this sense, maintains Ali, communication with formal and informal leaders is necessary to achieve organizational goals. Courage is also an Islamic virtue. Workers are willing to confront managers and will express their concerns openly.[61]

Given the extreme diversity in literacy rates, healthcare systems, educational institutions, technological advancement, management techniques, and forms of government, it is difficult to offer generalizations about managing people in Arab countries. The list below, however, offers some broad guidelines for doing business in the Middle East that most Americans would be wise to consider.[62]

Interacting With Arabs

1. Arabs have a tendency to use elaborate and ritualized forms of communication, especially during greetings. Even in markets, loud and boisterous bargaining is accepted and expected and accompanied with wide gestures and animated facial expressions. Many Americans are unnerved by this.

2. Arab women's bodies are not to be seen. American women should dress with their arms and legs covered.

3. As a sign of trust and friendship, Arab men may be seen holding hands. During greetings, men kiss each other on the cheeks.

4. Generally, Arabs have a smaller personal space than most Americans. They tend to stand very close while interacting, sometimes in order to smell their partner's breath. They expect intense eye contact.

5. During negotiations, Arabs will personalize arguments and appeal to emotions.

6. In general, Arabs are less private than Americans. Visiting and long conversations are expected.

7. Do not hesitate to praise an Arab's country, food, and art. But do not make comments of any kind about Arab women, especially an Arab's wife.

8. Do not appear detached or reluctant to accept favors. Unlike the Japanese, Arabs enjoy verbal interaction and expect it from others. Silence will be perceived as a sign that something is wrong.

CHAPTER SUMMARY

Doing business and managing people in a culture other than one's own is a daunting task indeed. This chapter has discussed how the principles presented throughout the text can be applied to the business world across cultures. An understanding of the cultural, microcultural, environmental, perceptual, sociorelational, verbal, nonverbal, and relational contexts of the host culture increases the probability of being an effective and productive manager across cultures. Five diverse cultures—Japan, Germany, Mexico, China, and the Middle East—are active participants in the global marketplace, each with its own unique way of doing business. The Japanese are subtle and indirect, Germans forthright and direct, Arabs expressive and intuitive, Chinese rooted in Confucian rules of hierarchy, and Mexicans collectivistic and hierarchical. Managers who understand the contexts of these cultures are in a much better position to do business. Finally, we have seen that several factors affect and facilitate intercultural conflict. Although conflict can never be eliminated, identifying these factors can help us reduce and manage conflict in our professional lives.

Visit the student study site at **www.sagepub.com/neuliep5e** *for e-flashcards, web quizzes, web resources and more.*

DISCUSSION QUESTIONS

1. How are the dominant cultural values of the United States reflected in U.S. management styles and U.S. company policies?

2. How might the U.S. management style of participative management affect a U.S. manager in Mexico? China?

3. How might the U.S. emphasis on time (i.e., monochronic) affect how you would do business in Mexico?

4. What considerations would you make in preparing for a presentation in a German or a Chinese company?

5. Your company has just established an account with a firm in Saudi Arabia. Your top salesperson is a young woman. Should you send her there? Why or why not?

KEY TERMS

cultural context   377

environmental context   380

organizational culture   377

perceptual context   381

power distance   379

REFERENCES

1. Trompenaars, F. (1994). *Riding the Waves of Culture: Understanding Diversity in Global Business.* Burr Ridge, IL: Irwin, p. 14.

2. Fishman, C. (2006). *The Wal-Mart Effect.* New York: Penguin.

3. Landler, M., & Barbaro, M. (2006, August 2). International Business; No, Not Always. *New York Times,* pp. A1, A3.

4. U.S. Census Bureau. (2010, October). *Top 10 Countries With Which the U.S. Trades.* http://www.census.gov/foreign-trade/top/dst/2010/10/balance.html; U.S. Census Bureau. (2010, October). *Top Trading Partners: Total Trade, Imports, Exports.* http://www.census.gov/foreign-trade/statistics/highlights/top/top1010yr.html.

5. U.S. Census Bureau. (2007). *Survey of Business Owners.* Washington, DC: Author. http://www.census.gov/econ/sbo/.

6. Stroh, L. K., Black, J. S., Mendenhall, M. E., & Gregersen, H. B. (2005). *International Assignments: An Integration of Strategy, Research, and Practice.* Hillsdale, NJ: Erlbaum.

7. Wasson, R. (2004). Going International: Getting the People Dimension Right. *Engineering Management Journal, 14,* 16–17.

8. Rosenzweig, P. M. (1994). *National Culture and Management* (Teaching Note 9–394–177). Boston: Harvard Business School.

9. Ibid.

10. Elenkov, D. S. (1997). Differences and Similarities in Managerial Values Between U.S. and Russian Managers. *International Studies of Management and Organization, 27,* 85–107.

11. This scene is adapted from Harris, P. R., & Moran, R. T. (1996). *Managing Cultural Differences.* Houston: Gulf.

12. Trompenaars, *Riding the Waves of Culture.*

13. Harris & Moran, *Managing Cultural Differences.*

14. Pew Global Attitudes Project. (2005, June 23). *American Character Gets Mixed Reviews: U.S. Image Up Slightly, but Still Negative: 16-Nation Pew Global Attitudes Survey.* Washington, DC: Pew Research Center. Available from http://pewglobal.org/files/pdf/247.pdf.

15. Ibid.

16. Ibid.

17. Trompenaars, *Riding the Waves of Culture.*

18. Axtell, R. E. (Ed.). (1993). *Do's and Taboos Around the World: A Guide to International Behavior.* New York: Wiley.

19. Ibid.

20. Morris, M. W., Williams, K. Y., Leung, K., Larrick, R., Mendoza, M. T., Bhatnagar, D., et al. (1998). Conflict Management Style: Accounting for Cross-National Differences. *Journal of International Business Studies, 29,* 729–748.

21. Some of these examples are from Axtell, R. E. (1993). *Gestures: The Do's and Taboos of Body Language Around the World.* New York: Wiley.

22. Trompenaars, *Riding the Waves of Culture.*

23. Adler, N. J. (1993). Competitive Frontiers: Women Managers in the Triad. *International Studies of Management and Organization, 23,* 3–24.

24. U.S. Department of State. (2007). *Background Notes: Japan.* Washington, DC: Bureau of East Asian and Pacific Affairs.

25. Grainger, R. J., & Miyamoto, T. (2003). Human Values and HRM Practice: The Japanese Shukko System. *Journal of Human Values, 9,* 105–115.

26. Dore, R. (2004). *Japanese Style Management: Has it Survived? Will it Survive?* Research Institute of Economy, Trade, and Industry IAA. http://www.rieti.go.jp/en/events/bbl/04090801.html.

27. Brown, W. S., Lubove, R. E., & Kwalwasser, J. (1994). Karoshi: Alternative Perspectives of Japanese Management Styles. *Business Horizons, 37,* 58–61.

28. Bolda, R. A. (1990). Correlates of Personal Productivity of Supervisors: Perceptions of American and Japanese Managers. *Current Psychology, 9,* 339–346.

29. Abramson, N. R., Lane, H. W., Nagai, H., & Takagi, H. (1993). A Comparison of Canadian and Japanese Cognitive Styles: Implications for Management Interaction. *Journal of International Business Studies, 24,* 575–588.

30. Brett, J. M., & Okumura, T. (1998). Inter- and Intracultural Negotiation: U.S. and Japanese Negotiators. *Academy of Management Journal, 41,* 495–510.

31. Rao, A., Hashimoto, K., & Rao, A. (1997). Universal and Culturally Specific Aspects of Influence: A Study of Japanese Managers. *The Leadership Quarterly, 8,* 295–313.

32. William Drake & Associates. (1997). *Japanese and Americans: Sources of Mutual Misunderstandings.* Available from www.culturebank.com/jpn027.html; William Drake & Associates. (1997). *The Japanese Seniority System.* Available from www.culturebank.com/jpn043 .html.

33. Central Intelligence Agency. (2011). *The World Factbook: Germany.*

34. William Drake & Associates. (1997). *Managing Business Relationships in Germany.* Available from www .culturebank.com/demo/demogermany/sld001.htm.

35. Glunk, U., Wilderom, C., & Ogilvie, R. (1996). Finding the Key to German-Style Management. *International Studies of Management and Organization, 26,* 93–108.

36. Hall, E. T., & Hall, M. R. (1990). *Understanding Cultural Differences.* Yarmouth, ME: Intercultural Press.

37. Ibid.

38. German Lessons. (1996). *The Economist, 340,* 59.

39. Ibid.; Drake & Associates, *Managing Business Relationships in Germany.*

40. Lewis, R. D. (1997). *When Cultures Collide.* London: Nicholas Brealey, p. 212.

41. U.S. Census Bureau: Foreign Trade Statistics, 2011; U.S. Central Intelligence Agency. (2011). *The World Factbook: Mexico.*

42. Pelled, L. H., & Xin, K. R. (1997). Work Values and the Human Resource Management Implications: A Theoretical Comparison of China, Mexico, and the United States. *Journal of Applied Management Studies, 6,* 185–199; Schuler, R. S., Jackson, S. E., Jackofsky, E., & Slocum, J. W. (1996). Managing Human Resources in Mexico: A Cultural Understanding. *Business Horizons, 39,* 55–62.

43. Crouch, E. C. (2004). *Mexicans and Americans: Cracking the Cultural Code.* Yarmouth, ME: Intercultural Press; Pelled & Xin, Work Values and the Human Resource Management Implications.

44. Ibid.; De Forest, M. E. (1998). Hecho en Mexico: Tips for Success. *Apparel Industry, 59,* 98–104; Schuler et al., Managing Human Resources in Mexico.

45. Ibid.; Crouch, *Mexicans and Americans: Cracking the Cultural Code.*

46. De Forest, Hecho en Mexico; Schuler et al., Managing Human Resources in Mexico.

47. De Forest, Hecho en Mexico.

48. Hamlin, K., & Yanping, L. (2010, August 16). China Overtakes Japan as World's Second-Biggest Economy. *Bloomberg News.* http://www.bloomberg.com/news/ 2010–08–16/china-economy-passes-japan-s-in-second-quarter-capping-three-decade-rise.html.

49. *Doing Business 2011: Making a Difference for Entrepreneurs.* (2011). The World Bank. Retrieved February 19, 2011, from http://www.doingbusiness.org/data/exploreeco nomies/china/.

50. Laroche, L. (2003). *Managing Cultural Diversity in Technical Professions.* Amsterdam: Butterworth-Heinemann.

51. Tang, J., & Ward, A. (2003). *The Changing Face of Chinese Management.* New York: Routledge.

52. Ibid.

53. Chen, P. P. W. (2004, July 30). China Business Etiquette: Gift Giving. *Executive Planet.*

54. Jreisat, J. E. (1992). Managing National Development in the Arab States. *Arab Studies Quarterly, 14,* 1–17.

55. Jreisat, Managing National Development in the Arab States; Wetzel, H. (2004). *Egypt Country Commercial Guide FY 2004.* Washington, DC: U.S. Department of State.

56. Ali, A. J. (1993). Decision-Making Style, Individualism, and Attitudes Toward Risk of Arab Executives. *International Studies of Management and Organization, 23,* 53–74; Ali, A. J. (1995). Cultural Discontinuity and Arab Management Thought. *International Studies of Management and Organization, 25,* 7–31.

57. U.S. Census Bureau. (2008, March). *Foreign Trade Statistics: Trade in Goods (Imports, Exports, and Trade Balance) With Kuwait;* U.S. Census Bureau. (2008, March). *Foreign Trade Statistics: Trade in Goods (Imports, Exports, and Trade Balance) With Qatar;* U.S. Census Bureau. (2008, March). *Foreign Trade Statistics: Trade in Goods (Imports, Exports, and Trade Balance) With Saudi.*

58. *Arab Names.* www.arab.net/arabnames.

59. This dialogue is adapted from a scene in Copeland, L. (Producer). (1983). *Managing the Overseas Assignment* [Motion picture]. San Francisco: Copeland Griggs.

60. Ali, Cultural Discontinuity and Arab Management Thought; Decision-Making Style, Individualism, and Attitudes Toward Risk of Arab Executives.

61. Ibid.

62. This figure is adapted from Harris & Moran, *Managing Cultural Differences,* and Lewis, *When Cultures Collide.*

Acculturation, Culture Shock, and Intercultural Competence

After reading this chapter, you should be able to

1. define acculturation,

2. identify and discuss the factors that facilitate or hinder acculturation,

3. define and name the stages of culture shock,

4. recognize and discuss the causes of culture shock,

5. assess your level of culture shock,

6. identify and discuss the four components of intercultural communication competence, and

7. assess your intercultural willingness to communicate.

Nothing so sensitizes us to our own culture as living outside it and then trying to return.

—John Condon and Fathi Yousef[1]

———

Having read the previous 11 chapters of this book, you may well be motivated to go out and interact with people from different cultures. Perhaps you are even ready to travel abroad! In either case, remember that intercultural communication assumes the principle of difference. Not all intercultural communication is successful. This chapter focuses on three important features associated with intercultural communication as they relate to traveling abroad to foreign cultures: (a) acculturation, (b) culture shock, and (c) intercultural communication competence. **Acculturation** is the process whereby you adapt to a new culture by adopting its values, attitudes, and practices. **Culture shock** is a multifaceted experience resulting from the stress associated with entering a new culture. **Intercultural communication competence** is defined as the degree to which you effectively adapt your verbal and nonverbal messages to the appropriate cultural context. When you communicate with someone from a different culture, you will have to adjust and modify the kinds of verbal and nonverbal messages you send. This process requires that you have some *knowledge* about the person with whom you are communicating, that you are *motivated* to communicate with him or her, and that you have the appropriate verbal and nonverbal *skills* in order to encode and decode messages. Each of these variables affects the success rate of your intercultural communication experiences. When individuals or groups of individuals enter a new culture, they are faced with a different set of values, different behavioral patterns, and a different verbal and nonverbal communication system. In most (perhaps all) cases, such people are affected by their new cultural surroundings.

ACCULTURATION

Acculturation is the term used to describe what happens when people from one culture enter a different culture. Many years ago, acculturation was defined by Redfield, Linton, and Herskovits as "those phenomena which result when groups of individuals having different cultures come into continuous first-hand contact with subsequent changes in the original culture pattern of either or both groups."[2] John Berry, well known for his work on acculturation, argues that in practice, when two different cultural groups engage in continuous contact, one of the two groups will induce more change than the other. For example, when immigrants enter the United States, they are probably going to experience more change than the people already living here. Berry also distinguishes between acculturation at the group level and at the individual level. He contends that the distinction is important because not all members of the group experience the same levels of acculturation.[3]

According to Berry, in pluralistic, diverse societies such as that of the United States, there are three factors that bring cultural groups together: mobility, voluntariness, and permanence. For example, regarding mobility, some groups experience acculturation because they have moved into a new culture—as is the case for immigrants and refugees such as the Hmong people of Laos, who came to the United States. Other groups experience acculturation because they have had a new culture thrust on them, as is the case for indigenous peoples such as Native Americans. Some groups enter acculturation voluntarily, such as Mexican immigrants entering the United States, whereas others experience acculturation involuntarily, as did African slaves brought to the United States. Finally, some groups will experience a relatively permanent acculturation change, as African Americans and Mexican Americans have, whereas others face only temporary acculturation, as do exchange students studying abroad or expatriates in temporary job transfers. Berry maintains that despite the sometimes dramatic differences in the circumstances of acculturating groups, the overall acculturation process is universal across groups.[4]

Acculturative Stress

Most people experience a degree of stress and strain when they enter a culture different from their own. Acculturation is often marked by physical and psychological changes that occur as a result of the adaptation required to function in a new and different cultural context. People adapting to new cultures face changes in their diet, climate, housing, communication, role prescriptions, and media consumption as well as the myriad rules, norms, and values of a new and (relatively) dissimilar culture. Moreover, such persons are isolated from familiar social networks and may experience problems with language, unemployment, and discrimination. The stress associated with such changes, known as **acculturative stress**, is marked by a reduction in one's physical and mental health.[5]

Many immigrant groups in the United States experience acculturative stress. A rather substantial body of research has documented the effects of acculturative stress on America's largest microcultural group, Hispanics. Miranda and Matheny point out that among Hispanics, acculturative stress is related to decreased self-efficacy expectations, decreased career aspirations, depression, and suicidal ideation (especially in Hispanic adolescents).[6] In their work with Hispanics, Julie and David Smart have observed that acculturative stress is associated with fatalistic thinking. Smart and Smart argue that acculturative stress has a lifelong effect on Hispanics' psychological well-being, decision-making abilities, occupational effectiveness, and physical health. Smart and Smart contend that for Hispanic immigrants, the most significant aspect of acculturative stress is the loss of social support from the family. They maintain that this loss is particularly intense for Hispanics because of their collectivistic orientation. In fact, Hispanic women may be more likely than men to suffer from acculturative stress because in their native culture, their roles are clearly prescribed. In the United States, an individualistic, equality-based society, women's roles are more open and unspecified.[7] Hovey, in his work, found that family dysfunction, separation from family, negative expectations for the future, and low income levels were significantly related to higher levels of acculturative stress.[8]

In an interesting line of research, Nwadiora and McAdoo investigated acculturative stress among Amerasian refugees in the United States. Amerasians are individuals born of American servicemen and Vietnamese or Cambodian women during the Vietnam War. Because of their mixed racial background, these children were considered half-breeds and social outcasts in their homeland. In 1987, Congress passed the Amerasian Homecoming Act, permitting all Amerasians and their immediate families (including wives, half-siblings, and mothers) to immigrate to the United States. Nwadiora and McAdoo report that Amerasians have faced pervasive prejudice in the United States, often by Asians, Europeans, and especially African Americans. In their research, they found that the Amerasians experienced acculturative stress in the areas of spoken English, employment, and limited formal education. They also report that gender and race had no significant impact on acculturative stress.[9]

In addition to the above factors, Berry argues that the degree of acculturative stress experienced by people adapting to new cultures varies according to the similarities and dissimilarities between the host culture and the native culture of the immigrants. To the extent that the cultures are more similar than different, less stress is experienced. Individual personal traits also play a role in the manifestation of acculturative stress. Berry notes that such characteristics as the amount of exposure one has had to the new culture; one's level of education; one's sex, age, language, race, and income; and one's psychological and spiritual strength all affect acculturative stress.[10] A well-educated woman from the United States may experience more acculturative stress than a well-educated man from the United States when entering a culture that does not recognize sexual equality (either socially or legally).

A MODEL OF ACCULTURATION

Acculturation is not unilateral; it is an interactive process between a culture and groups of people. When individuals or groups of individuals enter a new culture, they are often changed by the culture, but they also have an impact on the culture in return. For example, although Mexican immigrants face challenges imposed on them by the dominant culture, their presence has changed the United States' cultural milieu, especially in places such as Texas and California. Young Kim's model of cultural adaptation takes into account both individual and cultural factors that affect acculturation. Kim argues that acculturation is not a linear, one-way process; rather, there is an interaction between the stranger and the host culture. Kim argues that the role of communication, the role of the host environment, and the role of predisposition best explain the acculturation process.[11]

Factors Affecting Cultural Adaptation and Acculturation

Communication	Environment	Predisposition
Personal communication	Host receptivity	Preparedness
Social communication	Host conformity pressure	Ethnicity
Ethnic group strength	Personality	

In terms of the role of communication, personal communication refers to the individual's host communication competence—that is, the degree to which the newcomer can encode and decode verbal and nonverbal messages within the host environment. Kim argues that natives acquire this competence early in life, so it comes to them automatically. Host communication competence also refers to the degree to which the newcomer understands the host language's rules and norms, understands effective and appropriate conflict resolution strategies, and is motivated to initiate and develop host culture relationships. Social communication refers to the actual interaction between the newcomer and host persons. Participating in relationships, engaging in conflict resolution, and exposing oneself to the mass communication of the host culture can enhance and facilitate the acculturation process.[12]

Kim argues that the environment plays a key role in the acculturation process. The degree to which the host culture is receptive to strangers is important. Certain factions in the United States, for example, believe the country should close its borders to immigrants. Given the tensions in the Middle East, Americans sometimes face hostilities when they enter certain countries. Host conformity pressure is another factor. The extent to which natives within the host culture exert pressure on newcomers to conform to their culture's values, beliefs, and practices can facilitate or alienate the newcomers. In the United States, for example, people expect that newcomers will speak English. In fact, some members of the U.S. Congress have introduced legislation that would make English the official language of the United States. Ethnic group strength refers to the amount of influence the newcomer's group wields in the host culture. Clearly, some ethnic groups are more powerful politically, economically, and socially than others. Because of their numbers, Blacks and Hispanics have become powerful ethnic groups in the United States. Kim notes that as ethnic group strength increases, members of the ethnic group may encourage newcomers to maintain their native ethnic heritage and pressure them not to conform to the host culture. Hence, newcomers may feel pressure from the host culture to adapt while simultaneously facing pressure from their native ethnic group to preserve their ethnic heritage.[13]

Predisposition factors also affect acculturation. Kim argues that newcomers enter into their new culture with varying degrees of readiness. How much people know about their new culture, their ability to speak the language, the probability of employment, and their understanding of the cultural institutions will have a dramatic effect on their acculturation process. Newcomers' ethnicity will also play a role in the pace of their acculturation.

Kim uses the term *ethnicity* to refer to the inherited characteristics that newcomers have as members of distinct ethnic groups. Such characteristics include race and language. For example, because of their ethnicity, Japanese may have a more difficult time acculturating to the United States than would a person from Great Britain. Finally, Kim argues that there are certain personality characteristics that affect the individual's acculturation process. Age, for example, has been shown to affect acculturation. Generally, young persons adapt more quickly to new and different modes of behavior than do older persons, who may be set in their ways. Karmela Liebkind found that among Vietnamese refugees in Finland, younger generations maintained much more positive attitudes about acculturation than did older generations. Liebkind explains that the Finnish values and practices of gender equality and egalitarian parent/child relationships contrasted sharply with Southeast Asian values of hierarchical familial relationships and filial piety. In the traditional Southeast Asian family, children are taught to be loyal. They are obligated to show respect and obedience to their parents. Wives are expected to rear the children and serve their husbands. Not having been completely enculturated into Vietnamese society, the younger generations of the refugee Vietnamese families found it much easier than did their parents to acculturate into Finnish society.[14]

Modes of Acculturation

In order for acculturation to occur, there must be contact between the members of the host culture and the newcomers. Berry argues that such contact needs to be continuous and direct. He maintains that short-term accidental contact does not generally lead to much acculturation. Moreover, the purpose of contact between the two groups is an important consideration. Berry points out that acculturation effects may vary according to whether the purpose of contact is colonization, enslavement, trade, military control, evangelization, or education. The length of contact is also a factor, as are the social or political policies of the mainstream culture as they relate to the immigrant group (i.e., political representation, citizenship criteria, language requirements, employment opportunities, and so forth).[15]

Berry points out that an individual's level of acculturation depends in part on two independent processes: the degree to which the person approaches or avoids interaction with the host culture (i.e., out-group contact and relations) and the degree to which the individual maintains or relinquishes his or her native culture's attributes (i.e., in-group identity and maintenance). On the basis of these two factors, Berry has identified four modes of acculturation: (a) *assimilation,* (b) *integration,* (c) *separation,* and (d) *marginalization* (see Figure 12.1).

To the extent that the individual desires contact with the host culture (and the various microcultures) while not necessarily maintaining an identity with his or her native culture, **assimilation** occurs. According to Hardin Coleman, the individual loses his or her original cultural identity as he or she acquires a new identity in the host culture. During assimilation, the individual takes on the behaviors and language habits and practices the basic rules and norms of the host culture. There is an ongoing effort to approach the dominant culture while discontinuing the values, beliefs, and behaviors associated with the native culture. Coleman argues that the defining property of the assimilation mode is that the individual endeavors to acquire the values and beliefs of a single cultural group with the ultimate goal of becoming indistinguishable from other members of the host culture. The individual will seek interaction with members of the host culture and build social networks with them.[16]

| Figure 12.1 | Modes of Acculturation |

On the other hand, some people desire a high level of interaction with the host culture while maintaining identity with their native culture. This kind of acculturation is called **integration**. In this mode, the individual develops a kind of bicultural orientation that successfully blends and synthesizes cultural dimensions from both groups while maintaining an identity in each group. Coleman maintains that people practicing this mode of acculturation take part in activities that allow individuals from different groups to interact without the obstacle of social hierarchies. Presumably, integration is associated with less acculturative stress and conflict. To be sure, an individual's successful integration of cultural skills and norms does not mean that the person relinquishes his or her native cultural identity. In fact, Coleman contends that it is the development of the bicultural identity that leads to a successful life in a bicultural context. In other models of acculturation, this mode is called *pluralism* or *multiculturalism*. This mode of acculturation guides many of the social and legislative efforts in the United States' educational and affirmative action statutes.[17]

When individuals prefer low levels of interaction with the host culture and associated microcultural groups while desiring a close connection with, and reaffirmation of, their native culture, the mode of acculturation is called *separation*. Here, the individual resists acculturation with the dominant culture and chooses not to identify with the host cultural group. At the same time, the person retains his or her native cultural identity. Coleman argues that people choosing separation may harbor animosity toward the host culture as a result of social or historical factors. Such persons generally focus on the perceived incompatibility between their native culture and the host culture. Although the values and beliefs of the host culture are eschewed, the individual may take on selected behaviors of the host culture for purely functional reasons (e.g., to get a job). Coleman suggests that separated persons communicate almost exclusively with their own group while actively avoiding participation in situations with members of the host culture. Some African Americans and Native Americans, for example, prefer not to identify with the dominant White culture because of past racism and the country's history of slavery. In some models, the separation mode is labeled *segregation*.[18]

The fourth type of acculturation is *marginalization*. Marginalization occurs when the individual chooses not to identify with his or her native culture or with the host culture. In many instances, marginalized people give up their native culture only to find that they are not accepted by the host culture, to which they would choose to acculturate if given the opportunity. These persons experience alienation from both cultures. Often, they feel a sense of abandonment. Dysfunctional behaviors (e.g., alcoholism or drug abuse) are often seen in marginalized people. African Americans, Asian Americans, and Hispanic Americans often feel marginalized in U.S. culture. Acculturative stress is often found among marginalized groups.[19]

Another possible acculturation mode, articulated by Richard Mendoza, is **cultural transmutation**. In this mode, the individual chooses to identify with a third cultural group (microculture) that materializes out of the native and host cultural groups. For example, a youth may choose to join a gang or some other kind of microcultural outlet. Although similar to separation, cultural transmutation is different in that a new cultural identity is created. In other models of acculturation, this is called *fusion*. Gay and lesbian groups are a good example of the cultural transmutation mode of acculturation. In this mode, individuals have left their native heterosexual groups and have immigrated into homosexual contexts. Religious groups are another example of acculturative transmutation. Many religious communities merge the values, beliefs, and behaviors of diverse religions into a new religion.[20]

ACCULTURATION IN THE UNITED STATES

The two largest ethnic populations in the United States are Hispanics and Blacks. For these groups, acculturation refers to the degree to which they participate in the cultural traditions, values, beliefs, and norms of the dominant White society, remain immersed in their own unique cultural customs and conventions, or participate in both. As Hope Landrine and

Elizabeth Klonoff comment, some microcultural groups remain highly traditional, whereas others are highly acculturated. Highly traditional Hispanics and Blacks differ significantly from Whites in a variety of values and behaviors, whereas highly acculturated Hispanics and Blacks do not (see Figure 12.2).[21]

Social scientists are beginning to understand that the degree of acculturation for microcultural groups within the United States is associated with a variety of social and medical problems, such as alcoholism, cigarette smoking, drug abuse, and HIV/AIDS-related knowledge, attitudes, and behaviors.[22] Moreover, microcultural group acculturation is associated with methods of conflict resolution (e.g., belligerent behaviors), willingness to use counseling, career development and work habits, and educational achievement (i.e., increased absences, lower grades). The more marginalized or segregated the group, the more likely they are to experience physical and mental health problems and the less likely they are to seek out appropriate avenues to handle them. Landrine and Klonoff maintain that ethnic differences observed in the United States might be better understood as degrees of acculturation. According to Landrine and Klonoff, understanding a microcultural group's level of acculturation has the potential to diminish racist beliefs about ethnic differences and to increase our knowledge of such differences as a symptom or an exhibition of culture.[23]

Figure 12.2   Hispanics are the largest ethnic population in the United States.

In an effort to better understand maladaptive attitudes and behaviors among the various microcultural groups in the United States, researchers have devoted considerable effort to assessing levels of acculturation. The Acculturation Rating Scale for Mexican Americans (ARSMA) was first published in 1980.[24] The scale was recently revised and is designed to assess Mexican American acculturation according to Berry's four modes of acculturation—namely, integration, assimilation, separation, and marginalization.[25] It is designed to be completed by persons of Mexican or Hispanic origin.

Acculturation Rating Scale for Mexican Americans II

Directions: In the blank space to the left of each item, place a number between 1 and 5 that best applies to you: 1 = not at all, 2 = very little or not very often, 3 = moderately, 4 = much or very often, and 5 = extremely often or almost always.

_____ 1. I speak Spanish.

_____ 2. I speak English.

_____ 3. I enjoy speaking Spanish.

_____ 4. I associate with Anglos.

_____ 5. I associate with Mexicans and/or Mexican Americans.

_____ 6. I enjoy listening to Spanish music.

_____ 7. I enjoy listening to English-language music.

_____ 8. I enjoy Spanish-language TV.

_____ 9. I enjoy English-language TV.

_____ 10. I enjoy English-language movies.

_____ 11. I enjoy Spanish-language movies.

_____ 12. I enjoy reading books in Spanish.

_____ 13. I enjoy reading books in English.

_____ 14. I write letters in Spanish.

_____ 15. I write letters in English.

_____ 16. My thinking is done in English.

_____ 17. My thinking is done in Spanish.

_____ 18. My contact with Mexico has been . . .

_____ 19. My contact with the U.S.A. has been . . .

(Continued)

(Continued)

_____ 20. My father identifies or identified himself as "Mexicano."

_____ 21. My mother identifies or identified herself as "Mexicana."

_____ 22. My friends while I was growing up were of Mexican origin.

_____ 23. My friends while I was growing up were of Anglo origin.

_____ 24. My family cooks Mexican food.

_____ 25. My friends now are of Anglo origin.

_____ 26. My friends now are of Mexican origin.

_____ 27. I like to identify myself as an Anglo.

_____ 28. I like to identify myself as a Mexican American.

_____ 29. I like to identify myself as a Mexican.

_____ 30. I like to identify myself as an American.

_____ 31. I have difficulty accepting some ideas held by Anglos.

_____ 32. I have difficulty accepting certain attitudes held by Anglos.

_____ 33. I have difficulty accepting some behaviors exhibited by Anglos.

_____ 34. I have difficulty accepting some values held by some Anglos.

_____ 35. I have difficulty accepting certain practices and customs commonly found in some Anglos.

_____ 36. I have, or think I would have, difficulty accepting Anglos as close personal friends.

_____ 37. I have difficulty accepting some ideas held by some Mexicans.

_____ 38. I have difficulty accepting certain attitudes held by Mexicans.

_____ 39. I have difficulty accepting some behaviors exhibited by Mexicans.

_____ 40. I have difficulty accepting some values held by some Mexicans.

_____ 41. I have difficulty accepting certain practices and customs commonly found in some Mexicans.

_____ 42. I have, or think I would have, difficulty accepting Mexicans as close personal friends.

_____ 43. I have difficulty accepting ideas held by some Mexican Americans.

_____ 44. I have difficulty accepting certain attitudes held by Mexican Americans.

_____ 45. I have difficulty accepting some behaviors exhibited by Mexican Americans.

_____ 46. I have difficulty accepting some values held by Mexican Americans.

_____ 47. I have difficulty accepting certain practices and customs commonly found in some Mexican Americans.

_____ 48. I have, or think I would have, difficulty accepting Mexican Americans as close personal friends.

Scoring:

1. Sum your responses to the following items: 2, 4, 7, 9, 10, 13, 15, 16, 19, 23, 25, 27, and 30. Divide the sum by 13. This is your Anglo Orientation Score (AOS).

2. Sum your responses to the following items: 1, 3, 5, 6, 8, 11, 12, 14, 17, 18, 20, 21, 22, 24, 26, 28, and 29. Divide the sum by 17. This is your Mexican Orientation Score (MOS).

3. Sum your responses to the following items: 31, 32, 33, 34, 35, and 36. This is your Anglo Marginality (ANGMAR).

4. Sum your responses to the following items: 37, 38, 39, 40, 41, and 42. This is your Mexican Marginality (MEXMAR).

5. Sum your responses to the following items: 43, 44, 45, 46, 47, and 48. This is your Mexican-American Marginality (MAMARG).

Acculturative Types Generated by ARSMA-II:

Traditional Mexican = MOS scores $\geq$ 3.7 and AOS scores $\leq$ 3.24.

Integrated = AOS $\geq$ 3.5 and MOS $\geq$ 2.8.

Marginal = ANGMAR $\geq$ 17.34, MEXMAR $\geq$ 17, and MAMARG $\geq$ 15.

Separation = MEXMAR $\leq$ 11, ANGMAR $\geq$ 15, and MAMARG $\geq$ 15.

Assimilated = MOS $\leq$ 2.4 and AOS $\geq$ 4.

Approximately 13% of the population in the United States is African American. As with other microcultural groups, some African Americans are more acculturated than others. Hope Landrine and Elizabeth Klonoff have developed an instrument designed to measure levels of African American acculturation. Landrine and Klonoff argue that within the microcultural context, acculturation refers to the degree to which microcultural groups (e.g., African Americans, Asian Americans, Native Americans) participate in the traditional values, beliefs, and practices of the dominant White culture, remain immersed in their own cultural traditions, or blend the two traditions.[26]

African Americans who complete the instrument are asked to indicate their preference for things identified as being African American, their religious beliefs and practices, and their experience with traditional African American foods and games, as well as any relevant childhood experiences, superstitions, interracial attitudes and cultural mistrust of the White majority, experiences with "falling out," adherence to Black family values, and family practices. This scale is designed for African Americans in the United States and is not applicable to other microcultural groups. The two scales discussed here are valid indices of acculturation for Hispanics and African Americans and indicate that cultural diversity can be measured reliably. Such measurements give us a better understanding of an individual's perceptual context. The more we know about a person's individual level of acculturation, the better able we are to provide culturally competent services to him or her.

African American Acculturation Scale

Directions: On a scale ranging from 1 to 7, indicate the extent to which you agree or disagree with the statement: 1 = totally disagree, 2 = disagree, 3 = slightly disagree, 4 = don't know, 5 = slightly agree, 6 = agree, and 7 = totally agree.

_____ 1. Most of the music I listen to is by Black artists.

_____ 2. I like Black music more than White music.

_____ 3. The person I admire most is Black.

_____ 4. I listen to Black radio stations.

_____ 5. I try to watch all the Black shows on TV.

_____ 6. Most of my friends are Black.

_____ 7. I believe in the Holy Ghost.

_____ 8. I believe in heaven and hell.

_____ 9. I like gospel music.

_____ 10. I am currently a member of a Black church.

_____ 11. Prayer can cure disease.

_____ 12. The church is the heart of the Black community.

_____ 13. I know how to cook chitlins.

_____ 14. I eat chitlins once in a while.

_____ 15. Sometimes I cook ham hocks.

_____ 16. I know how long you're supposed to cook collard greens.

_____ 17. I went to a mostly Black elementary school.

_____ 18. I went (or go) to a mostly Black high school.

_____ 19. I grew up in a mostly Black neighborhood.

_____ 20. I avoid splitting a pole.

_____ 21. When the palm of your hand itches, you'll receive some money.

_____ 22. There's some truth to many old superstitions.

_____ 23. IQ tests were set up purposefully to discriminate against Black people.

_____ 24. Most tests (such as the SAT and tests to get a job) are set up to make sure Blacks don't get high scores on them.

_____ 25. Deep in their hearts, most White people are racists.

_____ 26. I have seen people "fall out." I know what "falling out" means.

_____ 27. When I was a child, I used to play tonk. I know how to play bid whist.

_____ 28. It's better to move your whole family ahead in this world than it is to be out for only yourself.

_____ 29. Old people are wise.

_____ 30. When I was young, my parent(s) sent me to stay with a relative (aunt, uncle, grandmother) for a few days or weeks, and then I went back home again.

_____ 31. When I was young, I took a bath with my sister, brother, or some other relative.

Scoring: Sum your responses to the above 31 items. Your score must range between 33 and 231.

Scores 33–60 = Acculturated.

Scores 66–85 = Mostly acculturated.

Scores 99–130 = Bicultural (slightly acculturated).

Scores 165–185 = Bicultural (slightly traditional).

Scores 198–200 = Mostly traditional.

Scores 200–231 = Traditional.

SOURCE: The African American Acculturation Scale II, from H. Landrine & E. A. Klonoff. (1995). The African American Acculturation Scale II. *Journal of Black Psychology, 21*, 124–153. Copyright © 1995 Association of Black Psychologists. Used by permission of Sage Publications.

CULTURE SHOCK

When people move to a new culture, they take with them the values, beliefs, customs, and behaviors of their old culture. Often, depending on the degree of similarity between the old and the new culture, the values, beliefs, customs, and behaviors of the native culture clash with those of the new culture. This can result in disorientation, misunderstandings, conflict, stress, and anxiety. Researchers call this phenomenon *culture shock*. Winkelman defines culture shock as a multifaceted experience that results from the numerous stressors that occur when coming into contact with a different culture.[27] Anyone can experience culture shock, although some are more prone to it than others. Winkelman maintains that culture shock can occur with immigrant groups—such as foreign students and refugees, international business exchanges, Peace Corps volunteers, and social workers entering new communities during crises—as well as with members of microcultural groups within their own culture and society. Expatriate professors teaching abroad often describe their experiences using the term *education shock*.

Anthropologist Kalervo Oberg was the first to apply the term *culture shock* to the effects associated with the tension and anxiety of entering into a new culture combined with the sensations of loss, confusion, and powerlessness resulting from the forfeiture of cultural norms and social rituals.[28] Likewise, Winkelman points out that culture shock stems from the challenges associated with new cultural surroundings in addition to the loss of a familiar cultural environment.[29] Culture shock appears to be a psychological and social process that progresses in stages, usually lasting as long as a year. Most models of culture shock include four stages. The first model of culture shock, developed by Oberg nearly 50 years ago, incorporates a medical metaphor and terminology, beginning with the incubation stage, followed by crisis, leading to recovery, and finishing with full recovery.[30] Smalley's model begins with a fascination stage, and then moves through hostility, adjustment, and biculturalism. Richardson's four-stage model includes elation, depression, recovery, and acculturation. Kealey's model incorporates exploration, frustration, coping, and adjustment phases (see Table 12.1).[31]

Most models of culture shock describe the process curvilinearly, or by what Lysgaard called the "U-curve hypothesis."[32] Elaborating on the U curve, Professor Kim Zapf asserts that culture shock begins with feelings of optimism and even elation that eventually give way to frustration, tension, and anxiety as individuals are unable to interact effectively with their new environment. As they develop strategies for resolving conflict, people begin to restore their confidence and eventually recover and reach some level of acculturation.[33]

The initial stage of culture shock, usually called something like the *tourist stage* or *honeymoon stage,* is characterized by intense excitement and euphoria associated with being somewhere different and unusual (see Figure 12.3). Winkelman asserts that this stage is typical of that experienced by people who enter other cultures temporarily during honeymoons, vacations, or brief business trips.[34] The stresses associated with cultural differences are tolerated and may even seem fun and humorous. During the tourist phase, the newcomers' primary interaction with their new cultural environment is through major cultural institutions, such as museums, hotels, Western restaurants, and so forth.

Table 12.1 Culture Shock Models

Oberg (1954)	Smalley (1963)	Richardson (1974)	Kealey (1978)
1. Incubation	1. Fascination	1. Elation	1. Exploration
2. Crisis	2. Hostility	2. Depression	2. Frustration
3. Recovery	3. Adjustment	3. Recovery	3. Coping
4. Full recovery	4. Biculturalism	4. Acculturation	4. Adjustment

Figure 12.3 Stages of Culture Shock

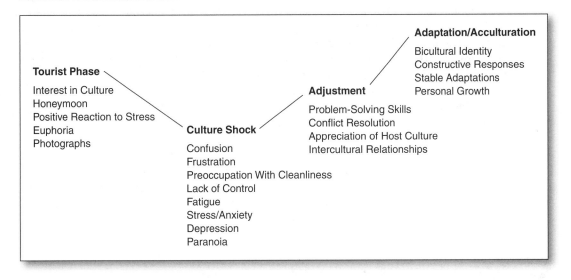

Tourist Phase

Interest in Culture
Honeymoon
Positive Reaction to Stress
Euphoria
Photographs

Culture Shock

Confusion
Frustration
Preoccupation With Cleanliness
Lack of Control
Fatigue
Stress/Anxiety
Depression
Paranoia

Adjustment

Problem-Solving Skills
Conflict Resolution
Appreciation of Host Culture
Intercultural Relationships

Adaptation/Acculturation

Bicultural Identity
Constructive Responses
Stable Adaptations
Personal Growth

This phase may last weeks or months but is temporary. In some instances, the tourist phase may be very short, as when newcomers are confronted with drastic changes in climate or hostile political environments. Eventually, the fun and excitement associated with the tourist phase give way to frustration and real stress, or active *culture shock*. Failure events once considered minor and funny are now perceived as stressful. Winkelman maintains that culture shock is partially based on the simultaneous effects of cognitive overload and behavioral inadequacy that are rooted in the psychological and physical stresses associated with confronting a new environment. The new environment requires a great deal of conscious energy that was not required in the old environment, which leads to cognitive overload and fatigue. People also experience role shock in that the behaviors associated with their role in their native culture may be dramatically different in the new culture. Finally, people may experience personal shock in the form of a loss of intimacy with interpersonal partners. In describing the second phase of culture shock, Winkelman notes,

> Things start to go wrong, minor issues become major problems, and cultural differences become irritating. Excessive preoccupation with cleanliness of food, drinking water, bedding, and surroundings begins. One experiences increasing disappointments, frustrations, impatience, and tension. Life does not make sense and one may feel helpless, confused, disliked by others, or treated like a child.[35]

Rhinesmith notes that during the culture shock phase, people feel helpless, isolated, and depressed. Paranoia—in which newcomers are convinced that their troubles are deliberate attempts by the natives to disrupt their lives—is also a typical response to culture shock. In this phase, people may develop irrational fears of being cheated, robbed, or even assaulted.[36] The degree to which one experiences culture shock varies from person to person. Walt Lonner has identified six factors that affect the nature of culture shock experienced: (a) control factors, (b) interpersonal factors, (c) organismic/biological factors, (d) intrapersonal factors, (e) spatial/temporal factors, and (f) geopolitical factors. Churchman and Mitrani have added three additional factors: (a) the degree of similarity between one's native and new culture, including the physical environment; (b) the degree and quality of information about the new environment; and (c) the host culture's attitude and policies toward immigrants (see Figure 12.4).[37]

Some people never recuperate from the crisis stage of culture shock and return home or isolate themselves from the host culture by restricting their interaction with it, such as by fostering only intracultural relationships (e.g., in a military base or university setting). When the lines of communication with the host culture are severed, there is little hope of acculturation or recovery from the crisis stage. The third phase of culture shock is typically called the **adjustment phase,** or reorientation phase. Here, people eventually realize that the problems associated with the host culture are due not to deliberate attempts by the natives but, rather, to a real difference in values, beliefs, and behaviors. At this stage, people actively seek

Figure 12.4   Factors That Affect Culture Shock

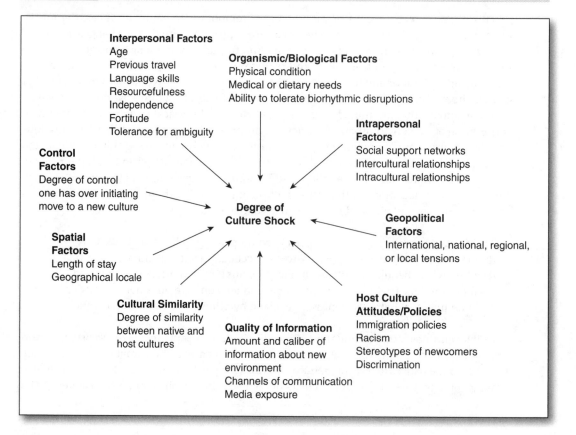

Interpersonal Factors
Age
Previous travel
Language skills
Resourcefulness
Independence
Fortitude
Tolerance for ambiguity

Organismic/Biological Factors
Physical condition
Medical or dietary needs
Ability to tolerate biorhythmic disruptions

Intrapersonal Factors
Social support networks
Intercultural relationships
Intracultural relationships

Control Factors
Degree of control one has over initiating move to a new culture

Degree of Culture Shock

Geopolitical Factors
International, national, regional, or local tensions

Spatial Factors
Length of stay
Geographical locale

Cultural Similarity
Degree of similarity between native and host cultures

Quality of Information
Amount and caliber of information about new environment
Channels of communication
Media exposure

Host Culture Attitudes/Policies
Immigration policies
Racism
Stereotypes of newcomers
Discrimination

out effective problem-solving and conflict resolution strategies. They begin to develop a positive attitude about solving their problems. As Winkelman notes, the host culture begins to make sense, and pessimistic reactions and responses to it are lessened as people recognize that their problems are due largely to their inability to understand, accept, and adapt.[38] Typically, the adjustment phase is gradual and slow, and often people relapse into mini-crisis stages. The final stage of culture shock is labeled the *adaptation* or *acculturation stage*. At this point, individuals actively engage the culture with their new problem-solving and conflict resolution tools with some degree of success.

Young Kim argues that to the extent that people acculturate to their new culture, they experience cultural transformation. They possess a degree of functional fitness in which the external demands of the host culture are met with appropriate and consistent internal responses. Moreover, they develop a level of competency in communicating with the natives. As a result of their successes, people also acquire psychological health, take on an intercultural identity, and foster a sense of integration with their host environment.[39]

STUDENT VOICES ACROSS CULTURES

Jessica Bahrke

When I moved to Madrid, I was on a high for about a month. Everything was new and exciting—the people, the food, the culture—everything different and exhilarating. During this time, I took every opportunity to visit sights, museums, experience the never-ending night life, and eat as many tapas as possible. This honeymoon period lasted for about 4 weeks before I really started to immerse myself in the Spanish culture. It took that long to realize that I was more or less living as a tourist on an extended vacation. It took about 4 weeks for the culture shock to sink in.

Before I left the States, I thought I had taken every preparation I could to prevent culture shock. I honestly thought that I had mentally prepared myself and would be able to avoid the vast majority of the common struggles people go through when entering a new culture. I still feel as though my preparation allowed me to handle the shock better, but I was not able to avoid it altogether. A simple trip to the grocery store would leave me frustrated and upset. How could a country possibly survive without cooking spray? And, more importantly, how was I to keep my eggs from sticking to the pan? Being from the dairy state of Wisconsin, I would gag at the thought of not refrigerating milk and eggs; however, no one seemed to be getting sick. There was no epidemic of salmonella going around Spain. After speaking with the locals and building up a lot of courage, I was eventually able to stomach these items.

Not only did the differences in food leave me with small, daily aggravations, simple greeting practices left me outside my comfort zone. Every time I would meet a new friend or acquaintance, I would extend my hand instinctually, expecting to feel a hand grip mine in return. Instead, I would be tugged into an unexpected embrace and kissed once on each cheek before I realized what was going on. It wasn't as if I was unaware that this was customary in Europe—of course I had read about this—but it always went against my nature to do it. Even though this introductory practice became commonplace, it never grew into a natural instinct during my time there.

W-Curve Models of Reentry Culture Shock

As mentioned above, most models of culture shock contain four phases in the U-curve tradition. But many people who have lived outside their native culture argue that they experience a kind of **reentry shock** when they return to their native culture. Furnham and Bochner's "W-curve" model of culture shock contains two U curves—the initial culture shock experienced when the traveler enters a new culture and a reentry shock U curve (see Figure 12.5). In other words, when people return home after an extended stay in a foreign culture, they experience another round of culture shock, this time in their native culture. Furnham and Bochner note that students returning from study abroad often report a reentry-shock phenomenon. Some students fear that they will be treated differently by their "stay-at-home" peers, friends, and parents when they return. In addition, because they have successfully acculturated themselves to a foreign culture, they essentially have to reacculturate to their native culture.[40] Students frequently report that the nature of long-term international travel transforms them. When they return home, they are different; they have taken on new perspectives and see the world with a different outlook. Students lament that communicating their experiences abroad to their friends and families at home is often difficult.

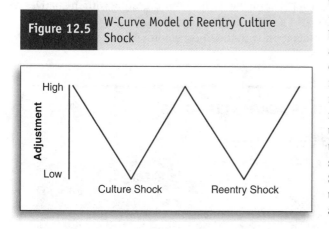

Figure 12.5 W-Curve Model of Reentry Culture Shock

Strategies for Managing Culture Shock

If you are traveling to a new culture for the first time, it is likely that you will experience some kind of culture shock. The level of intensity you experience will vary. In addition, the duration of your culture shock will depend on your ability to manage it. Probably the best piece of commonsense advice is to do your homework and be prepared. Successful management of culture shock depends on an awareness of its symptoms and the degree of its severity. Winkelman maintains that sometimes people falsely attribute their problems to sources other than culture shock. He argues that there is a tendency to deny that one is experiencing it. His advice is that one should accept the fact that virtually all atypical problems that occur during acculturation are caused by or exacerbated by culture shock.[41] Professor Kim Zapf has developed a questionnaire, called the Culture Shock Profile, designed to assess the intensity of culture shock you are experiencing. Please keep in mind that everyone experiences some degree of culture shock when entering a new culture for some length of time. Zapf recommends that the Culture Shock Profile be taken several times during the first year of your move—specifically, after the first month, sometime during about your fourth or fifth month, and then after one year. If managed appropriately, most culture shock is significantly reduced after a year.[42]

Self-Assessment 12.1

Culture Shock Profile

Directions: Below is a list of 33 terms that may or may not describe how you feel about your experiences in your new culture. On a scale of 0 to 3, indicate the frequency with which you experience the feeling: 0 = none, 1 = slight, 2 = moderate, and 3 = great.

I feel:

_____   1. Enthusiastic

_____   2. Impatient/irritable

_____   3. A desire to resign

_____   4. Happy/content

_____   5. Energetic

_____   6. Rejected

_____   7. Purposeful/directed

_____   8. Pessimistic/hopeless

_____   9. Contemptuous of others (natives)

_____ 10. Angry/resentful

_____ 11. A need to complain

_____ 12. Creative

_____ 13. Confident/self-assured

_____ 14. Ready to cry

_____ 15. Challenged

_____ 16. Cynical

_____ 17. A sense of discovery

_____ 18. Helpless/vulnerable

_____ 19. Optimistic/hopeful

_____ 20. Inadequate/self-doubt

_____ 21. Isolated/homesick

_____ 22. Physically ill

_____ 23. I need to "get out"

(Continued)

(Continued)

_____ 24. Confused/disoriented

_____ 25. Excited/stimulated

_____ 26. Accepted

_____ 27. A sense of loss

_____ 28. Overwhelmed/bewildered

_____ 29. Afraid/panic

_____ 30. Depressed/withdrawn

_____ 31. Frustrated/thwarted

_____ 32. Exhausted/sleep difficulty

_____ 33. Apathetic/"I don't care"

Scoring: To determine your level of culture shock, reverse your score for Items 1, 4, 5, 7, 12, 13, 17, 19, 25, and 26. If your original score was a 0, reverse it to a 3. If your original score was a 1, reverse it to a 2. If your original score was a 2, reverse it to a 1, and if your original score was a 3, reverse it to a 0. After reversing the scores for those 10 items, sum the entire 33 items. Scores must range from 0 to 99. The higher your score, the more culture shock you are experiencing, and the more you should engage in some of the strategies listed in this section.

SOURCE: Zapf, M. K. (1993). Remote Practice and Culture Shock: Social Workers Moving to Isolated Northern Regions. *Social Work, 38,* 694–705.

INTERCULTURAL COMMUNICATION COMPETENCE

One of the fundamental goals of this book is to help you become a competent intercultural communicator. *Intercultural communication competence* is defined as the degree to which you effectively adapt your verbal and nonverbal messages to the appropriate cultural context.[43] When you communicate with someone from a different culture, in order to be interculturally competent, you will have to adjust and modify the kinds of verbal and nonverbal messages you send. This process requires that you have some *knowledge* about the person with whom you are communicating, that you are *motivated* to communicate with him or her, and that you have the appropriate verbal and nonverbal *skills* in order to encode and decode messages.

Interculturally competent people successfully and effectively adapt their verbal and nonverbal messages to the appropriate cultural context. For the most part, competence is something that is perceived about another person, rather than something an individual inherently possesses. In other words, an individual may appear competent to one person but not to another. Moreover, intercultural competence varies from situation to situation. That is, a particular American may be quite competent while interacting with Chinese people and relatively incompetent when interacting with Germans. Verbal and nonverbal appropriateness and effectiveness are two important qualities of intercultural competence. According to Brian Spitzberg, appropriate behaviors conform to the rules, norms, and expectancies of the cultural context.[44] For example, when greeting a Japanese person in Japan, you are expected to bow. The rules associated with bowing are determined by one's status (e.g., age, sex, occupation, education). The person of lower status bows lower and longer than the person with higher status and typically does not make direct eye contact. Effective behaviors are those that successfully perform and accomplish the rules and norms.[45] For example, to the extent to which you are able to bow correctly, your behavior will be perceived as effective and competent. As we have seen throughout this book, the appropriateness and effectiveness of verbal and nonverbal messages varies considerably across cultures. Behaviors considered appropriate in one culture may not be wholly appropriate in another culture.

A MODEL OF INTERCULTURAL COMPETENCE

Brian Spitzberg and his colleague Bill Cupach argue that there are three necessary and interdependent ingredients of communication competence: (a) knowledge, (b) motivation, and (c) behavior.[46] The model of intercultural competence presented in this text includes these three dimensions along with a fourth component, situational features (see Figure 12.6). In this model, intercultural competence is the potential outcome of four interdependent components of the intercultural communication encounter. Each component influences and is influenced by the other three.

Figure 12.6   Model of Intercultural Competence

The Knowledge Component

The **knowledge component** of intercultural competence consists of how much one knows about the culture of the person with whom one is interacting. To the extent that people have knowledge about other cultures, they are more likely to be perceived as competent (although there is no guarantee!). Consider your own general cultural awareness. Below is a self-report instrument designed to assess your level of cultural awareness.[47]

Self-Assessment 12.2

Cross-Cultural Awareness

Directions: The scale consists of 15 items concerning what you know or don't know about other cultures.

Respond to each item on a scale of 1 to 5: 1 = definitely no, 2 = not likely, 3 = not sure, 4 = likely, and 5 = definitely yes. Be as honest with yourself as possible in completing the scale.

_____ 1. I can accurately list three countries that are considered collectivistic.

_____ 2. I can accurately identify three countries that have large power distance.

_____ 3. I can conduct business in a language other than my own.

_____ 4. I know the appropriate distance at which to stand when interacting with people in at least two other cultures.

_____ 5. I know the appropriate touch rules in at least two other cultures.

_____ 6. I know in what countries I can use first names when conducting business.

_____ 7. I can name the (political/governmental) leaders of four other countries.

_____ 8. I understand and can practice appropriate gift giving in three other countries.

_____ 9. I can identify some gestures appropriate in the U.S.A. that are considered obscene in other countries.

_____ 10. I understand sex-role differences in at least two other countries.

_____ 11. I can name three countries that are considered polychronic.

_____ 12. I understand the proper protocol for exchanging business cards in at least two other countries.

_____ 13. I understand the business philosophies of Japan and China.

_____ 14. I can name the United States' top three trading partners.

_____ 15. I can name the currencies in four other countries.

Scoring: Sum the 15 responses. Scores must range from 15 to 75. The higher your score, the more culturally aware you are. Scores at or above 50 indicate a relatively healthy degree of cultural awareness.

In order to be perceived as culturally knowledgeable, minimally, one should have some comprehension of the other person's dominant cultural values and beliefs. In addition, one should know whether the person is from an individualistic or collectivistic, high- or low-context, large or small power distance, and high or low uncertainty avoidance culture. In the model of intercultural competence, *verbal and nonverbal scripts* are also a part of the knowledge component. Communication theorist Charles Berger argues that verbal and nonverbal scripts (or plans) guide communication action. Scripts are like blueprints for communication that provide people with expectations about future communicative encounters with others. Berger and Jordan have argued that knowledgeable communicators develop and maintain a repertoire of scripts that enable them to comprehend and predict their actions and the actions of others. Berger and Jordan have demonstrated that people store scripts in long-term memory. According to Berger and Jordan, when anticipating interaction with others, communicators establish goals. They search their long-term memory for instances when they have tried to accomplish similar goals and then access a script or plan that was successful in achieving those goals in the past. The frequency and similarity with which a particular script has been used facilitates access to it. In never-before-encountered situations, people may possess vicariously based scripts. Perhaps one has witnessed a similar event by watching a film or by reading a comparable account.[48] The more plans one has, the better equipped one is to enact them.

Cognitive simplicity and rigidity refers to the degree to which individuals process information about persons from different cultures in a simplistic and rigid manner. Young Kim includes this dimension in her model of intercultural conflict. According to Kim, people with simplistic and rigid cognitive systems tend to engage in gross stereotyping. Moreover, such individuals may have narrowly defined and inflexible categories. Narrow categorizers tend to make more negative and more confident judgments about other people, particularly those from other cultures. Such persons probably think dogmatically (i.e., are narrow-minded). Metaphorically, a person with a simple and rigid cognitive system sees the world with blinders on, like a racehorse. Obviously, the competent communicator would possess an open and flexible cognitive system. The person with a simple and rigid system would not be perceived as competent.[49]

As discussed in Chapter 5, *ethnocentrism* is the extent to which one perceives one's own group as the center of everything and judges other groups with reference to it. Ethnocentrics tend to create and reinforce negative attitudes and behaviors toward out-groups. Judgments about in-groups and out-groups almost always are biased in favor of the in-group at the expense of the out-group. Furthermore, ethnocentric groups see themselves as righteous and exceptional and view their own standards as universal and moral. Out-groups are seen as immoral, subordinate, and impotent. Ethnocentrism is clearly an obstacle to intercultural communication competence. The ethnocentric person most likely possesses narrow categories and a simple and rigid cognitive system.[50] In his research, Rich Wiseman found that ethnocentrism was the strongest predictor of general cultural understanding. That is, higher levels of ethnocentrism were associated with less general cultural understanding. Higher levels of ethnocentrism were also related to less positive regard for other cultures.[51]

The Affective Component

The **affective component** of intercultural communication is the degree to which one approaches or avoids intercultural communication—that is, one's level of motivation to interact with others from different cultures. A central feature here is intercultural communication apprehension (ICA). ICA is defined by Neuliep and McCroskey as the fear or anxiety associated with either real or anticipated interaction with persons from different cultures.

Persons high in ICA tend to avoid interacting with others from different cultures.[52] As mentioned in Chapter 1, because they are seen as strangers, people from different cultures may seem unusual and novel. This difference can create tension and anxiety, which, in turn, can lead to avoidance. On the other hand, some people may be positively predisposed to initiate intercultural interactions even when they are completely free to choose whether or not to communicate. This predisposition, labeled by Jeffrey Kassing, is called **intercultural willingness to communicate**.[53] You can assess your individual level of intercultural willingness to communicate by completing the Intercultural Willingness to Communicate Scale.

Self-Assessment 12.3

Intercultural Willingness to Communicate Scale

Directions: Below are six situations in which a person might choose to communicate or not to communicate. Assume that you have completely free choice. Indicate the percentage of times you would choose to communicate in each type of situation. Keep in mind that you are reporting not the likelihood that you would have an opportunity to talk in these instances but, rather, the percentage of times you would talk when the opportunity presented itself. Indicate in the space to the left what percentage of time you would choose to communicate: 0 = never, 100 = always.

_____ 1. Talk with someone I perceive to be different from me

_____ 2. Talk with someone from another country

_____ 3. Talk with someone from a culture I know very little about

_____ 4. Talk with someone from a different race than mine

_____ 5. Talk with someone from a different culture

_____ 6. Talk with someone who speaks English as a second language

Scoring: Your score must range from 0 to 600. Scores below 300 indicate a general unwillingness to communicate interculturally. Scores above 350 indicate a slight willingness to communicate interculturally. Scores above 400 indicate a moderate level, and scores above 500 indicate a high willingness to communicate interculturally.

SOURCE: Adapted from Kassing, J. W. (1997). Development of the Intercultural Willingness to Communicate Scale. *Communication Research Reports, 14,* 399–407.

Young Kim has argued that one's ability to cope with stress also affects one's approach–avoidance tendencies. Because of the potentially inordinate uncertainty of intercultural communication, anxiety levels may be high as well, leading to increased stress. Some people handle stress well, whereas others do not. Gudykunst and Kim maintain that to be an effective intercultural communicator, one needs to tolerate ambiguity to a certain degree. The more that one is able to manage stress and endure ambivalence, the more likely one is to initiate intercultural communication and to be an effective and competent intercultural communicator.[54] The knowledge component and the affective component of intercultural competence are interdependent in that the more knowledge one has, the more likely one is to approach situations involving intercultural communication. The increase in knowledge generally leads to an increase in motivation. Likewise, the more motivation one has, the more likely one is to pursue interaction with people from different cultures, thereby learning more about them and their culture and increasing one's knowledge.

The Psychomotor Component

The **psychomotor component** of intercultural communication is the actual enactment of the knowledge and affective components. The elements of the psychomotor component are (a) verbal and nonverbal performance and (b) role enactment.[55] Verbal performance is how people use language. A person may know a great deal about the language of the host culture but not be able to engage in a conversation. Many foreign exchange students in the United States come here not to learn more about English but to practice using it in actual conversations. An American student who recently returned from a year's stay in Japan reported that she had been paid handsomely for hourly conversations with Japanese. People would come to her apartment and pay her simply to converse in English about trivial subjects for 60 minutes. These Japanese had all the knowledge they needed about English but wanted to sharpen their performance skills. Knowing and being able to use a second language certainly increases one's perceived competence when interacting interculturally. Language scripts and plans that reduce uncertainty are of particular importance. The psychomotor function is where one puts the scripts and plans into action. If one does not speak the language of the host culture, then at the very least, one should know some of the basic greetings, requests, and routines used frequently in that language.

Nonverbal performance is also an important part of the psychomotor component. Here, the individual needs to pay close attention to the nuances of the kinesic, paralinguistic, haptic, olfactic, and proxemic codes of the other culture. As with verbal knowledge and performance, one may have knowledge of a particular culture's nonverbal mannerisms but may not be able to execute them. Hence, before traveling to a foreign country, it might be wise to polish and refine your repertoire of nonverbal skills. For example, before traveling to Japan, you might practice bowing with family members or friends. Keep in mind also that how you smell will affect how others perceive you. Many cultures feel that Americans smell antiseptic because of our frequent use of soaps, perfumes, and so forth. As mentioned in Chapter 8, we have a tendency to mask the natural odor of the human body, and this custom seems strange to many other cultures.

Role enactment refers to how well one executes the appropriate verbal and nonverbal messages according to one's relative position and role in the host culture.[56] The behaviors that professors in the United States enact in the classroom may be misinterpreted or seen as improper in classrooms in other cultures. Managers must be particularly careful about the types of strategies they employ across cultures. Men and women should know how their sex roles vary across cultures. American women returning from abroad frequently comment on how badly they were treated. The freedoms U.S. women have gained throughout this century are not shared by women across the globe. A female student who had recently returned from a semester of study in southern Italy recounted her experience:

> I couldn't believe how the men acted toward me and my friends. When we would walk through town, they would whistle and hiss at us. They would try to touch us and acted like all we wanted to do was sleep with them. It was simply expected. Everyone told us that this was how they treated women and to just get used to it.

As we have seen throughout this text, the verbal and nonverbal behaviors expected for certain sex and occupation roles vary considerably across cultures. In particular, understanding these two role positions is key to becoming interculturally competent.

Situational Features

The fourth component of intercultural competence is the actual situation in which intercultural communication occurs. Remember that a person may be perceived as competent in one situation and not in another. Perceived competence varies with the situation. Some of the **situational features** that may affect competence include, but are not limited to, the *environmental context, previous contact, status differential,* and *third-party interventions.* Recall from Chapter 4 the influence of the environment on communication. Some situations may have higher information loads than others, which may affect your motivation and ability to enact appropriate verbal and nonverbal behaviors. Highly loaded situations may increase anxiety and reduce your motivation to approach another. In addition, you should have some knowledge of the host culture's perception of time and space. If you are lucky enough to be invited into someone's home, keep in mind that the use of space in homes varies dramatically across cultures. In some of her work, Young Kim discusses the importance of previous contact and status differences.[57]

Because of the dynamic nature of competence, any previous contact you may have had with a person from another culture may enhance your perception of competence. Competence and trust take time to establish and build, and your competence will grow as you interact more with the people of your host culture. Conversations with persons from other cultures provide a particularly rich source of data for you. The more contact you can have with these people, the more likely you are to learn about them (knowledge) and feel comfortable (affective) interacting with them, thus enabling you to master your verbal and nonverbal skills (psychomotor).

Although you may have sufficient knowledge about another culture and be motivated to interact, status differences may require you to take on multiple modes of behavior. Certain verbal and nonverbal strategies may be more or less appropriate depending on whether you are interacting with someone of lower, equal, or higher status. In the United States, we have a tendency to minimize status differences. In other cultures, as we learned in Chapter 2, one's status determines the order of speakers and the types of codes to use in a given situation. Because your status may be high in one situation and low in another, you should be mindful of how the communication will vary accordingly.[58]

The addition of a third party may noticeably change the dynamics of the situation and, hence, your competence. All of a sudden, your status may go up or down, as might the status of the person with whom you are interacting. The sex of the third party may also alter the situational features. Topics that were just a moment ago appropriate may now be unfit for discussion. The competent communicator keeps a sharp eye on the changing characteristics of the situation and adapts his or her verbal and nonverbal communication accordingly. The model of intercultural competence provided in Figure 12.6 depicts the knowledge, affective, psycho-motor, and situational features as interdependent. This means that as one component changes, the others are affected as well. Generally, as knowledge increases, one's motivation to approach increases. As motivation increases, one is more likely to engage in behaviors. If the behaviors are successful, one learns more about intercultural communication, which serves to further increase motivation. And the cycle continues.

AN INTEGRATED MODEL AND MEASURE OF INTERCULTURAL COMMUNICATION COMPETENCE

For the past 10 years or so, Lily Arasaratnam has been developing what she calls an integrated model and measure of intercultural communication competence. Like others, Arasaratnam maintains that being a competent intercultural communicator involves knowing about other cultures, an approach tendency, and the application of appropriate and effective communication behaviors. Arasaratnam believes that effective and appropriate behavior can be best judged and determined from the perspectives of both the communicator enacting the behavior and the other person with whom intercultural communication occurs. Moreover, Arasaratnam contends that a person who is competent in one type of intercultural exchange probably possesses characteristics that enable him or her to communicate competently in other intercultural exchanges as well.

In related research, Arasaratnam and Doerfel discovered that those who were identified as competent intercultural communicators possessed five qualities in common: (a) empathy, (b) intercultural experience/training, (c) approach tendencies, (d) a global attitude, and (e) listening skills. Arasaratnam and Doerfel arrived at these five characteristics via interviews with persons from 15 different countries who were asked to describe a competent intercultural communicator. Arasaratnam and Doerfel interviewed persons from the United States, Bahamas, Bosnia, Burkina Faso, China, Egypt, Ghana, India, Indonesia, Ivory Coast, Japan, Malaysia, Nigeria, Norway, and the Philippines. Specifically, they wanted to identify those traits in competent intercultural interactants that transcend the cultural context and cultural identity.[59]

Empathy, of course, involves the extent to which one can infer the cognitions and motivations of another. As we saw in Chapter 9, complete empathy is impossible. Here, empathy also includes the ability to sense, accurately perceive, and appropriately respond to one's personal, interpersonal, and social environment. Approach tendencies involve the individual's interest in and effort to talk, understand, and extend help. This includes the anticipation of or actual engagement in intercultural communication. Intercultural experience and training involves the actual study of intercultural communication. Respondents in the study reported that taking a course in intercultural communication led to competence. Regarding the listening aspect, competent intercultural communicators are perceived as such because they are willing to spend time listening and learning and they know about cultural matters and are good at relating to different cultures. The global attitude dimension describes individuals who are open to others, better at communicating, show interest in differences and are aware of them, and have a level of exposure to these differences that makes them able to discern them. For example, are they speaking from their own cultural perspective or trying to communicate in the other's cultural mode or speaking in a cultural mode that is neutral or not specific to either culture? Based on these five characteristics, Arasaratnam developed a scale designed to measure one's intercultural communication competence.[60]

The Intercultural Communication Competence Scale[61]

Directions: The following items may or may not describe how you think, feel, and behave when interacting with people from different cultures. In the space to the left of each item, indicate the degree to which you (5) strongly agree, (4) agree, (3) are neutral, (2) disagree, or (1) strongly disagree with the statement. There are no right or wrong answers. It's best to record your initial response and not think too much about it.

_____ 1. I often find it difficult to differentiate between similar cultures (e.g., Asians, Europeans, Africans, etc.).

_____ 2. I feel a sense of belonging to a group of people based on relationship (i.e., family, friends) instead of cultural identity (i.e., people from my culture, people from other cultures).

_____ 3. I find it easier to categorize people based on their cultural identity than their personality.

_____ 4. I often notice similarities in personality between people who belong to completely different cultures.

_____ 5. If I were to put people in groups, I would group them by their culture rather than by their personality.

_____ 6. I feel that people from other cultures have many valuable things to teach me.

_____ 7. I feel more comfortable with people from my own culture than with people from other cultures.

_____ 8. I feel closer to people with whom I have a good relationship, regardless of whether they belong to my culture or not.

_____ 9. I usually feel closer to people who are from my own culture because I can relate to them better.

_____ 10. I feel more comfortable with people who are open to people from other cultures than with people who are not.

_____ 11. Most of my close friends are from other cultures.

_____ 12. I usually change the way I communicate depending on whom I am communicating with.

_____ 13. When I interact with someone from a different culture, I usually try to adopt some of his or her ways.

_____ 14. Most of my friends are from my own culture.

_____ 15. I usually look for opportunities to interact with people from other cultures.

Scoring: Reverse your responses for Items 1, 2, 7, 8, 9, and 14. For these six items, if your original response was a 5, reverse it to a 1; if your original score was a 4, reverse it to a 2; if your original score was a 3, leave it a 3; if your original score was a 2, reverse it to a 4; and if your original score was a 1, reverse it to a 5. After reversing your scores for these items, sum all 15 items. Your score must range between 15 and 75. Higher scores (above 55) indicate more intercultural communication competence. Lower scores (below 35) indicate less intercultural communication competence.

CHAPTER SUMMARY

Leaving your native culture for a new one can be one of the most rewarding, yet challenging experiences of a lifetime. Upon relocating to a new culture, everyone goes through a process of acculturation—that is, a process of cultural change that results from ongoing contact between two or more culturally different groups. For some, this process can be particularly difficult, whereas for others, it is relatively easy. Acculturation is in large part a function of how much interaction one chooses to have with members of the new culture and how much of the old culture one desires to maintain. Virtually everyone experiences some degree of culture shock when entering a new culture for an extended period of time. Culture shock results in feelings of disorientation, misunderstandings, conflict, stress, and anxiety. Often, a traveler experiences the same feelings upon returning home. In addition to discussing its causes and symptoms, this chapter has offered several strategies for assessing and managing culture shock. Although culture shock sounds awful, having an understanding of its causes, symptoms, and effects is the first step in alleviating the severity you might experience. Generally speaking, most students who travel abroad experience only minor levels of culture shock.

Finally, one of the foremost goals of this book is to help you become a competent intercultural communicator. As defined in this chapter, *intercultural communication competence* is the degree to which you effectively adapt your verbal and nonverbal messages to the appropriate cultural context. This chapter has presented a model of intercultural competence that includes knowledge, affective, psychomotor, and situational components. In order to be a competent intercultural communicator, you must have some *knowledge* about the person with whom you are communicating, you need to be *motivated* to communicate with people who are different from you, and you need to engage in appropriate and effective verbal and nonverbal *skills* in order to encode and decode messages. You also need to be sensitive to the situational features that influence the verbal and nonverbal messages you send. It is hoped that you, after having read this text, are more knowledgeable about culture, are more motivated to enter into new cultures and establish relationships with persons from different cultures, and have gained some communication skills. Although challenging, intercultural communication is one of the most rewarding life experiences you will ever encounter.

Visit the student study site at **www.sagepub.com/neuliep5e** *for e-flashcards, web quizzes, web resources and more.*

DISCUSSION QUESTIONS

1. What factors do you think would most affect you if you were to travel to another culture?
2. Why do some groups in the United States assimilate more than others?
3. What groups do you think are the most assimilated in the United States?
4. How might the dominant culture of the United States help diverse groups assimilate?
5. Are there good reasons for groups not to assimilate to U.S. culture?

KEY TERMS

acculturation   406

acculturative stress   407

adjustment phase   420

affective component   427

assimilation   410

cultural transmutation   411

culture shock   406

integration   410

intercultural communication
   competence   406

intercultural willingness to
   communicate   428

knowledge component   426

psychomotor component   429

reentry shock   422

situational features   430

REFERENCES

1. Condon, J. C., & Yousef, F. (1975). *An Introduction to Intercultural Communication*. Indianapolis, IN: Bobbs-Merrill. (Quote on p. 270)

2. Redfield, R., Linton, R., & Herskovits, M. (1936). Memorandum on the Study of Acculturation. *American Anthropologist, 38*, 149–152.

3. Berry, J. W., & Sam, D. T. (1997). Acculturation and Adaptation. In J. W. Berry, M. H. Segall, & C. Kagitcibasa (Eds.), *Handbook of Cross-Cultural Psychology: Social Behavior and Applications* (Vol. 3, pp. 291–326). Boston: Allyn & Bacon.

4. Ibid.

5. Nwadiora, E., & McAdoo, H. (1996). Acculturative Stress Among Amerasian Refugees: Gender and Racial Differences. *Adolescence, 31*, 477–488.

6. Miranda, A. O., & Matheny, K. B. (2000). Sociopsychological Predictors and Acculturative Stress Among Latino Adults. *Journal of Mental Health Counseling, 22*, 306–318.

7. Hovey, D. (2000). Psychosocial Predictors of Acculturative Stress in Mexican Immigrants. *Journal of Psychology, 134*, 490–502; Smart, J. F., & Smart, D. W. (1995). Acculturative Stress of Hispanics: Loss and Challenge. *Journal of Counseling and Development, 73*, 390–397.

8. Hovey, J. D. (2000). Psychological Predictors of Acculturative Stress in Mexican Immigrants. *Journal of Psychology, 134*, 490–502.

9. Nwadiora & McAdoo, Acculturative Stress Among Amerasian Refugees.

10. Berry, J. W. (1987). *Understanding the Process of Acculturation for Primary Intervention*. Unpublished manuscript, Department of Psychology, Queen's College, Kingston, Ontario, cited in Nwadiora & McAdoo, Acculturative Stress Among Amerasian Refugees.

11. Kim, Y. Y. (1997). Adapting to a New Culture. In L. A. Samovar & R. E. Porter (Eds.), *Intercultural Communication: A Reader* (8th ed., pp. 404–417). Belmont, CA: Wadsworth.

12. Ibid.

13. Ibid.

14. Liebkind, K. (1996). Acculturation and Stress: Vietnamese Refugees in Finland. *Journal of Cross-Cultural Psychology, 27*, 161–180.

15. Berry, J. W. (1990). Psychology of Acculturation. In R. A. Dienstbier (Ed.), *Nebraska Symposium on Motivation 1989* (pp. 201–234). Lincoln: University of Nebraska Press.

16. Berry, Psychology of Acculturation; Coleman, H. L. K. (1995). Strategies for Coping With Cultural Diversity. *Counseling Psychology, 23*, 722–741.

17. Coleman, Strategies for Coping With Cultural Diversity; Cuellar, I., Arnold, B., & Maldonado, R. (1995). Acculturation Rating Scale for Mexican-Americans II: A Revision of the Original ARSMA. *Hispanic Journal of Behavioral Sciences, 17*, 275–305.

18. Ibid.

19. Cuellar et al., Acculturation Rating Scale for Mexican-Americans II.

20. Coleman, Strategies for Coping With Cultural Diversity; Cuellar et al., Acculturation Rating Scale for Mexican-Americans II; Mendoza, R. H. (1989). An Empirical Scale to Measure Type and Degree of Acculturation in Mexican-American Adolescents and Adults. *Journal of Cross-Cultural Psychology, 20*, 372–385.

21. Landrine, H., & Klonoff, E. A. (1995). The African-American Acculturation Scale II: Cross Validation and Short Form. *Journal of Black Psychology, 21*, 124–153.

22. DeLeon, B., & Mendez, S. (1996). Factorial Structure of a Measure of Acculturation in a Puerto Rican Population. *Educational and Psychological Measurement, 56*, 155–166.

23. Landrine & Klonoff, The African-American Acculturation Scale II.

24. Cuellar, L., Harris, C., & Jasso, R. (1980). An Acculturation Scale for Mexican-Americans: Normal and Clinical Populations. *Hispanic Journal of Behavioral Sciences, 2*, 199–217.

25. Cuellar et al., Acculturation Rating Scale for Mexican-Americans II.

26. Landrine & Klonoff, The African-American Acculturation Scale II.

27. Winkelman, M. (1994). Cultural Shock and Adaptation. *Journal of Counseling and Development, 73,* 121–127.

28. Oberg, K. (1954). *Culture Shock* (Bobbs-Merrill Series in Social Science, A-329). Indianapolis, IN: Bobbs-Merrill; Oberg, K. (1960). Culture Shock: Adjustments to New Cultural Environments. *Practical Anthropology, 4,* 177–182.

29. Winkelman, Cultural Shock and Adaptation.

30. Oberg, *Culture Shock*; Oberg, *Culture Shock: Adjustments to New Cultural Environments.*

31. These models are briefly reviewed in Zapf, M. K. (1993). Remote Practice and Culture Shock: Social Workers Moving to Isolated Northern Regions. *Social Work, 38,* 694–705; see also Kealey, D. J. (1978). Adaptation to a New Environment. In Canadian International Development Agency (Ed.), *Pre-Departure Documentation Kit* (pp. 48–55). Hull, Quebec: CIDA Briefing Centre; Richardson, A. (1974). *British Immigrants and Australia: A Psychosocial Inquiry.* Canberra: Australian National University Press; Smalley, W. A. (1963). Culture Shock, Language Shock, and the Shock of Self-Discovery. *Practical Anthropology, 10,* 49–56.

32. Lysgaard, S. (1995). Adjustment in a Foreign Society: Norwegian Fulbright Grantees Visiting the United States. *International Social Science Bulletin, 7,* 45–51.

33. Zapf, Remote Practice and Culture Shock.

34. Winkelman, Cultural Shock and Adaptation.

35. Ibid., p. 122.

36. Rhinesmith, S. (1985). *Bring Home the World.* New York: Walsh.

37. Churchman, A., & Mitrani, M. (1997). The Role of the Physical Environment in Culture Shock. *Environment and Behavior, 29,* 64–87; Lonner, W. (1986). Foreword. In A. Furnham & S. Bochner (Eds.), *Culture Shock: Psychological Reactions to Unfamiliar Environments* (pp. xv–xx). London: Methuen.

38. Winkelman, Cultural Shock and Adaptation.

39. Kim, Adapting to a New Culture.

40. Furnham, A., & Bochner, S. (Eds.). (1986). *Culture Shock: Psychological Reactions to Unfamiliar Environments.* London: Methuen.

41. Winkelman, Cultural Shock and Adaptation.

42. Zapf, Remote Practice and Culture Shock.

43. Gudykunst, W. B., & Kim, Y. Y. (1997). *Communicating With Strangers: An Approach to Intercultural Communication.* New York: McGraw-Hill; Spitzberg, B. H. (1997). A Model of Intercultural Competence. In L. A. Samovar & R. E. Porter (Eds.), *Intercultural Communication Reader* (8th ed., pp. 379–391). Belmont, CA: Wadsworth.

44. Spitzberg, A Model of Intercultural Competence.

45. Ibid.

46. Spitzberg, B. H., & Cupach, W. R. (1984). *Interpersonal Communication Competence.* Beverly Hills, CA: Sage.

47. This scale is loosely adapted from Goodman, N. R. (1994). Cross-Cultural Training for the Global Executive. In R. W. Brislin & T. Yoshida (Eds.), *Improving Intercultural Interaction: Models for Cross-Cultural Training Programs* (pp. 34–54). Thousand Oaks, CA: Sage.

48. Berger, C. R., & Jordan, J. (1992). Planning Sources, Planning Difficulty, and Verbal Fluency. *Communication Monographs, 59,* 130–149.

49. Kim, Y. Y. (1990). *Explaining Interethnic Conflict: An Interdisciplinary Overview.* Paper presented at the annual convention of the Speech Communication Association, Chicago, IL.

50. See, for example, Hewstone, M., & Ward, C. X. (1985). Ethnocentrism and Causal Attribution in Southeast Asia. *Journal of Personality and Social Psychology, 48,* 614–623; Islam, M. R., & Hewstone, M. (1993). Intergroup Attribution and Affective Consequences in Majority and Minority Groups. *Journal of Personality and Social Psychology, 64,* 936–950; Segall, M. H. (1979). *Cross-Cultural Psychology: Human Behavior in Global Perspective.* Monterey, CA: Brooks/Cole; Sumner, W. G. (1906). *Folkways.* Boston: Ginn.

51. Wiseman, R. L., Hammer, M. R., & Nishida, H. (1989). Predictors of Intercultural Communication Competence. *International Journal of Intercultural Relations, 13,* 349–370.

52. Neuliep, J. W., & McCroskey, J. C. (1997). The Development of Intercultural and Interethnic Communication Apprehension Scales. *Communication Research Reports, 14,* 145–156.

53. Kassing, J. W. (1997). Development of the Intercultural Willingness to Communicate Scale. *Communication Research Reports, 14,* 399–407.

54. Kim, Y. Y. (1991). Intercultural Communication Competence: A Systems-Theoretic View. In S. Ting-Toomey & F. Korzenny (Eds.), *Cross-Cultural Interpersonal Communication* (pp. 259–275). Newbury Park, CA: Sage; Gudykunst & Kim, *Communicating With Strangers.*

55. Gudykunst & Kim, *Communicating With Strangers*; Spitzberg, A Model of Intercultural Competence.

56. Gudykunst & Kim, *Communicating With Strangers.*

57. Kim, Explaining Interethnic Conflict.

58. Ibid.; Gudykunst & Kim, *Communicating With Strangers.*

59. Arasaratnam, L. A., & Doerfel, M. L. (2005). Intercultural Communication Competence: Identifying Key Components From Multicultural Perspectives. *International Journal of Intercultural Relations, 29,* 137–163.

60. Arasaratnam, L. A. (2009). The Development of a New Instrument of Intercultural Communication Competence. *Journal of Intercultural Communication, 20.*

61. Ibid.

Glossary

acculturation: The process of cultural change that results from ongoing contact between two or more culturally different groups

acculturative stress: The anxiety and tension associated with acculturation

adaptors: Mostly unconscious nonverbal actions that satisfy physiological or psychological needs, such as scratching an itch

adjustment phase: Third stage of culture shock, in which people actively seek out effective problem-solving and conflict resolution strategies

affect displays: Nonverbal presentations of emotion, primarily communicated through facial expressions

affective component: Approach–avoidance tendencies during intercultural communication; the extent to which one experiences intercultural communication apprehension and one's willingness to communicate

affective style: Communication manner where the process of interaction is emphasized, placing the burden of understanding on both the speaker and the listener; relies heavily on nonverbal cues

African Americans: Microcultural group in the United States whose ancestors were brought to the United States as slaves

Amish: A microcultural religiously oriented group whose members practice simple and austere living

analogic communication: Nonverbal communication

Arab: A person with ancestries originating from Arabic-speaking countries or areas of the world

arranged marriage: Marriage that is initiated and negotiated by a third party rather than by the bride and groom

assertiveness: An individual's ability to make requests, actively disagree, and express positive or negative personal rights and feelings

assimilation: The degree to which an individual takes on the behaviors and language habits and practices the basic rules and norms of the host culture while relinquishing ties with the native culture

built environment: Adaptations to the terrestrial environment, including architecture, housing, lighting, and landscaping

carpentered-world hypothesis: Learned tendency by those living in industrialized cultures to interpret nonrectangular figures as rectangles in perspective

categorization: Classifying or sorting of perceived information into distinct groups

chronemics: The use of time

collectivism: Cultural orientation where the group is the primary unit of culture. Group goals take precedence over individual goals.

communication: The simultaneous encoding, decoding, and interpretation of verbal and nonverbal messages between people

communication apprehension: The fear or anxiety associated with either real or anticipated communication with another person or group of persons

context: The cultural, physical, social, and psychological environment

contextual style: Role-centered mode of speaking where one's choice of messages is influenced by one's relative status in the conversation

cultural context: An accumulated pattern of values, beliefs, and behavior held by an identifiable group of people with a common verbal and nonverbal symbol system

cultural transmutation: Mode of acculturation in which the individual chooses to identify with a third cultural group (microculture) that materializes out of the native and host cultural groups

culture: An accumulated pattern of values, beliefs, and behaviors shared by an identifiable group of people with a common history and verbal and nonverbal symbol system

culture shock: The effects associated with the tension and anxiety of entering a new culture, combined with the sensations of loss, confusion, and powerlessness resulting from the forfeiture of cultural norms and social rituals

decay: Memory loss due to lack of use

denotative meaning: The literal meaning of a word; the dictionary meaning

dialect: A language variety associated with a particular region or social group

digital communication: Verbal communication

direct style: Manner of speaking where one employs overt expressions of intention

dynamic: Something considered active and forceful

Ebonics: From the terms *ebony* and *phonics,* a grammatically robust and rich African American speech pattern whose roots are in West Africa

elaborate style: Mode of speaking that emphasizes rich, expressive language

elaborated code: A cultural context wherein the speakers of a language have a variety of linguistic options open to them in order to explicitly communicate their intent via verbal messages

emblems: Primarily hand gestures that have a direct verbal translation; can be used to repeat or to substitute for verbal communication

environmental context: The geographical and psychological location of communication within some cultural context

episodic long-term memory: A component of long-term memory where private individual memories are stored

ethnocentric attributional bias: The tendency to make internal attributions for the positive behavior of the in-group while making external attributions for its negative behavior; also called the ultimate attribution error

ethnocentrism: The tendency to place one's own group (cultural, ethnic, or religious) in a position of centrality and worth, and to create negative attitudes and behaviors toward other groups

exacting style: Manner of speaking where persons say no more or less than is needed to communicate a point

fixed-feature space: Space bounded by immovable or permanent fixtures, such as walls

gender: A socially constructed and learned creation usually associated with one's sex; masculinity and femininity. People are born into a sex group but learn to become masculine or feminine. The meaning of gender stems from the particular culture's value system.

GENE: Self-report instrument designed to measure generalized ethnocentrism

generative grammar: The idea that from a finite set of rules, a speaker of any language can create or generate an infinite number of sentences, many of which have never before been uttered

haptics: Nonverbal communication through physical contact or touch

high context: Cultural orientation where meanings are gleaned from the physical, social, and psychological contexts

high load: A situation with a high information rate

Hispanic: Defined by the U.S. government as a person of Cuban, Mexican, Puerto Rican, South or Central American, or other Spanish culture or origin, regardless of race

Hmong: Microculture belonging to the Sino-Tibetan language family and culturally similar to the Chinese. The Hmong, whose name means "free people" or "mountain people," fought for the United States during the Vietnam War, and many have immigrated to the United States since the end of the war.

horizontal collectivism: Cultural orientation where the self is seen as a member of an in-group whose members are similar to one another

horizontal individualism: Cultural orientation where an autonomous self is valued but the self is more or less equal to others

illusory correlation principle: When two objects or persons are observed to be linked in some way, people have a tendency to believe they are always linked (or correlated).

illustrators: Primarily hand and arm movements that function to accent or complement speech

indirect style: Manner of speaking wherein the intentions of the speakers are hidden or only hinted at during interaction

individualism: Cultural orientation where the individual is unique and individual goals are emphasized over group goals

informal space: Space defined by the movement of the interactants

information rate: The amount of information contained or perceived in the physical environment per some unit of time

in-group: A membership group whose norms, goals, and values shape the behavior of the members. Extreme in-groups see the actions of an out-group as threatening.

instrumental style: Sender-focused manner of speaking that is goal and outcome oriented. Instrumental speakers use communication to achieve some goal or purpose.

integration: Mode of acculturation in which the individual develops a kind of bicultural orientation that successfully blends and synthesizes cultural dimensions from both groups while maintaining an identity in each group

intentionality: During communication, the voluntary and conscious encoding and decoding of messages

interactive: A process between two people

intercultural communication: Two persons from different cultures or co-cultures exchanging verbal and nonverbal messages

intercultural communication apprehension: The fear or anxiety associated with either real or anticipated communication with a person from another culture or co-culture

intercultural communication competence: The ability to adapt one's verbal and nonverbal messages to the appropriate cultural context

intercultural willingness to communicate: Predisposition to initiate intercultural interaction with persons from different cultures even when completely free to choose whether or not to communicate

interference: During recall, when new or old information blocks or obstructs the recall of other information

involuntary membership group: A group to which a person belongs and has no choice but to belong, such as sex, race, and age groups

involuntary nonmembership group: A group to which a person does not belong because of ineligibility

kinesics: General category of body motion, including emblems, illustrators, affect displays, and adaptors

knowledge component: The extent of one's awareness of another culture's values and so forth; also, the extent to which one is cognitively simple, rigid, and ethnocentric

language: A systematic set of sounds, combined with a set of rules, for the sole purpose of communicating

language variety: The way a particular group of people uses language

LGBT: Persons who consider themselves lesbian, gay, bisexual, or transgendered

long-term memory: Cognitive storage area where large amounts of information are held relatively permanently

low context: Cultural orientation where meanings are encoded in the verbal code

low load: A situation with a low information rate

membership group: A group to which a person belongs where there is regular interaction among members who perceive themselves as members

memory: The storage of information in the human brain over time

microculture: An identifiable group of people who share a set of values, beliefs, and behaviors and who possess a common history and a verbal and nonverbal symbol system that is similar to but systematically varies from the larger, often dominant cultural milieu

minority group: A subordinate group whose members have significantly less power and control over their own lives than do members of the dominant or majority group

monochronic time orientation: Cultural temporal orientation that stresses the compartmentalization and segmentation of measurable units of time

morpheme: Smallest meaningful unit of sound; a combination of phonemes

Muslim: A person who practices Islam

muted groups: Microcultures whose members are forced to express themselves (e.g., speak, write) within the dominant mode of expression

nonmembership group: A group to which a person does not belong

nonverbal expectancy violations theory: Theory that posits that people hold expectations about the nonverbal behavior of others. When these expectations are violated, people evaluate the violation positively or negatively, depending on the source of the violation.

olfactics: The perception and use of smell, scent, and odor

organizational culture: An organized pattern of values, beliefs, behaviors, and communication channels held by the members of an organization

out-group: A group whose attributes are dissimilar from those of an in-group and that opposes the realization of in-group goals

out-group homogeneity effect: The tendency to see members of an out-group as highly similar while seeing the members of the in-group as unique and individual

paralanguage: Characteristics of the voice, such as pitch, rhythm, intensity, volume, and rate

perception: The mental interpretation of external stimuli via sensation

perceptual context: The attitudes, emotions, and motivations of the persons engaged in communication and how they affect information processing

perceptual filters: Physical, social, and psychological processes that screen and bias incoming stimuli

Personal Report of Communication Apprehension (PRCA): Self-report instrument designed to measure communication apprehension

personal style: Manner of speaking relying on the use of personal pronouns that stresses informality and symmetrical power relationships

phoneme: Smallest unit of sound, as in a consonant or vowel

polyandry: The practice of having multiple husbands

polychronic time orientation: Cultural temporal orientation that stresses the involvement of people and the completion of tasks as opposed to strict adherence to schedules. Time is not seen as measurable.

polygamy: The practice of having multiple spouses

polygyny: The practice of having multiple wives

power distance: The extent to which members of a culture expect and accept that power is unequally distributed

process: Anything ongoing, ever changing, and continuous

proxemics: The perception and use of space, including territoriality and personal space

psychomotor component: The extent to which one can translate cultural knowledge into verbal and nonverbal performance and role enactment

reentry shock: The effects associated with the tension and anxiety of returning to one's native culture after an extended stay in a foreign culture

reference group: A group to which a person may or may not belong but with which the person identifies in some way in terms of values and goals

regulators: Nonverbal acts that manage and govern communication between people, such as stance, distance, and eye contact

relational empathy: Shared meaning and harmonization that is the result of the interaction of two people

responsiveness: An individual's ability to be sensitive to the communication of others, including providing feedback, engaging in comforting communication, and listening

restricted code: A cultural context wherein the speakers of a language are limited as to what they can say or do verbally. A restricted code is a status-oriented system.

role: One's relative hierarchical position or rank in a group. A role is a prescribed set of behaviors that is expected in order to fulfill the role. Roles prescribe with whom, about what, and how to interact.

semantic long-term memory: A part of long-term memory where general information such as how to read and write and the meanings of words is stored

semifixed-feature space: Space bounded by movable objects, such as furniture

sensation: Gathering of visual, auditory, olfactic, haptic, and taste stimuli/information

sensory receptors: Eyes, ears, nose, mouth, and skin

sex: A designation of people based on biological genital differences

sex role: A prescribed set of behaviors assigned to different sexes

short-term memory: Cognitive storage area where small amounts of information are held for short periods of time, usually less than 20 seconds

situational features: The extent to which the environmental context, previous contact, status differential, and third-party intervention affect one's competence during intercultural communication

social identity: The total combination of one's group roles; a part of the individual's self-concept that is derived from the person's membership in groups

social stratification: A culture's organization of roles into a hierarchical vertical status structure

sociocommunicative style: Degree of assertiveness and responsiveness during communication

sociorelational context: The roles that one assumes within a culture; the role relationship between interactants (e.g., brother/sister). Roles are defined by verbal and nonverbal messages.

Spanglish: Hybrid language combining the phonological features (i.e., sounds) and syntactic structures (i.e., grammar) of English and Spanish

Standard English: The variety of English spoken in the United States that is considered correct

stereotype: Usually negative but sometimes positive perceptions we have of individuals based on their membership in groups

Stereotype Content Model: A model that proposes that all stereotypes are based on social perceptions of warmth and competence

stereotype threat: When a stereotyped group believes the stereotype about them may be true

succinct style: Manner of very concise speaking often accompanied by silence

symbol: An arbitrarily selected and learned stimulus representing something else

terrestrial environment: The physical geography of the Earth

third culture: That which is created when a dyad consisting of persons from different cultures come together and establish relational empathy

transactional: The simultaneous encoding and decoding process during communication

uncertainty: The amount of unpredictability during communication

uncertainty avoidance: The degree to which members of a particular culture feel threatened by unpredictable, uncertain, or unknown situations

uncertainty reduction theory: Theory whose major premise is that when strangers first meet, their primary goal is to reduce uncertainty

universal grammar: The idea that all languages share a common rule structure or grammar that is innate in human beings, regardless of culture

vertical collectivism: Cultural orientation where the individual sees the self as an integral part of the in-group but the members are different from one another (e.g., status)

vertical individualism: Cultural orientation where an autonomous self is valued and the self is seen as different from and perhaps unequal to others

voluntary membership group: A membership group to which a person belongs out of choice, such as a political party or service organization

voluntary nonmembership group: A membership group to which a person does not belong by choice

Photo Credits

The photographs appearing in the *Student Voices Across Cultures* feature are used by permission and courtesy of the following individuals:

Page 30: Jennifer Seidemann

Page 50: Pengfei Song

Page 79: Ahmed I. Alshaya

Page 123: Stephen Rupsch

Page 159: Sebastian Friedemann

Page 183: Amanda Garrity

Page 186: Morgan Leah Johnson

Page 227: Ala Aldahneem

Page 240: Chen Chen

Page 290: Lindsey Novitzke

Pages 317: Karen Henao-Carbonell

Page 346: Mohammed I. Alshaya

Page 369: Rodrigo Villalobos

Page 421: Jessica Bahrke

The following chapter opening photos are used by permission:

Chapter 1, Page 1: Digital Vision/ Digital Vision/Thinkstock

Chapter 2, Page 45: Jupiterimages/Photos.com/ Thinkstock

Chapter 3, Page 93: ©iStockphoto.com/Shelly Perry

Chapter 4, Page 131: ©iStockphoto.com/ John Sigler

Chapter 5, Page 167: Michael Blann/Lifesize/ Thinkstock

Chapter 6, Page 205: ©iStockphoto.com/Karen Moller

Chapter 7, Page 235: Jupiterimages/Comstock/ Thinkstock

Chapter 8, Page 267: ©iStockphoto.com/Chris Gramly

Chapter 9, Page 311: ©iStockphoto.com/ Michael Monu

Chapter 10, Page 351: ©iStockphoto.com/ Willie B. Thomas

Chapter 11, Page 373: ©iStockphoto.com/ Joshua Hodge Photography

Chapter 12, Page 405: MM Productions/ Lifesize/Thinkstock

The following photos appearing within the chapters are used by permission:

Figure 1.2, Page 16: Thinkstock Images/ Comstock/Thinkstock

Figure 1.3, Page 21: ©iStockphoto.com/Shmulitk

Figure 1.4, Page 22: Andrea Chu/Digital Vision/ThinkStock

Figure 2.3, Page 78: ©iStockphoto.com/Juanmonino

Figure 2.4, Page 82: Photo courtesy of Tevaprapas Makklay

Figure 3.1, Page 107: Comstock Images/ Comstock/Thinkstock

Figure 3.2, Page 112: ©iStockphoto.com/Diane Diederich

Figure 3.3, Page 117: ©iStockphoto.com/Josef Muellek

Figure 3.4, Page 120: ©Steve Raymer/Corbis

Figure 4.1, Page 140: ©iStockphoto.com/ TommL

Figure 4.2, Page 143: Jupiterimages/ iquidlibrary/Thinkstock

Photo 5.1, Page 171: Jupiterimages/Photos.com/ Thinkstock

Photo 5.2a, Page 172: John Foxx/Stockbyte/ Thinkstock

Photo 5.2b, Page 172: Jupiterimages/Photos .com/Thinkstock

Photo 5.2c, Page 172: Brand X Pictures/Brand X Pictures/Thinkstock

Figure 5.5a, Page 182: Jupiterimages/Photos. com/Thinkstock

Figure 5.5b, Page 183: Thinkstock/Comstock/ Thinkstock

Figure 5.6, Page 187: Jupiterimages/Polka Dot/Thinkstock

Figure 6.1, Page 208: Wikimedia Photo/ Paul M. Walsh

Figure 6.2, Page 212: Stockbyte/ Stockbyte/ Thinkstock

Figure 6.4, Page 225: Ryan McVay/ Digital Vision/Thinkstock

Figure 7.2, Page 241: Thinkstock/Comstock/ Thinkstock

Figure 7.3, Page 242: Comstock Images/ Comstock/Thinkstock

Figure 8.1, Page 274: ©iStockphoto.com/Steve Cole

Figure 8.6a, Page 280: ©iStockphoto.com/ zilli

Figure 8.6b, Page 280: © Can Stock Photo Inc. /3650308

Figure 8.7, Page 283: Jupiterimages/Brand X Pictures/Thinkstock

Figure 9.5, Page 343: Stockbyte/Stockbyte/ Thinkstock

Figure 10.2, Page 355: Library of Congress. Photograph by John F. Vachon, U. S. Farm Security Administration

Figure 10.4, Page 368: BananaStock/ BananaStock/Thinkstock

Figure 11.1, Page 377: Digital Vision/Digital Vision/Thinkstock

Figure 12.2, Page 412: ©iStockphoto.com/

Name Index

Abramson, N. R., 388–389, 404
Adams, J., 2–3
Adams, K., 232
Adams, T. M., 98, 127
Adler, N. J., 386, 403
Adler, R. B., 232
Adorno, T. W., 203
Ahmad, K., 233
Aiello, J., 141, 164
Alexander, J. F., 121, 129
Ali, A. J., 399–400, 401, 404
Almaney, A., 283, 308
Altman, I., 136, 137, 148, 154–155, 164, 165
Alwan, A., 283, 308
Ambady, N., 273, 278, 281, 306, 307, 308
Ambah, F. S., 233
Amman, J., 110
Amole, D., 287, 308
Anders, G., 127
Andersen, J. F., 91
Andersen, P. A., 77, 82, 91, 289, 299, 309, 310
Anderson, C. M., 348
Andre, C., 44
Angeloni, E., 43
Anger-Elfenbein, H., 278, 307
Arasaratnam, L. A., 431–432, 435
Archer, D., 273, 275, 276–278, 307
Ardener, E., 127
Ardener, S., 127
Ardila, A., 102, 127
Argyle, M., 308
Armstrong, K., 349
Arnold, B., 415, 434
Aronson, J., 192–193, 203
Assmar, E., 52, 89
Atoon, P., 99 (table)
Auman, C., 203
Austin, W., 231

Awwad, E., 52, 89
Axtell, R. F., 43, 274, 307, 383, 403

Badea, C., 202
Bailey, G., 262, 266
Baker, R. L., 292, 309
Balaghi, S., 232
Banchero, R., 127
Barbaro, M., 403
Barkan, E. R., 118, 129
Barkowitz, P., 308
Barnes, M. K., 349
Bar-On, D., 52, 89
Barrett, G., 265
Barrett, L. E., 96, 126
Barry, E., 42
Basho, 255
Basit, T., 219, 232
Basso, K., 43
Batarfi, K. M., 309
Beavin, J., 43
Beavin, J. B., 14
Becker, C. B., 255, 265
Becker, G. S., 332, 349
Bem, S. L., 220, 232
Benoist, A., 203
Berger, C. R., 29, 43, 44, 313–316, 320–322,
    348, 427, 435
Berlo, D. K., 11 (table), 43
Berman, J. J., 88, 231
Bernstein, B., 247–248, 252, 265
Bernstein, M. J., 282, 308
Berry, J. W., 174, 175, 201, 202, 215, 232,
    406–407, 408, 410, 413, 434
Best, D. L., 221–223, 232
Bhatnagar, D., 383–384, 403
Bhawuk, D. P. S., 56, 89
Bichler, S., 164

Billings, A., 109, 128
Billington, R., 44
Birdwhistell, R. L., 279, 307
Bishop, R. J., 136, 164, 307, 308, 309
Black, J. S., 403
Blake, J., 272–273, 307
Boas, F., 23
Bochner, S., 422, 435
Bolda, R. A., 387–388, 404
Bond, M. H., 69, 70–71, 82, 90, 91, 201
Borden, G. A., 164
Bothwell, R. K., 308
Bowers, J. W., 11 (table), 43
Bowles, P., 165
Bradac, J. J., 11 (table), 43
Braithwaite, C. A., 44, 64, 90, 287, 308
Brake, S., 308
Braly, K. W., 184–185, 202
Brett, J. M., 390, 404
Brewer, M. B., 209, 231
Briggs, M. T., 203
Brigham, J. C., 282, 308
Brinkman, H., 309
Brislin, R. W., 164, 181, 201, 435
Brittingham, A., 129
Brockmeier, J., 177, 201
Broome, B. J., 324–325, 326–327, 348
Brown, W. S., 387, 404
Bruner, J. S., 194, 203
Bruno, R., 43
Buch, B. B., 128
Buerger, C., 158–159, 166, 296, 309
Buerger, C. M, 232
Burd, S., 165
Burgoon, J. K., 165, 300–303,
    301 (table), 305, 310
Burnett, M., 193, 203
Buss, A. H., 44
Buss, D. M., 338, 340–342, 341 (table), 349
Butterfield, E. C., 178, 201
Byrne, D., 327–328, 349
Byrnes, D., 293, 309

Cabral, M., 272–273, 307
Cahn, D., 352, 371
Calabrese, R. J., 44, 313–316, 321–322, 348
Calvert, C., 151–152, 165
Calvert, S. L., 338, 349
Cameron, D., 4, 42, 129
Campbell, D. T., 209, 231
Caprariello, P. A., 202

Carbaugh, D., 43, 44, 90, 128, 265, 266
Carroll, J., 42
Casas, J. M., 105, 127
Casmir, F., 348
Casteel, B., 289, 308, 309
Castle, S., 203
Caudle, E., 336–338, 349
Chan, A., 279–281, 307
Chan, D. K. S., 90
Chan, S., 232
Chan, T.-S., 91
Chang, H.-C., 60, 90
Chang, K. S., 218, 232
Chapanis, A., 201
Chapman, J. W., 165
Chase, C. H., 201
Chemers, M., 136, 137, 164
Chen, H., 343, 349
Chen, P. P. W., 404
Chen, V., 126
Chen, X. P., 90
Chesebro, J., 129
Chesla, C., 44
Chew-Sanchez, M. I., 91
Choi, M., 155–156, 165, 307, 308
Choi, S.-C., 89
Choi, S. H., 90
Choi, Y. S., 273, 306, 307
Chomsky, N., 236, 240–241, 243, 245,
    264, 270, xv
Chua, E. G., 368–369, 372
Chun, Y., 219, 232
Churchman, A., 420, 435
Claire, T., 202–203
Classen, C., 291, 292, 309
Clutter, A. W., 102, 127
Cocks, R., 308
Cocroft, B., 371
Cohen, D., 54, 89
Colcombe, S. J., 203
Cole, M., 180, 201
Coleman, H. L. K., 410–411, 434
Colloff, P., 262, 266
Conaway, W. A., 164
Condon, J., 71, 72, 74, 75, 76, 90, 91
Condon, J. C., 232, 252, 265, 307, 406, 434
Cook, C. T., 336, 349
Cooley, C., 11 (table), 43
Coon, H. M., 49, 51, 56, 89
Copeland, L., 89, 166, 232, 266, 404
Coren, S., 201

Correa, T., 337–338, 349
Cottone, R. R., 333, 349
Craig, E., 44
Cran, W., 266
Croizet, J. C., 202–203
Crouch, E. C., 395–396, 404
Crouch, N., 100–101, 102, 127
Cruz, B., 103, 127
Cua, A. S., 44
Cuddy, A. J. C., 188–191, 193, 202, 203
Cuellar, I., 415, 434
Cuellar, L., 434
Cunningham, S., 127
Cupach, W. R., 425, 435

Darwin, C., 279, 307
Dasen, P. R., 174, 175, 201, 202, 215, 232
Davin, D., 229, 233
DeAndrea, D. C., 349
De Forest, M. E., 395, 396, 404
DeJesus, J., 285, 308
De le Cruz, G. P., 129
DeLeon, B., 434
DeMenthe, B., 91
Demoulin, S., 202
Deschamps, J. -C., 50, 51, 89
DeVargas, M. C., 307
Devine, P. G., 185, 202
DeVito, J. A., 308
Diacoyanni-Tarlatzis, I., 279–281, 307
Dienstbier, R. A., 434
Dixon, J. A., 308
Dixon, R., 89
Dodge, B., 129
Doerfel, M. L., 431, 435
Doggett, L. E., 297–298, 309
Dollard, J., 292, 309
Dolphin, C. Z., 308
Domino, G., 71, 90
Dong, X., 165
Dore, R., 387, 403
Dovidio, J. F., 286, 308
Dowell, W., 165
Drake, W., 390–391, 394 (table), 404
D'Souza, D., 203
Duck, S., 115, 128, 327, 349
Duffy, J., 128
Dugan, S., 81, 91
Duley, M. I., 225–226, 233
Duncan, B. L., 194, 203
Dunne, M., 335, 349

Dunning, D., 191, 202
Durga, R., 178, 201

Eckert, P., 266
Edwards, M. I., 233
Ekman, P., 272, 279–281, 307
Elenkov, D. S., 379–403
Elfenbein, H. A., 281, 308
Elliot, A. J., 185, 202
Elliot, D., 345, 350
Ellis, D. G., 232
England, J., 7
England, J. T., 42
Enns, J. T., 201
Enriquez, L., 101, 127
Entwistle, D. R., 282, 308
Esteve, A., 233
Evans, C. A., 338, 349

Farb, P., 268, 306
Farr, J., 198, 203
Fedarko, K., 265
Feingold, C. A., 281, 308
Feinstein, M. H., 201
Ferman, S., 282, 308
Fernandez, C., 180, 201
Fernea, E., 309
Fernea, R., 309
Ferreira, M. C., 52, 89
Fischer, R., 52, 89
Fisher, B. A., 11 (table), 43, 52, 232
Fisher, S., 138–139, 164
Fishman, C., 403
Fiske, S. T., 188–191, 202
Flores, L. A., 309
Ford, J. K., 198, 203
Fortenberry, J. D., 129
Fought, C., 104, 127
Fought, J., 266
Fox, K., 293–296, 309
Frances, S., 153, 165
Francoeur, R. T., 291, 293, 309
Frantz, C. M., 193, 203
Frenkel-Brunswik, E., 203
Friesen, W., 272, 279–281, 307
Fuller, D. B., 98, 127
Furnham, A., 422, 435

Gaertner, L., 61, 90
Gage-Brandon, A. J., 350
Gagnon, J. H., 105, 127

Galanes, G. J., 232
Gallois, C., 281, 307–308
Gandhi, M., 352
Gandy, O. H., 152–153, 165
Gao, G., 361, 372
Gao, X., 343, 349
Garcia, W., 372
Garfield, J. L., 201
Gates, G. J., 129
Gay, J., 180, 201
Gayle, A. R., 88
Gedro, J., 122, 129
Gee, C. B., 334–335, 349
Geertz, C., 154
Geiselman, R. E., 308
Gelfand, M. J., 56, 89
George, J. M., 91
Gergen, K. J., 312, 348
Gershenfeld, M. K., 210, 232
Giacalone, R. A., 82, 91
Gibbons, B., 290–291, 292, 309
Gibson, M. A., 121, 129
Gifford, R. K., 191, 202
Gilbert, A. N., 309
Gilbert, G., 202
Gil de Zuniga, H., 337–338, 349
Gilovich, T., 191, 202
Giridharadas, A., 3, 42
Gittler, J. B., 371
Glazer, S., 52, 89
Gleitman, L. R., 241–243, 265
Glick, P., 202
Gluck, P., 272–273, 307
Glunk, U., 392, 404
Gluszek, A., 286, 308
Gogek, F. M., 232
Gonzales, A., 126
Goodman, C. C., 194, 203
Goodman, N. R., 435
Gordon, L., 202
Gordon, M. J., 262, 266
Goss, B., 11 (table), 43, 201, 264
Gould, S. J., 279, 307
Graetz, K., 61, 90
Grainger, R. J., 386–387, 403
Green, E. G. T., 50, 51, 89
Gregersen, H. B., 403
Gregor, T. A., 165
Groshkopf, E. L., 295, 321, 348
Guan, S. J., 196, 203

Gudykunst, W. B., 29, 32, 43, 44, 55, 65, 67,
    83–84, 89, 90, 91, 181, 182, 196, 197, 201,
    202, 203, 211–212, 231, 232, 248–249, 251,
    252, 254, 265, 266, 286–287, 308, 310, 315,
    316–318, 329, 330 (table)–331 (table), 348,
    349, 368–369, 371, 372, 435
Guenena, N., 227–228, 233
Guensburg, C., 129
Guerrero, L. K., 308
Guidetti, M., 272, 307
Guimond, S., 202
Guo, C., 343, 349
Gutierrez, R., 233

Haas, S., 349
Hagino, G., 165
Hahlweg, K., 335, 349
Hale, J. L., 310
Halford, W. K., 335, 349
Hall, E. T., 11 (table), 22–24, 34, 43, 46, 62–63, 88,
    90, 139–140, 141, 156–157, 164, 165, 166,
    250, 255, 265, 298, 308, 309, 310, 368,
    392–393, 394 (table), 404
Hall, J. A., 278, 283–284, 288–289, 307, 308
Hall, M. R., 250, 255, 265, 392–393,
    394 (table), 404
Hall, R., 164
Halverson, R., 88, 164
Hamilton, D. L., 191, 201–202
Hamlin, K., 404
Hammer, M. R., 362–364, 372, 435
Hannah, M. T., 71, 90
Harb, C., 52, 89
Harms, L. S., 24
Haroun, M., 219, 232
Harris, C., 434
Harris, M., 126
Harris, P. R., 74, 90, 158, 164, 165, 274–275, 283,
    289, 296–297, 307, 308, 309, 310, 380–381,
    394 (table), 403, 404
Harris, R., 91
Harris, R. J., 180, 201
Hart, A., 193, 203
Hart, W. B., 43
Hasegawa, T., 286–287, 308
Hashimoto, K., 390, 404
Hashimoto, M., 308
Hattie, J., 89
Hayes J., 124
Heath, J., 265

Hecht, M. L., 77, 82, 91, 299, 308, 310
Heider, K., 279–281, 307
Hensley, D. I., 180, 201
Herbenick, D., 129
Herdt, G. H., 220, 232
Herrick, J., 219, 232
Herskovits, M., 406, 434
Hess, T. M., 203
Hesselink, R. C., 155, 165, 308
Hessini, L., 223, 232
Hewstone, M., 435
Heyman, S., 55, 67, 89, 90
Hill, C. L., 181, 201, 202
Hill, S. E., 340, 349
Hinsley, A. W., 337–338, 349
Hintz, S. M., 197, 198, 203
Hodson, G., 91
Hoffman, J., 345, 350
Hofstede, G., 76–77, 80, 84–85, 91, 169, 195,
        200, 203, 220, 232
Hofstede, G.-J., 200
Hollis, A. C., 166
Holt, R., 90
Honeycutt, J. M., 58, 89
Hoobler, G. D., 77, 82, 91, 299, 310
Hooker, R., 253, 265
Hostetler, J. A., 109, 110, 111, 128
House, T., 197, 203
Houston, M., 126
Hovey, J. D., 434
Howard, M. C., 332, 335, 336, 349
Howard, R. W., 201
Howes, D., 291, 292, 309
Hsin-Yui, Y., 308
Hsu, F. L. K., 68, 72, 74, 89, 90
Huber, R., 110, 128
Hugenberg, K., 282, 308
Hui, C. H., 51, 89
Huo, Y. J., 80–81, 91
Hutchison, R., 116, 128
Hymes, D., 265

Ikonen, T., 52, 89
Ilcan, S. M., 96, 126
Imada, T., 51, 89
Ishii, S., 348
Ishikawa, Y., 308
Islam, M. R., 435
Iuzzini, J., 90
Iwao, S., 90, 224, 225, 233, 249–250, 265

Iwawaki, S., 281, 307–308
Izard, C. E., 280–281, 307

Jackofsky, E., 404
Jackson, D., 14, 43
Jackson, R. L., II, 43
Jackson, S. E., 404
Jackson, T., 343, 349
Jaeger, R., 164
Jaggi, V., 195–196, 203
Jahn, J., 108, 128
Jasso, R., 434
Jefferson, T., 292
Johnson, D. W., 231
Johnson, F. R., 231
Jones, A., 128
Jones, S. B., 310
Jones, T. S., 309
Jordan, J., 427, 435
Jourard, S. M., 289, 309
Jreisat, J. E., 404
Judd, C. M., 181, 201, 202

Kagitçibasi, C., 89, 90, 434
Kao, H. S. R., 71, 90
Kassea, B. R., 52, 89
Kassing, J. W., 428, 435
Katsurada, E., 233
Katz, D., 184–185, 202
Katzner, K., 264, 265
Kaya, N., 287, 308
Kealey, D. J., 435
Keaton, S. A., 58, 89
Keberlein, M., 74, 91, 215–216, 232
Keberlein, M. C., 307
Keberlein, M. C. G., 166
Keesing, R. M., 46, 88
Kemmelmeier, M., 49, 51, 56, 89
Kent, S., 144–146, 165
Kilmann, R. H., 371
Kim, H. S., 361, 372
Kim, K. S., 55, 89, 90
Kim, M., 218–219, 232
Kim, M. S., 309
Kim, U., 89, 90
Kim, Y. Y., 29, 43, 44, 83–84, 91, 181,
        182, 197, 201, 202, 203, 211–212, 231,
        232, 252, 265, 315, 348, 353–354, 355,
        357, 371, 408–409, 421, 427, 428–429,
        430, 434, 435

King, P., 259
Kinzler, K. D., 285, 308
Kitao, K., 43
Kline, S., 343–344, 350
Klonoff, E. A., 412, 415–417, 434, 435
Klopf, D. W., 203, 216, 232, 309, 327, 348
Kluckhohn, C., 19, 43, 164
Kluckhohn, F., 71, 90
Kluckhohn, F. R., 136, 137, 164
Knapp, M. L., 278, 283–284, 288–289,
    307, 308
Knopf, R., 135, 164
Knutson, K. P., 88
Kochman, T., 107, 128, 251, 265
Koester, J., 91, 141, 164, 265, 266
Kohl, J. V., 291, 293, 309
Kokdemir, D., 154, 165
Kolata, G., 105, 127
Koltz, R., 164
Konkka, A., 98, 127
Korzenny, F., 435
Koslow, J., 98–99
Krabbenhoft, M. A., 273, 306, 307
Kraiger, K., 198, 203
Kramarae, C., 127
Kravitz, J., 308
Kraybill, D. B., 114, 128
Kroeber, A., 19
Kroeber, A. I., 43
Kroonenberg, P., 281, 307–308
Krueger, K., 158–159, 166, 232, 296, 309
Kulick, D., 129, 265
Kurogi, A., 357, 371
Kwalwasser, J., 387, 404
Kwan, V. S. Y., 202
Kwon, K. H., 338, 349

Lachman, J. L., 178, 201
Lachman, R., 178, 201
Ladefoged, P., 284
Landler, M., 403
Landrine, H., 411–412, 415–417, 434, 435
Landy, F., 198, 203
Lane, C., 152, 165
Lane, H. W., 388–389, 404
Lang, J. T., 135, 136, 139, 140, 148, 164, 165
Lanter, J. R., 282, 308
Laroche, L., 404
Larrick, R., 383–384, 403

Larson, C., 9
Larson, C. U., 43
Laumann, E. Q., 105, 127
Laungani, P. D., 6, 42, 96, 126, 208, 225, 231,
    233, 346, 350
Laurenceau, J.-P., 333, 349
Leap, W., 124, 129
Lee, H. O, 361, 372
Lee, J. H., 129
Lee, Y. T., 43
Leeds-Hurwitz, W., 43
Le Guerer, A., 291, 309
Leung, K., 81, 82, 91, 383–384, 403
Levande, D., 219, 232
Levin, S., 336–338, 349
Levine, T. R., 349
Levinson, D. J., 195, 203
Lewis, I. M., 203
Lewis, R. D., 391 (table), 394, 394 (table)
Lewis, W., 42
Lewis-Smith, J., 333, 349
Leyens, J.-Ph., 202
Libby, S., 232
Liberman, M., 265
Liebkind, K., 409, 434
Lim, S. S., 155–156, 165
Lin, S. L., 361, 372
Lind, E. A., 80–81, 91
Lindsay, R. C. L., 308
Linton, R., 406, 434
Littlejohn, S. W., 307
Liu, I., 180, 201
Lobel, T. E., 232
Lonner, W. J., 201, 202, 232, 309,
    340, 341 (table), 349, 420, 435
Lor, H., 345, 350
Lubove, R. E., 387, 404
Lukens, J., 197, 203
Lustig, M. W., 91, 141, 164, 265, 266
Lynn, R., 203
Lysgaard, S., 435

Ma, Y., 43
MacDermid, S. M., 219, 232
MacKaye, W. R., 110, 128
Mackie, D. M., 202
MacNeil, R., 259, 266
Mahoney, B., 308
Mahoney, J., 114, 128

Maldonado, R., 415, 434
Malpass, R., 201, 202, 232, 309, 340, 341 (table), 349
Malpass, R. S., 282, 308
Mandelbaum, P., 233
Manders, A., 164
Mantzur, A., 232
Marquez, C. M., 229–230, 233
Marsh, A., 281, 308
Marsh, A. A., 278, 307
Martin, J. N., 309
Martin, M. M., 176, 201, 348
Martin, S. E., 253, 255, 265
Mashraki-Redhatzur, S., 232
Matheny, K. B., 407, 434
Matlin, M., 173, 178–179, 201
Matsui, Y., 224–225, 233
Matsumoto, D., 307
Matsumoto, T., 357, 371
Matsumoto, Y., 55, 89, 90
Mayo, Y. Q., 127
McAdoo, H., 407–408, 434
McCaa, R., 233
McCann, R. M., 58, 89
McCloud, L., 43
McCroskey, J. C., 15–16, 18, 29, 30, 32, 33, 43, 44, 195, 196, 197, 198, 203, 216, 232, 321, 324, 325, 348, 428, 435
McDaniel, E., 289, 309
McLaughlin, M. W., 128
McLuhan, M., 2
McNall, M., 116, 128
McNamara, T. F., 257, 266
McNeil, D., 270
Meem, D. T., 121, 129
Mehrabian, A., 133, 134, 163–164
Mendelbaum, D. G., 307
Mendenhall, M. E., 403
Mendez, S., 434
Mendoza, M. T., 383–384, 403
Mendoza, R. H., 411, 434
Mendoza-Denton, N., 266
Mendoza-Romero, J., 127
Merkel, A., 4
Merton, R. K., 231
Meyer, M. J., 44
Meyer, S. J., 44
Meyers, B., 126
Michael, E. T., 127

Miike, Y., 43
Miller, G. A., 176, 201, 245
Miller, G. R., 11 (table), 43
Millson, C., 180, 201
Miranda, A. O., 407, 434
Mitrani, M., 420, 435
Miyagawa, S., 265
Miyake, K., 285, 308
Miyamoto, T., 386–387, 403
Mochizuki, M., 165
Moellendorf, S., 112–113, 128, 274, 307
Molinsky, A. L., 273, 306, 307
Moon, S., 338, 349
Moore, H., 146–148, 165
Moran, R. T., 74, 90, 158, 164, 165, 274–275, 283, 289, 296–297, 307, 308, 309, 310, 380–381, 394 (table), 403, 404
Moran, S. V., 274–275, 283, 289, 296–297, 307, 308, 309, 310
Morris, M. W., 383–384, 403
Morris, R., 94, 126
Morrison, T., 164
Mortenson, S. T., 90
Motley, M. T., 43
Mullen, R. T., 155, 165, 308
Murray, H. A., 164

Naftali, O., 153–154, 165
Nagai, H., 388–389, 404
Nakayama, T. K., 309
Napier, R. W., 210, 232
Nasir, N. S., 128
Nelson, T. D., 202
Neuberg, S. L., 193, 203
Neuliep, J. W., 29, 30, 32, 33, 43, 44, 149 (figure), 195, 196, 197, 198, 201, 203, 213, 232, 246 (figure), 275 (figure), 277 (figure), 295, 320, 321, 322, 324, 348, 428, 435
Ng, W. J., 308
Nicoladis, E., 272, 307
Nieto, R. D., 102, 127
Nisbett, R. E., 170–172, 201
Nishida, H., 435
Nishida, T., 55, 89, 90, 315, 329, 330 (table)–331 (table), 348, 349
Norton, M. I., 202
Nuriy, O. E., 105, 127
Nwadiora, E., 407–708, 434
Nyrop, R. F., 164

Oberg, K., 418, 435
Oetzel, J. G., 91, 352, 353, 357, 361, 365–366, 371, 372
Ogilvie, R., 392, 404
Ogura, M., 136, 164, 307, 308
O'Hair, D., 201, 264
Okumura, T., 390, 404
Orr, E., 52, 89
Osborne, P., 272–273, 307
O'Sullivan, M., 279–281, 307
Otsubo, Y., 91
Oyama, N., 61, 90
Oyserman, D., 49, 51, 56, 89

Páez, D., 50, 51, 89
Paik, S., 218, 232
Pajewski, A. M., 101, 127
Pan, X., 357, 371
Park, B., 181, 201, 202
Park, M., 44
Pearce, S., 128
Pedersen, D. M., 149–151, 153, 165
Pelled, L. H., 395, 404
Pels, T., 219, 232
Pempek, T. A., 338, 349
Penasa, A. G., 307
Peng, F., 197, 203
Pennock, J. R., 165
Perea, A., 81, 91
Peters, M., 307
Peterson, M. F., 81, 91
Pettigrew, T. F., 203
Pexman, P. M., 182, 202
Philipsen, G., 258, 266
Phipps, C. A., 162, 166
Pimentel, E. E., 229, 233
Pinker, S., 238, 241–242, 243, 264, 265
Pirttilä-Backman, A. M., 52, 89
Pittan, J., 281, 307–308
Pliscott, K., 88, 164
Polyani, M., 168, 200
Poortinga, Y. H., 174, 175, 201, 202, 215, 232
Porter, L. E., 182, 185–187, 191–192, 202
Porter, R. E., 44, 127, 128, 232, 265, 266, 308, 349, 371, 372, 434, 435
Posner, R. A., 332, 349
Powell, A., 128
Powell, K., 128

Pratt, S., 64, 90, 251–252, 257, 265, 266
Pretty, K., 345, 350
Proctor, R. F., 232

Quinn, D. M., 203
Quittner, J., 165

Rahhal, T. A., 203
Rahim, M. A., 371
Rao, A., 390, 404
Rapoport, A., 139, 164
Ray, H., 193, 203
Redfield, R., 406, 434
Redford, P., 52, 89
Reece, M., 129
Reick, S., 136, 164
Reiling, D., N., 111, 128
Reisberg, L., 165
Reiter, M. J., 334–335, 349
Remland, M. S., 309
Renkens, S., 345, 350
Resnick, R. P., 127
Reuning, H., 174, 201
Rhinesmith, S., 419, 435
Rhodes, G., 308
Richardson, A., 435
Richardson, E., 266
Richmond, V. P., 321, 324, 325, 348
Rickford, J. C., 106–107, 128
Ridley, C. R., 181, 201, 202
Rieck, S., 307, 308
Rifkin, J. M., 103, 127
Risen, J. L., 191, 202
Rissland, E. L., 201
Rivera-Sanchez, M., 155–156, 165
Roberts, J. M., 165
Rodgers, B., 129
Rodriguez, R., 9
Rogan, R. G., 361, 372
Rogers, E. M., 43
Rogoff, B., 179–180, 201
Rokeach, M., 67, 68, 90
Roman, M., 104
Rosch, E., 181, 201
Rosenberg, M., 42, 88
Rosenzweig, P. M., 376, 403
Ross, B. M., 180, 201
Rothbaum, F., 349–350
Rouse, J. M., 155, 165, 308

Rozin, P., 293, 309
Rubin, D. L., 308
Rubin, M., 202
Rush, K., 187, 202
Rushton, J. P., 203
Rustemli, A., 154, 165
Ryan, D. J., 320, 321, 322, 324348

Safra, J. E., 164
Sagar, A. H., 194, 203
Sagy, S., 52, 89
Salzmann, Z., 237, 238, 264, 265, 244245
Sam, D. L., 434
Samhan, H. H., 119, 129
Samovar, L. A., 44, 127, 128, 232, 265, 266, 308,
    349, 371, 372, 434, 435
SanAntonio, P. M., 257, 266
Sanders, J., 315, 348
Sanders, S. A., 129
Sanford, R. N., 203
Sapir, E., 237–238, 264, 307
Saunders, J. B., 37, 44
Schaefer, R. T., 95–96, 105, 106, 126, 127,
    182, 192, 202, 209, 232
Schick, V., 129
Schiefelbein, B., 164
Schilling-Estes, N., 266
Schimmack, U., 281, 307
Schlabach, D., 128
Schlatter, E., 129
Schlesinger, A. M., Jr., 2, 3, 9, 42, 43
Schneider, D. M., 164
Schoen, L. M., 180, 201
Schofield, J. W., 194, 203
Schuler, R. S., 404
Schultz, W., 164
Schwartz, S. H., 68, 71, 90, 310
Schwirtz, M., 42
Searchinger, G., 264, 265, 306–307, 308
Sears, C. R., 182, 202
Sedikides, C., 61, 90
Seelye, H. N., 43, 90
Segall, M. H., 174, 175, 195, 201, 202, 203,
    215, 232, 434, 435
Sek-Hong, N., 71, 90
Seklecki, R., 43
Seward, P., 165
Shanks, T., 44
Shapiro, J. R., 193, 203

Shapiro, R. B., 372
Shaw, A. S., 349
Shin, H. B., 43
Shoemaker, M. W., 164
Shriver, E. R., 282, 308
Shulruf, B., 89
Shuper, P. A., 91
Shuter, R., 39, 44
Shutts, K., 285, 308
Siegel, B. J., 88
Sieke, K., 142, 165
Silver, J., 307
Simmel, G., 292, 309
Sims, A., 124, 129
Singelis, T. M., 56, 89
Singer, J. A., 90
Sinnen, R., 345, 350
Slater, M. D., 81, 91
Slobin, D., 241, 264
Slocum, J. W., 404
Smalley, W. A., 435
Smallwood, M., 77, 82, 91, 310
Smart, D. W., 407, 434
Smart, J. F., 407, 434
Smith, A. G., 265
Smith, E. R., 202
Smith, P. B., 81, 91
Smitherman, G., 127, 258–259, 266
Smits, S., 307
Smucker, P. G., 296, 309
Sodetani, L. L., 315, 348
Sonoda, K. T., 315, 348
Sorenson, J. H., 137–138, 164
Sorrentino, R. A., 91
Spear, T., 232
Spelke, E. S., 285, 308
Spencer, S. J., 192–193, 203
Spencer-Oatey, H., 81, 91
Spinner-Halev, J., 40, 44
Spitzberg, B., 29, 32
Spitzberg, B. H., 44, 425, 435
Srinivasan, R., 164
Stafford, L., 334, 335, 349
Stavans, I., 102, 103, 127
Steele, C. M., 192–193, 203
Stefanone, M. A., 338, 349
Stein, H. F., 132, 133, 163, 164
Stephan, C. W., 307
Stephan, W. G., 307

Stepp, C. S., 165
Stevens, S. S., 11 (table), 43
Stigler, J. W., 180, 201
Stillings, N. A., 201
Stoddart, D. M., 291, 309
Stokols, D., 164, 165
Storti, C., 90, 253, 265
Stowell, J., 251, 265
Strodtbeck, F., 71, 90
Stroh, L. K., 403
Stumpf, S., 91
Sugihara, Y., 233
Sullivan, C., 333, 349
Suminski, S., 128
Summers, C. J., 129
Sumner, W. G., 32, 44, 203, 208–209,
    231, 435
Sung, K., 219, 232
Synnott, A., 291–292, 309

Tajfel, H., 192, 202, 209, 231
Takagi, H., 388–389, 404
Takai, J., 357, 371
Tan, S., 308
Tang, J., 397–398, 404
Tang, S., 165
Tavassoli, N. T., 176–177, 201
Taylor, D. M., 182, 185–187, 191–192,
    195–196, 202, 203
Taylor, K., 308
Taylor, P. L., 336–338, 349
Teck, B., 103, 127
Teitelbaum, S., 308
Terry, C., 142, 165
Thao, K., 115–116, 117, 128, 129, 164,
    218, 232, 307
Thomas, K. W., 371
Thompson, C. A., 348
Thorne, R., 164
Ting-Toomey, S., 44, 55, 67, 81, 89, 90, 91,
    248–249, 251, 252, 254, 265, 352, 353,
    357, 361, 365–368, 371, 372, 435
Tocqueville, de, A., 206, 231
Todrank, J., 293, 309
Toguchi, Y., 90
Tohsaku, C. K., 264
Triandis, H. C., 49–50, 54, 55, 56, 88, 90,
    164, 209, 231
Trice, A. D., 187, 202

Trompenaars, F., 374, 380, 381–382, 382 (figure),
    384–385, 385 (figure), 403
Troy, A. B., 333, 349
Trubisky, P., 361, 372
Tsang, B., 349–350
Tschudy, K., 128
Turkle, S., 152, 165
Turner, J., 209, 231
Tyler, T. R., 80–81, 91
Tyson, C., 98, 127
Tyson, E. H., 98, 127
Tyson, J. L., 128

Ueda, A., 142, 143–144, 165
Ui, M., 224–225, 233
Unsworth, S. J., 182, 202

Vandehey, K., 158–159, 166, 232, 296, 309
Vandello, J. A., 54, 89
van den Berghe, P. L., 42
Vander Leest, J, 9
Vasquez, G., 233
Velasquez, M., 44
Vevea, J. L., 90
Vinsel, A. M., 164
Voronov, M., 90
Vue, S., 43

Wagenheim, B. R., 127
Wagley, C., 126
Walker, A. M., 91
Waller, J., 42
Waller, R., 232
Wan, K. -C., 82, 91
Wang, Q., 177, 201
Wang, S. S., 338, 349
Wang, X. M., 228, 233
Ward, A., 397–398, 404
Ward, C. X., 435
Ward, L. M., 201
Warren, N., 201
Warsh, H., 112–113, 128, 307
Wassef, N., 227–228, 233
Wasson, R., 403
Watzlawick, P., 14, 43
Weber, J., 231–232
Weber, M. J., 287, 308
Weber, S., 266
Weber, S. N., 97–98, 106, 108–109, 127, 128

Weider, D. L., 64, 90, 251–252, 257, 265, 266
Weisler, S. E., 201
Welch, K., 43
West, D., 348
Westfahl, G., 164
Westin, A. F., 148–149, 154, 165
Wetzel, H., 404
White, G. F., 137–138, 164
Whitehead, C., 244
Whorf, B., 237, 264
Wibisono, A. K., 164
Wilcox, R., 91
Wilder, D. A., 181, 201
Wilderom, C., 392, 404
Williams, H., 309
Williams, J. E., 221–223, 232
Williams, K. Y., 383–384, 403
Winkelman, M., 417–418, 419, 422, 435
Winland, D. N., 114, 128
Wiseman, R. L., 315, 348, 427, 435
Wohlwill, J. F., 164
Wolfe, C. T., 203
Wolfram, W., 261, 266
Wolter, A., 307, 309
Wood, J., 232
Wood, J. T., 254, 265
Worchel, S., 231
Wortley, W., 174, 201
Wright, T. J., 372
Wrzesniewski, A., 293, 309
Wyndham, C. H., 175, 201
Wyndham, L., 2

Xin, K. R., 395, 404
Xu, J., 202

Yamaguchi, S., 90
Yamamoto, T., 165
Yang, D., 164
Yang, K.-S., 51, 89
Yang, Z., 361, 372
Yanping, L., 404
Yee-Jung, K. K., 372
Yermolayeva, Y. A., 338, 349
Yokochi, Y., 357, 371
Yoon, G., 89, 90
Yoshida, M., 180, 201
Yoshida, T., 142, 165, 435
Yoshimaru, K., 112–113, 128, 307
You, Y., 44
Young, S. G., 282, 308
Yount, K., 228, 233
Yousef, F., 71, 72, 74, 75, 76, 90, 91, 232, 307, 406, 434
Yu, A. B., 51, 89
Yum, J. O., 253, 255–256, 265, 329–332, 349
Yurkovich, D., 88, 164

Zanna, M. P., 90, 202, 203
Zapf, M. K., 418, 422–424, 435
Zhang, J., 70–71, 90
Zhang, Y., 91
Zhao, G. M., 228–229, 233
Zhong, M., 348
Zukerman, M., 283, 308

Subject Index

Accents, 259, 285, 286
Acculturation
   culture shock, 417–424
   defined, 406–407
   factors affecting, 408
   model of, 408–411
   modes of, 410–411
   in U.S., 118, 411–417
Acculturation Rating Scale for Mexican
      Americans (ARSMA), 413–415
Acculturative stress, 407–408
Activities, values about, 74
Adaptable environment, 140
Adaptors, 283
Adjustment phase, 420–421
Affect displays, 278–281
Affective component, 29, 427–429
Affective style, 254–257
African Americans, 105–109
   languages/dialects of, 106–109, 258–259
   as microcultural group, 96, 98
   polygyny and, 336
   privacy and, 148, 152–153
   self-rating acculturation scale, 416–417
   statistics on, 8, 105–106
   stereotypes of, 184, 185
Age, values about, 74, 75
Allocentric, 55
Amerasians, 407–408
Amish, 109–114
   greeting rituals and, 274
   nonverbal communication and, 113–114
   as trilingual, 98–99
   verbal communication and, 112–113
Analogic communication, 270
Animism, 117–118
Anxiety uncertainty management (AUM) theory,
      316–320

Appalachian English, 261
Arab Americans, 118–121
Arab League, 398
Arranged marriages, 116
Assertiveness, 321
Assimilation, 118, 410, 413
Asymmetrical reciprocity, 331
Audience-based communication, 16
Australia, 15, 115, 137, 138, 141, 275, 278
Austria, 58, 79, 141
Authoritarian collectivism, 218
Authoritarianism, 77
Autobiographical memory, 177

Bali, 155
Batek Negrito, 296
Black language, 106–109
   origins of, 108–109
Body language, 12, 21, 24
Bororo people, 293
Brazil
   land use in, 137–138
   management practices in, 375
   microcultural groups in, 96
   privacy in, 154–155
Bride price, 74, 116, 118, 344, 345
Bride trafficking, 345
Bride wealth. See Dowry
Britain. See United Kingdom
Buckley Amendment, 152
Buddhism, 136
Built environment, 139–141

Cajun English, 261
Calendars, 297–298
California English, 261–262
Cameroon, 52
Canada, 346, 381

Carpentered-world hypothesis, 175–176

Caste, 3, 40, 96, 208, 215–216, 274

Categorization, mental economy and, 181–182

Catholicism, 95, 102

Cell phones, 3

Chicano English, 103–104

China
  attitudes toward Americans, 381
  collectivism in, 50
  divorce rate in, 346
  fight/flight gestures in, 278
  greeting rituals n, 274
  human rights in, 4
  intermediaries in, 75
  land use in, 137
  language style in, 255–256
  management practices in, 396–398
  marriage in, 96, 345
  memory/retrieval and, 180–181
  one-child policy of, 47
  parent-child relationship in, 365
  power distance in, 81, 82
  privacy in, 153–154
  relationships in, 329–330
  romance/love gestures in, 276
  self-identity in, 72, 74
  sex roles and, 228–229
  values in, 69–71

Chinese language, 240, 248, 284–285

Christianity, 137

Chronemics, 23, 297–298

Civil Rights Act of 1964, 122

Cognitive rigidity, 427

Cognitive simplicity, 427

Collectivism, 35
  in Amish society, 111–112
  communication consequences, 55–56
  conflict styles and, 367–368
  defined, 49
  horizontal, 58, 60
  individualism vs., 50–53
  measuring, 56, 58–59
  patterns across the U.S., 54 (table)
  real-life application, 50
  self-assessment of, 57
  vertical, 58, 60

Collectivist cultures
  families in, 218
  nonverbal communication in, 299
  privacy and, 156
  role stratification and, 215

Colloquialisms, 6, 15, 112, 118, 383

Common good approach, 39

Communication
  analogic, 270
  conflict styles of, 362–364, 366–368
  context-based, 15–16
  cultural dimension, 14–15
  defined, 10–15, 11 (table)
  dynamic dimension, 11–12, 15
  effectiveness of, 318
  intentionality and, 13–14
  interactive-transactive, 12
  process dimension, 10–11
  properties of, 11 (table)
  symbolic dimension, 12–13
  ubiquitous dimension, 14

Communication apprehension, 15–18
  defined, 15
  self-assessment of (PRCA-24), 17–18

Competitiveness, 51

Conflict. See Intercultural Conflict

Confucianism, 39–40, 171, 329, 331, 332, 397

Costa Rica, 51

Cult of ethnicity, 9

Cultural context, 46–48
  defined, 25

Cultural continua, 47

Cultural relativism, 23

Cultural transmutation, 411

Culture
  cognition and, 170–187
  common history element of, 20
  defined, 19
  natural disasters and, 137–139
  natural environment and, 135–137
  as software of the mind, 169–170, 172
  value/belief/behavior pattern element of, 19–20
  verbal codes element of, 20–21

Culture shock, 417–424
  factors affecting, 420 (figure)
  models of, 418 (figure)
  real-life application, 421
  self-assessment of, 423–424
  stages of (figure), 419
  strategies for managing, 422
  W curve model of reentry, 422 (figure)

Culture shock profile, 422–424

Dassanetch, 296

Denmark, 174

Denotative meaning, 271–272

Desana, 296
Dialects, 258, 259–262
    a-prefixing, 261
    r-dropping, 261
    r-less, 260 (figure), 261
Digital communication, 270
Digital quality, of verbal communication, 28
Direct vs. indirect styles, 249–251
Diversity, within U.S., 8–9
Divorce/dissolution, 345–347
Dogon people, 296
Dowry, 38, 224, 225, 226, 346
Dynamic, communication as, 11–12, 15

Ebonics, 106–107, 109, 258–259
Economic benefit of intercultural
        communication, 7
Ecuador, 186
Egypt, 51, 227–228
Elaborated code, 63, 248
Elaborate language style, 251–252
E-mail, 3
Emblems, 272–278
Empathy, 324, 326–327, 431
    relational, 326–327
    third culture and, 326–326
Endogamy, 96
Environmental context, 25–26
    built environment, 139–141
    climate, 135–136
    defined, 25
    housing, 141–148
    information load and, 133–135
    land use, 137–138
    natural disasters, 138–139
    of organization, 380–381
    privacy, 148–156
    terrestrial environment, 135
    time orientation, 156–162
    views on natural environment, 136–137
Episodic long-term, 177
Equality norm, 56
Equity norm, 56
Ethics
    of intercultural communication, 36–41
    intercultural conversation, 36–37
Ethnicity, 409
Ethnic violence, 4
Ethnocentrism, 23, 195–199, 427
    attributional bias, 195–196
    contemporary conceptualization, 196

defined, 32–33
GENE scale, 33 (table)–34 (table)
intercultural communication and, 196–197
interpersonal communication and, 197
as perceptual filter, 320
racism and, 198–199
self-assessment of
    in workplace, 197–198
Exogamy, 96, 218

Face, 75, 79, 81
    self-assessment of, 358
Face negotiation theory, 357
Facework, 81, 357–358
    behaviors, 359 (table)
Facial expressions
    cross-racial identification of, 281–282
    of emotion, 278–281
Fairness, 39
Family Educational Rights and Privacy Act, 152
Finland, 324, 341, 342, 409
Fixed-feature space, 139–140
Flexible environment, 140
Foreign Service Institute (FSI), 23
Forgetting, 178–179
France
    collectivism in, 51
    Hmong in, 115
    human rights in, 4
    indirect language style in, 250
    individualism in, 51, 63
    obscene gestures in, 276
Fusion, 411

Gayspeak, 124
Gender
    defined, 220
    sex vs., 220
    stereotypes and, 221–223
Generative grammar, 245–247
GENE scale, 33 (table)–34 (table)
Geography of thought, 170–172
Germany
    affect displays in, 279
    individualism in, 63
    management practices in, 374–375, 391–394
    time orientation in, 159
Ghana, 180
Global village concept, 2
Greece, 49, 57, 141, 190, 209, 280, 289, 341, 382
Group membership, 75

Groups
    family, 217–219
    in-groups and out-groups, 208–209
    membership/nonmembership, 75, 207–208
    reference, 209–210
    roles in, 210–217
    sex and gender, 219–220
    voluntary and involuntary, 207–208
Guatemala, 158
    Ladinos in, 74, 215, 275

Haiku, 136, 255
Hangul, 219, 238
Haptics, 288–289
Harmony, 50
Hate crimes, 114, 123, 124
Healthy communities, 7
Hebrew alphabet, 237
High load, defined, 133
High vs. low context
    characteristics of, 62–63
    communication consequences of, 64
    conflict and, 368–369
    defined, 62
    intercultural conversation, 64–65
    nonverbal behavior and, 300
    nonverbal expectancies, 303
    self-assessment of, 65–67
Hinduism, 40
Hip hop/rap music, 98, 99
Hispanics/Latinos, 100–105
    defined, 100
    demographics of, 8, 100, 101
    languages of, 102–104
    self-rating acculturation scale, 413–415
    stereotypes of, 104–105
    values of, 101–102
Hmong, 114–118
    communication and, 116–118
    families and, 218
    marriage and, 116, 344–345
    obscene gestures among, 275–276
Hogan and ramada, of Navajo, 144–146
Hong Kong, 3, 69, 190, 280, 382
Housing, cross-cultural comparisons of, 141–148
Hsu's Postulates of Basic American Values, 68
Human communication
    apprehension, 15–18
    nature of, 10–15
    properties of, 9–10

Human information processing
Human information processing model, 172–174
Human nature orientation, 75–76

Idiocentric, 55
Illusory correlational principle, 191–192
Illustrators, 272–278
India
    attitudes toward environment in, 136
    caste system in, 40, 96, 208, 215–216
    divorce rate in, 346
    marriage in, 38, 96, 345
    personal dress in, 297
    personal space in, 288
    power distance in, 77, 78
    sex roles in, 225–226
Individualism
    collectivism vs., 50–53
    communication consequences, 55–56
    conflict styles and, 366–367
    defined, 48
    horizontal, 56, 58, 60
    measuring, 56, 58–59
    regional patterns across the U.S., 54 (table)–55
    self-assessment of, 57
    traits associated with
    vertical, 58, 60
Individualistic cultures, 48–49
    families in, 218
    nonverbal communication in, 299
    privacy and, 156
    role stratification in, 215, 216
Indonesia, 135, 141
Informal space, 140
Information load, 133–135
In-groups, 32, 49–50, 55–56, 106, 181,
        187, 208–209
Instrumental style, 254–257
Integration, 410–411
Intentionality, 13–14
Interactive, communication as, 12
Intercultural communication
    benefits of, 6–8
    defined, 10
    as discipline, 22–24
    ethics of, 36–41
    fundamental assumptions about, 32–36
    model of, 24 (figure)–28
    real-life application, 30
    uncertainty and, 28–29

Intercultural communication apprehension (ICA), 29–32, 428–429
  defined, 30, 320
  self-assessment of, 31 (table)
  Intercultural communication competence, 424–432
  affective component of, 29, 427–429
  behavioral component of, 29
  cross-cultural awareness self-assessment, 426
  defined, 424
  knowledge component of, 426–427
  model of, 425 (figure)–431
  psychomotor component of, 429–430
  scale for measuring, 431–432
  situational features and, 430–431
Intercultural Communication Competence Scale, 432
Intercultural conflict
  collectivism and, 367–368
  communication styles, 360–361
  conflict style inventory, 362–364
  defined, 352–353
  face/facework and, 357–359
  high and low context and, 368–369
  individualism and, 366–367
  intercultural conversation, 355–357, 361–362
  model of, 353 (figure)–357
  real-life application, 369–370
  situational model of, 364–366
Intercultural management, 375–385
  cultural context of, 377–378
  environmental context of, 380–381
  intercultural conversation, 378–379, 383–385
  intercultural relations and, 385–401
  perceptual context of, 381
  sociorelational context of, 381–382
  verbal/nonverbal codes in, 382–383
Intercultural marriage, 332–333
Intercultural relationships
  arranged marriages, 344–345
  Eastern vs. Western, 329–332
  empathy and, 324, 326–327
  factors affecting, 313 (figure)–329
  intercultural conversation, 322–324
  maintaining, 334–337
  maintaining, through Internet, 337–338
  marital dissolution/divorce, 345–347
  marital relationships, 332–333
  mate selection/desirability, 338–344
  real-life application, 317
  similarity and, 327–329

Intercultural willingness to communicate, 428–429
Interference, 178–179
Intermediaries, 75, 332, 345
Internet, relationship maintenance and, 337–338
Interracial marriage, 332–333
Intimate distance, 140–141
Involuntary membership groups, 207
Involuntary nonmembership groups, 207–208
Iran, 276, 289, 345
Iraq, 289
Islam, 119–120
  family life and, 219
  personal appearance and, 296–297
  polygyny and, 335–336
Israel, 52
Italy, 136, 141, 289

Jamaica, Rastafarian movement in, 96
Japan
  affect displays in, 279
  alphabet in, 238
  attitudes toward environment in, 136
  cultural variability in, 47
  divorce rate in, 346
  fight/flight gestures in, 278
  greeting rituals in, 273–274
  housing in, 142–144
  land use in, 138
  language practices of U.S. companies in, 257
  language style in, 249–250, 253, 255
  management practices in, 386–391
  marriage in, 345
  memory/retrieval and, 180
  nonverbal expression in, 35
  personal dress in, 297
  romance/love gestures in, 276
  sex roles in, 224–225
  silence in, 287
  social distance and, 141
  student-teacher relationships in, 28, 81
  time orientation in, 158
  touch in, 289
Jargon, 259
Java, 154, 155
Jews, stereotypes of, 184
Johnson, Lyndon B., 122
Judaism, 95, 137

Kalahari Bushmen, 174
Kenya, 274, 288, 289
Kinesics, 24, 272–283
  See also Body language
Korea, 21
  contextual language style in, 253
  family life in, 218–219
  management practices in, 375
  role relationships in, 212, 213 (figure), 216
  touch in, 289

Language
  elaborated codes of, 63, 249
  ethnic identity and, 257–262
  generative grammar, 245–247
  official, 9
  phonemes, 239
  real life application, 240
  restricted codes and, 247–248
  Sapir-Whorf hypothesis and, 237–238, 245
  structure of, 238–247
  syntax, 238, 240, 247
  universal grammar and, 240–244
  universals of, 244–245
  verbal codes, 20–21
  See also Language styles
Language styles
  direct *vs.* indirect, 249–251
  elaborate *vs.* succinct, 251–252
  instrumental *vs.* affective, 254–257
  intercultural conversation, 250–251, 253–254, 256–257
  personal *vs.* contextual, 252–254
Language variety, 259, 261
Laos, 96, 135
Latinos. *See* Hispanics/Latinos
Lesbian, gay, bisexual, and transgendered (LGBT), 121–124
  gayspeak, 124
  gestures concerning, 276, 278
  real-like application, 124
  relationship maintenance, 335
Long-term memory, 177
Long-term reciprocity, 331
Low load, defined, 133

Machismo, 104–105
Malawi, 137
Malaysia, 79

Marakwet housing, 146–148
Marginalization, 411
Marriage
  arranged, 96, 116, 344–345
  dissolution of, 345–347
  endogamy, 96
  exogamy, 96, 218
  intercultural/interracial, 332–333
  odor groups and, 296
  polyandry, 336
  polygamy, 74, 332
  polygyny, 332, 335–336
Masai, 28, 158–159, 210, 296
Mate selection (across cultures), 338–344
  self-assessment, 339–340
Mediated voyeurism, 152
Mehinacu Indians, 154–155
Memory
  cross-cultural differences in, 179–181
  episodic, 177
  forgetting, 178–179
  long-term, 177
  semantic, 177–178
  short-term, 176–177
Mexico
  dominant verbal code in, 20–21
  fight/flight gestures in, 278
  management practices in, 375, 394–396
  memory/retrieval and, 180
  obscene gestures in, 275
  power distance in, 77, 79
  romance/love gestures in, 276
  sex roles and, 229–230
Microcultural context, 25
Microcultures, 22
  defined, 94
  defining characteristics of, 95–97
  muted groups as, 97–99
  in U.S., 95, 99–124
  See also African Americans; Amish; Arab
    Americans; Hispanics/Latinos; Hmong;
    Lesbian, gay, bisexual, and transgendered
    (LGBT)
Middle East, management practices in, 398–402
Midwest accent, 262
Mindfulness, 318
Minority groups, 95
Misogyny, 98
Monochronic time, 156–162

Monogamy, 332
Monophthong, 262
Morocco, 155, 223–224, 288
Morphemes, 239
Muslims, 95, 381
  See also Islam
Muted groups, 97–99

Native Americans, 22, 35, 64, 251–252,
  257, 286, 407
Natural disasters, 137–139
  as cultural/social event, 138–138
Nature orientation, 75–76
Navajo housing, 144–148
Nepal, fight/flight gestures in, 278
New Guinea, 220, 244
New Zealand, collectivism in, 51
Nigeria, 4, 74, 137, 287
Nommo, 108–109
Nonfluencies, 284
Nonverbal accents, 278, 281
Nonverbal code, 23–24, 28
  among Amish, 113–114
  among Hmong, 118
  channels of, 272–303
  definitions of, 21, 269–270
  dimensions of cultural variability, 298–305
  power distance and, 82
  psychomotor component and, 429
  real-life application, 290
  verbal code vs., 270–280
  See also Language; Verbal code
Nonverbal expectancy violation (NEV) theory,
  300–305
  assumptions of, 300–302
  cross-cultural conversation, 304–305
  cultural contexts and, 303
  reward valence and, 302–303
Nonverbal symbols, 12, 15, 21–22
Northern Ireland, 96
Norway, 79, 135

Occulesics, 299–300
Olfactics, 34, 290–296
Ongee people, 293
Organizational culture, 377–378
Other-face need, 357, 360 (figure)–361
Out-group homogeneity effect, 191, 192
Out-groups, 32, 55–56, 106, 181, 187, 208–209

Pakistan, 96, 141, 345
Palestine, 52
Pancultural self, 60–61
Paralinguistics, 299
Paralanguage, 283–287
Particularism, 331
Perception, cross-cultural differences in,
  19, 174–179
Perceptual context, 26–27, 28, 62
  of organization, 381
Perceptual filters, 173–174
Personal distance, 141
Personal Report of Communication
  Apprehension (PRCA-24), 17–18
Personal Report of Olfactory Perception and
  Sensitivity (PROPS), 294–295
Personal vs. contextual language styles, 252–254
Peru, 276
Philippines, power distance in, 77
Phonemes, 239
Physical appearance and dress, 296–297
Physical context, 14, 25, 62, 149, 300, 317, 368
Physiological filters, 173
Plateau Tonga, 335
Polyandry, 336
Polychronic time, 157–162
Polygamy, 74, 332
Polygyny, 332, 335
  African-Americans and, 336
  Muslims and, 335–336
Population statistics, 2
Positional roles, 74
Power distance, 76–83
  communication, affect on, 80–82
  defined, 76–77
  intercultural conversation, 83
  intercultural management and, 379
  nonverbal communication and, 299–300
  privacy and, 156
  real-life application, 79
  role stratification and, 216
  self-assessment of, 80
Privacy, 148–156
  cross-cultural comparisons of, 153–155
  defined, 148
  online, 155–156
  self-assessment of, 150–151
  types of, 148–149
  U.S. perceptions of, 151–153

Procedural memory, 177, 178
Process, communication as, 10–11
Protestantism, 95
Proxemics, 24, 287–288
Psychological context, 25
Psychological filters, 174
Psychomotor component, 429–430
Public distance, 141
Puerto Rico, touch in, 289

Racism, 198–199
Rap music, 98, 99 (table)
Rastafarians, 96
Reciprocity, 75, 331
Reference groups, 209–210
Regulators, 282–283
Relational empathy, 326–327
Responsiveness, 321–322
Restricted code, 62–63
Rights, fundamental, 38
Ritual, 40
Roles
    communication and, 211
    cross-cultural variations in, 211–213 (figure)
    defined, 210
    differentiation of, 215
    enactment of, 429–430
    formal vs. informal, 211
    intercultural conversation, 213, 214, 216–217
    relationships, 210–213
    stratification and, 213, 215–216
Roman Catholicism, 102
Russia, 135
    divorce rate in, 346–347
    managerial values in, 379

Sapir-Whorf hypothesis, 237–238, 245
Saudi Arabia
    greeting rituals n, 274–275
    personal space in, 288
    power distance in, 79
    sex discrimination in, 97
    sex roles in, 226
    touch in, 289
Scandinavia, 63, 141, 157, 297
Scotland, social distance in, 141
Self-concept, 192, 210, 281, 312, 318, 357
Self-esteem, 48, 55, 192, 195, 209, 210, 312, 318
Self-face need, 357, 360 (figure), 361

Self-identity, 72, 74
Semantic long-term memory, 177–178
Semantic memory, 177
Semi-fixed feature space, 140
Sensation
    cross-cultural differences in, 174–179
    defined, 173
    perceptual filters of, 173–174
Sensory receptors, 175
Separation, 411
Serer Ndut, 293
Serial monogamy, 332
Sex roles
    across cultures, 223–230
    among Amish, 111–112
    among Hmong, 118
    among Marakwet, 147–148
    among Native Americans, 144
    Bem's, 220
    within families, 74
    real-life application, 227
Sex vs. gender, 220
Shame, 49, 50, 71, 124, 283
Short-term memory, 176
Shunning, 113
Sign language, 95
Silence, 34–35, 251, 284, 286–287
    among Japanese, 35, 64, 303
    among Koreans, 35
    among Native Americans, 21, 64
    LGBT persons and, 123
    in low-context culture, 63
Similarity, 316, 327–329
    attitudinal, 327–328
    attraction and culture, 328–329
Singapore, 51, 156, 382
Situational-based communication, 16
Slang, 259
Social-consultative distance, 141
Social context, 25
Social distance, 141
Social identity, 98, 211, 257, 286
Social justice, 39
Social networking, 3
Social stratification, 213, 215–216
Sociocommunicative style
    defined, 312
    orientation, 321–322
    self-assessment of, 324, 325

Sociological filters, 174
Sociorelational context, 27–28, 62
    defined, 206–207
    of organization, 381–382
South Africa, 97, 141
South Korea, 37–38, 219
South Yemen, 135
Spain, 30, 101, 136, 141, 159, 421
Spanglish, 102–103
    examples of, 103 (table)
Sri Lanka
    attitudes toward environment in, 136
    greeting rituals n, 274
    land use in, 137–138
    personal space in, 288
    touch in, 289
Standard American English (SAE), 109, 259
Stereotype Content Model (SCM), 188–191
Stereotypes
    of African Americans, 184, 185
    gender, 187, 221–223
    of groups in U.S., 7 (table)
    of Hispanics, 104–105
    of Jews, 184
Stereotype threat, 192–193
Stereotyping, 182–195
    defined, 182
    intercultural conversation, 194–195
    real-life application, 183–184, 186
    reasons for, 191–193
    social expectations and, 194–195
    in U.S., 185–188
Subculture, 95
Succinct language style, 251–252
Supernatural orientation, 76, 102
Swahili, 243–244
Sweden, 58, 141
Switzerland, 63
Symbols, 12–13, 20–21
Syntax, 238, 240, 247

Taiwan, 21, 51, 115, 278, 289
Tanala people, 335
Tanzania, collectivism in, 51
Technology, effect on information
        dissemination, 2–3
Terrestrial environment, 135
Texas English, 262
Thailand, touch in, 289

Third culture, 326–327, 411
Time orientation, 156–162
    consequences of mon-/polychronic, 158–159
    intercultural conversation, 159–160
    monochronic vs. polychronic, 156–157
    real-life application, 159
    self-assessment of, 161–162
Tolerance, personal growth through, 7–8
Tourist phase, 418–419
Traitlike communication, 16
Transactive, communication as, 12
Tuareg, 155
Turkey, 96, 137–138, 154

U-curve hypothesis, 418
Uncertainty
    anxiety uncertainty management theory,
        316–320
    intercultural communication and, 28–29
Uncertainty avoidance, 83–87
    defined, 84
    intercultural conversation, 86–87
    real life application, 30
Uncertainty reduction theory (URT), 313–316
    axioms of, 314 (figure)–316
    socio-communicative style and, 312
United Kingdom
    individualism in, 63
    land use in, 138
    power distance in, 81
    social distance in, 141
    touch in, 289
United States
    acculturation in, 411–417
    attitudes toward environment in, 137
    conflict style in, 364
    individualism in, 51, 58, 63
    interracial marriage in, 332–333
    managerial values in, 379
    memory/retrieval and, 180
    microcultures in, 95, 99–124
    obscene gestures in, 275
    parent-child relationship in, 365
    perception of sensory stimuli in, 174
    personal language style in, 252
    power distance in, 82
    privacy perceptions in, 149, 151–153
    reciprocity in, 75
    romance/love gestures in, 276

social distance in, 141
social stratification in, 216
stereotypes in, 7 (table)
student/teacher role relationship in,
    212–213 (figure)
time orientation in, 157
touch in, 289
Universal grammar, 240–244
Universalic orientation, in relationship, 331
Uruguay, 278
Utilitarianism, 38

Value orientations, 67–76
American, 68
Chinese, 69–71
Condon and Yousef's, 72–76
Klukhohn and Strodbeck's, 71–72
Schwartz's universals, 71
Values
of Amish, 111
of Hispanics/Latinos, 101–102
of Southeast Asians, 409
universal, 71

Venezuela, 51, 141
Verbal code, 20–21
nonverbal code *vs.,* 270–280
See also Language; Nonverbal code
Violence against women
after natural disasters, 138
dowry deaths, 38
in Egypt, 228
Virtues approach, 39
Vocal attractiveness, 285
Voluntary membership groups, 207
Voluntary nonmembership groups, 207–208
Voyeurism, 151–152

Wal-Mart, 374–375
Win-win conflict resolution, 366
Wisconsin v. Yoder, 110
Working memory, 176
Workplace discrimination, 122

Xenophobia, 4

Zaire, 136

About the Author

James W. Neuliep (PhD, University of Oklahoma, 1985) is professor of Communication and Media Studies at St. Norbert College in DePere, Wisconsin, where he teaches courses in intercultural communication, interpersonal communication, small group communication, and communication theory. Neuliep is the author of the best-selling book *Intercultural Communication: A Contextual Approach* (4th ed., Sage), *Communication Theory: Applications and Case Studies* (Allyn & Bacon), *Replication Studies in the Social Sciences* (Sage), and *Replication Studies in the Social Sciences II* (Select Press).

Neuliep has authored dozens of papers and articles, mostly dealing with intercultural communication. Several of his papers have been presented on *Top Three* panels. Neuliep and Jim McCroskey created and developed the Generalized Ethnocentrism (GENE) Scale and the Personal Report of Intercultural Communication Apprehension Scale, which are used widely in intercultural communication research. Neuliep's original research has appeared in *Communication Education*, *Communication Quarterly*, *Communication Reports*, *Communication Research Reports*, *Communication Studies*, *Human Communication Research*, *Journal of Intercultural Communication Research*, *Psychological Reports*, and *Journal of Social Behavior and Personality*, among others.

Neuliep is a past editor of the *Journal of Intercultural Communication Research*. He has served or is serving on the editorial boards of *Communication Monographs*, *Communication Reports*, *Communication Studies*, *Journal of Communication*, *Journal of Intercultural Communication Research*, *Journal of Applied Communication Research*, *Journal of Social Behavior and Personality*, and *Communication Quarterly*. Neuliep has served as an ad hoc reviewer for *Communication Education*, *European Journal of Social Psychology*, *Journal of International and Intercultural Communication*, *Human Communication Research*, *Psychological Reports*, and *Western Journal of Communication*. Neuliep is past chair of the Intercultural Communication Division of the International Communication Association (ICA) and a former member of ICA's Board of Directors. Neuliep often serves as a paper reviewer, panel chair, and panel respondent for ICA's Intercultural Communication Division and the National Communication Association's Division of International and Intercultural Communication.

At St. Norbert College, Neuliep is the recipient of the Leonard Ledvina Award for Excellence in Teaching and the Donald King Award for Outstanding Scholarship. He is one of only a few professors in the 110-year history of St. Norbert College to receive both awards.

SAGE Research Methods Online
The essential tool for researchers